Preface

T0181494

This book contains all of the papers presented at the 11th International Conference on Field Programmable Logic and Applications (FPL 2001), hosted by The Queen's University of Belfast, Northern Ireland, 27–29 August 2001. The annual FPL event is the longest-standing international conference covering programmable logic, reconfigurable computing, and related matters. It was founded in 1991, and has been held in Darmstadt, Glasgow, London, Oxford (thrice), Prague, Tallinn, Vienna, and Villach. FPL brings together experts, users, and newcomers from industry and academia, in an informal and convivial atmosphere that encourages stimulating and productive interaction between participants.

The size of the FPL conference has been growing rapidly, the number of participants increasing from 144 in 1999 to 240 in 2000. The number of papers submitted in 2001 was in line with the previous year, and our goal for 2001 was to sustain the growth in participation. The 117 submitted papers came from 24 different countries: USA (26), UK (24), Germany (14), Spain (12), Japan (7), France (4), Greece and Ireland (3 each), Belgium, Canada, Czech Republic, Finland, Italy, The Netherlands, Poland, and Switzerland (2 each), and Austria, Belarus, Brazil, Iran, Mexico, Portugal, South Africa, and Sweden (1 each). This illustrates the position of FPL as a genuinely international event, with by far the largest number of submissions of any conference in this field. As in previous years, each submitted paper was subjected to thorough reviewing. As a result, 56 regular papers and 15 posters were accepted for presentation. Another three keynote papers were invited.

We thank all the authors who submitted papers, and also thank the members of the program committee and the additional referees who carefully reviewed the submissions. We thank Reiner Hartenstein for publicizing the event, Axel Sikora for coordinating the industrial input, Thomas Hoffmann and Ulrich Nageldinger for their assistance with the software for the reviewing process and the general handover from the previous year. We also acknowledge the cooperation given by Alfred Hofmann of Springer-Verlag, which has now been the official publisher for eight consecutive years. Financial support is vital to the organization of any conference, and we acknowledge considerable assistance from the Industrial Development Board for Northern Ireland, which sponsored the conference banquet, Amphion Semiconductor, which sponsored the industry night, and Quicksilver Technology, which supported the Michal Servit award. Finally, we thank the many staff who have assisted at Queen's University of Belfast, particularly Sakir Sezer and Victoria Stewart for their help in local organization, Richard Turner and Tim Courtney for their general assistance, and Paula Matthews for her considerable effort on all aspects of administration.

June 2001

Gordon Brebner
Roger Woods

Organization Committee

General Chair: Roger Woods, Queen's University of Belfast, UK
Program Chair: Gordon Brebner, University of Edinburgh, UK
Publicity Chair: Reiner Hartenstein, Univ. of Kaiserslautern, Germany
Local publicity: Sakir Sezer, Queen's University of Belfast, UK
Industrial liaison: Axel Sikora, BA Lörrach, Germany
Spouse programme: Victoria Stewart, Queen's University of Belfast, UK

Programme Committee

Peter Athanas, Virginia Tech, USA
Neil Bergmann, University of Queensland, Australia
Gordon Brebner, University of Edinburgh, UK
Michael Butts, Cadence Design Systems, USA
Andre DeHon, California Institute of Technology, USA
Carl Ebeling, University of Washington, USA
Hossam ElGindy, University of New South Wales, Australia
Manfred Glesner, Darmstadt University of Technology, Germany
John Gray, Independent Consultant, UK
Herbert Gruenbacher, Carinthia Tech Institute, Austria
Stephen Guccione, Xilinx Inc, USA
Yoshiaki Hagiwara, SONY Corporation, Japan
Reiner Hartenstein, University of Kaiserslautern, Germany
Brad Hutchings, Brigham Young University, USA
Tom Kean, Algotronix Consulting, UK
Andreas Koch, Technical University of Braunschweig, Germany
Dominique Lavenier, IRISA, France
Wayne Luk, Imperial College, London, UK
Patrick Lysaght, University of Strathclyde, UK
George Milne, University of Western Australia, Australia
Toshiaki Miyazaki, NTT Laboratories, Japan
Kiyoshi Oguri, Nagasaki University, Japan
Michel Renovell, LIRMM, Montpellier, France
Jonathan Rose, University of Toronto, Canada
Zoran Salcic, University of Auckland, New Zealand
Hartmut Schmeck, University of Karlsruhe, Germany
John Schewel, Virtual Computer Corporation, USA
Stephen Smith, Quicksilver Technology, USA
Lothar Thiele, ETH Zurich, Switzerland
Kjell Torkelson, Celoxica Ltd, UK
Stephen Trimberger, Xilinx Inc, USA
Ranga Vemuri, University of Cincinnati, USA
Roger Woods, Queen's University of Belfast, UK

Additional Referees

Alfred Blaickner, Carinthia Tech Institute, Austria
Karam Chatha, University of Cincinnati, USA
George Constantinides, Imperial College, UK
Tim Courtney, Queen's University of Belfast, UK
Colin Cowan, Queen's University of Belfast, UK
Oliver Diessel, University of New South Wales, Australia
Rolf Enzler, ETH Zurich, Switzerland
Alberto Garcia-Ortiz, Darmstadt University of Technology, Germany
Thomas Hoffmann, University of Kaiserslautern, Germany
Thomas Hollstein, Darmstadt University of Technology, Germany
Leandro Soares Indrusiak, Darmstadt University of Technology, Germany
Philip James-Roxby, Xilinx Inc, USA
Wen-Ben Jone, University of Cincinnati, USA
Lukusa Didier Kabulepa, Darmstadt University of Technology, Germany
Sang-Seol Lee, Wonkwang University, South Korea
Ralf Ludewig, Darmstadt University of Technology, Germany
Maire McLoone, Queen's University of Belfast, UK
Oskar Mencer, Imperial College, UK
Madhubanti Mukherjee, University of Cincinnati, USA
Takahiro Murooka, NTT, Japan
Kouichi Nagami, NTT, Japan
Brent Nelson, Brigham Young University, USA
Abdulfattah Obeid, Darmstadt University of Technology, Germany
Erwin Ofner, Carinthia Tech Institute, Austria
Iyad Ouaiss, University of Cincinnati, USA
Cameron Patterson, Xilinx Inc, USA
Christian Plessl, ETH Zurich, Switzerland
Thilo Pionteck, Darmstadt University of Technology, Germany
Marco Platzner, ETH Zurich, Switzerland
Philip Power, Queen's University of Belfast, UK
Tanguy Risset, IRISA, Rennes, France
Michel Robert, LIRMM, Montpellier, France
Bernd Scheuermann, University of Karlsruhe, Germany
Sakir Sezer, Queen's University of Belfast, UK
Yuichiro Shibata, Nagasaki University, Japan
Tsunemichi Shiozawa, NTT, Japan
Noriyuki Takahashi, NTT, Japan
Lok Kee Ting, Queen's University of Belfast, UK
Lionel Torres, LIRMM, Montpellier, France
Herbert Walder, ETH Zurich, Switzerland
Mike Wirthlin, Brigham Young University, USA
Peter Zipf, Darmstadt University of Technology, Germany

Michal Servit Award Committee

Wayne Luk, Imperial College, London, UK
Reiner Hartenstein, University of Kaiserslautern, Germany
Gordon Brebner, University of Edinburgh, UK (chair)
Stephen Smith, Quicksilver Technology, USA (sponsor)
Roger Woods, Queen's University of Belfast, UK

Steering Committee

Manfred Glesner, Darmstadt University of Technology, Germany
John Gray, Independent Consultant, UK
Herbert Gruenbacher, Carinthia Tech Institute, Austria
Reiner Hartenstein, University of Kaiserslautern, Germany
Andreas Keevalik, University of Tallin, Estonia
Wayne Luk, Imperial College, London, UK
Patrick Lysaght, University of Strathclyde, UK
Roger Woods, Queen's University of Belfast, UK

Table of Contents

Synthesis

Encryption

Runtime Reconfiguration 1

Graphics and Vision

Invited Keynote 2

Place and Route 2

Networking

Processor Interaction

Applications

Methodology 1

DSP 2

Loops and Systolic

Image Processing

Invited Keynote 3

Runtime Reconfiguration 2

Faults

Methodology 2

Arithmetic

Short Papers 1

Short Papers 2

Technology Trends and Adaptive Computing

Michael J. Flynn and Albert A. Liddicoat

Computer Systems Laboratory,
Department of Electrical Engineering Stanford University,
Gates Building 353 Serra Mall, Stanford, CA 94305, USA
`flynn@ee.stanford.edu` and `liddicoat@stanford.edu`
`http://www.arith.stanford.edu`

Abstract. System and processor architectures depend on changes in technology. Looking ahead as die density and speed increase, power consumption and on chip interconnection delay become increasingly important in defining architecture tradeoffs. While technology improvements enable increasingly complex processor implementations, there are physical and program behavior limits to the usefulness of this complexity at the processor level. The architecture emphasis then shifts to the system: integrating controllers, signal processors, and other components with the processor to achieve enhanced system performance. In dealing with these elements, adaptability or reconfiguration is essential for optimizing system performance in a changing application environment. A hierarchy of adaptation is proposed based on flexible processor architectures, traditional FPL, and a new coarse grain adaptive arithmetic cell. The adaptive arithmetic cell offers high-performance arithmetic operations while providing computational flexibility. The proposed cell offers efficient and dynamic reconfiguration of the arithmetic units. Hybrid fine and coarse grain techniques may offer the best path to the continued evolution of the processor-based system.

1 Introduction

Deep-submicron technology allows billions of transistors on a single die, potentially running at gigahertz frequencies. According to the Semiconductor Industry Association (SIA) projections[1] the number of transistors per die and the local clock frequencies for high-performance microprocessors will continue to grow exponentially over the next decade. Physical constraints and program behavior limit the usefulness of the increased hardware complexity. Physical constraints include interconnect and device limitations as well as power consumption. Program behavior including program control, data dependencies, and unpredictable events, limit the available computational parallelism. Increasing instruction level parallelism and clock rates have met diminishing returns on system performance [2] [3] [4]. Memory access time and bandwidth create a "memory wall"[5] that impedes true system level performance improvements. As systems become more complex the computational integrity of the system becomes increasingly important. Reliability, testability, serviceability, fault diagnosis, process recovery, and fail-safe computation must be reconsidered.

G. Brebner and R. Woods (Eds.): FPL 2001, LNCS 2147, pp. 1–5, 2001.

A systems based approach to architecture is a promising avenue. By integrating controllers and signal processors with a flexible base, processor concurrency can be enhanced while minimizing interconnect limitations. The effectiveness of this system-oriented architecture depends on the adaptability and configurability of the system elements. Reconfiguration at the processor level is an old technology. A write-able control store (WCS) was conceived to add robustness and adaptability to the processor. Using WCS instruction set emulation, adaptable arithmetic operations, diagnostics, and self-test are possible. This form of reconfiguration did not come without a price. The area needed to store microcode was limited and meeting performance objectives with WCS implementations posed a challenge. Additionally, systems themselves provided an obstacle for updating the WCS. Even with the robustness and adaptability WCS ceased being a general application tool and retreated to the special niche of internal processor system support.

More robust forms of adaptability evolved in the meantime. Today, field programmable logic (FPL) is a mature technology with broad applicability. FPL is used for protocol management, matrix operations, cryptography, and for circuit emulation. Some of these more broadly based applications are very similar to those of the WCS technology. But looking ahead FPL is being challenged by technological changes just as WCS was in the past. The SIA predicts that 20 billion transistors per die will be available by 2014. Due to the projected process scaling, die area will be of little concern in the coming decade. As technology scales, interconnect delay and power consumption become the dominant performance limiting constraints. Furthermore, the design emphasis shifts to the system as opposed to the processor. FPL must accommodate these changes to remain the preferred reconfiguration technology.

One critical facet of process scaling is that the interconnect delay does not scale with feature size. If all three dimensions of the interconnect are scaled down by the same scaling factor, the interconnect delay remains roughly unchanged. This is due to the fact that the fringing field component of wire capacitance does not vary with feature size [4]. Thus interconnect delay decreases far less rapidly than gate delay and proves more significant in the deep-submicron region. In an effort to minimize interconnect resistance, typically the interconnect height is scaled at a much slower pace than the interconnect width. Consequently, the aspect ratio rises gradually as process parameters are scaled. The increased aspect ratio reduces the interconnect resistance, but it also increases coupling capacitance from 20% at 0.7 micron to 80% at 0.18 micron. Cross talk between adjacent wires poses a serious problem and the die wire congestion will ultimately determine the interconnect delay and power consumption.

Just as long lines limit memory access time and create a "memory wall" for processors, long global interconnects create an "interconnect wall" for FPL. To avoid this wall we make two observations: 1) many (but certainly not all) FPL system applications are arithmetic intensive, and 2) global interconnects must be minimized.

Arithmetic operations are fundamental to many of the most important commercial and military applications of signal processors, wireless and wired communications processors, and graphics and video oriented processors. Efficient execution of arithmetic operations is fundamental to signal processing and communications.

A hierarchy of adaptable blocks may satisfy the diverse requirements of re-configurable computing. Fine grain re-configurable cells such as those used in field programmable gate arrays (FPGAs) may be used for traditional re-configurable applications. A coarse grain array of adaptive arithmetic cells (AACs) is proposed to advance the execution and reconfiguration performance of signal processing applications. Each AAC consists of a small re-configurable multiplier-type array. By properly configuring the input gates to the multiplier partial product array (PPA), the AAC may be dynamically configured to perform various elementary arithmetic operations such as reciprocal, divide, square root, log, exponentiation, and the trigonometric functions. The execution time of the arithmetic operation is comparable to that of a multiplication operation.

A relatively small number of programmable input gates to the PPA determine the AAC operation. Therefore, the cell's state information may be contained in one large internal register improving the reconfiguration time of the computing element. Additionally, multiple configurations may be stored within each cell allowing for cycle-by-cycle reconfiguration.

2   Adaptive Arithmetic

There are many ways to incorporate flexibility into functional units. At one extreme the functional unit may be implemented using conventional field programmable gate arrays, and at the other extreme application specific integrated circuits (ASICs) might be used. The proposed approach combines aspects from both of these techniques to form a coarse grain adaptive arithmetic cell. The AAC consists of a functional unit that flexibly uses a multiplier array to realize rapid approximations to a broad variety of elementary functions. The approximation precision ranges from 10-20 bits depending on the size of the PPA and the function realized. Schwarz [6] developed the methodology to compute elementary function approximations using a standard multiplier PPA. The approximation theory was based on the work of Stefanelli [7] and Mandelbaum [8] [9]. Additional techniques have been proposed to enhance the precision of the functional approximations[10].

AACs are combined to extend the precision of the initial approximation or to realize composite functions such as polynomial evaluation. Each of the cells operates synchronously at the typical processor cycle time.

These cells are interconnected using a combination of conventional FPGA technology and special neighbor cell interconnections. Neighbor cells should be tightly coupled so that higher-order functional evaluation or extended precision computations may occur with data flow between adjacent cells.

Using a small number of arithmetically robust cells has several advantages. First, the AAC requires only a small amount of state information thus enabling dynamic and efficient reconfiguration with minimal stored information. Secondly, each AAC executes complete multiply-add operations or function approximations at the processor speed. Finally, a small number of robust cells imply increased intra-cell data communication and less inter-cell data communication. Inter-cell data communication requires longer and slower programmable interconnect channels.

Multiplier optimization is an important factor in AAC performance. An exhaustive study of PPA topology was conducted by Al-Twaijry [11]. This work includes a performance analysis based on the physical layout of both planar array structures and tree structures. Furthermore, Al-Twaijry develops a CAD tool to enable optimum placement and routing of counters in a PPA tree in order to produces a multiplier layout with the fastest possible execution time.

Recent research has shown that for any continuous function of x it is possible to realize the function $f(x)$ to n bits of precision with multiple tables requiring much less total area than would be required by a single lookup table with 2^n entries [12] [13] [14] and [15]. These lookup table approaches, while theoretically quite different from the PPA computation, may be combined with the AAC computation to accelerate the convergence of the function approximation.

3   Non-arithmetic Applications

While the multiplier PPA clearly suits most arithmetic intensive applications, its usefulness in non-arithmetic applications is less clear. Surely there remains a central role for the traditional FPGA, although its performance may suffer relatively due to the dominance of the interconnect delay. It may also be possible to broaden the applicability of the PPA structure to at least some non-numeric applications. The basic elements of the counters within the PPA are two exclusive-OR gates and a 2 out of 3 detector. If a storage element is added to the counter, then the generalized array could be configured for match detection (content addressed memory) or even pattern matching. The essential difference of this approach from the FPGA is the dedicated interconnet structure and the more limited internal functional vocabulary. The generalized PPA is an optimization which improves speed at the expense of functionality.

4   Conclusions

Re-configurable computing technologies must be extended beyond current cell limitations to match the expected changes in technology. Interconnect delay is the dominant delay in deep sub-micron technologies. Furthermore, with the ability to design integrated circuits with more than 20 billion transistors, power consumption becomes the limiting constraint after real time performance objectives have been met.

A shift from processor design to system design is evident. The integration of intellectual property brings an important advantage to FPL. Specifically, FPL will play an important role in the areas of system validation, testing, scaling and implementation. System integration requires effective floorplanning and management of the processors and the hierarchy of adaptable blocks.

Adaptive arithmetic cells based on small PPAs can play a useful role in providing flexible functional units that can be re-configured for specific system or application requirements. An ensemble of these cells may be used to improve the precision of the approximations or to compute composite functions. The AAC may be dynamically reconfigured in less than one cycle to perform any of the basic elementary arithmetic functions. Recent and future research that improves the multiplier execution time directly applies to the proposed AAC. The adaptive arithmetic approach increases system performance and flexibility while remaining robust in light of impending technological changes.

References

1. The National Technology Roadmap for Semiconductors, tech report, Semiconductor Industry Association, San Jose, CA, 1997.
2. Dubey, P., and Flynn, M.: "Optimal Pipelining, Parallel and Distributed Computing," Vol. 8, No. 1, January 1990, pp. 10-19.
3. Hung, P., and Flynn, M.: "Optimum ILP for Superscalar and VLIW Processors," tech report, Stanford University, EE Dept., CSL-TR-99-737, 1999
4. Bakoglu, H.: Circuit, Interconnections, and Packaging for VLSI, Addision-Wesley, Reading, Mass., 1990.
5. Wulf W., and McKee S.: "Hitting the Memory Wall: Implications of the Obvious," ACM Computer Architecture News, Vol. 13, No. 1, March 1995, pp. 20-24.
6. Schwarz, E.: High Radix Algorithms for Higher-Order Arithmetic Operations, PhD thesis, Stanford University, January 1993.
7. Stefanelli, R.: "A Suggestion for a High-Speed Parallel Binary Divider," IEEE Trans. on Computers, C-21(1):42:55, January 1972.
8. Mandelbaum, D.: "A Method for Calculation of the Square Root Using Combinatorial Logic," Journal of VLSI Signal Processing, December 1993, pp. 233-243.
9. Mandelbaum, D.: "A Fast, Efficient, Parallel-Acting Method of Generating Functions Defined by Power Series," IEEE Trans. on Parallel and Distributed Systems, January 1996, pp. 33-45.
10. Liddicoat, A., Flynn, M.: "Reciprocal Approximation Theory with Table Compensation," In SPIE's 45th Annual Conference, July 2000.
11. Al-Twaijry, H.: Technology Scaling Effects on Multipliers, PhD thesis, Stanford University, November 1998.
12. DasSarma, D., and Matula, D.: "Faithful Bipartite ROM Reciprocal Tables," In Proc. 12th IEEE Symp. Computer Arithmetic, July 1995, pp. 17-28.
13. DasSarma, D., and Matula, D.: "Faithful Interpolation in Reciprocal Tables," In Proc. 13th IEEE Symp. Computer Arithmetic, July 1997, pp. 82-91.
14. Takagi, N.: "Generating a Power of an Operand by a Table Look-Up and a Multiplication," In Proc. 13th IEEE Symp. Computer Arithmetic, July 1997, pp. 126-131.
15. Takagi, N.: "Powering by a Table Look-Up and a Multiplication with Operand Modification," IEEE Trans. on Computers, C-47(11):1216-1222, November 1998.

Prototyping Framework for Reconfigurable Processors

Sergej Sawitzki[1,2], Steffen Köhler[1], and Rainer G. Spallek[1]

[1] Institute of Computer Engineering
Dresden University of Technology
01062 Dresden, Germany
Phone: +49 351 463-8243, Fax: +49 351 463-8324
{sawitzki,stk,rgs}@ite.inf.tu-dresden.de
[2] Philips Research Laboratories
Prof. Holstlaan 4 (WL01)
5656 AA Eindhoven, The Netherlands
Phone: +31 40 274-2704, Fax: +31 40 274-4639
Sergei.Sawitzki@philips.com

Abstract. During the last decade it has been shown that reconfigurable computing systems are able to compete with their non-reconfigurable counterparts in terms of performance, functional density or power dissipation. A couple of concept and prototyping studies have introduced the reconfigurability within general purpose microprocessor world. This paper introduces a prototyping environment for the design of simple reconfigurable microprocessors. The work differs from the previous approaches in the fact that a systematical way (concerning both hardware and software sides) to design, test and debug a class of reconfigurable computing cores instead of one particular application is discussed. First experiments with a simple 8 bit prototype have shown that the reconfiguration allows performance gains by a factor 2–28 for different applications. The study has discovered some directions for further architectural improvements.

1 Introduction

The idea of hardware reconfigurability within general purpose computing systems has been introduced in early sixties [1]. The availability of the first field-programmable gate arrays (FPGA) in 1985 created a technological base for the practical implementation of such systems. Since that time about one hundred different custom computing machines (CCM) were developed and successfully tested [2]. Some studies have explored the usage of reconfigurable resources within general purpose microprocessors. The basic idea is to combine the flexible and well-known instruction flow oriented programming model with the adaptability of the underlying hardware to achieve performance gains, improve the effectiveness of computation or cost/performance ratio. The spectrum reaches from novel instruction sets and microarchitectures [3,4] to the extensions of the

G. Brebner and R. Woods (Eds.): FPL 2001, LNCS 2147, pp. 6–16, 2001.

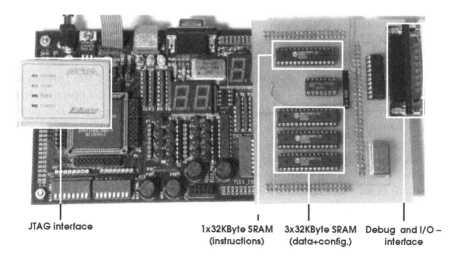

JTAG interface   1x32KByte SRAM   3x32KByte SRAM   Debug and I/O –
                                      (instructions)   (data+config.)   interface

Fig. 1. Prototyping Hardware

commercial processor architectures [5,6]. For a remarkable amount of computational tasks it is possible to achieve sound performance estimates with simulations and prototyping. The prototyping of reconfigurable microprocessors however introduces additional complexity because it is not possible to consider the hardware structure (i.e. instruction set or data path architecture) as given and unchangeable. The prototyping study introduced in this paper attempts to find a systematic approach to design and test of small reconfigurable processor cores.

The rest of this paper is organized as follows. Section 2 discusses different approaches to the integration of reconfigurable resources within modern microprocessors. Section 3 introduces the prototyping concept and environment. Section 4 describes the results achieved. Section 5, finally, draws some conclusions and shows potentials for the further work.

2   Reconfigurable Processors

The design space for the general purpose microprocessors is roughly characterized by two aspects: instruction set architecture (ISA, which is the part of the machine visible to programmer) and hardware structure (implementation and technological aspects interesting for hardware designer). Introducing the reconfigurability to this design space affects both aspects as follows:

– reconfigurable logic must augment the hardwired resources and fit into the existing instruction-flow-driven processing scheme (pipeline, bus structure, interrupt processing etc.) The granularity and the grade of reconfigurability are both implementation and technology dependent

- the communication mechanism between fixed and reconfigurable resources requires special instructions (ISA extensions) or additional features for existing instructions (e.g. memory-mapped or interrupt driven communication)

The analysis of existing concepts suggests that the approach of the ISA extension is more suitable for fine-grained reconfigurable logic which operates synchronously to the global clock. Interrupt driven or memory-mapped communication is usually preferred by the loosely coupled reconfigurable coprocessors. Although the reconfigurability can be applied to nearly every part of the microprocessor core (cache, pipeline, register set, control unit etc.) the most promising results were achieved with flexible data-paths and functional units.

PRISC [5] is an extension to a RISC CPU which uses additional three-address instructions to control the reconfigurable unit. Each reconfigurable instruction has to be accomplished within one clock cycle. The simulations with SPECint benchmark set attest PRISC performance gains of up to 2.5 compared with MIPS processor of similar complexity.

Spyder [4] is a VLIW (128 bit) processor which is able to adapt the structure of its functional units to the different instruction mixes as required by the particular application. The FPGA prototype running at 8 MHz has achieved speed-ups of 3–50 for some algorithms compared to the MicroSPARC clocked at 85 MHz.

Garp [6] introduces the fine-grained reconfigurable extension to the MIPS architecture. The communication is controlled by some special instructions. The communication mechanism allows both global processor clock as well as local reconfigurable array clock to be used for synchronization purposes. Simulations have shown that an 133 MHz Garp implementation would be able to achieve 2–24 times the performance of the 167 MHz UltraSPARC workstation for some encryption, image processing and sorting applications.

Only a few concepts of reconfigurable microprocessors have ever existed as prototypes. This fact can be particulary addressed to the opinion that a complex architecture is required to run the "real-world" applications, so it seems obvious to take an existing commercial implementation and look for the suitable reconfigurable extension for it. Expensive details like cache, large register sets, branch prediction logic etc. however cannot be considered (at least with acceptable effort) within the prototyping environment based on FPGA or CPLD technology, so the simulation is usually the only way to obtain some performance estimates. In many cases, however, prototyping and implementation are possible even with cheaper and less complicated resources.

3   Prototyping Platform

The prototyping of the reconfigurable microprocessors introduces some requirements to the test environment:

Flexibility. The development process often requires frequent changes to the "device under prototyping", the prototyping engine must be able to change the configurations quickly (within several seconds or minutes). This fact sets some constraints to the bandwidth of the reconfiguration and memory interfaces.

Table 1. Communication Protocol

Code	Command
10000000	Reset
10000001	Run
10000010	Stop
10000011	Single step
00000000	Get status info
01000000	Register write
01000001	Program counter write
01000010	Data memory write
01000011	Instruction memory write
00100000	Register read
00010000	Program counter read low byte
00010001	Program counter read high byte
00001000	Data memory read
00000100	Instruction memory read low byte
00000101	Instruction memory read middle byte
00000110	Instruction memory read high byte

Scalability. The amount of logic resources in middle-range FPGA devices does not yet suffice for the implementation of wide (32 or 64 bit) data-paths. For this reason the system must allow accurate performance estimates for processors with wider data-paths based on the data for 8, 12 or 16 bit.

Observability. The current state of the processor must be visible for both hardwired and reconfigurable part. Due to this fact, a hardware interface with additional registers and a software protocol to control this interface are required.

Multi-FPGA engines like RPM [7] and Transmogrifier-2 [8] are usually used for the prototyping of complex digital systems. Such engines consist of several FPGA or CPLD devices, communication chips, dedicated SRAM and DRAM modules, clock management and interfacing circuitry. The main disadvantage of these boards (in addition to the fact that they are very expensive) is the necessity to split the design over several reconfigurable chips. For the prototyping of embedded cores a single-FPGA board suffices in most cases. For this work Altera's UP1 Education Board [9] was chosen as the basic equipment because of the low cost and high performance of FLEX 10K FPGA family known from previous projects. The UP1 board uses JTAG interface to configure the FLEX10K20 FPGA from the host workstation (alternatively, the configuration can be read from the on-board PROM). Unfortunately, UP1 does not provide any on-board memory except 12 KBit embedded RAM within FLEX10K20 memory cells. For this reason, a dedicated daughter card with 4x32 KByte SRAM was developed. Although JTAG could be used as debugging interface for the circuitry implemented with FPGA, it is unable to control the SRAM, so an extended capability port (ECP) interface was integrated on the daughter card and is used for debugging and control purposes reducing the role of JTAG to configuration download.

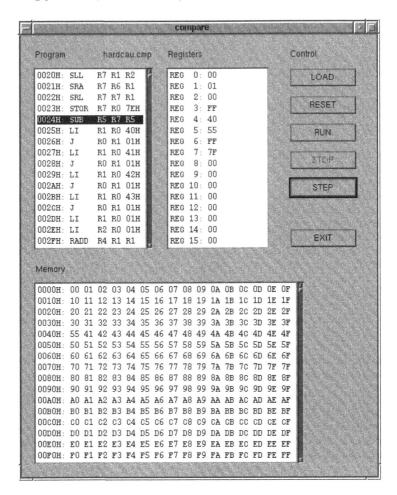

Fig. 2. Graphical User Interface

Another minor change to the board structure was an additional exchangeable clock oscillator (basically only one oscillator operating at 25 MHz is provided on-board). Fig. 1 shows the hardware part of the prototyping environment.

The corresponding software environment is running on the host workstation providing all functions required to control the execution and the system state. A dedicated graphical user interface (GUI, Fig. 2) provides following functionality:

– reset the system to the initial state
– download program code and data to the SRAM memory. All information to be downloaded is coded in hexadecimal and can be stored in ASCII format as shown below:

Table 2. Example Instruction Set

Fixed Instr.	Meaning	Reconf. Instr.	Meaning
ADD	Addition	MADD	Multiply then Add
AND	Bitwise And	MSUB	Multiply then Subtract
BE	Branch on Equal	ADSU	Add and Subtract
BL	Branch On Less Than	SADD	Shift then Add
BLU	Branch On Less Than Unsigned	SSUB	Shift then Subtract
COMP	Binary Complement	ADDC	Add then Compare
J	Jump	MULA	Multiply then Add
LI	Load Immediate	MUMU	Multiply and Multiply
LOAD	Load	ADAD	Add and Add
NOR	Bitwise Nor		
SLL	Shift Left Logical		
SRA	Shift Right Arithmetic		
SRL	Shift Right Logical		
STOR	Store		
SUB	Subtraction		
XNOR	Bitwise Xnor		

```
# Instruction memory section
# Format: I<i-mem address>:<instr-code>
I0000:05005    # LI R5,5
I0001:06006    # LI R6,6
I0002:07007    # LI R7,7
I0003:80177    # ADD R1,R7,R7
I0004:88265    # AND R2,R6,R5
# Data memory section
# Format: D<d-mem address>:<data word>
D0040:55
D4101:0A
```

This file can be created manually or using a retargetable assembler tool
 – execute the program either until termination or in single-step mode. It is
   possible to define the breakpoints within the program for debugging

The GUI uses a dedicated protocol to communicate with the prototyping hardware via the ECP interface. Table 1 summarizes the commands of this protocol. This set sufficed for the test examples discussed below, however, it is easily extendable. Despite the relatively poor bandwidth of the ECP interface, it is possible to read all necessary status information of the system (program counter, register and memory values) within several microseconds, so no appreciable response delays could be notified even while working in the single-step mode. Overall, the chosen hardware platform incorporates several thousands programmable logic gates, RAM, adaptable clock oscillators and a possibility to interface with external I/O channels via daughter card. Augmented by the control and interaction features of the software environment it provides simple but yet powerful framework for the experimentation with embedded reconfigurable processor cores.

4   Experimental Results

The CoMPARE processor was chosen as a test example to obtain some preliminary results. CoMPARE is a RISC-like architecture with a reconfigurable extension that maintains close compatibility with the conventional programming model. To simplify the design neither caches nor FPU and only 16 instructions and 16 registers on 8 bit wide, three-stage-pipelined datapaths are considered. CoMPARE uses a reconfigurable processing unit (RPU), which is a conventional ALU augmented by a look-up-table (LUT) based configurable array unit (CAU) used to implement additional, customized instructions. The hardwired instructions in the ALU are always available, but it only needs to provide the most basic instructions (Table 2, left). Additional operations useful to accelerate different applications are provided by the CAU. It has been shown, that about 10 such reconfigurable instructions (Table 2, right) suffice to improve the performance of a broad application range (cryptography, data compression, digital signal processing, simulation) by the factor of 2–28. The details of the CoMPARE microarchitecture together with RPU schematics can be found in [10].

To get the prototype running on FLEX10K FPGA, the VHDL behavioural model was rewritten in Altera Hardware Description Language (AHDL) and synthesized within Altera MAX+plus II CAD environment. Since the register file is the most logic consuming part of the design, the amount of general purpose registers was reduced from 16 to 8 for the prototyping purposes. Two different concepts were tested for the CAU:

– using embedded array blocks (EAB) provided by the FLEX10K as LUTs. The EABs can be read and written word-wise during the circuit operation providing the ideal base to test the dynamic reconfiguration. The only limitation for the complexity of the reconfigurable operations in this case is the amount of memory available (12 KBit). By organizing memory into different logical pages it is possible to use several configurations contexts simultaneously.
– providing the "hardwired" CAU for each application. In this case, the circuitry to be implemented in the CAU is the part of the AHDL processor description and (once the synthesis run is complete) cannot be changed. Thus, adapting the processor to another application means downloading a completely new FPGA configuration.

10 reconfigurable custom instructions (Table 2) were implemented in both ways discussed above. Although the first approach stands for more flexibility and lower reconfiguration times (about 100 ns are required to exchange one word of the

configuration context), the second one is usually achieving better timing performance. This can be easily explained by the fact, that EAB access time is a constant value in the first case whereby different subcircuits for the "hardwired" CAU are involved within global netlist optimization process and can reduce the critical path of the whole design in the second case. The highest clock rate (about 12 MHz) were achieved with the MADD instruction, on average, the prototype has achieved the clock rate of 10 MHz with approximately 2 W power dissipation (nearly 50% caused by the SRAM). Using FPGA of higher speed grade and hand-tuning some design units would probably allow to achieve the performance of 20 MHz. Following computational kernels were successfully tested and confirmed the simulation data obtained with VHDL behavioral model:

FFT. The butterfly computation (basic operation of the fast Fourier transform, FFT) consists of several multiplications, additions and subtractions which can be partially executed in parallel. Such instructions are implemented in several digital signal processors (DSP) as single cycle instructions to accelerate such algorithmic cores [11] and can easily be implemented by the RPU. 3 extended instructions MADD, MSUB, and ADSU (Multiply then Add, Multiply then Subtract, and Add and Subtract respectively) were used to accelerate the execution by a factor of 28.

Arithmetic coding. According to the compression ratio, arithmetic coding provides better results than the better known Huffman encoding. The corresponding algorithm however is computationally intensive, requiring many additions, multiplications and bit shift operations to be executed for each character from the input data stream. Executing two additions and two multiplications in parallel combined with shifting allows to achieve speedup by a factor of nearly 20.

Neural nets simulation. During the computer simulation of (already trained) artificial neural networks the simulator has to compute the activation and output functions of all neurons. A sum of weighted input values has to be compared with the activation value for each neuron in every time step. Acceleration of several orders of magnitude are achievable by massively parallel execution on systems implementing neurons in hardware (like the FPGA board described in [12]). Some CAU instructions for the sum of products computation improve the simulation performance by a factor of at least 17.

Image dilatation. Many image processing filters includes computational masks which are applied to the each pixel of the image. Dilatation filter applies boolean operations to the pixels adjacent to one for which the "filtered" value should be produced. By defining reconfigurable instructions, which can compute several pixels in parallel, it is possible to achieve speedup by a factor of 3.

The experimental results suggest that CoMPARE achieves 2–4 the performance of the MIPS R2000. The performance gain through the usage of the CAU (compared to the similar embedded core without CAU) falls into the range of 2–28. Table 3 summarizes the synthesis results for different design units (LC stands for logic cell, which consists of one 4-bit look-up-table and one flipflop with some additional logic, e.g. preset, carry chain etc.) The communication and debugging interface consumes about 14% of the logic resources which seems much at the

Table 3. Cell complexity of the prototype

Design Unit	LC count	
	"stand-alone" synthesis	% of FLEX10K20
Fetch and Decode Unit (FDU)	119	10
Register file	364	32
Load and Store Unit (LSU)	35	3
Arithmetic and Logic Unit (ALU)	192	17
Datapath Control Unit (DCU)	54	5
Configurable Array Unit (CAU)	max. 226	max. 19
Debugging Interface	162	14

first glance. Considering the fact that FLEX10K20 is one of the smallest devices in the family, however, this effort does not have to be treated as critical. The advantages of this debugging concept overcompensate its logic consumption:

- once implemented and tested, the communication interface allows to find and eliminate the design errors more efficiently than simulation runs
- testing new custom instructions becomes impossible without the detailed information provided by the communication protocol. Conventional processors allows detailed simulations and tests with each instruction and (theoretically) all possible short instruction sequences, so at least side-effects caused by timing hazards and pipelining can be minimized. The instruction set of a reconfigurable microprocessor however can depend on the particular application so the debugging interface as one described above proves to be much more reliable
- extendable concept leaves enough room for future extensions

The basic disadvantage of the most FPGA architectures is the fact that the routing channels perform poor with bit-parallel data paths, so a couple of wires have to be routed "around the chip" decreasing the overall timing performance.

5   Conclusions and Further Work

This work has introduced a systematical approach to development and prototyping of simple reconfigurable microprocessors. A low-cost prototyping environment featuring Altera UP1 board with dedicated daughter card and corresponding software were used to build and test an 8-bit microprocessor core and evaluate two different concepts of the reconfigurability. The results suggest that custom instructions which use reconfigurable resources improve the performance of the processor core by the factor of 2–28. Keeping the core simple (e.g. omitting cache, out-of-order and similar techniques) still provides acceptable performance at lower cost and leaves some space for other architectural improvements.

Currently, an 12-bit version of the CoMPARE core is under development. Extending the data path by 4 bits will allow some real-time sound processing applications to be tested to compare the performance of the prototype with commercial digital signal processors. Hand-tuning the most timing-critical design units (CAU and debugging interface) should improve the performance of the prototype. The implementation of a new instruction set architecture targeting signal processing domain will be the next test example for the prototyping environment. The study has shown some limitations which should be considered in case of future improvements:

- logic resources of FLEX10K20 circuit do not suffice for more complex designs, so a larger FPGA should be considered
- ECP interface provides enough bandwidth for prototyping and debugging purposes. For computational intensive or real-time tasks, however, more powerful communication concept (e.g. compact PCI) should be considered
- "hardwired" processor core consumes reconfigurable resources of the FPGA which could be used for custom computing. New circuits like Atmel's FP-SLIC [13] which combines a microcontroller core and an FPGA on a single chip seem promising for the further studies

In the nearest future, a retargetable assembler tool we be completed to simplify the programming of the "processors under test". A concept of the compiler to support reconfigurable microprocessors based on the SUIF kit [14] is currently under development. The completion of these software tools will round up the prototyping environment and allow advanced experiments with different reconfigurable architectures.

References

1. G. Estrin. Organization of computer systems: The fixed plus variable structure computer. In *Proceedings of the Western Joint Computer Conference*, pages 33–40, New York, 1960. American Institute of Electrical Engineers.
2. S. A. Guccione. List of FPGA-based computing machines. http://www.io.com/~guccione/HW_list.html, Last Update March 1999, 1999.
3. M. Wirthlin, B. Hutchings, and K. Gilson. The Nano processor: A low resource reconfigurable processor. In D. Buell and K. Pocek, editors, *Proceedings of FCCM'94*, pages 23–30, Napa, CA, April 1994. IEEE.
4. C. Iseli. *Spyder: A Reconfigurable Processor Development System*. PhD thesis, Département d'Informatique, École Polytechnique de Lausanne, 1996.
5. R. Razdan. *PRISC: Programmable Reduced Instruction Set Computers*. PhD thesis, Harvard University, Cambridge, Massachusetts, May 1994.
6. J. Hauser and J. Wawrzynek. Garp: A MIPS processor with a reconfigurable coprocessor. In J. Arnold and K. Pocek, editors, *Proceedings of FCCM'97*, pages 24–33, Napa, CA, April 1997. IEEE.
7. P. Barroso, S. Iman, J. Jeong, K. Öner, M. Dubois, and K. Ramamurthy. RPM: a rapid prototyping engine for multiprocessor systems. *IEEE Computer*, (28):26–34, February 1995.
8. D. Lewis, D. Galloway, M. van Ierssel, J. Rose, and P. Chow. The Transmogrifier-2: A 1 million gate rapid prototyping system. In *In Proceedings of ACM Symposium on FPGAs*, pages 53–61, Monterey, CA, February 1997. ACM.

9. Altera Corporation. *University Program Design Laboratory Package User Guide*, August 1997. Version 1.
10. S. Sawitzki, A. Gratz, and R. Spallek. CoMPARE: A simple reconfigurable processor architecture exploiting instruction level parallelism. In K.A.Hawick and J.A.Heath, editors, *Proceedings of the 5th Australasian Conference on Parallel and Real-Time Systems (PART'98)*, pages 213–224, Berlin Heidelberg New York, 1998. Springer-Verlag.
11. Hyperstone Electronics GmbH. *Hyperstone E1-32/E1-16. 32-Bit-Microprocessor User's Manual*, 1997. Revision 03/97.
12. J. Eldredge and B. Hutchings. Density enhancement of a neural network using FPGAs and run-time reconfiguration. In K. Pocek and J. Arnold, editors, *Proceedings of FCCM'94*, pages 180–188, Napa, CA, April 1994. IEEE.
13. Atmel Corporation. *AT94K Series Field Programmable System Level Integrated Circuit Advance Information*, 1999. Revision 1138B-12/99.
14. C. Wilson. *The SUIF Guide*. Stanford University, 1998.

An Emulator for Exploring RaPiD Configurable Computing Architectures*

Chris Fisher, Kevin Rennie, Guanbin Xing, Stefan G. Berg, Kevin Bolding,
John Naegle, Daniel Parshall, Dmitriy Portnov, Adnan Sulejmanpasic, Carl Ebeling

Department of Computer Science and Engineering
University of Washington
Box 352350
Seattle, WA 98195-2350

Abstract. The RaPiD project at the University of Washington has been studying configurable computing architectures optimized for coarse-grained data and computation units and deep computation pipelines. This research targets applications in the signal and image-processing domain since they make the greatest demand for computation and power in embedded and mobile computing applications, and these demands are increasing faster than Moore's law. This paper describes the RaPiD Emulator, a system that will allow the exploration of alternative configurable architectures in the context of benchmark applications running in real-time. The RaPiD emulator provides enough FPGA gates to implement large RaPiD arrays, along with a high-performance streaming memory architecture and high-bandwidth data interfaces to a host processor and external devices. Running at 50 MHz, the emulator is able to achieve over 1 GMACs/second.

1 Introduction

The explosion of mobile and embedded applications has sparked interest in configurable computing as a way to achieve high performance with low power consumption at a reasonable cost. The performance and power consumption demands of these applications is growing faster than the rate of improvement in technology as described by Moore's law. The RaPiD project has been exploring a configurable computing architecture called RaPiD (Reconfigurable Pipelined Datapath) that is optimized for the domain of signal and image processing. The goal of RaPiD architectures is to attain the highest performance for the lowest cost and power by taking advantage of the characteristics of this application domain. As such, RaPiD attains performance closer to that of ASICs than traditional FPGA-based computing, but retains sufficient flexibility to be able to perform a wide range of computations common in signal processing.

The RaPiD architecture leverages several key attributes of this domain of application. RaPiD is optimized for arithmetic operations over data values comprising

---

* This research was supported by the National Science Foundation Experimental Systems Program (EIA-9901377)

G. Brebner and R. Woods (Eds.): FPL 2001, LNCS 2147, pp. 17-26, 2001.

many bits. There is tremendous saving to using compute units optimized for the word length used by the computation. The RaPiD datapath supports deep pipelining to achieve a high degree of parallelism. Systolic algorithms in particular are well suited to the RaPiD architecture. The RaPiD datapath implements I/O using multiple, independent data streams. These streams are either connected directly to external streaming devices, or to a streaming memory system. Finally, RaPiD takes advantage of the regular, repetitive nature of computations in this domain to generate the datapath control signals via a very efficient configurable control path.

In earlier papers, we described the performance and cost of the RaPiD architecture and the programming model used to program applications [1, 2]. Our studies show that RaPiD can achieve performance of over 1.5 billion multiply/accumulate operations/second for a number of important applications using a moderately sized array running at 100MHz.

We have thus far relied on simulations to study the RaPiD architecture and while these are useful for developing compilation tools and applications and for preliminary performance analyses, they do not replace "real iron" for providing a proof of concept. Many architectures that make sense on paper turn out to have many unforeseen problems when actually constructed. The next step was to construct an experimental RaPiD system as a proof of concept of the architecture. Although we had originally thought to implement RaPiD using semi-custom VLSI, we decided instead to build an emulator for two reasons.

First, it became clear that RaPiD arrays would be used as components of large systems on a chip. For example, in a mobile device, the RaPiD array would handle the demanding parts of the applications such as the radio front end and image compression/decompression while other components would handle the more complex, but computationally less demanding parts of the application. Such a RaPiD component would be customized to the set of computations required by the system as a whole.

By building a fixed RaPiD array, we would be precluded from experimenting with and demonstrating the effectiveness of different versions of the RaPiD architecture customized to different sets of applications. Although the "general-purpose" RaPiD array that we defined as part of our earlier work was applicable to a range of different computations, customization increases the applicability of the RaPiD architecture by the ability to incorporate specialized functional units and customize the data widths, bus structure and other parameters of the architecture. An emulator for the RaPiD architecture allows us to explore and demonstrate customized versions of the RaPiD array for different applications.

Second, building a fixed implementation of the RaPiD architecture would effectively freeze the architecture and keep us from trying out new ideas. As we understand the strengths and weaknesses of the architecture, we want to explore ways to improve it. In particular, RaPiD has a very optimized control architecture that allows it to drive thousands of control signals from a 32-bit instruction. This efficiency costs RaPiD some flexibility. For example, in cases where the components must be time-multiplexed to implement a large dataflow graph, the control may exceed the 32-bit instruction size. With an emulator, we can build a demonstration system as a proof of concept, and continue to develop the RaPiD architecture at the same time with no deadline for incorporating new ideas into the system.

2 The RaPiD Datapath Architecture

A typical RaPiD datapath contains hundreds of functional units, ranging in complexity from simple registers to multipliers, barrel shifters and memories. These functional units are arranged linearly, as shown in Fig.1, and connected together using configurable interconnect based on segmented buses. Both the functional units and the buses in this configurable architecture are word-based instead of bit-based. Although the linear structure of the architecture may appear to be limiting, there is a wealth of research that shows how to map multidimensional algorithms to linear arrays [3, 4, 5] if memories are embedded in the datapath to hold an extra dimension of data.

Each functional unit receives data values from selected buses in the configurable interconnect, performs a computation specified by a set of control signals, and outputs results in the form of data values and status bits. For example, an ALU receives two data words from two selected buses in the interconnect, performs the arithmetic or logical instruction specified by the control, and writes the result to another selected bus. The status outputs allow for data-dependent control to be generated. For example, the zero status bit could be used to select one of two values to be stored in a register.

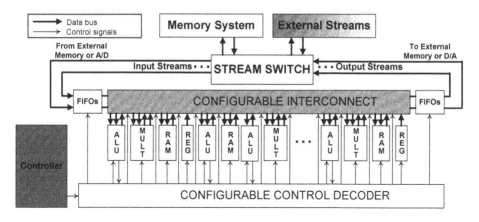

Fig. 1. Overall structure of a RaPiD architecture

A variety of functional units can be included in a RaPiD architecture. General-purpose functional units like ALUs, multipliers, shifters, and memories are the most common, but for specific domains, a special-purpose functional unit that performs a single function (i.e. has no control inputs) might make the most efficient use of silicon. For other domains, a highly configurable functional unit might be the right choice. For example, a functional unit could be constructed of FPGA-like logic blocks to support bit-oriented computations like those found in encryption algorithms. Memories within the datapath provide space for temporary variables, constant tables, and configurable-length delay lines. Like other functional units, memories have control inputs that govern read/write and address selection.

The configurable interconnect consists of a set of segmented buses that run along the entire length of the datapath. Some bus segments are connected by bus connectors that can be configured to connect adjacent segments into longer segments, with optional pipelining. All buses have the same width, which matches the data width operated on by the functional units. Each input to a functional unit selects one of the buses in the interconnect using a multiplexor that is operated by a set of control signals. Data outputs are driven onto buses selected by control signals.

The operation of the RaPiD datapath is determined by control signals that determine what operations each functional unit performs and how data is routed by the configurable interconnect between the functional units. The setting of the entire set of control bits for one clock cycle is called a *datapath instruction* and a RaPiD program sequences through a series of datapath instructions to perform the desired computation. A typical RaPiD datapath contains on the order of 100 functional units, requiring more than 5000 control signals to specify the operation of the function units and to route data through the interconnect.

Perhaps the most challenging problem posed by configurable architectures is generating the control signals driving the computational datapath. The high degree of parallelism combined with configurability results in a large number of potential control signals. Generating and driving these control signals at datapath clock rates is extremely expensive both in area and power. RaPiD solves this problem by dividing the control signals into *hard* and *soft* control signals. The hard control signals are traditional configuration signals provided by distributed static RAM cells that are changed only infrequently when the architecture is reconfigured for a different application. Hard control determines the underlying datapath structure that does not change.

Soft control signals in contrast potentially change every clock cycle as directed by a control program. RaPiD takes advantage of the highly correlated nature of the control signals and uses an efficient decoding structure to generate hundreds of soft control signals from a 32-bit instruction. The compiler configures an instruction format for each application to provide the most efficient encoding of the soft control signals. Soft control signals can also incorporate status signals generated in the datapath to implement data-dependent operations such as maximum and absolute value.

RaPiD is programmed using a programming language called RaPiD-C that is specialized for pipelined, parallel algorithms. RaPiD-C programs are compiled into configuration bit-files and controller programs by the process described in Fig.2. The compiler analyzes the RaPiD-C program, partitioning it into a datapath that performs the data operations and a control program, which generates the control signals that operate the datapath. RaPiD-C programs use a zero-delay model to simplify the problem of describing a parallel computation. In this model communication and operations take zero time so that arbitrarily many operations can be chained in a single clock cycle. For example, sixteen numbers can be added together using 15 adders in one cycle. The pipelining and retiming phase adds sufficient registers to meet clock frequency constraints. Finally, the resulting netlist is placed and routed onto the RaPiD data and control path.

To support the emulation system, the tool flow was augmented by the blocks highlighted in Fig.2. First the datapath netlist is partitioned over multiple FPGAs, producing a netlist for each one. The programmer specifies the partitioning by indicating which pipeline stages are to be placed in each chip. Since nets that pass between chips must have at least one register to maintain high-speed operation (50 Mhz) the partitioner adds a dummy element that adds a minimum register constraint to the nets that cross chip boundaries. The retimer automatically places the necessary number of registers to these nets. The resulting netlist is split at these registers into the netlists for each FPGA, which are placed and routed using the usual Xilinx tools.

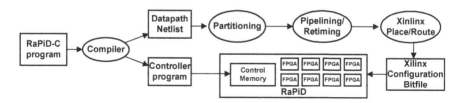

Fig. 2. CAD tool flow for compiling programs to the RaPiD Emulator

3 The RaPiD Emulator

The emulation system contains two boards: a StrongArm development board[8] that serves as a host, and the custom RaPiD emulation board. The emulation board contains 13 Xilinx Virtex FPGAs[7], nine of which are used to emulate the RaPiD datapath, two for a stream-based SDRAM memory subsystem, and one each for a stream switch and control generator. Fig. 3 shows a structural diagram of the major chips on our board.

The emulator datapath is sized to accommodate a 32-cell RaPiD datapath with each cell containing one multiplier, three ALUs, three memories, and six datapath registers. Although the computational elements are easily accommodated by the FPGAs, the configurable interconnect, comprising 14 16-bit busses and 4000 tri-state drivers, is too expensive to implement directly.   Instead, only the interconnect used by an application is configured into the datapath.   This maintains all the dynamic multiplexing of the interconnect, but eliminates the buses that are not used by the application and all the tristate drivers. The routing of the application onto the RaPiD configurable interconnect must be performed independently to validate its feasibility.

Fig.3 shows how the elements of the RaPiD architecture in Fig.1 are implemented on the emulator using the shading from Fig.1 for reference. The RaPiD datapath is partitioned across eight Virtex XCV300 parts, each of which can emulate four typical RaPiD cells. The Control Generator, comprising four parallel programmed controllers, is mapped to a single Virtex part that sends datapath instructions to Datapath Switch Interface. The Datapath Switch Interface chip contains the interface between the datapath and all the control and data streams. It is also responsible for stalling the datapath if any input stream is empty or if any output stream is full.

The clock on the emulation board has sixteen settings ranging from 4Mhz-100Mhz. The printed circuit board has ten controlled impedance signal planes with fourteen total layers. All significant signals were designed with the goal of 100Mhz operation, although the actual maximum speed that the emulator will achieve is probably closer to 50Mhz due to a combination of the control generator design complexity and our FPGAs' speed-grade. Fig. 5 shows a photograph of the emulation board.

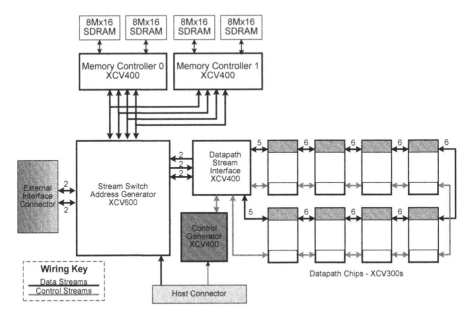

Fig. 3. RaPiD Emulator Board

The host for the emulation system is a StrongArm development board from Intel. The host board contains a 220Mhz SA-1100 StrongArm processor with 32 MB of DRAM. The emulation board is connected to the StrongArm via the Xbus, which is a buffered version of the StrongArm's memory bus and runs about 10 million 32-bit transactions per second, or approximately 40MB/sec. The Xbus is connected to three chips on the emulator board: the Stream Switch, the Control Generator, and the Configuration CPLD. There are three different logical interfaces from the StrongArm to the emulator board, all implemented using memory-mapped registers: a configuration interface, a debug interface, and a data interface.

The configuration interface is divided into two sections: FPGA configuration and RaPiD System configuration. FPGA configuration can be done two ways: From the StrongArm over the Xbus using the Configuration CPLD, or from a PC via the JTAG port in conjunction with the Xilinx Parallel Download Cable. Configuring all 13 FPGAs takes 2½ minutes using the JTAG port but only 1/2 second using the Xbus interface. The RaPiD System is configured by writing directly to memory and registers in the emulation components which are all mapped into the StrongArm address space.

The debug interface is implemented using specially designed Debug FIFOs, which can be halted and single stepped. The data at the head of these FIFOs is also available through the debug interface. The system is debugged by single stepping the FIFOs and examining the data as it flows through the system.

The host data interface allows the host to source or sink data streams connected to Xbar, as well as read and write the memory system on the emulation board. The StrongArm can read/write data streams at the rate of two 16-bit words per Xbus transaction.

3.1 Streaming Memory System

A high-performance computing platform can succeed only if coupled with a high-bandwidth memory system. The RaPiD architecture requires a sustained data bandwidth of up to three data values per cycle, and this is provided by the emulation board using four interleaved SDRAM modules, each of which can provide one access per cycle for same-page data accesses. For most memory access patterns, these four memory modules can provide an average of over three accesses per cycle.

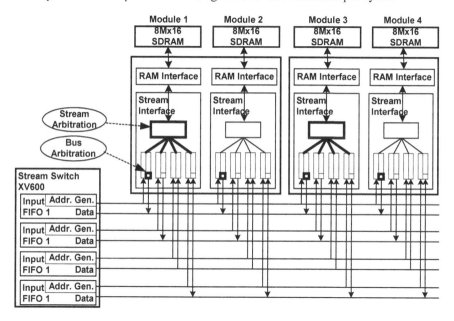

Fig. 4. Architecture of the streaming memory system

All access to the memory is provided by four streams, which are configurably connected to the datapath through the Stream Switch Chip. Each memory stream has an address and data stream: The address stream is generated by an address generator programmed to implement the address patterns described in a RaPiD-C program. For read streams, the address stream is sent to memory and the data is returned via the data stream and delivered to the datapath. For write streams, the address stream is sent to memory along with the data stream. Two of the four memory streams are read streams, one is a write stream and one is configured as either a read or write stream.

Fig.4 shows how the four streams are connected to the memory system. Each stream is connected to all four memory modules and each address sent to memory is consumed by the module specified by that address. These addresses are queued up within the module and presented to the SDRAM interface. Since each memory module is connected to all four streams, the Stream Interface must arbitrate between the addresses from each stream. This arbitration gives priority to addresses that reference a page that is already open, but ensures that no stream is starved. Data returned by a read is the queued up for transfer back to the originating stream using a data bus that is shared by all the memory modules. Arbitration of this data bus is necessary to prevent collisions between memory words that are returned from the different modules. This arbitration is more difficult than the SDRAM arbitration, because the memory modules are distributed and operate independently.

This arbitration is performed using placeholders to keep track of read transactions that are being processed by other memory modules. For example, let us assume that addresses A1, A2 and A3 are generated by one of the read input streams and that the data for A1 and A3 are stored on Module 1, whereas the data for A2 is stored on Module 2. The Stream Interface on Module 1 will internally store A1, *, A3 as the sequence of memory transactions to process for the read input stream and the Stream Interface on Module 2 will store *, A2, *, where * denotes a placeholder for a transaction processed on another Stream Interface. After the Stream Interface on Module 1 has returned A1 on the data bus, it knows because of the placeholder that another module will use the bus to return the next data value. After data has been returned by Module 2 for A2, which Module 1 can see by snooping the data bus, Module 1 knows that it is its turn to return data for A3. These placeholders are an efficient distributed mechanism that avoids any explicit bus arbitration because every module knows on every cycle whether or not it owns the bus. This mechanism also ensures that the input data is returned in the same order as the requests.

A special memory test was configured into the Stream Switch FPGA to verify the correctness and performance of the memory system. Correctness was tested using a set of worst-case memory access patterns that stressed the arbitration logic of the stream interfaces and the steam queues. In this test, all four streams were active simultaneously and shared the entire address space. These tests run for several hours, reading and writing each of the 32 million memory locations thousands of times, using a variety of address and data patterns.

The second phase of the memory test measured the performance of the memory system using different access patterns. These tests show that streaming accesses of unit stride achieve a bandwidth of .97 accesses per cycle, if there is little or no contention. That is, if the four streams are allocated to different memory modules, a total bandwidth of 3.88 accesses per cycle is achieved. If either the stride or contention is increased, the bandwidth decreases gradually as page crossings in the SDRAM increase. Although we have yet to perform a comprehensive performance analysis of the memory system for complex patterns, our preliminary tests confirm that for common data access patterns for linear and two-dimensional data structures, the streaming memory system should deliver the required data bandwidth of an average of 3 accesses per cycle.

3.2 Streaming Data Interface

All data is communicated within the RaPiD architecture via data streams. These streams are buffered using small FIFOs wherever there may be a stall, for example at the memory interface or the input/output streams of the RaPiD datapath. These FIFOs have little affect on performance since performance is affected mostly by throughput and not latency. The streams use an asynchronous communications protocol for flow-control based on two signals: DataValid and TakingData. The sender asserts DataValid whenever valid data exists on its output. The receiver asserts TakingData on any cycle when it can accept a new piece of data. Data is actually transferred on a cycle only if both DataValid and TakingData are asserted. The advantage of this protocol is that there is no round trip communication.

The primary responsibility of the Stream Switch is to connect together data streams from four places: the host processor, the data path, the memory system and an external interface. This external interface allows data streams produced by devices like cameras and A/Ds to be connected directly to the RaPiD array via a connector.

Data streams are routed through the Xbar switch with a standard cross bar architecture. The host processor configures connections by sending instructions to the crossbar control that indicate the source, the destination, and the desired state of the connection (e.g. connected, disconnected, enabled, disabled). Logic in the control unit interprets the instruction and updates a register table that contains the status of all connections in the system. The Xbar switch in turn uses the data contained in the register table to route the data. The registers are memory mapped and can be read as status information by the host processor for debugging purposes.

4 Project Status

The RaPiD emulator board is now operational and the first RaPiD application, a simple FIR filter, was recently compiled and executed on the emulator. The next step is to port other applications to the emulator, including an multi-antenna OFDM modem demonstration system and a passive atmospheric radar application. At the same time, we are beginning to extend our tools to allow the generation of custom RaPiD arrays and are investigating alternative control structures for more flexible operation.

References

1. Ebeling, C. and Cronquist, D. C. and Franklin, P. and Berg, S., "Mapping applications to the RaPiD configurable architecture", Field-Programmable Custom Computing Machines (FCCM-97), April 1997, pp. 106-15.
2. Darren C. Cronquist, Paul Franklin, Chris Fisher, Miguel Figueroa, and Carl Ebeling. "Architecture Design of Reconfigurable Pipelined Datapaths," Twentieth Anniversary Conference on Advanced Research in VLSI, 1999.
3. Kung, H. T. "Let's design algorithms for VLSI systems". Tech Report CMU-CS-79-151, Carnegie-Mellon University, January, 1979.
4. Moldovan, D. I. and Fortes, J. A. B., "Partitioning and mapping algorithms into fixed size systolic arrays", IEEE Transactions on Computers, 1986, pp.1-12.
5. Lee, P. and Kedem, Z. M., "Synthesizing linear array algorithms from nested FOR loop algorithms", IEEE Transactions on Computers, 1988, pp.1578-98.

Fig. 5. Photograph of the RaPiD emulator board. The board is shown about 1/3 scale.

6. Gold, B. and Bially, T., "Parallelism in fast Fourier transform hardware", IEEE Transactions on Audio and Electroacoustics, vol. AU-21 no.1, Feb. 1973, pp. 5-16.
7. Xilinx. "Virtex and Virtex-E Overview."
   http://www.xilinx.com/xlnx/xil_prodcat_product.jsp?title=ss_vir (16 Mar. 2001).
8. Intel. "StrongARM SA-110 Multimedia Development Board with Companion SA-1101 Developement Board". Order Number: 278253-001 Jan. 1999. ftp://download.intel.com/design/strong/datashts/27825301.pdf (16 Mar. 2001).

A New Placement Method for Direct Mapping into LUT-Based FPGAs

Joerg Abke and Erich Barke

Institute of Microelectronic Circuits and Systems,
University of Hannover, Appelstr. 4,
D-30167 Hannover, Germany
{abke, barke}@ims.uni-hannover.de,
http://www.ims.uni-hannover.de/~abke

Abstract. In this paper, we present a new placement method which provides short implementation times for today's high capacity FPGAs within a direct mapping environment. We show that using additional component information is beneficial for faster logic block placement. The new placement method reduces the placer's run time by taking the module in- and output interconnections into account.

1 Introduction

Within the last decade, **F**ield-**P**rogrammable **G**ate **A**rrays (FPGAs) evolved to high performance devices which address a wide range of applications. These include the substitution of Application Specific Integrated Circuits as well as tools for functional design verification [5], [8] and rapid prototyping [10]. Despite the tremendous success of FPGAs, the demand for short implementation times and fast verification cycles becomes more and more critical due to increasing design complexity [2].

Traditional implementation techniques as partitioning, gate-level synthesis, technology mapping, placement and routing in a sequential way do not keep pace with high-capacity FPGAs and multi-million gate complexities [15]. Two main reasons prevent FPGA implementation tools from delivering good results in a reasonable amount of time. First, regular structures, especially in data path designs, are broken within the synthesis process which flattens the design hierarchy. Second, partitioning and placement are known to be very complex processes. Furthermore, they do not exploit information about regularity or hierarchy. Thus, they need long execution times [16].

1.1 Related Work

Several approaches have addressed the issue of FPGA placement. Most of them stem from VLSI placement methods using **S**imulated **A**nnealing (SA) [9]. A tool set targeting placement and routing is **V**ersatile **P**lace and **R**oute (VPR) that is proposed in [3] and described in detail in [4]. VPR uses an extended bounding

G. Brebner and R. Woods (Eds.): FPL 2001, LNCS 2147, pp. 27–36, 2001.
© Springer-Verlag Berlin Heidelberg 2001

box cost function for SA which models routing channel capacities separately for horizontal and vertical direction and uses a factor for multi-terminal nets. Furthermore, VPR adapts its annealing parameters according to the design size. VPR's cooling schedule is driven by the acceptance rate of moves. This speeds up SA significantly without compromising excellent placement results.

In contrast to the majority of methods the placement strategy in [6] is solely based on a constructive and deterministic algorithm. It takes user defined placement hints for any circuit component and processes the design from the innermost sub-circuit to the outermost. This leads to a linear time complexity and very fast execution times. For larger circuits a floorplanner is proposed. However, the overall placement results strongly depend on the user's knowledge of the target technology.

Recent approaches, like ultra-fast placement [16], overcome the problem of long run times by using clustering at at least one level. However, the cluster assignment is mostly driven by weighting net length or fan-out evaluation.

In this paper, we present a new approach for placing logic-elements into FPGAs within a direct mapping environment combining ideas from all formerly cited approaches. In order to speed up the placement step for direct mapping, our approach uses structural design information and makes use of hints for intermodule connections. The direct mapping flow starts at **R**egister **T**ransfer (RT)-level. A configurable module generator implements soft- as well as hardmacros directly into FPGAs. The soft macros are generated according to the LPM (**L**ibrary of **P**arameterized **M**odules) standard [12]. The mapping environment is not limited to RTL modules. It is also able to map flattened gate-level netlists. Both inputs, the module's configuration and the flattened netlists are described in structural Verilog [19].

1.2   Paper Organization

The paper is organized as follows: Section 2 gives a brief overview of the direct mapping approach CoMGen (**Co**nfigurable **M**odule **Gen**erator). In Section 2.1 the placement problem for direct mapping is formulated. Section 3 provides the placement algorithm for CoMGen. Using this algorithm we obtained several experimental results which are given in Section 4. Section 5 concludes this paper and presents an outlook on further research activities.

2   Direct Mapping Approach

Our direct mapping approach addresses the demands for implementing both RTL components and structural netlist parts in a short development cycle. Direct mapping means in this case implementation of structural netlists on RT-level by using topological information of the components. Long implementation times for dedicated module generators [13] are overcome by CoMGen due to its configuration capabilities. CoMGen is not limited to a specific FPGA, instead, it targets any LUT-based FPGA. The generator works on a generic logic block model which is derived from [14] and further extended in [1], where the mapping phase is explained in detail. Special FPGA features like carry logic, embedded memory blocks and wide gate functions are handled specifically. To illustrate this, the carry logic mapping for the Xilinx XC4000 family is fully integrated into CoMGen.

The mapped network of LUTs und flip-flops is input to the packing, decomposition and placement steps. These steps interface to an external floorplanner. Hereby, information about the ideal shape of the respective component is shared. Currently, the floorplanner from [15] is used. It arranges all components within the FPGA and determines their absolute position as well as the size of a rectangular shape. Additionally, it assigns a signal flow direction to each component.

2.1   Problem Formulation

The placement problem within this approach can be formulated as follows. Find a legal assignment for any logic block within a given rectangular shape. The found logic block assignment has to be routable. Additionally, hard-macros (e.g. fast carry path, embedded memory blocks) as part of the module have to be placed within the assigned shape. Hard-macros can be part of parameterizable soft-macros. Currently, we incorporate fast carry path support in CoMGen. Further FPGA related macro support can be easily added to CoMGen. Hard-macros must not overlap with others nor with a logic block. The placement has to satisfy the floorplanner constraints like shape size and signal flow direction.

None of the related placement algorithms addresses all these constraints. Especially meeting the floorplanning criteria in order to enhance the whole FPGA implementation containing all modules is a new challenge.

3   CoMGen's Placement Algorithm

The placement is separated into three phases. The first one accomplishes the initial placement. The second and third placement steps are optional. They optimize the initial placement using Simulated Annealing. The Simulated Annealing placement is mainly needed to smooth the constructive placement results according to the shape dimensions which are determined by the floorplanner. For flattened gate-level netlists recent publications have identified SA as the appropriate algorithm for logic block placement [4], [16]. The constructive part is described in detail in Section 3.2 and the iterative one can be found in Section 3.3.

3.1   Wire-Length Calculation

The objective of our placement is to minimize the wire-length. In order to identify the best approximation for different module structures and under varying constraints several experiments have been made. The minimum spanning tree

(MST) approximates the routing architecture of island-style FPGAs with homogeneous routing channel capacity very well. The minimum spanning tree estimation is too computational intensive for iterative approaches. However, there are single run estimations with time complexities of $O(m \log n)$ or $O(m + n \log n)$ depending on the implemented method. It gives a good approximation for the wire-length [11]. We denote the wire-length by MST approximation normalized per CLB as MST_{CLB} for evaluation of the final placement of different experiments as

$$MST_{CLB} = \frac{\sum_{i=1}^{\#Nets} MST_i}{\#CLBs},$$

where MST_i is the length of the minimum spanning tree of net i.

The following cost functions have been incorporated in the new method:

Center (C)
The center of the terminals for all nets connected to the logic block is calculated. The Manhattan distance of a block and the center of the respective nets serves as an objective function. This function does not reflect the net's topology but it is fast to calculate. Additionally, it can be incrementally recalculated.

Bounding box (BB)
The half-perimeter of the bounding box of the net terminals is calculated. An incremental calculation is implemented as proposed in [4] because we target mainly data path modules with less than four terminals for each net.

Local wire-length (LWL)
Our experiments have shown, that five neighboring net terminals are important to evaluate the movement of a respective block. Thus, $\#Nets$ is limited to five. This reduces the calculation complexity significantly.

Static wire-length (SWL)
The run time complexity of LWL can be further reduced. For static wire-length approximation the next neighbors are determined only once. These nets are taken into account for all wire-length estimations.

Global wires (e.g. clocks) are generally distributed via special low-skew nets within an FPGA [23]. Thus, they do not require segmented routing resources. Hence, the placement algorithm identifies those nets and does not incorporate them into the cost evaluation.

3.2   Constructive Part

For initial placement, a constructive algorithm, a random placement or a simple placement can be used. For predefined soft macros, the places of the module's primary inputs and outputs are specified as pragma statements in its module description file. The specification is done according to the floorplanner's signal flow model. The constructive placement phase utilizes this information in order to support inter-module routing.

```
Set U of all unplaced logic blocks
Set B of all unplaced logic blocks but next candidates
Logic block LB has to be placed
While (U != empty) {
    if (B == empty) {
        if (U != empty) {
            LB = select_lb(U);
            if (LB == 0)
                LB = primIO_connected_crit_path(U);
            U -= LB;
        }
    }
    else {
        LB = select_lb(B);
        B -= LB;
    }
    place(LB);
    B += nearest_neighbors(LB);
    U -= nearest_neighbors(LB);
}
```

Fig. 1. Pseudo-Code of Constructive Placer

For the constructive placement, we use a greedy algorithm which is described as pseudo-code in Fig. 1. The `select_lb` function orders the logic blocks descending in the respective set using the following function:

$$P = \frac{\sum\limits_{Net\ i} w_{i,L_i>0}}{\sum\limits_{Net\ i} w_i} \quad , \quad w_{i,L_i>0} = \begin{cases} w_i, & L_i > 0 \\ 0, & L_i = 0 \end{cases}$$

where w_i is defined as $w_i = \frac{1}{N_i L_i}$. N is the number of net terminals and L is the number of already placed net terminals. $w_{i,P>0}$ equals w_i iff $P_i > 0$. Thus, if at least one terminal of the respective net is placed, the fraction is incorporated in the sum.

Within the function `place`, the ideal placement position is calculated as the center of the net terminals. The final position for the logic block is selected among all legal positions with the same Manhattan distance to the ideal one. The best selection is evaluated by one of the formerly described cost functions. If two or more legal positions are determined as best, the one next to the shape's edge is selected. If no ideal placement position is found, an evaluation according to the given cost function is started.

The function `nearest_neighbors` determines the unplaced logic blocks next to LB. Only nets with a terminal count below a given limit are considered in order to prevent global nets (i.e. clock, enable) from taking part in the evaluation.

The constructive placement for hard macros is similar to the logic block placement, despite that if a position for the hard macro is found within the shape and it overlaps with other logic blocks, the logic blocks must be placed again.

3.3   Iterative Part

Simulated Annealing has been used for iterative placement on FPGAs very frequently. It is well described in many contributions [3], [7], [9]. In contrast to VPR [4], the cooling scheme differs in our approach. VPR uses a temperature update schedule which depends on the acceptance rate [3]. We use a linear temperature update for simplification. Further research will be done on different update schedules. The radius of the swapping distance of logic blocks D_{limit} is defined as $D_{limit} = \delta T$ with the temperature T. δ is a parameter which can be specified for each module individually. The cost function can be selected from a set of implemented cost functions given in Section 3.1. The experimentally determined best parameter set including the cost function for any module is given as pragma statement in the module description.

4   Experimental Results

The experiments have been obtained on a SUN Ultra 2, UltraSparc-IIi processor with 200 MHz and 768MByte main memory. The final routing and pad placement was accomplished by Xilinx' M3.1 implementation software [22].

4.1   Default Parameter Set

Several experiments have been run in order to identify a good default parameter set for the annealing with respect to each cost function. Table 1 shows the set of

Table 1. Parameter Set for Different Cost Functions

Cost function	$Costinc_{start}$	δ	$D_{limit_{max}}$	T_{min}
Center	14%	14%	10	0.0
Bounding Box	3%	10%	10	0.0
Local wire-length	5%	16%	5	0.0
Static wire-length	5%	16%	5	0.0

parameters for the available cost functions. The second column shows the start value of the accepted increase of costs $Costinc_{start}$. The third column denotes the fraction of temperature for the swapping distance while the fourth gives the maximum of the radius. The fifth column gives the minimum temperature.

4.2   Placement Phases

In order to select a default parameter set for arbitrary netlists we combined different functions and placement procedures. Its parameters provide a good trade-off between run time and placement quality. Due to our three phases approach, a

Table 2. Combined Placement Phases

Combination	c7552		braun32x32		booth32x32	
1st, 2nd, 3rd phase	MST_{CLB}	run time	MST_{CLB}	run time	MST_{CLB}	run time
R, SA(BB),—	9.47	19.34s	9.47	55.93s	16.51	127.18s
R, SA(BB),—	9.37	38.01s	8.26	112.68s	16.51	127.18s
R, SA(BB), SA(SWL)	9.29	20.53s	9.44	58.01s	15.36	68.56s
R, SA(BB), SA(LWL)	9.19	33.55s	9.32	96.17s	14.57	127.54s
R, SA(Cen),—	9.62	11.96s	9.66	30.74s	19.87	40.51s
R, SA(Cen), SA(SWL)	9.41	12.67s	9.58	32.43s	18.13	43.20s
R, SA(Cen), SA(LWL)	9.13	26.11s	9.35	72.07s	16.63	104.89s
C(BB),—,—	12.56	1.98s	5.15	6.22s	20.52	9.23s
C(BB), SA(SWL)	10.66	10.32s	5.11	22.28s	18.14	39.03s
C(BB), SA(Cen)	9.53	12.45s	5.89	33.01s	18.35	45.10s
C(BB), SA(Cen), SA(SWL)	9.24	20.6s	5.85	49.34s	15.56	74.83s
C(BB), SA(Cen), SA(LWL)	9.17	26.62s	5.83	73.86s	15.19	110.16s
C(BB), SA(BB),—	9.23	20.88s	5.99	76.15s	15.69	70.11s
C(BB), SA(BB), SA(SWL)	8.97	28.89s	5.92	95.52s	14.42	99.92s
C(BB), SA(BB), SA(LWL)	8.98	34.82s	5.91	115.61s	14.00	133.40s
Combination	s35932		s35932 $N < 256$		c6288	
1st, 2nd, 3rd phase	MST_{CLB}	run time	MST_{CLB}	run time	MST_{CLB}	run time
R, SA(BB),—	14.23	418.00s	15.78	63.26s	7.53	16.45s
R, SA(BB),—	13.72	833.72s	15.01	119.12s	7.17	33.54s
R, SA(BB), SA(SWL)	14.22	432.18s	15.74	65.82s	7.48	17.78s
R, SA(BB), SA(LWL)	14.18	3227.57s	15.68	73.05s	7.36	26.13s
R, SA(Cen),—	14.44	56.83s	14.44	43.99s	7.11	12.16s
R, SA(Cen), SA(SWL)	14.35	62.74s	14.22	45.38s	7.09	12.60s
R, SA(Cen), SA(LWL)	14.20	2920.54s	14.00	52.54s	7.05	20.73s
C(BB),—,—	21.78	33.30s	20.71	14.92s	8.84	2.26s
C(BB), SA(SWL),—	20.55	79.98s	17.93	23.71s	8.13	7.26s
C(BB), SA(Cen),—	14.56	81.05s	14.54	48.61s	6.54	12.71s
C(BB), SA(Cen), SA(SWL)	14.43	127.87s	14.15	57.97s	6.46	17.44s
C(BB), SA(Cen), SA(LWL)	14.35	2916.13s	14.15	57.29s	6.44	21.03s
C(BB), SA(BB),—	14.29	585.65s	14.56	67.98s	6.37	18.13s
C(BB), SA(BB), SA(SWL)	14.26	622.16s	14.47	77.44s	6.30	22.74s
C(BB), SA(BB), SA(LWL)	14.23	3411.27s	14.47	76.32s	6.27	26.35s

R　　　　random placement
C(BB)　　constructive placement(cost func.: bounding box)
SA(Cen)　Simulated Annealing (cost func.: center)
SA(BB)　 Simulated Annealing (cost func.: bounding box)
SA(LWL)　Simulated Annealing (cost func.: local wire-length)
SA(SWL)　Simulated Annealing (cost func.: static wire-length)
$N < 256$　nets with more than 256 terminals have been ignored

Table 3. Optimized Placement Phases

Phase	Algorithm	$Costinc_{start}$	δ	$D_{limit_{max}}$	$\#Iter_{LB_{max}}$	T_{min}
1.	C(BB)	-	-	-	-	-
2.	SA(Cen)	14%	14%	10	1000	0.0
3.	SA(SWL)	0%	16%	5	100	0.0

default combination of constructive and iterative methods has to be identified. For this, a series of experiments for different circuits has been made. The results are given in Table 2. The sequential benchmark s35932 is listed twice. First, we took all net terminals into account. Second, for s35932 N < 256, we omitted nets for all cost functions with more than 256 terminals because of the circuit's sequential nature. The results show that for regular data path circuits like the Braun multiplier the single constructive phase outperforms any iterative optimization in run time. For the wire-length optimization it gets ahead of all except one which gives slightly better results. For all other circuits a good compromise of run time and placement quality can be found. Its parameters are given in Table 3 where $\#Iter_{CLB_{max}}$ denotes the maximum numbers of iterations per logic block.

4.3   Routability

A main issue of FPGA placement is the routability of the logic block arrangement due to the limited routing resources which are channel oriented for most FPGAs. In order to ensure routability a series of experiments has been run. A set of 28 benchmark circuits from the ISCAS 85/89 suites has been placed by our placement algorithm on the smallest FPGA constrained by a rectangular shape. All circuits were routed successfully on FPGAs of the XC4000XL series from Xilinx [23].

However, these results do not ensure the routability of all circuits in any case. For this, we exemplarily investigated the routability by dropping the placement quality for a circuit that contains the highest routing congestion and occupies a whole FPGA. A 32 by 32 Booth multiplier has been selected for this using 97.6% of a 36 by 36 logic block shape using an XC4036 device. A placement with a value of 33.5 for MST_{CLB} was no longer routable since the constructive placement obtained a value of 20.4 which could be further improved by Simulated Annealing to 13.6.

4.4   CoMGen Placer vs. Xilinx Par

Since our approach targets generated modules as well as arbitrary netlists, we compared both to the commercial Xilinx placement tool **par** in Version 3.3.06. Figure 2 depicts the component delay results obtained for different circuits for our implemented placer using the default parameter set (see Table 2). All circuits are gate-level netlists except the circuit **Braun 32x32 gen**. This is a predefined soft macro with pragma statements for module specific optimization parameters. The run time for placing the circuits by our placer and by M3.3 is given in Figure 3. All results show that our proposed placer is faster and yields better results in terms of component delay compared to the commercial one. Basically, CoMGen does not sacrifice results for its configurability in comparison to the dedicated generators. Unfortunately, this can not be shown here due to limited space.

5   Conclusion

In this paper, we proposed a new placement method within a direct mapping environment for FPGAs. This mapping environment mainly addresses implementation times. Placement is sped up by an effective and efficient constructive part. This part takes advantage of the module mapping idea. The placement

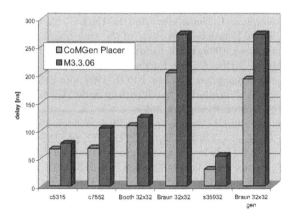

Fig. 2. Component Delay for CoMGen's Placer and Xilinx M3.3.06

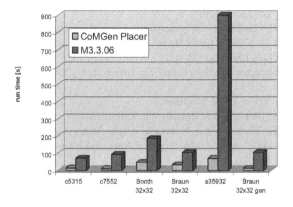

Fig. 3. Run Times for CoMGen's Placer and Xilinx M3.3.06

strategy is the first known method supporting the module's interconnect as well as taking advantage of the signal flow assignments. The placement results are better in terms of run time and placement quality for both module and gate-level netlists. Additionally, the VPR cooling schedule will be incorporated into the proposed placement tool in order to compare both cooling schemes. Our further research covers the mapping of finite state machines. Furthermore, we investigate parameter sets for placement of all modules defined in LPM.

References

1. J. Abke, and E. Barke, "CoMGen: Direct Mapping of Arbitrary Components into LUT-Based FPGAs, *Field-Programmable Logic and Applications, The Roadmap to Reconfigurable Computing*, FPL 2000, pp. 191–200. Springer.

2. K. Harbich, J. Stohmann, L. Schwoerer, and E. Barke, "A Case Study: Logic Emulation - Pitfalls and Solutions", In *Proc. of the 10th IEEE Int'l. Workshop on Rapid System Prototyping*, 1999, IEEE Computer Society, pp. 160–163.
3. V. Betz, and J. Rose, VPR: A New Packing, Placement and Routing Tool for FPGA Research, *ACM Symp. on FPGAs*, FPGA 1997, pp. 213–222.
4. V. Betz, J. Rose, and A. Marquardt, "Architecture and CAD for Deep-Submicron FPGAs", *Kluwer Academic Publishers*, 1999.
5. M. Butts, J. Batcheller, and J. Varghese, "An Efficient Logic Emulation System". *Proc. of the Int'l. Conf. of Circuit Design*, ICCD 1992, pp. 138–141.
6. S. W. Gehring, S. H.-M. Ludwig, "Fast Integrated Tools for Circuit Design with FPGAs", *ACM Symp. on FPGAs*, FPGA 1998, pp. 133–139.
7. S. Kirkpatrick, C. D. J. Gelatt, and M. Vecchi, "Optimization by Simulated Annealing", Technical report, 1982, IBM Thomas J. Watson Reseearch Center.
8. H. Krupnova, and G. Saucier, "FPGA-Based Emulation: Industrial and Custom Prototyping Solutions". In *Field-Programmable Logic and Applications, The Roadmap to Reconfigurable Computing*, FPL 2000, pp. 68–77. Springer.
9. C. Sechen, "VLSI Placement and Global Routing Using Simulated Annealing". *Kluwer Academic Publishers*, 1988.
10. D. M. Lewis, D. R. Galloway, M. van Ierssel, J. Rose, and P. Chow "The Transmogrifier-2: A 1 Million Gate Rapid Prototyping System", *ACM Symposium on FPGA*, FPGA 1997, pp. 53–61.
11. T. Lengauer "Combinatorial Algorithms for Integrated Circuit Layout", *Wiley Teubner*, 1990.
12. "LPM 220: Description of LPM Modules", http://www.edif.org/lpmweb/documentation/220cells.pdf.
13. J. Stohmann and E. Barke, "An Universal CLA Adder Generator for SRAM-Based FPGAs". *Field-Programmable Logic: Smart Applications, New Paradigms and Compilers*", FPL 1996, pp. 44–54, Springer.
14. J. Stohmann and E. Barke, "A Universal Pezaris Array Multiplier Generator for SRAM-Based FPGAs". *Int'l Conf. on Computer Design*, ICCD 1997, pp. 489–495.
15. J. Stohmann, K. Harbich, M. Olbrich, and E. Barke. "An Optimized Design Flow for Fast FPGA-Based Rapid Prototyping", *Field-Programmable Logic and Applications, From FPGAs to Computing Paradigm*, FPL 1998, pp. 79–88, Springer.
16. Y. Sankar, J. Rose, "Trading Quality for Compile Time: Ultra-Fast Placement for FPGAs", *ACM Symp. on FPGAs*, FPGA 1999, pp. 157–166.
17. R. Tessier, "Fast Place and Route Approaches for FPGAs", Ph.D. thesis, Massachusetts Institute of Technology, 1998.
18. R. Tessier, "Frontier: A Fast Placement System for FPGAs", *Proc. of the 10th IFIP Int'l Conf. on VLSI*, 1999.
19. D. E. Thomas and P. R. Moorby, "The Verilog Hardware Description Language", *Kluwer Academic Publishers*, 4th edition, 1998.
20. N. Togawa, M. Yanagisawa, T. Ohtsuki; "Maple-opt: A Performance-Oriented Simultaneous Technology Mapping, Placement, and Global Routing Algorithm for FPGA's", *IEEE Trans. on CAD*, Sep. 1998, Vol. 17, No. 9, pp.803–818.
21. W.-J. Sun, C. Sechen, "Efficient and Effective Placement for Very Large Circuits", *IEEE Trans. on CAD*, Mar. 1995, Vol. 14, No. 3, pp.349–359.
22. Xilinx, Inc. "Alliance Series 3.1i Software Documentation", 2000.
23. Xilinx, Inc. "The Programmable Logic Data Book", *Xilinx Inc.*, San Jose, 2000.

fGREP - Fast Generic Routing Demand Estimation for Placed FPGA Circuits

Parivallal Kannan, Shankar Balachandran, and Dinesh Bhatia

Center for Integrated Circuits and Systems
Erik Jonsson School of Engineering and Computer Science
University of Texas at Dallas
PO Box 830688, Richardson, TX 75083, USA
{parik, shankars, dinesh}@utdallas.edu

Abstract. Interconnection planning is becoming an important design issue for large FPGA based designs and ASICs. One of the most important issues for planning interconnection is the ability to predict the routability of a given design. In this paper, we introduce a new methodology, fGREP, for *ultra-fast* estimation of routing demands for placed circuits on FPGAs. Our method uses logic block fanout as a measure of available routing alternatives for routing a net. Experimental results on a large set of benchmark examples show that our predictions closely match with the detailed routing results of a well known router, namely VPR[1]. fGREP is simultaneously able to predict the peak routing demand (channel width) and the routing demands for every routing channel. It is currently used for post-placement estimation of routing demands, but can be used during the placement process also. fGREP can be used with any standard FPGA place and route flow.

1 Introduction

Routing of nets for FPGAs is a hard and very time consuming task. In commercial CAD tools, the majority of the design time is spent performing routing of nets. With changing size and complexity of FPGA devices, CAD tools are faced with challenges related to good convergence of mapped designs in an acceptable time frame. Most complex FPGAs have more than a million gates and the complexity of the designs is constantly rising. With such enormous sizes, the problem related to FPGA based design are no different from those in the custom and semi-custom ASIC arena, i.e. confidence of routability, good performance, reasonable total mapping time and more. Prediction of wiring requirements and managing overall CAD to ensure wireability of a circuit is one problem that demands the most attention. In this paper, we have studied the problem of interconnection prediction for large FPGAs. Although our method demands a fully placed circuit as an input to our estimation techniques, it can be very easily embedded within a placement tool for optimizing routability based cost during placement iterations. The execution time overheads of our method are very low. Thus our method can be used post-placement to ensure routability of the placed circuit prior to actual routing.

G. Brebner and R. Woods (Eds.): FPL 2001, LNCS 2147, pp. 37–47, 2001.

2   Prior Work

Interconnection prediction and related problems are being actively investigated for various design styles and technologies. Most of the recent literature has addressed interconnection prediction keeping Rent's rule[2] in consideration. Rent's rule establishes an empirical relationship between the *number of pins* N_p and the *number of logic blocks* N_g in a logic design. It shows that a log-log plot between the two parameters form a straight line and empirically yield a relationship

$$N_p = K_p N_g{}^\beta \tag{1}$$

Here, β is the Rent's constant, and K_p is a proportionality constant. K_p is also the average number of interconnections per block. Van Marck et. al. [3] used Rent's rule to describe local variations in interconnect complexity. Sadowska et. al. [4] used Van Marck's results and modified the VPR placement cost function (originally linear wirelength based) to account for interconnection complexity. Wei [5] has used Rent's rule to arrive at a statistical model for predicting routability for hierarchical FPGAs prior to placement.

El Gamal [6] proposed a stochastic model for estimating the channel densities in mask programmable gate arrays. The model assumes a normal distribution of interconnection within channels. Brown [7] et. al. extended this model by taking into account the FPGA routing architecture and various flexibilities associated with programmable switching elements. Both the models predict routing resource requirements in the post placement stage of design. Although our work addresses the prediction of routing resources in the post placement stage, it avoids complex evaluation of conditional probabilities, thus making the entire evaluation very fast. Wood [8] et. al. used boolean satisfiability with BDDs to estimate routability for FPGAs. The representation of routing channels as a satisfiability problem makes the entire process very cumbersome and difficult to evaluate. The time spent in routability estimation sometimes exceeds the time required to perform incremental routing. This makes the model very impractical for even small size problems.

Some other works that indirectly address the routing resource prediction or evaluation include the congestion minimization techniques due to Wang and Sarrafzadeh[9], simultaneous place and route by Nag and Rutenbar[10], and wireability analysis for gate arrays by Sastry and Parker[11].

In general, routing estimation methods should be very fast, have high accuracy, be capable of predicting both global and local routing requirements, and conform as much as possible to actual routed results from standard routers. In the following sections we explain fGREP, our new routing demand estimation methodology, and show that the estimates produced by fGREP are very close to the actual *detailed routes* produced by VPR's router.

3   Preliminaries

3.1   FPGA Physical Design Tool: VPR

VPR is a well known FPGA physical design tool suite, capable of targeting a broad range of FPGA architectures. The placer in VPR is simulated annealing based and optimizes a cost function containing a wirelength estimate among other things. VPR's router is based on the PathFinder [12] negotiated congestion algorithm. The router has to be given a track width, W as an input. In the absence of W, the router has no way of predicting the track width and so starts with $W = 12$, tries to route the circuit and performs a binary search on W, trying to find the optimum value for W. This repeated routing attempts make the routing process time consuming.

3.2   FPGA Architecture and Design Flow

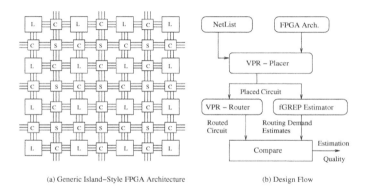

(a) Generic Island–Style FPGA Architecture   (b) Design Flow

Fig. 1. *Island Style FPGA Architecture and fGREP Design Flow with VPR*

Fig 1(a) shows a conventional island style FPGA architecture commonly used for research purposes. The logic blocks are marked L, the connection boxes as C and the switch boxes as S. The routing matrix is composed of the routing channels and the switch boxes. Each routing channel consists of a number of routing tracks. The number of tracks in a channel is called the track width and is commonly represented by W. fGREP produces estimates on a channel by channel basis and hence considers channels as routing elements. Hence the terms routing element and routing channel are used interchangeably.

Fig 1(b) portrays the design flow of fGREP using VPR. VPR's placer produces a placement solution for the given netlist and FPGA architecture. The placement solution forms an input to both fGREP and VPR's router. VPR's router produces a detailed route for the optimum value of track width W_{vpr}, which is found by the binary search method as explained earlier. fGREP's output is a routing demand value $D_i \in \Re$ for each channel E_i. The maximum value of D_i is the estimated peak routing demand or the track width W_{est}. This is directly compared with W_{vpr}. The individual D_i values are compared with the channel occupancy values of VPR's detailed route, to bring out the local estimation accuracy of fGREP. It is to be noted that fGREP is completely independent of the placer and router, and the same design flow can be used with the VPR's placer and router replaced with any other placer and router.

4   Routing Estimation Model

4.1   Routing Demand

The routing estimation model of fGREP is based on the concept of routing flexibility over all the routing elements. First we define routing flexibility and routing demand in their general sense. In section 4.3, we define them in the context of fGREP.

Routing flexibility of a net N_i is defined as the number of different routes possible for the net. Let P^i be the set of all possible routes for net N_i. Each net exacts a certain routing demand on the routing elements used by its paths. Let $P_k^i \subseteq P^i$ be those paths that use the routing element E_k. Formally, the routing demand on E_k due to the net N_i is defined as,

$$D_k^i = \frac{|P_k^i|}{|P^i|} \tag{2}$$

Similarly, all the nets in the given circuit exact routing demands on all the routing elements in the device. Hence the total routing demand due to all the nets on a routing element E_k is defined as,

$$D_k = \sum_{i=1}^{\#nets} D_k^i \tag{3}$$

4.2   Bounding Box Considerations

For a variety of reasons it is preferable to limit the range of influence of a net. Usually the route of a net is limited to within the bounding box of the net. The bounding box of a net is the smallest possible rectangle covering all the terminals of the net. This is done to reduce both wirelength and routing resource utilization. [9] shows that a placement with minimum wirelength has minimum total congestion. Also, minimizing the wirelength is preferred as it has a direct impact on performance. Taking these facts into consideration, we limit the range of all nets to their bounding boxes. Hence Eqn 2 is rewritten as,

$$D_k^i = \begin{cases} 0 & \text{if } E_k \text{ outside the bounding box of net } N_i \\ \frac{|P_k^i|}{|P^i|} & \text{otherwise} \end{cases} \tag{4}$$

This concept is similar to and is drawn from earlier works [13, 14]. In these works, a list of possible paths for each net is enumerated and the routing demands on the individual routing elements are calculated. In practice, the number of paths enumerated is usually far less than the total number of paths possible. This affects the accuracy of the routing demands. The main difference in our work is that we theoretically calculate the routing demands on all routing elements, instead of actually trying to enumerate the list of possible paths. Our formulation produces accurate routing demands at far lesser runtimes. We explain our method in the following sections.

4.3   fGREP Routing Demand

The routing fabric of an FPGA can be represented by a graph $G(V, E)$. The vertices V represent the channels on the FPGA and the edges E represent the switch-boxes connecting them. There exists an edge (v_i, v_j) if there is a switch-box connecting the two channels i and j.

Consider a vertex v_i on the routing graph. The level l_{ij} of any other vertex v_j is defined as the level of v_j in the breadth first search (BFS) tree with v_i as the root. The level-set L_{ik} is defined as all the vertices in level k on the BFS tree with v_i as the root.

$$L_{ik} = \{v_j \in V | l_{ij} = k\} \tag{5}$$

Definition 1. *We define a path p_{ij} from the root v_i to a vertex v_j as a set of connected vertices $\{v_i, p_{ij}^2, p_{ij}^3, \cdots, p_{ij}^k, \cdots, v_j \mid 2 \leq k \leq l_{ij} - 1, p_{ij}^k \in L_{ik}\}$.*

Such paths represent the shortest distance paths (non-returning paths) on the FPGA routing fabric. Since these paths also use the smallest number of routing elements, they are commonly produced by most routers.

Theorem 1. *If all possible unique paths, of large lengths, originating from a vertex v_i and expanding outwards, were to be enumerated, then the ratio of the number of paths that contain any vertex v_j to the total number of paths will be at least $\frac{1}{|L_{ik}|}$, where k is the level of v_j.*

Proof. Let v_i be the root vertex. Consider all the vertices at some level k from v_i. The level-set at k is L_{ik}. The number of vertices in L_{ik} is the number of alternatives available for paths coming from levels greater than k. Let Φ_{k+1} be the total number of paths at level $k + 1$, all of them proceeding towards v_i. Since the paths are all equally distributed about the periphery of the level k, they are also equally distributed over the vertices in L_{ik}. Hence each vertex in L_{ik} will be used by $\frac{\Phi_{k+1}}{|L_{ik}|}$ paths. Hence the ratio of the number of paths using a vertex in L_{ik}, to the total number of paths is $1/|L_{ik}|$.

Since $|L_{ik}|$ represents the number of alternatives that may be available for a net at the level k, the routing demand on each routing element in the level-set L_{ik} is $1/|L_{ik}|$.

Consider Fig 2(a). It shows a hypothetical routing graph, on which v_i is the current root vertex. The vertices at the same level from v_i are all shown to be connected by dotted lines. For example, vertices marked Level 2 are all at a distance of 1 from the root vertex and those vertices form the level-set L_{i2}. The number of alternatives available for paths going out of v_i is 4 here. Thus the demand on the nodes at level 2 is $1/|L_{i2}| = 1/4$.

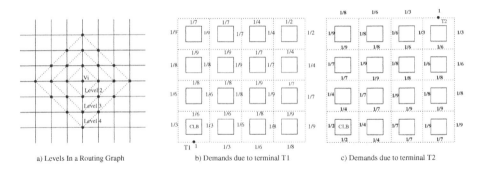

a) Levels In a Routing Graph   b) Demands due to terminal T1   c) Demands due to terminal T2

Fig. 2. *Levels (a) and Routing Demands With Bounding Box Constraint (b), (c)*

4.4   Routing Demand with Bounding Box

We now explain the effect of the bounding box on the routing demands. Consider a two terminal net with terminals t_1, t_2 represented by vertices v_1 and v_2 respectively on the routing graph. For reasons detailed in Section 4.2, we calculate the routing demands due to the terminals on the routing elements that are contained in the bounding box only.

Figures 2(b,c) show the terminals and the bounding box of the two terminal net, on the FPGA layout. The routing demands on the channels due to each of the terminals is also shown. The routing demands are obtained by considering only those channels inside the bounding box. The number of channels $|L_k|$ in each level k are calculated using breadth first search and the demands for all the channels in that level are assigned $1/|L_k|$. For all other channels outside the bounding box, the demands are assigned zero.

4.5   Demands due to a Net : Interaction of Multiple Terminals

This section deals with the interaction of multiple terminals and the effect of such in-teraction on the demand values of the routing elements. By the method detailed above, we get as many demand values for each routing element as there are terminals in the net. Since we are considering the demands due to the whole net, we have to compose the demands in such a way that it captures the concept of a net, as opposed to different independent terminals. We do that by assigning the contribution of the nearest terminal as the routing demand of the net. This has the effect of creating regions of influence around each terminal, where it contributes to the routing demand. For those routing elements that are equidistant from more than one terminal, the higher of the routing de-mands due to the terminals is assigned. This is done because the higher routing demand due to some terminal will mask out any lower demand due to any other terminal, when considering the net as a whole.

In Fig 3, we have shown the interaction of the terminals of a two terminal net. The routing demands of each channel are marked next to the channels. The entries in regular typeface are those due to terminal t_1 and those in boldface are due to terminal t_2. Note the entries with circles on them. These elements are equidistant from both the terminals. We assign the maximum of the demands due to two terminals for them, which in this case happens to have the same value of $1/9$.

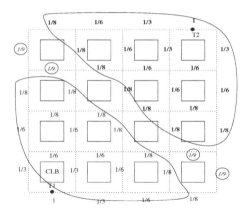

Fig. 3. *Interaction of Multiple Terminals*

The expression for the routing demand on a routing element r_i due to a net n_j is

$$D_i^j = \begin{cases} 0; \text{ if } r_i \text{ outside the bounding box of net } n_j \\ \max(\text{demand due to nearest terminals}); \text{ otherwise} \end{cases} \quad (6)$$

4.6 Interaction of Multiple Nets

The demand on a routing element r_i due to all the nets is the sum of demands due to every individual net.

$$D_i = \sum_{j=1}^{\#nets} D_i^j \quad (7)$$

This value is calculated for all the routing elements in the FPGA layout.

5   Algorithm and Complexity Analysis

The algorithm for calculating the routing demands for all channels is listed in Figure 4. The innermost loop performing the BFS is of the order $|E|$, the number of routing elements in the routing graph. The combined complexity of the outer two loops is of the order $|T|$, where T is the set of all terminals in the netlist. Thus the overall complexity is of the order $O(|E| \cdot |T|)$.

6   Experimentation

We have implemented the fGREP system for a generic FPGA architecture as defined in [1]. The implementation was done in C and was executed on a standard Pentium 800MHz system running Linux. To evaluate the quality of the estimation, we use the FPGA physical design suite VPR. For a fair comparison, VPR was also run on the same

---

Procedure fGREP(netlist N, target architecture A, placement):
    Build routing graph $G(V, E)$ from target architecture A;
    Read Netlist and placement information;
    Create and clear global_demand for all routing elements;
    for each net $n_i \in N$ do
        Calculate the bounding box of the net;
        Create and clear demand_for_net and level_for_net;
        for each terminal t_{ij} of net n_i
            Set t_{ij} as the root for BFS;
            Mark all routing elements in the bounding box as unvisited;
            while unvisited nodes in the bounding box exist
                Find the number of children C in the next level;
                Calculate demand due to t_{ij} as $1/C$;
                for each child
                    if level_for_net(child) > bfslevel(child)
                        Update demand_for_net and level_for_net;
                    end if;
                end for; –end of one bfs level
            end while; –end of bfs search for one terminal
        end for; –end of all terminals
        Add demand_for_net to global_demand;
    end for;–end of all nets
    return global_demand;
End Procedure fGREP

Fig. 4. Routing Estimation Procedure

machine. Most of the runtime options to VPR were set to their default values. The only changes made were to set the number of I/O pads per row(column) to 1 ($io\_rat = 1$) in the FPGA architecture description file, 4lut_sanitized.arch and set the router option to search for routes only inside the bounding box ($bb\_fac = 0$). The FPGA architecture has 4-input LUTs, switch-box flexibility $F_s = 3$, and connection-box flexibility $F_c = 1$.

VPR is first run in *place_only* mode for all the circuits to get the placement. VPR places the circuits in the smallest possible rectangular area, subject to pad constraints. The fGREP estimator then uses VPR's placement information and produces estimates for all the routing channels. Then, VPR is run in the *route_only* mode to produce actual global and detailed routes. VPR's router performs a binary search on the track widths, starting with $W_{vpr} = 12$, to find a feasible route and the lowest possible track width. The fGREP estimates and the VPR's routed results are compared on a channel-by-channel basis and the mean and standard deviation of the differences, over all the channels are calculated. In order to make make fair comparison with VPR, the router is again executed with the *route_only* option and the optimal value of W_{vpr} found by VPR earlier, and the runtimes are noted down as T_{vpr}. This ensures that the runtimes reported in our experiments, as stated in next section, are from a single run of the VPR router and not multiple runs due to binary search for finding smallest feasible W_{vpr}.

	fGREP	VPR Detailed	VPR Global
Total #of Tracks	201.87	217	147
% Diff in Tracks	6.97%	0	32.26%
Total Runtime	478s	2852s	-

Table 1. *Comparison of fGREP with VPR - Summary of Results*

We used the 20 largest circuits from the standard ISCAS-89 benchmark set. The benchmarks and their characteristics are tabulated in the first 4 columns in Table 2. The benchmarks range in size from 1263 to 8384 CLBs and 1072 to 8444 nets. Extensive experimentation results for all the ISCAS-89 benchmarks are available in [15].

7   Results

The results are tabulated in Table 2. The column headed by $N \times N$ is the dimension of one side of the placement. W_{est}, W_{vpr} and W_{gvpr} are respectively the peak channel width predicted by fGREP, optimum peak channel width found by VPR's detailed router and optimum peak channel width found by VPR's global router. T_{est} is the runtime for fGREP in seconds. T_{vpr} is the runtime for VPR's detailed router to route on a device with a maximum channel width of W_{vpr}. The runtimes for the global router were similar to T_{vpr} and are not tabulated. The column headed by $Mean$ lists the mean of the difference between routing demand of fGREP and that of VPR's detailed router, over all the channels. The column headed by σ lists the standard deviation of the differences. It should be noted that the peak demands W_{vpr} and W_{est} are local values that define the required channel widths based on actual routing and estimated values. The $Mean$ and σ highlight a more global picture across the complete routing architecture. In vast majority of cases, the local values as obtained by the VPR router closely match the estimated values through out the FPGA. This is also supported by very small values for the $Mean$ and σ.

It can be seen that fGREP's estimates are very close to the actual routed results of the VPR's router. For most of the circuits, the difference is of the order of one track, for the maximum channel width W. fGREP is 5 to 20 times faster than the detailed router. Note that this comparison is done between the runtimes of fGREP and that of running VPR with a specific maximum channel width. Under normal circumstances, the maximum channel width is not available to VPR and the runtimes are many times higher. Table 1 summarizes these observations. In Table 1, the percentage difference in tracks is with respect to VPR's detailed router results.

8   Conclusion and Future Work

In this paper we have described a post placement routing demand estimation method for field-programmable gate arrays. Our method avoids costly computations that are associated with other techniques that use stochastic [7], [6], [11], and satisfiability based [8] techniques. In most cases our method is correctly able to predict the peak (local) routing demand (also called as channel width) and the routing demand for each and every channel in the FPGA. The computation is very fast and hence can provide a quick check on the feasibility or non-feasibility of the routing. As shown in the Table 2, the difference between the actual peak demand and the estimated demand is not more than one in majority of the cases. The $Mean$ and σ gives even greater confidence where we are assured that our prediction is pretty much how the overall routing would be performed. The difference of 6.97 % in track estimation as reported in Table 1 amounts to no more than a difference of one track in prediction. It is also interesting to note that the channel width reported by VPR running in global routing mode (W_{gvpr}) is far less than actual results, even though high execution times are spent in finding the global routes.

As future work we are extending this work to generate a placement method that will assure routable designs with very high degree of confidence. Extensions to various FPGA architectures is a natural extension of this work.

Circuit	#Cells	#Nets	#Pads	NxN	W_{est}	W_{vpr}	W_{gvpr}	T_{est}	T_{vpr}	Mean	σ
alu4	1523	1536	22	40	9.974	11	7	4.956	38	1.447	1.086
apex2	1879	1916	41	44	10.539	12	8	4.751	59	1.652	1.276
apex4	1263	1271	28	36	11.956	13	9	2.560	43	1.879	1.396
bigkey	1708	1935	426	107	7.466	9	6	46.748	101	0.587	0.746
clma	8384	8444	144	92	11.059	13	8	118.280	549	1.697	1.247
des	1592	1847	501	126	8.072	8	6	26.840	76	0.593	0.652
diffeq	1498	1560	103	39	8.087	8	6	2.352	23	1.114	0.813
dsip	1371	1598	426	107	7.558	7	6	55.887	181	0.429	0.688
elliptic	3605	3734	245	62	10.461	11	7	19.430	237	1.381	1.041
ex1010	4599	4608	20	68	10.728	12	8	32.923	131	1.609	1.196
ex5p	1065	1072	71	33	12.974	14	10	1.855	35	1.853	1.461
frisc	3557	3575	136	60	11.762	14	9	15.307	150	1.662	1.269
misex3	1398	1411	28	38	10.018	11	6	3.097	45	1.508	1.143
pdc	4576	4591	56	68	16.162	16	11	35.321	460	2.132	1.523
s298	1932	1934	10	44	7.590	8	6	9.317	60	1.143	0.814
s38417	6407	6434	135	81	8.899	8	6	28.148	203	1.104	0.823
s38584.1	6448	6484	342	86	8.942	9	6	44.173	248	1.136	0.851
seq	1751	1791	76	42	10.384	12	8	4.073	53	1.680	1.249
spla	3691	3706	62	61	11.865	15	9	19.888	132	1.973	1.438
tseng	1048	1098	174	44	7.375	6	5	2.280	28	0.948	0.732

Table 2. *fGREP Results for the 20 Biggest ISCAS-89 Circuits*

References

[1] Vaughn Betz and Jonathan Rose, "VPR: A New Packing, Placement and Routing Tool for FPGA research," in *Field-Programmable Logic and Applications*. Sep 1997, pp. 213–222, Springer-Verlag, Berlin.

[2] H. B. Bakoglu, *Circuits, Interconnections, and Packaging for VLSI*, Addison Wesley, Reading, MA, 1990.

[3] H. Van Marck, D. Stroobandt, and J. Van Campenhout, "Toward an Extension of Rent's Rule for Describing Local Variations in Interconnection Complexity," in *Proceedings of the 4th International Conference for Young Computer Scientists*, 1995, pp. 136–141.

[4] G. Parthasarathy, M. Marek-Sadaowska, and A. Mukherjee, "Interconnect Complexity-aware FPGA Placement Using Rent's Rule," in *To appear in, Proc. Intl. Workshop on System Level Interconnect Prediction (SLIP)*, April 2001.

[5] Wei Li, "Routability Prediction for Hierarchical FPGAs," in *Proc. Great Lakes Symposium on VLSI*, 1999.

[6] Abbas A. El Gamal, "Two-Dimensional Stochastic Model for Interconnections in Master Slice Integrated Circuits," *IEEE Trans. CAS.*, Feb 1981.

[7] S.Brown, J.Rose, and Z.G.Vranesic, "A Stochastic Model to Predict the Routability of Field Programmable Gate Arrays," *IEEE Transactions on CAD*, pp. 1827–1838, Dec 1993.

[8] R.G. Wood and R.A. Rutenbar, "FPGA Routing and Routability Estimation via Boolean Satisfiability," in *ACM International Symposium on FPGAs FPGA98*. June 1998, ACM.

[9] M. Wang and M. Sarrafzadeh, "Congestion Minimization During Placement," in *Proceedings of the 1999 International Symposium on Physical Design (ISPD)*, 1999.

[10] Sudip K. Nag and R.A. Rutenbar, "Performance-driven Simultaneous Placement and Routing for FPGAs," *IEEE Transactions on CAD*, June 1998.

[11] S. Sastry and A.C. Parker, "Stochastic Models for Wireability Analysis of Gate Arrays," *IEEE Trans. on CAD*, Jan 1986.

[12] Larry McMurchie and Carl Ebeling, "PathFinder: A Negotiation-Based Performance-Driven Router for FPGAs," in *ACM Symp. on FPGAs, FPGA95*. ACM, 1995, pp. 111–117.

[13] S. Brown, J. Rose, and Z.G. Vranesic, "A Detailed Router for Field Programmable Gate Arrays," *IEEE Transactions on CAD*, May 1992.

[14] G. Lemieux and S. Brown, "A Detailed Router for Allocating Wire Segments in FPGAs," in *ACM Physical Design Workshop*, April 1993, pp. 215–226.

[15] Parivallal Kannan, Shankar Balachandran, and Dinesh Bhatia, "fGREP Results for ISCAS-89 Benchmarks," Tech. Rep., CICS, University of Texas at Dallas, 2001, http://www.eac.utdallas.edu/pubs/rep1_01.pdf.

Macrocell Architectures for Product Term Embedded Memory Arrays

Ernie Lin and Steven J.E. Wilton

Department of Electrical and Computer Engineering
University of British Columbia,
Vancouver, B.C., Canada,
{erniel|stevew}@ece.ubc.ca
http://www.ece.ubc.ca/~stevew

Abstract. We examine ways to increase product term usage efficiency and propose several new sharing architectures that addresses this problem. We also present a technology mapping algorithm for product term based FPGA embedded memory arrays. Our algorithm, pMapster, is used to investigate the effects of macrocell granularity and macrocell sharing on the amount of logic that can be packed into a product term embedded memory array.

1 Introduction

On-chip memory has become an essential component of modern FPGAs. FPGAs are being used to implement entire systems, as opposed to smaller glue-logic type subcircuits that FPGAs have traditionally been used to implement; large systems typically require storage and memories, something that smaller subcircuits usually do not. Though memory could be implemented off-chip, on-chip storage can lead to higher clock frequencies and relaxed I/O pin requirements.

On-chip storage architectures can be classified as either fine-grained or coarse-grained. In fine-grained architectures, such as the Xilinx 4000, each look-up table can be configured as a tiny RAM, and many of these RAMs can be combined to create larger user memories [1]. Coarse-grained architectures use large memory arrays embedded in the FPGA. For example, Altera APEX20KE FPGAs have between 12 and 216 2-Kbit arrays [2], while Xilinx Virtex-E FPGAs have between 16 and 144 4- Kbit arrays [3].

The coarse-grained approach to memory architecture results in significantly denser memory implementations, due to less overhead per bit of memory [4]. However, this approach requires the FPGA manufacturer to partition the chip into memory and logic regions when the FPGA is designed. Since circuits have widely-varying memory demands, this "average case" partitioning may result in poor device utilization for logic-intensive applications. Specifically, if the on-chip memory is not utilized completely or not at all, the chip area devoted to these unused memory arrays is wasted.

G. Brebner and R. Woods (Eds.): FPL 2001, LNCS 2147, pp. 48–58, 2001.

However, this chip area need not be wasted if these unused arrays are used to implement logic. Unused arrays could be configured as large ROM multiple-input, multiple-output lookup tables. Wilton [5] proposes an algorithm, SMAP, which packs logic into unused memory arrays. Cong and Xu's EMB_Pack [6] is another example of an algorithm that packs logic into memory arrays.

A recent innovation in on-chip storage is the addition of a product term mode for FPGA memories. Heile and Leaver [7] describe one such product term based architecture, found in the Altera APEX20K family of FPGAs. Product term memories can either operate as regular RAM (which can be used for storage or implementing logic), or as a collection of macrocells that implement logic in a manner similar to PLAs. In the Altera APEX20K architecture, an array operating in product term mode can implement between 16 outputs of two product terms each, to one output of 32 product terms. The number of outputs is variable as long as the total number of product terms implemented by the macrocells does not exceed 32 [2].

In the product term memory in [7], the OR plane is implemented using a collection of macrocells. Compared to traditional PLA architectures, this results in a far less flexible mechanism for combining product terms. To compensate for this, a sharing mechanism is provided, by which product terms can be shared between macrocells. The structure of this sharing mechanism is critical; if it is too flexible, it will slow the memory unacceptably, while if it is not flexible enough, it will limit the achievable logic density. In this paper, we present several alternative sharing schemes, and quantify their ability to implement logic.

In order to perform this evaluation, we require a technology mapping tool that can pack logic into the memory arrays. Traditional PLA mappers [8,9] are not sufficient, since they don't take into account the specific OR plane (macrocell) architecture. Krishnamoorthy details an algorithm targeting a product term memory [10], however, it does not take into account the product term sharing mechanism. Thus, a second contribution of this paper is a new algorithm, pMapster, which is flexible enough to map logic to product term memories with a variety of sharing mechanisms.

2   Macrocell Architectures

In this section we present several alternate parameterized macrocell architectures.

2.1   Base Architecture

The Altera APEX20K product term architecture uses the large embedded RAM arrays to implement an AND array similar to that found in a PLA [11]. The column outputs are connected to macrocell structures that implement the OR array function of a PLA. Each macrocell implements a sum of a fixed number of product terms, usually two. In cases where more than two product terms are needed to implement a function, adjacent macrocells can be cascaded such that multiple macrocell outputs are OR'ed together. This is done through a structure called the parallel expander.

There is also extra logic inside the macrocell that permits the macrocell to compute the XOR of the two product terms instead of an OR. Finally, the output of the macrocell can be programmably configured to be registered or non-registered. Figure 1 shows a schematic of a simplified APEX20K macrocell.

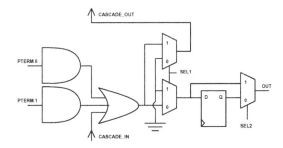

Fig. 1. A simplified APEX20K macrocell

2.2 Architectural Enhancements

Granularity of the Macrocell: When implementing functions of a large number of product terms, many macrocells need to be cascaded (using the parallel expander) to implement the desired number of product terms. However, this incurs an incremental delay for every macrocell that is cascaded. A solution is to increase the number of product terms per macrocell (the granularity of the macrocell) so that functions with more product terms can be more efficiently implemented. Unfortunately, increasing the granularity also decreases the efficiency with which smaller functions are implemented. Figure 2 illustrate the granularity enhancements.

Sharing Macrocell Outputs: In the APEX20K, each macrocell can either direct the sum of the product terms to the macrocell's output or to the next macrocell via the parallel expander, but not both simultaneously. This may lead to product terms being used inefficiently.

In cases where the product term block must implement a number of functions which are incrementally similar, having a macrocell capable of sharing its output with the next macrocell may be useful. Macrocells can then be chained together to efficiently implement these functions. Figure 3a) shows how a macrocell with output sharing could be useful. Figure 3b) is a schematic of a basic macrocell with the enhanced output circuitry.

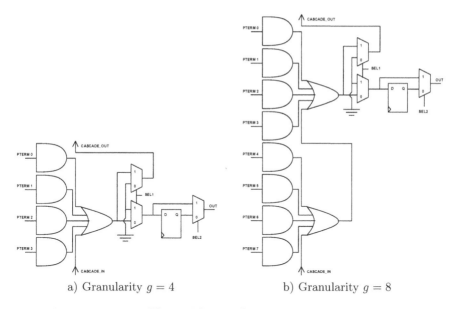

a) Granularity $g = 4$

b) Granularity $g = 8$

Fig. 2. Macrocell granularity

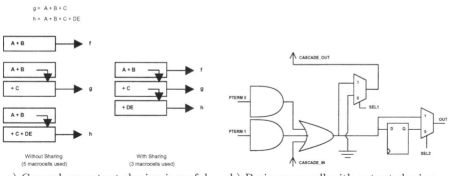

a) Case where output sharing is useful

b) Basic macrocell with output sharing

Fig. 3. Sharing macrocell outputs

Multiple Parallel Expanders: Since each macrocell has only one connection to the adjacent macrocell, product terms generated in one macrocell can only be used by at most two macrocells (the generating macrocell and the macrocell adjacent to it, assuming macrocell output sharing exists). In certain cases, this could lead to an inefficient use of macrocells since certain product terms may be repeated. Increasing the number of parallel expanders could increase product term usage efficiency, since product term repetition can be reduced.

In cases where the product term block must implement a number of functions which are similar, although not necessarily incrementally similar as in the previous example, having a macrocell capable of sharing with the next 2, 4, 6, or more macrocells may be useful. A macrocell can then be used to generate the common product terms (in a set of functions) and share them with several other macrocells. Figure 4a) shows how this could be useful. Figure 4b) shows a basic macrocell with enhanced parallel expanders.

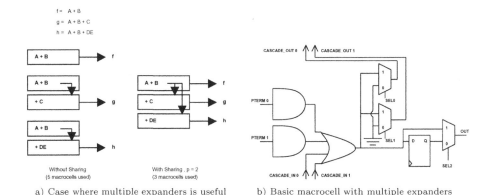

a) Case where multiple expanders is useful   b) Basic macrocell with multiple expanders

Fig. 4. Multiple parallel expanders

3   Mapping to Product Term Memory: pMapster Algorithm

In order to take advantage of the above architectural enhancements, a new technology mapping tool, pMapster, was implemented.

3.1   Basic Algorithm

The objective of our algorithm is to determine which nodes in a circuit are suitable for implementation as product terms, and to remove them from the network. The removed nodes are implemented using product term memory, and the remaining nodes are implemented using 4-LUTs.

The algorithm is outlined in Figure 5. Each internal node in the network is considered as a potential seed node. For each potential node, we repeatedly collapse fanin nodes into the seed. For nodes with multiple fanins, we choose the fanin as to minimize the number of inputs and product terms of the resultant collapsed node.

If the fanin has only one output (the seed node), we can remove the fanin as we collapse it. If the fanin has more than one fanout (ie. feeds a node other than the seed node), then we can still remove the fanin node, as long as we use an output of the memory array to implement the fanin signal. In this way, we can collapse beyond the maximum fanout-free cone rooted at the seed node.

Fanin nodes are collapsed into the seed until the number of product terms, inputs, or outputs in the memory is exceeded. We then repeat the algorithm for each seed node, and choose the seed node that results in the maximum number of nodes being deleted.

3.2   Extending the Algorithm to Handle Sharing

The algorithm in Figure 5 assigns output signals to the output macrocells in the memory arbitrarily. When using the product term sharing architectures outlined in section 2, however, the manner in which the outputs are assigned to macrocells can affect the number of macrocells required. This is shown in Figure 6.

In order to take this into account, we first assign the outputs to macrocells arbitrarily, as in Figure 5. We then use a greedy swapping algorithm to improve the assignment. In order to evaluate the fitness of a given assignment, we step through each output in order and determine if an output can be shared with any of its neighbouring outputs. In the example shown in Figure 6, we can see that output (A + B) shares product terms with output (A + B + C). Thus, if placed adjacent to each other, they could share their common product terms.

We also need to keep track of how many neighbouring outputs we consider, since clearly if an output requires more than one macrocell to implement it, that "steals" one or more of the available parallel expanders. Therefore, a "macrocell distance" is calculated which determines how many outputs are to be considered. Figure 7 shows the pseudocode of the fitness function.

Using the above fitness function, the algorithm rearranges the output assignment by randomly swapping two outputs. If the new assignment results in a lower overall cost, the move is accepted, otherwise, it is not. This is repeated n^2 times, where n is the number of outputs being considered. We experimented with varying values of repetitions, and found that increasing the number of repetitions to n^3 did not improve the results.

4   Experimental Results and Discussion

To evaluate the proposed macrocell architectures, we used 17 large benchmark circuits from the Microelectronics Corporation of North Carolina (MCNC) benchmark suite. Initially, all circuits were optimized using SIS and technology mapped into 4-LUTs using FlowMap.

We first examined the effect of macrocell granularity, as defined in section 2.2. We fixed the total number of product terms (columns of the memory) at 32, but varied how many of the product terms are associated with each macrocell. The number of inputs (literals) to each memory was held at 32. Clearly, the more product terms per macrocell, the wider the function that can be implemented by each macrocell. On the other hand, more product term per macrocell means

```
map_one_array():

for each node in the network {
    n = numNodesFaninNet(node);
    if(n> numNodes(bestSolution)) {
        networkCopy = copy(network);
        numDeleted = process_seed(node, networkCopy);
        if(numDeleted > bestSolution) {
            bestSolution = numDeleted;
            record cut nodes and deleted nodes;
        }
    }
}
remove selected nodes from the network;
```

```
process_seed():

while(!done) {
    bestScore = HUGE;
    for each fanin of seed {
        calculate newInputs;
        if(newInputs < MAX_INPUTS)
            calculate newPTerms, newMacrocells;
        if(newPTerms < MAX_PTERMS) && (newMacrocells < MAX_MACROCELLS) {
            score = calculateScore(fanin);
            if(score < bestScore) {
                bestScore = score;
                record this fanin as candidate;
                atLeastOneFanin = true;
            }
        }
    }
    if(atLeastOneFanin) {
        collapse fanin into all seeds;
        if(numFanout(fanin) > 1)
            add fanin to seeds;
    }
    else
        done = true;
    count inputsUsed, ptermsUsed, macrocellsUsed;
}
return cut nodes and deleted nodes;
```

Fig. 5. Pseudocode listing for pMapster Algorithm

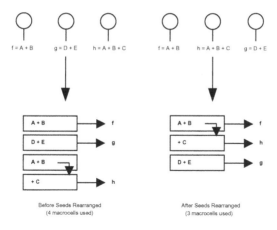

Fig. 6. How rearranging seeds leads to better use of macrocells when sharing is possible

```
for i=0 to array_size(seeds) {
    cur = seeds[i];
    distance = 0;
    j = 1;
    while(distance < numOfExpanders) && ((i+j) < array_size(seeds)) {
        dest = seeds[i+ j];
        if(cur is shared with dest)
            dest->pterms = numCube(dest) - numCube(cur);
        else
            dest->pterms = numCube(dest);

        distance += numMacrocells(dest->pterms);
        j++;
    }
}

for i=0 to array_size(seeds) {
    cur = seeds[i];
    ptermsUsedThisArrangement += cur->pterms;
    macrocellsUsedThisArrangement += numMacrocells(cur->pterms);
}
```

Fig. 7. Pseudocode listing for finding the fitness of a particular arrangement of seeds

there are fewer macrocells (and hence outputs) in the memory. Figure 8 shows the number of logic blocks that can be packed into memory arrays, as a function of the number of arrays, for four different granularities. As can be seen, the amount of logic that can be packed into the arrays decreases as the granularity (number of product terms per macrocell) increases. The best choice is to have two product terms per macrocell.

Second, we considered the ability of the parallel expanders (sharing architecture) to increase the amount of logic that can be implemented by each memory. We assumed an architecture in which each memory has 32 inputs (literals) and 16 macrocells of two product terms each. The number of parallel expanders was varied from 1 to 8. For comparison, we also included the non-sharing base architecture. As shown in Figure 9, as we increase the number of parallel expanders, the amount of logic we can pack into each memory increases slightly.

Finally, we compared the overall packing density for two cases: (1) using SMAP alone (which implements logic in the memory arrays by configuring them as ROMs) and (2) using a combination of SMAP and the pMapster algorithm. In the second case, we use both SMAP and pMapster on each memory array, and choose the better of the two results (recall that each memory array can be configured to operate as a ROM or as a collection of pterms). Figure 10 shows that the combination of the two algorithms works better than SMAP alone, especially as the number of arrays increases.

We estimate that adding product term capability to an embedded memory array increases its area by approximately 18.4%. However, adding product term capability also increases the amount of logic that can be packed in the array by between 13.4% to 39.8%. Thus having product term capability is a worthwhile feature.

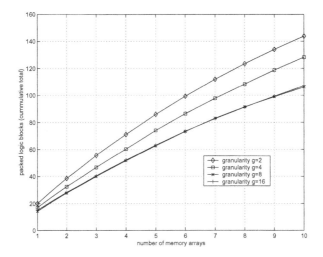

Fig. 8. The effect of granularity on the number of packed logic blocks

	Number of Memory Arrays									
	1	2	3	4	5	6	7	8	9	10
no sharing	20.4	38.8	56.0	71.5	86.3	99.6	111.9	123.1	133.3	142.6
sharing, p=1	20.5	39.1	55.9	71.6	86.6	100.5	112.5	123.8	133.8	143.3
sharing, p=2	20.5	39.1	56.0	71.7	86.8	100.8	113.0	124.1	134.4	143.9
sharing, p=4	20.6	39.2	56.0	71.7	86.8	100.8	113.0	124.2	134.5	144.0
sharing, p=8	20.6	39.2	56.1	71.8	86.9	100.9	113.1	124.3	134.6	144.0

Fig. 9. The effect of sharing on the number of packed logic blocks (numbers are geometric means over all benchmarks)

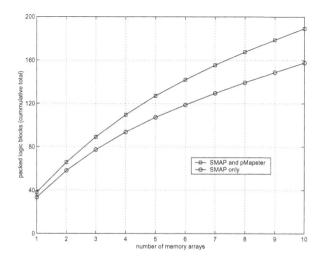

Fig. 10. A performance comparison between SMAP and SMAP with pMapster

5   Conclusions

In this paper we have proposed a new architecture for facilitating the sharing of product terms between adjacent macrocells. In order to evaluate this new architecture, a new technology mapping tool, pMapster, was created to take advantage of this enhancement. Experimental results show that product term sharing did not substantially increase the amount of logic that could be packed into each memory array. In fact, compared with no sharing and over 10 memory arrays, the amount of packed logic increased by only 1% with eight parallel expanders. We also examined how macrocell granularity affected packed logic and found that increasing granularity also decreased the amount of logic that was packed into the memory array because of decreased flexibility in the number of macrocell outputs. Lastly, we examined how pMapster could enhance SMAP's performance since SMAP does not perform as well at higher numbers of memory arrays. We found that pMapster (working with SMAP) increased the amount of packed logic by between 13.4% and 39.8% for each memory array and by 20.1% over 10 arrays.

Acknowledgments

This work was supported by the British Columbia Advanced Systems Institute and the Natural Sciences and Engineering Research Council of Canada.

References

1. Xilinx, Inc., XC4000E and XC4000X Field Programmable Gate Arrays Datasheet, ver. 1.6, May 1999.
2. Altera Corp., APEX20K Programmable Logic Device Family Datasheet, ver. 3.3, Jan. 2001.
3. Xilinx, Inc., Virtex-E 1.8V Field-Programmable Gate Arrays Datasheet, ver. 1.3, Feb. 2000.
4. Ngai, T., Rose, J., and Wilton, S. J. E., "An SRAM Programmable Field-Configurable Memory," in Proceedings of the IEEE 1995 Custom Integrated Circuits Conference, pp.499–502, May 1995.
5. Wilton, S. J. E., "SMAP: Heterogeneous Technology Mapping for Area Reduction in FPGAs with Embedded Memory Arrays", in Proceedings of the ACM/SIGDA International Symposium on Field-Programmable Gate Arrays, Feb. 1998.
6. Cong, J. and Xu, S., "Technology Mapping for FPGAs with Embedded Memory Blocks", in Proceedings of the ACM/SIGDA International Symposium on Field-Programmable Gate Arrays, Feb. 1998.
7. Heile, F. and Leaver, A., "Hybrid Product Term and LUT Based Architectures Using Embedded Memory Blocks", in Proceedings of the ACM/SIGDA International Symposium on Field-Programmable Gate Arrays, pp. 13–16, Feb. 1999.
8. Anderson, J. H. and Brown, S. D., "Technology Mapping for Large Complex PLDs", in Proceedings of the 35th ACM/IEEE Design Automation Conference, pp. 698–703, 1998.
9. Cong, J., Huang, H., and Yuan, X., "Technology Mapping for k/m-Macrocell Based FPGAs", in Proceedings of the ACM/SIGDA International Symposium on Fireld-Programmable Gate Arrays, pp 51-59, Feb. 2000.
10. Krishnamoorthy, S., Swaminathan, S., and Tessier, R., "Area-Optimized Technology Mapping for Hybrid FPGAs," in Proceedings of the International Conference on Field Programmable Logic and Applications, August 2000.
11. Heile, F., "Programmable Logic Array Device with Random Access Memory Configurable as Product Terms," U.S. Patent No. 6020759, Feb. 2000.

Gigahertz Reconfigurable Computing Using SiGe HBT BiCMOS FPGAs

Bryan S. Goda[1], Russell P. Kraft[2], Steven R. Carlough[3], Thomas W. Krawczyk Jr.[4], and John F. McDonald[2]

[1]United States Military Academy
West Point, NY, 10996 USA
[2]Rensselaer Polytechnic Institute
Troy, NY, 12180 USA
kraftr2@rpi.edu, mcdonald@unix.cie.rpi.edu
IBM, Inc.
[3]Poughkeepsie, NY USA
scarloug@us.ibm.com
[4]Sierra Monolithics, Inc
Redondo Beach, CA, 90277 USA
tkrawczyk@monolithics.com

Abstract. Field programmable gate arrays (FPGAs) are flexible programmable devices that are used in a wide variety of applications such as network routing, signal processing, pattern recognition and rapid prototyping. Unfortunately, the flexibility of the FPGA hinders its performance due to the additional logic resources required for the programmable hardware. Today's fastest FPGAs run in the 250 MHz range. This paper proposes a new family of FPGAs utilizing a high-speed SiGe Heterojunction Bipolar Transistor (HBT) design, co-integrated with CMOS in an IBM BiCMOS process. This device is bit-wise compatible with the Xilinx 6200, with operating frequencies in the 1 to 20 GHz range. All logic and routing in this new design is multiplexer based, eliminating the need for pass transistors, the main roadblock to high speed in today's FPGAs.

Introduction

A field programmable gate array consists of an array of reconfigurable logic blocks surrounded by segmented programmable interconnect (Fig. 1) [1]. Design entry and simulation is done in software and used to create the configuration file that defines the FPGA's logic function. Once programmed, the design is tested, validated, and optimized. The flexibility of the FPGA allows it to reconfigure hardware resources to satisfy the instantaneous needs of a digital system. This can be done in a few milliseconds and an unlimited number of times. However, the relatively slow operating speeds of current FPGAs (currently 70-250 MHz for designs of moderate complexity), prevents their use in high-speed digital systems. Logic implemented in an FPGA is less dense and slower than in its gate array implementation [1]. This is mainly due to the large amount of wiring resources needed (up to 85% of chip area),

G. Brebner and R. Woods (Eds.): FPL 2001, LNCS 2147, pp. 59-69, 2001.

and memory to store the on-chip configuration (up to 10%), leaving only a small fraction of the chip area for active circuitry (as little as 5%).

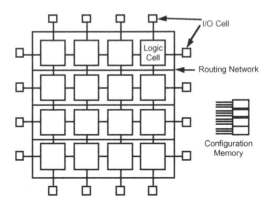

Fig. 1. Typical FPGA Design

The logic cell is the basic building block of an FPGA. These cells can implement either combinational or sequential logic. A matrix of programmable interconnect surrounds the basic logic cells, with programmable I/O on the outside boundaries. The configuration memory holds the programming bits that determine the function of the logic cell, the cell interconnect, and what inputs and outputs will flow in and out of the logic cells.

An example of an FPGA's programmable interconnect is depicted in Fig. 2a, demonstrating how points 2 and 3 would be interconnected. FPGAs utilize pass transistors (Fig. 2b) to route signals based on configuration bits stored in memory. The pass transistor is a simple switch that can act as an AND gate if two are connected in series or an OR gate if connected in parallel. The equivalent circuit of a pass transistor is effectively a low-pass filter (Fig. 2c) and studies have shown that the smallest delay between two Configurable Logic Blocks (CLB) in the Xilinx 4000 FPGA family is approximately 1 ns [2], [3]. The delay in the FPGA's programmable interconnect is significantly greater than that of a simple wire, because of the considerable resistance and capacitance introduced by routing signals though pass transistors. This resistance and capacitance reduces the noise margin, creates charge-sharing problems, and makes predicting delay difficult. Connection delays often exceed the delay of the of the logic block and is therefore one of the fundamental limits on FPGA performance. The slow operating speed and poor bandwidth caused by the interconnect delay limits the FPGA's widespread use [1].

Description of Designed FPGA

The FPGA created here was designed to be the functional equivalent of a Xilinx 6200 part. The Xilinx 6200 is a family of fine-grained, sea of gates FPGAs. A sea of gates can be described as a large array of simple cells. This device is designed to work with a microprocessor to implement functions normally placed on an ASIC. The XC6200 can provide high gate counts for data path or regular array type designs. The XC6200 is composed of a large array of configurable cells that contain a computation unit and a routing area so inter-cell communications can take place. The XC6200 is configured by a six-transistor SRAM control store that can be quickly reconfigured an unlimited number of times, including partial reconfiguration. Data transfers can be 8, 16, or 32 bits wide that allow circuits on the FPGA to be saved and then later restored with the same internal state. The chip itself is fabricated in a 3-metal n-well CMOS process. Industry standard schematic capture, synthesis and simulation can be done in such packages as Viewlogic, Mentor Graphics, and Synopsys.

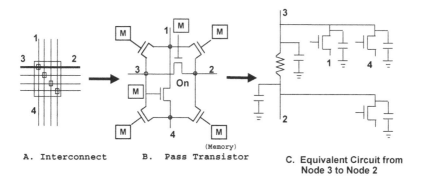

A. Interconnect   B. Pass Transistor   C. Equivalent Circuit from Node 3 to Node 2

Fig. 2. Interconnect Device Implementation and Delay Model

Functional Unit

Fig. 3 shows that basic layout of a XC6200 functional unit [4]. The X1 input controls whether the Y2 or Y3 output will be selected. The inputs to Y2 and Y3 can be an outside input (X2, X3), its complement, or a stored bit from a D flip-flop (or its complement).

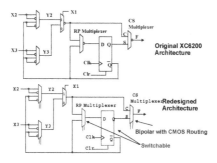

Fig. 3. Original and Redesigned Versions of XC6200

The Register Protect (RP) multiplexer controls what signal gets into the D flip-flop and the Chip Select (CS) multiplexer controls whether the logic output (C) or the stored bit (S) are output (F). It is important to notice that the functional unit design consists of 5 multiplexers and 1 D flip-flop, with no pass transistors. The Clear is an asynchronous signal that resets the D flip-flop, which is especially useful at startup. The clock controls when a bit will be stored. Only when the clock is high can a bit be stored in the D flip-flop. Once the functional unit is surrounded with routing resources it will become a flexible building block of programmable logic. Fig. 3 also shows the slightly modified circuit that was implemented as part of this research into the high-speed version of the FPGA. CMOS and bipolar HBTs were both used strategically in an effort to balance speed requirements as well as power consumption limits and real estate area in the circuit layout.

Design Details

Changes from the original XC6200 design were required in order to increase the clock rate as well as add extra flexibility in configuration storage. A fast switching logic design scheme that uses differential signals and 250 mV logic levels was found to be most appropriate for this application.

Current Mode Logic

The FPGA was designed using IBM's SiGe HBT BiCMOS process with (differential) current mode logic (CML) for fast logic circuit response. The process and circuits have been well documented [5], [6], [7], [8], [9]. Fig. 4 depicts a typical CML XOR implementation in 7 transistors and 3 resistors. Signal A and its complement come in on level 1 (0 and -0.25 V) and Signal B and its complement comes in on level 2 (-0.95 and -1.2 V). The difference between levels is slightly more than one V_{BE} (0.85 V). The tail resistor at the bottom of the current steering tree is connected to a reference current mirror that fixes the current through the circuit (0.7 mA). Suppose $\overline{A}=1$ and $\overline{B}=1$. Current will flow down the far left side of the tree, drawing the 'A XOR B' line down to –250 mV, while no current will be flowing in the other parts of the tree. Since there is no current flowing in the '$\overline{\text{A XOR B}}$' path, the voltage level will remain at V_{cc}. The opposite output will result if $\overline{A}=1$ and B=1, so current will be flowing down the far right side of the tree. The four possible input patterns implement the XOR function in CML. This logic was used throughout the FPGA design.

Context Memory Switching

A fast FPGA should be complimented with fast programmability otherwise many cycles are wasted during reconfiguration. Fast memory reduces the latency but it is not expected that configuration memory will constantly be changing as fast as possible. This would create excess current load and heat dissipation problems. The proposed FPGA design includes 8 memory planes, with each memory plane containing a different configuration for the FPGA. A CMOS multiplexer used to select between the memory planes allows the FPGA to page between up to eight different tasks extremely quickly and efficiently. Furthermore, the memory planes may be loaded or saved to the external system while processing continues uninterrupted in the FPGA. For the test chip designs, 2 memory planes were constructed on-chip with a 2:1 CMOS multiplexer to switch inputs (Fig. 5). The CMOS 2:1 multiplexer consists of 4 pairs of pass transistor logic with a one pair control line (S) that can be switched to allow a new FPGA personality to be programmed.

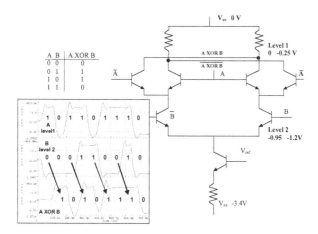

Fig. 4. Full Differential Current Mode Logic XOR Cell

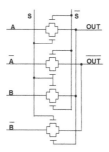

Fig. 5. CMOS 2:1 Multiplexer

One of the most interesting features of the XC6200 is the ability to reprogram parts of the chip while other parts of the chip are active. This is possible due to the fine-grained architecture of the XC6200. If multiple planes of memory can be accessed by each CLB, switching between each plane could apply different functions on the inputs. Allowing for a generous 1 ns between context switches, a CLB could reprogram itself a billion times per second if the memory planes were available and an application required this unusual capability.

With the world's fastest FPGA architecture, adding SRAM would cut down on the speed and computational ability of the bipolar logic (a tradeoff). If multiple memory planes were stacked in a 3-D arrangement, the fast signals could stay on a CLB plane while the slower CMOS signals can be routed throughout a 3-D architecture (Fig. 6).

The wires on the CLB plane could be shorten, since there would be no need for configuration memory on the CLB plane, only CMOS routing transistors. The CLBs could be packed closer together, creating less delay between CLBs. The memory planes could vary in size to support the application, with only a multiplexer needed to route the correct configuration plane to the CLB plane. This is an extension of chip stacking technologies used in commercial memory products and current 3-D integrated circuit design research sponsored by the US Defense Advanced Research Projects Agency MARCO program with active investigations at the Massachusetts Institute of Technology and Rensselaer Polytechnic Institute. One of the main goals is significant reductions in interconnect lengths through 3-D circuit design.

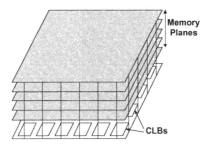

Fig. 6. 3-D Chip Stacking

Results

This research effort has culminated in two small layouts going to fabrication. Working circuits from the first have been tested and have been confirmed. Initial testing of clock signals has verified simulations. The second layout further optimized the design by building on experience gained from the first design and fabrication. Configuration memory and several more CLBs were included in the second layout and fabrication. Although the wafers had not yet been received from the fab line, initial testing on the first wafers and simulation results of the second design are very encouraging. The wafers are expected to be available at the end of March 2001, but not soon enough to have experimentally measured results included in this paper.

Fig. 7 shows the layout of a portion of the first test design, including a Mux, CLB, buffer, and clock divide-by-8 circuit. Fig. 8 is an actual photomicrograph of the same circuit on the fabricated wafer.

Fig. 9 shows the 400 mV output from the test chip (7-6b) along with the 8/1 divide output. The initial simulation was for an operating frequency of 5.1 GHz. The measured result was 4.2 GHz, a difference of 19%. The initial simulation was redone, this time to include parasitics and a temperature of 50° C, yielding a result of 4.31 GHz. The difference between measured and simulated was down to 2.3%.

A simulation in Fig. 10 shows CLB 1 ANDing two 10 GHz signals, CLB 2 XORing the same two signals, and CLB 3 ORing the outputs of CLBs 1 and 2. The simulation demonstrates that different logic functions can be implemented at high speeds and the output can drive other CLBs. Further simulation at higher speeds result in distorted waveforms since transistors are unable to switch fast enough to maintain the design noise margin of 200 mV. The most important point is that HBT CML can be used to implement all of the logic functions. CML multiplexers pass signals with delays of about 12-14 ps in the 50 GHz SiGe HBT process. A nice feature of multiplexers is that they can function as repeaters that can reshape rise and fall times.

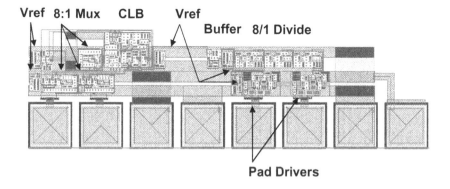

Fig. 7. Test Circuit Layout

Fig. 8. Photo Image of Test Circuit Chip

This CLB is an excellent example of the BiCMOS process, taking advantage of the speed of bipolar combined with the low power consumption of CMOS. Fig. 11 is a schematic of the basic CLB cell with routing and configuration memory. Two sets of configuration RAM are used to set different CLB personalities. The different RAMs are selected through a 2:1 multiplexer, which is controlled by a single bit. The high-speed bipolars are used in the top level of the 8:1 multiplexers, sending three high-speed signals to the CLB. The signals are then mixed to produce the desired output, which is then routed to any of 5 output multiplexers (North, South, East, West, Magic).

Implementing memory on-chip has a number of advantages over off-chip memory. Switching between memories can be done rapidly and memory can be accessed faster [10], [11]. If the memory/logic interface is not flexible enough, many circuits will be unroutable; if too flexible then the chip will be slow and consume extra chip area. For ease of design the memory was built around the high-speed bipolar section, routing the necessary configuration bit information directly into the CMOS/Bipolar mixed tree from the outside in.

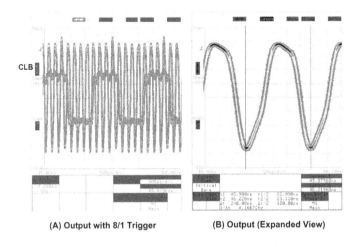

(A) Output with 8/1 Trigger   **(B) Output (Expanded View)**

Fig. 9. Output From Test Chip

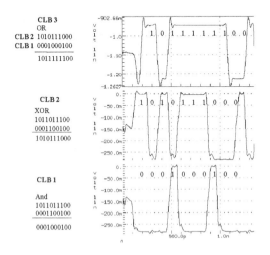

Fig. 10. 10 GHz Three CLB Simulation

Fig. 12 is a layout of the 6th generation of the CLB. It has 2 sets of 24-bit SRAM, the CLB logic, and the local routing resources. This layout measures 360 μm x 225 μm and serves as the basic large building block for the FPGA. The different layers of metal are shown to demonstrate the care that must be taken in wiring this design.

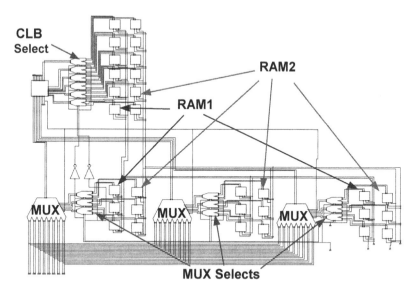

Fig. 11. CLB Schematic

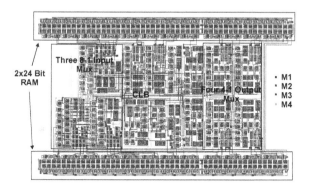

Fig. 12. 6th Generation CLB Layout

Analysis and Conclusion

The design of an FPGA that runs at 5 GHz for designs of moderate complexity using CML in SiGe technology combined with low power CMOS in the same process has been investigated. The Xilinx XC6200 was chosen for emulation due to its public domain bit stream and implementation in multiplexer logic and flip-flops. The core of the XC6200 has been demonstrated to be feasible and the major parts work at speed at room temperature. Further research into the drawbacks of high power consumption has devised a method of using a CMOS switch to turn off current mirrors on unused gates in a given configuration and integrating CMOS directly into the bipolar current tree. Furthermore, power saving modes have been developed to sacrifice speed for less power consumption.

The current SiGe HBT BiCMOS 0.5-micron 5HP process available from IBM has a maximum transistor frequency of 50 GHz. The next process from IBM, 7HP, is billed as a 0.18-micron process with a maximum frequency close to 120 GHz. Using the 7HP process on the next layout version of this design will achieve the goal of operating frequencies approaching 20 GHz. Although processes and speeds for both CMOS and HBT devices continue to improve, current commercial CMOS devices have f_T around 25 GHz while SiGe devices are more than 4 times faster at 120 GHz.

One of the largest areas of future work will be integrating the existing XC6200 tools to work with the SiGe FPGA. At the 1999 First NASA/DOD Workshop on Evolvable Hardware, a discussion group concluded that the software supporting the evolvable hardware is the major hindrance towards advancement. Although the XC6200 is not being manufactured anymore, there are many independent programmers that are still creating tools for the XC6200. Work in this area will help continue the independent development of the XC6200.

References

1. Smith, M.: 'Applications-Specific Integrated Circuits' (Addison-Wesley, Reading Massachusetts, 1997)
2. Dehon, A.: 'Reconfigurable Architectures for General-Purpose Computing.' A.I. Technical Report No. 1586, Artificial Intelligence Laboratory, MIT, 1996
3. Singh, S., Rose, J., Chow, P., Lewis, D.: 'The Effect of Logic Block Architecture on FPGA Performance,' *IEEE Journal of Solid-State Circuits,* Vol. 27, No. 3, March 1992, pp. 281-287
4. 'Xilinx Series 6000 User Guide' (Xilinx Inc., San Jose CA., 1997).
5. Rabaey, J.: 'Digital Integrated Circuits, A Design Perspective,' (Prentice Hall, Upper Saddle River, NJ, 1996)
6. Carlough, S., Campbell, P., Steidl, S., Garg, A., Maier, C., Greub, H., McDonald, J., Ernest, M.: 'Wiley Encyclopedia of Electrical and Electronics Engineering Vol. 17' (Wiley, New York, Feb 1999)
7. Garg, A., Le Coz, L., Greub, H., Iverson, R., Philhower, F., Campbell, P., Maier, C., Steidl, S., Kraft R., Carlough, S., Perry, J., Krawczyk, T., McDonald, J.: 'Accurate High-Speed Prediction for Full Differential Current-Mode Logic: The Effect of Dielectric Anisotropy,' *IEEE Transactions of Computer-Aided Design of Integrated Circuits and Systems,* Vol. 18, No. 2, Feb 1999, pp. 212-219
8. Goda, B., McDonald, J., Carlough, S., Krawczyk, T., Kraft, R.: 'SiGe HBT BiCMOS FPGAs for Fast Reconfigurable Computing,' *IEE Proceedings of Computers and Digital Techniques,* Vol. 147, No. 3, May 2000, pp.189-194
9. Greub, H., McDonald, J., Yamaguchi, T.: 'High-Performance Standard Cell Library and Modeling Technique for Differential Advanced Bipolar Current Tree Logic,' *IEEE Journal of Solid-State Circuits,* Vol. 26, No. 5, May 1991, pp. 749-762

10. Wilton, S., Rose, J., Vranesic, Z.: 'The Memory/Logic Interface in FPGA's with Large Embedded Memory Arrays,' *IEEE Transactions on VLSI Systems*, Vol. 7., No. 1, Mar 1999, pp. 80-91

11. Wilton, S.: 'Heterogeneous Technology Mapping for Area Reduction in FPGA's with Embedded Memory Arrays,' *IEEE Transactions on Computer Aided Design of Integrated Circuits and Systems*, Vol. 19, No. 1, Jan 2000, pp. 56-67

Memory Synthesis for FPGA-Based Reconfigurable Computers*

Amit Kasat, Iyad Ouaiss, and Ranga Vemuri

Department of ECECS, ML 30, University of Cincinnati
Cincinnati, OH 45221-0030, U.S.A.
{akasat,iouaiss,ranga}@ececs.uc.edu

Abstract. For data intensive applications like Digital Signal Processing, Image Processing, and Pattern Recognition, memory reads and writes constitute a large portion of the total design execution time. With the advent of on-chip memories, a rich hierarchy of physical memories is now available on a Reconfigurable Computer (RC). An intelligent usage of these memories can lead to a significant improvement in the latency of the overall design. This paper presents an automated heuristic-based memory mapping framework for RCs. We use a Tabu search guided heuristic, *Rectangle Carving*, to map a single data structure onto several instances of a memory type on the RC. We also introduce control logic to resolve potential memory access conflicts and to make the details of memory mapping transparent to the accessing logic.

1 Introduction

FPGAs have been the focus of attention because of the quick turn-around design time. Most designers utilize FPGAs as a prototyping platform where the focus is on functionality. However, with the increasing pressure on time to market, the tremendous increase in the density and complexity of programmable devices, and the flexibility offered by such devices, FPGAs have become a viable alternative to ASIC implementations in many situations. Thus, the performance of designs mapped to FPGA-based platforms has become equally important.

Contemporary FPGA architectures provide a large number of fast physical memories on the device. Xilinx Virtex *BlockRAMs* [1], Altera FLEX 10K *Embedded Array Blocks* [2], and Altera APEX E *Embedded System Blocks* [3] are some of the examples.

With many variations in properties of physical memories, the mapping of data structures in the design is a non-trivial task. Physical memories have multiple ports through which the storage space can be accessed in parallel. There are multiple configurations possible for each port that can be used to minimize wastage of storage space. Also, different types of memories present on a RC provide different read and write latencies. A memory mapper should take all these factors into account.

---

* This work is supported in part by the US Air Force, Wright Laboratory, WPAFB, under contract number F33615-97-C-1043.

The rest of the paper has been arranged as follows. Section 2 discusses some related research. Section 3 describes various features of an RC architecture and the model for input design. Section 4 describes what constitutes mapping of data structures and gives a formal definition of the mapping problem. It also presents details about Tabu Search adapted for the problem. Section 5 presents the heuristic algorithm used to perform the actual mapping. Section 6 describes control logic generation for memory mapping. Various constraints in mapping are presented in Section 7 and the components of the cost function for tabu search in Section 8. We present the results in Section 9.

2 Related Work

As outlined in [4], the process of mapping *data structures to physical memory* can be divided into two steps: *(i)* translating the storage requirements into *logical memories (LMs)*, i.e. forming the data structures needed by the design, and *(ii)* mapping the LMs onto the *physical memories* of the hardware; i.e. assigning the data structures to the memory banks.

In memory synthesis for ASICs, the problem is that of mapping various data structures onto a predefined set of library components. The optimization goals include minimizing the number of different physical memory components used, thus minimizing the overall area; and placing the chosen components so as to minimize routing requirements and signal delay. An ILP approach has been used in [5,6] to group registers to form multi-port memory modules. [7] concentrates on minimizing the area while finding a legal packing of the logical segments into the physical segments.

However, in the case of RCs, the resources available are already fixed. The goal is to optimize performance while satisfying the constraints posed by the RC. [8] and [9] consider single and dual ported memories in FPGAs, but not both at the same time.

In [10], an ILP formulation considers all instances simultaneously and gives optimal mapping. However, as the problem size increases, it takes a long time to converge. In [11], mapping is done in two stages (*global* and *detailed*) to simplify the ILP formulation. However, if an LM is bigger than an instance, it is split in some predefined manner during the first stage. This may prevent the mapper to find the optimal solution.

3 Problem Formulation

3.1 Reconfigurable Platform Description

A generic RC has a set of programmable devices (FPGAs), a set of physical memories, and an interconnection network for communication between various FPGAs and memory banks.

The various physical memories on a RC can be grouped into different clusters, called *memory types*, on the basis of similarities in some of their invariant attributes: A fixed connection already exists between instances of a memory type and its *local_pe*. *Read and Write Latencies* are the number of clock cycles required to perform corresponding operations on that *memory type*. *Num_ports* is the number of ports available on *each* instance of this memory type. The storage space can be accessed through any of these ports in parallel. *Max_storage_bits* is the maximum number of bits of data that can be stored in an instance of this memory type. *Configuration* of a port is the way in which storage space is accessed through that port. It is specified by *(width,depth)* pair. Each word has *#width* bits and there are a total of *#depth* words. *Num_configurations* is the number of different ways in which a port of an instance of this memory type can be configured. *Num_instances* gives the total number of elements of this memory type which are available on the RC. A signal from *local_pe* needs to traverse through *pins_trav* number of pins to access the memory. It represents the proximity of the memory bank to the logic area and is predominant in determining the maximum clock frequency.

3.2   Input Design Description

An LM is modeled as a rectangle; the number of words is represented by the depth of the rectangle while the width represents the number of bits in each word. Each rectangle has a weight, specified by a pair of integers *(num_reads, num_writes)* . The higher the weight of an LM, the greater the influence of the LM on the overall design latency.

4   Tabu Search Formulation

Tabu Search (TS) [12], is a general purpose *meta-heuristic* for solving combinatorial optimization problems. This paper uses Tabu Search to perform memory mapping.

We view an LM as a *complete rectangle*. If split, the complete rectangle can be decomposed into *sub-rectangles*. A mapped sub-rectangle is specified by a tuple of 6 values as shows below:

$$sub\_rectangle = \{phy\_mem\_num, port\_num, depth, width, start\_depth, start\_width\}$$

Physical_mem_num specifies the physical instance to which this sub-rectangle has been mapped. *Port_num* specifies which port of that physical instance will be used to access this sub-rectangle. *depth* and *width* are the dimensions of the sub-rectangle indicating how much of the LM has been mapped to this port. *Start_depth* and *start_width* specify the position of the top-left corner of the sub-rectangle with respect to the complete rectangle. Together, the last four parameters exactly specify which part of the LM is mapped through this sub-rectangle. This information is helpful in automating the initialization of physical instances on the RC. We define the mapping of an LM to be a set of sub-rectangles, one corresponding to each part into which the memory task has been split.

For a mapping to be valid, we require that all its sub-rectangles be mapped to physical instances of the *same memory_type*. We further require that no two sub-rectangles share the same port. If different parts of an LM are mapped to two physical memories whose *local_pes* are not the same, the address and data bus will need to be routed to both PEs. This can greatly deteriorate the quality of the solution. Even if the *local_pe* is the same, memories might differ in read/write latencies. Thus, different parts of the same LM will be available to the logic in different clock cycles. Furthermore, if two sub-rectangles contain different bits of the same word of an LM and get mapped to the same port, more than one read will be required to access the word completely. Our assumption excludes such scenarios without deteriorating the solution.

4.1 Problem Definition

Given

- **Set** $\mathcal{L} = \{l : logical\_memory\}$. $\mathcal{L}$ specifies the input design.
- **Set** $\mathcal{T} = \{t : memory\_type\}$.
- **Set** $\mathcal{P} = \{pm : physical\_mem\_instances | \forall pm : \exists_1 t \in \mathcal{T}\}$. $\mathcal{T}$ and $\mathcal{P}$ are part of the target architecture.
- If logic partitioning information is available, the target architecture specification will also have num_fpgas and **set** $\mathcal{I} = \{i_{f_1 f_2} | 0 \leq f_1, f_2 < num\_fpgas\}$. Each element of $\mathcal{I}$ specifies the number of interconnect pins available between the corresponding FPGA pair.

The objective is to produce another set
$\mathcal{M} = \{m : memory\_mapping \mid \forall l \in \mathcal{L}, \exists_1 l \leftrightarrow m\}$ **such that**
$\{\forall pm \in \mathcal{P}, satisfies(Constraints_{pm})\}$ and $\{\forall i \in \mathcal{I}, satisfies(Constraints_i)\}$

4.2 Memory Mapping Adaption for Tabu Search

The TS operates on an array (of size #LM) of mappings.

- **Neighborhood Moves:** Since the neighborhood space is very large and totally random, we randomly choose a small number of LMs. We heuristically re-map the chosen LMs while mappings for the remaining LMs are retained.
- **Tabu Attributes:** We consider two attributes for each LM re-mapped during an iteration of TS: *from_bank* and *to_bank* are *memory_types* to which the LM was mapped before and after the move. Any move which contemplates to undo a recently made move (by moving the LM to the *from_bank* or from the *to_bank*) will be tabued for the next few iterations, called the *tabu tenure*. Tabu status can be over-ridden if the contemplated solution is better than the best encountered so far (*aspiration criterion*).
- **Residence and Transition Frequency:** These are long-term memories of the TS. Residence Frequency stores the total number of iterations for which a LM was mapped to a bank type. It indicates the suitability of mapping the LM to that bank type. Transition Frequency holds the number of times a

LM was re-mapped from one bank type to another. LMs with high transition frequency generally are smaller in size and their re-mapping causes localized search. Suitably rewarding or penalizing high residence and/or transition frequency can lead to search *intensification* or *diversification* respectively.

- **Restart:** This is a form of medium term memory. After a fixed number of iterations, an average cost of all the solutions explored in the current region is compared with the best cost found so far. If the average cost is significantly higher, chances of finding a new best solution in this region are very small. All memories are reset at restart, and search is restarted with a new random solution.

5   Heuristic: Rectangle Carving

At every iteration, Tabu Search decides which LMs are to be re-mapped and onto which memory type. However, the new mapping for an LM on its memory type is found by a heuristic called *Rectangle Carving* (Figures 1 and 2). The algorithm reads in an LM as a rectangle. It maintains a list of sub-rectangles which are to be mapped. As part of a sub-rectangle is mapped, new ones are carved out of its unmapped part and added to the list. The algorithm continues until all sub-rectangles have been mapped.

```
Algorithm: Map_LM
    Input:
        M : Logical Memory
        B : Bank Type
    Output:
        S : Solution, a set of mapping to ports
begin
    C, R, N : Rectangle
    L :List of Rectangles to map
    P :Physical Port
    U, FORCE :Bool
    R ← Rectangle(M.depth, M.width);
    S ← ∅;
    L ← [R];
    /*initialize L with the rectangle corresponding to M */
    while (L ≠ ∅) loop
        R ← L.first();
        P ← random_port(B);
        U ← port_usable(P, M);
        FORCE ← (max_fails_reached);
        C ← carve_rectangle(R, P, FORCE);
        if (FORCE or (is_valid(C) and U) ) then
            gen_new_subrect (R, C, L);
            L ← L − [R];
            S ← S ∪ {C};
        end if
    end while
end
```

Fig. 1. *Algorithm Map LM*

```
Algorithm: Carve_Rectangle
    Input:
        R :Rectangle to map
        P :Physical Port
        FORCE :Bool
        /*indicates if mapping to be done forcefully*/
    Output:
        C :Rectangle
        /* Carved from R, can be mapped onto P */
begin
    Fitness :Array of fitness, of size #configs
    N :A subset of Port Configurations
    N ← {n|n ∈ Configurations of P
        ∧ n.width ≥ P.curr_config.width}
    for each(n ∈ N) loop
        get_assignable_rect(R, P, n);
        Fitness_n ← func(assignable_depth,
            assignable_width, R);
        save_best_assignable_rectangle();
    end for
    if (BestFitness > 0) then
        C ← Rectangle(best_assignable_depth,
            best_assignable_width);
        P.curr_config ← best_config;
    else
        /* Failed to carve out a rectangle */
        if (FORCE) then
            /* Forcefully assign R to C */
            C ← R;
        else
            /* Try in future iterations */
            C ← NULL;
        end if
    end if
end
```

Fig. 2. *Algorithm Carve Rectangle*

In each iteration, the algorithm tries to map the first sub-rectangle in the list. It randomly picks one of the ports of an instance of a given bank. *port_usable*

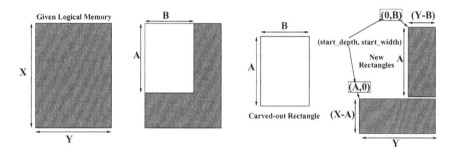

Fig. 3. *Rectangle Carving Process*

performs a check to see if this port has already been assigned to some other sub-rectangle.

Carve_rectangle considers a *subset of configurations* of the selected port and calculates a fitness of mapping the rectangle to each configuration. The fitness depends upon how much of the rectangle can be mapped, whether the rectangle has to be split, and how much storage space would be wasted. We consider only those configurations which have width larger than that required by the already mapped sub-rectangle, if any.

If the carved-out rectangle is smaller than the given rectangle, *at most* two new sub-rectangles, shown in Figure 3, are created out of the unmapped parts. While splitting, we intuitively try to keep all bits of a word in the same rectangle, i.e. depth-wise splitting is preferred over width-wise splitting. The port's configuration is updated to accommodate the new as well as any old rectangles mapped to this port. The overall complexity of mapping an LM to mem_type t is $O(\#Ports_t \times (\#LM + \#config_t))$.

6   Control Logic

6.1   Arbitration

If more than one compute_task access a physical port, arbitration logic is required to serialize any parallel accesses. Also, if several LMs are sharing the same port, tasks accessing either of them will have to be arbitered. If an LM is split across ports, all compute_tasks accessing at least one of these ports will have to be arbitered. All ports whose accessors need to be arbitered are combined together to form a *logical port* for arbitration purpose. A scalable arbiter logic for RCs is presented in [13]. Handshake signals (Request/Acknowledge) are introduced between the arbiter and all corresponding arbitered tasks.

6.2   Address Translation and Enable Logic

An address translation mechanism is required to handle the *mismatch* between the *logical address* coming from the task and the *physical address* location where

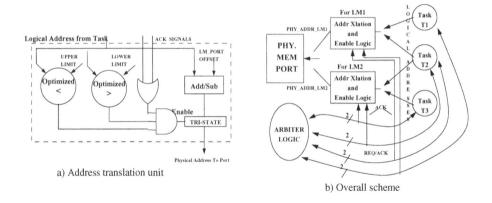

a) Address translation unit

b) Overall scheme

Fig. 4. *Overall Scheme*

that word is placed. If multiple LMs are sharing a port, then only one LM can be placed starting at physical address location 0 of the port. All other LMs will be placed at an *offset*.

One address translation unit (Figure 4a) is required for each *LM-port* pair. *Logical_starting_addr* is the address of the first word of the sub-rectangle of the LM mapped to this port. *Physical_starting_addr* is the address of the physical location where the sub-rectangle is mapped. The difference between the two is added as *lm_port_offset* to the logical address to obtain the actual physical address. Note that the offset value can also be negative. The translated address is given to the input of a tri-state buffer, output of which goes directly to the address port. The enable of this tri-state is controlled by the *lm_port_enable* signal. To assert it, at least one task should be accessing the LM. This is checked by OR*ing* the acknowledge signals generated by the arbiter for tasks accessing the LM. In addition, the logical address coming from the task should be in the range which has been mapped to this port.

6.3   Putting It Together

As shown in Figure 4b, each compute task has address/data ports for each LM it accesses. We assume that when a task is not accessing a particular LM, its corresonding ports are tri-stated. In the case of simultaneous accesses to an LM, the arbiter ensures that only one of the accessing tasks drives the input. If this address is valid for the port and the tri-state logic is enabled, the translated address is sent to the address port. The data bus is directly connected between all accessing tasks and the data port.

7   Constraints

Architectural constraints are dictated by the RC onto which the design has to be mapped.

- **Physical Memory Sizes:** The mapper should ensure that the sum of bits consumed by all LMs assigned to a physical instance does not exceed the maximum capacity of that instance.
- **Interconnect Constraints:** The mapper should ensure that there are enough pins available between each FPGA pair for routing all the address, data, and arbitration signals.
- **Mapping Constraints:** Mapping Constraints are a reflection of the limitations in the ways in which an LM can be mapped. We require that two sub-rectangles of the same LM should not be mapped to the same port.

Design Constraints should be looked upon as broad guidelines being provided by the user based on design requirements. *Sharing of ports between LMs* can lead to better utilization of storage capacity. It also leads to address and data bus sharing between various logical memories. However, the number of compute tasks which need to be arbitered might increase. This will introduce additional delay in memory access, extra arbitration signals to be routed and a bigger area requirement for the arbiter. The user can specify a *Latency Constraint* in the form of an upper limit of the overall read/write latency of the design.

8   Cost Function and Estimation

Tabu Search evaluates a solution by calculating a cost of the current solution. The overall cost function is a weighted sum of the following factors:

- **Latency:** The total number of clock cycles required to perform all read and write operations.
- **Arbitration Cost:** The number of tasks which need to be arbitered at any *logical port* is equal to the sum of number of tasks accessing the LMs. Arbiters of different sizes are pre-synthesized and their areas used while evaluating a solution.
- **Clock Frequency:** Any signal which needs to be routed across chips becomes the bottleneck in operating at high frequency. We take the maximum number of pins traversed by any signal in the design to be an indication of maximum operating clock frequency of the design.
- **Blocks Processed:** Processing multiple sets of data without reconfiguring the device involves introducing a counter for address offset. This is done by packing multiple sets of data in the same memory space. Unused memory instances of the same type can be grouped with used instances to pack more sets of data.
- **Address Translation and Enable Logic:** The size of the logical address bus as well as that of the offset is known. Thus the total area required can be estimated.

Design Name	#LM	Total Words	Exec Time (sec)
DCT1	15	112	17.9
FFT	12	80	15.0
DCT2	10	48	15.4
Laplace	14	509	17.0
MeanValue	13	1200	17.4
LUD	13	1343	17.4
Rand100	100	3513	142

Table 1. *Memory Mapping Results*

Des Num	Num LM	Num Ports	ILP Cost	Heu. Cost	% Diff.
1	8	18	422	422	0.0
2	18	39	770	777	0.9
3	32	63	1292	1319	2.0
4	27	29	1302	1381	5.7
5	27	37	1327	1411	5.9
6	39	95	1584	1622	2.3
7	42	77	1841	1872	1.6
8	49	99	1997	2280	12.4
9	18	52	3139	3143	0.1
10	32	60	4702	4931	4.6

Table 2. *ILP versus Heuristic Results*

– **Address and Data Bus Routing:** Since only one LM can be accessed through a logical port at a time, sharing of the address and data buses between LMs is done. For each logical port, the maximum address and data width required is calculated based on the biggest and widest memory present in it.

9   Results

Table 1 shows results of memory mapping for some benchmark examples. The target architecture is assumed to have one FPGA. There are 3 instances of on-chip memories of size 4096 bits each, with 5 configurations varying in width from 1 to 16 and a read/write latency of 1 clock cycle each. There is one instance of off-chip memory having 2K words, 16-bit wide, single-ported with read latency of 3 and write latency of 1. The total number of words in all LMs is given in Column 3. The last column shows the execution time of the heuristic approach on a SUN Sparc station running at 336MHz with 1344MB of RAM.

Table 2 presents comparison between ILP [10] and heuristic approaches. Designs are characterized by the number of LMs and target architectures by the total number of ports available over all instances of physical memories. As expected, the ILP approach gives better results in terms of lower cost function. However, in many cases, even though a solution was found, the ILP approach did not converge while the heuristic execution time was very small (52 seconds for the largest design). On average, the cost of the heuristic solution is within 3.5% of the ILP cost.

Figure 5 shows different runs of the mapper for the same set of designs and target architectures. Each graph displays two sets of data, one for which sharing of port between LMs was permitted and the other in which it was not. In the portsharing case, bigger logical_ports are formed, leading to sharing of address and data pins between various LMs. This also enabled the mapper to find a constraint satisfying solution very quickly. In fact, for the last 3 designs, no-portsharing constraint prevented the mapper from finding a constraint satisfying solution. We also observe that in each case where a solution was found, portsharing gives lower read/write latencies; this is expected as more LMs are packed into faster physical memories.

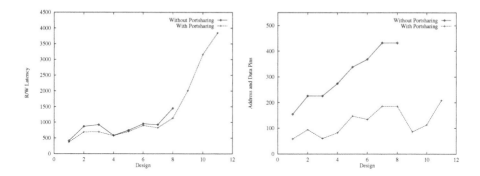

Fig. 5. *Read/Write Latency and Pins Utilized*

References

1. Xilinx Corporation. *"Using Virtex BlockRAMs"*, 1999.
2. Altera Corporation. *"FLEX 10K Embedded Programmable Logic Family Data Sheet"*, May 2000.
3. Altera Corporation. *"APEX 20K Programmable Logic Device Family Data Sheet"*, March 2000.
4. P. Jha and N. Dutt. "High-Level Library Mapping for Memories". In *ACM Transactions on Design Automation of Electronic Systems*, pages 566–603. ACM Press, July 2000.
5. M. Balakrishnan. "Allocation of Multiport Memories in Data Path Synthesis". In *IEEE Transactions on Computer-Aided Design of Integrated Circuits and Systems*, volume 7, pages 536–540, April 1998.
6. I. Ahmad and C. Y. Chen. "Post-Process for Data Path Synthesis". In *Proceedings of International Conference on Computer Aided Design*, pages 276–279. ACM Press, 1991.
7. D. Karchmer and J. Rose. "Definition and Solution of the Memory Packing Problem for Field-Programmable Systems". In *Proceedings of International Conference on Computer Aided Design*, pages 20–26. ACM Press, November 1994.
8. S. Wilton. *"Architectures and Algorithms for Field-Programmable Gate Arrays with Embedded Memory"*. PhD thesis, University of Toronto, 1997.
9. W. Ho and S. Wilton. "Logical-to-Physical Memory Mapping for FPGAs with Dual-Port Embedded Arrays". In *International Workshop on Field Programmable Logic and Applications*, pages 111–123, September 1999.
10. I. Ouaiss and R. Vemuri. "Hierarchical Memory Mapping During Synthesis in FPGA-Based Reconfigurable Computers". In *Design Automation and Testing*

Conference of Europe, pages 284–293, Berlin, Germany, September 2000. Springer-Verlag.

11. I. Ouaiss and R. Vemuri. "Global Memory Mapping During Synthesis in FPGA-Based Reconfigurable Computers". In *Reconfigurable Architectures Workshop*, pages 284–293, San Francisco, September 2000. Springer-Verlag.

12. F. Glover and M. Laguna. *"Tabu Search"*. Kluwer Academic Publishers, 1997.

13. I. Ouaiss and R. Vemuri. "Resource Arbitration in Reconfigurable Computing Environments". In *Proceedings of Design Automation and Test in Europe*, pages 560–566. IEEE Computer Society Press, April 2000.

Implementing a Hidden Markov Model Speech Recognition System in Programmable Logic

Stephen J. Melnikoff, Steven F. Quigley & Martin J. Russell

School of Electronic and Electrical Engineering, University of Birmingham, Edgbaston, Birmingham, B15 2TT, United Kingdom
s.j.melnikoff@iee.org, s.f.quigley@bham.ac.uk,
m.j.russell@bham.ac.uk

Abstract. Performing Viterbi decoding for continuous real-time speech recognition is a highly computationally-demanding task, but is one which can take good advantage of a parallel processing architecture. To this end, we describe a system which uses an FPGA for the decoding and a PC for pre- and post-processing, taking advantage of the properties of this kind of programmable logic device, specifically its ability to perform in parallel the large number of additions and comparisons required. We compare the performance of the FPGA decoder to a software equivalent, and discuss issues related to this implementation.

1 Introduction

The decoder part of a speech recognition system, i.e. the part that converts a pre-processed speech waveform into a sequence of words or sub-word units, is highly computationally demanding.

Current systems work best if they are allowed to adapt to a new speaker, the environment is quiet, and the user speaks relatively carefully; any deviation from this "ideal" will result in significantly increased errors. At present it is not clear whether these problems can be overcome by incremental development of the current algorithms, or whether more fundamental changes are needed. In either case, it is likely that the result will place increased computing demands on the host computer. Hence, as is the case for graphics, it may be advantageous to transfer speech processing to some form of co-processor or other hardware implementation.

Research has been carried out in the past on such implementations, generally using custom hardware. However, with ever more powerful programmable logic devices being available, these chips appear to offer an attractive alternative.

Accordingly, this paper describes the current findings of research into implementing the decoder part of a speech recognition system on a programmable logic device, targeting in particular an FPGA. We describe our most recent implementation, which follows on from the preliminary findings described in [1].

The paper is organised as follows. Section 2 explains the motivation behind the research; this is followed in section 3 by an overview of speech recognition theory and

G. Brebner and R. Woods (Eds.): FPL 2001, LNCS 2147, pp. 81-90, 2001.

Hidden Markov Models. In section 4, we look at current commercial recognition ASICs, before describing the structure of the system in section 5, followed by details of the implementation and discussion of the results in section 6. Section 7 summarises the conclusions drawn so far, and section 8 describes issues that will need to be considered when working on future implementations.

2 Motivation

The increased computational power that a dedicated speech co-processor within a PC would provide could be utilised to improve the quality of the recognition. With more power at the user's disposal, it might be possible to make the system speaker-independent, and less susceptible to errors caused by a noisy environment (e.g. by using real-time noise compensation).

The results described below suggest that a hardware recogniser can perform speech-to-text transcription significantly faster than real time. At its simplest, this could be used for offline transcription, where a recording of speech could very quickly be converted to text.

Also, Viterbi decoding (described below) is often given as an example of a dynamic programming problem. Lessons learnt from a successful FPGA implementation of this could prove applicable to dynamic programming algorithms in non-speech applications.

It should be noted that the unique properties of speech mean that it only needs to be sampled at 100 Hz, giving us up to 10ms to perform all necessary processing. While this may beg the question as to whether we need to perform these calculations using dedicated hardware at all, we can take advantage of this free time to increase the accuracy of the system by improving the algorithm or speech model, so as to do in hardware what it would not be possible to do in software in the same amount of time.

3 Speech Recognition Theory

3.1 Overview

The most widespread and successful approach to speech recognition is based on the Hidden Markov Model (HMM) [2], [4], and is a probabilistic process which models spoken utterances as the outputs of finite state machines (FSMs). The notation here is based on [2].

3.2 The Speech Recognition Problem

The underlying problem is as follows. Given an observation sequence $O = O_0, O_1 ... O_{T-1}$, where each O_t is data representing speech which has been sampled at fixed intervals, and a number of potential models M, each of which is a representation of a particular spoken utterance (e.g. word or sub-word unit), we would like to find the model M which best describes the observation sequence, in the sense that the probability $P(M|O)$ is maximised (i.e. the probability that M is the best model given O).

This value cannot be found directly, but can be computed via Bayes' Theorem [4] by maximising $P(O|M)$. The resulting recognised utterance is the one represented by the model that is most likely to have produced O. The models themselves are based on HMMs.

3.3 The Hidden Markov Model

An N-state Markov Model is completely defined by a set of N states forming a finite state machine, and an $N \times N$ stochastic matrix defining transitions between states, whose elements $a_{ij} = P(\text{state } j \text{ at time } t \,|\, \text{state } i \text{ at time } t\text{-}1)$; these are the *transition probabilities*.

With a Hidden Markov Model, each state additionally has associated with it a probability density function $b_j(O_t)$ which determines the probability that state j emits a particular observation O_t at time t (the model is "hidden" because any state could have emitted the current observation). The p.d.f. can be continuous or discrete; accordingly the pre-processed speech data can be a multi-dimensional vector or a single quantised value. $b_j(O_t)$ is known as the *observation probability*.

Such a model can only generate an observation sequence $O = O_0, O_1 \ldots O_{T-1}$ via a state sequence of length T, as a state only emits one observation at each time t. The set of all such state sequences can be represented as routes through the state-time trellis shown in Fig. 1. The $(j,t)^{\text{th}}$ node (a state within the trellis) corresponds to the hypothesis that observation O_t was generated by state j. Two nodes $(i,t\text{-}1)$ and (j,t) are connected if and only if $a_{ij} > 0$.

As described above, we compute $P(M|O)$ by first computing $P(O|M)$. Given a state sequence $Q = q_0, q_1 \ldots q_{T-1}$, where the state at time t is q_t, the joint probability, given a model M, of state sequence Q and observation sequence O is given by:

$$P(O, Q | M) = b_0(O_0) \prod_{t=1}^{T-1} a_{q_{t-1} q_t} b_{q_t}(O_t) , \tag{1}$$

assuming the HMM is in state 0 at time $t = 0$. $P(O|M)$ is then the sum of all possible routes through the trellis, i.e.

$$P(O | M) = \sum_{\text{all } Q} P(O, Q | M) . \tag{2}$$

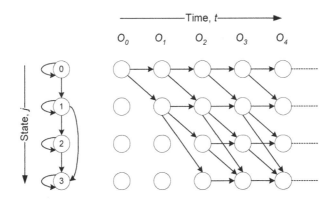

Fig. 1. Hidden Markov Model, showing the finite state machine for the HMM (*left*), the observation sequence (*top*), and all the possible routes through the trellis (*arrowed lines*)

3.4 Viterbi Decoding

In practice, the probability $P(O|M)$ is approximated by the probability associated with the state sequence which *maximises* $P(O,Q|M)$. This probability is computed efficiently using Viterbi decoding.

Firstly, we define the value $\delta_t(j)$, which is the maximum probability that the HMM is in state j at time t. It is equal to the probability of the most likely partial state sequence $q_0, q_1 ... q_t$, which emits observation sequence $O = O_0, O_1 ... O_t$, and which ends in state j:

$$\delta_t(j) = \max_{q_0, q_1 \cdots q_t} P(q_0, q_1 ... q_t; q_t = j; O_0, O_1 ... O_t | M). \tag{3}$$

It follows from equations (1) and (3) that the value of $\delta_t(j)$ can be computed recursively as follows:

$$\delta_t(j) = \max_{0 \le i \le N-1} [\delta_{t-1}(i) a_{ij}] \cdot b_j(O_t), \tag{4}$$

where i is the previous state (i.e. at time t-1).

This value determines the most likely predecessor state $\psi_t(j)$, for the current state j at time t, given by:

$$\psi_t(j) = \arg\max_{0 \le i \le N-1} [\delta_{t-1}(i) a_{ij}]. \tag{5}$$

At the end of the observation sequence, we backtrack through the most likely predecessor states in order to find the most likely state sequence. Each utterance has an HMM representing it, and so this sequence not only describes the most likely route through a particular HMM, but by concatenation provides the most likely sequence of HMMs, and hence the most likely sequence of words or sub-word units uttered.

4 Speech Recognition ASICs and Cores

In order to better appreciate how this implementation compares to existing commercial speech recognition hardware and firmware, a few examples are given below.

4.1 ASICs

Sensory RSC-300 & RSC-364. These two chips [6] are based on an 8-bit 14MHz RISC microprocessor, and use a pre-trained neural network to perform speaker-independent speech recognition. They can store 6 speaker-dependent words in on-chip RAM, with the RSC-300 using off-chip storage to enable no limit on vocabulary size (subject, of course, to access times). They boast speaker-independent recognition accuracy of 97%, with 99% for speaker-dependent, and a response time of 83ms.

These devices are designed for use in "consumer electronics products," with similar chips targeted for use in toys.

Sensory Voice Direct 364. This device is also based on a neural network, but is purely speaker-dependent. It can operate under the control of a separate microprocessor, permitting a 60-word vocabulary, or on its own which limits it to 15 words. It is capable of 99% accuracy, with a response time of less than 500ms.

Philips HelloIC. This device [5] uses a 16-bit fixed point DSP to allow both speaker-dependent and independent speech recognition, with a vocabulary of 15 words. It operates at 30MHz, and is capable of "noise robustness" and echo cancellation.

DSPs. Some DSPs have dedicated logic for Viterbi decoding. For example, the Texas Instruments TMS320C54x family [7] has a Compare, Select, and Store Unit which is used for the add-compare-select part of the decoding process. As with comparable FPGA cores, however, this is designed more for signal processing applications than speech recognition.

4.2 FPGA Cores

A comparable FPGA core is TILAB's Viterbi Decoder core [8]. On a Virtex XCV50-6, it requires 495 slices, and runs at 56MHz - but only accepts 6-bit inputs. This is because Viterbi decoding was originally designed for signal processing applications, specifically for the decoding of convolutional codes; hence the core is best suited to that kind of application, and not speech, which tends to require larger data widths.

Xilinx also has a decoder core [9], again designed for signal processing rather than speech recognition, which provides a choice between a parallel version, requiring 1000-2000 Virtex-II slices running at 90-130 MHz, and a serial one, requiring around 500 slices operating at 200 MHz.

5 System Design

5.1 System Structure

The complete system consists of a PC, and an FPGA on a development board inside it. For this implementation, we used already pre-processed speech waveforms.

The waveforms are quantised, and the resulting data sent to the FPGA, which performs the decoding, outputting the set of most likely predecessor states. This is sent back to the PC, which performs the simple backtracking process in software.

5.2 FPGA Implementation Structure

The structure of the implemented design is shown in Fig. 2. The HMM Block contains the processing elements which compute $\delta_t(j)$, the probability of the observation sequence up to time t and the "best" partial state sequence terminating in state j at time t; and the most probable predecessors $\psi_t(j)$. The $\delta_t(j)$ values are then passed to the Scaler, which scales the data in order to reduce the required precision, and discards values which have caused an underflow.

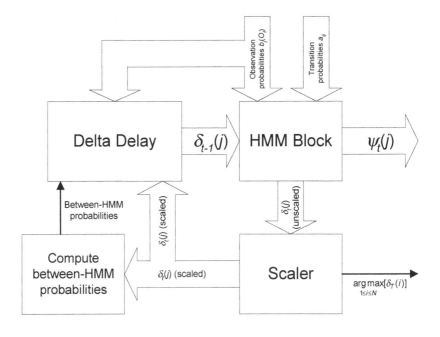

Fig. 2. System structure. The HMM Block contains the processing elements - nodes - which compute $\delta_t(j)$, the probability of the observation sequence up to time t and the "best" partial state sequence terminating in state j at time t; and the most probable predecessors $\psi_t(j)$

In order to keep the design as simple as possible, no language model is being used. As a result, the probability of a transition from one HMM's exit state to another's entry state is the same for all HMMs. This value is computed by a dedicated block, which passes it to Delta Delay. Delta Delay is used at initialisation to set the values of $\delta_0(j)$, and thereafter routes the scaled values of $\delta_t(j)$ back to the HMM Block, while ensuring that the various data streams are properly synchronised.

The node is the basic processing unit for performing Viterbi decoding, and each one processes the data corresponding to one state of an HMM. As every node depends only on the outputs of nodes produced in the previous time frame, and not the current one, the nodes can all be implemented in parallel.

The structure of the nodes is very similar to that used in previous parallel implementations, and is shown in Fig. 3. All calculations are performed in the log domain. This makes the system particularly appropriate for FPGAs, as it reduces all the arithmetic to addition-type operations (in this case, addition, comparison and subtraction), for which FPGAs tend to have dedicated logic.

The most likely predecessor $\psi_t(j)$ information is stored off-chip, and processed in software, as it requires more storage than is available on the FPGA, and does not demand much processing power.

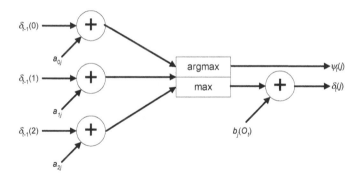

Fig. 3. Node structure. Each node processes the data corresponding to one state of an HMM. As every node depends only on the outputs of nodes produced in the previous time frame, and not the current one, the nodes can all be implemented in parallel

5.3 Data Format

For this implementation, we used a simple model consisting of 49 monophones - i.e. just vowels and consonants - of 3 states each, with no language model, which gave a recognition accuracy of 50%. The data for this model was calculated using the HTK speech recognition toolkit [3], based on a set of recorded speech waveforms from the TIMIT database. The speech observations themselves consisted of 8-bit values, treated as addresses into 256-entry 15-bit-wide look-up tables, one for each node.

6 Implementation and Results

The design described above was implemented on a Xilinx Virtex XCV1000, sitting on Celoxica's RC1000-PP development board. The RC1000 is a PCI card, which features 8Mb of RAM, accessible by both the PC and FPGA, 8-bit data ports in each direction with handshaking control, and two 1-bit data lines.

The RC1000 was used within a PC with a Pentium III 450MHz processor. C++ software was written to do pre- and post-processing, and was also capable of carrying out all the same calculations as the FPGA, in order to compare performance. The code was written so as to be as functionally similar to the VHDL as possible, with the exception that scaling was found to be unnecessary.

6.1 Implementation Overview

The design was implemented in three versions, each able to process a different number of HMMs in parallel. The first attempted to process all 49 HMMs in parallel, but did not fit into the XCV1000, requiring 100% of the FPGA's slices, which along with a $\delta_t(j)$ data bus over 2000 bits wide resulted in a design which could not be routed.

In order to substantially reduce the required resources, a second version was implemented which cut the number of parallel HMMs to 7, with the other modules in the system reduced in size accordingly. The final design required 70% of the slices, and routed successfully.

However, this implementation was still not satisfactory, as there was a significant bottleneck when it came to reading from and writing to off-chip RAM. In addition, any future implementation based on a more complex algorithm (e.g. continuous HMMs) would have no more space on the FPGA with which to perform additional calculations as required.

In order to overcome these problems, a third version was designed which dealt with just one HMM at a time, reducing the resource usage, and matching the internal bandwidth with that available for accessing the RAM, thereby reducing the delay incurred by the second implementation.

6.2 Data Storage

We previously [1] compared the use of off-chip RAM, on-chip distributed RAM and on-chip Block RAM, and in this implementation, we use all three. The observation probabilities form the largest block of data - nearly 70Kb. This amount is too large to store on the FPGA, and in any case we do not need it all at once, so the data is stored in the RAM banks on the RC1000 board, and the relevant parts loaded in when a new observation is received.

The transition probabilities are somewhat smaller at 830 bytes, and so are stored in Block RAM. The between-HMM probabilities occupy even less space, and are stored in distributed RAM.

6.3 Hardware

7-HMM Implementation. The implementation tools (Xilinx Foundation Design Manager 2.1i SP6) reported a maximum clock frequency of 31MHz. The design required 26 cycles to process a single observation, but because the internal data bus was larger than the off-chip RAM data bus, further delays were incurred: 36 cycles to read in the observation probabilities $(b_j(O_t))$ from RAM and 20 to write the predecessor information $(\psi_t(j))$ back to RAM. As some of the RAM accesses could take place while data was being processed, a total of 77 cycles were required.

Hence from these figures, we expected a complete observation cycle to take around 2.7µs. Experiments showed the average time (taken to be the mean time to process each observation value and write the results to RAM) to be 2.1µs.

1-HMM Implementation. This design returned a maximum clock frequency of 86.4MHz. This higher value is partly due to greater use of pipelining and relationally-placed macros, and gives a predicted time per observation of 2.5µs.

The narrower data width led to a longer pipeline - 117 cycles. However, the effective delay due to RAM accesses was reduced, as data from RAM could enter the pipeline as soon as it was read, rather than being buffered first as was done in the previous implementation.

6.4 Comparison with Software

The equivalent processing was performed in software on the same PC as used above. The average time per observation (taken as the time required to compute the most likely predecessor information otherwise done by the HMM Block, and the between-HMM probabilities) was found to be 790µs.

For the 7-HMM implementation, this gives a speedup over software of 370, and we predict that the 1-HMM implementation will give a speedup of at least 310.

7 Conclusion

We have implemented a simple monophone HMM-based speech recogniser, using an FPGA to perform the decoding, and a host PC to send it the speech observations, and process the results. We have also implemented the decoder in software in order to compare performance.

Our findings so far are that while the FPGA can easily outperform the PC, the degree to which the algorithm can be parallelised within the FPGA is limited by the bandwidth restriction between the FPGA and RAM, leading to a less parallel implementation than originally planned. However, this implementation is expected to operate at a comparable speed to its predecessor, while leaving more space free on the device for use in the future.

8 Further Issues

- **Types of HMM:** We mention above that the speech data is quantised; such discrete HMM-based systems tend to perform poorly in term of accuracy. A better approach is to use continuous HMMs, where the data is processed to extract feature vectors, with the observation probability distribution based on Gaussian mixtures.
- **Real-time recognition:** This system is essentially an off-line transcription system, in that the speech data is sent to the FPGA and processed as fast as is possible, and backtracking does not take place until the (known) end of the speech. Since, for a real-time continuous speech recognition system, the length of the speech data is not known in advance, other methods exist for initiating backtracking. The pre- and post-processing can be done in software in real time.

References

1. Melnikoff, S.J., James-Roxby, P.B., Quigley, S.F. & Russell, M.J., "Reconfigurable computing for speech recognition: preliminary findings," *FPL 2000, LNCS #1896*, pp.495-504.
2. Rabiner, L.R., "A tutorial on Hidden Markov Models and selected applications in speech recognition," *Proceedings of the IEEE*, 77, No.2, 1989, pp.257-286.
3. Woodland, P.C., Odell, J.J., Valtchev, V. & Young, S.J. "Large vocabulary continuous speech recognition using HTK," *ICASSP '94*, 2, pp.125-128.
4. Young, S., "A review of large-vocabulary continuous-speech recognition," *IEEE Signal Processing Magazine*, 13, No.5, 1996, pp.45-57.
5. http://www.speech.philips.com/ud/get/Pages/vc_home.htm
6. http://www.sensoryinc.com/
7. http://dspvillage.ti.com/docs/dspproducthome.jhtml
8. http://www.xilinx.com/ipcenter/catalog/search/alliancecore/tilab_viterbi_decoder.htm
9. http://www.xilinx.com/ipcenter/catalog/search/logicore/viterbi_decoder.htm

Implementation of (Normalised) RLS Lattice on Virtex

Felix Albu[1], Jiri Kadlec[2], Chris Softley[3], Rudolf Matousek[2], Antonin Hermanek[2]
Nick Coleman[3], Anthony Fagan[1]

[1]University College Dublin, Ireland
felix@ee.ucd.ie
[2]UTIA Prague, Czech Republic
Kadlec@utia.cas.cz
[3]University of Newcastle upon Tyne, UK
C.I.Softley@ncl.ac.uk

Abstract. We present an implementation of a complete RLS Lattice and Normalised RLS Lattice cores for Virtex. The cores accept 24-bit fixed point inputs and produce 24-bit fixed point prediction error. Internally, the computations are based on 32bit logarithmic arithmetic. On Virtex XCV2000E-6, it takes 22% and 27% of slices respectively and performs at 45 MHz. The cores outperform (4-5 times) the standard DSP solution based on 32 bit floating point TMS320C3x/4x 50MHz processors.

Introduction

The lattice algorithms solve the least-squares problem in a recursive form. They require less arithmetic operations than RLS (order N) [2]. They offer a number of advantages over conventional LMS transversal algorithms such us faster rate of convergence, modular structure and insensitivity to variations in the eigenvalue spread of the input correlation matrix. Another feature of the lattice-based algorithms is their good performance when implemented in finite-precision arithmetic [2]. However, the high computational load of division or square-root operations is one of the reasons why these algorithms are usually not used in real-time applications. They need floating point-like precision, and this has been a severe restriction for FPGA use. FPGA offers a viable alternative to programmable DSP processors or ASIC for some applications (see for example [7,8]). As an alternative to floating-point, the logarithmic number system offers the potential to perform real multiplication, division and square-root at fixed-point speed and, in the case of multiply and divide, with no rounding error at all. These advantages are, however, offset by the problem of performing logarithmic addition and subtraction. Hitherto this has been slower or less accurate than floating-point, or has required very cumbersome hardware. Following the discovery of new arithmetic techniques at Newcastle, however, it is possible to perform logarithmic addition and subtraction with speed and accuracy equivalent to that of floating-point [1,3]. The patented solution developed by the HSLA project team under Dr. Coleman, yields a drastic reduction in the size of the look-up tables

G. Brebner and R. Woods (Eds.): FPL 2001, LNCS 2147, pp. 91-100, 2001.

required compared to those needed for conventional linear interpolation of both functions. This is achieved by the parallel evaluation of a linear approximant and an error correction term. Furthermore, it has been shown that a modified form of LNS operation is possible, which delivers considerably better precision in applications involving underflow. This "Extended Precision LNS" is described in [4]. Coleman's approach leads to a suitable solution for the FPGA implementation. It avoids the need for a barrel shifter, implementation of which is area-costly and ineffective in an FPGA. The LNS ALU provides one of the first hardware solutions to this problem. For a description of the ALU see [5]. We present results of the implementation based on this 32-bit logarithmic ALU designed in Handel C for the Celoxica DK1 toolset [6]. The core takes just 8% of the XILINX Virtex XCV2000E-6 device. It operates at 53MHz and implements all the basic operations of logarithmic arithmetic (ADD, SUB, MUL, DIV and SQRT), with precision equal to or better than:
– the standard IEEE 32-bit floating point used in new DSPs
– the TI 32-bit floating point standard used in the TMS320C30/C40 devices.

The block diagram for our implementation is presented in Fig.1. In the next two sections we present the Lattice RLS algorithm based on *A Posteriori* errors and the Normalised *A Posteriori* Error Lattice RLS algorithm.

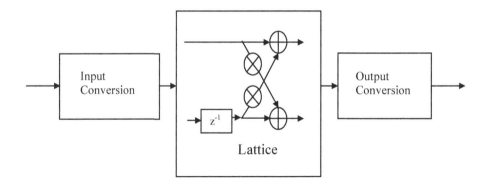

Fig. 1. Block diagram of LNS Lattice implementation

Lattice RLS Algorithm

Table 1 presents the Lattice RLS (LRLS) Algorithm based on *A Posteriori* errors [2]:

Initialisation
Do for $i = 0,1,..., N$
$$\delta(-1,i) = \delta_D(-1,i) = 0, \xi_{b_{min}}^d(-1,i) = \xi_{f_{min}}^d(-1,i) = \varepsilon$$
$$\gamma(-1,i) = 1, e_b(-1,i) = 0$$

Do for $k \geq 0$

$$\gamma(k,0)=1, e_b(k,0)= e_f(k,0)= x(k), e(k,0)= d(k)$$

$$\xi^d_{b_{min}}(k,0)= \xi^d_{f_{min}}(k,0)= x^2(k)+ \lambda\xi^d_{f_{min}}(k-1,0)$$

For each $k \geq 0$, do for $i = 0,1,..., N$

$$\delta(k,i)= \lambda\delta(k-1,i)+ \frac{e_b(k-1,i)e_f(k,i)}{\gamma(k-1,i)}$$

$$\gamma(k,i+1)= \gamma(k,i)- \frac{e_b^2(k,i)}{\xi^d_{b_{min}}(k,i)}$$

$$k_b(k,i)= \frac{\delta(k,i)}{\xi^d_{f_{min}}(k,i)}$$

$$k_f(k,i)= \frac{\delta(k,i)}{\xi^d_{b_{min}}(k-1,i)}$$

$$e_b(k,i+1)= e_b(k-1,i)- k_b(k,i)e_f(k,i)$$

$$e_f(k,i+1)= e_f(k,i)- k_f(k,i)e_b(k-1,i)$$

$$\xi^d_{b_{min}}(k,i+1)= \xi^d_{b_{min}}(k-1,i)- \frac{\delta^2(k,i)}{\xi^d_{f_{min}}(k,i)}$$

$$\xi^d_{f_{min}}(k,i+1)= \xi^d_{f_{min}}(k,i)- \frac{\delta^2(k,i)}{\xi^d_{b_{min}}(k-1,i)}$$

Feed-forward Filtering

$$\delta_D(k,i)= \lambda\delta_D(k-1,i)+ \frac{e(k,i)e_b(k,i)}{\gamma(k,i)}$$

$$v_i(k)= \frac{\delta_D(k,i)}{\xi^d_{b_{min}}(k,i)}$$

$$e(k,i+1)= e(k,i)- v_i(k)e_b(k,i)$$

Table 1. The Lattice RLS Algorithm based on *A Posteriori* Errors.

$e_f(k,i)$ represents the instantaneous *a posteriori* forward prediction error, $e_b(k,i)$ represent the instantaneous *a posteriori* backward prediction error, $\xi_{f_{min}}(k,i)$ and $\xi_{b_{min}}(k,i)$ are the minimum in least-squares sense of the forward and backward prediction errors respectively. The coefficients $k_f(k,i)$ and $k_b(k,i)$ are called the forward and backward reflection coefficients. $\gamma(k,i)$ is a conversion factor between *a priori* and *a posteriori* errors and $v_i(k)$ are the feedforward multiplier coefficients.

The Normalised LRLS Algorithm

Table 2 presents the Normalised *A Posteriori* Error LRLS Algorithm [2] :

Initialisation
Do for $i = 0,1,..., N$
$$\bar{\delta}(-1,i)= 0, \bar{\delta}_D(-1,i)= 0, \bar{e}_b(-1,i)= 0$$
$$\sigma_x^2(-1)= \lambda\sigma_d^2(-1)= \varepsilon$$
Do for $k \geq 0$
$$\sigma_x^2(k)= \lambda\sigma_x^2(k-1)+ x^2(k)\,\text{(Input signal energy)}$$
$$\sigma_d^2(k)= \lambda\sigma_d^2(k-1)+ d^2(k)\,\text{(Reference signal energy)}$$
$$\bar{e}_b(k,0)= \bar{e}_f(k,0)= x(k)/\sigma_x(k)$$
$$\bar{e}(k,0)= d(k)/\sigma_d(k)$$
For each $k \geq 0$ do for $i = 0,1,..., N$
$$\bar{\delta}(k,i)= \bar{\delta}(k-1,i)\sqrt{\left(1-\bar{e}_b^2(k-1,i)\right)\left(1-\bar{e}_f^2(k,i)\right)}+\bar{e}_b(k-1,i)\bar{e}_f(k,i)$$
$$\bar{e}_b(k,i+1)= \frac{\bar{e}_b(k-1,i)-\bar{\delta}(k,i)\bar{e}_f(k,i)}{\sqrt{\left(1-\bar{\delta}^2(k,i)\right)\left(1-\bar{e}_f^2(k,i)\right)}}$$
$$\bar{e}_f(k,i+1)= \frac{\bar{e}_f(k,i)-\bar{\delta}(k,i)\bar{e}_b(k-1,i)}{\sqrt{\left(1-\bar{\delta}^2(k,i)\right)\left(1-\bar{e}_b^2(k-1,i)\right)}}$$
Feedforward filter
$$\bar{\delta}_D(k,i)= \bar{\delta}_D(k-1,i)\sqrt{\left(1-\bar{e}_b^2(k,i)\right)\left(1-\bar{e}^2(k,i)\right)}+\bar{e}(k,i)\bar{e}_b(k,i)$$
$$\bar{e}(k,i+1)= \frac{1}{\sqrt{\left(1-\bar{e}_b^2(k,i)\right)\left(1-\bar{\delta}_D^2(k,i)\right)}}\left[\bar{e}(k,i)-\bar{\delta}_D(k,i)\bar{e}_b(k,i)\right]$$

Table 2. The Normalised *A Posteriori* Error LRLS Algorithm

The reconstructed $e(k, N+1)$ is the standard prediction error and it must be up to the numerical rounding identical to the prediction error produced by the normal RLS lattice. Only this reconstructed prediction error can be reasonably compared with the prediction error produced by other RLS algorithms.

$$e(k, N+1) = \left(\overline{e}(k, N+1) \prod_{j=0}^{N} \sqrt{(1 - \overline{e}_b^2(k, j))} \prod_{j=0}^{N} \sqrt{(1 - \overline{\delta}_D^2(k, j))} \right) \sigma_d(k) \tag{1}$$

The "chain" of 2 x N supplementary multiplications can be performed by Extended-LNS. Only the final single re-scaling needs the standard LNS multiplication and returns us to the "real" domain.

Results

The Lattice RLS Algorithm based on *A Posteriori* Errors and the Normalised *A Posteriori* Error LRLS Algorithm were used to identify a system with impulse response **h**=[0.1 0.3 0.0 –0.2 –0.4 –0.7 –0.4 –0.2]. The input signal was generated as a first-order AR process with the eigenvalue spread of the correlation matrix of 20 [2]. The forgetting factor was $\lambda = 0.96$ and the parameter $\varepsilon = 0.01$. The standard deviation of the input was 1 and the standard deviation of measurement noise was 0.01. Results for the double implementations of LRLS and NLRLS are identical. However, the finite implementations have slightly different performances (Fig.2).

In order to compare the numerical properties of the different implementations we used a procedure similar to that described in [4]. An input noise signal was generated. Starting from time 500 the noise signal is changed to a sine, thereby creating non-persistent excitation and hence poorly conditioned operation. An accurate standard for comparison of the outputs was obtained by presenting this input data to the IEEE double precision floating-point versions of each filter.

Figs. 3-4 present the absolute sum of errors for the output results of the identification of a 30th order FIR regression model by this filter, with exp. weighting factor 0.9. The two algorithms have different numerical properties and each has errors in a different range [2]. Some time after the start of non-persistent excitation at time 500, however, each implementation could become unstable, with the accumulation of successively larger errors. We notice that FLOAT-LRLS and the LNS-LRLS errors start to grow very much after 100 samples of the non-persistent excitation. In the same time ELNS-NLRLS and LNS-NLRLS start to drift at about 200 samples of the non-persistent excitation. These results are comparable to the RMGS and NL RMGS RLS reported in [4]. Therefore LNS enables at no substantial cost to go to the normalised version of the algorithm and gain the robustness in the comparison with the un-normalised version. The normalised lattice is particularly suitable for extended LNS implementation because of its normalised internal variables.

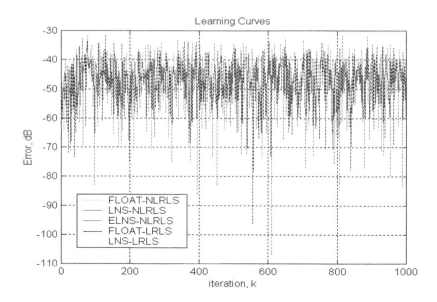

Fig. 2. The learning curves for FLOAT 32bit and LNS implementations of Lattice RLS and Normalised Lattice RLS Algorithms

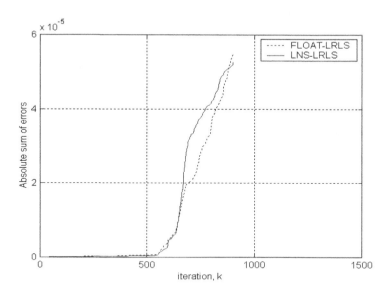

Fig. 3. The absolute sum of errors for FLOAT and LNS implementation of the Lattice RLS Algorithm.

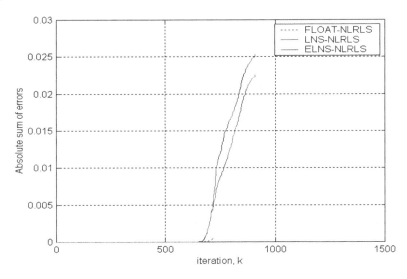

Fig. 4. The absolute sum of errors for ELNS, FLOAT and LNS implementation of the Normalised Lattice RLS Algorithm

Comparison of LNS FPGA Implementation with TMS320C30/C40

The instruction counts for 8th order filters are presented in Tables 4-6. In counting FLP operations, additions and subtractions were recorded from LRLS or NLRLS algorithm equations. The number of multiplications and divisions is about twice the number of additions and subtraction operations. Therefore these algorithms are suitable for LNS implementation. Clock cycles for each type of operation are presented in Table 3. int2* and *2int indicate the functions for conversion to/from int domain to/from log or floating point domain. The conversion to/from log domain is based on evaluation of the rational polynomial approximation of log and antilog in the range (-1,1) conversion. The log ALU is used for the conversion. For details see [5].

	add	sub	mul	div	Sqrt	Int2*	*2int
C3X/4X	4	4	4	62	92	2	2
Log	10	10	1	1	1	100	60

Table 3. Comparison of LNS and FLOAT execution time (clock cycles)

The LNS multiplication, division and square-root operations are implemented by fixed-point addition, subtraction, right shift and are extremely efficient. LNS addition and subtraction, implemented as described in [1], requires a number of table-lookups. In the current arrangement these tables are located in four external banks of SRAM, and hence require several cycles to access [5]. Future FPGA implementations will use the on-chip RAM, which will yield a substantial decrease in the latency of these operations.

	add	sub	mul	div	int2*	*2int	Cycles	Speedup
C3X/4X	17	48	74	64	2	1	**4,530**	**1**
Log	21	44	74	64	2	1	**1,048**	**3.9**
Log/par	21	44	24	16	2	1	**950**	**4.3**

Table 4. Clock cycle counts (LRLS algorithm) TMS320C30/40 in comparison with FPGA.

	add	sub	mul	Div	sqrt	int2*	*2int	Cycles	Speedup
C3X/4X	18	72	167	26	50	2	1	**7,246**	**1**
Log	24	66	167	26	50	2	1	**1,403**	**4.6**
Log/par	24	66	48	0	16	2	1	**1,224**	**5.3**

Table 5. Clock cycle counts (NLRLS algorithm) TMS320C30/40 in comparison with FPGA.

Tables 4-5 compare the clock cycles for processing of one input/output sample for the 8-th order filter.

The last line of the tables, denoted Log/par, indicates additional savings and speedup gained by parallel execution of mul, div and sqrt operations in the FPGA. This is illustrated in the following example.

```
par
{ lsub(lxifmin[lj], ltemp2, lxifmin[lj+1],zsl);

    { ltemp5= lm(lkappab[lj], lef);

      ltemp6= lm(lkappaf[lj], loldeb[lj]);

      ltemp1=ld(leb[lj], lxibmin[lj]);

    }

}
```

This small section of code is taken from the Handel C implementation. It outlines the style of parallel programming of the LNS ALU. The subtract operation lsub() executes in parallel with 2 instances of the HW macros for logarithmic multiplication lm() and one for division ld(). It is possible, because the log. mult is just 32bit integer add and divide is 32bit integer subtract. Macro lsub() is in fact an interface to a parallel HW module. The HW receives operands through a set of channels. After 9 to 12 clock cycles, the 32bit LNS results and status are returned by a second set of channels. We "programme" the Lattice algorithm as a HW module communicating with the large single LNS ADD/SUB module. All other operations are created in parallel, distributed logic. Our Virtex XCV2000E-6 implementations of LRLS and NLRLS algorithms work at 45MHz clocks and takes 22% and 27% of slices respectively on this device.

Algorithms were coded in Handel-C 2.1 and Celoxica DK1. The reported performance has been achieved by this path:

1. Celoxica DK1 (using the Handel C2.1 compatible code) with export to VHDL.
2. Synplify 5.3 from Synplicity to create EDIF.
3. XILINX Alliance 3.3i tools to place and route from the EDIF netlist for the FPGAs.
4. The Virtex XCV2000E-6 on the RC1000 board [6] was used for the implementation.
5. MSVC code was used for interfacing of RC1000 board to Matlab. See [5] for details.

Conclusions

The LNS implementation of the LRLS algorithms in an FPGA offers better speed than C30/C40 DSP floating-point and provides a low-cost, efficient solution for different system-on-chip applications. The resulting RLS Lattice cores operate with 24-bit precision fixed point input/output signals. Therefore, the internal conversion to the log domain and the internal LNS operations can be hidden from the user. Our Virtex XCV2000E-6 implementation works with 45MHz clocks and if compared with 50MHz TI C30/C40 DSP, it provides significant speedup without any loss of precision.

The analyzed 8-th order Normalised RLS Lattice filter works on this FPGA device at 36.7 kHz, while 50MHz C30/C40 allows just 6.9 kHz. This gives the sustained performance 12 Mflops for Virtex (input domain conversion is counted just one operation) and 2.3 Mflops for C30. Both RLS lattice algorithms have efficient LNS implementation because of numerous divisions or square-roots operations. The un-normalised LRLS algorithm is less complex than the normalized one. However, the sampling rate is just about 20% faster (47kHz for the same FPGA). We have demonstrated that the Normalised RLS Lattice has superior robustness to the non-persistent excitation. These algorithms could be used in applications like echo cancellation, noise reduction, channel equalization. Our future work will be focused in implementing these algorithms using multiple pipelined logarithmic ALUs.

Acknowledgment

The authors wish to thank the referees for their helpful suggestions. This work has been performed under the EU ESPRIT 33544 HSLA Long-term research project (http://napier.ncl.ac.uk/HSLA), coordinated by the University of Newcastle, UK.

References

[1] J.N. Coleman, E.I.Chester, 'A 32-bit Logarithmic Arithmetic Unit and Its Performance Compared to Floating-Point', *14th Symposium on Computer Arithmetic'*, Adelaide, April 1999

[2] Paulo S.R. Diniz, Algorithms and Practical Implementation, Kluwer Academic Publishers, 1997

[3] J.N.Coleman, E.Chester, C.Softley and J.Kadlec "Arithmetic on the European Logarithmic Microprocessor", IEEE Trans. Comput. Special Edition on Computer Arithmetic, July 2000. Vol. 49, No. 7, p702-715.

[4] Coleman J. N., Kadlec J.: Extended Precision Logarithmic Arithmetics. In Proceedings of the 34-th IEEE Asilomar Conference on Signals, Systems and Computers, Monterey USA. November 2000.

[5] J. Kadlec, A. Hermanek, Ch.Softley, R. Matousek, M. Licko "32-bit Logarithmic ALU for Handel C 2.1 and Celoxica DK1 (53 MHz for XCV2000E-6 based RC1000 board)" Results will be presented at Celoxica user conference (In Stratford, UK, 2-3. April, 2001. Download from: http://www.celoxica.com/programs/university/academic_papers.htm

[6] RC1000-PP Hardware Reference Manual, Celoxica, United Kingdom http://www.celoxica.com/products/boards/DATRHD001.2.pdf

[7] R.L. Walke, R.W.M.Smith, G. Lightbody, "20 GFLOPS QR processor on a Xilinx Virtex-E FPGA", SPIE, San Diego, 2000, U.S.A

[8] R.L. Walke, J. Dudley, "An FPGA based digital radar receiver for Soft Radar", 34th Asilomar Conference on Signals, Systems, and Computers, Monterey, 2000, California, U.S.A

Accelerating Matrix Product on Reconfigurable Hardware for Signal Processing

[*] Abbes Amira, Ahmed Bouridane, and Peter Milligan

School of Computer Science
The Queen's University of Belfast
Belfast BT7 1NN, Northern Ireland
[*] A.Abbes@qub.ac.uk

Abstract. This paper investigates how some of the new features of the Xilinx Virtex FPGA may be used to support efficient and optimised implementation of matrix product based on Multiply and Accumulate (MAC) such operations are frequently used in signal applications. The principle new features that have been investigated are the Block RAM and the fully digital Delay-Locked Loop (DLL). The approach used for the matrix multiplication algorithm employs the idea used in the modified Booth encoder multiplication using Wallace Trees addition. Preliminary performance results and comparisons with similar algorithms implemented on multi-FPGA platforms have shown better performance for the proposed architecture.

1. Introduction

As Field Programmable Gate Arrays (FPGAs) have grown in capacity, improved in performance, and decreased in cost, they have become a viable solution for performing computationally intensive tasks, with the ability to tackle applications for custom chips and programmable digital signal processing (DSP) devices [8], [9]. One of the very well known applications in signal processing is beamforming, which is useful in many types of applications including ultrasound medical imaging, sonar processing and antenna imaging [5], [9], [4].

Generally, beamforming is a spatial filtering operation performed on the data received by an array of sensors, such as antennas, microphones, or hydrophones. It provides a system with the ability to "listen" directionally even when the individual sensors in the array are omnidirectional. Beamforming not only causes the system to be more sensitive to signals coming from a specific direction, but also attenuates the noise and interferences coming from other directions [4].

One method used to perform beamforming is delay-sum, or time-delay, beamforming. In this method, the spatial filtering results from the coherent (in-phase) summing of the signals received by the sensors in the array. A signal's propagation time between sensors in the water for sonar processing applications can be calculated using knowledge of the signal's propagation speed through water, the distance between sensors, and the signal's direction of arrival. With this information, signals received by the array are added *in-phase* by taking appropriately delayed samples from a sample memory for each sensor. Signals approaching from directions other

G. Brebner and R. Woods (Eds.): FPL 2001, LNCS 2147, pp. 101–111, 2001.

than the direction of interest are not coherently summed and are thus attenuated compared to signals arriving from the direction of interest. Delay-sum beamforming has the important characteristic that the beams formed are "broadband" since they are sensitive to a wide range of frequencies (as opposed to being tuned to specific frequencies). Despite (or even because of) its simplicity, delay-sum beam-forming is still commonly used in many sonar applications. The following pseudo-code represents the delay-sum beam-forming calculation for a single beam:

formBeam(b) {response = 0; for (s=0;s<numSensors;s++)
response = response + shade[b][s] x dataSamples[s][delayFunction(b,s)];}[4]

The calculation is basically a multiply-accumulate (MAC) operation which applies a windowing function, represented by the *shade* array, to the appropriately delayed versions of the received signal for all of the sensors. The *dataSamples* array represents a fixed-size buffer which holds a running history of the last N samples received by each sensor. The function *delayFunction()* returns the location of the sample to sum, using the beam's direction and the sensor's position to ensure that signals coming in the beam's direction are coherently summed [4].

It is the aim of this work to develop a matrix multiplier for performing the beamfoming technique based on matrix multiplication. The multiplier is basically based on the Modified Booth encoder and Wallace trees Multiplication (MBWM). The proposed architecture in this paper has been designed and targeted to the Xilinx XCV1000E of the Virtex-E family, which has the following important features [7]:

- Fast, and high-density;
- Flexible architecture that balances speed and density;
- Availability of the internal Block SelectRAM memories, and
- Built-in clock-management circuitry.

The composition of the rest of the paper is as follows. The mathematical model for the matrix multiplier based on the MBWM is given in section 2. Existing architectures suitable for beamforming computation are described in section 3. Section 4 is concerned with the proposed architecture of matrix multiplier using the multiply accumulate principle. Section 5 gives the design report with analysis. Concluding remarks are given in section 6.

2. Mathematical Model for Matrix Product Based on MBWM

2.1 Modified Booth-Encoder Multiplication

As the beamforming algorithm can be formulated as matrix product multiplication, the beamforming variables can be specified as follows: C = *response*, A = *shade [b][s]* and B = *dataSamples[s][delayFunction(b,s)]*, S=*numSensor*=N=*matrix size* and the following equation can be obtained:

$$C = AB \qquad (1)$$

Such that

$$C_{ij} = \sum_{k=0}^{N-1} A_{ik} B_{kj} \qquad (2)$$

If the elements of the matrix B is represented using the 2's complement number representation, then:

$$B_{kj} = -b_{kj,n-1} 2^{n-1} + \sum_{m=0}^{n-2} b_{kj,m} 2^m \qquad (3)$$

where $b_{kj,m}$ is the mth bit of B_{kj}, (which are zero or one). $b_{kj,n-1}$ is the sign bit, where n is the word length.

Equation (3) can be rewritten as follows:

$$B_{kj} = \sum_{m=0}^{(n/2)-1} (b_{kj,2m-1} + b_{kj,2m} - 2b_{kj,2m+1}) 4^m \qquad (4)$$

or:

$$B_{kj} = \sum_{m=0}^{(n/2)-1} (D_m) 4^m \qquad (6)$$

where: $D_m = \sum_{m=0}^{(n/2)-1} (D_m) 4^m$, $b_{kj,-1} = 0$ and $D_m \in \{-2,-1,0,1,2\}$

By substituting (6) into (2), the product coefficients C_{ij} can be computed as follows:

$$C_{ij} = \sum_{k=0}^{N-1} A_{ik} \sum_{m=0}^{(n/2)-1} (D_m) 4^m \qquad (7)$$

such as:

$$C_{ij} = \sum_{k=0}^{N-1} \sum_{m=0}^{(n/2)-1} (A_{ik} D_m) 4^m \qquad (8)$$

The product coefficients C_{ij} are given by equation (9) as follows:

$$C_{ij} = \sum_{k=0}^{N-1} \sum_{m=0}^{(n/2)-1} (PP_{ik,m}) 4^m \qquad (9)$$

where : $PP_{ik,m} = (A_{ik} D_m)$,   based on the modified booth encoder algorithm [6] as explained in Table 1.

2.2 Background on Wallace Trees

One level of Wallace trees is composed of arrays of 3-2 adders (or compressors). The logic of the 3-2 adder is the same as a full adder except the carry-out from the previous bit has now become an external input. For each bit of a 3-2 adder, the logic is:

$$S[i] = A1[i] \oplus A2[i] \oplus A3[i]$$
$$C[i] = A1[i]A2[i] + A2[i]A3[i] + A3[i]A1[i]$$

Table 1. Modified Booth algorithm

$b_{ki,2m+1}$	$b_{ki,2m}$	$b_{ki,2m-1}$	D_m	$PP_{ik,m}$
0	0	0	0	0
0	0	1	1	$+ A_{ik}$
0	1	0	1	$+ A_{ik}$
0	1	1	2	$2 A_{ik}$
1	0	0	-2	$-2 A_{ik}$
1	0	1	-1	$- A_{ik}$
1	1	0	-1	$- A_{ik}$
1	1	1	0	0

For the whole array, $S + 2C = A1 + A2 + A3$, where S and C are partial results. They can be combined during a final addition phase to compute the sum. The total inputs across an entire level of a 3-2 adder array is the same as the bit-width of the inputs [3], [6].

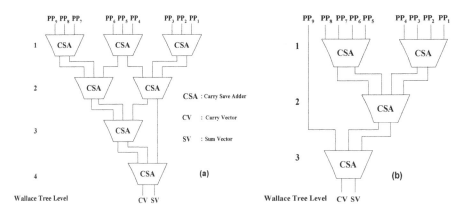

Fig.1 (a) An array of 3-2 adders. (b) An array of 4-2 adders.

In some Wallace tree designs, 4-2 adder arrays have also been used because they reduce the number of compressor levels required. For each bit of a 4-2 adder, the logic is:

$$S[i] = A1[i] \oplus A2[i] \oplus A3[i] \oplus A4[i] \oplus Cin[i]$$
$$C_{out}[i] = (A1[i]A2[i] \oplus A2[i]A3[i]) + A3[i]A1[i]$$
$$C[i] = (A1[i] \oplus A2[i] \oplus A3[i] \oplus A4[i])Cin[i] + (\overline{A1[i] \oplus A2[i] \oplus A3[i] \oplus A4[i]})A4[i]$$

For the whole array, $S + 2C = A1 + A2 + A3 + A4$, Fig. 1 shows the layout of array examples using 3-2 or 4-2 adders [3], [6].

3. Existing Matrix Multipliers Suitable for Performing the Beamforming Technique

Classical matrix multiplication algorithms, which can be used to perform the beamforming technique, will be presented in this section.

3.1 Clemson's University [1]

The work carried out at Clemson's University which is the most promising contribution concerning the implementation of matrix product on the FPGA is concerned with two algorithms. The design has been pipelined on eight FPGA chips on a GigaOps board in a parallel fashion.

- **Algorithm 1**
  In this algorithm, a separate column of the B matrix is loaded in the SRAM associated with each FPGA (if there are more than one multiply-accumulate parts on a chip, the same number of columns of B are loaded into the SRAM for each FPGA). Therefore, there are $8*N$ (where N is the number of the multiply-accumulate parts per FPGA) columns of the B matrix loaded in the SRAM. Each row of the A matrix is broadcast by the host so that each chip receives the same value of A. Each row value of A is matched with the appropriate value from the B matrix as inputs to the multiply-accumulate part. Once one row has been broadcast and matched in the multiply-accumulate part with one or more columns of the B matrix, the result is eight or more values of the C matrix. When the entire A matrix has been broadcast, the result is eight or more columns of the C matrix. By repeating this process for the remaining columns of the B matrix, the entire C matrix is computed [1].
- **Algorithm 2**
  The eight FPGAs used are split up into four modules of two FPGAs each (Y and X). Because communication between FPGA's in a module is trivial, a module can be looked at as one larger FPGA. This algorithm attempts to minimize the number of times the A matrix is broadcast by loading multiple columns of the B matrix in each SRAM. Instead of putting a multiply-accumulate part on each FPGA, multiplication and summation parts are split up between FPGA's in a module. Therefore, instead of eight (or more) individual multiply-accumulate parts on the board, four pipelined multiply-accumulate parts have been performed on the board. The multiplier is put on the Y FPGA and the summation part on the X FPGA. The SRAM for the Y FPGAs is loaded with multiple columns of the B matrix and the rows of the A matrix are broadcast to the Y FPGAs. Each row value is matched with the appropriate column value for each column loaded into the SRAM. Therefore, each row value broadcasted

is matched with N column values, where N is the number of columns loaded into each SRAM [1].

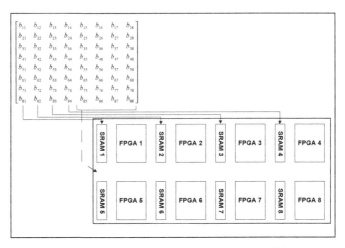

Fig.2 Matrix multiplication algorithm at Clemson's University

3.2 Brigham Young's University [4]

The application of time-delay sonar beamforming and its implementation on a multiboard FPGA system is discussed in [4]. Additionally, they show that their proposed FPGA system has a six to twelve times performance advantage over the existing systems. This performance advantage is due to the simplicity of the core calculation using a multi-FPGA system [4].

4. Proposed Architecture for Matrix Multiplier

Equation (9) can be mapped into the proposed system. Fig.3 shows the design philosophy for an implementation of matrix product on the Viretx-E FPGA. The proposed system exploits some of the Viretx FPGA features such as Block SelectRAM and the fully digital Delay-Locked Loop (DLL). Virtex-E FPGAs incorporate large Block SelectRAM memories. These complement the distributed SelectRAM memories that provide shallow RAM structures implemented in CLBs. Block SelectRAM memory blocks are organised in columns, starting at the left (column 0) and right outside edges and inserted every 12 CLB columns. Each Block selectRAM cell is a fully synchronous dual-ported (true Dual Port^{TM}) 4096-bit RAM with independent control signals for each port. The data widths of the two ports can be configured independently, providing built-in bus -width conversion.

The BlockRAM (*RAMB4_n_n*) available on the FPGA chips as an internal memory can be used to download the coefficients of the two matrices *A* and *B* using dual port option available on this type of memory, where *n* is word-length of the data. The multiplication of two N x N matrices can be performed using N BlockRAMs to store the matrix coefficients. As FPGAs and the matrix product grow in size, quality on-chip clock distribution becomes increasingly important. Clock skew and clock delay impact on device performance and the task of managing clock skew and clock delay with conventional clock trees becomes more difficult in large devices [7]. The Virtex series of devices resolve this potential problem by providing up to eight fully digital dedicated on-chip Delay-Locked Loop (DLL) circuits which (a) provide zero propagation delay, (b) low clock skew between output clock signals distributed throughout the device and (c) allows the user to retrieve the coefficients of the A row and B column from the RAMB_n_n without delay.

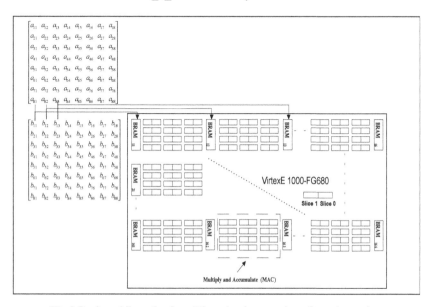

Fig.3 Design philosophy for a Virtex implementation of matrix product

• **Multiply-Accumulate Part**

The heart of this algorithm is the multiply-accumulate component. This part takes two values (one row value from the A matrix and one column value from the B matrix), multiplies them and adds the result to the running total. Once N multiplications and additions have been completed, the result is one value of the C matrix. The MAC has been used in this algorithm is basically based on the MBWM as shown in Fig.4.

It is worth mentioning that the system produces N x N matrix results C after O $(2N)$ clock cycles based on the multiple accumulate technique and therefore the entire computation can be carried out after O $(2N)$ clock cycles and requires N (MACs) (see Table.2).

Table.2 Pipeline Diagram of Integer MAC for the computation of the inner product (one C coefficient) $\sum_{i=0}^{3} A_{i1} B_{1i}$ (for k=1). (PP) Booth Encoder Partial Products, (W$_1$: Wallace tree level 1), (W$_2$: Wallace tree level 2), (W$_3$: Wallace tree level 3), (CPR) Compressor.

Cycle #	1	2	3	4	5	6	7	8	Result
Input 1	PP	W$_1$	W$_2$	W$_3$	CPR				
Input 2		PP	W$_1$	W$_2$	W$_3$	CPR			
Input 3			PP	W$_1$	W$_2$	W$_3$	CPR		
Input 4				PP	W$_1$	W$_2$	W$_3$	CPR	Final Addition

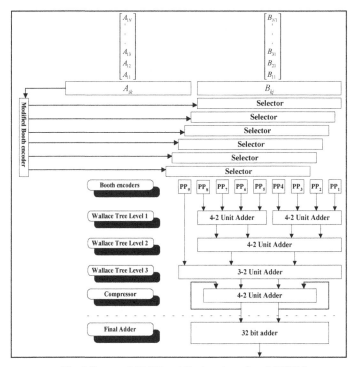

Fig.4 Proposed MAC architecture based on MBWM.

The algorithm performances concerning the number of FPGAs used together with the type of memory exploited are shown in Table.3.

Table.3 Algorithm performances and criteria of comparison

Architectures		Proposed architecture	Structure [1]	Structure [4]
Number of FPGAs used		1	8	4
Type of memory used	Internal	RAMB4_8_8	-	-
	External	-	SRAM	SRAM

It can be seen that the proposed architecture provides better performances, requiring a single FPGA chip and using the internal memory. The benefit by using this structure is to avoid the disadvantages of multi-FPGA system, problems of communication across chips, longer delays, more complex hardware, and so on. Another benefit for the proposed architecture is the possibility to use the external memory available on board for another task.

5. Results and Analysis

The proposed architecture described above has been implemented using a Xilinx Virtex XCV1000E FPGA series board with Target Package: fg680. The design was carried out using Relative LoCations (RLOC) attributes and using mixed schematic-VHDL to obtain efficient placement. The most relevant feature of the CLB in the Virtex-E FPGA is the dedicated carry logic to implement fast, efficient arithmetic functions. Dedicated carry logic provides fast arithmetic carry capability for high-speed arithmetic functions. The full adder structure suitable for the Virtex-E FPGA implementation is shown in Fig.5. The mapping fashion for the 4-2 adders on the Virtex-E CLBs used for the Wallace addition is illustrated in Fig. 6 [2].

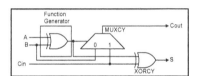

Fig.5 Full adder based Virtex-E FPGA, Virtex Carry Logic

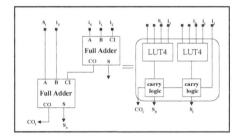

Fig.6. 4 -2 adder mapped to a Virtex CLB

The design is modular, regular and can be implemented for larger matrix product and input data word lengths. The circuit developed has O $(2N)$ as computation time complexity and requires less area (a O (N)) when compared with existing systolic architectures. Table 4 illustrates the performance obtained for the proposed architecture for the case of $N= 4$ and $n=8$. In comparison with *PAM-Blox* matrix multiplier - proposed at Stanford University and implemented on XC4K device [9] where the number of CLBs is divided by two to perform a logical comparison- and the standard matrix multiplier based on MAC (Multiplier + Adder)- the author's architecture using the same design strategies-, the design shows significant improvements when implemented on a single FPGA structure, requiring a single global clock, less area/speed ratio and reduced numbers of hardware slices for the logic operations used. In addition, each MAC requires 135 CLB slices and the Mac's distribution is shown in Fig. 7, which depends on the Block SelectRAM distribution on the FPGA chip.

Table 4. Design parameters for the design implementation, $(N=4, n=8)$

Design Parameters	CLBs	RAMB4_8_8	Speed (MHz)	(Area/Speed) Ratio
Proposed architecture	296	4	60	4.93
MAC (Multiplier + Adder)	270	4	46	5.87
PAM-Blox matrix multiplier [9]	954/2=477	-	33	14.45

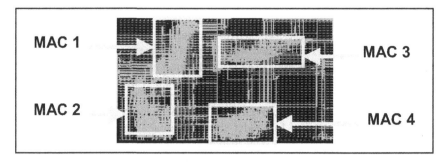

Fig.7. Matrix product implementation on Virtex-E 1000, Mac's distribution

6. Conclusion

Due to the flexibility of the Virtex-E FPGAs, the extra features provided such as Block SelectRam and CLKDLL, their communications and functions which can be specialised to provide higher performance than multi-DSP systems for some applications such as the matrix multiplier designs discussed above. A novel system for matrix multiplication computation based on MBWM suitable for this purpose has been presented in this paper. The proposed architecture is modular, regular and requires a single FPGA chip with lower time complexity when compared with existing structures.

References

[1]   W.B. Ligon III, S. McMillan and al., "A re-evaluation of the practicality of floating-point operation on FPGAs." IEEE Symposium on FPGAs for Custom Computing Machines, pp.206-215, April 15-17, 1998.

[2]   J. Poldre, K. Tammemaee, "Reconfigurable Multiplier for Virtex FPGA Family." Lecture notes in computer science, Vol.1673, pp.359-364, 1999.

[3]   D.A. Patterson, J.L. Hennessy, and D. Goldberg, "Computer Architecture, A Quantitative Approach." Appendix A, second ed. Morgan Kaufmann, 1996.

[4]   P. Graham and B. Nelson "FPGA-Based Sonar Processing." Proceedings of the sixth ACM/SIGDA international symposium on Field Programmable Gate Arrays (FPGA 1998), February 22-25 2001, Monterey, CA, USA.

[5]   A. Amira, A. Bouridane, P. Milligan and P. Sage   "A High Throughput FPGA Implementation of A Bit-Level Matrix Product." Proceedings of the IEEE Workshop on Signal Processing Systems Design and Implementation (SIPS), pp 356-364, October 2000, Lafeyette, LA, USA.

[6]   C.S. Wallace "A Suggestion for Fast Multiplier." IEEE Transaction On Electronic Computers, VOL.13, pp14-17, February 1964.

[7]   URL:www.xilinx.com

[8]   O. Mencer, M. Morf and M.J. Flynn, "*PAM-Blox*: High Performance FPGA Design for Adaptive Computing." IEEE Symposium on FPGAs for Custom Computing Machines (FCCM), 1998 Napa Valley.

[9]   A. Amira, A. Bouridane and P. Milligan "*RCMAT*: a Reconfigurable Coprocessor for Matrix Algorithms." Proceedings of the Ninth ACM/SIGDA International Symposium on Field-Programmable Gate Arrays (FPGA 2001), Monterey, pp 228, February 11-13 2001, Monterey, CA, USA.

Static Profile-Driven Compilation for FPGAs

Srihari Cadambi[1] and Seth Copen Goldstein[2]

[1] C&C Research Laboratories, NEC USA, Princeton, NJ, USA
cadambi@nec-lab.com
[2] Carnegie Mellon University, Pittsburgh, PA, USA
seth@cs.cmu.edu

Abstract. We describe a static profiling methodology to extract hot-spots from netlists. Hot-spots are small regular sub-circuits the optimization of which has a big impact on the final result. We have built a tool that can extract and characterize hot-spots from large netlists very quickly. The tool can be used to direct human attention on portions of circuits that need hand-optimization, as well as to automatically direct efforts of FPGA tools. We show impressive throughput improvements when compiling to the PipeRench reconfigurable architecture and use hot-spots to enable fast architectural design space exploration for FP-GAs by predicting the FPGA CLB structure that produces the best final area-delay. Our prediction is fairly accurate and only takes a few hours as compared to weeks for an exhaustive analysis. We also demonstrate better results when targeting FPGAs with heterogeneous CLBs.

1 Introduction

Owing to their flexibility, performance and fast application design times, FPGAs are increasingly used in diverse applications. This popularity is making them more complex and heterogeneous in nature. In addition, designs targeted to FPGAs are getting larger. However, FPGA CAD tools are still slow.

A crucial problem in FPGA CAD is constrained netlist optimization. FPGA tools are responsible for the optimization, mapping, placement and routing of a netlist on a target FPGA given constraints such as area and delay. This is a complex problem. Instead of treating the netlist to be optimized as a global entity, this work suggests using static profiling to quickly identify the portions of the netlist that are the most important. These important portions, or *hot-spots*, can then be manually optimized by a designer or given priority by the tools. We will show that different kinds of hot-spots exist given different optimization criteria. We will also demonstrate how they may be used to aid FPGA compilation.

Earlier efforts have focused on regularity extraction [10,11,12] and regularity-preserving transformations [13]. Our work is not confined to extracting and maintaining regularity in netlists. Instead, we characterize regular patterns in terms of their impact on the optimization constraint and heavily optimize such patterns anytime during the CAD tool flow. Further, in this work, we target our techniques specifically to FPGA CAD.

G. Brebner and R. Woods (Eds.): FPL 2001, LNCS 2147, pp. 112–122, 2001.

The remainder of the paper is organized as follows. In Section 2, we explain hot-spots and how they may be identified. In Section 3, we describe how the static profiler may be used to focus human attention on small sub-circuits in netlists that have a big impact. We show how hot-spots can be used to aid FPGA architecture exploration in Section 4, describe the integration of the static profiler within FPGA tool flow in Section 5, and conclude in Section 6.

2   Hot-Spots

Many netlists, especially those with datapaths, have simple patterns that occur repeatedly. Some of these patterns may have properties that are significant from the point of view of an optimization constraint (for example, they may lie on the critical path). When a single instance of the pattern is optimized, it induces significant improvement throughout the netlist with minimal effort. Such a pattern is a *hot-spot*[1]. Unlike the case of software optimization, where a hot-spot has a simple metric (execution time per line of code), it is possible to define different metrics resulting in the detection of different kinds of hot-spots. For example, we find sub-circuits with similar functionality and connectivity that when optimized reduce the overall area. Another case is finding dissimilar sub-circuits that are all on the critical path.

Common Definitions A netlist is represented by a directed graph: the *nodes* correspond to the hardware functional blocks (eg., gates), and the edges to *wires*, or *nets*. Each wire has a single source and multiple destinations, called *pins*. Each wire also has a *width* that represents that number of bits used to specify the value on the wire.

A subgraph or sub-circuit is any connected subset of nodes of the graph. The number of inputs of a subgraph G is the number of distinct nets whose sources are outside G. The number of outputs of a subgraph G is the number of distinct nets at least one of whose destinations is outside G.

For pin p of net n in netlist P, the signal slack is the difference between the actual signal arrival time and the latest possible signal arrival when p becomes critical. The *criticality* cr_p^n of pin p of net n is

$$cr_p^n = 1 - \frac{slack_p^n}{max\_slack_P} \tag{1}$$

where $slack_p^n$ represents the slack of pin p of net n, and max_slack_P represents the maximum slack among all the pins in netlist P.

A single-sinked directed acyclic graph (SSDAG) is a subgraph that has a single primary output but one or more internal outputs. SSDAGs can be used to represent a large number of electrical circuits. An SSDAG is characterized by several properties such as the number of its inputs, outputs, its size, widths of wires and criticalities of pins within.

---

[1] This is similar to the 90:10 "rule" in software, which states that 90% of a program's execution time is spent in 10% of the code.

An *equivalence relation* may be defined between two SSDAGs. This determines if the SSDAGs are to be considered similar or not. For instance, the equivalence relation between SSDAGs p_i and p_j, $R(p_i, p_j)$, may imply that p_i and p_j are functionally isomorphic. On the other hand, if $R(p_i, p_j)$ implies that the number of inputs and outputs of p_i and p_j are equal, then p_i and p_j may be functionally different but are still equivalent under R.

A *template* is an SSDAG equivalence class, i.e., it is a set of SSDAGs which are equivalent under a given equivalence relation R:

$$T = \{p_i \mid \forall (i, j), \ R(p_i, p_j)\} \tag{2}$$

The number of SSDAGs in a template is referred to as its *frequency*.

In order to build a tool that focuses on important portions of a netlist, hotspots have to be extracted and characterized. In [1], we published an algorithm to extract all possible SSDAGs from a DAG. Here, we present characterization schemes to evaluate the extracted SSDAGs and use them during FPGA compilation.

Characterization Given an equivalence relation R, extraction produces a set of templates from a netlist each consisting of SSDAGs equivalent under R. Characterization is then used to evaluate each template and identify which are of importance.

Characterization is based on the given optimization constraints (such as area or delay minimization) and several properties of a template, including structural properties (such as the size, number of inputs and outputs of each SSDAG in the template, etc), functional properties (such as the Boolean or arithmetic function), architecture specific properties (such as how well the template matches a given resource on an FPGA architecture), and others. For a certain optimization objective, the characterization value of a template, represented by F_T, is a function of the template properties. The user can parameterize the static profiler by specifying different F_T's. This specification is done using a template for a general form of F_T[2]. The set of all templates produced by static profiling is sorted based on F_T, and the top few templates are selected as hot-spots.

Example: Area-Delay Hot-Spots In FPGAs, minimizing the area-delay product is a direct indicator of the performance achievable. We define a pin as being critical if its criticality before place and route is more than the average criticality of all pins in the netlist[3].

The criticality of a template is defined as the total number of critical pins contained by the SSDAGs in the template. Templates that have a high frequency *and* contain a lot of critical pins are good area-delay hot-spots since optimizing instances of such templates improves area (because of the regularity) and delay

---

[2] However, in our current implementation, F_T is not a parameter: it is hard-coded by the user into the profiler.

[3] Such pins are more likely to encounter timing problems during place and route.

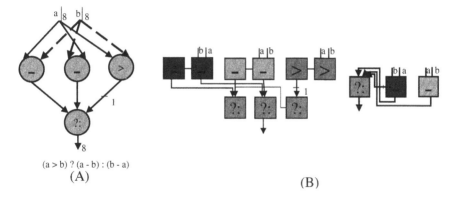

Fig. 1. (A) Hot-spot extracted from Optical Flow, used in 3-D image rendering. The inputs are all 8-bit wide. (B) Layout depicted using the resources on the PipeRench architecture [2] mapped by the DIL compiler (left); Compact hand-created layout (right).

(because of the presence of critical pins). If f_T is the frequency, A_T the area and cr_T the criticality of template T, the characterization function to extract area-delay hot-spots is

$$F_T = f_T * A_T * cr_T \qquad (3)$$

3   Using Hot-Spots in the DIL Compiler

In this section, we show how the profiler can be used to quickly direct human attention on the most important portions of a large netlist. We use the DIL reconfigurable compiler [2] for this experiment. The input to the DIL compiler is a high-level language [3] and the target is the PipeRench reconfigurable architecture [2,4]. Most of the input designs to the DIL compiler consist of word-wide operations, such as those found in multimedia applications. DIL places and routes them on PipeRench while minimizing the resources used [2].

In order to enhance the efficiency of compilation, while not looking for a globally optimal solution, the static profiler was used to quickly extract hot-spots, an example of which is shown in Figure 1(A). The layout obtained by the compiler for this hot-spot and the more optimal hand-layout are shown in Figure 1(B). Creating a hand-layout is easy for this small circuit, but not for the entire netlist. The profiler thus helps focus attention on those parts that benefit most from hand layouts.

In order to extract such sub-circuits we use the following characterization function:

$$F_T = f_T * A_T \ (if \ T \ has \ 1 - bit \ wires)$$
$$= 0 \ (otherwise) \qquad (4)$$

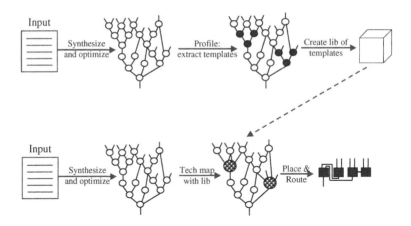

Fig. 2. Using the static profiler with the DIL compiler. High ranking templates are converted into preplaced macros and used during subsequent compilation.

F_T is high for regular SSDAGs that cover a large part of the netlist *and* contain 1-bit wide wires. SSDAGs that contain 1-bit wires can be heavily optimized using special circuitry in PipeRench, an optimization that is time-consuming for the compiler to perform globally. The 1-bit wires are marked in Figure 1(A) and shown as interconnects between the processing elements in the subtractors and comparators in Figure 1(B).

The top few extracted SSDAGs are hand-compacted and inserted into a newly created library of macros. This macro library is used during subsequent compilation: i.e., the optimized hand layout from the macro library is used for each instance of the hot-spot. Shown in Figure 2, this is similar to technology mapping, except the static profiler helps decide what parts of the netlist should be hand-optimized and converted into macros.

Table 1 shows some properties of the macros used in 6 applications in which we selected and optimized a single macro. All of the macros were among the top few ranked templates provided by the profiler. In every case except ATR, we found a good macro high up in the list. For ATR however, the first six macros could not be compacted. This is because the profiler finds regular patterns with 1-bit wires in them, the presence of which is a necessary but not sufficient condition for compaction. Thus, the user actually has to try compacting the top few templates provided by the profiler. However with the characterization function we used, all hot-spots were within the top few patterns ranked by the profiler.

The overall results obtained by using hot-spots are shown in Table 2. The number of processing elements represents the raw functional resource usage. The total number of pipeline stages synthesized is indicative of the number of functional and routing resources used.

Table 1. Properties and profiler rankings of macros found and used in different applications. Each application had a single macro that was used.

Benchmark (netlist)	Macro Properties			Coverage of netlist	Profiler Ranking
	Inputs	Outputs	Size		
Optical-flow	1	1	4	68.4%	1
IDEA	3	1	2	42%	1
Quantize	3	1	2	40.1%	2
FIR	3	1	2	32.3%	2
Cordic	4	1	3	23.7%	1
ATR	3	1	2	10.8%	7

Table 2. Improvement seen in the number of pipeline stages and processing elements used for the PipeRench reconfigurable architecture [2] targeted by the DIL compiler.

Benchmark (netlist)	Processing Elements			Pipeline Stages		
	No Macros	With Macros	Imp.	No Macros	With Macros	Imp.
Optical flow	3200	2166	32.3%	542	388	28.4%
IDEA	4338	3974	8.4%	973	702	27.9%
Quantization	3670	3218	14%	1395	1143	18%
FIR	1274	1180	7.4%	370	318	14.1%
Cordic	621	548	11.8%	81	75	7.4%
ATR	1753	1739	0.8%	512	482	5.9%

4   Using Hot-Spots in FPGA Architecture Exploration

In the previous section, we demonstrated how the static profiler is useful for directing human attention on sub-circuits that have a big impact. In this section, we illustrate its use in making FPGA architecture exploration faster.

FPGA Architectural Model and Experimental Setup In [5], the authors described a cluster-based FPGA architecture. A cluster is a group of LUTs and high-speed local interconnect. Packing critical wires into clusters improves the final compiled clock speed. Typical FPGA tools first pack gates and LUTs into clusters and then perform place and route. A cluster is characterized by: (i) the number of LUTs inside (*cluster size*), N (ii) size of each LUT, K (iii) number of inputs, I (iv) number of outputs, O (v) type of interconnect (vi) fraction of routing tracks in the adjacent routing channel that each CLB pin can connect from and to, FC_{input} and FC_{output}.

We base our experiments on those performed in [5]. The cluster size and inputs, N and I, alone are varied. The number of outputs O is always assumed to be equal to N. K is fixed at 4, which is determined as optimal in [5]. For all other parameters of the cluster and the routing architecture, we make the same assumptions as [5].

The benchmarks used for all the experiments were taken from three different sources: MCNC benchmarks, the LGSynth93 benchmark suite and random benchmarks generated by CircGen[6]. Benchmarks are first optimized and decomposed into 4-feasible netlists using SIS[7], and subsequently mapped to 4-input LUTs using FlowMap[8].

The Problem and Solution The problem is to predict the size and number of inputs of the cluster that yields the lowest area-delay product when the design is compiled. This is crucial when designing new FPGA architectures or when fine-tuning existing architectures to a new set of applications. The conventional method of approaching this is to exhaustively compile each application over all cluster sizes and determine the best cluster[5]. However, we use the static profiler to analyze the netlist instead and quickly predict the best cluster.

We attempt to identify the single most recurring cluster in the netlist. In order to do this, the equivalence relation is set as follows: two SSDAGs are equivalent if they have the same number of LUTs (N) and external inputs (I). Note that the number of outputs is assumed to be equal to N. Such an equivalence relation will result in the identification of templates where each template corresponds to a specific cluster type.

We determine the characterization function F_T used to identify the best template using the following properties of a cluster of size N:

- As N increases, more critical pins in the netlist may be subsumed into clusters, resulting in better delay.
- Intra-cluster delay increases with N, as a large cluster requires large multiplexers to implement its internal interconnect.
- The overall area of all mapped clusters increases linearly with N[5].
- Cluster I/O increases with N, creating routability issues. This increases the final routing area, as well as the final delay owing to potentially long wires.

Based on the above, we construct a function F_T to model the area and delay of a cluster represented by template T:

$$F_T = F(N, cdelay(N), (I + O), cr_T) = \frac{cr_T^a * (b - I - O) * (c - N)}{cdelay(N) + d} \quad (5)$$

where N is the size in LUTs, $cdelay(N)$ is the combinational delay inside a cluster of size N (which was determined experimentally), I and O are the number of external inputs and outputs and cr_T the criticality of the template T. N and $(I + O)$ model the logic area and routing area while cr_T and $cdelay(N)$ model the delay behavior when the instances represented by T are clustered.

The unknowns in F_T were determined empirically: we "trained" the function using 30 different benchmarks taken from MCNC, LGSynth93 and from the randomly generated set of CircGen. For each benchmark, an exhaustive run (similar to the one performed in [5]) was used to determine the actual best cluster parameters. This was the reference for the training. The trained equation was then directly used to obtain a fast prediction for new benchmarks.

The parameters a, b, c and d were thus empirically determined to be $a = 3$, $b = 100$, $c = 30$ and $d = 300$. It may be inferred from $a = 3$ that the number of

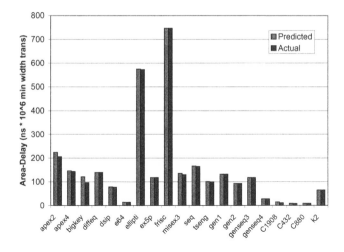

Fig. 3. Architecture Exploration Using the Static Profiler.

critical nets encapsulated is by far the most important parameter in determining the best cluster.

We now use this equation to predict the best cluster size for benchmarks that were not part of our training set. Figure 3 shows a comparison of the area-delay of the correct best cluster (determined exhaustively using VPR) and the area-delay of the cluster predicted using the profiler. It may be seen that the error in the area-delay between the predicted cluster and the actual best cluster is within 5% for most benchmarks. Further, the geometric mean of the predicted cluster sizes was 4.96, while the exhaustively determined cluster size for producing the minimal average area-delay was 5. Using the profiler is significantly faster: our running time on an UltraSparc II was about 10 hours for 30 training benchmarks, while the corresponding running time for exhaustive analysis, similar to the one performed in [5], for the complete set of benchmarks is about 2 weeks.

5   Compiling to Heterogeneous FPGA Architectures

In this section, we illustrate how the profiler may be used to automatically direct FPGA compilation. We also show the use of non-intuitive equivalence relations.

Our goal is to use the static profiler in an FPGA tool and improve the area-delay product for architectures with heterogeneous clusters. Heterogeneous clusters are similar to the clusters described in Section 4, except their LUTs are not all of the same size. A "3344" heterogeneous cluster, for instance, is a cluster with four LUTs, two of which are 3-LUTs and the other two are 4-LUTs. Many commercial architectures use heterogeneous clusters. Such clusters present more constraints and make compilation difficult. It is therefore important to identify hot-spots and focus on them first.

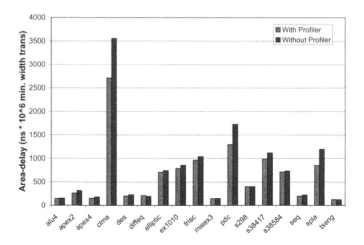

Fig. 4. Area-delay improvements from using the static profiler.

The tool flow and other FPGA architectural assumptions were similar to the previous experiment. We used VPR [9] and augmented the mapper T-VPack with the static profiler. Given a heterogeneous cluster $C(N, L_T, I)$, where L_T describes the type of LUTs in the cluster, area-delay hot-spots were extracted using the following equivalence relation: a pair of SSDAGs are equivalent if they have the same number of inputs, the exact same LUT types and at least one critical pin. Thus, if $C(N, L_T, I)$ is the target cluster, the profiler identifies the template with most instances (and critical pins) that matches C. The netlist is annotated with instances of this template and provided to the mapper, which preferentially packs all instances of the template into clusters.

Figure 4 shows a comparison of the final area-delay product with and without the static profiler when targeting 3344 clusters. When the static profiler is used to identify area-delay hot-spots, a sizeable improvement is seen in almost all the cases. The area is modeled in terms of minimum-width transistors, and the delay is in nanoseconds[5].

In contrast, we found that homogeneous clusters offer little in terms of hot-spots since they have fewer architectural constraints, which makes them an easier compiler target. Hence the profiler is of little use when targeting such clusters.

6 Conclusions

In this paper, we describe hot-spots in netlists and how they may be used to focus human attention and help FPGA CAD tools prioritize their efforts. Hot-spots are small regular sub-circuits that have a big impact. Focusing on hot-spots in large netlists helps lower CAD tool running times and improves efficiency of both tools and human designers. We show how hot-spots may be characterized and used to improve FPGA compilation.

The static profiler can be used to quickly focus human attention on those parts of the netlist that are the most important. In the DIL compiler for the PipeRench reconfigurable architecture, an area improvement of up to 29% was seen when profiler-suggested sub-circuits were optimized. We have also shown that such a tool can be used for fast FPGA architecture exploration. By using the profiler with a proper hot-spot characterization function many netlists could be analyzed and the results used to predict the best FPGA cluster, orders of magnitude faster than conventional, exhaustive architectural exploration schemes. Finally, we demonstrated that the profiler could guide FPGA compilation automatically by incorporating it within the FPGA tool flow. When the profiler was used together with the T-VPack and VPR tools, a large improvement was seen in the final area-delay product when compiling to heterogeneous FPGAs.

Acknowledgments We wish to thank the reviewers for their helpful comments. This work was supported by DARPA, under contract DABT63-96-C-0083.

References

1. Srihari Cadambi, Seth Copen Goldstein: CPR: A Configuration Profiling Tool. IEEE Symposium on FPGAs for Custom Computing Machines (1999) 104–113.
2. S C Goldstein, H Schmit, M Moe, M Budiu, S Cadambi, R Laufer, R Taylor: PipeRench: A Coprocessor for Streaming Multimedia Acceleration. 26th Annual Internation Symposium on Computer Architecture (1999) 28–39.
3. Mihai-Dan Budiu, Seth Copen Goldstein: Fast Compilation for Pipelined Reconfigurable Fabrics. Proc. ACM/SIGDA Seventh International Symposium on Field Programmable Gate Arrays.
4. S Cadambi, J Weener, S C Goldstein, H Schmit, D E Thomas: Managing pipeline-reconfigurable FPGAs. Proc. ACM/SIGDA Sixth International Symposium on Field Programmable Gate Arrays (1998).
5. Alexander (Sandy) Marquardt, V Betz, J Rose: Speed and Area Trade-offs in Cluster-Based FPGA Architectures. IEEE Tran. on VLSI Systems (2000) 84–93.
6. M Hutton, J P Grossman, J Rose, D Corneil: Characterization and Parameterized Random Generation of Digital Circuits. Proc. 33rd ACM/SIGDA Design Automation Conference (1996).
7. R K Brayton, R Rudell, A Sangiovanni-Vincentelli, A R Wang: MIS: A Multiple-level Logic Optimization System. IEEE Tran. on CAD (1987) 1062–1081.
8. Jason Cong, Yuzheng Ding: FlowMap: An Optimal Technology Mapping Algorithm for Delay Optimization in Lookup-Table Based FPGA Designs. IEEE Transactions on CAD (1994) 1–12.
9. V Betz, J Rose: VPR: A New Packing, Placement and Routing Tool for FPGA Research. Proc. International Workshop on Field Programmable Logic and Applications (1997).
10. D S Rao, F J Kurdahi: On Clustering for Maximal Regularity Extraction. IEEE Trans. on CAD 12, 8 (1983) 1198–1208.
11. S R Arikati, R Varadarajan: A Signature-Based Approach to Regularity Extraction. Proc. Int'l Conf. on CAD (1997) 542–545.

12. Amit Chowdhary, Sudhakar Kale, Phani Saripella, Naresh Sehgal, Rajesh Gupta: A General Approach for Regularity Extraction in Datapath Circuits. Proc. Int'l Conf. on CAD (1998).
13. Thomas Kutzchebauch, Leon Stok: Regularity Driven Logic Synthesis. Proc. Int'l Conf. on CAD (2000).

Synthesizing RTL Hardware from Java Byte Codes

Michael J. Wirthlin[1], Brad L. Hutchings[1], and Carl Worth[2]

[1] Brigham Young University, Provo UT 84602
[2] USC Information Sciences Institute, 4350 N. Fairfax Dr., Arlington VA 22203

1 Introduction

A structural design tool called JHDL was developed to aid in the design of high-performance pre-placed circuit macros for FPGAs [1]. This tool was successfully used to design and field several high-performance reconfigurable computing systems. Examples of systems developed with this tool include a multi-FPGA sonar beamforming system and an automatic target recognition system. In these examples, the reconfigurable systems developed with JHDL achieve at least an order of magnitude performance improvement over programmable processors by exploiting parameterized module generators.

While JHDL has successfully been used to design complex module generators and data-path, its structural design style can be awkward when designing complex control circuitry. Designing state machines within JHDL requires the use of a companion FSM generator tool or manual design of the state machine with discrete gates. To simplify the process of creating control circuitry (or any circuitry that does not require the benefits of module generators), hardware synthesis capability has been added to the JHDL environment. This synthesis environment generates hardware from RTL-style descriptions written in Java and under the JHDL design environment. The goals of this work are as follows:

1. Fully integrate synthesis capability into the JHDL design suite,
2. Support a mixed structural/behavioral design style where the user could specify part of the circuitry structurally (e.g., optimized datapath), and specify other parts of the circuitry behaviorally (the related control),
3. Allow fine control over the bit widths to be used in various parts of the synthesized circuit,
4. Allow the designer to schedule behavioral operations,
5. Synthesize circuitry without using an external logic synthesis tool.

An important component of this work is the ability to synthesize hardware from the compiled Java byte codes rather than using the original Java text. Using the conventional Java compiler for the front end of the synthesis tool moves much of the syntax and semantic checking and basic optimizations to the compiler. Hardware synthesis from Java byte codes is not unique to this work - several other projects synthesize hardware from Java byte codes. The GALADRIEL and NENYA projects [2] use Java byte codes as the design specification and generate

G. Brebner and R. Woods (Eds.): FPL 2001, LNCS 2147, pp. 123–132, 2001.
© Springer-Verlag Berlin Heidelberg 2001

synthesizable VHDL. The Forge-J tool[3][1] from Xilinx generates hardware from byte codes of behavioral Java descriptions. The main similarity between our work and the other efforts highlighted above is the focus on synthesizing hardware from Java byte codes. However, unlike the other related synthesis projects, the work reported here was heavily constrained by the requirement to work in the existing JHDL context. This created a different set of goals and resulted in a behavioral synthesis tool with substantially different capabilities.

2 Behavioral Modeling in JHDL

JHDL is a Java-based object-oriented circuit tool that gives the designer fine control over both the structure and placement/floorplan of a circuit[1]. This approach has been extremely effective for designing high-performance data paths and writing reusable parameterized module generators. In addition, JDHL provides hardware debugging capabilities that allow users to observe and control running hardware using an easy-to-use simulator-like user interface.

Although JHDL is primarily a structural design tool, the JHDL simulator supports behavioral modeling. Users are able to create behavioral models in Java and simulate them with structural JHDL circuits based on library primitives. The behavioral simulation environment in JHDL is similar to system modeling environments that use high-level languages to create complex testbenches [4].

Behavioral simulation models are used within JHDL for several reasons. First, behavioral models are created for all library primitives. The underlying simulation model of each JHDL primitive is written in Java under the appropriate JHDL interfaces. Second, behavioral models are created for testbenches. User designs can be simulated under complex operating environments by creating testbench models for user designs. Third, behavioral models can be used as a reference for complex structural circuits. Users specify the behavior of a complex circuit or module generator in Java and use the model throughout the design process to insure the structural circuit matches the intended behavior. Such behavioral models exist for many module generators and are frequently used as an alternative for structural simulation models to reduce simulation time.

2.1 Creating Behavioral Models in JHDL

Circuits are designed in JHDL by creating Java classes that extend the *Logic* class within the JHDL framework. The internal structure of these circuits is defined in the constructor of the class. In the constructor, instances of library elements are created (i.e. using **new**) and wired together as necessary. Once the circuit has been created structurally in the constructor, it can be simulated using the JHDL simulator, viewed in the schematic browser or converted to the appropriate technology format using the tech-mapper.

As described above, JHDL circuits may be defined by behavioral descriptions rather than with structure. Such circuits extend the *Logic* class but do not create

---

[1] Formerly from LavaLogic.

circuit structure in the constructor. Instead, these classes define behavior in two special methods named `propagate()` and `clock()`. The `propagate()` method models combinational circuitry and is called every time an input signal to the circuit changes. The `clock()` method models sequential circuitry and is called on each positive edge of the clock.

The JHDL behavioral modeling environment supports two basic classes of types. These types include traditional Java primitive types (i.e. `int`, `boolean`, `float`, etc.) and the *Wire* class. The *Wire* class is used directly to create instances (*wires*) that support concurrent assignment[2]. These wires are used to structurally interconnect circuits via their ports and for behavioral modeling within `clock()` and `propagate()` functions. Users can use both wires and Java variables in behavioral descriptions; the essential semantic difference between the two being that assignments to variables occurs sequentially and immediately, while assignment to wires is performed in parallel (again, from the simulator point of view) after the relevant `clock()` or `propagate()` method exits[3]. Because there is no operator overloading in Java, assigning a value to a wire is performed with a *put()* function, while retrieving a value from a wire is performed with a *get()* function. For synthesis purposes, assignments to wires within a `propagate()` method result in concurrent combinational circuitry while within a `clock()` method each wire assignment results in a register.

Figure 1 illustrates a JHDL behavioral model of an up-down counter (some parts of the circuit description have been simplified to avoid unneeded detail). In Line 1 of Figure 1, the user defined class inherits from *Synthesizable* which indicates to JHDL that this description is behavioral and may be synthesized to hardware (if this were to be a structural description, the user-defined class would extend from the *Logic* class). Lines 2-6 of the figure are the JHDL format for declaring the interface of the up-down counter. This is similar to the entity declaration of a VHDL model. Note that all JHDL circuits, both structural and behavioral, require a port interface declaration. This circuit contains four ports: resetPort (1 bit), enablePort (1 bit), up_dnPort (1 bit) and countPort (4 bits). Note that the declaration allows the user to control the bit width of the counter output. In general, users can control internal bit widths of operators by assigning them to JHDL class types that allow users to specify bit width. If sequential assignment is required (variables), the *BitVector* class may be used; if concurrent assignment is required, the *Wire* class can be used to control bit width.

The `clock()` function is defined in Lines 7-25. When the `clock()` function is invoked by the simulator, the first step is to query the *wires* attached to the ports of the counter for their current values (lines 8-11). With the wires values assigned to variables, the function checks to see if the reset signal is asserted (line 12) and if so, assigns 0 to the count variable. If reset is not asserted, then the enable signal is checked to see if it is asserted, if so, the count variable

---

[2] The semantics of concurrent assignment are defined by the JHDL simulator.

[3] This is somewhat analogous to the differences between VHDL variables and signals.

```
1   public class UpDownCounter extends Synthesizable {
2     public static CellArray cell_array[] = {
3       in("resetPort", 1),
4       in("enablePort", 1),
5       in("up_dnPort", 1),
6       out("countPort", 4)};
7     public void clock() {
8       int count = countPort.get();
9       boolean reset = resetPort.getB(),
10              enable = enablePort.getB(),
11              up_dn = up_dnPort.getB();
12      if (reset) {
13        count = 0;
14      } else {
15        if (enable) {
16          if (up_dn)
17            count++;
18          else
19            count--;
20        } else {
21          count = countPort.get();
22        }
23      }
24      countPort.put(count);
25    }
26 }
```

Fig. 1. UpDownCounter.java: A Behavioral description using `clock`

is either incremented if the up_dn signal is asserted (line 17), or decremented if
the up_dn signal is negated (line 19). If the enable signal was not asserted, then
the count variable is simply assigned its original value (line 21). The final step
of the `clock()` function is to assign the current value of the count variable to
the wire attached to the countPort (line 24). Note that there are many different
equivalent ways to specify an up-down counter in JHDL, the style presented here
is just one possibility.

3   Synthesis Strategy

The goal of this synthesis project is to provide hardware synthesis capability
within the existing behavioral modeling environment of JHDL. To integrate synthesis within JHDL, this synthesis tool will generate hardware that matches the
behavior of any given `propagate()` or `clock()` method defined by the user. Note
that this synthesis approach does *not* attempt to synthesize any arbitrary Java
code. Rather, this synthesis tool will synthesize hardware only within the semantic limits of the `propagate()` or `clock()` methods. While this may be more

limited than other Java-based synthesis environments, this approach allows us to exploit the existing JHDL tool flow and tightly integrate synthesized behavioral circuits with high-performance structural circuits constructed by JHDL module generators. This added synthesis capability allows designers to define the data-path of the circuit using high-performance module generators optimized for the FPGA technology and specify the control using high-level language constructs.

Conventionally, most synthesis tools work directly from the program text. This synthesis environment, however, works directly from the Java .class files containing the binary Java byte codes. Class files were chosen for this project for several reasons.

1. Existing compilers can be leveraged to do most of the front-end error checking, analysis and optimization.
2. Class files are not limited to Java and can be generated from other languages making it relatively easy to reuse the synthesis software with other language front-ends.
3. Class files contain nearly all of the important semantic information contained in the original Java source, including function and class variable names, and local variable names. It is relatively easy to infer loops, if-then-else structures, etc. directly from the class file.

4   Synthesis Steps

Synthesizing behavior within the `clock()` and `propagate()` methods within the JHDL framework involves several steps. These steps include compiling the Java into byte codes, disassembling the Java byte codes, creating dataflow and control flow graphs from the byte codes, dataflow analysis on the graphs and technology mapping. These steps are summarized in Figure 2.

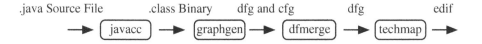

Fig. 2. JHDL Synthesis Flow.

4.1   Compiling Java Source Files into Byte Codes

As suggested above, the first step of the synthesis process involves the use of the `javacc` Compiler. A behavioral JHDL description is compiled into the standard Java byte codes [5] by invoking a platform independent Java compiler. If the behavioral model is syntactically correct, a valid .class file is created that contains the Java byte codes needed for the next step in the synthesis process. As suggested earlier, all syntax and semantic checking are done by the Java compiler, not the synthesis tool.

4.2   Disassemble Class Files

The next step of this synthesis tool is to disassemble the *.class* file containing the Java byte codes and symbol information. The format of Java *.class* files is widely available[5] and contains all the information necessary for extracting data flow and control flow from the behavioral descriptions.

4.3   Generating Control Flow and Data Flow Graphs from JHDL Class Files

A control flow graph (CFG) and data flow graph (DFG) of the Java behavior can be extracted directly from the disassembled class file. The CFG and DFG are created through static analysis of the byte codes in the appropriate class method.

Control Flow Graph The CFG is a directed graph with vertices representing basic blocks and edges representing control flow paths between the basic blocks. A special Decision vertex represents the forking behavior of `if-then` and `switch` conditional branching behavior. The control flow graph is generated by identifying the basic blocks of the appropriate class method and determining the control flow paths between basic blocks. Basic block boundaries are easily identified by searching for control byte codes (branches, jumps, switches, return, etc.). The control flow paths are determined by examining the target byte codes of each control instruction. Figure 3 illustrates the CFG for the UpDownCounter example seen in Figure 1.

Data Flow Graph The dataflow graph (DFG) is a directed-acyclic graph (DAG) representing the operations and data dependencies found within each basic block. Vertices within the DFG represent variables, operators and method invocation and edges represent the data dependencies between the vertices. The DFG is created by statically analyzing the byte codes of the basic block. Each byte code is responsible for creating a vertex (i.e. operator) and edges (i.e. data dependancies) in the DFG. Figure 3 illustrates the DFG for basic blocks 0 of the UpDownCounter.

Static analysis is performed on the basic block by emulating byte codes. The emulator steps sequentially through each byte code in the basic block and manipulates its operand stack as the conventional JVM would. Rather than pushing and popping operand values, this emulator pushes and pops dataflow graphs. When operator byte codes are reached, intermediate dataflow graphs are popped from the stack, merged and placed back onto the stack. Once the complete set of byte codes has been emulated, a set of dataflow graphs is available

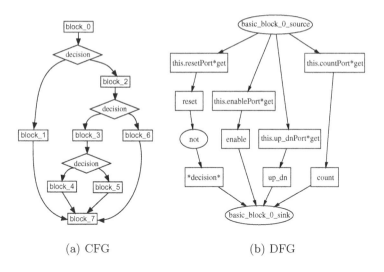

(a) CFG   (b) DFG

Fig. 3. DFG and CFG For UpDownCounter.

for each variable used in the basic block. Consider the following Java expression and its associated byte codes:

a = a + b * c	iload 4
	iload 5
	iload 6
	imul
	iadd
	istore 4

The emulator begins by pushing a single vertex graph onto the stack representing variables **a**, **b** and **c**. When the `imul` byte code (integer multiplication) is reached, the emulator will pop the top two vertices (**b** and **c**) from the stack and push a new graph back onto the stack. This new graph contains a new multiply vertex with input arcs from the two vertices **b** and **c**. The `iadd` byte code will pop the top two graphs from the stack (the multiply graph and **a** graph), combine them with an add vertex and place it back onto the stack. The istore byte code "stores" the result of the expression (i.e. our dataflow graph) into the memory location associated with variable **a**. Figure 4 illustrates the state of the stack as the emulator executes byte codes.

4.4   Merge DFG and CFG Graphs

The DFG and CFG created in the previous section represent the program behavior without any assumptions regarding the timing of the operations and move-

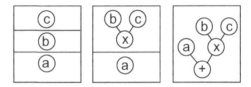

Fig. 4. Sample DFG Generated by Emulating JVM Stack.

ment of data (i.e. these graphs represent unscheduled data flow and control flow). In this synthesis environment, no scheduling step is necessary – all operations within the `clock()` method occur within a single clock cycle. Further, the operations in the `propagate()` method have no reference to the clock and should be synthesized as purely combinational logic. To synthesize logic for these methods, the CFG and DFG generated earlier must be converted into a single acyclic dataflow graph representing the dataflow semantics of these methods.

To generate a DAG, all cycles in the CFG must be removed. Cycles in the CFG arise from the feedback in loops (both `for` and `do-while`). In this early implementation, only loops with bounded iteration counts are supported. For bounded loops, the feedback in the CFG can be removed by unrolling the loop and creating a new control flow vertex for each loop iteration. Once any feedback in the CFG is removed, a single acyclic dataflow graph is created by combining the dataflow graphs of each basic block. For control flow vertices appearing in series within the CFG, the corresponding dataflow graphs are concatenated – the outputs of the first basic block feed the inputs of the second basic block. Control flow vertices appearing in parallel (i.e. appearing as children of the same decision vertex) represent mutually exclusive execution paths. To combine the dataflow of mutually exclusive control paths, a multiplexer must be added for each variable/signal to resolve the execution path.

4.5   Generating Hardware from the DFG

The FPGA circuit is created directly from the DFG – circuit operators are created for the operators in the DFG and physical wires are created for edges. Before proceeding with this technology mapping, several preprocessing steps are necessary. These steps include signal width resolution, constant value instantiation and multiplexer cleanup.

The signals within the DFG do not contain sufficient type information for synthesis. Within the byte codes, signals are usually represented as Java integer or long values (`int` or `long`). In most cases, these signals are not 32 or 64 bits as specified by the Java integer and long types. To determine the actual bit widths, the synthesis tool must examine the port interface of the behavioral circuit and the size of internal wires specified by the user. Using this information, intermediate bit widths can be inferred. For example, in lines 3-6 of the UpDownCounter in Figure 1, the bit-widths of each port signal are specified. In this port declaration, the `countPort` signal is specified as 4 bits. Using this information, the bit-width of the integer variable `count` is calculated at 4 bits rather than the 32 bits of the Java integer type.

After determining bit-widths of internal signals, the DFG is ready for the technology mapping step. The DFG is sorted in a topological order and each vertex is visited and replaced with its corresponding FPGA circuit library. Signal vertices are replaced with the appropriate signal wires, constants are replaced with a constant wire and operators are replaced with their corresponding operator library element. As the vertices are visited, intermediate wires are created and added to provide communication between the dependent operators and signals. Figure 5 illustrates the circuit generated by the UpDownCounter example.

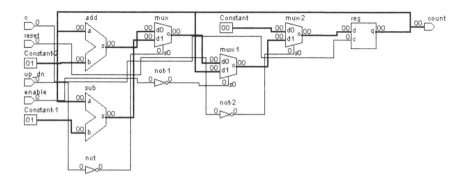

Fig. 5. Final Circuit Schematic For UpDownCounter.

5   Summary and Conclusions

The project has been successful in meeting its goals: modest synthesis capability has been integrated into JHDL and we have demonstrated that hardware can be synthesized directly from Java byte codes. The current JHDL tool now supports a mixed structural/behavioral design environment where designers control which description format they are using through inheritance. JHDL directly generates hardware without the need for an intermediate commercial CAD tool. Circuits generated from this synthesis tool have been netlisted through the JHDL netlisters and have been verified to operate correctly in FPGA hardware. The ability to include behavioral descriptions in JHDL circuits simplifies the process of developing the control circuitry and other behavioral descriptions within JHDL.

The major strengths of this synthesis tool are its ease of use, ability to operate without an external synthesis tool and close interaction with the JHDL design environment. Although this is a significant improvement to the JHDL design suite, work on additional behavioral synthesis capabilities continues. As synthesis and other capabilities are added to JHDL, designers will be able to specify and synthesize FPGA designs from a wide range of styles.

References

[1] B. Hutchings, P. Bellows, J. Hawkins, S. Hemmert, B. Nelson, and M. Rytting. A cad suite for high-performance FPGA design. In K. L. Pocek and J. M. Arnold, editors, *Proceedings of the IEEE Workshop on FPGAs for Custom Computing Machines*, pages 12–24, Napa, CA, April 1999. IEEE Computer Society, IEEE.

[2] J. M. P. Cardoso and H. C. Neto. Macro-based hardware compilation of Java bytecodes into a dynamic reconfigurable computing system. In K. L. Pocek and J. M. Arnold, editors, *Proceedings of the IEEE Workshop on FPGAs for Custom Computing Machines*, pages 2–11, Napa, CA, April 1999. IEEE Computer Society, IEEE.

[3] Don Davis, Steve Edwards, and Jonathan Harris. Forge-J. Technical report, Xilinx Corporation, 2000.

[4] Stan Y. Liao. Towards a new standard for system-level design. In *Proceedings of the 2000 International Workshop on Hardware/Software Codesign (CODEN)*, pages 2–6. IEEE, 2000.

[5] Jon Meyer and Troy Downing. *Java Virtual Machine*. O'Reilly & Associates, March 1997.

PuMA++: From Behavioral Specification to Multi-FPGA-Prototype

Klaus Harbich, Erich Barke

Institute of Microelectronic Circuits and Systems
Design Automation Group
University of Hannover, Appelstr. 4
D-30167 Hannover, Germany
{harbich,barke}@ims.uni-hannover.de

Abstract. In this paper we present a new design flow for efficient hardware implementation of behavioral system specifications at algorithmic level into heterogeneous multi-FPGA (**F**ield-**P**rogrammable **G**ate **A**rrays) rapid prototyping systems. We discuss the benefits of coupling the high-level synthesis tool CADDY-II and the partitioning and mapping environment PuMA, which is designed for optimized implementation of RT-level (**R**egister-**T**ransfer) netlists into multi-FPGA architectures. With our new approach, rapid prototyping and in-circuit verification in earliest design phases are enabled. Due to short implementation times and precise back annotation accomplished by a close coupling of the tools, more design iterations and thus better design space exploration is possible.

1 Introduction

Since a couple of years, rapid prototyping systems and logic emulators based on FPGAs [2, 5, 7, 14, 16, 13] have become very popular in digital design verification. In such systems, a digital circuit is mapped into programmable devices implementing a hardware prototype, which can be connected to an existing target hardware for real-world in-circuit functional verification. The main drawbacks of these systems are that only structural gate-level netlists or some restricted behavioral code at RT-level can be processed by the software. In addition turn-around-times are still far too long for today's design complexities.

If emulation technology could be used at higher abstraction levels, which means earlier in the design phase, and turn-around times would be shorter, emulation would evolve to an even more powerful technology. Doncev, Leeser and Tarafdar [8] stated "Truly Rapid Prototyping Requires High Level Synthesis". They used commercial tools for first investigations, affirming our vision that providing the designer with a virtual prototype for behavioral specifications at the algorithmic level allows faster and better design space exploration.

The remainder of the paper is structured as follows: In Section 2 we give a brief introduction into high-level synthesis and introduce the high-level synthesis tool CADDY-II. Section 3 gives information about the partitioning and mapping environment *PuMA*, which directly processes the output of CADDY-II. In Section 4

G. Brebner and R. Woods (Eds.): FPL 2001, LNCS 2147, pp. 133-141, 2001.

we propose our new approach of coupling both tools to accomplish an environment for the implementation of behavioral specifications into FPGA-based rapid prototyping systems. Section 5 gives an overview on the status of our work. Experimental results are given in Section 6. Finally, Section 7 gives concluding remarks.

2   High-Level Synthesis System CADDY-II

This section focuses on the principal methods used by the high-level synthesis system CADDY-II. The goal of high-level synthesis is the translation of a behavioral circuit description at algorithmic level into a Register-Transfer data-path with an appropriate controller. CADDY-II uses behavioral VHDL for the algorithmic input specification and structural VHDL for the synthesized RT-description. The underlying synthesis approach is only summarized here and can be found in more detail in [10] and [4]. The main synthesis steps used in the CADDY-II system are allocation, scheduling, binding and datapath generation.

Allocation is the selection of a suitable set of component types to be used in the design, including the number of components of each type. The components are provided in a library, which contains e.g. different types of adders, multipliers and ALUs with different functionality, area consumption, execution time and other properties. The component properties strongly depend on the underlying target technology, e.g. different ASIC technologies in general or different FPGA types, as in our specific application. In case of a target architecture based on Xilinx FPGAs, the area consumption of a component is represented by its CLB (Configurable Logic Block) usage. Area and timing constraints can be specified by the designer. They are automatically considered during allocation. Especially, the overall area limit of the target architecture can be taken into account. During allocation, an exhaustive design space exploration is carried out, controlled by the user specified constraints and a global heuristic function, which estimates the area and the execution time for each generated component allocation. Moreover, an appropriate clock frequency is determined for each set of allocated components.

During scheduling the design's performance is optimized with respect to the previously allocated components. Scheduling comprises two tasks, assigning operations of the input specification to control steps as well as to component types. Different components of the same type are scheduled according to their properties, e.g. scheduling fast multipliers to the critical path and slower ones to non-critical paths. In order to avoid local inferior design decisions, a global heuristic estimation function, based on the probabilities of scheduling operations to given control steps, is applied.

The estimation function further calculates the cost of all possible component type assignments. Moreover, timing and interface constraints are considered during scheduling. Data transfer operations, representing inter-chip communications, can additionally be specified in the input specification and annotated with the delay introduced by inter-chip communications. If no valid schedule can be obtained under the given resource constraints, the current allocation is rejected and a new allocation is selected automatically. As a result, the sequential timing behavior of the design is fixed after scheduling is completed.

Binding is the mapping of operations onto component instances, the allocation of an optimized number of registers and multiplexors and the mapping of variables onto the allocated registers. Because only the type of the component has been assigned during scheduling, the actual assignment of operations to component instances is performed during binding. Main optimization goal of the binding step is the minimization of the design's area by applying resource sharing – where applicable – in order to allow multiple non-concurrent operations or variables sharing the same hardware resources.

The final step is datapath generation. According to the previously executed synthesis steps an appropriate interconnection-structure is created and a finite state machine is generated, which controls the data-path. A structural VHDL RT-level description (netlist) is generated for the datapath whereas a behavioral VHDL RT-level description is used for the controller. Additionally, the determined schedule of the design is provided as a DFG (**D**ata **F**low **G**raph).

3   PuMA

After CADDY-II has synthesized the behavioral VHDL description into a structural RT-level netlists, we use the partitioning and mapping tool *PuMA* for automatic partitioning, mapping, floorplanning and placement. These four tasks are combined within one process with tight data exchange between the interacting sub-processes.

An RT-level netlist is translated into a hierarchical design database [12] preserving the original circuit hierarchy, the circuit components and their interconnections. Each RT-level component is directly mapped into the FPGA's logic blocks by a module generator system in order to satisfy designer's demand on minimum CLB consumption or on maximum design clock rate. Additionally, components exceeding an FPGA's pin or CLB capacity are automatically decomposed. After mapping, each RT-level component is described at CLB level. In case of decomposed components, for each part a separate CLB description is generated. All information about mapping and decomposition, like CLB count and cut lines, is added to the database and is used by the partitioning program.

Partitioning is performed at RT-level, where each element - even adders and multipliers - is represented by a single node or in case of decomposed components by only a few nodes. This yields very short run times, even if traditional partitioning algorithms are used, since netlist complexity is very low. Another advantage is that area consumption can unambiguously be measured in terms of CLBs and not in terms of Equivalent Gates, since all components are already mapped. Due to the generator-based placement approach a precise timing estimation is possible, which is very important for back annotation to ensure a correct scheduling during high-level synthesis (see Section 6.1).

The exact measurement in terms of CLBs further allows highest CLB utilization within the FPGAs. However, high utilization aggravates the placement and routability problem. We overcome this difficulty by integrating an automatic FPGA-specific floorplanner into the *PuMA* design flow, which directly interacts with the partitioner and the module generators. When the partitioner has assigned the components to the multi-FPGA architecture, the floorplanner determines FPGA-by-FPGA optimized shapes for each component and arranges the blocks with respect to the design-internal signal flow. This guarantees short interconnections between the components and simplifies routing (see Section 6.2).

Based on these floorplans the module generators perform a structure-driven placement considering inherent knowledge about individual component properties, component's shape and component-internal signal flow. This combination of floorplanning and generator based placement leads to high density and regular CLB distributions, which tremendously speed up the final routing step accomplished by FPGA vendor tools (see Section 6.3). Note, that *PuMA* is capable to handle heterogeneous FPGA architectures. A detailed description of the *PuMA* environment is given in [19].

4   The Overall Approach

The main idea of our approach is to provide the designer as early as possible with a virtual prototype in order to enable exhaustive design space exploration. Algorithmic system specifications can be synthesized easily by CADDY-II into structural RT-level netlists. *PuMA* is specialized on implementing such netlists into multi-FPGA architectures. It is obviously a good idea to couple both tools. The main question is, how to do this to gain most benefits.

A library of arithmetic components based on the LPM 2 2 1 standard (**L**ibrary of **P**arameterized **M**odules) [17] is the basis for all synthesis steps. All components specified in this library can be directly implemented into the FPGA target technology by the partitioning and mapping environment *PuMA*. Very precise models in terms of delay and area have been derived from an exhaustive set of arbitrary component implementations, as reported exemplarily in Section 6.1. These models are provided to the high-level synthesis tool CADDY-II, which is only allowed to use components out of this library.

All information available during high-level synthesis, like information about timing-critical components, simultaneously active components, shared components, etc. can be passed to *PuMA* by annotation of the components within the netlist.

4.1   Advantages of Annotation

For an efficient hardware implementation of RT-level netlists with respect to the prototype's performance, detailed information about timing-critical parts of the design has to be considered during partitioning. In traditional approaches, this information is derived from a very time consuming analysis of the circuit's structure. Additional problems like the GFP (**G**eneral **F**alse **P**ath) have to be solved [9, 18, 3] during traditional timing-optimized partitioning. Within our concept this information is passed by CADDY-II to the partitioner, which results in tremendous savings of run time as well as precision.

4.2   Advantages of Back Annotation

One major problem during high-level synthesis is the correct consideration of implementation dependent communication delay caused by partitioning, as shown in Fig. 1. Due to different delays of on-chip and inter-chip connections, partitioning and decomposition of components may invalidate the original schedule, given in Fig. 2 on the left hand side. In this context, two different kinds of implementation-dependent delay have to be distinguished.

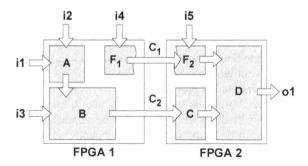

Fig. 1. Back annotation of partitioning effects

First, inter-chip connections caused by placing connected components into different FPGAs introduce additional interconnection delay as shown for components B and C. The additional delay can extend the clock cycle beyond the given clock cycle time, although the corresponding operation could be postponed without any effect on the circuit's performance. A postponed operation could either be chained with another operation during the next clock cycle or the operation is not on the critical path so that an additional clock step would not extend the schedule's length.

Second, inter-chip connections caused by decomposition of a component into several parts -which are assigned to two or more different FPGAs- extend the execution time of the corresponding component by the additional interconnection delay, as shown for the component parts F_1 and F_2.

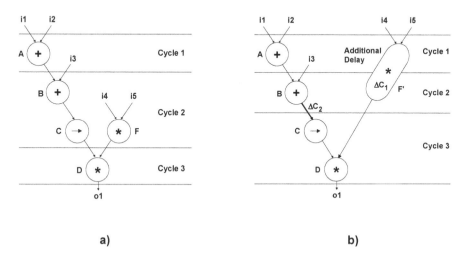

a)   b)

Fig. 2. a) Original schedule, b) refined schedule with extended component F'

Therefore, the additional communication delay can have a strong impact on the timing of the entire design and should be considered during high-level synthesis by back annotating the determined delays. Inter-chip connections between different components are represented as delay-annotated edges between operation pairs in the

DFG. All annotated edges within the DFG are handled during scheduling similarly to user-specified timing constraints. Thus, succeeding operations are postponed, if the additional interconnection delay violates the clock cycle time.

Inter-chip connections caused by decomposed components are handled differently. The additional delay is considered during synthesis by temporarily extending the component's delay within the synthesis library. Thus, partitioned components are scheduled according to their extended delay and might be active during multiple clock cycles in order to do not violate the clock cycle time.

As a result, back annotation provides an iterative refinement process of the design. The refined schedule is given on the right hand side in Fig. 2. As mentioned before, all additional inter-chip delay is assumed to be annotated to the edges, but the additional delay due to decomposition of component F is handled by extending its execution time introducing the new component $F'=F_1\cup F_2$. During refinement of the original schedule component F' is scheduled for two cycles, starting its operation one clock cycle earlier. Due to the delay ΔC_2 the shift operator has to be moved to clock cycle 3 in order to fulfill the clock cycle constraint.

The presented refinements are not possible in the traditional rapid prototyping design flow, because a fixed RT-level architecture is chosen and high-level synthesis is not included in the iteration loop.

5   Status of Work

The tools CADDY-II and *PuMA* are already implemented and working as reported in [4,19]. The exchange format for annotation is defined and implemented whereas the back annotation format is currently under development. The consideration of timing and scheduling constraints from high-level synthesis within *PuMA's* partitioner is implemented. We are currently integrating the high quality floorplanning and placement tool FRONTIER [20] into *PuMA* in order to evaluate our floorplanning approach. In addition, the dedicated module generators are going to be replaced by CoMGen [1] in order to increase configuration flexibility. Minor extensions to CADDY-II have to be made in order to enable incremental scheduling.

6   Experimental Results

6.1   Component Models

As mentioned, CADDY-II needs a precise library of available components in terms of area and timing estimation according to the component's parameters such as operand width. The component's area can be easily calculated, whereas the timing estimation is much more sophisticated. Due to the generator approach used within *PuMA*, we found very precise and scalable analytical estimation functions by implementing various components of arbitrary size into Xilinx' XC4013PQ208-5, which is used in our Quickturn System Realizer emulation system.

The functions describe the combinational (CLB) delay as well as the routing delay of the components with accuracy between 1% in best case and 5% in worst case. Only in case of decomposition of a component into multiple FPGAs, the additional inter-chip delay is not considered and may lead to violations of the schedule. However, our concept still offers the possibility of back annotation, although the probability of such cases is decreasing with each new FPGA generation.

6.2   Signal-Flow-Driven Floorplanning

Due to the integrated signal-flow-driven floorplanner the generators have the opportunity of placing the CLBs within given rectangular shapes according to the signal flow assigned to each component. An example of benchmark filter2a is given on the left hand side in Fig. 3. Please notice that arrows represent the component's signal flow direction. In this example, the XC4085 is utilized by only 31% intentionally in order to increase visibility and to show the poor average utilization, which is reached in today's emulation systems by the traditional implementation approach. Fig. 3 shows on the right hand side the pre-placed and fully routed *PuMA* implementation of example filter2a. Please notice that the floorplan can be recognized even within the routing! This is caused by the local routing due to the generator-based pre-placement.

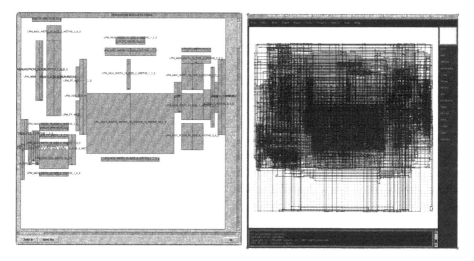

Fig. 3. Floorplan of example filter2a (XC4085) and fully pre-placed and routed implementation

We realized in almost all cases, that the component's internal connections have been routed within the given rectangular shapes and only interconnections between connected components are routed outside the shapes (Fig. 3, right hand side).

This is the main reason, why the delay models are so precise, we gain much shorter routing times and last but not least gain much better overall routability. Contrary to *PuMA*, the traditional simulated-annealing-based approach of Xilinx' tool produces the typically cloud-like result, as shown in Fig. 4 on the left hand side, which is only acceptable for low FPGA utilization. The more the utilization grows, the poorer the achieved placement results are and the longer the execution time gets, as described in Section 6.3.

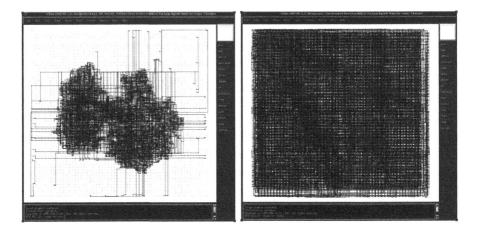

Fig. 4. Traditional placement and routing and routability for high CLB utilization

6.3   Signal-Flow-Driven Placement

Depending on the floorplan's quality, we have proven [11] that FPGA utilization up to 90% is realistic and that such implementations are still routable in acceptable time, in contrast to traditional approaches. An implementation of a 54x54 bit Pezaris multiplier, using 92% of an XC4085 FPGA, is given in Fig. 4 on the right hand side. With our approach the full implementation (mapping, placement, routing) took about three hours.

Placing exactly the same CLB-netlist without our placement information with Xilinx' tool took two hours. This would be still acceptable. However, after six days of routing the tool failed with 600 nets still not routed. Please recognize the very even routing density for the *PuMA* implementation. This is accomplished by considering the component's internal structure during placement, which is not possible in traditional approaches. This example highlights the potential of our approach.

7   Conclusion

The presented results point out the benefits of coupling high-level synthesis and direct implementation of RT-level circuit descriptions into FPGA-based rapid prototyping or logic emulation systems. The overall turn-around-time, which the most critical problem in rapid prototyping and logic emulation, is reduced dramatically, although *PuMA* is only a university software prototype, which is yet not specifically tuned for run time.

We are encouraged by [6, 8, 14, 15] and our previous work, that the overall concept will speed up the design process as well as improve design quality due to better design space exploration. Shortening the design process additionally offers the opportunity of better design verification without extending time-to-market.

8   References

1.   J. Abke, E. Barke; "CoMGen: Direct Mapping of Arbitrary Components into LUT-Based FPGAs", FPL '00: 10th International Workshop on Field Programmable Logic and Applications, 2000, pp. 191-200
2.   http://www.aptix.com/Products/index.html
3.   J. Bell, K. Sakallah, J. Whittemore; "False Path Analysis in Sequential Circuits", PATMOS '98, Lyngby, 1998, Denmark, pp. 245-253
4.   O. Bringmann, W. Rosenstiel; "Cross-Level Hierarchical High-Level Synthesis", DATE '98: Design Automation and Test in Europe, 1998, pp. 451-456
5.   M. Butts, J. Batcheller, J. Varghese; "An Efficient Logic Emulation System", ICCD '92: IEEE International Conference on Computer Design, 1992, pp. 138-141
6.   T. Buchholz, G. Haug, U. Kebschull, G. Koch, W. Rosenstiel; "Behavioral Emulation of Synthesized RT-level Descriptions Using VLIW Architectures", RSP '98: 9th IEEE International Workshop on Rapid System Prototyping, Leuven, 1998, pp. 70-74
7.   P. K. Chan, M. Schlag, M. Martin; "BORG: A Reconfigurable Prototyping Board Using Field-Programmable Gate Arrays", FPGA '92: 1st International Symposium on Field Programmable Gate Arrays, 1992, pp.47-51
8.   G. Doncev, M. Leeser, S. Tarafdar; "Truly Rapid Prototyping Requires High Level Synthesis", RSP '98: 9th IEEE International Workshop on Rapid System Prototyping, 1998, pp. 101-106
9.   D. Du, S.Yen, S. Ghanta; "On the General False Path Problem", DAC '89: 26th Design Automation Conference, 1989, pp. 555-560
10. P. Gutberlet, W. Rosenstiel; "Timing Preserving Interface Transformations for the Synthesis of Behavioral VHDL", EURO-DAC '94:   European Design Automation Conference, 1994, pp. 618-623
11. K. Harbich, J. Abke, E. Barke: "*PuMA*: An Optimised Partitioning and Mapping Environment for Rapid Prototyping of Structural RT-level Circuit Descriptions", DATE 2000: 3rd Design Automation and Test in Europe, 2000, Paris, University Booth
12. K. Harbich, H. Hoffmann, E. Barke; "A New Hierarchical Graph Model for Multiple FPGA Partitioning", WDTA '98: 1st IEEE Workshop on Design, Test and Application, 1998, pp. 101-104
13. http://www.ikos.com/products/virtualwires.pdf
14. U. Kebschull, G. Koch, W. Rosenstiel: "The Weaver Prototyping Environment for Hardware-Software-Codesign and Codebugging", DATE '98: Design, Automation and Test in Europe, 1998, Design Track, pp. 239-242
15. R. Kress, A. Pyttel, A. Sedlmeier; "FPGA-Based Prototyping for Product Definition", FPL '00: 10th International Workshop on Field Programmable Logic and Applications, 2000, pp. 78-86
16. D. M. Lewis, D. R. Galloway, Marcus van Ierssel, J. Rose, P. Chow; "The Transmogrifier-2: A 1 Million Gate Rapid Prototyping System", FPGA '97: 5th International Symposium on Field Programmable Gate Arrays, 1997, pp. 53-61
17. http://www.edif.org/lpmweb/
18. S. Raman, L. Patnaik; "Performance-Driven MCM Partitioning Through an Adaptive Genetic Algorithm", IEEE Transactions on VLSI Systems, Vol. 4, No. 4, December 1996, pp. 434-444
19. J. Stohmann, K. Harbich, M. Olbrich, E. Barke; "An Optimized Design Flow for Fast FPGA-Based Rapid Prototyping ", FPL '98: 8th International Workshop on Field Programmable Logic and Applications, 1998, pp. 79-88
20. R. Tessier; "Frontier: A Fast Placement System for FPGAs", IFIP '99: 10th International Conference on VLSI, 1999, Lisbon

Secure Configuration of Field Programmable Gate Arrays

Tom Kean

Algotronix Consulting, PO Box 23116, Edinburgh EH8 8YB, United Kingdom
tom@algotronix.com

Abstract. Although SRAM programmed Field Programmable Gate Arrays (FPGA's) have come to dominate the industry due to their density and performance advantages over non-volatile technologies they have a serious weakness in that they are vulnerable to piracy and reverse engineering of the user design. This is becoming increasingly important as the size of chips - and hence the value of customer designs - increases. FPGA's are now being used in consumer products where piracy is more common. Further, reconfiguration of FPGA's in the field is becoming increasingly popular particularly in networking applications and it is vital to provide security against malicious parties interfering with equipment functionality through this mechanism.

1 Introduction

In recent years, SRAM programmed FPGA's have established a major competitive presence in market areas previously dominated by mask programmed ASIC technology. For example, SRAM programmed FPGA's such as Xilinx's Spartan family are being promoted for use in consumer products. At the high end FPGA's with a density of several million gates are available. Upgrading of products containing FPGA's by downloading bitstreams in the field is an increasingly attractive option as more and more applications are connected to networks. All of these market trends increase the need for protection of FPGA bitstream information. Consumer products are particularly susceptible to competition from low cost illegal 'cloned' copies. The costs of developing a multi-million gate FPGA design are significant and, therefore, it is desirable to prevent design reverse engineering. Unlike cloning, design reverse engineering for competitive analysis is not, in itself, illegal. In the case of network connected equipment it is important to protect against malicious interference with the download process: maliciously created FPGA configurations can even cause physical damage to the FPGA chip.

The SRAM FPGA bitstream security problem arises because an attacker can probe the connection between the FPGA and the external non-volatile memory during configuration and obtain a copy of the programming bitstream. Many solutions to the problem have been proposed over the last fifteen years [1]. Most have significantly reduced the convenience of using FPGA's or had easily exploitable security loopholes

G. Brebner and R. Woods (Eds.): FPL 2001, LNCS 2147, pp. 142-151, 2001.

and none have been successful commercially.   A major selling proposition of anti-fuse FPGA vendors has been the superior design security offered by their technology [2]. Only within the last few months has a major manufacturer introduced a 'mainstream' SRAM programmed FPGA chip with security features: Xilinx's Virtex II [3].

2   Approaches to Bitstream Security

2.1 Ignorance Is Bliss

Until the introduction of Virtex II, the advice from the major SRAM FPGA vendors was that to protect against design piracy by copying bitstream information the best approach was to configure the FPGA before the product left the factory and maintain the configuration in the field using a battery back up when the main power supply to the equipment containing the FPGA was switched off. While theoretically providing a high level of security this was never a practical option for most applications due to the relatively high power consumption of FPGA chips. Battery back up reduces the reliability of the equipment, increases its cost and requires provision for battery replacement in the field.

The conventional approach to preventing design reverse engineering by 'decompiling' the bitstream was for manufacturers to keep the configuration memory layout of the devices secret and only release it under Non-Disclosure Agreement - 'security through obscurity'. FPGA CAD software vendors such as NeoCad nevertheless managed to reverse-engineer FPGA programming bitstreams for the major Xilinx devices. Recently, Xilinx has started to offer Jbits software to support dynamic reconfiguration of mainstream devices [4] which provides an API to bitstream information. With the introduction of Jbits the 'security through obscurity' defence is paper thin and it is only a matter of time before bitstream to EDIF de-compilers become readily available on the internet. At the time of writing there are unconfirmed reports that such software is already in circulation.

2.2 Encapsulation

In October 2000 Atmel announced a secure version of their FPSLIC chip [5]. An FPSLIC is a 'system level integration' device containing an FPGA and a microcontroller. A degree of physical security is achieved by packaging the non-volatile configuration memory with the FPSLIC chip.   This constitutes a significant inconvenience to would-be pirates but will not deter a professional adversary. It is relatively easy to remove external packaging around an integrated circuit: this is routinely done by IC vendors to support failure analysis. Once the external packaging is removed it is straightforward to probe the individual IC chips and determine configuration information.

A further downside of this approach to design security is that it restricts the choices for reconfiguring the device. For example, in many systems it may be preferable to share a single large FLASH memory between multiple programmable chips. It may also be desirable to have a larger memory than strictly required in order that multiple configurations can be stored.

2.3 User Defined Key

One of the earliest suggested mechanisms for providing bitstream security to an FPGA is contained in a US patent assigned to Pilkington Microelectronics [6]. The suggestion in this patent is quite straightforward: CAD software encrypts the bitstream prior to storing it in the serial EPROM. The encryption key used is then loaded into a non-volatile key register built from EPROM cells on the FPGA device. When the product is powered up in the field the FPGA can decrypt the encrypted bitstream from the external memory using the key stored in the non-volatile on chip register. This approach protects against both design piracy (since the bitstream stored in the serial EPROM will only configure an FPGA with the correct key stored in its on chip register) and reverse engineering (since the externally available bitstream is encrypted).

The primary disadvantage of this approach is that it requires non-volatile memory within and hence non-standard processing of the FPGA device which increases cost. Copy prevention also requires a different bitstream and encryption key to be generated for each device and therefore complicates the user's manufacturing flow.

A variant of the Pilkington scheme is used by Xilinx in their recently announced Virtex II family. Instead of providing on-chip EPROM memory to store the cryptographic key the key is stored in a key register with its own power supply pins. An external battery maintains the state of this register when the equipment is powered off. Since only the key register is battery backed up very little power is required compared with backing up the entire configuration memory and a small watch battery is sufficient. A key-register only battery backup scheme was independently suggested in a UK patent application filed by Algotronix Ltd. in 1999 [7].

Although the key-register only backup scheme is much preferable to backing up the entire configuration memory it still adds cost to the system and reduces overall reliability. Vibration and shock are of concern because even a momentary loss of power will delete the key. Battery lifespan is affected by self-discharge and lifespan on a printed circuit board may be less than in an environmentally protected location such as inside a watch particularly if humidity is high. In general, provision will have to be made for service personnel to change batteries in the field. This must be done as preventative maintenance since any loss of battery back up power when the equipment is lost will make the equipment inoperative.

2.4 Secure Serial Memory

Various schemes have been suggested in which a special 'secure' serial EPROM containing encryption circuitry communicates with an FPGA containing decryption circuitry. Such schemes are disclosed in US Patent 5,970,142 assigned to Xilinx [8] and US Patent 5,915,017 assigned to Altera [9]. Schemes based on special secure EPROM's can provide protection against copying the bitstream as it passes between an FPGA and a secure serial EPROM however they have problems with other modes of attack. In so called 'man in the middle' attacks in which an attacker interposes circuitry under her control between the FPGA and the serial EPROM in order to eavesdrop on and make malicious changes to information passing between the FPGA and serial EPROM. In a 'spoofing' attack an attacker designs circuitry to 'impersonate' an FPGA in order to 'spoof' the secure serial EPROM into providing information in a form she can decrypt.

It is possible to design a secure protocol between a secure serial EPROM and an FPGA (although the prior art references cited do not achieve this) but it appears to be a fundamental requirement that the secure EPROM be able to determine that it is communicating with a 'real' FPGA and not 'hostile' circuitry pretending to be an FPGA. The most practical way of the secure serial EPROM confirming the identity of the FPGA is a cryptographic protocol based on secret data known to the FPGA which can be verified by the serial EPROM. Thus, effective schemes based on secure memories also depend on being able to store a secret key in a non-volatile manner on the FPGA.

Since there are alternative methods of providing effective bitstream security using conventional memories given a cryptographic key stored on the FPGA there is little reason to incur the additional inconvenience and expense of schemes based on special secure memories.

2.5 Manufacturer Defined Key

In a scheme supported by Actel in their 60RS family of SRAM programmed FPGA's [10] a fixed key is implanted into the FPGA during manufacture. The method of implanting the key is not specified in the limited documentation available. This fixed key is believed to be the same for all devices and is known to the CAD software which creates a bitstream encoded according to the key. When the FPGA loads the encoded bitstream it decrypts it according to the fixed key prior to storing it in configuration memory.

This scheme provides security against design reverse-engineering but not against 'cloning' since every FPGA has an identical key. Further, there is an 'all the eggs in one basket' issue in that if the fixed secret key is determined then *all* user designs are affected - thus it is worth an attacker's time to devote considerable effort to determining the secret key. The attacker's task may be made much easier by the fact that key information is embedded in the CAD software as well as the FPGA artwork - decompiling or tracing software is a much easier task than reverse engineering IC artwork.

2.6 Hardware Token Based Schemes

Another possibility which has been suggested is anti-piracy schemes analogous to the 'dongles' or hardware tokens used to protect PC software (for example, the FreeCores proposal [11]). In these schemes a separate chip, normally a CPLD, is provided and connected to user I/O on the FPGA. The FPGA is configured normally from a serial EPROM and the user design on the FPGA then makes contact with the user design on the CPLD. A challenge-response mechanism is provided so that the design on the FPGA can determine that the design on the CPLD is as expected. For example, the FPGA design and the CPLD design might implement identical Linear Feedback Shift Registers, the FPGA then clocks the CPLD a random number of times and compares its output with the output of its own LFSR. If the two do not match the user design on the FPGA determines that it is installed in 'cloned' equipment and disables itself.

The advantage of this scheme is that it requires no hardware support on the FPGA. It relies on the fact that CPLD's are based on non-volatile memory and hence have physical protection against piracy and attempts to extend the protection to a connected SRAM programmed FPGA. However, the scheme provides no additional protection beyond 'security by obscurity' against reverse engineering the bitstream. Dongle based protection schemes for PC software are regularly cracked by de-compiling the software binary and disabling the code which accesses the dongle. It would be relatively straightforward to circumvent the piracy protection offered by this approach using a similar technique. In general, it appears impossible to offer strong piracy protection without reverse engineering protection.

A further disadvantage of this scheme is the cost of the external CPLD and the FPGA resources required to implement the security circuitry within the user design.

While this approach makes some sense where piracy is a concern and the FPGA provides no built in security it is insecure and expensive compared with schemes based on encryption circuitry within the FPGA configuration logic.

2.7   Desirable Features in a Bitstream Security System

Based on this description of the prior art some desirable characteristics of FPGA bitstream protection schemes are apparent.
1.   The scheme should provide strong protection against both reverse engineering and 'cloning'.
2.   No additional components should required on the customer board, so there is no cost penalty.
3.   There should be no effect on the reliability of the user board or need for additional service in the field.
4.   The user should not have to maintain a database of encryption keys in order to allow for future changes to the design.
5.   There should be no significant complication to the manufacturing flow for products containing the FPGA.

6. No changes should be required to the CAD tools or design flow. In particular, no information which could compromise the security of the scheme should be embedded in CAD tools or their supporting files.
7. The scheme should be compatible with standard CMOS processing.
8. The scheme should be based on well understood and standardized cryptographic algorithms and usage modes to allow easy analysis of threats and should not depend on 'security through obscurity'.
9. The scheme should be upward compatible with standard programming modes and standard non-volatile memories. It should allow for design upgrades in the field and design changes during prototyping.

3 A New Bitstream Security System

Figures 1 and 2 illustrate a new FPGA bitstream security scheme proposed by Algotronix [7] which removes most of the difficulties with prior art schemes. The scheme is based on two observations:
1. Flash memory has largely superseded EPROM: thus most modern FPGA's are configured from non-volatile memories which can be programmed in-system by the FPGA itself.
2. If the FPGA is configured within the FPGA customer's facility then there are no security implications to transferring unencrypted bitstreams to the FPGA.

Figure 1, shows the initial configuration of the FPGA within the customer facility. This is achieved during the manufacturing of the board containing the FPGA and involves downloading an unencrypted bitstream via a JTAG interface. The FPGA then encrypts the bitstream based on an on-chip secret key which is unknown even to the FPGA customer and programs it into an external in-system programmable FLASH EPROM. Header bits on the bitstream file are used to indicate its status, for example, insecure bitstream to be converted to a secure bitstream, secure bitstream, insecure bitstream to be left insecure. With this scheme the FPGA CAD tool flow is not concerned with the encryption process and there is no need for the customer to protect or manage cryptographic keys.

This is only one illustration of how initial programming can be achieved - as with conventional FPGA's it is expected that a variety of modes will be available. Another option would be to pre-program the serial EPROM's with an unencrypted bitstream prior to board assembly and on initial power-on for the FPGA to read in that bitstream, encrypt it and reprogram the serial EPROM with the encrypted bitstream. Similarly, the FPGA may be programmed by a microprocessor on the customer board and return encrypted data to the microprocessor which the microprocessor then uses to overwrite the initial unencrypted data in its memory system.

Figure 2 shows the situation when an FPGA is powered up 'in the field': by examining the header bits it determines that the bitstream is secure and therefore decrypts it using the internally stored key prior to loading it into configuration memory. Although the figure shows encrypted data coming from an adjacent serial EPROM it could equally be provided by a microprocessor or another FPGA in a configuration 'daisy-chain'.

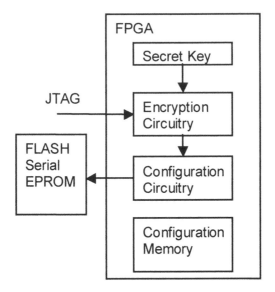

Fig. 1. Initial Programming of Secure FPGA.

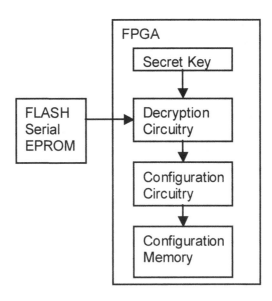

Fig. 2. Normal Configuration of Secure FPGA in the field

Standard ciphers operating in cipher-block-chaining (CBC) mode can be used to implement the encryption and decryption functions. The choice of cipher is not critical but triple-DES is a reasonable option. CBC mode removes any patterns which would otherwise be present in highly regular data such as FPGA bitstreams, it also provides a cryptographic checksum which can be used to detect tampering with the file. If tampering is detected the FPGA takes appropriate action such as clearing the configuration memory and disables FPGA output pins.

As described so far this security scheme requires a non-volatile key register within the FPGA chip. This could be implemented using a battery backed key register as in Virtex II, however this is not the preferred approach for the reasons outlined above. Instead, it is suggested that laser programmed fuses are used to implant a random key on each chip during the manufacturing process. This is a standard low-cost option at many foundries and has been used in support of redundancy schemes for commodity DRAM chips for many years.

4   Simplified Piracy Protection

An extension to the scheme outlined above [12] removes the need for laser programmed fuses and provides a high degree of resistance to reverse engineering and piracy while maintaining a completely conventional CMOS flow.

This extension is based on the novel observation that in order to deter piracy it is not necessary to absolutely prevent 'cloning' an FPGA design, only to make it uneconomic to offer a product based on cloned FPGA's. That is, in the vast majority of cases, the problem is that a pirate can compete with the original designer of a piece of equipment by offering 'cloned' equipment at similar or lower cost in the market: not that a pirate could make a small number of units of cloned equipment.

Assume that instead of a non-volatile memory containing the encryption key each FPGA had the same encryption key embedded into the design artwork through changes in one of the masks used in fabrication. The approach of hiding a small amount of secret data in a much larger database is termed steganography and can be a highly secure way of storing an encryption key given the small number of bits involved (less than 200) and the 100's of millions of polygons in an FPGA design database. In fact, arguably, it is harder for a pirate to determine the value of an encryption key when it is hidden in this way than if it is configured into EPROM memory or stored in SRAM. This system provides strong protection against reverse engineering (since the design is encrypted when it is transferred to the FPGA) but no protection against 'cloning' (since every FPGA will successfully load the design).

Based on this analysis prior art systems came to the conclusion that each FPGA chip should have a unique key. However, this is not necessary if the goal is to make 'cloning' uneconomic rather than impossible. Suppose there were five possible keys and FPGA's were supplied with no markings indicating which key was in a particular

FPGA. The design owner can use any FPGA since the FPGA will create an encrypted bitstream itself based on whatever internal key it contains. However, a pirate using a naive approach would have to buy, on average, five FPGA's in order to find one which would load a particular pirated design.

More sophisticated pirates might attempt to sort the FPGA's according to their key and resell those they could not use or obtain copies of the design encrypted with all five possible keys and choose the appropriate configuration for a particular FPGA. FPGA manufacturers can counter these more sophisticated schemes in a variety of ways. Firstly, keys can be used in manufacturing for a limited time and then replaced: in this case it may be impossible for a pirate buying 'new' FPGA's from distribution to find one that will accept a design copied from equipment in the field which will contain an FPGA manufactured several months earlier. Secondly, FPGA's can be supplied with different keys in different geographic areas. Thirdly, large customers can be supplied with FPGA's with keys not supplied through 'distribution'. All these approaches make it less likely that a pirate will be able to obtain FPGA's compatible with a cloned design. Lastly, the number of possible FPGA keys can be increased.

Each key variant will involve changes to a particular mask in the FPGA, this represents an additional expense and inconvenience in the manufacturing flow. However, these costs are acceptably small. High volume products will run on multiple fab lines in any case and will, therefore, have multiple mask sets. Also, masks do not last forever and must be replaced from time to time.

5 Summary

Lack of design security has long been the skeleton lurking in the closet of the SRAM FPGA industry. Until recently, customers were willing to live with this problem in order to benefit from the ease of use of programmable logic. Recently, however industry trends have forced manufacturers to address the issue. Provision of strong security technology removes one of the few remaining advantages of antifuse FPGA's and unlocks additional areas of the ASIC marketplace.

Whereas customers may have been willing to ignore security deficiencies when no leading supplier offered a solution now that one, albeit imperfect, system is available bitstream security is likely to become a standard, must-have, feature for all vendors. Similar situations have occurred many times in the past with security technologies: for example, today, all new cars in Europe are sold with engine immobilisers and all e-commerce websites offer Secure Sockets Layer (SSL) security for credit cards.

The proposed security technology offers key advantages compared with alternative schemes: it does not affect system reliability, it does not require additional components, it is compatible with standard CMOS processing, it does not require support from CAD software and it is based on standardised cryptographic protocols.

References

1. Dipert, B., "Cunning Circuits Confound Crooks", EDN Magazine, October 12, 2000.
2. Actel Corporation, "Protecting your Intellectual Property from the Pirates", presentation at DesignCon '98. Available from www.actel.com.
3. Xilinx Inc., "Using Bitstream Encryption", in Chapter 2 of the Virtex II Platform FPGA Handbook available from www.xilinx.com.
4. Steven A. Guccione, Delon Levi and Prasanna Sundararajan, "Jbits: A Java-based Interface for Reconfigurable Computing". Proceedings 2nd Annual Military and Aerospace Applications of Programmable Devices and Technologies Conference (MAPLD).
5. Atmel Corp., "Atmel Introduces Secure FPLSIC", Press Release, Atmel Corp, Oct 12, 2000.
6. Austin, K., US Patent 5,388,157 "Data Security Arrangements for Semiconductor Programmable Devices"
7. Algotronix Ltd., "Method and Apparatus for Secure Configuration of a Field Programmable Gate Array", PCT Patent Application PCT/GB00/04988.
8. Erickson, C., US Patent 5,970,142 "Configuration Stream Encryption"
9. Sang, C., et al, US Patent 5,915,017 "Method and Apparatus for Securing Programming Data of Programmable Logic Device"
10. Actel Corp., "60RS Family SPGA's", Advanced Data Sheet. Available from www.actel.com.
11. Kessner, D., "Copy Protection for SRAM based FPGA Designs", Application Note, Free IP Project, http://www.free-ip.com/copyprotection.html.
12. Algotronix Ltd., "Method of using a Mask Programmed Key to Securely Configure a Field Programmable Gate Array", Unpublished pending patent application.

Single-Chip FPGA Implementation of the Advanced Encryption Standard Algorithm

Máire McLoone , John V. McCanny

DSiP™ Laboratories, School of Electrical and Electronic Engineering,
The Queen's University of Belfast, Belfast BT9 5AH, Northern Ireland
Maire.McLoone@ee.qub.ac.uk, J.McCanny@ee.qub.ac.uk

Abstract. A single-chip FPGA implementation of the new Advanced Encryption Standard (AES) algorithm, Rijndael is presented. Field Programmable Gate Arrays (FPGAs) are well suited to encryption implementations due to their flexibility and an architecture, which can be exploited to accommodate typical encryption transformations. The FPGA implementation described here is that of a fully pipelined single-chip Rijndael design which runs at a data rate of 7 Gbits/sec on a Xilinx Virtex-E XCV812E-8-BG560 FPGA device. This proves to be one of the fastest single-chip FPGA Rijndael implementations currently available. The high Block RAM content of the Virtex-E device is exploited in the design.

Keywords: FPGA Implementation, AES, Rijndael, Encryption

1 Introduction

On the 2nd October 2000 the US National Institute of Standards and Technology (NIST) selected the Rijndael algorithm [1], developed by Joan Daemen and Vincent Rijmen, as the new Advanced Encryption Standard (AES) algorithm. It proved to be a fast and efficient algorithm when implemented in both hardware and software across a range of platforms. Rijndael is to be approved by the NIST and replace the aging Data Encryption Standard (DES) algorithm as the Federal Information Processing Encryption Standard (FIPS)[2] in the summer of 2001. In the future Rijndael will be the encryption algorithm used in many applications such as:

- Internet Routers
- Remote Access Servers
- High Speed ATM/Ethernet Switching
- Satellite Communications
- High Speed Secure ISP Servers

- Virtual Private Networks (VPNs)
- SONET
- Mobile phone applications
- Electronic Financial Transactions

In this paper a single-chip FPGA implementation of the Rijndael algorithm is presented. The fully pipelined design is implemented using Xilinx Foundation Series 3.1i software on the Virtex-E XCV812E FPGA device [3]. A 10-stage pipelined

G. Brebner and R. Woods (Eds.): FPL 2001, LNCS 2147, pp. 152-161, 2001.
© Springer-Verlag Berlin Heidelberg 2001

Rijndael design requires considerable memory; hence, its implementation is ideally suited to the Virtex-E Extended Memory range of FPGAs, which contain devices with up to 280 RAM Blocks (BRAMs).

The fastest known Rijndael FPGA implementation is by Chodowiec, Khuon and Gaj [4], which performs at 12160 Mbits/sec. Their design is implemented on 3 Virtex XCV1000 FPGA devices. Dandalis, Prasanna and Rolim [5] also carried out an implementation on the XCV1000 device, achieving an encryption rate of 353 Mbits/sec. A partially unrolled design by Elbirt, Yip, Chetwynd and Paar [6] on the same device performed at a data-rate of 1937.9 Mbits/sec. The fastest Rijndael software implementation is Brian Gladman's [7] 325 Mbit/sec design on a 933 MHz Pentium III processor. Whereas, an earlier paper [8] described a high-speed generic Rijndael design, which supported three key lengths, this paper assumes a 128-bit data block and a 128-bit key and concentrates on using an optimum number of Block RAMs to attain high throughput.

Section 2 of this paper describes the Rijndael Algorithm. The design of the fully pipelined Rijndael implementation and the exploitation of the Block RAMs on the Virtex E device are outlined in Section 3. Performance results are given in section 4 and conclusions are provided in section 5.

2   Rijndael Algorithm

The Rijndael algorithm is a substitution-linear transformation network [9]. It can operate on 128-bit, 192-bit and 256-bit data and key blocks. The NIST requested that the AES must implement a symmetric block cipher with a block size of 128 bits, hence the variations of Rijndael which can operate on larger data block sizes will not be included in the actual FIPS standard. An outline of Rijndael is shown in Fig. 2.1.

Rijndael comprises 10, 12 and 14 iterations or rounds when the key lengths are 128, 192 and 256 respectively. The transformations in Rijndael consider the data block as a 4 column rectangular array of 4-byte vectors (known as the *State* array), as shown in Fig 2.2. A 128-bit plaintext consists of 16 bytes, B_0, B_1, B_2, B_3, B_4... B_{14}, B_{15}. Hence, B_0 becomes $P_{0,0}$, B_1 becomes $P_{1,0}$, B_2 becomes $P_{2,0}$ ... B_4 becomes $P_{0,1}$ and so on. The key is also considered to be a rectangular array of 4-byte vectors, the number of columns, N_k, of which is dependent on the key length. This is illustrated in Fig 2.3. This paper assumes a 128-bit key and therefore a similar rectangular array is considered for the key as for the data block. The algorithm design consists of an initial data/key addition, nine rounds and a final round, which is a variation of the typical round. The Rijndael key schedule expands the key entering the cipher so that a different sub-key or *round key* is created for each algorithm iteration. The Rijndael round comprises four transformations:

-     ByteSub Transformation   - ShiftRow Transformation
-     MixColumn Transformation   - Round Key Addition

The ByteSub transformation is the *s-box* of the Rijndael algorithm and operates on each of the State bytes independently. The s-box is constructed by finding the multiplicative inverse of each byte in GF(2^8). An affine transformation is then applied, which involves multiplying the result by a matrix and adding to the hexadecimal number '63'.

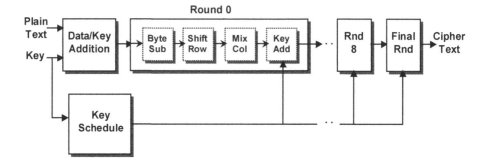

Fig.2.1. Outline of Rijndael Encryption Algorithm

$P_{0,0}$	$P_{0,1}$	$P_{0,2}$	$P_{0,3}$
$P_{1,0}$	$P_{1,1}$	$P_{1,2}$	$P_{1,3}$
$P_{2,0}$	$P_{2,1}$	$P_{2,2}$	$P_{2,3}$
$P_{3,0}$	$P_{3,1}$	$P_{3,2}$	$P_{3,3}$

	$N_k = 4$			$N_k = 6$		$N_k = 8$	
$K_{0,0}$	$K_{0,1}$	$K_{0,2}$	$K_{0,3}$	$K_{0,4}$	$K_{0,5}$	$K_{0,6}$	$K_{0,7}$
$K_{1,0}$	$K_{1,1}$	$K_{1,2}$	$K_{1,3}$	$K_{1,4}$	$K_{1,5}$	$K_{1,6}$	$K_{1,7}$
$K_{2,0}$	$K_{2,1}$	$K_{2,2}$	$K_{2,3}$	$K_{2,4}$	$K_{2,5}$	$K_{2,6}$	$K_{2,7}$
$K_{3,0}$	$K_{3,1}$	$K_{3,2}$	$K_{3,3}$	$K_{3,4}$	$K_{3,5}$	$K_{3,6}$	$K_{3,7}$

Fig. 2.2. State Rectangular Array   **Fig. 2.3.** Key Rectangular Array

In the ShiftRow transformation, the rows of the State are cyclically shifted to the left. Row 0 is not shifted, row 1 is shifted 1 place, row 2 by 2 places and row 3 by 3 places. The MixColumn transformation operates on the columns of the State. Each column is considered a polynomial over $GF(2^8)$ and multiplied modulo x^4+1 with a fixed polynomial $c(x)$, where,

$$c(x) = \text{'03'}x^3 + \text{'01'}x^2 + \text{'01'}x + \text{'02'} \tag{1}$$

The Round keys are derived from the cipher key and are also represented as an array of 4-byte vectors. Each round key is bitwise XORed to the State in Round Key Addition. In the final round the MixColumn transformation is excluded.

2.1 Key Schedule

The Rijndael key schedule consists of first expanding the cipher key and then from this expansion, selecting the required number of Round keys. Assuming a 128-bit key, the number of rounds in the algorithm is 10 and the number of round keys required is

11. The expanded key is a linear array of 4-byte words, W[0] to W[43]. The first four words contain the cipher key as illustrated in Fig. 2.4. Each remaining word, W[i] is derived by XORing the previous word, W[i–1] with the word, W[i–4]. For words in positions, which are a multiple of four, a transformation is applied to W[i–1]. Firstly, the bytes in the word are cyclically shifted to the left. For example, a word [a,b,c,d] becomes [b,c,d,a]. Next, each byte in the word is passed through the Rijndael ByteSub transformation and finally, the result is XORed with a round constant.

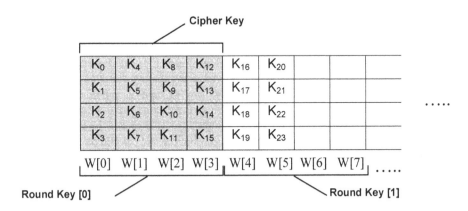

Fig. 2.4. Expanded Key Array with $N_k = 4$

The round constants required for each of the ten rounds are described in [1]. In the Round key selection process, Round key [0] is taken to be W[0] to W[3], Round key [1] as W[4] to W[7] and so on as shown in Fig. 2.4 above.

2.2 Decryption

The decryption process in Rijndael is effectively the inverse of its encryption process. It comprises an inverse of the final round, inverses of the rounds, followed by the initial data/key addition. The data/key addition remains the same as it involves an xor operation, which is its own inverse. The inverse of the round is found by inverting each of the transformations in the round. The inverse of ByteSub is obtained by applying the inverse of the affine transformation and taking the multiplicative inverse in $GF(2^8)$ of the result. In the inverse of the ShiftRow transformation, row 0 is not shifted, row 1 is now shifted 3 places, row 2 by 2 places and row 3 by 1 place. The polynomial, $c(x)$, used to transform the State columns in the inverse of MixColumn is given by,

$$c(x) = \text{`0B'}x^3 + \text{`0D'}x^2 + \text{`09'}x + \text{`0E'} \tag{2}$$

Similarly to the data/key addition, Round Key addition is its own inverse. During decryption, the key schedule does not change, however the round keys constructed are now used in reverse order. Round key 0 is still utilized in the initial data/key addition and round key 10 in the inverse of the final round. However, round key 1 is now used in the inverse of round 8, round key 2 in the inverse of round 7 and so on.

3 Design of Pipelined Rijndael Implementation

The Rijndael design described in this paper is fully pipelined, with ten pipeline stages. A number of different architectures can be considered when designing encryption algorithms [6]. These are described as follows. Iterative Looping (IL) is where only one round is designed, hence for an *n*-round algorithm, *n* iterations of that round are carried out to perform an encryption. Loop Unrolling (LU) involves the unrolling of multiple rounds. Pipelining (P) is achieved by replicating the round and placing registers between each round to control the flow of data. A pipelined architecture generally provides the highest throughput. Sub-Pipelining (SP) is carried out on a partially pipelined design when the round is complex. It decreases the pipeline's delay between stages but increases the number of clock cycles required to perform an encryption.

The main consideration in this design is the memory requirement. The Rijndael s-box - the ByteSub transformation – is utilised in each round and also in the key schedule. This transformation can be implemented as a look-up table (LUT) or ROM. This will prove a faster and more cost-effective method than implementing the multiplicative inverse operation and affine transformation. Since the State bytes are operated on individually, each Rijndael round alone requires sixteen 8-bit to 8-bit LUTs – a total of 160 LUTs. The Virtex-E Extended Memory range of FPGAs is utilized for implementation as it contains devices with up to 280 BlockSelectRAM (BRAM) memories. An outline of the Virtex-E architecture is provided in Fig 3.1 [3].

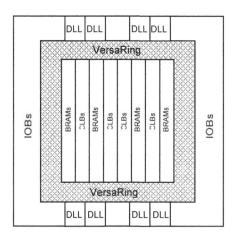
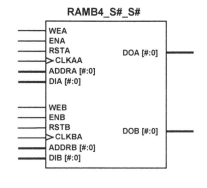

Fig. 3.1. Virtex-E Architecture Overview   **Fig. 3.2.** Dual-port Block SelectRAM

A single BRAM can be configured into two single port 256 x 8-bit RAMs, as illustrated in Fig. 3.2 [3]; hence, eight BRAMs are required for each round. When the write enable of the RAM is low ('0'), transitions on the write clock are ignored and data stored in the RAM is not affected. Hence, if the RAM is initialized and both the input data and write enable pins are held low then the RAM can be utilized as a ROM or LUT.

In the key schedule, forty words are created during expansion of the key and every fourth word is passed through the ByteSub transformation with each byte in the word being transformed. Hence, forty 8-bit to 8-bit LUTs or twenty BRAMs can be utilised in its implementation. However, since the round keys are constructed in parallel to the Round operations, only two BRAMs are required. The s-box is only used in the construction of the first word of every Round key (a Round key comprises four words) and each BRAM is used in the construction of two bytes of a word. Therefore an iterative process is used to access the two BRAMs and the Round keys are constructed as they are required by each Rijndael Round. The design assumes that the same key is used in any one data transfer session. The construction of every fourth word, which incorporates the BRAM, is shown in Fig 3.3. As described in Section 2, words which are not a multiple of four are created by XORing the previous word with the word four positions earlier.

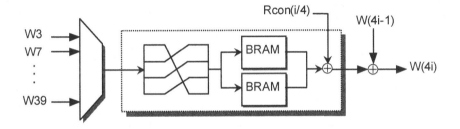

Fig. 3.3. Construction of every Fourth Word in Rijndael Key Schedule

Therefore, in the fully pipelined Rijndael design, a total of 82 ROMs are utilised – 80 ROMs are required for the 10 rounds and a further 2 for the key schedule.

The same design methodology as above can be applied to decryption. The inverse of the ByteSub transformation used in an inverse round operation can also be implemented as a LUT. However, the values in this LUT are different to those required for encryption. During decryption, the values of the LUTs utilized in the key schedule do not change and the round keys are used in reverse order. Therefore, if data decryption is carried out, it is necessary to wait 20 clock cycles before the respective decrypted data appears (10 clock cycles for the construction of the round keys and 10 clock cycles corresponding to the number of rounds in the design). In encryption the latency is only 10 clock cycles. The values contained in the encryption and decryption ROMs are outlined in Appendix 1. Some applications may require a design that can perform both encryption and decryption. One method would involve doubling the number of BRAMs utilized. However, this would prove costly on area. A simple solution [10] is to add two further ROMs to the design outlined here, one containing the initialization values for the LUTs required during encryption, the other containing the values for the LUTs required during decryption. Therefore, instead of initializing each individual BRAM as a ROM, when the design is set to encrypt, all the BRAMs are initialized with data read from the ROM containing the values required for encryption. When the design is set to decrypt, the BRAMs are initialized with data from the ROM containing the values required for the decryption operation.

4 Performance Results

The outlined Rijndael design is implemented using Xilinx Foundation Series 3.1i software and Synplify Pro V6.0. Data blocks can be accepted every clock cycle and after an initial delay the respective encrypted/decrypted data blocks appear on consecutive clock cycles.

The Rijndael encryptor design, implemented on the Virtex-E XCV812E-8BG560 device, utilizes 2679 CLB slices (28%) and 82 BRAMs (29%). Of IOBs 385 of 404 are used. The design uses a system clock of 54.35 MHz and runs at a data-rate of 7 Gbits/sec (870 Mbytes/sec). This result proves to be one of the fastest single-chip Rijndael FPGA implementations currently available, as illustrated in Table 4.1 below. The only faster FPGA implementation is that of Chodowiec, Khuon and Gaj, which has a throughput of 12.16 Gbit/sec. However, this design is implemented over a total of 3 Virtex XCV1000 devices.

Table 4.1. Specifications of Rijndael FPGA Implementations

	Device	Type	Area (CLB Slices)	No. of BRAMs	Throughput (Mbits/sec)
Chodowiec, Khuon, Gaj[4] *Over 3 Devices*	XCV1000	P	12600	80	12160
McLoone, McCanny	XCV812E	P	2679	82	6956
Elbirt *et al*[6]	XCV1000	SP	9004	-	1938
Dandalis *et al*[5]	XCV1000	IL	5673	-	353
Gladman [7]	PentiumIII	-	-	-	325

The high performance of the Rijndael design presented is achieved for a number of reasons:

- The design is fully pipelined with data blocks being accepted on every clock cycle.
- The use of dedicated Block RAMs: The complex and slow operations involved in the ByteSub transformation, the multiplicative inverse calculations over $GF(2^8)$ and matrix multiplication and addition, are replaced with simple LUTs.
- The layout of the Virtex-E architecture: From Fig 3.1, it is evident that the BRAMs are located in columns throughout the chip, with each memory column extending the full height of the chip. Each Rijndael round involves

implementation on both CLBs and BRAMs. Therefore, having an architecture where these are located in close vicinity to one another throughout the chip will improve overall performance.

The Rijndael decryptor design is also implemented on the XCV812E-8BG560 FPGA device. It utilises 4304 slices (45%) and 82 BRAMs. It performs at a rate of 6.38 Gbit/sec using a system clock of 49.9 MHz. The variance in the encryption and decryption performances is due to the different multiplier constants required by each design. In encryption the multiplier constants are simply 0x01, 0x01, 0x02 and 0x03 (hexadecimal) while those used in decryption are 0x0B, 0x0E, 0x09 and 0x0D.

5 Conclusions

A high performance single-chip FPGA implementation of the Rijndael algorithm is described in this paper. The encryptor design performs at a data-rate of 7 Gbits/sec, which is 3.5 times faster than existing single-chip FPGA implementations and 21 times faster than software implementations. The decryptor design also achieves a fast throughout of 6.4 Gbits/sec. The pipelined Rijndael design is well suited to the Virtex-E Extended Memory FPGA, since this device can accommodate the 82 BRAMs required in its implementation. The NIST is set to replace DES as the FIPS in the summer of 2001. It will replace DES in applications such as IPSec protocols, the Secure Socket Layer (SSL) protocol and in ATM cell encryption. In general, hardware implementations of encryption algorithms and their associated key schedules are physically secure, as they cannot easily be modified by an outside attacker. Also, the high speed Rijndael encryptor core should prove beneficial in applications where speed is important as with real-time communications such as SONET OC-48 networks and satellite communications.

Acknowledgements

This research has been supported by Amphion Semiconductor Ltd. and by a University Research Studentship, which incorporates funding by the European Social Fund.

References

1. J. Daemen, V.Rijmen ; The Rijndael Block Cipher: AES Proposal ; First AES Candidate Conference (AES1) ; August 20-22, 1998
2. NIST; Advanced Encryption Standard (AES) FIPS Draft Publication; URL: http://csrc.nist.gov/encryption/aes/ : 28 February, 2001
3. Xilinx Virtex[TM]-E Extended Memory 1.8V Field Programmable Gate Arrays ; URL: http://www.xilinx.com : November 2000.
4. P. Chodowiec, P. Khuon, K. Gaj; Fast Implementations of Secret-Key Block Ciphers Using Mixed Inner- and Outer- Pipelining; FPGA 2001, 11-13 February 2001, California.
5. A. Dandalis, V.K. Prasanna, J.D.P. Rolim ; A Comparative Study of Performance of AES Candidates Using FPGAs; The Third Advanced Encryption Standard (AES3) Candidate Conference, 13-14 April 2000, New York, USA.

6. A.J. Elbirt, W. Yip, B. Chetwynd, C. Paar; An FPGA Implementation and Performance Evaluation of the AES Block Cipher Candidate Algorithm Finalists; AES3 Conference, 13-14 April 2000, New York, USA.
7. Brian Gladman: The AES Algorithm (Rijndael) in C and C++: URL: http://fp.gladman.plus.com/cryptography_technology/rijndael/index.htm: April 2001.
8. M. McLoone, J. V. McCanny; High Peformance Single-Chip FPGA Rijndael Algorithm Implementations; Cryptographic Hardware and Embedded Systems – CHES 2001;
9. K. NechBarker, Bassham, Burr, Dworkin, Foti, Roback; Report on the Development of the Advanced Encryption Standard (AES); URL: http://csrc.nist.gov/encryption/aes/ : 2 October, 2000.
10. M.McLoone, J.V. McCanny: Apparatus for Selectably Encrypting and Decrypting Data: UK Patent Application No. 0107592.8: Filed March 2001.

Appendix 1

The Hexadecimal values contained in the LUT utilised during encryption are outlined below. For example, an input of '00' (hexadecimal) would return the output, '63', an input of '07' would return the output, 'C5', an input of '08' would return the output, '30' and so on.

	0	1	2	3	4	5	6	7
0	63	7C	77	7B	F2	6B	6F	C5
1	CA	82	C9	7D	FA	59	47	F0
2	B7	FD	93	26	36	3F	F7	CC
3	04	C7	23	C3	18	96	05	9A
4	09	83	2C	1A	1B	6E	5A	A0
5	53	D1	00	ED	20	FC	B1	5B
6	D0	EF	AA	FB	43	4D	33	85
7	51	A3	40	8F	92	9D	38	F5
8	CD	0C	13	EC	5F	97	44	17
9	60	81	4F	DC	22	2A	90	88
A	E0	32	3A	0A	49	06	24	5C
B	E7	C8	37	6D	8D	D5	4E	A9
C	BA	78	25	2E	1C	A6	B4	C6
D	70	3E	B5	66	48	03	F6	0E
E	E1	F8	98	11	69	D9	8E	94
F	8C	A1	89	0D	BF	E6	42	68

	8	9	A	B	C	D	E	F
0	30	01	67	2B	FE	D7	AB	76
1	AD	D4	A2	AF	9C	A4	72	C0
2	34	A5	E5	F1	71	D8	31	15
3	07	12	80	E2	EB	27	B2	75
4	52	3B	D6	B3	29	E3	2F	84
5	6A	CB	BE	39	4A	4C	58	CF
6	45	F9	02	7F	50	3C	9F	A8
7	BC	B6	DA	21	10	FF	F3	D2
8	C4	A7	7E	3D	64	5D	19	73
9	46	EE	B8	14	DE	5E	0B	DB
A	C2	D3	AC	62	91	95	E4	79
B	6C	56	F4	EA	65	7A	AE	08
C	E8	DD	74	1F	4B	BD	8B	8A
D	61	35	57	B9	86	C1	1D	9E
E	9B	1E	87	E9	CE	55	28	DF
F	41	99	2D	0F	B0	54	BB	16

The Hexadecimal values contained in the LUT utilised during decryption are as outlined below. For example, an input of '00' (hexadecimal) would return the output, '52', an input of '07' would return the output, '38', an input of '08' would return the output, 'BF and so on.

	0	1	2	3	4	5	6	7
0	52	09	6A	D5	30	36	A5	38
1	7C	E3	39	82	9B	2F	FF	87
2	54	7B	94	32	A6	C2	23	3D
3	08	2E	A1	66	28	D9	24	B2
4	72	F8	F6	64	86	68	98	16
5	6C	70	48	50	FD	ED	B9	DA
6	90	D8	AB	00	8C	BC	D3	0A
7	D0	2C	1E	8F	CA	3F	0F	02
8	3A	91	11	41	4F	67	DC	EA
9	96	AC	74	22	E7	AD	35	85
A	47	F1	1A	71	1D	29	C5	89
B	FC	56	3E	4B	C6	D2	79	20
C	1F	D0	A8	33	88	07	C7	31
D	60	51	7F	A9	19	B5	4A	0D
E	A0	E0	3B	4D	AE	2A	F5	B0
F	17	2B	04	7E	BA	77	D6	26

	8	9	A	B	C	D	E	F
0	BF	40	A3	9E	81	F3	D7	FB
1	34	8E	43	44	C4	DE	E9	CB
2	EE	4C	95	0B	42	FA	C3	4E
3	76	5B	A2	49	6D	8B	D1	25
4	D4	A4	5C	CC	5D	65	B6	92
5	5E	15	46	57	A7	8D	9D	84
6	F7	E4	58	05	B8	B3	45	06
7	C1	AF	BD	03	01	13	8A	6B
8	97	F2	CF	CE	F0	B4	E6	73
9	E2	F9	37	E8	1C	75	DF	6E
A	6F	B7	62	0E	AA	18	BE	1B
B	9A	DB	C0	FE	78	CD	5A	F4
C	B1	12	10	59	27	80	EC	5F
D	2D	E5	7A	9F	93	C9	9C	EF
E	C8	EB	BB	3C	83	53	99	61
F	E1	69	14	63	55	21	0C	7D

JBits™ Implementations of the Advanced Encryption Standard (Rijndael)

Scott McMillan and Cameron Patterson

Xilinx, Inc.
2100 Logic Drive
San Jose, California 95124-3400
{Scott.McMillan,Cameron.Patterson}@xilinx.com

Abstract. The Rijndael algorithm has been selected as the new Advanced Encryption Standard. Several JBits implementations of this algorithm are described which target the Virtex™ FPGA family. As illustrated by sample code, JBits provides a concise means of creating structured datapaths. JBits design abstractions include conventional ones (such as hierarchical modules, ports, nets and buses) and ones that do not appear in structural HDLs (such as layered placement and routing APIs). Unlike mainstream design flows, JBits also permits the exploration of hardware/software tradeoffs for operations such as changing keys and modes, and dynamically modifying the width of key and data blocks. This can significantly reduce the FPGA resource utilization.

1   Introduction

In 1997, the United States National Institute of Standards and Technology began the process of defining a new algorithm to replace the aging Data Encryption Standard [1]. DES has served well for nearly 25 years, but has several deficiencies that become more problematic each year:

- It is vulnerable to an exhaustive key search attack. Triple-DES alleviates this concern but with a significant increase in computation.
- The block size (64 bits) is insufficient for high bandwidth applications.
- Software implementations of DES are inefficient, due to the bit-level operations.

The specification for the Advanced Encryption Standard (AES) includes key size options of 128, 192 or 256 bits, a block size of 128 bits, and efficient implementation in software platforms ranging from smart cards to 64 bit processors. Fifteen algorithms were initially proposed as AES candidates. Five candidates remained by August 1999. A detailed analysis of the security and efficiency of these candidates led to the selection of the Rijndael algorithm in October 2000 [2]. Rijndael's simple design and low memory requirements makes it particularly well suited to resource-constrained environments such as smart cards. A large number of software and FPGA implementations of Rijndael have already been produced during the selection process.

FPGA circuits for Rijndael make effective use of embedded block RAM. However, we are not aware of any FPGA implementations that perform dynamic circuit

G. Brebner and R. Woods (Eds.): FPL 2001, LNCS 2147, pp. 162–171, 2001.

specialization of the key, mode or block size. As was shown for the DES and Serpent algorithms, dynamic specialization can increase throughput without increasing pipeline latency [3,4]. For example, the fastest reported static implementation of DES in an XCV300E-8 achieves 12 Gbits/sec (189 MHz) with 48 pipeline stages [5], while a key-specific DES core would achieve 12.8 Gbits/sec (200 MHz) in an XCV200E-8[1] with 33 pipeline stages [3]. In practice, power consumption may limit clock rates. Dynamic specialization of DES has a power and area advantage, since the key-specific circuit is about half the size of the static circuit.

This paper describes and compares various implementations of Rijndael that target the Virtex architecture. The JBits system [6] is used for design capture and most of the design implementation. Although many associate JBits with low-level design, we will illustrate high-level design abstractions that have recently been added to JBits. These include block, port, net and bus classes available in other module generation systems [7,8,9,10]. Several non-standard physical abstractions also exist, such as layered placement and routing APIs. This layering obviates the need for constraints, since the designer can always resort to a lower layer if a higher level of abstraction does not achieve the desired result. The bottom layer still provides direct manipulation of the bitstream.

2   The Rijndael Algorithm

Rijndael was strongly influenced by the design of the Square block cipher [11]. Unlike DES and several other AES candidates, Rijndael is not based on a Feistel network. Rather, the round transformation can be described in terms of arithmetic in the finite field $GF(2^8)$ [12]. This allows all operations to be performed on byte-wide data.

The plaintext and its intermediate transformations to ciphertext are referred to as the *State*. A *RoundKey* sequence is derived from the cipher key by a key expansion algorithm, which is not described here. Both the State and RoundKey are represented as byte matrices with 4 rows. The bytes are labeled with (row, column) indices, where $(0,0)$ is in the upper left corner. The number of columns in the State matrix is denoted by Nb, which is equal to the block size divided by 32. The number of columns in the key matrix is given by Nk, which is equal to the key size divided by 32. Both Nb and Nk may be independently set to 4, 6 or 8. The number of rounds (Nr) is a function of Nb and Nk, and varies from 10 to 14.

Rijndael uses four basic transformations:

ByteSub(State) Each State byte is replaced with a substitution table consisting of the multiplicative inverse in $GF(2^8)$, followed by an affine mapping over $GF(2)$.

ShiftRow(State) The rows of the State are cyclically shifted, where the shift offsets for each row are a function of Nb. For Nb = 4 or 6, row i is rotated i bytes to the left.

MixColumn(State) Each column of the State is treated as a polynomial $a(x)$ over $GF(2^8)$, and is multiplied with a fixed polynomial $c(x)$. This can be considered as a matrix multiplication.

---

[1] The DES circuit will actually fit in an XCV150.

AddRoundKey(State, RoundKey) A bitwise XOR is performed between corresponding State and RoundKey bytes.

A round applies these transformations in the above order. The last round, however, omits the MixColumn step. The complete Rijndael cipher is described with the pseudocode given in Figure 1.

```
Rijndael(State, CipherKey) {
    KeyExpansion(CipherKey, RoundKey);
    AddRoundKey(State, RoundKey[0]);
    for (int i = 1;  i < Nr;  i++) {
        ByteSub(State);
        ShiftRow(State);
        MixColumn(State);
        AddRoundKey(State, RoundKey[i]);
    }
    ByteSub(State);
    ShiftRow(State);
    AddRoundKey(State, RoundKey[Nr]);
}
```

Fig. 1. The Rijndael Cipher

3   Rijndael Implementations

Two versions of Rijndael were implemented on the Virtex device using JBits. The first design, discussed in Section 3.1, attempts to minimize resource usage. This version operates on one column of cipher block data at a time and utilizes the BRAMs (Block RAMs) to implement 8 bit lookup tables. The second design also makes use of the BRAMs, but unrolls and operates on one round at a time. This version provides a performance increase at the expense of additional BRAM utilization, and will be discussed in Section 3.2.

Both of these designs use the T tables described in [12]. These tables are recommended for efficient implementation on 32 bit processors, and also map nicely to Virtex BRAM resources. Unfortunately, this approach limits unrolling of the Rijndael rounds. It also bases the device choice on BRAM availability rather than CLB requirements. However, it is reasonable to assume that many applications will have additional circuitry that can utilize these CLBs.

Figure 2 provides pseudocode for our Virtex implementation, which rearranges the Rijndael steps shown in Figure 1. The key expansion is performed in software and the RoundKey sequence is downloaded with JBits. In addition, all rounds are treated in a uniform way, but some operations are masked with the firstRound and final-Round control flags. The modified Rijndael transformations are:

```
Rijndael_Virtex(State, CipherKey) {
    for (int i = 0;  i < Nr + 1;  i++) {
        ShiftRow(State, firstRound);
        ByteSub/MixColumnMultiply(State, firstRound, finalRound);
        MixColumn/AddRoundKey(State, RoundKey[i]);
    }
}
```

Fig. 2. The Virtex Rijndael Cipher

ShiftRow(State, firstRound) The transformation is unchanged, but it is moved to the top of the transformation list. ShiftRow is masked out during the first round where only AddRoundKey should be performed.

ByteSub/MixColumnMultiply(State, firstRound, finalRound) These operations are combined in sets of BRAM tables. Portions of this transformation are masked out during the first and final rounds.

MixColumn/AddRoundKey(State) These transformations are combined in a 5 input XOR operation. Although they are never masked out, the output of the Byte-Sub/MixColumnMultiply during the first and final rounds ensures that the MixColumn addition is not performed in these rounds.

A goal was to have the same footprint for both the encryption and decryption circuits. This allows JBits to switch between encryption and decryption modes without the concern of modifying resources not owned by the Rijndael core. For example, S-Box tables are not needed in the ByteSub/MixColumnMultiply transformation for encryption. An encryption-specific circuit would allow extraction of the appropriate S-Box tables from the T tables, but a decryption-specific circuit would not. Since identical footprints are desired, the S-Box tables are instantiated in both designs.

Parameter	Possible Values
Mode	Encryption, Decryption
Nb	4, 6, 8
Nk	4, 6, 8
Key	Any Value

Table 1. Run-Time Reconfigurable Rijndael Parameters

JBits provides true run-time reconfiguration (RTR) [13]. This capability is exploited in the Rijndael implementation by providing the run-time parameters given in Table 1. These parameters need not be specified until just before the bitstream is generated. The key can be modified at any time, after which the bitstream may be partially reconfigured using the JBits Java Run-Time Reconfiguration (JRTR) utility [14]. Figure 3 shows how to modify the key using JBits. Subsequent JRTR calls would be needed to configure the device with the new key.

```
/* Lower 16 bits of expanded key (expKey) in Bram(2,1). */
expKey = initKeyLower(cipherKey, Nb);
jbits.setBram(2, 1, 0, 16, expKey, expKey.length);
/* Higher 16 bits of expanded key (expKey) in Bram(3,1). */
expKey = initKeyUpper(cipherKey, Nb);
jbits.setBram(3, 1, 0, 16, expKey, expKey.length);
```

Fig. 3. JBits Key Expansion and Bitstream Modification

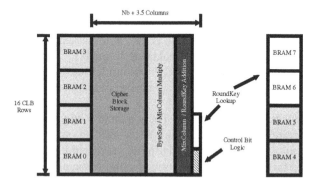

Fig. 4. Rijndael Layout in Virtex

3.1 An Area Efficient Implementation

Figure 4 depicts the layout of the area efficient Virtex design. Data flows in a circular pattern through the pipelined stages. The ShiftRow operation is not shown because it is implemented as a permutation of wires in the CipherBlockStorage module and does not require logic resources. A normal round would first apply the ShiftRow operation. Data is then shifted out one column at a time and transformed with the Byte-Sub/MixColumnMultiply and MixColumn/RoundKeyAddition blocks. Finally the data is shifted back into the left side of the CipherBlockStorage module and the cycle starts over.

This implementation requires 7 clock cycles for each round including the first AddRoundKey, or 77 clock cycles for a 128 bit data block. The CipherBlockStorage module will be expanded to the right by 2 (if Nb = 6) or 4 (if Nb = 8). This expansion changes the total clock cycles required for encryption or decryption. For Nb = 6, the total clock cycles increases to 99 and for Nb = 8, it increases to 121.

The encryption and decryption modes can both be implemented using the footprint in Figure 4. The only differences between the two modes lies in the key expansion (which is done in software), the BRAM lookup tables values, and the ShiftRow routing permutation. The key can be modified at any time using partial reconfiguration, as shown in Figure 3. Although this capability could be extended to the other modifications necessary to change modes, this decision must be made before placing the circuit.

```
public void implement(int cipherKey[], boolean encryption) {
    cbsp = new CipherBlockStorageProperties();
    cbsp.setIn_clk(clk);
    cbsp.setIn_dataIn(dataIn);
    cbsp.setIn_dataShiftRow(dataShiftRowOut);
    cbsp.setIn_dataColumn(dataColIn);
    cbsp.setIn_finalRound(finalRound);
    cbsp.setIn_shiftRow(shiftRow);
    cbsp.setOut_dataOut(dataOut);
    cbs = new CipherBlockStorage("CipherBlockStorage", cbsp);

    srpp = new ShiftRowPermutationProperties();
    srpp.setIn_dataShiftRowIn(dataOut);
    srpp.setOut_dataShiftRowOut(dataShiftRowOut);
    srp = new ShiftRowPermutation("ShiftPermutation", srpp);
}
```

Fig. 5. RTPCore Connectivity Sample Code

Figure 5 illustrates defining connections in a JBits RTPCore. A properties object is optionally used to specify the connections. Some of the connections for the first level in the RTPCore hierarchy are given. Figure 6 shows these connections in a diagrammatic form.

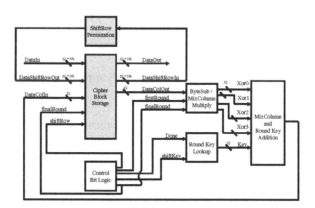

Fig. 6. Rijndael Connectivity in Virtex

RTPCores also provide placement abstractions, as shown in Figure 7. This `Mix-ColumnRoundKey` module uses placement directives to specify the relative juxtaposition of submodules. Tedious and error-prone coordinate calculations are not required. The first instance must be placed in one of the four corners of the parent's bounding box. A `LUT5` module takes up one slice of a CLB, so the first 16 `LUT5` cores will be placed in a right hand column of slices. The `lut5_16` instance is placed to the left of all previous instances, and each subsequent instance is placed above this one until the process repeats with `lut5_32`. Figure 8 shows the resulting pattern.

```
public void implement() {
    for (i = 0;  i < dataCol.getWidth();  i++) {
        lut5 = new LUT5("lut5_"+i, lut5Properties);
        if (i == 0)
            addChild(lut5, Place.LOWER_RIGHT);
        else if ((i%16) == 0)
            addChild(lut5, Place.LEFTOF_ALL_PREV_ALIGN_BOTTOM);
        else
            addChild(lut5, Place.ABOVE_PREV_ALIGN_RIGHT);
    }
}
```

Fig. 7. RTPCore Placement Sample Code

lut5_47	lut5_31	lut5_15
lut5_46	lut5_30	lut5_14
•	•	•
•	•	•
•	•	•
lut5_33	lut5_17	lut5_1
lut5_32	lut5_16	lut5_0

Fig. 8. RTPCore Placement Sample Result

This design provides a compact, easy to implement, and versatile implementation of Rijndael. The encrypt/decrypt mode, data/key block sizes, and key value may be changed at run-time. It also fits in an XCV50, which is the smallest Virtex device. All of the BRAM resources and about 30% of the CLB resources are used in the XCV50. This leaves the majority of CLBs available for ancillary functions.

3.2   A Higher Performance Implementation

Figure 9 shows the layout of a Virtex implementation with a single round unrolled. Dataflow is similar to the area efficient version except that the transformations are performed on an entire data block at a time, rather than one column at a time. In CBC mode, one data block will flow from left to right through the transformations and back again. In ECB, there can be multiple blocks in the pipeline, which results in three times the throughput of CBC mode.

This implementation requires 44 clock cycles to perform all rounds of the transformation, and is the same for all block sizes. Different values of Nb change the size requirements of the implementation as in the area efficient implementation, but the cycle time is not changed. Increasing Nb therefore improves throughput.

The parameters available for this implementation are the same as those in the previous design. The only modification required to the original implementation was a duplication of the transformations across each column and a change in the layout of the CipherBlockStorage block. This allowed for quick development and debug phases.

Because of BRAM requirements, this design requires an XCV1000 or XCV300E when Nb = 4. Having Nb > 4 requires the Virtex-E family. As with the previous implementation, CLB resources are available for additional circuitry.

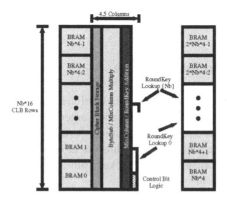

Fig. 9. Rijndael Layout in Virtex With One Round Unrolled

3.3   Timing and Area Comparison

Table 2 shows the timing reported by the standard Xilinx tools for the above implementations. This is compared with two case studies in the AES selection report [2]. The differences in area and the comparable timing results are partly explained by the case studies not using BRAM. However, the case studies were unable to completely unroll all rounds in the Rijndael cipher. In fact, the area utilization displayed without feedback represents 5 unrolled rounds and takes up the majority of the XCV1000 CLB space.

Table 3 shows CPU requirements for performing a key change. The key schedule time also includes the JBits "set" calls needed to make the actual key modifications to the bitstream. The other measure, in the table, involves the time JRTR takes to generate the Virtex partial reconfiguration packets necessary to update the key on the actual FPGA. As a datum point, the size of the Virtex command packets ranged from 8 to 16 Kbits during testing of key modifications. As a result of these small packet sizes, hardware reconfiguration times are insignificant and are not included.

Version	Throughput	CLB Slices	BRAMs
Area Efficient (w/ Feedback)	250 Mbps	240	8
Unrolled (w/ Feedback)	300 Mbps	288	32
Unrolled (w/o Feedback)	900 Mbps	288	32
Case Study (w/ Feedback) [2]	300 Mbps	5300	0
Case Study (w/o Feedback) [2]	1938 Mbps	11000	0

Table 2. Timing and Area Comparison (Nb = Nk = 4)

Version	Key Schedule	Generate Partial Virtex Packets (JRTR)
Area Efficient (XCV50)	31 ms	32 ms
Unrolled (XCV1000)	121 ms	32 ms

Table 3. Key Change CPU Times (PII, 450 MHZ, Windows NT 4.0, JDK 1.2.2)

4   Conclusions and Future Work

Although JBits-based dynamic circuit specialization has previously focused on increasing the speed of algorithms such as DES and Serpent, the techniques have been used here to decrease Rijndael's resource utilization. A reduction in area also addresses the important issues of power and cost. Encoding the key, mode and block size parameters in the configuration bitstream frees up package pins, which are scarce resources when the block size is 128 bits or more.

Code fragments have shown that JBits now provides high-level design abstractions that are on par with those used in structural HDLs. Unlike mainstream HDLs, JBits also supports hardware/software co-design including dynamic reconfiguration. Compared with the coordinate calculations required in HDLs and most module generators, RTPCore placement directives provide an easier means of specifying packing, placement and floorplanning. Net and bus objects are simply passed as arguments to the JBits router. Alternatively, the RTPCore can generate EDIF for verification and implementation by conventional tools.

Speed is being addressed by work in progress that completely unrolls and pipelines the Rijndael algorithm for Nb = Nk = 4. The design requires an XCV1000, and utilizes all of the BRAMs and nearly all the CLBs. Throughput in ECB mode should comfortably meet the bandwidth requirements for SONET OC-192c optical networks.

Acknowledgments

Advice and assistance from the other members of the JBits project at Xilinx and Virginia Tech is greatly appreciated. This work was supported by the U.S. Defense Advanced Research Projects Agency, under contract DABT63-99-3-0004.

References

1. National Institute of Standards and Technology. Announcing request for candidate algorithm nominations for the Advanced Encryption Standard (AES). *Federal Register*, 62(117):48051–48058, Sep 1997.
2. James Nechvatal, Elaine Barker, Lawrence Bassham, William Burr, Morris Dworkin, James Foti, and Edward Roback. Report on the development of the Advanced Encryption Standard (AES). Available at http://www.nist.gov/aes/round2/r2report.pdf, Oct 2000.
3. Cameron Patterson. High performance DES encryption in Virtex FPGAs using JBits. In Kenneth L. Pocek and Jeffrey M. Arnold, editors, *IEEE Symposium on Field-Programmable Custom Computing Machines (FCCM 2000)*, pages 113–121, Apr 2000.
4. Cameron Patterson. A dynamic FPGA implementation of the Serpent block cipher. In Çetin Koç and Christof Paar, editors, *Second International Workshop on Cryptographic Hardware and Embedded Systems (CHES 2000)*, pages 141–155. Springer-Verlag Lecture Notes in Computer Science, Volume 1965, Aug 2000.
5. Steve Trimberger, Raymond Pang, and Amit Singh. A 12 Gbps DES encryptor/decryptor core in an FPGA. In Çetin Koç and Christof Paar, editors, *Second International Workshop on Cryptographic Hardware and Embedded Systems (CHES 2000)*, pages 156–163. Springer-Verlag Lecture Notes in Computer Science, Volume 1965, Aug 2000.
6. Steve Guccione, Delon Levi, and Prasanna Sundararajan. JBits: Java based interface for reconfigurable computing. In *Second Annual Military and Aerospace Applications of Programmable Devices and Technologies (MAPLD'99)*, The Johns Hopkins University, Laurel, Maryland, Sep 1999.
7. Oskar Mencer, Martin Morf, and Michael J. Flynn. PAM-Blox: High performance FPGA design for adaptive computing. In Kenneth L. Pocek and Jeffrey M. Arnold, editors, *IEEE Symposium on Field-Programmable Custom Computing Machines (FCCM'98)*, pages 167–174, Apr 1998.
8. Peter Bellows and Brad Hutchings. JHDL: An HDL for reconfigurable systems. In Kenneth L. Pocek and Jeffrey M. Arnold, editors, *IEEE Symposium on Field-Programmable Custom Computing Machines (FCCM'98)*, pages 175–184, Apr 1998.
9. Michael Chu, Nicholas Weaver, Kolja Sulimma, André Dehon, and John Wawrzynek. Object oriented circuit-generators in Java. In Kenneth L. Pocek and Jeffrey M. Arnold, editors, *IEEE Symposium on Field-Programmable Custom Computing Machines (FCCM'98)*, pages 158–166, Apr 1998.
10. S. Mohan, R. Wittig, S. Kelem, and S. Leavesley. The core generator framework. In *Fifth Canadian Workshop on Field-Programmable Devices (FPD'98)*, Jun 1998.
11. Joan Daemen, Lars R. Knudsen, and Vincent Rijmen. The block cipher Square. In Eli Biham, editor, *Fast Software Encryption (FSE 97)*, pages 149–165. Springer-Verlag Lecture Notes in Computer Science, Volume 1267, 1997.
12. Joan Daemen and Vincent Rijmen. AES proposal: Rijndael. In *The First Advanced Encryption Standard Candidate Conference*, Aug 1998. Available at http://www.nist.gov/aes.
13. Steven A. Guccione and Delon Levi. Run-time parameterizable cores. In Patrick Lysaght, James Irvine, and Reiner Hartenstein, editors, *Ninth International Conference on Field-Programmable Logic and Applications (FPL'99)*, pages 215–222. Springer-Verlag Lecture Notes in Computer Science, Volume 1673, Aug 1999.
14. Scott McMillan and Steven A. Guccione. Partial run-time reconfiguration using JRTR. In R.W. Hartenstein and H. Grunbacher, editors, *Tenth International Conference on Field-Programmable Logic and Applications (FPL 2000)*, pages 352–360. Springer-Verlag Lecture Notes in Computer Science, Volume 1896, Aug 2000.

Task-Parallel Programming of Reconfigurable Systems*

Markus Weinhardt[1] and Wayne Luk[2]

[1] PACT GmbH, Leopoldstr. 236, 80807 Munich, Germany
[2] Department of Computing, Imperial College, London SW7 2BZ, UK

Abstract. This paper presents task-parallel programming, a style of application development for reconfigurable systems. Task-parallel programming enables efficient interaction between concurrent hardware and software tasks. In particular, it supports description of communication and computation tasks running in parallel to allow effective implementation of designs where data transfer time between hardware and software components is comparable to computation time. This approach permits precise specification of parallelism without requiring hardware design knowledge. We present language extensions for task-parallel programming, inspired by the occam and Handel languages. A compilation scheme for this method is described: the four main stages are memory mapping, channel implementation, software generation and hardware synthesis. Our techniques have been evaluated using video applications on the RC1000-PP hardware platform.

1 Introduction

The reconfigurable computing community has recognized the need for efficient tools which enable software developers with no hardware design experience to take advantage of reconfigurable technology. Compilers have been developed [1, 2] which translate a high-level program into both machine code for a host processor and configuration bitstreams for a field-programmable accelerator. They can automatically parallelize regular algorithms, such as signal and image processing applications, and map them to appropriate platforms.

While being successful at exploiting fine-grain parallelism within the hardware part of an application, these compilers do not usually exploit parallelism between hardware and software, or between (coarse-grain) hardware tasks. Host/coprocessor communication cannot normally overlap with computation, which causes significant inefficiency for loosely coupled reconfigurable systems [3, 4] on which copying data across system busses, like the PCI bus, often takes longer than the hardware computation itself.

These shortcomings are addressed by the proposed approach. The contributions of this paper include: (a) explaining how the task-parallel programming style can capture patterns of efficient interactions between hardware and software tasks, (b) presenting a compilation scheme for task-parallel programs, and (c) describing an implementation of task-parallel programming for the RC-1000PP hardware platform, and evaluating its performance.

---

* This work was supported by a European Union TMR training project, the UK Engineering and Physical Sciences Research Council, Celoxica Limited, and Xilinx Inc.

G. Brebner and R. Woods (Eds.): FPL 2001, LNCS 2147, pp. 172–181, 2001.
© Springer-Verlag Berlin Heidelberg 2001

```
                                   frame fr_in, fr_out;
frame fr_in, fr_out;               configure_FPGA();
while (1) {                        while (1) {
  get_frame(fr_in);                  get_frame(fr_in);
  proc_frame(fr_in, fr_out);         copy_to_hardware(fr_in);
  put_frame(fr_out); }               run_hw_coprocessor();
                                     copy_to_host(fr_out);
            (a)                      put_frame(fr_out); }
                                              (b)
```

Fig. 1. Video processing loop: (a) software only, (b) call to hardware coprocessor added.

Section 2 first reviews the sequential coprocessing model and its shortcomings for reconfigurable computing. Next, Section 3 presents the task-parallel programming model. Section 4 outlines the compilation techniques used to generate a host program and FPGA bitstreams. Finally, performance results for video processing applications are given in Section 5, before we conclude the paper in Section 6.

2   Sequential Coprocessing Model

Typical hardware/software compilers for sequential programs, such as [1, 2, 5], attempt to accelerate an application by synthesizing dedicated hardware *coprocessors* for computationally-intensive parts of the program. The coprocessors are often implemented using FPGAs, and the respective parts of the host program are substituted by coprocessor calls. The amount of program code performed by a coprocessor can range from a few instructions to loops, functions and larger computational kernels.

The hardware/software partitioning determines which input data have to be transferred to the reconfigurable hardware, and which results to be returned to the host processor. The amount of communication, and thus the duration of these transfers, are determined by the partitioning and are beyond the user's direct control. Often the transfer time outweighs the speedup achieved by the coprocessor. Hence this model is only effective if the computation to communication ratio is high (for instance, for specialized bit-level functions which are not supported by standard microprocessors [5]), or for closely-coupled systems which combine reconfigurable hardware and a processor kernel on the same chip [6, 7] and thus have a much smaller communication overhead.

Furthermore, the semantics of the sequential input program constrains the execution order of software instructions, hardware coprocessors, and the data transfers. Only fine-grain parallelism is possible if local analyses detect independent operations. For instance, consider the program fragment of a typical video processing loop in Figure 1(a). The function get_frame repeatedly reads a video frame in fr_in, proc_frame performs some processing on it resulting in fr_out, and put_frame stores or displays the result. A typical hardware/software compiler generates the host program in Figure 1(b) to perform the computation-intensive function proc_frame in hardware. Since all function calls in the loop depend on their predecessor, the execution phases cannot overlap. For instance, copy_to_host needs to wait until the coprocessor execution is finished, thus leaving the host processor idle. The coprocessor waits until the next software iteration calls run_hw_coprocessor. Hardware and software executions alternate, wasting valuable processing time.

Note that pipelining the loop, ie. starting `get_frame` for a new iteration before `run_hw_coprocessor` and `put_frame` for previous iterations have finished, could change the program's semantics. Pipelining is illegal since `fr_in` could depend on `fr_out`: for instance if `get_frame` just copies `fr_out` back to `fr_in`. On the other hand, if `get_frame` reads, for instance, from a file, pipelining only increases the latency of the application, but does not change its functionality.

We conclude that the application developer often needs to specify conditions explicitly, for instance whether an increased latency is acceptable; this is not possible in a purely sequential programming language. Task parallelism, described in the next section, enables us to keep programming as general and simple as possible, but as specific as necessary to allow an efficient implementation.

3   Task-Parallel Programming

Different methodologies for parallel programming have been suggested. They mainly differ in the way processors (or processes) access memory: either they all have access to the same memory space (shared memory), or they use individual memories (distributed memory). The uniform memory space makes shared memory systems simpler to program. However, some provisions to prevent two processes from writing to the same memory cell at the same time are needed.

Parallel processors based on distributed memory can be programmed using the Communicating Sequential Processes (CSP) model [8] and its implementation as the *occam* programming language. In occam, parallel processes do not share variables. They run independently in parallel and synchronize through channel communication. The versatility of occam has been noted for specifying both hardware and software components [9]; occam has also been used in hardware/software partitioning [10]. We propose a language and compiler similar to Handel-C [4, 11], which facilitates description of overlapping computation and communication in parallel. It captures both shared memory parallelism and distributed memory parallelism in hardware. The main innovations are that our system can: (a) support both hardware and software descriptions, (b) treat array data as a single entity for channel communications, and (c) provide automatic optimised allocation of array data to memory banks.

Our approach, best described as *task-parallel programming*, is specialized for loosely-coupled reconfigurable systems. Since the host and the coprocessor run independently and do not share memory, we use two dedicated communicating processes to model the software and hardware part of an application. Channel communications are translated to transfers over the system bus. We extend the channel concept to entire data arrays, like the image frames in the example of Section 2. For them, DMA transfer instructions are generated as explained in the next section. In addition to this hardware/software parallelism, the software and hardware parts may contain parallel sub-tasks. They can be programmed using shared memory methods. As opposed to the sequential coprocessing model in Section 2, our approach enables task-level parallelism. Data transfers and the hardware/software partitioning — which have a crucial impact on system performance — are explicit and thus predictable and controllable.

```
#define V 240
#define H 320                          static void hardware() {
chan unsigned char                        unsigned char fr_in1[V][H],
  chan_fr_in[V][H],                         fr_in2[V][H], fr_out1[V][H],
  chan_fr_out[V][H];                        fr_out2[V][H];
                                          while (1) {
static void software() {                     par { /* first parallel task */
  unsigned char fr_in[V][H];                    {/* sequential snd_chan,rcv_chan */
  unsigned char fr_out[V][H];                     snd_chan(chan_fr_out, fr_out2);
  while (1) {                                      rcv_chan(chan_fr_in, fr_in2); }
  /* sequential block with 2 par */             smooth_frame(fr_in1, fr_out1);
    par {                                     }
      get_frame(fr_in);                    par { /* second parallel task */
      rcv_chan(chan_fr_out, fr_out);          {/* sequential snd_chan,rcv_chan */
    }                                           snd_chan(chan_fr_out, fr_out1);
    par {                                       rcv_chan(chan_fr_in, fr_in1); }
      snd_chan(chan_fr_in, fr_in);        smooth_frame(fr_in2, fr_out2);
      put_frame(fr_out);                  } } }
    } } }
```

Fig. 2. Task-parallel program for video smoothing. Since the two parallel tasks in hardware execute one after the other, they can share hardware for the smooth_frame process.

Figure 2 shows an example task-parallel program which applies image smoothing to each video frame. The special functions software and hardware represent the main software and hardware processes, and the intention is to maximize the available parallelism by having a double buffer between them. Both processes are initialized at program start-up and execute concurrently. They communicate over the channels chan_fr_in and chan_fr_out, globally declared by the keyword chan. The statements snd_chan and rcv_chan perform unbuffered channel communications and also synchronize the processes like occam channels. Either of the processes stalls until a send command is met by a receive command on the same channel and vice versa. Following Handel-C, statements enclosed within a block by curly brackets execute sequentially unless the keyword par immediately precedes the block.

According to these rules, the program in Figure 2 executes as follows. The software process contains a loop as in Figure 1, but the frame processing itself is not specified in it. Instead, the process gets a new input frame and receives a previous result frame from hardware via chan_fr_out at the same time. Then it sends the new input frame over chan_fr_in and outputs the result frame. The hardware process also has a main processing loop, but it uses two pairs of arrays for input and output frames. It pipelines the transfer of a new frame, its processing, and the transfer back. While the image smoothing operator smooth_frame transforms fr_in1 into fr_out1, concurrently snd_chan sends an old transformed frame (fr_out2) back to the software process, and rcv_chan receives a new frame in fr_in2.

Figure 3 shows these processing phases with the software process mapped to the host, the hardware process mapped to the FPGA, and each array of the hardware process mapped to its own memory bank. These mappings are automatically performed as described in the next section. Note that the first two output frames are undefined: the pipeline is only filled up in the third iteration. Concurrent computation and communication, however, require twice as much storage – memory for fr_in2 and fr_out2 will not be needed if computation and communication take place sequentially.

first parallel task: second parallel task:

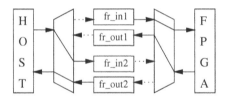   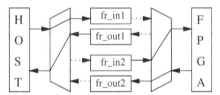

Fig. 3. Two parallel tasks running one after the other described in Figure 2. Active links are indicated by solid arrows, and inactive links by dotted arrows.

```
static void
hardware() {
  unsigned char fr1[V][H],
    fr2[V][H], fr3[V][H];
  unsigned int minmax1[2],
    minmax2[2], minmax3[2];
  while (1) {
  /* sequential block with 3 par */
    par { {
    /* sequential snd_chan,rcv_chan */
        snd_chan(chan_fr_out, fr1);
        rcv_chan(chan_fr_in, fr1); }
      comp_minmax(fr3, minmax3);
      stretch(fr2, minmax2, fr2);
    }
```

```
    par {
    {
        snd_chan(chan_fr_out, fr2);
        rcv_chan(chan_fr_in, fr2); }
      comp_minmax(fr1, minmax1);
      stretch(fr3, minmax3, fr3);
    }
    par {
    {
        snd_chan(chan_fr_out, fr3);
        rcv_chan(chan_fr_in, fr3); }
      comp_minmax(fr2, minmax2);
      stretch(fr1, minmax1, fr1);
    } } }
```

Fig. 4. Main hardware task of histogram stretching.

The task-parallel program in Figure 2 follows a pattern which can easily be generalized to cover two or more hardware sub-tasks in parallel. To illustrate this generalization, consider another video processing algorithm, histogram stretching [12]. Unlike smoothing, histogram stretching is not a local transformation. It scans the entire frame twice: first to determine the minimum and maximum greyscale values, and second to "stretch" the pixel values over the entire greyscale range. The hardware implementation in Figure 4 performs these two processing phases in parallel on different frames, using the internally vectorized tasks comp_minmax and stretch. The data transfer can also be performed in parallel with these tasks. This results in three processing phases which use three frame arrays and small arrays for the minima and maxima in a cyclic manner, delaying the output by three frames. Note that stretch can read and write to the same array since it processes each pixel independently of the surrounding pixels.

4   Compilation

Figure 5 shows an overview of the compilation process. The target hardware architecture that we adopt contains memory banks, to which arrays of data can be mapped. After memory mapping, the communication channels are implemented, involving both software and hardware. Finally, the hardware is synthesized, producing a netlist, and the software program is generated. In case we target a single-processor host, software sequentialization is necessary, too. We describe these compilation phases below.

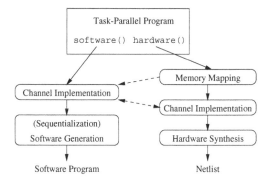

Fig. 5. Compilation overview.

Memory Mapping This phase determines where program variables are stored on the reconfigurable accelerator. Scalar variables are directly mapped to FPGA registers, and arrays to local off-chip RAM [2]. We allocate arrays to memory banks using an optimization technique [13], which determines a bank number and an offset value for each array. The allocation is subject to the following additional constraint: if array A is transferred to or from the host while array B is accessed by the FPGA, then A and B cannot be stored on the same bank since a memory bank can never be accessed by the host bus and the FPGA at the same time. The restriction also applies if A and B are accessed in different hardware sub-tasks concurrently since we want to optimize the memory accesses of the hardware tasks independently, see paragraph *Hardware Synthesis* below. Arrays only used in hardware can also be allocated to banks not accessible from the host, like on-chip RAM.

The arrays `fr_in1/fr_out1` and `fr_in2/fr_out2` in Figure2, and `fr1/minmax1`, `fr2/minmax2`, and `fr3/minmax3` in Figure 4 are examples which must be allocated to different memory banks to overlap data transfer and hardware computation. As mentioned above, Figure 3 shows the memory allocation for the video smoothing algorithm on a system with four memory banks.

Channel Implementation The compiler replaces `snd_chan` and `rcv_chan` calls in both software and hardware by data transfer functions for the targeted accelerator board. Since only one physical communication channel (the system bus) exists, the consistency of the logical channels used in the program must be checked, too. We therefore identify each channel transfer in the main hardware task, and assign a unique ID value for each of them which is sent to the software process before performing the actual channel communication. The statements `snd_to_sw` in hardware and `rcv_from_hw` in software initiate a handshake protocol transferring the ID. On the software side, the consistency of the logical channels are checked, and the program aborts if an inconsistency is detected.[1]

---

[1] Note that the consistency could be checked statically at compile time for simple, regular programs, and sequences of channel transfers could be combined, reducing the number of communications.

```
main() {
  unsigned char fr_in[V][H];
  unsigned char fr_out[V][H];
  unsigned char id;
  configure_hw();
  start_hardware();
  while (1) {
    rcv_from_hw(id);
    assert(id==0 || id==2);
    if (id == 0)
      DMA_to_host(bank("fr_out2"),
        offset("fr_out2"), fr_out);
    else /* id == 2 */
      DMA_to_host(bank("fr_out1"),
        offset("fr_out1"), fr_out);
    get_frame(fr_in);
    wait_DMA_finished();
    snd_to_hw();
    rcv_from_hw(id);
    assert(id==1 || id==3);
    if (id == 1)
      DMA_to_hw(fr_in, bank("fr_in2"),
        offset("fr_in2"));
    else /* id == 3 */
      DMA_to_hw(fr_in, bank("fr_in1"),
        offset("fr_in1"));
    put_frame(fr_out);
    wait_DMA_finished();
    snd_to_hw(); } }
```
(a)

```
static void hardware() {
  unsigned char fr_in1[V][H],
    fr_in2[V][H], fr_out1[V][H],
    fr_out2[V][H];
  while (1) {
    par {
      {
        snd_to_sw(0);
        rcv_from_sw();
        snd_to_sw(1);
        rcv_from_sw();
      }
      smooth_frame(fr_in1,
        fr_out1);
    }

    par {
      {
        snd_to_sw(2);
        rcv_from_sw();
        snd_to_sw(3);
        rcv_from_sw();
      }
      smooth_frame(fr_in2,
        fr_out2);
    }
  }
}
```
(b)

Fig. 6. Generated (a) software and (b) hardware for program in Fig. 2.

For scalar data, the synthesized hardware design ensures that the correct FPGA register is used for the transfer. For array transfers, the transfer instruction of the software process (Figure 2) does not contain enough information. It only specifies the used channels, but the array in the hardware process to which a transfer refers must be known, too. Since software controls DMA, the array's bank number and offset, as determined by the memory mapping, are necessary to generate the correct DMA instruction. We use the ID numbers by the hardware to generate conditional statements containing the correct DMA instruction, depending on the hardware state. After the DMA transfer is finished, an acknowledgment is sent to the hardware (snd_to_hw, rcv_from_sw). The hardware process synchronizes with software using these functions, but the array send and receive functions themselves are removed since the DMA transfers are under software control. The FPGA circuit only has to release those memory banks currently not used.

Figure 6 shows (a) the resulting software main function and (b) the hardware description, ready for synthesis, for the task-parallel program in Figure 2. ID numbers 0 and 2 indicate transfers to the host on channel chan_fr_out, and ID numbers 1 and 3 indicate transfers to the accelerator on channel chan_fr_in. In hardware, each channel communication is substituted by a snd_to_sw/rcv_from_sw pair. In software, rcv_from_hw reads the ID number before the assert statement checks channel consistency, and snd_to_hw sends the acknowledgement to the hardware. The remaining components of main are explained in the next section.

Software Generation The generated software program contains code to configure and start the hardware process on the FPGA, followed by the code in the `software` function with channel communication substituted as defined above.[2] In case we target a single-processor host, we have to generate a sequential host program or use multiple software threads. We can restrict the parallelism allowed in the software process to DMA transfers running in parallel with other host computations. These can be implemented in a sequential program by placing the other computations between DMA start and stop instructions.

Figure 6(a) shows the result of this technique. By placing `get_frame` and `put_frame` in between `DMA_to_host` or `DMA_to_hw` and `wait_DMA_finished`, they execute concurrently with the DMA transfers.

Hardware Synthesis Hardware synthesis generates circuitry to evaluate expressions. Assignments to FPGA registers, memory accesses and host communications are generally performed in the order of the input program. Components in a `par` block, however, are started at the same time and only synchronized at the end of the block. Hence in Figure 6(b) the arrays are transferred in parallel with `smooth_frame`. Since there is only one physical host communication channel, our compiler requires that no channel communications occur in parallel: otherwise the transfers have to be serialized in a way consistent with the software.

As mentioned in Section 3, write conflicts must be prevented in shared memory parallel programs. For hardware synthesis, we could detect these conflicts by defining that all assignments in all processes take one clock cycle. This approach can be supported by the Handel-C language. It is also possible to parallelise appropriate subtasks by, for instance, pipeline vectorisation [2].

One way to reduce deadlock problems is to restrict hardware sub-tasks to communicate through shared variables rather than synchronous channels. Only one sub-task can access an array of variables for an entire sub-task execution, and only scalar variables in the main hardware task can be read. Together with the memory mapping constraints, these conditions guarantee that a subtask has exclusive access to the memory banks that it requires. All synchronization is limited to the main hardware task, and the sequentially specified sub-tasks can be synthesized independently, using optimization techniques such as vectorization which have been developed for sequential programs [2]. These enable additional fine-grain parallelism within sub-tasks.

In the histogram stretching example of Figure 4, the minimum and maximum values computed by `comp_minmax` are allocated to arrays rather than to scalar variables in order to synthesize and vectorize `comp_minmax` and `stretch` independently.

5   Implementation and Results

We are currently extending our SUIF Pipeline Compiler prototype [2] for task-parallel programs. It targets Celoxica's RC1000-PP [4] board which contains a single FPGA and up to four banks of 2 MB memories accessible to both the FPGA and the host bus.

---

[2] Since we currently do not consider run-time reconfiguration or multi-FPGA architectures, there is only one configuration bitstream which is downloaded at program start-up.

Implementation	(1) Vidcap		(2) SimpleAvi		(3) Ideal	
	smooth	stretch	smooth	stretch	smooth	stretch
Sequential Coprocessing	4.7 fps	4.8 fps	32 fps	36 fps	65 fps	82 fps
Task parallel	4.9 fps	4.9 fps	45 fps	45 fps	108 fps	164 fps
Speedup	4%	3%	41%	27%	66%	100%

Table 1. Performance for skeletonization program.

We use annotations instead of the extended syntax used in Section 3 so that the SUIF standard C compiler [14] can be used without frontend changes. The only extensions to the hardware synthesis are channel communication and parallel sub-tasks.

The following presents preliminary performance estimates for the smoothing and histogram stretching algorithms on the RC1000-PP board. The effect of overlapping sub-tasks is obviously application specific. For instance, the sub-tasks of the histogram stretching example take 3.1 ms and 6.1 ms per frame when the design runs at 25 MHz. Concurrent execution reduces the run-time from 9.2 ms to 6.1 ms, a speedup of 51%.

We can make more general statements about the speedup achieved by overlapping software and hardware: $Speedup = (t_{SW} + t_{FPGA})/max(t_{SW}, t_{FPGA})$ where t_{SW} is the duration of an iteration of the software process (including DMA transfers), and t_{FPGA} is the duration of a hardware iteration. The maximum speedup of 100% is achieved if $t_{SW} = t_{FPGA}$.

This improvement can make the difference between non real-time and real-time performance. Table 1 shows estimated frame rates and speedups for smoothing and histogram stretching using the coprocessor model and our task parallel approach. We consider three software systems: (1) *Vidcap*, a relatively slow program capturing and displaying video frames from a camera (about 200 ms/frame); (2) SimpleAvi which retrieves and displays AVI files (about 20 ms/frame); and (3) an efficient ideal system with 6.1 ms/frame. The results show that the speedup is limited for Vidcap since the software time largely outweighs the hardware time. The situation is better for SimpleAvi, achieving 41% for smoothing. Only a fast system with balanced hardware and software workloads can achieve the maximum speedup.

6   Conclusion and Future Work

This paper describes task-parallel programming for reconfigurable systems. It combines shared memory and distributed memory parallel programming techniques and extends them for loosely-coupled hardware/software systems. Using video processing as example, we show how easily applications can be specified using parallel software and hardware tasks. The developer does not require specific hardware design knowledge since the compiler is capable of mapping the program efficiently to host processor and reconfigurable accelerator. Our system specifically enables the overlapping of software, data transfer and hardware computations by using communication channels, as well as the parallel execution of coarse-grain hardware tasks. The compilation scheme of task-parallel programs is based on optimization and vectorization techniques previously developed for sequential programs. Run-time estimates for a commercially available accelerator board show the effectiveness of our method.

Future work includes optimizing the channel implementation and supporting general parallel software tasks. Additionally, we intend to combine task-parallel programming with run-time reconfiguration for multi-FPGA systems or partially reconfigurable FPGAs. Just as communication latency can be hidden by overlapping communication with computation, reconfiguration latency can be hidden by overlapping reconfiguration and computations, or by pre-configuring currently unused resources, possibly in a speculative way. Finally, the stylized communication patterns for task-parallel programs, shown in Figure 2 and Figure 4, indicate the potential for automation; the objective is to arrange parallel tasks to have similar lengths of execution time.

References

[1] M. B. Gokhale and J. M. Stone. NAPA C: compiling for a hybrid RISC/FPGA architecture. In *Proc. FPGAs for Custom Computing Machines*. IEEE Computer Society Press, 1998.

[2] M. Weinhardt and W. Luk. Pipeline vectorization. *IEEE Transactions on Computer-Aided Design of Integrated Circuits and Systems*, February 2001.

[3] D. A. Buell, J. M. Arnold, and W. J. Kleinfelder. *Splash 2 - FPGAs in a Custom Computing Machine*. IEEE Computer Society Press, 1996.

[4] *Celoxica Limited*. Homepage http://www.celoxica.com.

[5] P. M. Athanas and H. F. Silverman. Processor reconfiguration through instruction-set metamorphosis. *IEEE Computer*, 26, March 1993.

[6] J. R. Hauser and J. Wawrzynek. Garp: A MIPS processor with a reconfigurable coprocessor. In *Proc. FPGAs for Custom Computing Machines*. IEEE Computer Society Press, 1997.

[7] C. R. Rupp, M. Landguth, T. Garverick, E. Gomersall and H. Holt. The NAPA adaptive processing architecture. In *Proc. FPGAs for Custom Computing Machines*. IEEE Computer Society Press, 1998.

[8] C. A. R. Hoare. *Communicating Sequential Processes*. Prentice-Hall International, 1985.

[9] C. A. R. Hoare and I. Page. Hardware and software: The closing gap. *Transputer Communications*, 2(2), June 1994.

[10] E. Barros and A. Sampaio. Towards provably correct hardware/software partitioning using occam. In *Proc. Int. Workshop on Hardware/Software Codesign*. IEEE Computer Society Press, 1994.

[11] I. Page and W. Luk. Compiling Occam into FPGAs. In *FPGAs*. Abingdon EE&CS Books, 1991.

[12] H. R. Myler and A. R. Weeks. *Computer Imaging Recipes in C*. Prentice Hall, 1993.

[13] M. Weinhardt and W. Luk. Memory access optimization and RAM inference for pipeline vectorization. In *Field Programmable Logic and Applications*, LNCS 1673. Springer, 1999.

[14] The Stanford SUIF Compiler Group. Homepage http://suif.stanford.edu.

Chip-Based Reconfigurable Task Management

Gordon Brebner[1] and Oliver Diessel[2]

[1] Division of Informatics
University of Edinburgh
Mayfield Road, Edinburgh EH9 3JZ
United Kingdom
[2] School of Computer Science & Engineering
University of New South Wales
Sydney, NSW 2052
Australia

Abstract. Modularity is a key aspect of system design, particularly in the era of system-on-chip. Field-programmable logic (FPL), particularly with the rapid increase in programmable gate counts, is a natural medium to host run-time modularity, that is, a dynamically-varying ensemble of circuit modules. Prior research has presumed the use of an external processor to manage such an ensemble. In this paper, we consider on-chip management, implemented in the FPL itself, based upon a one-dimensional allocation model. We demonstrate an algorithm for on-chip identification of free FPL resource for modules, and an approach to on-chip rearrangement of modules. The latter includes a proposal for a realistic augmentation to existing FPGA reconfiguration architectures. The work represents a key demonstration of how FPL can be used as a first-order computational resource, rather than just as a slave to the microprocessor.

1 Introduction

Field-programmable logic (FPL) continues to grow in importance as a digital implementation medium in markets that are driven by diminishing lead times, a hunger for performance, rapidly changing standards and the need to be capable of rapidly differentiating or personalising products. It has become impractical to design whole systems from scratch, so a modular design approach is used instead. Common functions are identified and parameterized, and then a system is composed of many modules, some of them interacting, others operating quite independently. This methodology suits the nature of FPL which, as a general-purpose digital circuit implementation medium, is a natural platform for hosting the variety of circuit modules that comprise a system. Moreover, it is useful that only those modules that need to be active at some time need be configured on the reusable resource.

This motivates the need for allocation of the logic resource amongst the various modules and for a mechanism to recycle or reclaim and reallocate logic resources, as computational requirements dictate. It is also conceivable (although

G. Brebner and R. Woods (Eds.): FPL 2001, LNCS 2147, pp. 182–191, 2001.

few examples exist so far) that FPL-based systems can be shared in time and/or space amongst several concurrent independent users or tasks.

Most SRAM-based field-programmable gate array devices are composed of a two-dimensional grid of configurable logic cells embedded in a hierarchical routing network. In general, this structure does not easily lend itself to a systematic, modular view of circuits that can be pursued both at design and execution time. Aside from basic wiring considerations, just the fact that the resource is two-dimensional is a major complication for run-time module management. One approach to handling this is to superimpose a one-dimensional management strategy. With such a (column-oriented) scheme, individual modules occupy the complete height of the FPGA but have a variable width. The regions of the array associated with different modules can be easily separated and managed independently. Several such one-dimensional or striped FPGA systems and devices have been proposed (for example, DISC [15], GARP [9], PipeWrench [13], even Xilinx Virtex chips). As new modules arrive, it is then simply necessary to find a region of sufficient free columns. I/O can generally be readily provided at pins adjacent to the tasks needing it at the top and bottom edges of the array, and inter-module communication can be provided by abutting modules or by routing signals via an interconnecting bus.

To obtain good utilisation from one-dimensional FPGA-based systems, effective and efficient allocation methods are needed to cope with arbitrary arrival and departure sequences for differently sized modules. Traditionally this is done by an allocator executing on an attached host [1,2,3]. In this paper, however, we discuss on-chip module management methods that do not require an external host, being implemented on the array itself. This eliminates a computational load and communication bottleneck from an auxiliary processor and also provides a decentralised means of scalably allocating FPGA resources.

In high-load applications or environments, utilisation can be improved by defragmenting or partially rearranging the executing modules to collect sufficient free columns to allocate to an incoming module. The results of previous experiments suggest that rearranging modules by moving them on-chip provides the greatest boost to utilisation by minimising reconfiguration overheads [6]. In this paper, we therefore present on-chip methods both for identifying space for arriving modules and also for compaction of the space used by existing modules. In the latter case, we suggest a specific and realistic architectural enhancement that facilitates the efficient on-chip movement of modules.

2   One-Dimensional Task Model

We take a high-level view of the capability and operation of reconfigurable systems. Since we are interested not just in the static circuitry requirements of modules, but also their dynamic computational functions, we shall refer to *tasks* from now on. There are various published examples of the use of tasks in various guises, and their management at run time. The desire to reallocate FPL resources during operation has a number of origins, including the desire to redistribute the components that are to be computed between hardware and software in response to performance objectives.

In this paper, we consider a system model that does not require a controlling host. Traditional host-based CCMs are not excluded from consideration — it is just that the host is no longer required for detailed task management. In a 'closed' system, for which the set of tasks and the possible sequences of operation are known, an optimal bespoke on-chip controller can be constructed to manage the task reconfigurations. This has been investigated in the past by several researchers [11,14, for example]. We consider 'open' systems here, seeking a general dynamic solution to task management.

Since the approach is one-dimensional, each task will be allocated the entire height of the array, and as many contiguous columns as are needed to lay out the circuit. The array is thus partitioned into vertical slices of variable width corresponding to the various tasks, and so the model can be seen as one-dimensional with variable-width contiguous blocks either allocated to tasks or free.

The block of logic resource used by each task is composed of three parts, layered vertically, as illustrated in Fig. 1. Some of the logic associated with the

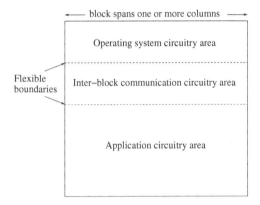

Fig. 1. Basic structure of a task block (in practice, application circuitry area would be much larger relative to the others)

task will be devoted to system functions such as assisting in the management of tasks. A second component is envisaged to be associated with communications between the task and other tasks or its environment (devices, host or network). The third, and typically most substantial, part comprises the computational circuitry for performing the task. As with all system overheads, there is a need to keep the space associated with the first two components small and to ensure that their operation does not reduce the performance of the task significantly.

Tasks are typically configured by loading a configuration bitstream onto the FPGA. Usually such streams are loaded sequentially so, short of exploiting compression techniques, the amount of data that must be loaded for a task is assumed to be proportional to the area of the task. In the one-dimensional model, the area of the task is proportional to its width.

As tasks arrive and leave, fragmentation of the free space occurs, and consolidation of the free space by rearranging the executing tasks is desirable. Host-based task rearrangement methods rely on moving executing tasks by reloading them at their new location, and methods that minimize the (additional) configuration delays to the moving tasks are therefore sought. Previous attempts have focused on finding feasible rearrangements that minimize the delay to individual tasks. Here, we describe a one-dimensional simplification of a two-dimensional method known as ordered compaction [5]. In this method, a subset of the executing tasks is squashed together towards one side of the array until there is no free space left between them. Their relative order is preserved, and a single free block is created adjacent to the compacted tasks. When carried out by an external host, each task is moved in sequence, with the reconfiguration of each task in turn carried out serially. Compton *et al* proposed a novel adaptation of the Xilinx 6200 series FPGA that allows a column (using our task arrangement) of configuration bits to be relocated in a constant number of steps [4]. Their structure supports the relocation of a single task under host control in time proportional to its width. We improve on this using an on-chip method that enables tasks to be moved in parallel, thereby reducing overheads and improving the efficacy of compaction.

3   On-Chip First-Fit Allocation

In this section, we present an on-chip implementation of a search algorithm that finds a free block of a required column width, if such a block is available. An integer value is input to the circuit, to specify the number of columns required, and an integer value is output from the circuit, indicating the column where a block was found or equal to zero if no block was found. The basic circuitry used is an inverted variant of the string pattern matching circuitry that has been studied by numerous researchers since the advent of programmable logic technology [8,10, for example]. The variance arises from the fact that the pattern is shifted past the 'text', in this case, the pattern string representing a unary encoding of the column width required (e.g., 11111 for five columns), and the text string representing the current status of the array, having length equal to the array width, with 1's denoting used columns (occupied by tasks) and 0's denoting unused columns (free). In our design, the text string bits are not stored explicitly, instead being encoded by circuitry variants.

The matching circuitry is contained in the system part of each column of the array as illustrated in Fig. 2. The pattern string is shifted through this circuitry from the rightmost column to the leftmost column (the direction of the data flow being arbitrary, but in this case implying finding the first fit from the right-hand side of the array). A 'hit' signal line runs from left to right, the output value at the right being zero until a pattern match is detected, that is, a suitable free block has been detected. Each column's circuitry is dynamically configured with

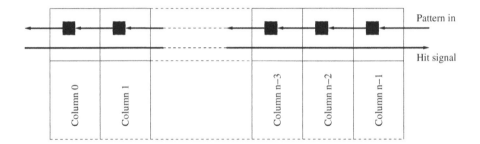

Fig. 2. Matching circuitry distributed over array columns

one of two layouts, depending on whether the column is used or unused, as shown in Fig. 3. The reconfiguration occurs when a block is allocated or deallocated.

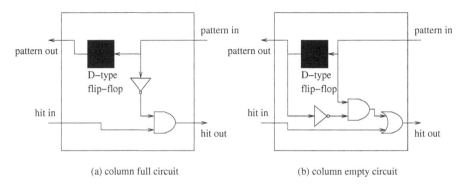

(a) column full circuit   (b) column empty circuit

Fig. 3. Per-column matching circuitry variants

The operation of the pattern-matching circuitry involves a very simple control circuit, to be located in a system circuitry area immediately to the top-right of the array area available for allocation. This control circuit contains a counter wide enough to count to the maximum number of columns available for allocation (note that it is allowable for this maximum, and hence the size of the counter to be dynamically reconfigurable). The operation of the control circuit is as follows:

1. The counter is set to the number of columns sought as part of the search request.
2. A single zero is shifted into the pattern chain.
3. While the counter is non-zero, a one is shifted into the pattern chain, and the counter is decremented.
4. Decrement the counter.
5. While the hit line is zero **and** the counter is non-zero, a zero is shifted into the pattern chain and the counter is decremented.

On completion, if the hit line is zero, no available block has been found. Otherwise, the counter indicates the column number (labelled from zero at the left end of the array) of the rightmost column of the block found. The basic run time of this circuitry is $O(k + n)$, where k is the size of the required block, and n is the number of columns in the array.

Note that this control circuit is in the simplest form possible. To improve the running time, some optimisations could be made at the expense of more circuitry. First, Step 2. can be omitted if a zero was shifted in as the last pattern bit of the previous match. Second, Step 5. could be shortened, in the case where no match is found, if the counter is only decremented as far as the number of columns sought minus the maximum number of columns. (In fact, if the counter was equipped with testing for other than zero contents, Step 4 could be eliminated.) The run time of the optimised circuitry would be improved to $O(n)$.

However, we believe that it is appropriate to use the simplest possible circuit because the matching algorithm can run in parallel with both the task circuits present on the array and any agent requesting the search. In this sense, the run time is 'free', at the expense of a small amount of programmable logic resource.

4   On-Chip Ordered Compaction

The circuitry described in the previous section provides an efficient means of finding free blocks when they exist. In general, the total number of columns required might be available, but not in a contiguous block. This means that two enhancements are necessary. First, the matching process must be extended to find non-contiguous columns and to indicate where they are located. Second, a compaction process must be introduced to create a block of the required size. Due to limitations of space, we just outline the necessary extension to the matching process, since the more profound implications arise from the compaction process.

The basic modification to the matching process is that the pattern string is shortened by one bit each time it passes through an unused column. This can be implemented simply by having the circuitry at an unused column forward a zero rather than a one, just when it sees the leading one of the pattern (i.e., a one which was preceded by a zero). A hit will have occurred when the pattern has been reduced to a single bit, and enters an unused column. This causes a hit signal to be propagated back to the right-hand side. It indicates that there are sufficient free columns to form the required block size. The run time of this matching process is the same as for the contiguous case above.

Unlike the contiguous-space case, where the location of the free block can immediately be inferred when the hit signal is received, the situation is more complex here. While it is easy for an external controller to maintain a bitmap of the free and occupied columns, or for the array to provide one by shifting it out to the right, we consider a purely internal mechanism for free space compaction that is targeted at the underlying configuration mechanisms of typical FPGAs.

Fig. 4 shows an example of what might be required, where three free sub-blocks must be combined to produce a free block. The essential operation is to shift the necessary number of rightmost used blocks to the left, thereby creating a large enough free block. It is easy to envisage how the required shifting of con-

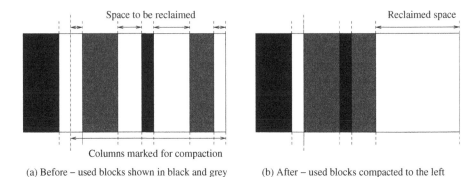

(a) Before – used blocks shown in black and grey   (b) After – used blocks compacted to the left

Fig. 4. Example of compaction requirement

figuration information can be achieved by sequentially reloading configuration bitstreams using an external agent or, more adventurously, an internal agent on the array.

However, we wish to point out a more efficient possibility, targeted at exploiting the nature of contemporary FPGA technologies, but requiring minor physical changes to the device architecture. Our suggestion therefore represents a possible and feasible future option for FPL.

The basic idea is to map two-dimensional block shifts onto one-dimensional configuration data shifts. Reflecting upon the past and continuing architectural heritage of FPGA devices, this should be convenient since in many architectures configuration is carried out by passing a serial bitstream through a shift register formed over all cells of the array. This persists in features such as the partial reconfiguration capability of the Xilinx Virtex family, where each column still has a shift register nature.

Here, we postulate the existence of (additional) configuration shift registers spanning FPGA rows and advocate the addition of extra gating along the register, in order to allow partial shifts within the register, as required for block compaction. The structure of a typical row shifter needed to support our on-chip compaction mechanism is depicted in Fig. 5. Assuming the required block width is k, the algorithm for identifying and compacting the tasks on chip is as follows:

1. The head of the search string sets up a 'shift mask' by marking all columns as it travels left until a hit is generated or all columns have been searched. This mask covers the columns in the space to be reclaimed.
2. If no hit is generated, the mask is cleared and we are done (the pending task cannot be accommodated).
3. For k cycles do:
   (a) If the leftmost column of a moving task coincides with the leftmost column of the shift mask, then clear the fragment of the shift mask covered by that task (it has reached its destination).
   (b) Shift columns one place left into all columns covered by the shift mask (the mask bits drive the column select lines shown in Fig. 5).

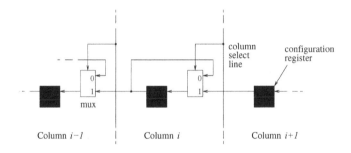

Fig. 5. Configuration shift register in a typical row.

Step 1. requires $O(n)$ cycles in the background as previously discussed. Step 2. can be completed in a single cycle if a long line is dedicated to the operation, or also takes $O(n)$ cycles operating in the background. Step 3(a). can be accomplished in a single cycle with appropriate propagation from the left end of the mask to the right end of the task. Step 3(b). requires a single cycle for all columns shifting in parallel. Note that the used/unused nature of the column, which is implicit in part of the operating system circuitry for the task, is shifted with the task. The algorithm thus needs $O(n + k)$ cycles in total.

Considering the run time of the on-chip compaction process, the major benefit derives from the fact that all necessary blocks can be shifted in parallel, in contrast to a conventional sequential approach. The time required for shifting is upper-bounded by the *width* of the free block requested. This time can be contrasted with a sequential approach, where the required time would be equal to the sum of the *areas* of the blocks moved. The latter would be smaller in some cases, for example where one or more small blocks are being shifted relatively long distances. However, a particular benefit of the proposed scheme is that it has a run time directly related to the size of request made and that is independent of the current array usage.

If we assume the FPGA device is provided with column-oriented configuration shift registers to facilitate rapid one-dimensional task configuration, the enhancement suggested above requires the addition of a wire segment and a 2-input multiplexer between each horizontal pair of registers, as well as a select line and select logic for each column. The cost of this additional hardware could be reduced by forming a single snake over all columns of the array and simply providing column select logic to support task compaction. Compaction would then take time proportional to the *area* of the incoming task, and moving tasks would be delayed by the area of the free space to their left that is to be reclaimed. It should be noted that these delays are also bounded by the area of the incoming task and that the greater delays associated with this scheme can significantly erode the benefits of compaction. Instead, we sought to minimize the delays associated with task rearrangement by making full use of the available on-chip bandwidth for moving tasks in parallel.

Since information about which columns are used and unused resides at the appropriate physical positions in the array, there is no need for an external agent, nor the major complication of indirecting shift operations through any superimposed layers of mapped access to the configuration memory.

Aside from moving configuration information for blocks, there are some other task management issues to be considered. Where inter-block communication circuitry is present, this must be adjusted appropriately. However, depending upon the inter-task communications method adopted, this could be as simple as eliminating the wire segments spanning empty columns. Also, to allow other blocks and external interfaces to continue operation while a block is being moved, there must be buffering of data sent to the block [7]. Our solution bounds the maximum buffer space needed by a task during its lifetime since, at most, it moves from one end of the array to the opposite end. We can therefore determine whether a task should be admitted to the system based on the available buffer space and its maximum possible requirement.

5   Conclusions and Future Work

In this paper, we have built on two threads of prior research related to the management of tasks on a reconfigurable resource. The first thread, pursued by both authors amongst others, has concerned use of a separate processor resource to perform management of a dynamically-varying collection of tasks. The second thread has concerned the use of reconfigurable logic itself to oversee a static collection of tasks with static scheduling. This work, by focusing on the more challenging aspect of each thread, has demonstrated that reconfigurable logic can be used as a first-order computational resource. We have also proposed a realistic extension to the reconfiguration hardware of FPGAs that would enable very efficient partial reconfiguration geared towards task management.

Various challenges to building on this initial basis lie ahead. First, we will be applying the technique in a practical case study, that of autonomously managing a collection of reconfigurable function units made available to a microprocessor core. Second, we will be investigating the extension of the one-dimensional task management strategies to two-dimensional strategies, seeking to find ways of efficiently implementing proven software algorithms in reconfigurable logic.

More profoundly, we are also interested in what exercises like this, where programmable logic is the first-order computational mechanism, reveal about the computational power of this medium. In particular, we are exploring the relationship between the reconfigurable mesh (RMESH) theoretical model [12] and the capabilities of FPGAs. For instance, in contrast to our FPGA algorithm, a word-model RMESH algorithm for finding a suitable free block requires just a constant number of steps. We intend investigating practical techniques to overcome the differences between the models.

In summary, we intend our work to illuminate reconfigurable computing at several levels, including: physical architectures; dynamic modularisation; and computational models.

References

1. K. Bazargan, R. Kastner, and M. Sarrafzadeh. Fast template placement for recon-figurable computing systems. *IEEE Design and Test of Computers*, 17(1):68 – 83, Jan.–Mar. 2000.
2. G. Brebner. A virtual hardware operating system for the Xilinx XC6200. *Proc. 6th International Workshop on Field Programmable Logic and Applications*, Springer LNCS 1142, 1996, pages 327–336.
3. J. Burns, A. Donlin, J. Hogg, S. Singh, and M. de Wit. A dynamic reconfigura-tion run-time system. *Proc. 5th Annual IEEE Symposium on FPGAs for Custom Computing Machines*, IEEE, 1997, pages 66 – 75.
4. K. Compton, J. Cooley, S. Knol, and S. Hauck. Abstract: Configuration reloca-tion and defragmentation for reconfigurable computing. *Proc. 8th Annual IEEE Symposium on FPGAs for Custom Computing Machines*, IEEE, 2000, pages 279 – 280.
5. O. Diessel and H. ElGindy. Run–time compaction of FPGA designs. *Proc. 7th International Workshop on Field Programmable Logic and Applications*, Springer LNCS 1304, 1997, pages 131 – 140.
6. O. Diessel and H. ElGindy. On scheduling dynamic FPGA reconfigurations. *Proc. Fifth Australasian Conference on Parallel and Real–Time Systems*, Springer, 1998, pages 191 – 200.
7. H. ElGindy, M. Middendorf, H. Schmeck, and B. Schmidt. Task rearrangement on partially reconfigurable FPGAs with restricted buffer. *Proc. 10th International Workshop on Field Programmable Logic and Applications*, Springer LNCS 1896, 2000, pages 379 – 388.
8. B. K. Gunther, G. J. Milne, and V. L. Narasimhan. Assessing document relevance with run–time reconfigurable machines. *Proc. 4th Annual IEEE Symposium on FPGAs for Custom Computing Machines*, IEEE, 1996, pages 10 – 17.
9. J. R. Hauser and J. Wawrzynek. Garp: A MIPS processor with a reconfigurable coprocessor. *Proc. 5th Annual IEEE Symposium on FPGAs for Custom Computing Machines*, IEEE, 1997, pages 12 – 21.
10. E. Lemoine and D. Merceron. Run time reconfiguration of FPGA for scanning genomic databases. *Proc. 3rd Annual IEEE Symposium on FPGAs for Custom Computing Machines*, IEEE, 1995, pages 90 – 98.
11. P. Lysaght, G. McGregor, and J. Stockwood. Configuration controller synthesis for dynamically reconfigurable systems. *IEE Colloquium on Hardware–Software Cosynthesis for Reconfigurable Systems*, IEE, 1996, pages 1 – 9.
12. R. Miller, V. K. Prasanna-Kumar, D. I. Reisis, and Q. F. Stout. Parallel compu-tations on reconfigurable meshes. *IEEE Transactions on Computers*, 42(6):678 – 692, June 1993.
13. H. Schmit. Incremental reconfiguration for pipelined applications. *Proc. 5th Annual IEEE Symposium on FPGAs for Custom Computing Machines*, IEEE, 1997, pages 47 – 55.
14. N. Shirazi, W. Luk, and P. Y. K. Cheung. Run–time management of dynamically reconfigurable designs. *Proc. 8th International Workshop on Field Programmable Logic and Applications* Springer LNCS 1482, 1998, pages 59 – 68.
15. M. J. Wirthlin and B. L. Hutchings. Sequencing run–time reconfigured hardware with software. *Proc. Fourth International ACM Symposium on Field Programmable Gate Arrays*, ACM, 1996, pages 122 – 128.

Configuration Caching and Swapping

Suraj Sudhir, Suman Nath, and Seth Copen Goldstein

Carnegie Mellon University
{ssudhir,sknath,seth}@cs.cmu.edu

Abstract. Speedups of coupled processor-FPGA systems over traditional microprocessor systems are limited by the cost of hardware reconfiguration. In this paper we compare several new configuration caching algorithms that reduce the latency of reconfiguration. We also present a cache replacement strategy for a 3-level hierarchy. Using the techniques we present, total latency for loading the configurations is reduced, lowering the configurable overhead.

1 Introduction

Configurable computing systems can exhibit significant performance benefits over conventional microprocessors by mapping portions of executable code to a reconfigurable function unit (RFU). In such a system, native code sequences are replaced with configurations, which are loaded into the RFU using new instructions (rfuOps). In order to achieve speedups two requirements must be satisfied. First, a significant portion of the program must be mapped to the RFU and must execute significantly faster on the RFU as compared to native execution on the core. Second, the cost of loading the configurations onto the RFU must be small enough not to obviate the advantage of running on the RFU. In this paper we address the latter problem.

Some of the independent techniques researchers have proposed for reducing configuration overhead include configuration prefetching [14] , configuration compression [9] and configuration caching [7]. In this paper we describe an improved algorithm for RFU configuration caching and a new strategy for multilevel caching.

We divide configuration-caching algorithms into two classes, *penalty based* and *history-based* algorithms. Penalty-based algorithms evict configurations in the cache based on their size, distance of last occurrence and frequency of occurrence. The simple Least-Recently Used [7] algorithm, for example, evicts the configuration that was accessed furthest in the past. History-based algorithms evict rfuOps[1] based not only on their individual properties, but also their order of execution. In short, the one that is predicted to occur farthest in future is evicted.

---

[1] We use 'rfuOp' to refer to either the instruction that loads the configuration to be executed or the configuration itself

G. Brebner and R. Woods (Eds.): FPL 2001, LNCS 2147, pp. 192–202, 2001.
© Springer-Verlag Berlin Heidelberg 2001

class	size	cost	optional
virtual memory	fixed	fixed	no
web caching	variable	variable	yes
VM w/ superpages	multiple	fixed	no
ideal config caching	variable	fixed	yes
required config caching	variable	fixed	no

Table 1. *Comparison between different caching problems*

In this paper, we propose an effective cache replacement algorithm and describe the performance of a realistic 3-level configuration-caching model. Our contributions are:

- We characterize the cache replacement problem in the context of reconfigurable computing systems and point out the theoretical complexity of achieving the optimal performance.
- We propose a lightweight history-based online algorithm that, based on simulation results, outperforms previous cache replacement algorithms.
- We extend the caching model to a three-level cache model and show how performance varies with defragmentation and the exclusion property.

The rest of the paper is organized as follows. In section 2, we describe the configuration caching problem. In section 3, we describe different FPGA models. paper. We describe our own cache replacement algorithms in section 4. In section 5, we present and analyze performance results obtained from our configuration caching algorithms in different models.

2   Configuration Caching

There are significant differences between configuration caching and other caching problems (see Table 1) making previously developed techniques unsuitable to the configuration caching problem. Configuration caching is variable-size caching: The total latency depends not only on the number of times a configuration is loaded but also on its size. It is therefore possible that few loads of a very large configuration will be costlier than many loads of a smaller configuration. Thus, it might make more sense to keep larger configurations in cache longer and to consider both size and frequency when making eviction decisions.

While there are various systems that support variable-size pages, such as the superpage-based virtual memory systems in HP PA-RISC, Compaq Alpha and others [2], they only permit page sizes that are in multiples of a unit size. We call this *multiple page-sizes*, rather than variable page-sizes. Figure 1 shows how latency increases and is less predictable when page sizes are constrained to be a power of two.

Another variable but optional caching problem is web caching. Web caching is optional because the replacement algorithm may choose not to cache a page. This is called the Variable-size Variable-cost Optional Paging Problem [6,13]. A reconfigurable system that optionally loads rfuOps is an *ideal* reconfigurable system. We call this problem an *optional caching problem*. In this paper we

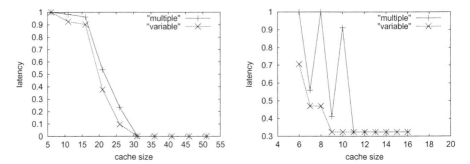

Fig. 1. *Comparison of the multiple-page size scheme which only allows page sizes that are a power of two, and the variable-page size scheme which allows pages of any size. On the left, gsm_d shows little difference in latency, whereas on the right, jpeg_e shows how latency can fluctuate for multiple page sizes.*

restrict ourselves to *required configuration caching*, i.e., all the rfuOps in the program must be loaded and executed.

In this paper we utilize a number of algorithms and conclusions developed for web caching. Besides the above differences between the two problems there are two more differences that affect the way techniques for web caching are extended to configuration caching. First, a web cache is much larger and can generally hold more pages making thrashing more likely in a configuration cache. Second, configuration cache replacement decisions must be made far more quickly than web cache replacement decisions. Thus, the configuration cache replacement algorithm needs to be implemented in hardware.

We begin our analysis with modified web caching algorithms LRU and Greedy-Dual as described in [4]. Both of these are penalty-based algorithms, i.e., they use past execution data in an order independent fashion to select a victim. We then propose a history-based technique which tracks the sequence in which rfuOps were executed to decide which rfuOp to evict at a given point of time.

3   FPGA Models

Different FPGA programming models have been proposed in literature. The three basic types are Single Context FPGAs, Multi-Context [10] FPGAs, and Partial Run-Time Reconfigurable (PRTR). According to [7] the PRTR FPGA has been found to be the best model and achieves speedups of more than 10 times that of single context FPGA models. However, even the basic PRTR model can suffer from thrashing caused by multiple configurations that are required frequently and must be loaded at the same address on the FPGA.

We describe our work in the context of two models based on the PRTR model, the *Location-independent* and the *Defragmentation* models[1]. In the Location-

---

[1] First proposed in [7], the Location-independent model is called the *Relocation* model and the Defragmentation model is called the *Relocation+Defragmentation* model

```
procedure SelectVictim( required_size)
 (min_cost, min_set)← (∞, nil)
 prefix ← nil
 last ← 1
 for i ← 1 to  rfu_count
    if (last > rfu_count – and required_size < size(prefix)) then
          break
    while (size(prefix) < required_size)
          if (defrag_mode  and rfuOp_last is not
             contiguous to rfuOp _last−1) then
                break
          prefix ← prefix ⋃ rfuOp_last
          last ← last +1
    endwhile
    if (cost(prefix) < min_cost) then
          min_cost = cost(prefix)
          min_set = prefix
          prefix ← prefix - rfuOp_i
    endif
 endfor
 return min_set
end procedure
```

Fig. 2. *SelectVictim algorithm to pick contiguous rfuOps. This algorithm returns the minimal set of contiguous rfuOps whose total size ≥ required size.*

independent model, a configuration can be dynamically allocated to any location of the chip at run time. However, once an rfuOp has been loaded it cannot be relocated. The Defragmentation model further improves chip area utilization by using a defragmenter to compact configurations on the fabric. It also permits rfuOps to be moved after being loaded. Including a defragmenter increases utilization of the fabric space, however, it also increases the total latency by adding the defragmentation cost.

4   Replacement Algorithms

In this section we describe cache replacement algorithms for different FPGA models. We break down the replacement algorithm into two phases. In the first phase a cost is computed for each configuration in the cache which is then used by phase two to determine which configurations to evict from the cache. All of the algorithms we present use the same phase two mechanism which we describe in Section 4.1. We then describe different cost computing algorithms in Section 4.2.

4.1   Victim Selection

The eviction policies for the Location-independent and the Defragmentation models are similar except that victims selected in the former must be physically contiguous on the fabric. Both models require that the set of rfuOps selected for eviction (*MINSET*) must have the minimum total eviction cost among all the rfuOps on the fabric. In the Location-independent model we call the set of evicted rfuOps the *contiguous MINSET*, where two rfuOps are contiguous if no other rfuOps lie physically between them in the fabric (though there may be a hole between them in which case it will just become part of the total freed space). Figure 2 shows the linear time procedure to find the MINSET. It maintains a sliding window of rfuOps, called *prefix*, from which it selects the victim. The operation *size(prefix)* and *cost(prefix)* are the total size and cost of all the rfuOps in the set *prefix*.

The complexity of this procedure is critical to the performance of the overall configuration caching algorithm. While an $O(\log n)$ hardware implementation based on parallel-prefix can be implemented, we use an alternate technique with $O(1)$ complexity which is competitive with the actual SelectVictim algorithm. The minimum cost victim with enough space after it is selected even if there are rfuOps occupying that space. Using the simplified SelectVictim strategy increases the latency, on average, by 3%.

Victim Eviction Strategies When one or more victims need to be evicted, two possible strategies may be used. The first strategy, which we call *full eviction* is to evict entire rfuOps. The second strategy, *partial eviction*, evicts only as much of the victim(s) as necessary.

Partial eviction performs well when a partially evicted rfuOp is needed again before it has been fully evicted by subsequent SelectVictim operations. Since part of the rfuOp is already on fabric, the load latency is reduced because only the remainder of the rfuOp needs to be loaded.

It can be shown that the partial eviction algorithm is the same as the general fixed-size virtual-memory caching problem where the smallest unit of configuration is analogous to a page in a fixed-page size virtual-memory system. In the full eviction model, on the other hand, the problem of variable-sized pages means that optimality cannot be assured by a polynomial time algorithm.

While partial eviction appears to reduce the amount of excess eviction it is not very helpful because the excess space on fabric will likely be used up by some other rfuOp that is loaded in future. Furthermore, tracking the partially loaded rfuOps is complex.

4.2   Replacement Algorithms for PRTR FPGAs

Here we present both history- and penalty-based algorithms to compute the cost of the resident rfuOps. This cost is used by SelectVictim, described above, to make room for a new rfuOp.

History-Based Algorithms This algorithm tries to predict the future sequence of rfuOps based on recent history. It maintains a *Next* table where Next[i] is the rfuOp that last followed i. The evicted rfuOp is determined by following

procedure
    HistoryBasedDecision*(rfuOp_to_load)*
R ← rfuOp_to_load
Next[prev_rfuOp] ← rfuOp_to_load
if rfuOp_to_load is on fabric **then**
    return
if there is enough space on fabric
  to load rfuOp_to_load **then**
    load rfuOp_to_load
    return
  Make the chain R, Next[R],
    Next[Next[R]],...
for each configuration C on fabric **do**
    C.cost ← -(distance of C on chain)
endfor
S_i ← SelectVictim(size(rfuOp_to_load))
Load rfuOp_to_load overwriting
  the configurations in S_i
end procedure

Fig. 3. *History-based Algorithm*

procedure
    PenaltyBasedDecision*(rfuOp_to_load)*
if rfuOp_to_load is on fabric **then**
  goto L1
if there is enough space on fabric
  to load rfuOp_to_load **then**
    load rfuOp_to_load
    goto L1
  S_i ← SelectVictim(size(rfuOp_to_load))
  Load rfuOp_to_load overwriting the
    configurations in S_i
L1:
  for each configuration C on fabric **do**
    C.cost ← C.cost–(FABRIC_SIZE
      –C.Size)
  endfor
  rfuOp.cost ← LARGE_CONSTANT
end procedure

Fig. 4. *Penalty-based Algorithm*

the Next pointers starting with the rfuOp being loaded, j, i.e., $j \rightarrow Next[j] \rightarrow Next[Next[j]] \ldots$ The rfuOp on the fabric that occurs furthest in this chain is predicted to occur furthest in future and will therefore be evicted.

Each rfuOp is assigned a cost which is negative of the smallest distance from j in the chain of next pointers. The rfuOp with the smallest cost is evicted. While the size of the rfuOp is not considered here, it is taken into account during phase two. As shown later, this algorithm works well despite the fact that it ignores the sizes of rfuOps in the chain. This agrees with [6].

Implementation of the algorithm in hardware requires a means to handle the chaining procedure. While a pointer jumping procedure would be expensive in hardware, it would execute with a complexity of O(log n). Here we describe an algorithm that predicts which rfuOp will occur furthest in the future without having to maintain or walk down a series of next links. The key idea is to keep information only about the RfuOps that are currently in the fabric. It maintains for each rfuOp, r,:

- FI(r) the first rfuOp to follow r that is in the fabric.
- FA(r) the last rfuOp to follow r that is in the fabric. FA(r) is only valid if r is resident in the fabric.

Using this information we can determine the rfuOp predicted to be needed farthest away in time when r is being loaded as: FA(FI(r)). For example, if the fabric currently holds rfuOps 1, 2, and 4 and we are about to load rfuOp 5, and the sequence of rfuOps upto this point is: ...,5,3,1,2,6,4, then FI(5) = 1 and FA(1) = 4.

To calculate FI and FA, we use two auxiliary items for each rfuOp: $S(r)$, a virtual sequence number, and $P(r)$, the rfuOp executed before r that is in the fabric. We also maintain a register, LastRfu, which holds the last rfuOp executed.

Before program execution, each rfuOp in the program is assigned a virtual sequence number such that $S(r) = r$. When an attempt is made to execute rfuOp R, one of three possibilities exists:

R **hits in the fabric:** We execute R and update the tables.

R **misses in the fabric and there is room for R:** We load R, execute R, and update the tables.

R **misses and we need to evict something:** We select FA(FI(R)) as the victim and invoke SelectVictim until there is room in the fabric. We load R, execute R, and update the tables.

Updating the tables requires that we update FI() for all the rfuOps in the program, FA() and P() for the rfuOps in the fabric, and S() for R.

FI: In parallel, for each rfuOp, i, in the program and $i \neq R$, if $(S(i) < S(R)$ and $S(R) < S(\text{FI}(i)))$, then set FI(i) = R. Finally, set FI(LastRfu) = R. In other words, if R occurs before FI(i) in the virtual sequence, make FI(R) = i.

FA: In parallel, for each rfuOp, i, in the fabric and $i \neq R$, if $(S(i) < S(\text{FA}(i))$ and $S(\text{FA}(i)) < S(R))$, then set FA(i) = R. Finally, set FA(R) = LastRfu. In other words, if R occurs after FA(i) in the virtual sequence, make FA(i) = R.

S: set $S(R) = S(\text{LastRfu}) + 1$ modulo some large number, e.g., 2^{16}.

P: If v is a victim, then in parallel, for each rfuOp, i, in the fabric and P(i) = v, P(i) = P(P(i)). This ensures that P(i) points to an rfuuOp still in the fabric.

If multiple victims need to be selected, they are found using the P entries. The update step can be done efficiently and is not on the critical path.

In all benchmarks, a significant portion of the rfuOp execution sequence constitutes a periodic pattern. This is because most of the speedup is achieved by implementing portions of a loop. In these cases the sequence information is as accurate as the algorithm in Figure 3. However, when the sequence is aperiodic the constant-time algorithm may differ from the algorithm in Figure 3. In some cases the simulation of the constant-time implementation proved to be better than that in Figure 3, in other cases the reverse was true. In all cases, the two are within 10% of each other and on average they are less than 2% of each other.

The strategy used by the history-based algorithm is not the same as most-recently used (MRU) unless the most recently accessed rfuOp is *always* the one that is accessed furthest in future. Consider the sequence of rfuOps 1 2 3 4 3 4 3 4...1 2 3 4 3 4..., with all rfuOps of size 1, and a fabric size of 3. The MRU algorithm will register evict 3 in order to load 4 and vice versa each time. On the other hand, the history-based algorithm does the following: the first time it loads 4 it will evict 3. Now FA(4) = 2, since FA(i) = P(LastRfu) when LastRfu is the victim. Also, FI(3) is 4. So when 3 is next loaded it will evict FA(FI(3)) = 2, avoiding the thrashing that happens with MRU. Furthermore, it can be seen that 2 really is the furthest in the sequence at this point, so the history-based algorithm makes a correct prediction, unlike the MRU, which on average increases latency by more than 160%.

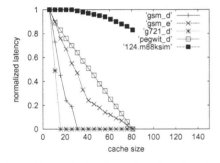

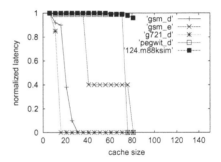

Fig. 5. *Effect of cache size for different benchmarks using the history-based algorithm*

Fig. 6. *Effect of cache size for different benchmarks using the penalty-based algorithm*

Penalty Based Algorithm Existing solutions to the variable page-size replacement problem, as described in Section 2, fall under the category of penalty-based algorithms. The algorithm we chose to implement for comparison is a modified form of the Greedy-Dual Size algorithm in [4]. It is used in web cache replacement and is shown to outperform other widely used web cache replacement algorithms.

Our penalty-based algorithm assigns costs to each rfuOp currently in the fabric. Whenever a configuration is accessed, its cost is set to some large constant and the cost of the other rfuOps on fabric are reduced by (fabric_size - configuration_size). Intuitively this penalizes smaller configurations more than the larger configurations. During replacement, we look for a configuration that has the smallest cost (that has been penalized most).

5   Performance Results

5.1   Experimental Setup

We used the SUIF [12] compiler with custom passes to automatically extract rfuOps from the program. We instrument the rfuOp-enabled code to generate traces which are then simulated on an extension of SimpleScalar [3] to obtain our results. We ran two benchmark applications from the SPECInt95 [5] and ten from the MediaBench [8] suites.

5.2   Experimental Results

In this section we present and analyze the experimental results for the algorithms proposed in Section 4. We found that in most benchmarks the latency decreased in a roughly linear fashion with increasing fabric size. This was truer for the history-based algorithm than the penalty-based algorithm. Figure 5 shows how the cache size affects the performance for a representative sample of the benchmarks, using the history-based algorithm. The history-based algorithm scales

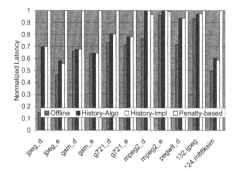
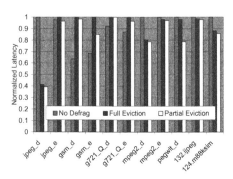

Fig. 7. *Performance of Replacement Algorithms*

Fig. 8. *Effect of Defragmentation*

well with changing cache size. On the other hand, as Figure 6 shows, the penalty-based algorithm scales poorly with cache size. To eliminate the effect of differing working sets we simulate each benchmark with an RFU that can hold half of all the rfuOps for that particular benchmark.

Performance of Replacement Algorithms To see how well our online algorithms perform, we compared their performance to that of the best of two offline algorithms: Belady's algorithm [1] or an approximation algorithm presented in [7]. The results for a location-independent FPGA are shown in Figure 7. History-Algo and History-Impl refer respectively to the theoretical model (using next-chains) and our implemented version of the history based algorithm. We also implemented the basic LRU algorithm. However, its performance was found to be vastly inferior to even the penalty-based algorithm.

Simulation results show that the history-based algorithm is more effective than the penalty-based one, and is consistently competitive with offline algorithms. The main reason for this is that the penalty-based algorithm evicts the rfuOp that occurred furthest *before* the current point, while the history-based algorithm replaces the one that it estimates to occur furthest *after* the current point. In fact, we find that the history-based algorithm tends to make choices similar to that of Belady's offline algorithm.

Effect of Defragmentation In Figure 8 we compare the history-based algorithm on a location-independent fabric with partial and full eviction on a fabric which implements defragmentation. Since the defragmentation cost is small, it has been ignored in simulation. The results are ambiguous as sometimes the extra power of defragmentation leads to worse behavior.

Partial eviction performs slightly better than the full eviction model, except for cases like jpeg_d and pegwit_d where an rfuOp is not required soon after its eviction. However, the implementation cost of partial eviction outweighs its small advantage.

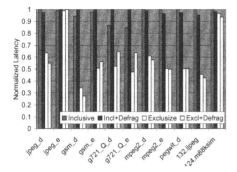
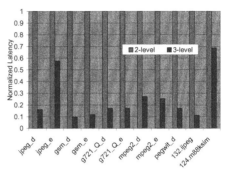

Fig. 9. *Performance of different three-level caching models*

Fig. 10. *Comparison of different caching models*

Performance of Three-Level Model Here we show the effect of introducing a configuration cache for the RFU.[2] To model the latency we used a 20:1 ratio for loading the cache from memory as compared to loading the fabric from cache.

Figure 9 shows that making the fabric and configuration cache exclusive always improves performance. This comes at the cost of an additional buffer to hold rfuOps that are evicted from fabric before they are loaded into the configuration cache. This buffer is necessary to maintain proper serialization of the operation. The Defragmentation model performs better than the Location independent model.

Comparison of the Effect of Different Models Figure 10 shows how performance improves significantly when we utilize the best three-level model, i.e., the one with the exclusion property, compared to the best two-level model. Most benchmarks showed a significant improvement in performance.

6   Conclusion

In this paper we have described algorithms for reducing reconfiguration overhead through effective replacement algorithms and configuration caching. We present an effective history-based algorithm with an efficient hardware implementation. We show that the added complexity of partial eviction does not yield significant performance improvement. Likewise, defragmentation increases the implementation complexity, but does not always improve performance.

There are still many avenues for further research. Our history-based algorithm considers only one preceding rfuOp, similar to a one bit prediction model in branch prediction. The algorithm can be extended to remember more than

---

[2] Space precludes describing our algorithms here, but a more complete description can be found in [11].

one preceding rfuOps, perhaps as a tree rather than a chain, and consider different possibilities before taking a replacement decision. Finally, we have not considered the case where the loading of the rfuOp into the fabric is optional.

Acknowledgments

We want to thank the reviews for their many helpful comments. This work was supported in part by an NSF CAREER award and Intel corporation.

References

1. L. A. Belady. A study of replacement algorithms for virtual storage computers. *IBM Systems Journal*, 5:78–101, 1966.
2. B.Jacob and T.Mudge. Virtual memory in contemporary microprocessors. In *Proceedings of IEEE MICRO*, volume 18, pages 60–75. IEEE, 1998.
3. Doug Burger, Todd M. Austin, and Steve Bennett. Evaluating future microprocessors: The simplescalar tool set. Technical Report CS-TR-1996-1308, University of Wisconsin-Madison, 1996.
4. P. Cao and S. Irani. Cost-aware www proxy caching. In *Proceedings of the 1997 USENIX Symposium on Internet Technology and Systems*, pages 193–206. USENIX, Dec. 1997.
5. http://www.spec.org/osg/cpu95. Specint95, 1995.
6. S. Irani. Page replacement with multi-size pages and applications to web caching. In *Proceedings of the 29th Symposium on the Theory of Computing*, pages 701–710, 1997.
7. S. Hauck K. C. Compton, Z. Li. Configuration caching techniques for fpga. In *IEEE Symposium on FPGAs for Custom Computing Machines*. IEEE, 2000.
8. W. H. Mangione-Smith M. Potkonjak, C. Lee. Mediabench: a tool for evaluating and synthesizing multimedia and communications systems. In *Proceedings of MICRO-30*, 1997.
9. E. J. Schwabe S. Hauck, Z. Li. Configuration compression for xilinx xc6200 fpga. In *IEEE Symposium on FPGAs for Custom Computing Machines*. IEEE, 1998.
10. A. Johnson S. Trimberger, D. Carberry and J. Wong. A time-multiplexed fpga. In *IEEE Symposium on FPGAs for Custom Computing Machines*. IEEE, 1997.
11. Sudhir, Nath, and Goldstein. Configuration caching and swapping. Technical report, CMU, 2001.
12. R. Wilson, R. French, C. Wilson, S. Amarasinghe, J. Anderson, S. Tjiang, S.-W. Liao, C.-W. Tseng, M. Hall, M. Lam, and J. Hennessy. SUIF: An infrastructure for research on parallelizing and optimizing compilers. In *ACM SIGPLAN Notices*, volume 29, pages 31–37, December 1994.
13. N. Young. Online file caching. Technical Report PCS–TR97–320, Dartmouth College, 1998.
14. S. Hauck Z. Li. Configuration prefetch for single context reconfigurable coprocessors. In *International Symposium on Field-Programmable Gate Arrays*, pages 65–74, Feb. 1998.

Multiple Stereo Matching Using an Extended Architecture

Miguel Arias-Estrada, Juan M. Xicotencatl

Computer Science Department
National Institute for Astrophysics, Optics and Electronics
Tonanzintla, Puebla, Mexico
ariasm@inaoep.mx

Abstract. In this paper, an FPGA based architecture for stereo vision is presented. The architecture provides a high-density disparity map in real time. The architecture is based on area comparison between an image pair using the sum of absolute differences. The architecture scans the input images in partial columns, which are then processed in parallel. The system performs monolithically on a pair of images in real time. An extension to the basic architecture is proposed in order to compute disparity maps on more than 2 images.

1   Introduction

In computer vision, stereo algorithms intend to recover depth information by combining information from two cameras separated by a distance previously established, but in some cases depth information is unreliable or insufficient for example in mobile robotics or surface recovering for automatic 3D-model acquisition. Furthermore, several applications like robotics and autoguided vehicles require real-time performance but, the process is computational expensive for conventional computers.

A functional real-time stereo system requires knowledge about the computational cost along the different stages of processing in the algorithm to found possible redundant calculation or characteristics that let us increase the processing speed or decrement hardware complexity. However, some stereo systems based on simplifications or assumptions on the input images are designed around heuristic considerations, but their hardware implementation is not straightforward. To avoid this problem, dedicated hardware for real-time stereo can be implemented based on higher structured algorithms like those found in area comparison. Several systems have been proposed based on similarity measurements like the Sum of Absolute Differences (SAD), Sum of the Squared Differences (SSD), and the coefficient of correlation [2][4][7].

The main problem in stereo disparity computation is the location of the possible correspondence points between image pairs. Dealing with all the possible

G. Brebner and R. Woods (Eds.): FPL 2001, LNCS 2147, pp. 203-212, 2001.

correspondence points goes beyond the computational capabilities of current computers because of the combinational explosion of the search.

FPGA implementation is attractive since a specific architecture can be designed for real time operation with an inherent capacity to work in parallel. Hishihara [1] developed a stereo vision system based on FPGAs with an algorithm adapted for hardware implementation. The algorithm is based on the sign of the Laplacian of Gaussian. Another approach is the INRIA PERLe-1 board [2], which uses a central processing nucleus with four memory banks. The system centred in the PART engine [3] for stereo computation is composed of 16 FPGAs with both global and local memory at each device. The FPGAs used in this system are of relatively high density and they are configured in a toroidal network. Again, the communication protocol and the architecture partition among FPGAs complicate the design.

In our work we propose a monolithic architecture, i.e. in a single chip, for real time stereo disparity computation based on area similarity then, an extension to the basic architecture is proposed. The present work is organised as follows: first an introduction to the stereo matching problem is discussed then, the basic architecture is presented and his extension discussed. Later, implementation details and preliminary results are presented. Finally a conclusion and further work are given.

2   Stereo Matching

The basic idea behind all stereo vision algorithms is to find which pixels in the two images are projections of the same physical locations in the three dimensional scene. Given a pixel in one image, it can generally match several pixels in the other image, but only one of these matches is correct.

There are two main techniques to process the stereo images: feature–based techniques and the area–based techniques. Area-based methods produce high-density disparity maps, they have extremely regular algorithmic structures and they can be used to propose a convenient hardware architecture, so they were chosen for our architecture.

2.1   Epipolar Geometry

In order to decrease the hardware complexity and the number of operations, the *epipolar restriction* is used. With the epipolar restriction, in an arrangement with two cameras with their principal axes in parallel, the epipolar lines are constrained to lie along scan lines or to lie along the columns. The stereo baselines are parallel to the scan lines or the columns and the image sensors are in the same plane, as show in figure 1. The difference in camera positions is purely a horizontal or vertical translation. Any pixel visible in an epipolar line of one image will appear at a shifted position in the corresponding epipolar line of the other image, assuming that the pixel is not hidden in the second image.

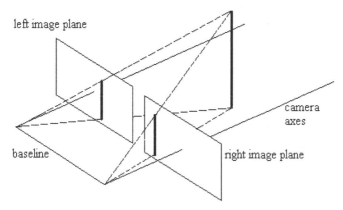

Fig. 1. Stereo camera arrangement shows an object and the corresponding images in the two cameras.

In general, if the sensors are in the same plane and the images obtained are conveniently aligned, i.e., epipolar lines coincide with scan lines or columns or both [5][8]. Then, it can be considered that between each pair of sensors in the arrangement the epipolar restriction is satisfied and the computation complexity is reduced. The design described in this paper can process multiple images obtained by multiple sensors with the described configuration.

2.2   Matching Algorithm, Description, and Implementation

First, given any two or more views of the same scene, at some image scale, a degree of similarity exists between the views, and in general, the coarser the scale the more similar the views become. These effects form the basis for matching area based stereo algorithms by the explanation that now follows. If a view is spatially quantised into smaller subregions, eventually any given subregion will begin to look more similar to its corresponding subregion in the other view. In this way, the similarity values are computed by comparing a fixed window in the reference image to a shifting window in the second image. The shifting window is moved over the first one by integer increments along the corresponding epipolar line and a curve of similarity values is generated for integer disparity values. The sum of absolute differences (SAD) computation technique was chosen in the architecture due to its low implementation complexity.

The area-based algorithm using the SAD can be resumed in equation 1:

$$\min_{d \in [0,D]} \left\{ \sum_{i=-n}^{n} \sum_{j=-m}^{m} |I_R(x+i, y+i) - I_L(x+i+d, y+i)| \right\} \qquad (1)$$

where: I_R and I_L are the right and left image respectively,
         x is an index on the columns,
         y is an index on the rows,
         d is the disparity index,
         n and m define the size of the correlation window and
         D is the maximum value for disparity

If equation 1 is applied to each pixel in the images, it can be rewritten as:

$$min \begin{bmatrix} \sum_{i=-n}^{n} \sum_{j=-m}^{m} |I_R(x+i,y+i) - I_L(x+i,y+i)| \\[2em] \sum_{i=-n}^{n} \sum_{j=-m}^{m} |I_R(x+i,y+i) - I_L(x+i+1,y+i)| \\[2em] \sum_{i=-n}^{n} \sum_{j=-m}^{m} |I_R(x+i,y+i) - I_L(x+i+2,y+i)| \\[1em] \vdots \\[1em] \sum_{i=-n}^{n} \sum_{j=-m}^{m} |I_R(x+i,y+i) - I_L(x+i+D,y+i)| \end{bmatrix} \qquad (2)$$

If for each disparity index exists a module to compute the window, then equation 2 suggests an implementation to the stereo architecture. However, the principal inconvenient for this implementation is that the modules require a large amount of memory to store the windows until the minimisation operation takes place. To solve this problem, it was noticed that the calculation of windows is a recursive computation, where adjacent pixels in overlapping windows are present, so it is not necessary to compute the complete similarity value for a pixel if the adjacent pixel have one already computed [7].

At this point, the main problem with the SAD matching technique is the size of the window, which need to be larger enough to include enough variations of intensity to make the matching, but small enough to prevent the effect of projective distortion [4]. If the window is too small and it does not cover sufficient variation of intensity, it gives a poor estimation because its SNR is low. On the other hand, if the window is too large and covers a region in which the depth of the points of the scene (i.e. the density) varies then the position of the SAD minimum can not present correct coincidence due to different projective distortions between the left and right images. In the literature, a recommend window size of 7×7 for real time applications [6].

3   Top Level Architecture

The architecture was developed based on an FPGA device, which is interfaced to two memory banks. The architecture is intended as a general engine for high-speed image processing. In order to maximise performance, the design minimise the number of accesses to the image memory banks storing temporal results in registers inside the FPGA. These registers contain the essential values to implement the pipeline in the architecture. The top level of the architecture is shown in figure 2.

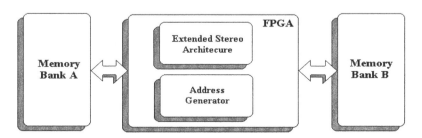

Fig. 2. FPGA based General-purpose engine for high-speed image processing and top level of the stereo matching system.

The main components of the architecture are two RAM memory banks, an address generator, and the stereo computation architecture. These components are described next:

Stereo Architecture. The stereo architecture reads pixels from the first RAM bank and processes them to obtain a dense disparity map. The resulting dense disparity map is send to the second RAM bank to storage.

Memory Banks. There are two memory banks. The first one contains the intensity images coded in 8-bit grey levels to be processed and is segmented in different spaces to store several images. Memory bank B receives the disparity data from the FPGA.

Address generator module. The address generator creates the addressing sequence to access the image pixels to read a window. The module also generates the addresses to the second memory bank to write the data computed by the architecture. The module generates the control signals for the architecture. The address generator is a specific purpose microprocessor with a small set of instructions. The next section describes the stereo architecture, which is the central part of the system.

3.1   Basic Stereo Architecture

Based on the discussion in section 2.2 and the considerations made in [7], it was implemented the *disparity basic module*. Figure 3 shows this module, here the *absolute-difference submodule* performs a similarity measurement between pixels from the reference image and pixels from the shifted image, the *computing columns submodule* sums the results from previous submodule to avoid the redundancy in the windows computations [2][7], and the *computing windows submodule,* obtains the sum of the results from the column submodule to form the window. Finally, a *minimum submodule* is added to compute the minimum value between the window generated in the module and the window formed in a previous module.

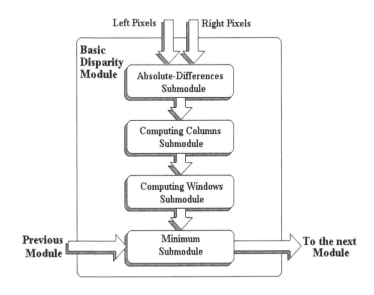

Fig. 3. The computing disparity basic module.

In figure 3, the Address Generator supplies the left and right pixels from the external memory and a previous disparity module calculates the window value at the input. In order to use the disparity module in a stereo architecture, it is necessary to assign a module for each disparity index and put them in cascade. Since pixels from external memory are multiplexed in the same input bus, a latch is used to separate them. Here, the pixels are read in partial columns from external memory to form the columns of the windows. In this way, in each module the columns are accumulated to compute the window values. To produce the movement between windows, the right pixels are delayed. The system architecture is shown in figure 4.

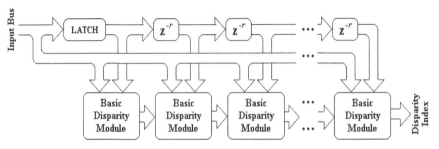

Fig. 4. System architecture for calculating disparity.

In figure 4, to calculate one 7-pixels column, four-column memory accesses ($r =4$) are needed. Pixel from column 8 is read but not used at this moment. It is stored in a register to be used in the computation of the next 7-pixels column that belongs to the next matching window in the next row [7]. In this way, the architecture can compute two disparity values at the same time. The communications between each module include the values that minimise the SAD criteria and the module number where the minimum value occurs. In the last module, the output is considered the disparity index.

3.2   Extended Architecture

There are stereo algorithms which can obtain accurate depth maps, but these techniques tend to be heuristics or they are computationally expensive that can not be implemented in hardware for real-time applications. In some applications, it can be necessary to process multiple stereo images from the same scene to obtain reliable depth maps. With this purpose, the basic stereo architecture is extended to compute more than one disparity map at the same time. This is possible since in the basic disparity module, almost all submodules yield temporal data that are erased or overwritten during windows computation except for the data in the computing window submodule. If pixels from the reference images and shifting images are multiplexed in time then added multiple computing window submodule to the basic module, it can process multiple stereo images. With this assumption the design area in the FPGA is maintained low. The disparity module with the additional computing window submodule is called *extended disparity module* and it is shown next

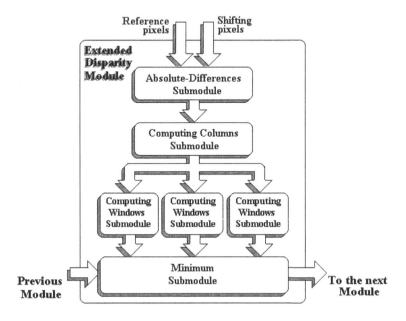

Fig. 5. Extended disparity module shown with three windows submodules. The module can have more than three of these submodules.

Figure 5 shows the extendend disparity module block diagram. In order to compute the different windows, successive cycles are assigned to it, i.e., in one cycle takes place the calculation for one window, in the next cycle take place the next window calculation, and so on. With this assumption, the system remains with low area requirements and uses the same configuration of the system shown in figure 5. In this context, a cycle means the calculation set to obtain the value of one window. The extended system is presented in figure 6.

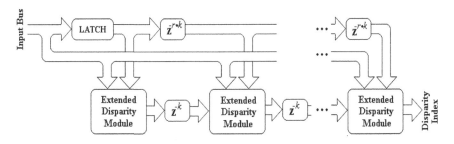

Fig. 6 Stereo system using the extended disparity modules

In the previous figure, k represents the number of stereo pairs to be processed. Delays between each pair of the extended modules are used to compensate the multiplexation in time of the pixels from the multiple images. At the output of the architecture the disparity indexes are multiplexed in time like the images.

4   Implementation and Results

The architecture was prototyped using VHDL and Foundation 2.1i tools, and synthesised for a XCV800HQ240-6 Virtex family device from Xilinx.

First, we will present the operation of the disparity module, the extended module just have extra signals that let choose among the computing windows submodules. The module was tested using a frequency of 50 MHz, but the maximum operation frequency for the basic module is 72 MHz.

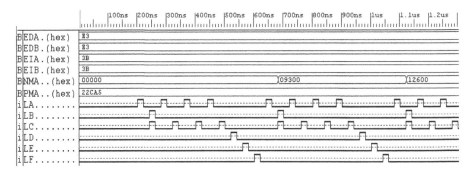

Fig. 7. Basic module simulation.

In figure 7, *EDA* and *EDB* are pixels from the reference images; *EIA* and *EIB* are pixels from the shifting images; *NMA* is the output to the next module, this signal contains the SAD value that minimises the criteria and its position, i.e., the disparity index. *PMA* is the input from signals that contain the disparity index and minimum value from the previous module. The disparity index is coded in the lower 5-bit in the *NMA* and *PMA* buses. Here, the *EDA*, *EDB*, *EIA,* and *IEB* signals have constant values to simplify the example. Every time that *LB* goes high the minimisation takes place. The *LA* and *LC* signals control the first two submodules and the *LD* and *LE* signals control the last submodule before minimisation.

The extended architecture was tested with $r= 4$, $k=1$, $D =16$ with a pair of stereo images (figure 8). The second stereo test compares the architecture results with the software implementation of the algorithm, software tests were implemented in MATLAB. As with other stereo techniques, which use the area correlation, a post-processing step is required. The postprocessing is done at present in software.

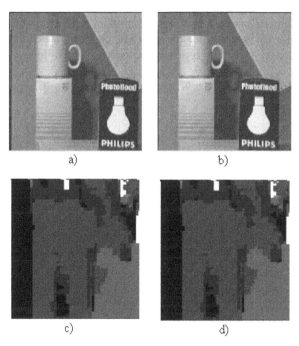

Fig. 8. Stereo pair images and results, a) and b) Original stereo pair, c) Software implementation in Matlab, d) post-synthesis simulation from the FPGA implementation.

Synthesis results for a XCV800HQ240-6 Xilinx FPGA device are summarised as follows: the extended architecture requires 4210 Slices or around 69Kgates (just the 46% of the total capacity of the device) to implement 16 disparity levels, operating at a frequency of 66 MHz. At this clock frequency, the architecture is capable of more than 71 disparity images computation per second for images which have a size of 320×240 pixels.

The optimesed structure can compute more than one hundred disparity maps. Individual modules and a simplified architecture with more modules are being validated in real applications. As a comparison with other architectures (DSP and software) for real-time stereo disparities reported in [9], our approach outperforms the fastest of them by a factor of 3.

5   Conclusions

An extended architecture for real-time stereo vision computation was presented. The proposed architecture is based on only one high density FPGA, which contains a parallel structure distributed in only one device. The basic processing modules are relatively simple and they do not require special operations to the memory banks or communication between modules. The architecture can achieve faster than real-time operation and it can easily be extended for larger images. The use of FPGAs as implementation media, permit fast development, and reconfigurability of the number of disparity modules. Furthermore, the modules can be reconfigured to implement other correlation criteria instead of the sum of absolute differences, to minimise noise and/or explore different performance for a specific application. All these possibilities are being evaluated in an FPGA coprocessing board for real-time 3D recovery and modeling.

References

1. H.K. Hishihara and T Poggio. *Stereo Vision for robotics*. In ISRR83 Conference, Bretton Woods, New Hamphshire, 1983.
2. O. Faugeras, B. Hotz H. Mathieu, T. Vieville, Z Zhang, P Fua, E. Theron, L. Moll, G. Berry, J. Vuillemin, P. Bertin, and C. Proy, *Real time correlation - based stereo: algorithm, implementations an applications.* INRIA Technical report #2013, August 1993.
3. Woodfill, John and Von Herzen Brian. *Real time Stereo vision on the PARTS reconfigurable Computer.* Interval Research Corporation report.
4. T. Kanade and M. Okutomi. A stereo matching algorithm with an adaptative window. Theory and experiments. *IEEE transactions on Pattern Analysis and Machine Intelligence,16(9): 920 - 932. September 1994.*
5. T. Kanade, H. Kano, S. Kimura, A. Yoshida, K. Oda. *Development of a video Rate Stereo Machine*. Robotics Institute. Carnagie Mellon University. 1996
6. Pascual Fua. *Combining stereo and Monocular Information to compute Dense Depth Maps that preserve depth discontinuities*. In Proceedings of the 12th International Joint Conference on Artificial Intelligence, pp. 1292 -1298, August 1991.
7. Miguel Arias-Estrada, Juan M. Xicotencatl, *A Real Time FPGA based Architecture for Stereo Vision*. SPIE Electronic Imaging 2001 – Photonics West, dedicated conference on Real Time Imaging V. San Jose, CA, Jan 2001.
8. Point Grey Research, Trinocular commercial cameras. *http://www.ptgrey.com*
9. K. Konolige. *Small Vision Systems: Hardware and Implementation*. Eighth International Symposium on Robotics Research, Hayama, Japan. October 1997.

Implementation of a NURBS to Bézier Conversor with Constant Latency[*]

Paula N. Mallón, Montserrat Bóo, and Javier D. Bruguera

Department of Electronic and Computer Engineering,
University of Santiago de Compostela, Spain

Abstract. In this paper, a FPGA implementation is presented to carry out the conversion process from NURBS to Bézier curves. It has a simple and regular timing schedule with a constant latency which reduces the area requirements with respect to previous implementations. The operation frequency obtained with the Xilinx tools, is around 13 MHz. The scheme we propose can be easily extended to process NURBS and Bézier surfaces.

1 Introduction

NURBS (Non-Uniform Rational B-Splines) are a standard in computer graphics for the representation of curves and surfaces [1], [2]. However, all the computer graphics hardware is focused on surfaces modelled by triangle meshes. So, NURBS surfaces are typically tessellated in software into triangles prior to transmission to the rendering hardware. The first step of NURBS tessellation is the conversion from NURBS to Bézier surfaces. After this, each Bézier surface is tessellated into triangles [3].

In this paper we present a FPGA implementation for the conversion from NURBS curves into Bézier curves. We have used the Xilinx XC4000–Series [4]. In contrast with previous implementations [5], the proposed architecture has a simple and regular timing schedule with a fixed number of cycles per conversion step. This implies a reduction of hardware requirements. On the other hand the critical path has been optimized resulting in an operating frequency of 13.39 MHz[1].

2 Conversion Algorithm from NURBS to Bézier Curves

In this section a brief introduction to NURBS and Bézier curves and the conversion algorithm are presented. A more detailed review is in [1] and [2].

---

[*] This work was supported in part by the *Secretaria Xeral de Investigacion e Desenvolvemento de Galicia* (Spain) under contract PGIDT99-PXI20602B.

[1] The same architecture has been implemented with Synopsys using a 0.35 μm MI-ETEC standard cell library [6] and the resulting operating frequency is 56 MHz.

G. Brebner and R. Woods (Eds.): FPL 2001, LNCS 2147, pp. 213–222, 2001.

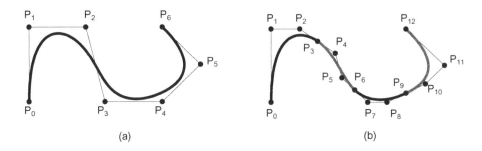

(a)   (b)

Fig. 1. B-Spline curves: (a) 3–degree NURBS curve (b) Decomposition into four 3-degree Bézier curves

2.1   B-Spline Curves: NURBS and Bézier

p–degree B-Spline curves are specified by a set of $n+1$ control points ($\{P_i\}$ with $i \in [0, n]$). These control points are fitted using $p-degree$ parametric functions. To complete the definition, a set of real and positive numbers, organized in a nondecreasing sequence named *knot vector* $U = \{u_0, \ldots, u_m\}$ ($u_i \le u_{i+1}$), are required. Each u_i ($i \in [0, m]$) is called *knot* and the number of knots in a knot vector is $m - 1 = n + p$. Each interval $[u_i, u_{i+1}]$ (with $u_i \ne u_{i+1}$) is called the i *knot span*. The number of knot spans is related to the number of different knots in the knot vector and their *multiplicity* s, that is, the number of times each knot appears in the knot vector.

Due to their flexibility, non uniform knot vectors, – characterized by different–sized spans –, are usually employed. The curves defined over these knot vectors are named **Non–Uniform Rational B-Splines** (NURBS). In Fig. 1(a) an example of a 3–degree NURBS curve is depicted. The curve approximates $n+1 = 7$ control points $\{P_0, \ldots, P_6\}$ and it is characterized by a knot vector $\{u_0, \ldots, u_{10}\}$ with $u_0 = \ldots = u_3, u_7 = \ldots = u_{10}$ and four knot spans. The definition of a p–degree NURBS curve is given by:

$$C(u) = \frac{\sum_{i=0}^{n} N_{i,p}(u)w_i P_i}{\sum_{i=0}^{n} N_{i,p}(u)w_i} \qquad u_{min} \le u \le u_{max} \qquad (1)$$

where $C(u)$ is a point of the curve for the parametric value u. $\{w_i\}$ are the weight factors for the control points and $\{N_{i,p}(u)\}$ are the p–degree B–Spline basis functions (usually, $p \le 7$). Each one of these basis functions $\{N_{i,p}(u)\}$ determines how strongly the control point P_i influences the curve at the parametric value u. Specifically, a NURBS curve is fully defined by its $n + 1$ control points and the corresponding knot vector. It is important to mention that, even when the generic Equation (1) implies $n + 1$ summations to compute each point of a p–degree curve, only $p + 1$ terms are non–zero. This is due to the fact that only $p + 1$ basis functions are non–zero for each parametric value u [2].

The other geometric representation we are going to introduce is the Bézier curve. A p-degree Bézier curve is specified by $p+1$ control points. In Fig. 1(b) four 3–degree Bézier curves are depicted (each one is indicated in a different colour). For example the first Bézier curve is defined by four control points: $\{P_0, P_1, P_2, P_3\}$. The general equation to define a p–degree Bézier curve is:

$$C(u) = \frac{\sum\limits_{i=0}^{p} B_{i,p}(u) w_i P_i}{\sum\limits_{i=0}^{p} B_{i,p}(u) w_i} \tag{2}$$

where $\{B_{i,p}(u)\}$ are the classical p–degree Bernstein polynomials. Only $p+1$ control points are required to define the curve.

2.2 Conversion Algorithm from NURBS to Bézier

A NURBS curve can be decomposed in sections each one corresponding with a knot span in the knot vector. Each section can be mathematically represented as a Bézier curve maintaining the original shape. As an example and according to the definitions presented in Sect. 2.1, Fig. 1 shows the decomposition of a 3–degree NURBS curve into its constituent 3–degree Bézier curves. Each Bézier curve is defined by $p+1=4$ control points.

The conversion process from NURBS to Bézier curves is summarized in Fig. 2. Initially we consider a p–degree NURBS curve defined over a general knot vector $U = \{\underbrace{u_0, \ldots, u_p}_{u_0 = \ldots = u_p}, u_{p+1}, \ldots, u_{m-(p+1)}, \underbrace{u_{m-p}, \ldots, u_m}_{u_{m-p} = \ldots = u_m}\}$ and a set of $n+1$ control points $\{P_{i,0}\}$. $p - s$ iterations are necessary for the conversion process in each section, such as, in iteration r a new set of $p - s - r + 1$ control points $\{P_{i,r}\}$ are obtained. The conversion process can be summarized as follows:

The first step is to analyze each one of the internal knots to determine its multiplicity. Each knot with multiplicity lower than the curve degree[2] has to be replicated in the knot vector until it appears p–times. After that, the new control points have to be computed. To obtain these points, a set of $p - s$ α coefficients are required (see Equation (3) in Fig. 2).

For each Bézier curve computation a subset of $p+1$ control points, $\{P_{k-p-s,0}, \ldots, P_{k-s,0}\}$, have to be considered. The first s points $\{P_{k-p-s,0}, \ldots, P_{k-p-1,0}\}$ are named *direct points* and do not have to be processed. The other control points have to be recomputed according to the Equation (4) in Fig. 2. It is important to note the recursive structure of this equation. As a consecuence, in each iteration r a set of $p - s - r + 1$ points are processed as shown in Fig. 3.

Next, the set of control points and the knot vector are rebuilt. The new control point set is formed by the direct points and the upper and lower diagonal of the triangular structure (Fig. 3), set $\{P_{k-p+r,r}\}$ and $\{P_{k-s,r}\}$ respectively. The upper diagonal together with the direct points define the actual Bézier curve and

---

[2] Multiplicity $s = p + 1$ could be possible only on the external knots.

l=p+1   /* *Index of the first knot in the knot vector* */
while (there are knot not analyzed) {
   s = multiplicity of knot u_k; k=l+s−1
   for $(i = k - p + 1; i \leq k - s; i{+}{+})$ /* *Calculation of α coeff.* */

$$\alpha_i = \frac{u_k - u_{k-s}}{u_{i+p} - u_{k-s}} \tag{3}$$

   for $(r = 1; r \leq p - s; r{+}{+})$ {   /* *New control points* */
      for $(i = k - p + 1; i \leq k - s; i{+}{+})$ {

$$P_{i,r} = \alpha_i(P_{i,r-1} - P_{i-1,r-1}) + P_{i-1,r-1} \tag{4}$$

} }
/* *Change the set of control points and the knot vector* */

$$P = \{P_{0,0}, \ldots, \underbrace{P_{k-p-s,0}, \ldots, P_{k-p-1,0}}_{direct\ points},$$

$$\underbrace{P_{k-p,0}, \ldots, P_{k-s,p-s}}_{upper\ diagonal}, \overbrace{P_{k-s,p-s-1}, \ldots, P_{k-s,0}}^{lower\ diagonal}, \ldots, P_{n,0}\}$$

$$U = \{\underbrace{0, \ldots, 0}_{p+1}, u_{p+1}, \ldots, \underbrace{u_{k-s+1}, \ldots, u_k}_{s}, \underbrace{u_k, \ldots, u_k}_{p-s} \ldots, u_{m-p-1}, \underbrace{1, \ldots, 1}_{p+1}\}$$

/* *Relabelling of set of control points and knot vector* */
   $P = \{P_{0,0}, \ldots, P_{n+(p-s),0}\}$ $U = \{u_0, \ldots, u_{m+(p-s)}\}$
   l=p−s+1   /* *Index of the next knot* */
}

Fig. 2. NURBS to Bézier conversion algorithm

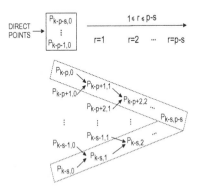

Fig. 3. Triangular recursive structure

the lower diagonal is necessary for the next iterations. Moreover, the knot u_k is inserted $p - s$ times in the knot vector. Finally, the set of control points and the knot vector are relabeled.

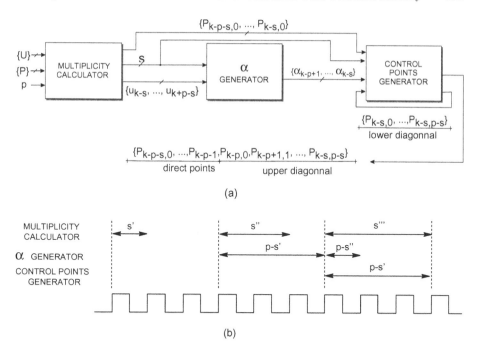

Fig. 4. (a) Block diagram of the architecture (b) Timing diagram (p=4)

3   Conversion Architecture

The algorithm for the NURBS to Bézier conversion and the proposed architecture have three steps (see Fig. 4(a)): knot multiplicity calculation, α coefficients computation and processing of the new control points.

In the *Multiplicity Calculator* module, the multiplicity of each knot in the knot vector is determined. This value is introduced in the α *Generator* in order to compute the required α values (Equation (3)). These values together with the multiplicity are introduced in the *Control Points Generator* to calculate the new control points (Equation (4)).

A timing diagram for a 4–degree NURBS curve is shown in Fig. 4(b). The figure is detailed for three knots u_6, u_7 and u_9 with multiplicities $s' = 1$, $s'' = 2$ ($u_7 = u_8$) and $s''' = 3$ ($u_9 = u_{10} = u_{11}$) respectively. Each module has $p - 1$ available cycles for its computations, where p is the curve degree. The first module only requires s cycles, that is, the multiplicity of the current knot, and the second and the third modules need $(p - s)$ cycles. In the remaining cycles the modules are idle. The total number of cycles for each Bézier curve computation is $3 * (p - 1)$. This easy and fixed timing schedule is an interesting alternative to other previous solutions [5].

For the implementation using the XC4000 Xilinx family a wordlength of 24 bits for the control points and 4 bits for the knots were employed. The implementation has been particularized for a NURBS curve with 18 control points.

Table 1. CLB count/Timing results

(a) Multiplicity Calculator

curve degree	# CLB				frequency(MHz)*
	FIFO queue	xor gates	counter	Total	
$p = 4$	78	1	2	95	67.12
$p = 3$	77	1	1	91	68.99
$p = 2$	74	1	1	80	77.16

(b) α Generator

# CLB					frequency(MHz)*
substractor	ROM	multiplier	CLA	Total	
3	4	27	24	61	41.97

(c) Control Points Generator

curve degree	# CLB		frequency(MHz)*
	QCPP	Total	
$p = 4$	342	1294	13.10
$p = 3$	342	809	13.36
$p = 2$	342	430	12.52

* With input/output pins

To evaluate the scalability of the proposed architecture, three diferent degrees ($p = 2, 3, 4$) have been implemented. The implementation results, number of CLBs and operating frequency, are summarized in Table 1.

3.1   Multiplicity Calculator

The general structure of the Multiplicity Calculator module is shown in Fig. 5. The FIFO queue contains all the knots which define the curve in process. The highest multiplicity value is the curve degree p, so, to compute each Bézier curve it is only necessary to take into account the knots stored in the first p positions. Each cycle, two knots are compared with a set of XOR gates. If the compared knots are equal, the multiplicity is incremented in the counter. The FIFO queue is shifted as shown in Table 2. Note that the number of shifts is different for the last cycle, the $p - 1$ cycle. This scheme is repeated until all the knots of the NURBS curve have been processed. After this, the system is ready to process the following NURBS curve.

The CLB count and frequency results are shown in Table 1(a). The FIFO queue only would need two CLBs per 4–bit knot. However, Xilinx tool tries to exploit the spatial locality of the system, so that each pair of bits of the same knot are not necessarily stored in the same CLB. This fact leads to a greater number of CLBs. The counter is the only element in this module which depends on the curve degree, and has been implemented as an incrementer. The remaining CLBs are used in the control unit.

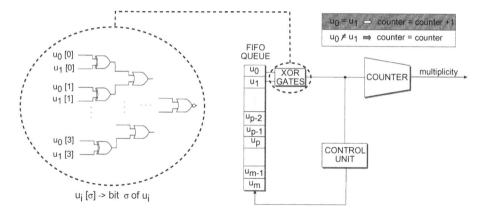

Fig. 5. Multiplicity calculator

Table 2. Control Unit (Multiplicity calculator)

input knots	i–cycle	FIFO shift	counter
$u_l = u_{l+1}$	$i \in [1,\dots,(p-2)]$	1 position	$counter + 1$
	$(p-1)$	2 positions	$counter + 1 = s$
$u_l \neq u_{l+1}$	$i \in [1,\dots,(p-2)]$	0 position	$counter$
	$(p-1)$	1 position	$counter = s$

3.2 α Generator

In this module the α coefficients are calculated. For a knot u_k with multiplicity s, the set of α coefficients to be calculated is $\{\alpha_{k-p+1},\dots,\alpha_{k-s}\}$ (see Fig. 2). Accordingly to Equation (3) and as $u_{k-p+1} = \dots = u_{k-s}$ and $u_{k-s+1} = \dots = u_k$ the α coefficients are calculated as: $\{\frac{u_k-u_{k-s}}{u_{k+1}-u_{k-s}},\dots,\frac{u_k-u_{k-s}}{u_{k+p-s}-u_{k-s}}\}$.

The architecture we propose is shown in Fig. 6. The division operation required to calculate the α coefficients is implemented as a reciprocal and a multiplication. The reciprocals are stored in a table of size $2^4 \times 16$–bits[3].

The substractors are implemented as prefix tree adders [7]. A 8×4–bits radix–4 signed–digit multiplier is used to obtain the α coefficients. The partial products are selected with a set of 4:1 mux and then added in a 4:2 CSA Wallace tree. A final 12–bits CLA is required to obtain the result in non redundant representation. Implementation results are shown in Table 1(b). The hardware complexity of this module is independent of the curve degree.

3.3 Control Points Generator

The control points are calculated using Equation (4). The architecture we propose is depicted in Fig. 7(a). It mainly consists of $(p-1)$ Q Control Point

---

[3] Implemented with a Xilinx's macrocells generation tool, CORE Generator.

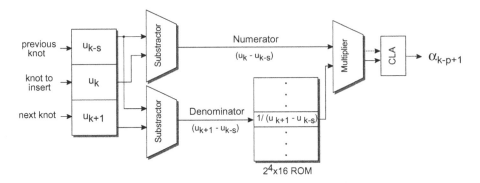

Fig. 6. Block diagram of the α Generator

Processors (QCPP), where the new control points are obtained. For a p–degree NURBS curve and a knot to insert u_k with multiplicity s, $2(p-s)-1$ new control points are obtained in consecutive $p - s$ cycles corresponding to the upper and lower diagonal of the triangular structure (see Fig. 3). The upper diagonal is obtained from the first processor $QCPP_0$ and the lower diagonal is picked up, in iteration r, from processor $QCPP_{p-s-r}$.

Each $QCPP_{i-(k-p+r-1)}$ processor uses as inputs $\{P_{(i-1)+(k-p+r-1),r-1}, \alpha_{i+1}, P_{i+(k-p+r-1),r-1}\}$ and computes the control point $P_{i+(k-p+r-1),r}$. Each time a knot is processed, the set of $p+1$ initial control points are located in the working set register: the s direct points which do not modify their values and the $p-s+1$ triangular points (the inputs to the triangular structure). The computed upper diagonal together with the direct points define the Bézier curve in process. The lower diagonal is stored in the working set register in order to consider the next computations.

Fig. 7(c) shows a timing diagram example for the conversion of a 4–degree NURBS curve. It is particularized for two knots u_5 and u_9 with multiplicities 1 and 3 respectively. Only $p - 1 = 3$ QCPPs are required. The columns show the inputs/outputs of each module. The upper diagonal ($QCPP_0$ output) is marked with circles whilst the lower diagonal is indicated with gray boxes. Note that the lower diagonal is obtained in a different $QCPP$ module each iteration. The processing of the first knot u_5 requires $p - s = 3$ cycles whereas for the second knot u_9 only $p - s = 1$ cycle is required and during the last 2 cycles the QCPPs are idle.

Fig. 7(b) details the QCPP processor architecture. Basically it consists of a 24–bits substractor and a 24×7–bits multiplier. The multiplier operand, the α coefficient, is recoded to a radix–4 signed digit representation and the partial products are added in a CSA tree. Finally, a 24–bits CLA is used to obtain the control point in non redundant representation. The results of the implementation are shown in Table 1(c). The number of CLBs is strongly dependent on the degree of the curve since the numbers of QCPPs is $p - 1$.

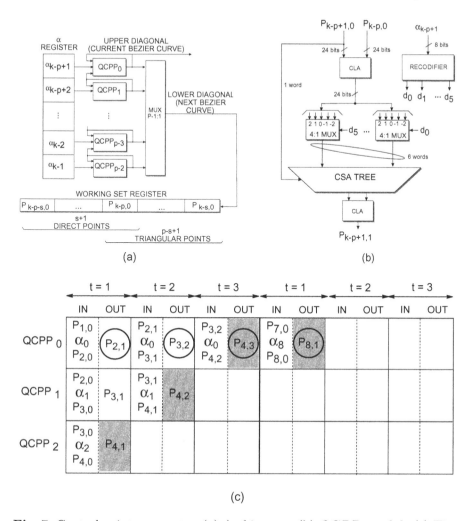

Fig. 7. Control points generator: (a) Architecture (b) $QCPP_0$ module (c) Timing

4   Architecture Evaluation

The architecture has been implemented, in a XC4044XL FPGA using the Xilinx tools, for three degree values, namely $p = 2$, $p = 3$ and $p = 4$. The resulting number of CLBs and operating frequencies are shown in Table 3. Note that the total number of CLBs is obtained as the number of CLBs in Table 1(a), (b) and (c) plus CLBs devoted to control. As said before, these values have been obtained considering a wordlength of 24 bits. Consideration of a different wordlength would result in different values.

Most of the CLBs are included in the *Control Points Generator* (see Table 1). As the number of QCPPs is determined by the curve degree, the number of CLBs

Table 3. Global architecture CLB count and timing

curve degree	# CLB	frequency(MHz)
$p = 4$	1545	12.77
$p = 3$	970	13.39
$p = 2$	624	15.47

of this module and of the global architecture is strongly dependent on the curve degree. On the other hand, the operating frequency is also determined by the *Control Points Generator* module.

Finally, to process a p–degree curve defined over $n + 1$ control points, $(\lceil \frac{n}{2} - 1 \rceil * (p - 1))$ cycles are necessary. It has to be pointed out that any of the three architectures can be employed to process curves with other degrees. In such a way that, to process a curve with larger degree, more cycles are needed while for a smaller degree some of the QCPPs would remain iddle.

5   Conclusions

In this paper we have presented a FPGA implementation to perform the conversion from NURBS to Bézier curves. This architecture has a modular structure that can be pipelined in three stages: in the first stage the knot vector is analyzed to determine the multiplicity of each knot, in the second stage the conversion coefficients α are calculated and in the last stage the new control points are obtained. The resulting architecture has a constant latency determined by the curve degree.

Three particular implementations for three different curve degrees have been presented but each one of them can be used to process curves with other degrees. Moreover, this scheme can be easily extended to perform the conversion from NURBS to Bézier surfaces.

References

1. Foley, J.D.: Computer Graphics: Principles and Practice. 2nd edn. Ed. Addison-Wesley (1996)
2. Piegl, L., Tiller, W.: The NURBS Book. 2nd edn. Ed. Springer (1997)
3. Kumar, S., Manocha, D., Lastra, A.: Interactive Display of Large–Scaled NURBS models. IEEE Transactions on Visualization and Computer Graphics, Vol. 2, No. 4, (1996) 323–336
4. Xilinx 4000 Series datasheet: http://www.xilinx.com/products/products.htm
5. Mallón, P. N., Bóo, M., Bruguera, J.D.: Parallel Architecture for Conversion of NURBS Curves to Bézier Curves. Proc. Int. Conf. Euromicro 2000. Workshop on Digital Systems Design. DSD2000 (2000) 324–331
6. MIETEC: Library Data Book 0.35 μ CMOS Technology
7. Hauck, S., Hosler, M. M., Fry, T. W.: High–Performance Carry Chains for FPGA's. IEEE Transactions on VLSI Systems, Vol. 8, No. 2, (2000) 138–147

Reconfigurable Frame-Grabber for Real-Time Automated Visual Inspection (RT-AVI) Systems

Sergio A. Cuenca, Francisco Ibarra, and Rafael Alvarez

Universidad de Alicante, Departamento de Tecnología Informática y Computación,
Campus de San Vicente, Alicante, Spain
sergio@dtic.ua.es, ibarra@dtic.ua.es, rias@alu.ua.es

Abstract. In most of the automated systems for visual inspection tasks, real time requirements constitute an important aspect to have in to account in the design of them. Often, a frame-grabber attached to a computer using MMX-optimised software libraries is not enough to satisfy the above requirements and it is necessary to use expensive specialised hardware and architectures. Reconfigurable hardware gives us the best of both worlds: the flexibility of software and the high performance of customised hardware. In this paper we present a reconfigurable frame-grabber concept to integrate complex real-time processing functions needed for high-speed line inspection applications directly onboard. This allows the efficient hardware-software co-design to achieve high-performance low-cost solutions.

1 Introduction

In order to implant RT-AVI systems on industrial environments it is necessary, on one hand, to satisfy requirements of real time, robustness and reliability, and on the other, requirements of economic profitability. A strong commitment exists between the first ones and the last one.

The final price of an application, and therefore its economic feasibility, will depend on the development costs and the cost of the image acquisition and processing hardware. The different nature of the working environments and activities make very useful the use of commercial software supporting real time capable hardware during the development tasks. Nowadays, most image processing systems are implemented using MMX-optimised software libraries [1,2], running on personal workstations. These kind of systems offer a good performance/cost ratio covering a wide spectrum of applications. However, for more demanding time requirements, e.g. web inspection, document imaging or quality control in high-speed line inspection, it is necessary to use specialised hardware and architectures [3,4,5,6]. This customised hardware usually increases the cost, reduces the flexibility and limits the applications of the system.

Some approaches based on FPL have been proposed. In the intelligent camera concept [7,8], an FPGA is directly connected to the video-data stream and outputs data to a low bandwidth output bus; this eliminates the need for external frame-grabber, but limits the processing to 1D operations followed by a

G. Brebner and R. Woods (Eds.): FPL 2001, LNCS 2147, pp. 223–231, 2001.

data compression algorithm. On-board hardware processing concept has been applied to several frame-grabbers [2,9], these include FPL parts to perform a limited number of basic pixel transformations like thresholding, gain and lighting correction, gray scale, or 1D filters. These boards are attached to the PCI bus eliminating the need of data compression and leaves to the host the more sophisticated operations.

Our proposal, reconfigurable frame-grabber for texture analysis (RCFG), enlarges the possibilities of this concept to support complex algorithms for textured surfaces inspection and takes advantage of the FPL reconfigurability to suit the algorithm particularities. The on-board processing allows supplying the main processor with elaborated data rather than the unprocessed frame and, in many cases, reducing the data bandwidth required between the acquisition system and the main processor. The RCFG integrates the processing functions on datastream thus providing higher parallelism possibilities to reduce the frame latency. On the other hand, using reconfigurable hardware (FPGAs), we can make this frame grabber more flexible while retaining high speed performance. In this way, we only have to reprogram the hardware to perform a different pre-processing operation to each frame or application; and if we consider the frame grabber attached to the main processor with a bidirectional bus, the functionality of the frame grabber could be changed on demand in milliseconds.

2   Algorithms

Texture is an important characteristic when considering automatic inspection for quality control. A wide variety of measures have been proposed related to texture properties. Among them, statistics measures are widely used in the classification and inspection of textured surfaces [10,11,12,13] but although the performance of such algorithms is usually very good [14], their structure is complex and the data flow process is large. Consequently, the computation cost is high and the implementation in high speed production lines is difficult. In this work we propose a reconfigurable frame-grabber concept that permits the efficient hardware implementation of first and second order histograms extraction for statistical-based texture analysis.

The statistics used are generally based on the distributions of pixel features like pixel intensity, edginess magnitude, edginess direction, or sum and difference of intensity between neighbour pixels. When characterizing textures, both the individual elements and the statistical features derived from them may be used. Some of the most common statistics used are: Maximum Probability (Mp), K moments (Mk), K Inv. moments(Imk), Energy(En), Entropy(Et), Skew (Sk), Kurtosis (Ku), Cluster Shade(Cs), Clust. Prominence(Cp), Haralick's Correlation (Hc), etc...

On the other hand, the histograms may be based on the probabilities of single occurrences (first order histograms) or joint occurrences (second order histograms).

Some examples of first order histograms are:

Grey level histogram (GLH) computes the grey level probabilities P(i) of the image, where; i=0, 1, 2...G, and G is the number of grey levels.

Edginess histogram (EH), in this case the gradient with displacement d is calculated for every pixel, and then the histogram of gradient magnitude or direction probabilities are computed.

Some second order histograms are:

Grey level coocurrence histogram (GLCH) is based on the coocurrence matrix [1], this is constructed from the image by estimating the pair wise statistics of pixel features. Each element (i,j) of the matrix represents an estimate of the probability that two pixels with a specified separation have levels of the feature i and j. This probability can be estimated as Pq,d(i,j)=P(i,j)= Cq,d(i,j)/N. Where Cq,d(i,j) is the number of cooccurrences, the separation is specified by a displacement d and an angle q, and N is the total number of cooccurrences. The coocurrence histogram has GxG bins, where G is normally reduced to 32 or 16 grey levels.

Grey level sum and difference histograms (GLSH, GLDH) are similar to coocurrence, these are the histograms of the sum and difference of all pixels dx and dy apart. Similar features to coocurrence can be extracted combining sum and difference histograms. The probability distribution of GLDH can also be used for texture classification [3]. In this way, DIFFX and DIFFY are the histograms of absolute grey level differences between neighbour pixels computed in horizontal and vertical directions, respectively, while DIFF2 accumulates absolute differences in vertical and horizontal directions and DIFF4 in all four principal directions respectively, in a single histogram.

For texture classification, all these algorithms are usually applied on square image sub windows, mainly with 32x32 or 64x64 pixels and G=256, 32, 16 grey levels.

3   Design and Implementation of the Proposed Architecture

3.1   Logical Design

The general task that the RT-AVI system has to perform could be described as follows: every frame of RxC pixels is divided in R/SxC/S sub-windows of SxS pixels, then N features are extracted from every pixel and H histograms of B bins are calculated for every sub window. When the frame has been processed, NxR/SxC/S histograms are transferred to the host for statistics calculation and classification. If we analyse the actual calculations made from image acquisition to statistics classification we find four clearly separated stages shown in figure 1: image pre-processing, histogram calculation, statistics calculation and finally texture classification. The first two stages involve intensive computation on integer data so these tasks can be easily carried out by the reconfigurable parts of the frame grabber. The sophisticated floating point calculations required in the third and fourth stages are left to the main processor because of its superior performance/cost ratio in these tasks.

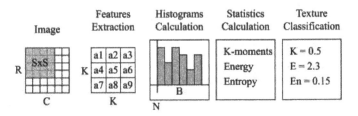

Fig. 1. Basic processing stages

A very simple and primitive solution would be as shown in figure 2. In this version we first read a frame from the camera and store it into the frame grabber's RAM; then we process that frame and calculate the histograms for each sub window, storing that histograms also on the on-board RAM; finally the host computer reads the histograms from the frame-grabber RAM and calculates statistics from them. This is far from optimal because it does not use any parallelism.

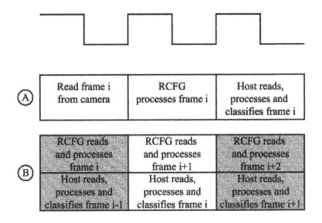

Fig. 2. Primitive solution with no parallelism (a) vs. parallel solution (b)

A better solution would try to improve performance by introducing parallelism at two different levels: camera - RCFG and RCFG - host. If we could process the frame line by line instead of the full frame at once, we would be processing the image at the same time we are reading it rather than after it has been read. Looking at the host, the RCFG does not need to wait until the host finishes the statistical calculations, instead it can be processing the next frame while the host processes the previous one.

To implement the parallelism between the camera and the RCFG we need to read the first K-1 lines before we start any processing since we need the lines above and below the one we are processing to implement the KxK convolution. Once we have read those lines we should pipeline this operation and keep processing a line while a new one is read. This requires some FIFOs to store these lines and maintain the pipelined execution. To parallelise the execution of the RCFG and the host, we must have, at least, two banks of onboard RAM so while the host reads the histograms for the previous frame the RCFG is writing the histograms for the next frame on a separate bank. Any single bank can be accessed by the host or the RCFG but not at the same time.

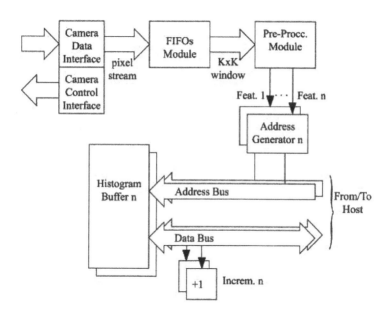

Fig. 3. Overview of the RCFG architecture

Figure 3 shows an overview of the architecture. Due to the simplicity of the pre-processing operations and taking advantage of the parallelism of the logical blocks of the FPGAs, the pixel data stream can be processed by fixed-point arithmetic units in a pipelined fashion. To provide greater flexibility we can assume the extraction of pixel features as a generic KxK convolution of the image pixels allowing simple additions, subtractions or even more complex pixel combinations involving more than just two pixels. K-1 FIFOs are required to pipeline these pre-processing operations. Using the pre-processing module several features can be extracted from every pixel allowing simultaneous calculation of different histograms for every subwindow.

Histogram computation is similar for both first and second order statistics. The histograms values (bins) are stored in external memories (Histogram Buffers); the pixel features previously extracted are used by the Address Generators to create the addresses of the bins that have to be incremented. An incrementer is used to carry out this operation and return the new bin value to the corresponding histogram buffer location. The Address Generators are critical components because they have to take into account the sub-window where the current pixel is included, hence all the histograms (N per sub-window) are calculated at the same time.

Several parameters of the architecture have to be set to perform the different measures, table 1 gives some of the possibilities. E.g. to implement GLCH with rotation invariant and taking windows of 32x32, the selected parameters are: S=32, N=4 (d=1 and q=0°, 45°, 90°, 135°), Preproc=Concatenation.

Table 1. Setting up the RCFG to perform different measures

Algorithm	S (window size)	N (num. of hist)	Preproc
GLH	64,32,16	1	IDENT
EH	64,32,16	1	SUB,CONV
GLCH	64,32,16	1 to 4	CONCAT
GLSDH	64,32,16	2 to 8	SUB,ADD
DIFF	64,32,16	1 to 4	SUB,ABS

3.2   Prototype Implementation

In order to validate the proposed architecture we are currently using a high performance prototyping board, the Celoxica RC-1000PP [15], and a line scan CCD camera, the DALSA Spark [8]. The Spark camera provides a resolution of 2048 pixels with 8-bit data @30MHz and a maximum line rate of 12KHz. The output is in EIA-644 (LVDS) format thus it can be directly attached to the RCFG by means of LVDS CMOS line drivers and receivers.

The RC-1000PP is a PCI board which carries a Xilinx Virtex V1000 FPGA device. This card is PCI compliant and is plugged into a PC computer (in our case a Pentium III) allowing simply interfacing between host and frame-grabber and bidirectional high rate data transfers. The on-board memory consists in four banks of asynchronous static RAM having 2Mbytes each and they can be accessed either in 8 or 32 bit mode. The card comes with a library of C functions that can be used by the host software to interface with the card (reading and writing to onboard memory, programming the FPGA, etc.). A fairly revolutionary language to specify the FPGA design is also included; this language is called

Handel C and is extremely similar to conventional C, though modified a little to allow hardware particularities. This language makes prototyping and design implementation extremely fast because it is mostly software oriented.

In the actual prototype we define the frame as a 1024x1024 256 levels grey scale image and is divided in 64x64 windows making a total of 256 windows. The histograms are stored as 32 bits values even though 16 bit values are more than enough but the RC-1000PP does not support 16 bits memory accesses. Thus 1Mb is required to store the processed frame and 256Kb are required to store the first order histograms of a single frame. The full process is divided into two stages; in the first stage (stage A) the FPGA writes the processed image in bank 0 and the histograms in bank 1 simultaneously, while the host reads banks 2 and 3 corresponding to the previous frame; in stage B the bank assignment is reversed and the FPGA writes to banks 2 and 3 and the host reads from banks 0 and 1. This division provides the required parallelism between host and FPGA. To achieve the desired parallelism between the FPGA and the camera a set of 6 on chip RAMs have been implemented, each consisting of 1024 positions of 8 bits. These RAMs are used alternatively on odd and even lines so the required pipelining is possible. The actual prototype implements the parallel version explained before, and is capable of performing a 3x3 convolution and storing the processed image and the histograms for the sub windows in 2 cycles per pixel (if we ignore pipelining start-up).

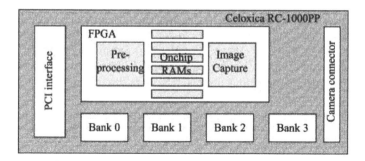

Fig. 4. The prototype architecture

3.3   Performance Comparison

The comparison has been made in a web inspection application using a line scan camera whose trigger is synchronised with the speed of the surface being analysed, being 5KHz the maximum line rate, 1 m/s the surface speed and 3 pixels/mm the required resolution.

Using a traditional frame-grabber, a frame consisting of 1024x1024 pixels is obtained every 205ms; if the frame-grabber has a double-buffering scheme such that the acquisition of the frame i is parallel to the transfer of the frame i-1 then the host has 205ms to process the frame i-1 (convolution, histograms, statistics calculation and classification of the 256 windows). If the time required to process frame i-1 is greater than 205ms then we start to loose lines from the next frame and we cannot perform 100

With the reconfigurable frame-grabber, the convolutions and histograms are calculated as the frame is captured so they take virtually no time and the host now has 205ms to perform the statistics and classifications, time that should be enough.

Table 2. Stage times for both implementations

Implementation	Capture	Conv + Hist	Statistics	Classification
Traditional	205ms	105ms	75ms	25ms
RCFG	205ms	0ms	75ms	130ms

4 Conclusion

The main proposal of this paper is the fact that by enhancing the frame grabber to perform first and second order histogram computations, a higher degree of parallelism is achievable. Because of the parallelism introduced between the frame grabber and the host, image acquisition, pre-processing and histogram calculation take virtually no time because they are simultaneous to the statistics computed by the host.

Nevertheless, the usage of reconfigurable hardware in the frame grabber provides extremely high speed computations with excellent flexibility allowing to change completely the functionality of the frame grabber simply by reconfiguring the FPGA and adjusting the image acquisition system to any new algorithms that may be developed in the main processor.

The degree of parallelism of this solutions depends greatly on the memory architecture of the system. We could greatly increase performance if we had more memory banks and therefore the possibility to calculate two or more histograms in parallel. When increasing the parallelism of the frame grabber the performance of the camera is critical since you may reach the point where you have to wait for the camera to provide pixels to continue computations.

References

1. Matrox, inc. http://www.matrox.com
2. Imaging Technology, inc. http://www.imaging.com

3. Baykut A. et al. Real-Time Defect Inspection of Textured Surfaces. Real-Time Imaging 6, 17-27, 2000.
4. Wei-Bin Chen and Gtan Libert. Real-Time Automatic Visual Inspection of High-speed Plane Products by Means of Parallelism. Real-Time Imaging 4, 379-388, 1998.
5. http://vetech.com
6. http://www.datacube.com
7. S.Hossain Hajimowlana, et. al. An In-Camera Data Stream Processing System for Defect Detection in Web Inspection Tasks. Real-Time Imaging 5, 23-34, 1999.
8. Dalsa inc. http:// www.dalsa.com/
9. I2S, inc. http://www.i2s-linescan.com/
10. R.M. Haralick. Computer and Robot Vision. Vol I. Addison-Wesley, New York, 1992.
11. P.C. Chen and T. Pavlidis, Segmentation by texture using a co-occurrence matrix and a split-and-merge algorithm, Computer Graphics and Image Processing 10, 172-182, 1979.
12. D. Harwood, T. Ojala, M. Pietikinen, S. Kelman and L.S. Davis, Texture classification by center-symmetric auto-correlation, using Kullback discrimination of distributions, Pattern Recognition Letters 16, 1-10, 1995.
13. K. Shiranita, T. Miyajima and R. Takiyama. Determination of meat quality by texture analisis. Pattern Recognition Letters, 19: 1319-1324, 1998.
14. T. Ojala, M. Pietikinen and D. Harwood. A comparative study of texture measures with classification based on feature distributions. Pattern Recognition 29(1): 51-59, 1996.
15. Celoxica, inc http://www.celoxica.com

Processing Models for the Next Generation Network

Jeff Lawrence

Intel Communications Group
Intel Corporation
12100 Wilshire Blvd
Suite 1800
Los Angeles
CA 90025
U.S.A.

Abstract. The nature of services and content within the Next Generation Network (NGN) and the way in which they are delivered to end-users
is changing. Content used to be text and some graphics. In the future it
will not only be text and graphics but it will also be voice, audio and
video. Entirely new classes of devices will proliferate in the home and
enterprise that will have varying display and input capabilities. Getting
services and content to these devices quickly, reliably and with low delay
will place new strains on the storage, transport and processing capabilities of the network.

Existing processing models will prove to be insufficient for the NGN. The
move from a text based world to a media rich world and the continually
increasing gap between processing cycles and bandwidth will drive the
demand for new processing models that are easily interconnected and
designed to support transparent scalable processing of text and other
signals.

A packet centric processor and logic-based architecture utilizing application processors, control processors, packet processors, signal processors,
neural processors, reprogrammable logic and application specific logic
can provide a continuum of optimized processing for the different phases
of an application or service running at wire or fiber speed. A shift to
this new architecture will have a profound impact on the capabilities of
the NGN and the types of content processing, content filtering and other
services that can be provided to users from servers, gateways, and service
platforms.

G. Brebner and R. Woods (Eds.): FPL 2001, LNCS 2147, pp. 232–232, 2001.

Tightly Integrated Placement and Routing for FPGAs

Parivallal Kannan and Dinesh Bhatia

Center for Integrated Circuits and Systems
Erik Jonsson School of Engineering and Computer Science
University of Texas at Dallas
PO Box 0688, Richardson, TX 75083, USA
{parik, dinesh}@utdallas.edu

Abstract. With increasing FPGA device capacity and design sizes, physical design closure is becoming more difficult, usually requiring multiple lengthy cycles of placement and routing. Increasing demands are being placed upon the placement method to produce routable solutions. Existing FPGA physical design methodologies treat placement and routing as two distinct steps resulting in significant loss of quality and increased design times. A tighter integration between placement and routing is expected to reduce the overall physical design time and produce better quality solutions. This paper presents a new methodology for tightly integrated placement and routing for FPGAs. It provides the capability to introduce the routing concepts to the placement stage itself, ensuring the placement is routability driven and that *desired good routes* exist for all nets, in the routing stage. This methodology has been implemented for XC6200 family of FPGAs, but can be used with any FPGA architecture.

1 Introduction

Placement and Routing are the two most important steps in physical design for *field programmable gate arrays* (FPGAs). Together, they are responsible for a major portion of the overall design time. As the device size and design complexity grows, it is becoming increasingly difficult to achieve physical design closure within a reasonable time frame. The placement process fixes the locations of the logic blocks of the design onto the FPGA device in a manner such that some cost function is optimized. The cost function of a typical placer usually includes parameters like area, total wirelength, delay etc. The goal of the routing process that follows placement is to produce routes for all the nets in the design using the routing resources available on the device. The possibility of a successful route depends on the quality of the router, the design complexity, the FPGA routing architecture and above all, the quality of the placement. The placement solution severely constrains the router's ability to explore and produce valid routes for all nets. For quick design closure, both the placement and routing should go hand in hand, supporting each other.

Traditionally, physical design methodologies and tools perform placement and routing sequentially and iteratively. There is very poor coordination between

G. Brebner and R. Woods (Eds.): FPL 2001, LNCS 2147, pp. 233–242, 2001.

the placer and router. This traditional approach of iterative place and route does not work well unless placement produces solutions that will route with high confidence. Only after a time consuming routing is performed, can the quality of the placement solution, in terms of routability be found. The designer has no alternative but to repeat the placement - routing cycle with perhaps different starting conditions and or constraints and hope for a closure. It is these repeated attempts of placement and routing that vastly increase the overall physical design time, which is seen by many as the main hurdle towards fast time to market.

We believe that a placement method that accurately captures the demand of routing resources and is able to supply such resources efficiently, will produce very high confidence in the overall routability of the design. Tighter integration with the router will ensure quicker design closure and cut down physical design time drastically. The anticipated physical design cycle will be a single, if need be lengthy, placement phase followed by a single routing phase that is certain to produce a completely routed solution. It would be nice if the runtime of the proposed physical design flow is comparable to a single run of a traditional placement followed by routing. Simultaneous place and route is sure to fit into this criteria but as shown in [1] the runtimes are very high and not practical for most applications. In this paper, we have addressed the problem of integrating routing within the placement stage, without incurring exceedingly large runtimes of simultaneous place and route.

Our method has the ability to produce placement solutions which guarantee the existence of *desired good routes* for all the nets in the design. By *desired good routes*, we mean routes with any or all of the desired qualities like short length, low delay, low routing element usage etc. Our method produces a highly routable placement similar to simultaneous place and route but with substantially lesser execution times. We put to use the distinguishing feature of FPGAs namely, fixed quantity and location of routing resources. We produce a set of alternate paths for each net, called *Route-Set* and each route-set produces a certain *routing demand* on all the routing elements it uses. We use simulated annealing to produce a placement solution with very low routing demand and hence high routability.

2   Background

There exists a large amount of previous work on FPGA placement and routing. VPR [2] is a well known academic FPGA physical design suite. VPR produces a placement using simulated annealing, with semi-perimeter net wirelength as its cost function and then routes the solution with different track widths, proceeding in a binary search fashion, until the router succeeds for some track width. In the real world, there is no such liberty, as the number of tracks per channel is fixed for a given FPGA architecture. Fast placement methods that trade-off some quality for speedup have been proposed. Notable among them is Ultra-Fast Placement for FPGAs [3]. It uses clustering techniques and then a hierarchical simulated annealing process to obtain a placement solution. A 50x speedup over pure simulated annealing is claimed at a 33% loss of quality. Again the cost function optimized is wirelength and we may end up with solutions that don't route at all. The speedup in placement, thereby produces no change to the overall physical design time.

Simultaneous place and route methodologies [1] have been proposed and have been shown to produce excellent results both for FPGAs and standard cell designs. For every placement iteration a complete detailed routing is performed and the number of unroutes is used as a part of the placer's cost function. Expectedly, this method is extremely time consuming, thereby beating the whole purpose of decreasing the physical design time. Another method is to include a routing estimator in the placement loop and use the estimated routability and routing costs to guide the placement. There has been a large number of reports about routability estimators. Several attempts [4] at using *Rent's Rule* for estimating routability for FPGAs have been reported. A stochastic model for interconnections is developed in [5] but no report of it being used for placement has been made. A boolean satisfiability based technique for routability estimation is reported in [6]. RISA [7] reports a routability method for standard cell designs, where the routing area is divided into sub-regions and demand-supply modeling of nets and routing resources is done on those sub-regions. [8] discusses about the stochastic models for routability developed in [9] and [10] adapted for FPGAs. Estimation methods typically do not have high accuracy and the final solution may still be unroutable. Many of these methods need an estimate of the wirelength and hence can only achieve a maximum accuracy as that of the wirelength estimators. Another major drawback with this approach is that they cannot be used to guide the placer towards producing solutions with *desired routes*, whatever that maybe.

3   Terminology

In this section we explain the terminology used in the subsequent sections. The important parameters that the methodology uses and their significance are discussed.

3.1   Problem Statement

Given a set of modules $M = \{m_1, m_2, \ldots, m_m\}$ and a set of nets $N = \{n_1, n_2, \ldots, n_n\}$ we associate with each module $m_i \in M$ a set of nets N_{m_i}, where $N_{m_i} \subseteq N$. Similarly, with each net $n_i \in N$ we associate a set of modules M_{n_i}, where $M_{n_i} = \{m_j | n_i \in N_{m_j}\}$.

The FPGA device can be represented as $G = (V, E)$, where V is the vertex set consisting of the basic cells (clbs) and E is the set of routing elements on the FPGA. The edge set could be directed for some FPGA architectures and may also have weights associated in case of multiple length routing elements. For simplicity, the clbs can be assumed to be arranged in a $F \times F$ two dimensional array. The vertex set is $V = \{V_{i,j} | 0 \leq i, j < F\}$.

The pure placement problem, without considering routability, is then to assign to each module $m_i \in M$ a unique location $v_j \in V$ such that an objective function is optimized.

A route R_i^k for a net n_k is defined as a connected set of routing elements $RE_i \subseteq E$, such that all the modules associated with the net n_k are connected. A route is defined to be a legal route if none of the routing elements RE_i are present in any other route.

The modified placement problem, considering routability, is then to assign to each module $m_i \in M$ a unique location $v_j \in V$ such that an objective function is optimized and there exist legal routes for all nets in N.

The definition of a legal route can be extended to attribute additional properties to each route, namely shortest route possible or shortest delay route possible and so on. These routes are called *desired good routes*. For example, if minimal delay is the desired property for all routes, then Figure 1a shows some examples of desired and undesired routes.

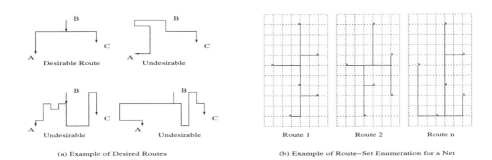

(a) Example of Desired Routes   (b) Example of Route–Set Enumeration for a Net

Fig. 1. *Desired Routes*

The placement problem considering routability can then be extended to ensure that desired good legal routes exist for all nets.

3.2   Route-Set

A route-set S_k for a net N_k is defined as a set of alternate routes produced for the net. That is, $S_k = \{R_1^k, R_2^k, \ldots, R_s^k\}$. The routes in a route-set may or may not be completely exclusive, that is they may or may not share routing elements. The routes in a route-set should ideally represent alternate paths for the same net, all having similar characteristics for the criterion that needs to be encouraged. For example, if high routability is desired, then the routes should all be approximations of steiner minimal trees. The generation of route-sets for each net is independent of the other nets and their route-sets. Hence fast algorithms can be devised for generating the route-sets. Figure 1(b) shows an example of a route-set for a multi-terminal net, with low routing element usage (and also wirelength reduction, in this case) as the goal.

Expectedly, not all routes in a route-set can always be optimal, with respect to the parameter being optimized. Better design space exploration can be obtained by including non-optimal routes also. Perhaps, a stronger constraint maybe enforced on critical nets. It is to be noted that this method differs from simultaneous place and route in that, the routes are produced without considering the effects of other nets. In simultaneous place and route, the routes produced have to be legal detailed routes and so the route generation is complicated and time consuming. The size of the route-set is an open issue. A smaller route-set will mean that it can be generated very fast and better run-times maybe expected. On the other hand, a larger route-set will mean better exploration of the design-space at an expense of additional runtime. Or, a smaller route-set but with routes of high generation cost (as in steiner minimal trees) maybe expected to give better quality results. We have not yet studied features like the size and composition of the route-set for optimal performance.

3.3   Routing Demand

Having defined the route-set, we proceed to define the *Routing Demand*, which is central to our methodology. The *routing demand* exacted by a net N_k on a routing element E_j is the inverse of the number of alternate routes available in its route set S_k. The number of alternate routes for a net N_k is

$$\text{alternate routes: } A_k = |S_k| \tag{1}$$

Therefore the *Routing Demand* on each routing element E_j in S_k is

$$\text{Routing Element Demand: } d_j^k = \frac{1}{A_k} \tag{2}$$

If any routing element is on more than one route in a route set, then the demand on it by that net is multiplied that many times as that for a routing element which appears only once. After the enumeration of the route-sets for all the n nets, the *routing element demand* on a routing element on the FPGA is,

$$RD_e = \sum_{\forall k: E_e \in S^k} d_e^k \tag{3}$$

The total Routing Congestion RC_{total} in the current placement is then calculated as the number of routing elements that have *routing element demand* $RD_e > 1.0$.

$$RC_{total} = |\{RD_e | \forall e \in E, RD_e > 1.0\}| \tag{4}$$

The maximum value of congestion $MC = Max(d_i)$ over all the routing elements represent the maximum congestion in the current placement.

4   Placement Method

4.1   Placement Schedule

We use simulated annealing [11] as the optimization process. The cost function for the annealer is a function of the estimated total wirelength WL_{total} of the current placement and the routing demand RC_{total}. The semi-perimeter wirelength model is used to estimate the total wirelength. The cost function is then,

$$cost = W_d \times RC_{total} + W_{wl} \times WL_{total} \qquad (5)$$

The annealer is characterized by the parameters, T_{start} the starting temperature or hot condition, T_{end} the lowest temperature or cold condition, the equilibrium condition at a given temperature and the next state function that perturbs the current solution to a neighboring state. The annealer parameters are problem dependent and have to be fine tuned for each and every problem. Many different methods exist which calculate these parameters in a problem independent manner. We use the methods explained in [12] and [13]. The initial solution is a random placement. A dry run of the annealing loop, where all the new solutions are accepted irrespective of the cost, is performed for about $100N_{cells}$ times, where N_{cells} is the number of cells. The standard deviation σ of the cost is calculated and the hot condition is set at $T_{hot} = 20\sigma$. The values of the cost components RC_{total} and WL_{total} obtained during the dry run are used to calculate the weights W_d and W_{wl}. A simple choice is to use the maximum values of the cost components obtained during the dry run for these constants, so that both the cost components are comparable. The equilibrium condition at a given temperature is set at $10N_{cells}^{1.33}$ moves per temperature. The stop or frozen condition is when no new solutions are accepted for ten successive equilibrium states.

In the inner metropolis loop of the annealer, the current solution is perturbed by randomly swapping two cells or by moving a cell to an empty location. The route-sets are updated for all the nets incident on the perturbed cells and the cost components are calculated. Since the generation of a route is independent of the other routes, the route-sets of the affected nets alone can be updated incrementally. If the move is accepted then the positions of the perturbed cells and the new routing information are frozen. If the move is rejected, then the cells are returned to their original location and the new route-sets are replaced with their previous values.

5   Experimentation

In order to test and demonstrate our methodology we have made use of the Xilinx XC6200 [14] family of devices. The XC6200 device has a very low number programmable logic gates per clb and also a very low routing element to logic block ratio which translates to high routing congestion, even for relatively small designs. The device enjoyed widespread attention for reconfigurable computing applications but was notoriously difficult to use because of its tough placement and routing requirements.

5.1 XC6200 Architecture

The XC6200 architecture is hierarchical. At the lowest level of the hierarchy lies a large array of simple cells. Each cell is individually programmable to implement a D-flipflop and one of any two input logic function, or a 2:1 multiplexer. The basic cell of a XC6200 family FPGA is shown in Figure 2(a). 16 such basic cells are grouped into a 4x4 block. 16 such 4x4 blocks form a higher level 16x16 block as in Figure 2(b). A 4x4 array of these 16x16 blocks forms a XC6216 device. Four such 6216 devices form a XC6264 device. The user configurable IOBs are located in the periphery of the device and there are two IOBs for each vertical and horizontal column of basic cells, located at both ends of the column.

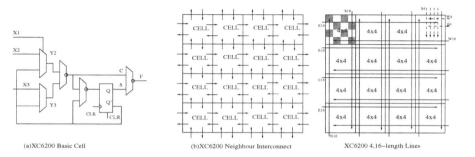

(a)XC6200 Basic Cell   (b)XC6200 Neighbour Interconnect   XC6200 4,16–length Lines

Fig. 2. *XC6200 family FPGA Architecture*

The XC6200 family devices have a hierarchical routing architecture, comprising of routing elements with different lengths. The cells in the basic 4x4 tiles are connected to their neighbors by 1–length neighbor interconnect lines, as in Figure 2(b). In a 4x4 block, 4–length lines called N4, S4, E4 and W4, depending upon their direction (North, South, East and West respectively), connect any cell to any other cell over which they pass. For clarity, a few of the 4 length lines are shown in Figure 2(b). Similarly, the 16x16 blocks have 16–length lines called N16, S16, E16 and W16 and they connect any 4 length boundary to another, over which they pass. At a higher level, there are chip length lines that connect any 16 length boundary to another, over which they pass.

5.2 CAD Flow

The input to the placer is the set of intermediate files obtained after techmapping from the Xilinx Xact6000 tool. The tool generates these files from an EDIF netlist. A flat netlist consisting of M unit sized modules and N nets is produced from these input files. As mentioned earlier, a proper choice of the route-set is necessary to get good results at a reasonable runtime. The exact structure of the routes that produce the optimal trade-off is unknown as yet. Our main goal with the XC6200 family was to get routability. So, each route in the route-sets should use as few routing elements as possible. Steiner minimal trees would be ideal. For various considerations, we implemented a single trunk steiner tree algorithm with linear time complexity. Other route structures are being investigated. The result of the placer is the location assignment for all the cells and the route-sets for all the nets in the design. A fast greedy algorithm is used to assign routes to the nets from their corresponding route-sets. A better method to do this assignment is being worked upon.

5.3   Evaluation Methodology

We compare the performance of our methodology with the Xact6000 [15] suite from Xilinx and with the well known FPGA physical design suite, VPR [2]. The Xact6000 suite from Xilinx is the primary physical design tool for the XC6200 family. The tool completes placement in a very short time but seldom succeeds to complete routing for most non-trivial designs. Unroutes typically range from 10% to more than 50% and manual intervention is almost always required to alter the placement for better routability. VPR uses simulated annealing for placement with semi perimeter wirelength as the cost function and the PathFinder [16] based negotiated algorithm for routing. VPR is designed for island style FPGAs and cannot be directly used for sea of gates FPGAs like the XC6200. We have approximated the XC6200 architecture and created a template file to be used with VPR. The model is not an exact representation of the XC6200 architecture but provides additional flexibilities to the router.

6   Benchmark Circuits

We used a set of benchmark circuits developed for the XC6200 device by [17]. They are portions of an image processing system, implementing wavelet based compression-decompression, and belong to the Honeywell ACS Benchmarks. The characteristics of the benchmark circuits are listed in table 1. These circuits range in size from small to big and form an interesting mix of circuits typically used in image processing applications.

7   Results

We were able to get $RC_{total} = 0$ for all of the circuits considered. The runtimes were within an hour, on a standard 800 MHz pentium PC. Table 1 shows the results obtained. For each circuit, the table lists the final RC_{total} value as RC, the maximum routing demand on the most congested routing element as MC, the area required, the final total semi-perimeter wirelength as W and the CPU time spent for placement and the final route assignment as T_{cpu}. Both Xact6000 and

VPR placed the circuits in the smallest possible area but failed to complete the routing. Furthermore, VPR was able to route the placement solution produced by our methodology.

The main reason for VPR's failure to route its own placement solution is that the VPR's placer always tries to place the circuit in the smallest possible area. This is because, the cost function is wirelength based and does not include any congestion or routability metric. Since our methodology includes congestion minimization as an integral part of the placement process, the placement solution occupies more area, to account for the very low number of routing resources available per logic block. Hence VPR's router was able to route these placement solutions.

Circuit	# Cells	# Nets	RC	MC	Area	W	T_{cpu}
ad12	37	35	0	1.0	64	264	110s
mlt8	350	385	0	1.0	1600	8796	971s
mt20	506	630	0	1.0	3600	17367	1191s
lfk2	1862	2147	0	1.0	16384	135887	1616s
comp	2187	2214	0	1.0	16384	143610	2015s

Table 1. *Results considering RC_{total} in cost-function*

The area requirement on the XC6200 device is very high, because of the very low number of available routing elements per logic gate and this increases the problem size, by increasing the search space many times. The same methodology can be expected to give better runtimes on routing element rich architectures.

8   Conclusion

A methodology to efficiently and accurately model routability for FPGAs has been developed and incorporated into a placement tool for the XC6200 family of FPGAs. Large improvements in routability have been achieved for a set of small to large circuits. 100% routability was achieved in all cases and the computation times were still reasonable. Complete physical design closure was obtained in roughly the same time needed for one traditional place and route iteration. More work is needed to investigate the properties of route-sets and runtime-quality trade-off studies are needed. Investigation into better algorithms for route-set generation would also be useful. Various interesting and useful extensions to the methodology, like adaptively changing the route-set exploration, adaptation to a hierarchical macro placement problem or general standard cell placement problem are possible and are being currently studied.

References

[1] Sudip K. Nag and R.A. Rutenbar, "Performance-Driven Simultaneous Placement and Routing for FPGAs," *IEEE Transactions on CAD*, June 1998.

[2] Vaughn Betz and Jonathan Rose, "VPR: A New Packing, Placement and Routing Tool for FPGA Research," in *Field-Programmable Logic and Applications*, Wayne Luk, Peter Y. K. Cheung, and Manfred Glesner, Eds. September 1997, pp. 213–222, Springer-Verlag, Berlin.

[3] Y. Sankar and J. Rose, "Trading Quality for Compile Time: Ultra-Fast Placement for FPGAs," in *ACM Symp. on FPGAs*. ACM, 1999, pp. 157–166.

[4] Wei Li, "Routability Prediction for Hierarchical FPGAs," in *Proc. Great Lakes Symposium on VLSI*, 1999.

[5] S. Brown, J. Rose, and Z.G. Vranesic, "A Detailed Router for Field Programmable Gate Arrays," *IEEE Transactions on CAD*, May 1992.

[6] R.G. Wood and R.A. Rutenbar, "FPGA Routing and Routability Estimation via Boolean Satisfiability," in *ACM International Symposium on FPGAs*. June 1998, ACM.

[7] Chih liang Eric Chang, "RISA: Accurate and Efficient Placement Routability Modeling," in *Proc. of ICCAD*, 1994.

[8] Pak K. Chan, Martine D.F. Schlag, and Jason Y. Zien, "On Routability Prediction for Field Programmable Gate Arrays," in *Proc. 30th DAC*, 1993June 1993.

[9] Abbas A. El Gamal, "Two-Dimensional Stochastic Model for Interconnections in Master Slice Integrated Circuits," *IEEE Trans. CAS.*, Feb 1981.

[10] S. Sastry and A.C. Parker, "Stochastic Models for Wireability Analysis of Gate Arrays," *IEEE Trans. on CAD*, Jan 1986.

[11] S. Kirkpatrick, C.D. Gelatt, and M.P. Vecchi, "Optimization by Simulated Annealing," *Science*, vol. 220, May 1983.

[12] M. D. Huang, F. Romeo, and Sangiovanni Vincentelli, "An Efficient Cooling Schedule for Simulated Annealing," in *Proc. of ICCAD*, 1986.

[13] V. Betz, J. Rose, and A. Marquard, *Architecture and CAD for Deep-Submicron FPGAs*, Kluwer Academic Publishers, Feb 1999.

[14] *XC6200 Field Programmable Gate Arrays*, 1997.

[15] *XACTstep Series 6000 v1.1.7*, 1997.

[16] Larry McMurchie and Carl Ebeling, "PathFinder: A Negotiation-Based Performance-Driven Router for FPGAs," in *ACM Symp. on FPGAs, FPGA95*. ACM, 1995, pp. 111–117.

[17] Mandeep Singh, "A Framework for Test and Validation of Adaptive Computing Systems," M.S. thesis, ECECS, University of Cincinnati, 1999.

Gambit: A Tool for the Simultaneous Placement and Detailed Routing of Gate-Arrays[*]

John Karro[1] and James Cohoon[2]

[1] Computer Science Program, Oberlin College, Oberlin, OH 44017
john.karro@oberlin.edu
[2] Department of Computer Science, University of Virginia, Charlottesville, VA 22903
cohoon@virginia.edu

Abstract. In this paper we present a new method of integrating the placement and routing stages in the physical design of channel-based architectures, and present the first implementation of this method: Gambit. Based on a graph coloring representation of the routing problem, we are able to produce circuit placements and detailed routes simultaneously, allowing routing constraints to influence decisions made in creating the placement. Gambit produces circuit mappings for both standard and three-dimensional FPGA architectures, and serves primarily as a proof-of-concept: the proposed algorithm will simultaneously perform placement and detailed routing for channel-based architectures. While the quality of Gambit mappings are not yet competitive with state-of-the-art tools in the literature, experimental results indicate that it does have the potential to become so.

1 Introduction

Given an abstract description of a circuit, it is no easy task to physically implement that description in hardware. The designer must map each of the components to a location on the chip, and then must run wires between component to provide the proper connections. All of this must be done with an eye towards keeping connections as small as possible, and towards minimizing the amount of chip area required for the design. The problems involved in finding an optimal solution are NP-complete, and researchers are continually developing new heuristics to produce high-quality solutions in a reasonable amount of time.

The task of physical design is frequently divided into several stages. For the popular FPGA architecture these include *technology mapping*, *placement*, *global routing* and *detailed routing*. Traditionally these have been performed in sequence, with the output of each becoming the input of the next. While such a division reduces the complexity of the problem, it has been argued that solving

[*] Research supported by the Virginia Aerospace Consortium Graduate Fellowship Program, the National Science Foundation under grants CDA 9634333, CDR 9224789, MIP 9107717, DUE 9554715, and DUE 9653413, and by the Department of Computer Science at the University of Virginia.

G. Brebner and R. Woods (Eds.): FPL 2001, LNCS 2147, pp. 243–253, 2001.
© Springer-Verlag Berlin Heidelberg 2001

the involved problems simultaneously would lead to superior results [7]. Thus there have been a number of proposals concerning the integration of stages [2, 7, 10, 11]. Many of these are aimed at integrating the placement and global routing stages; the integration of all three stages has proven considerably more difficult.

When working with channel-based architectures, the problem of detailed routing can be viewed as a graph-coloring problem [13]. Consider the Sharp methodology developed by Bapat and Cohoon [4], a technique for the integration of placement and global routing. We can integrate this graph-color representation into the methodology, allowing it to influence placement and global routing decisions. By heuristically maintaining a minimum coloring on our "routing" graph, and by making placement decisions that allow us to minimize the chromatic number of the developing graph, we can complete the Sharp algorithm and have a placement and a global routing that is guaranteed to be *fully* routable.

Gambit is our implementation of the proposed method. Developed as an extension of the Spiffy algorithm [7], a tool implementing Sharp partitioning for standard and three-dimensional FPGA architectures, Gambit produces in one step full circuit mappings that are heuristically optimized in terms of channel-width and net-length. While the results are not yet competitive against state-of-the-art tools such as Spiffy [7] or VPR [5], it is clear from the results that Gambit is on its way to becoming a state-of-the-art tool.

In the following paper we will discuss Gambit and the algorithm on which it is based. In Section 2 we present our problem statement and definitions, and in Section 3 we discuss details of Gambit. In Section 4 we discuss our experimental results, and in Section 5 we discuss our conclusions and the work we are currently pursuing with regard to Gambit.

It is also worth noting that while this paper concentrates on standard FPGAs, and algorithm generalizes, and has been implemented for, the newly proposed 3D-FPGAs [7, 9]. However, the techniques for doing so were straight forward, and not worth addressing here.

2   Problem Statement and Definitions

In Figure 1 we see the diagram of a Xilinx XC4000 FPGA architecture. In considering this diagram, we are concerned with five components. *Logic blocks* provide the functionality of the chip. *Channel wires* conduct signals. *Pins* carry signals from logic blocks to wires. *Connection-blocks* connect pins to wires. And *switch-blocks* connect wires. We use the term *routing blocks* to generically classify switch-blocks and connection blocks, the blocks used for signal routing. We use the term *channel* to denote the area between routing blocks through which a set of channels wires run. We denote the number of wires per channel as the *channel-width*, which must be uniform over all channels. Clearly, the smaller the channel-width, the smaller the FPGA.

In implementing a circuit on an FPGA, we program the functions of a circuit into the logic blocks, and we program the routing blocks to correctly provide connections. The challenge in doing this is to minimize the required size of

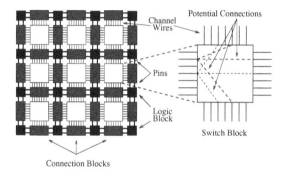

Fig. 1. A Xilinx XC4000 FPGA symmetrical architecture with a channel-width of seven.

the FPGA (by minimizing the required channel-width), and to maximize the performance of the FPGA (by minimizing the path connection lengths). This task is complicated by the restricted connection capacity of the switch-blocks. In order to simplify switch-block design, the designer is only allowed to connect certain subsets of wires touching the blocks. In Figure 2(a) we see the actual design of a switch-block, and in Figure 2(b) we see the possible connections such a design provides. Note that if wires are labeled sequentially from left to right or top to bottom in each channel, we have the option of connecting two wires if and only if they have the same label.

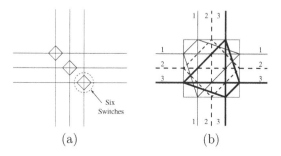

Fig. 2. (a) A Xilinx XC4000 switch-module and (b) its switch-module model.

While the restricted capacity of the switch-blocks complicates the design problem, it also allows us to divide the channel wires into equivalence classes. By labeling the wires in each channel as described, we know that a signal is restricted to using wires of the same label. As switch-blocks will not carry a signal between wires of different labels, there is no way for a signal to cross these "label boundaries." (While many routers assume that connection-blocks can be used as dog-legs, this does not seem to be the case.[5])

The existence of these equivalence classes allows the reduction of the problem of routing to a graph-coloring problem, as formulated by Wu and Marek-Sadowska [13]. Consider the global route of some circuit (that is, the assignment of signal paths to channels, but not to specific channel wires). In Figure 3(a) we see a sample global route, and in Figure 3(b) we see the corresponding *channel conflict-graph*. Such a graph has a node corresponding to each net, and two nodes share an edge if the corresponding nets share a channel in their global routes. By coloring the graph, we induce a legitimate detailed route. No two nodes that share an edge share a color, hence no two nets that share a channel are assigned to the same wire. By calculating a minimal graph coloring, we achieve an optimal detailed route given the global route.

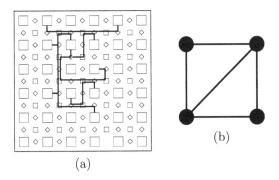

(a)   (b)

Fig. 3. (a) The global routings of four nets on an FPGA. (b) The corresponding conflict-graph. Note that even though the global routings require a channel-width of 2, the conflict-graph has a chromatic number of 3 – hence the detailed routing requires a channel-width of 3.

Our objective is to simultaneously create the placement, global routing and conflict-graph coloring in such a way as to minimize the number of colors used. We begin with the block/net description of a circuit, as produced by a standard technology-mapping tool. This gives us our list of functions to be programmed into logic-blocks and our list of pins that must be connected. We then wish to simultaneously develop our placement, global route and detailed route, allowing each of the developing solutions to influence the further development of the other two solutions.

3   Gambit

Built on Spiffy, a tool created by Karro and Cohoon [7], Gambit uses the same divide and conquer technique. However, Gambit augments the tool with a conflict-graph structure, incrementally building the graph as a course global route is created, and then uses the graph to influence future placement and global-routing decisions. Upon completion of the algorithm, the chromatic number of the graph has been heuristically minimized, leading to a full routing with small channel-width.

We begin the Gambit algorithm by imposing a $p \times q$ grid on the FPGA area. We partition the chip such that each logic block lies in exactly one area, with partition-lines running through switch-blocks. We then perform the following steps.

3.1   Partition

In the partition phase, we map the blocks to partitions, but not to specific logic-blocks. The goal in doing this is to minimize the number of partitions each signal must travel through in connecting the pins of a net. The stage is treated exactly the same as in the Spiffy algorithm, and simulated annealing is used to find a solution.

3.2   Route Selection

Given a placement, we now need to consider each net existing in multiple partitions and choose a *thumbnail* for it: a tree that dictates the path the net will take between partitions. In Figure 4(a) we see an example of a placement of a net into partitions. In Figures 4(b)-(d) we see different *thumbnails* that can be assigned to the net; each thumbnail is a different minimum-length tree that will determine how the net signal will travel between partitions.

In the Spiffy algorithm we select a thumbnail for each net by building a vector reflecting the use of edges, and assigning thumbnails in such a way as to minimize the variance over the elements of this vector. In Gambit, we choose a thumbnail for each net, but we also assign (or reassign) a color to each node so as to conform to the constraints of the conflict graph.

We begin our algorithm by clearing the colors of all nets that will need a thumbnail, and then count the "color availability" $\alpha(e, \kappa)$ of each thumbnail edge e and color κ. That is, consider thumbnail edge e and let $S(e)$ be the set of switch-blocks laying on the corresponding partition line. If $\mu(s)$ represents the colors of all nets currently used by switch-block s (or, more accurately, by the two sides of s relevant to the thumbnail edge), then no nets assigned to this thumbnail will be able to use any color in the set $\cap_{s \in S(e)} \mu(s)$. We define $\alpha(e, \kappa)$ as the number of switch-blocks in $S(e)$ that do not have a net of color κ assigned to them. Thus $\alpha(e, \kappa)$ is the number of nets of color κ that we can assign to a thumbnail using edge e before κ becomes a member of the set $\cap_{b \in S(e)} \mu(s)$ (the set of colors assigned to all blocks in $S(e)$).

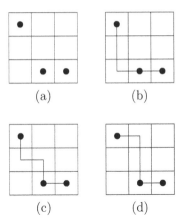

Fig. 4. (a) The placement of a net's blocks with respect to the partitions. (b) One possible thumbnail (minimum-length tree) connecting the net between partitions. (c) A second possible thumbnail. (d) A third possible thumbnail.

We use a greedy algorithm in which we order the nets by number of thumbnail choices. The nets with the least number of thumbnail choices will be assigned thumbnails first, thus preventing a net with a greater number of options from using up all the choices available to nets with few options. However, where we would arbitrarily break ties in Spiffy, in Gambit we pick the longest nets. The more switch-blocks a net must use, the more restricted will be its choice of colors.

When considering a net within the order, we examine each possible thumbnail and the partition edges that thumbnail crosses. For each of these thumbnails, we determine if there is some color κ that can legally be assigned to the net's conflict-graph node such that $\alpha(e, \kappa) > 0$ for every edge e in the thumbnail. If there is no color currently used by the conflict-graph that can be assigned to the node, we eliminate the thumbnail from consideration. Only if we eliminate all thumbnails do we introduce a new color. Introducing a color increases the total number of colors used by the graph (and hence the required channel-width), but allows us to reintroduce all of the net's thumbnails as candidates.

From this restricted set we pick our thumbnail as we did with Spiffy: in such a way so as to minimize the variance of the elements of the congestion vector for the partial solution. In addition, we assign the net ν a color. We pick a legal color κ that will maximize the value $min_{e \in \tau(\nu)} \alpha(e, \kappa)$, where $\tau(\nu)$ is the set of edges used by the thumbnail of net ν. We do this in order to avoid "using up" any color on any edge. This heuristic leaves more color options for future nets that might use of thumbnails sharing these edges. Having picked a color κ, we update the values of $\alpha(e, \kappa)$ for each $e \in \tau(\nu)$, and repeat the process for the next net. Upon termination of this phase, we have a thumbnail for each net and a color for each node in the conflict-graph.

3.3   Virtual Terminal Assignment

At this point, each net is placed with respect to the partitions, and is assigned a thumbnail that defines how its signal will travel between partitions. Now we look at the edges making up the thumbnail, and choose the exact spot on the corresponding partition line where the signal will cross. These points are known as *virtual terminals*. In Figure 5(a) we see a sample thumbnail, and in Figure 5(b) we see those points at which we could assign the net to cross the different partition lines. In an FPGA such points will take the form of switch-blocks, and define the edges of the conflict-graph. Any two nets entering the same side of a switch-block must share a channel, hence must be adjacent in the graph.

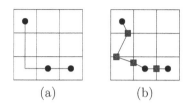

(a)   (b)

Fig. 5. (a) A placement and thumbnail for some net. (b) A possible assignment of virtual nodes along the thumbnail chosen for the net.

With Spiffy, the virtual terminal assignment problem is reduced to a minimum-cost perfect-matching problem and solved accordingly. The virtual terminal assignment for Gambit is very close in form to the virtual terminal assignment for Spiffy. The only additional constraints are that each net must be assigned to a switch-block that can accommodate the net's color, and that no two nets of the same color may be assigned to the same switch-block.

In the Spiffy algorithm we reduce the virtual terminal assignment to the bipartite matching problem. We do this by creating a complete bipartite graph P with a node for each net, a set of nodes for each available switch-block, and added edges between net-nodes and block-nodes. Edge weights reflect the distance between the net's terminals and the block. We ensure that no switch-block is overloaded by limiting the number of nodes in P corresponding to it.

In Gambit the limit on the number of colorings in the graph will implicitly limit switch-block overloading; there is no need to explicitly deal with the issue. Thus when creating nodes in P for each switch-block, instead of limiting the number of nodes by the ratio, we create one node for each color that can be used by the block. As the problem formulation requires that P be a complete bipartite graph, we must add a weighted edge from each of the net-nodes to each of the block-nodes. However, for any edge that connects a net of color κ with a switch-block node of color other than κ we add an infinite penalty to the weight of the edge, thus preventing the use of that edge in the matching solution. From the manner in which we assign our net colors, we know that if there are k nets using color κ then there must be k switch-blocks with color κ available. Therefore each net can be assigned to a switch-block without incurring a penalty.

After solving the matching problem, we have the virtual nodes for each net. This has the side-effect of introducing a (heuristically) minimal number of edges into the conflict-graph. As we have been coloring the graph on the fly, it is at this point useful to re-color the graph with a more efficient heuristic, which will likely reduce the number of colors required.

Following this, we are able to apply the algorithm recursively to each of the partitions. By developing a placement and global routing within each partition, while maintaining a "global" conflict-graph, we will end up with a placement and route for the chip whose conflict-graph will immediately induce a detailed route.

3.4   Base Case

At some point, we must halt the recursion and explicitly solve the base case. In Spiffy, the base case is dealt with using an integer programming technique. Gambit can use a similar approach, but where the Spiffy integer program needs to determine only the exact route the nets within the base case, the Gambit integer program must additionally determine a minimum coloring of the resulting conflict-graph. Ideally we would like Gambit to fully re-color the graph at each base case, but this is computationally infeasible. Instead we must re-color only the portion of the graph affected by the base case, leading to solutions of lesser quality, but ones that can be solved in a more reasonable amount of time.

Even with this concession, the base case is Gambit's major drawback. By adopting the base case of Spiffy to the Gambit algorithm, we have been saddled with a method that cannot handle the complexity of the total problem. In order to make Gambit into a truly competitive tool, a new approach to the base case will have to be developed.

4   Experimental Results

Gambit is presented as a proof-of-concept: using the conflict-graph structure, it is feasible to perform simultaneous placement and full routing. Raising the quality of Gambit's results to a competitive level will require further research. However, our experiments indicate that such research is worthwhile.

One aspect of Gambit not yet discussed is our selection of a graph-coloring heuristic. For our first implementation, we choose two common heuristics from the literature: Brelaz's Dsatur algorithm [6], and the graph interference algorithm frequently used with compilers [1]. In Table 1 we see the channel-widths achieved when mapping several standard benchmarks [5] to a Xilinx-4000 FPGA architecture. Results were compared against a verity of tools, including Locus-Route [12], GBP [13], TRACER [8], VPR [5], and the Alexander/Robins routing tool [3] In Table 2 we see that this version of Gambit is not competitive. (Though we note that these other tools allow dog-legging at connection blocks and thus they have an unrealistic advantage, as discussed in Section 2.)

The results do however serve as a proof-of-concept: with one tool we can generate full circuit mappings.

Table 1. Results of Gambit

Circuit	Dsatur		Graph Interference	
	Average Channel-Width	Best Channel-Width	Average Channel-Width	Best Channel-Width
busc	20.47 ± 0.6	18	14.2 ± 0.58	12
dma	26.20 ± 0.57	24	17.60 ± 0.5	15
bnre	36.53 ± 0.6	33	23.63 ± 0.5	21
dfsm	32.13 ± 0.80	29	20.23 ± 0.6	18
9symml	21.43 ± 0.59	19	16.23 ± 0.6	14
term1	16.10 ± 1.1	12	11.2 ± 0.7	9
apex7	17.60 ± 0.9	14	12.97 ± 0.8	11
alu2	30.30 ± 0.78	27	21.93 ± 0.6	19
too_large	30.00 ± 0.7	27	20.03 ± 0.7	18
example2	24.60 ± 1.0	21	18.06 ± 0.9	15
vda	42.33 ± 0.7	39	28.47 ± 0.5	26
alu4	42.70 ± 0.8	38	29.16 ± 0.7	27

Table 2. Other Tools

Placement Tool	Altor						Spiffy
G. Routing Tool	LocusRoute	GBP	OCG	Tracer	VPR	A/R	
D. Routing Tool	CGA	SEGA			SEGA		Upstart
9symml	9	9	9	9	6	7	8	8
alu2	12	10	11	9	9	8	9	9
alu4	15	13	14	12	11	10	11	10
apex7	13	13	11	10	8	10	10	6
example2	18	17	13	12	10	10	11	8
term1	10	9	10	9	7	8	8	6
too_large	13	11	12	11	9	10	10	9
vda	14	14	13	11	11	12	12	10
Total	104	96	93	83	71	75	76	66

While the use of Dsatur produces poor results, using the more sophisticated coloring algorithm within Gambit does lead to significant improvement, with a negligible increase in run time. Clearly we have improved our results, to the point where we even best some other tools on certain benchmarks – as shown in Table 3.

Table 3. Gambit v. Altor

Global R.	LocusRoute		GBP	OCG	Gambit
Detailed R.	CGA	SEGA			
9symml	9	9	9	9	14
alu2	12	10	11	9	19
alu4	15	13	14	12	27
apex7	**13**	**13**	**11**	10	11
example2	**18**	**17**	13	12	15
term1	**10**	**9**	**10**	9	9
too_large	13	11	12	11	18
vda	14	14	13	11	26
Total	104	96	93	83	139

From these tables, we see that Gambit is highly dependent on the choice of graph-coloring techniques used. We are in the process of implementing other techniques, and have high expectations of the results that this will produce. These results will be included in the final paper.

5   Conclusions and Future Work

The main contribution of this paper is the introduction of Gambit, a tool significant as a proof-of-concept: conflict-graphs can be used to simultaneously perform placement and routing for channel-based architectures. By modeling the FPGA as a colorable graph, we have essentially incorporated details of the switch-block structure into the placement decisions, allowing the interaction between the formally separate stages. While results are currently not competitive, we believe that with further research, Gambit has the potential to match the results of any tool in the literature.

In working on improving Gambit's results, we are currently pursuing two lines of research. First, we are working on a new approach to the base case, as discussed in Section 3.4. Spiffy's approach to the base case of the recursion did not extend well to the inclusion of the conflict-graph. We intend to develop a different approach to the problem, which will lead to a better tool.

It is also evident that the choice of graph-coloring algorithm is crucial to the quality of Gambit's results. We are currently exploring the use of more sophisticated coloring algorithms. Further, we are working on the characterization of the structure of conflict-graphs. It is our hope that we can exploit these properties shared by FPGA-induced graphs, leading to a better coloring heuristic. This in turn will lead to improved results and a faster execution time.

Our third direction of research is the generalization of Gambit to a larger class of channel-based architectures. Conceptually, the algorithm relies on the channels of the FPGA, hence it should be possible to apply the methodology to any architecture that is channel-based. Gambit exploits the "equivalence-class nature" of the channel wires, a property not necessarily shared with these other architectures. However, we are working towards a method of conflict-graph node-splitting which will allow us to compensate for that loss of structure.

Thus we present our conclusion: the use of conflict-graphs is a viable method in the integration of the placement and routing stages for channel-based architectures, and research into Gambit is worth pursuing.

References

[1] Aho, A.V., Sethi, R., and Jeffery, U.D. *Compilers: Principles, Techniques, and Tools*. Addison-Wesley Publishing Company, 1986.

[2] Alexander, M.J., Cohoon, J.P., Ganley, J.L., and Robins, G. Performance-oriented placement and routing for field-programmable gate arrays. *Proceedings of the European Design Automation Conference*, pages 80–85, 1995.

[3] Alexander, M.J. and Robins, G. New Performance-Driven FPGA Routing Algorithms. *IEEE Transactions on Computer-Aided Design of Integrated Circuits and Systems*, 15(12):1505–1517, December 1996.

[4] Bapat, S. and Cohoon, J.P. A parallel VLSI circuit layout methodology. *Proceedings of Sixth International Conference on VLSI Design*, pages 236–241, 1993.

[5] Betz, V. and Rose, J. VPR: A New Packing, Placement and Routing Tool for FPGA Research. *International Workshop on Field Programmable Logic and Applications*, pages 213–222, 1997.

[6] D. Brelaz. New methods to color the vertices of a graph. *Communications of the ACM*, pages 251–256, 1979.

[7] Karro, J. and Cohoon, J. A Spiffy Tool for the Simultaneous Placement and Global Routing of Three-Dimensional Field Programmable Gate Arrays. *Ninth Great Lakes Symposium on VLSI*, pages 226–227, March 1999.

[8] Lee, Y. and Wu, A. A performance and routability driven router for FPGA considering path delays. *Proceedings of the 32 IEEE/ACM Conference on Design Automation*, pages 557–561, 1995.

[9] Lesser, M., Meleis, W.M., Vai, M.M., and Zavracky, P.M. Rothko: A Three Dimensional FPGA Architecture, Its Fabrication, and Design Tools. *Field-Programmable Logic and Applications*, 1997.

[10] Nag, S.K. and Rutenbar, R.A. Performance-driven simultaneous place and route for FPGAs. *IEEE Transactions on Computer-Aided Design of Integrated Circuits and Systems*, 17(5):499–518, June 1998.

[11] Nakatake, S., Sakanushi, K., Kajitani, Y., and Kawakita, M. The channeled-BSG: a universal floorplan for simultaneous place/route with IC applications. *IEEE/ACM International Conference on Computer-Aided Design*, pages 418–25, 1998.

[12] Rose, J. Parallel Global Routing for Standard Cells. *IEEE Transactions on Computer Aided Design*, pages 1085–1095, October 1990.

[13] Wu, Y.L. and Marek-Sadowska, M. Orthogonal Greedy Coupling – A New Optimization Approach to 2-D FPGA Routing. *Proceedings of the ACM/IEEE Design Automation Conference*, pages 568–573, 1995.

Reconfigurable Router Modules Using Network Protocol Wrappers*

Florian Braun, John Lockwood, and Marcel Waldvogel

Applied Research Laboratory
Washington University in St. Louis
{florian,lockwood,mwa}@arl.wustl.edu

Abstract. The ongoing increases of line speed in the Internet backbone combined with the need for increased functionality of network devices presents a major challenge for designers of Internet routers. These demands call for the use of reprogrammable hardware to provide the required performance and functionality at all network layers. The Field Programmable Port Extender (FPX) provides such an environment for development of networking components in reprogrammable hardware. We present a framework to streamline and simplify networking applications that process ATM cells, AAL5 frames, Internet Protocol (IP) packets and UDP datagrams directly in hardware. We also describe a high-speed IP routing module "OBIWAN" built on top of this framework.

1 Introduction

In recent years, field programmable logic has become sufficiently capable to implement complex networking applications directly in hardware. The Field Programmable Port Extender has been implemented as a flexible platform for the processing of network data in hardware at multiple layers of the protocol stack. Layers are important for networks because they allow applications to be implemented at a level where the insignificant details are hidden. At the lowest layer, networks need to modify the raw data that passes between interfaces. At higher levels, the applications process variable length frames or packages as in the Internet Protocol. At the user-level, applications may transmit or receive messages in User Datagram Protocol (UDP) messages. An important application for the network layer is routing and forwarding packets to other network nodes.

2 Background

In the Applied Research Lab at Washington University in St. Louis, a rich set of hardware components and software for research in the field of ATM and active networking has been developed. The modules described in this paper are primarily targeted to this kit, though the design is written in portable VHDL and could be used in any FPGA-based system.

---

* This research was supported in part by NSF ANI-0096052 and Xilinx Corp.

G. Brebner and R. Woods (Eds.): FPL 2001, LNCS 2147, pp. 254–263, 2001.
© Springer-Verlag Berlin Heidelberg 2001

2.1 Switch Fabric

The central component of this research environment is the Washington University Gigabit Switch (WUGS, [1]). It is a fully featured 8-port ATM switch, which is capable of handling up to 20 Gbps of network traffic. Each port is connected through a line card to the switch. The WUGS provides space to insert extension cards between the line cards and the switch itself.

2.2 Field Programmable Port Extender

The Field Programmable Port Extender (FPX, [2]) provides reprogrammable logic for user applications. A configuration of the switch and the FPX is illustrated in figure 1(a). The FPX contains two FPGAs: the Network Interface Device (NID) and the Reprogrammable Application Device (RAD). The NID interconnects the WUGS, the line card and the RAD via a small switch. It also provides the logic to dynamically reprogram the RAD. The RAD can be programmed to hold user-defined modules. Hardware based processing of networking data is made possible that way. The RAD is also connected to two SRAM and two SDRAM components. The memory modules can be used to cache cell data or hold large tables. Figure 1(b) illustrates the major components on an FPX board.

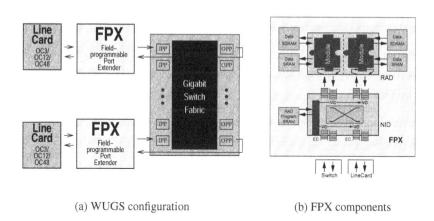

(a) WUGS configuration   (b) FPX components

Fig. 1. The Washington University Gigabit Switch (WUGS)

2.3 FPX Modules

User applications are implemented on the RAD as modules. Modules are hardware components with a well-defined interface which communicate with the RAD and other infrastructure components. The basic data interface is a 32-bit wide, Utopia-like interface. The data bus carries ATM header information, as well as the payload of the cells. The other signals in the module interface are used for congestion control and to connect to memory controllers to access the off-chip memory [3]. The complete module interface is documented in [4].

Usually, two application modules are present on the RAD. Typically, one handles data from the line card to the switch (ingress) and the other handles data from the switch to the line card (egress). As with the Transmutable Telecom System [5], modules can be replaced by reprogramming the FPGA in the system at any time. In the case of the FPX, this functionality occurs via partial reprogramming of the RAD FPGA. Modules can be replaced on the fly and independently of each other. A reconfiguration component performs a handshaking protocol with the modules to prevent loss of data.

3   Network Wrapper Concept

Network protocols are organized in layers. On the ATM data link layer, data is sent in fixed size cells. To provide variable length data exchange, a family of ATM Adaption Layers exists. The ATM Adaption Layer 5 (AAL5) is widely used to transport IP data over ATM networks. The Network layer uses IP packets to support routing through multiple, physically separated networks.

Components have been developed for the FPX that allow applications to handle data on different levels of abstraction. A similar implementation exists for IP over Ethernet and the corresponding network layers [6]. On the cell level, a Start of Cell (SOC) signal is given to an application module. For AAL5 frame based applications, Start-of-Frame (SOF) and End-of-Frame (EOF) signals indicate the beginning or the end of an AAL5 frame, respectively. An additional data-enable signal indicates whether valid payload data is being sent.

Translation steps are necessary between layers. A classical approach would be to create components for each protocol translation, for instance from cell level to AAL5 frame level. There would need to be a component for the reverse step as well, in our example from the frame level back to the cell level, i.e., segmentation. In a new approach, we combine these two translation units into one component, which has four interfaces

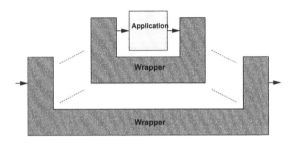

Fig. 2. Wrapper concept

as a consequence: two to support the lower level protocol and two to provide a higher level interface, respectively. Also the two units are connected to each other. This is useful to exchange additional information or to bypass the application. Latter is done in the cell processor (section 3.1).

When an application module is embedded into the new translation unit, it gets a shape like the letter U (figure 2). Regarding the data stream, the application only connects to the translating component, which wraps up the application itself. Therefore we will refer to the surrounding components as *wrappers*.

To support higher levels of abstraction, the wrappers can be nested. Since each has a well defined interface for an outer and an inner protocol level, they fit together within each other, as shown in(figure 2). As a result, we get a very modular design method to support applications for different protocols and levels of abstraction. Associating each wrapper with a specific protocol, we get a layered model comparable to the well known OSI/ISO networking reference model. This modularity gives application developers more freedom in their designs. They can choose the level of abstraction they needs for their specific application, while not needing to deal with the handling of complicated protocol issues, like frame boundaries or checksums.

3.1 Cell Based Processing

At the lowest level of abstraction, data is sent in fixed length cells. Applications or wrappers working on that protocol level typically process the ATM header and filter cells by their virtual channel. FPX Modules communicate with software via control cells, ATM cells with a well-defined structure used to perform remote configuration.

FPX Cell Processor The wrapper on the lowest level is the cell processor (figure 3). It performs every necessary step on the cell level that is common to all FPX modules. First of all, incoming ATM cells are checked against their Header Error Control (HEC) field, which is part of the 5 octet header. An 8 bit CRC is used to prevent errored cells from being misrouting. If the check fails, the cell is dropped.

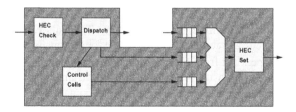

Fig. 3. Cell processor

Accepted cells are queried about their virtual channel information in the next step. The cell processor distinguishes between three different flows:

1. The cell is on the data VC for this module. In this case, the cell will be forwarded to the inner interface of the wrapper and thus to the application.
2. The cell is on the control cell VC and is tagged with the correct module ID. Control cells are processed by the cell processor itself.
3. None of the above, i.e. this cell is not destined for this module. These cells are bypassed and take a shortcut to the output of the cell processor.

The cell processor provides three FIFOs to buffer cells from either of the three paths. A multiplexer combines them and forwards the cells to their last stop. Just before they leave the cell processor, a new HEC is computed.

The control cell handling inside the cell processor is designed to be very flexible, thus making it easy for application developers to extend its functionality to fit the needs of their modules. Since user applications will typically support more types of control cells than the standard types, extendibility was an important goal in the design of the cell processor. A control cell processing framework handles common cases like data integrity.

3.2 Frame Based Processing

To handle data with arbitrary length over ATM networks, data is organized in frames, which are sent as multiple cells. Several adaption layers have been specified, which differ in the property of being connection-oriented or connectionless, in the ability to multiplex several protocols over one virtual channel and to reorder cells during transmission.

In the ATM Adaption Layer 5 (AAL5) [7, 8] datagrams or frames of arbitrary length are put into protocol data units (PDU). A PDU's length is always a multiple of 48 octets, because a PDU is sent as a multiple of ATM cells. One bit in the ATM header, the user bit of the PTI field, is used to indicate whether a cell is the last one of a PDU. The last 8 octets of the PDU are used by a trailer, which contains information about the actual length of the frame and a 32 bit CRC to ensure data integrity.

The frame processor is a wrapper module for the FPX to handle AAL5 frame data. Its interface is designed to give application modules a more abstract view of the data. The frame processor replaces the Start-of-Cell signal with three signals, namely Start-of-Frame (SOF), End-of-Frame (EOF) and Data-Enable (DataEn). As the name indicates, SOF indicates the transmission of a new frame. The Data-Enable signal indicates valid payload data. It can be seen as an enable signal for the data processing application. It is completely independent from the cell structure. Applications can therefore resize frames or append data very easily. Also generating new frames is now more convenient. After the EOF signal, two more words are sent, which contain the option and the length field and an indication whether the frame was transmitted correctly.

3.3 IP Packet Processing

The IP processor was developed to support IP based applications. It inherits the signalling interface from the frame processor and adds a Start-of-Payload (SOP) signal, to indicate the payload after the IP header. This wrapper serves three primary functions:

1. Checking the IP header integrity, i.e., the correctness of the header checksum. Corrupt packets are dropped.
2. Decrementing the Time To Live (TTL) field. As of RFC 1812 [9] all IP processing entities are required to decrement this field. Once this field reaches zero, the packet should not be forwarded any more. This is to prevent packets from looping around in networks due to mis-configured routers.
3. Recompute the length and the header checksum on outgoing IP packets.

An IP header has the length of 20 bytes, or 5 words.[1] The whole header must pass the header check before any decision about its integrity can be made. The IP Processor computes and then compares the header checksum. On a failure, the packet is not forwarded to the application. If the Time-To-Live field of an incoming packet is already zero, the packet is also dropped and an ICMP packet is sent instead. On outgoing IP packets the length field in the header and the header checksum are set accordingly. Therefore, a whole packet has to be buffered, before the actual length can be determined.

We have also implemented a processor to handle User Datagram Protocol (UDP) packets. This wrapper gives an indication to the embedded application when the data contains the payload of such a packet and handles the UDP checksum and length field. The UDP processor is used for an application that is not described in this paper.

4   IP Router OBIWAN

To demonstrate the functionality of our framework, we will now present a fully functional Internet Protocol router, which we call OBIWAN (Optimal Binary search IP lookup for Wide Area Networks). The router uses one external SRAM module and an internal bitmap. Routing entries can be configured with control cells as mentioned in section 3.1. The router extracts the destination IP address of incoming IP packets, which are encapsulated in AAL5 frames, buffers the data while the IP lookup is performed and forwards the packets with the VCI being replaced according to the next hop information. The WUGS switches the packets to one of the eight ports according to the new VCI. OBIWAN can operate at full line speed, i.e., 2.4 Gbps. It is designed to even work at the worst case, which is one IP packet in every ATM cell, or one lookup every 16 clock cycles. This provides a number of up to 6.25 million IP packets per second.

4.1   Lookup Algorithm

The lookup algorithm that we used for our implementation is a binary search over prefix lengths using hash tables. This algorithm is documented in detail in [10, 11]. The basic algorithm uses a hash table for each prefix length. A hash key and a value can be determined from the prefix and will be stored in the table. When a lookup is requested, the basic algorithm performs a binary search for the best matching prefix. It starts with the prefix length 16, and depending on a match it continues the search with a longer, i.e., 24 bits or a shorter, i.e., 8 bits length, until the longest matching prefix length has

---

[1] This applies to the vast majority of IP packets that do not contain any IP options.

been determined. The number of iterations, i.e., the depth of the binary search tree of the basic scheme is five.

Though the algorithm given above performs very well already, in terms of memory accesses, it still requires 3 simultaneous lookups to guarantee line speed operation. Reducing the number of memory accesses is our main goal in improving the algorithm above. This can be done by reducing the depth of the binary search tree. First, the algorithm combines two adjacent prefix length by expanding the shorter prefix to two more specific routing entries, which reduces the maximum depth of our search tree by one.

Many routing entries have a prefix length shorter or equal to 16 and our analysis of network traffic has shown, that around 50% of all routed IP packets will take one of these routes. These results led us to implement a bitmap for the first 16 prefix bits, which indicate, whether a longer prefix exists in the hash tables. This does not only reduce the binary search tree by another level, but also improves the lookup speed for every second IP packet significantly.

To reduce the overall memory consumption of the hash tables and to reduce the probability of collisions, we only use two relatively large hash tables. One for all prefix lengths from 17 to 24, and another one for the range 25 to 32. Our final configuration gives us two hash tables with four buckets per key each. The table for the shorter prefixes contains 64k entries with four buckets per word, the other 32k entries with two buckets per word. The key and value functions use a simple bit extraction algorithm, which is very efficient in hardware. Tests have shown, that this configuration is useful with real routing tables and does not give many collisions. Despite the fixed number of buckets per hash table entry, collisions can still be resolved by expanding a prefix to more entries, thus moving them to other locations in the table.

For each match in a hash table, the lookup algorithm should determine a next hop information. Since this information is only necessary at the very end of the lookup, we separated it from the hash tables and put them in a shadow-table to avoid unnecessary memory bandwidth usage.

4.2 Implementation

When IP packets first come into the router, the IP destination address is extracted and forwarded to the actual IP lookup engine. At the same time, the whole packet is stored in a FIFO (figure 4). The packet can only be forwarded when the next hop information, which is a new VCI, is available from the lookup engine. While the packet is written to the FIFO, the payload words are counted. The number is then put in a separate queue. On the output side of the router, the IP packets are forwarded, with the VCI being replaced, as soon as the next hop information is available from the IP lookup. There is also a queue for next hop information, in case the output port is congested and IP packets cannot be forwarded fast enough.

The actual IP lookup engine (figure 5) takes a destination IP address on its input and delivers a next hop information (VCI) on its output after some time. The IP lookup engine works strictly in order. The IP address is first checked against the internal bitmap, which is located in on-chip memory. As mentioned earlier, the bitmap contains the information, if the longest prefix for this address has at most 16 bits. Therefore the

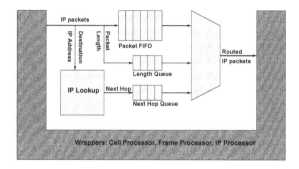

Fig. 4. IP router module OBIWAN

bitmap is $2^{16} = 64kb$ in size. If there is no longer prefix than 16 bits, the next step, the binary search over hash table lookups, is skipped and a next hop address is forwarded. A next hop address encodes the location of the next hop information in SRAM. Otherwise the IP address is forwarded to one of two engines, which perform the binary search.

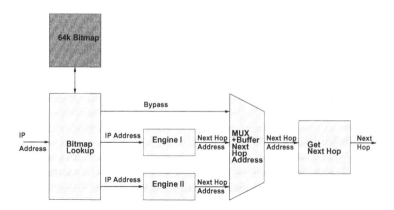

Fig. 5. IP routing lookup (block diagram)

The binary search units (figure 6) start with a prefix length of 24 bits, compute a key/value pair for the hash table and set the address for memory access. Because of buffers at the chip boundaries and inside the lookup engine, it takes 6 clock cycles, until the data from memory can be evaluated. During that time, some pre-computations are done: the next possible longer and shorter prefix lengths are determined, the corresponding key/value pairs and memory addresses are computed and stored. When the data words are finally available, the values of all buckets are compared to the value corresponding to the current IP address. On a match, the address for the longer prefix is selected for the next iteration, otherwise the address for the shorter prefix is chosen.

A match also updates the next hop address for the best matching prefix, which initially points to the 16 bit prefix of the IP address. After a total of 3 iterations, the next hop address is forwarded to retrieve the next hop information for the current IP address.

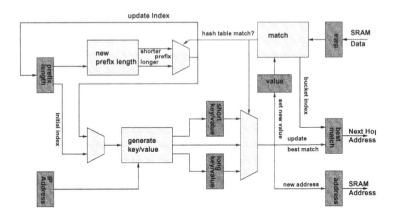

Fig. 6. Binary search on hash tables

Before we can read the next hop information from memory, we have to reorder the next hop addresses, coming from three different locations. Since some next hop addresses bypass the binary search, they may arrive out of order. The next hop information is read from a shadow table in memory.

5   Implementation Results

Our framework and the IP router are designed for the FPX. The system clock on the FPX is 100 MHz and the FPGA used is a Xilinx Virtex E 1000-7. The following table gives the size (in lookup tables) and the maximum speed of our components on the FPX hardware.

Wrapper/Module	LUTs	Speed (MHz)
Cell Processor	760	118
Frame Processor	312	116
IP Processor	680	109
OBIWAN	1196	111

6   Conclusions

We have presented a framework for IP packet processing applications in hardware. Although our current implementation was directed for use in the Field Programmable Port

Extender, the framework is very general and can be easily adapted to other platforms. We introduce the concept of U-shaped wrappers, where each handles a particular protocol level. Unlike the traditional pre-/postprocessor separation, the U shape allows to put components logically together, increasing the flexibility and reducing the number of cross-dependencies. The common interface between layers also lowers the learning curve.

The framework is useful for application developers, who are designing in the area of IP networking and ATM. We also presented a fully functional IP router, which runs at 2.4 Gbps (OC-48) and is based on our framework. The entire router consisting of all components (control cell processor, memory interface, frame processor, and OBIWAN router) have been synthesized for a Xilinx Virtex and fit within 17% of an XCV1000E FPGA. This indicates that the layering employed does not adversely affect size or performance. Besides the basic router, there is still plenty of space for future, application-defined functions, such as hardware-accelerated active networking or security processing.

References

[1] Tom Chaney, J. Andrew Fingerhut, Margaret Flucke, and Jonathan S. Turner. Design of a gigabit ATM switch. Technical Report WU-CS-96-07, Washington University in St. Louis, 1996.

[2] John W. Lockwood, Jonathan S. Turner, and David E. Taylor. Field programmable port extender (FPX) for distributed routing and queuing. In *Proceedings of FPGA 2000*, pages 137–144, Monterey, CA, USA, February 2000.

[3] John W. Lockwood, Naji Naufel, Jonathan S. Turner, and David E. Taylor. Reprogrammable Network Packet Processing on the Field Programmable Port Extender (FPX). In *Proceedings of FPGA 2001*, Monterey, CA, USA, February 2001.

[4] David E. Taylor, John W. Lockwood, and Sarang Dharmapurikar. Generalized RAD Module Interface Specification on the Field Programmable Port Extender (FPX). http://www.arl.wustl.edu/arl/projects/fpx/references, January 2001.

[5] Toshiaki Miyazaki, Kazuhiro Shirakawa, Masaru Katayama, Takahiro Murooka, and Atsushi Takahara. A transmutable telecom system. In *Proceedings of Field-Programmable Logic and Applications*, pages 366–375, Tallinn, Estonia, August 1998.

[6] Hamish Fallside and Michael J. S. Smith. Internet connected FPL. In *Proceedings of Field-Programmable Logic and Applications*, pages 48–57, Villach, Austria, August 2000.

[7] Juha Heinanen. Multiprotocol encapsulation over ATM adaptation layer 5. Internet RFC 1483, July 1993.

[8] Peter Newman et al. Transmission of flow labelled IPv4 on ATM data links. Internet RFC 1954, May 1996.

[9] Fred Baker. Requirements for IP version 4 routers. Internet RFC 1812, June 1995.

[10] Marcel Waldvogel, George Varghese, Jon Turner, and Bernhard Plattner. Scalable high speed IP routing table lookups. In *Proceedings of ACM SIGCOMM '97*, pages 25–36, September 1997.

[11] Marcel Waldvogel. *Fast Longest Prefix Matching: Algorithms, Analysis, and Applications*. Shaker Verlag, Aachen, Germany, April 2000.

Development of a Design Framework for Platform-Independent Networked Reconfiguration of Software and Hardware

Yajun Ha[1,2], Bingfeng Mei[1,2], Patrick Schaumont[1], Serge Vernalde[1], Rudy Lauwereins[1], and Hugo De Man[1,2]

[1] IMEC, Kapeldreef 75, Leuven 3001, Belgium,
yjha@imec.be,
http://www.imec.be
[2] Katholieke University Leuven, Department of Electrical Engineering, Kasteelpark Arenberg 10, Leuven 3001, Belgium

Abstract. The rapid development of the Internet opens wide opportunities for various types of network services. Development of new network services need the support of a powerful design framework. This paper describes such a design framework that can help service providers to build platform independent hardware-software co-designed services. Those new services consist of both software and hardware components, which can be reconfigured through the network. The new design framework can be considered as a Java framework with a hardware extension. Part of the measurement results and an application demonstrator are given.

1 Introduction

Many of us are familiar with software networked reconfiguration, of which Java technology is a good example. But in some applications, especially quality of service (QoS) oriented ones, it is required to extend networked reconfiguration to hardware [5].

Enabling hardware to be networked reconfigurable brings new challenges to the network service designers and EDA tool vendors. Of those challenges, support for platform independent hardware design becomes a very important and difficult requirement.

A lot of industry and academic efforts have already been put in the development of design tools for network-oriented reconfiguration. On the one hand for the industry category, design frameworks like Java [1] can support platform independent designs, but only with software components. Xilinx Online [8] is devoted to enable any network connected Xilinx programmable system that can be modified after the system has been deployed in the field. But basically, it is a vendor specific approach, not a platform-independent one. On the other hand for the academic category, virtual hardware and circlets concepts had been raised by Brebner[2][3]. The goal of circlets is to find a virtual description of circuits and integrated circlets with applets, which is quite similar to us. But the abstraction level that circlets work at is at logic level, and it needs too much mapping efforts in a resource limited terminal. JHDL [4] proposes to use general-purpose programming languages Java for FPGA design. Their work is focused on using

G. Brebner and R. Woods (Eds.): FPL 2001, LNCS 2147, pp. 264–274, 2001.
© Springer-Verlag Berlin Heidelberg 2001

Java to describe hardware, but not to solve platform-independent issues for networked hardware reconfiguraion. JBits [12] is currently developed in Xilinx, and it is a set of Java classes that provide an API to access Xilinx FPGA bitstreams. It is expected that networked hardware reconfiguration will be benefited from JBits.

This paper describes an extended Java design framework. In the design framework, service providers can build platform independent hardware-software co-designed services. Section 2 introduces the challenges and the proposed solutions for the networked reconfiguration. An overview of the platform independent design framework is then described. Next we introduce two of the main components of the framework: the hardware virtual machine and the virtual SW/HW interface. In that two sections, experimental results of hardware bitstream and bytecode sizes are compared, and performance measurement of the virtual SW/HW interface is given. Finally, a web MPEG player is introduced to demonstrate the design flow of this framework.

2   Problem Definition

In networked reconfiguration, the reconfiguration task is done in two steps and in two geographic sites: (1) a design is described on the server side. (2) clients pick up the design description from the server and implement it on their local reconfigurable platforms. Different clients use different reconfigurable platforms, that include CPU, FPGA and interface.

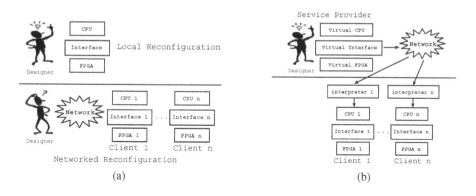

Fig. 1. Challenges and solutions for the networked reconfiguration. (a) Challenges   (b) Solutions.

But how do the challenges relate to networked reconfiguration? Let us first make a comparison between local reconfiguration and networked reconfiguration (see fig. 1(a)). In local reconfiguration, designers know exactly what CPU, interface and FPGA their platforms use. But in networked reconfiguration, this is not the case. Designers and implementation platforms are isolated in two geographic sites, and designers do not know the implementation platform details of their clients.

To cope with this problem, a design framework is being built to provide the service designer a simpler design environment. In the framework, the service designers only need to design towards to a single virtual platform. To build that single virtual platform, three abstractions are necessary for each of the three main platform components (CPU, Interface, FPGA) as shown in fig. 1(b). This means that we need a virtual representation of the CPU, interface, and FPGA. Since virtual CPUs like Java virtual machines [1] have already been commercially available, our current work is focused on developing a virtual FPGA and a virtual interface.

3   Design Framework Overview

An overview of the design framework will be given in this section by going through a complete design flow. The design flow consists of server and client components.

3.1   Design Flow on the Service Provider Side

On the service provider side, as the first stage, the service is represented by a functional model. This functional model will be partitioned into three sub-models in a hardware/software codesign environment as CoWare [9]. One sub-model describes the application software part. Another describes the application hardware part. The third describes the interface between the partitioned hardware and software sub-models. This interface sub-model contains both a software part and a hardware part.

The software sub-model and the software part of interface go through various phases of software development, which generates the detailed source code to implement the two sub-models. The detailed source code is then precompiled into software bytecode by a software virtual machine precompiler.

The hardware sub-model and the hardware part of interface are fed into a hardware design environment. After behavioural synthesis, the sub model for the hardware will be transformed into a structural register transfer level (RTL) hardware description. The hardware bytecode can be obtained by floorplanning this netlist on the abstract FPGA model.

Both hardware and software bytecodes are sent to the service bytecode binder, which produces the combined service bytefiles.

3.2   Design Flow on the Client Side

On the client side, the received service bytefile is first demultiplexed to software and hardware bytecode respectively. Software bytecode is interpreted by the software virtual machine and turned into *native application software code* that runs on the native CPU. On the other hand, the hardware bytecode is interpreted by the hardware virtual machine, and turned into *native FPGA bitstreams* that will configure the native FPGA. A HW/SW interface will first be defined via the virtual interface API calls. Through this defined interface, native FPGA bitstreams will be sent to the FPGA for reconfiguration. The reconfigured FPGA can then be used as a hardware accelerator. The native application software code interacts with the FPGA accelerator through the virtual interface.

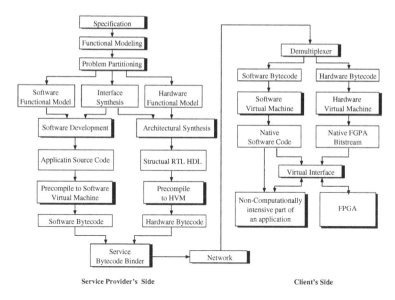

Fig. 2. Design flow in the framework

4   Hardware Virtual Machine

Initially, as for a choice of FPGA design flow for networked hardware reconfiguration, there are three options for the FPGA mapping tools [6]. Firstly, the mapping tools can be totally put on the service provider side. This is the strategy Xilinx Online [8] adopted. It is easy to implement in theory, but very troublesome in maintenance. As a second choice, the mapping tools can be totally put in the client's side. It is an easy way both for implementation and maintenance (from the point of view of the service provider), but too expensive for the terminals. Finally, as a third choice, mapping tools can be separated into two parts, partially on the service provider side (Map_S), and partially on the client side (Map_C). Let us define the Map_C block as *hardware virtual machine* (HVM), while Map_S block as *HVM-compiler*. As benefits of this approach, service providers only need to maintain a single or few FPGA CAD tools to distribute and update their new services, while at the same time, the client does a reasonable portion of the mapping task.

4.1   Logic vs RTL HVM

Once we decide to use the HVM approach for the service deployment, the next question is at which level should the HVM separate the design flow. A traditional FPGA design flow is shown in fig. 3. By separating the design flow at different levels, different HVMs can be obtained.

The level that a HVM belongs to is mainly depended on the level of abstract FPGA model that the HVM used. On the server side, each design will first be mapped on a abstract FPGA model, and then interpreted by its corresponding HVM on the client side. We will introduce two different level abstract FPGA models in the next two paragraphs.

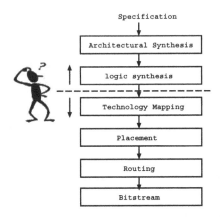

Fig. 3. Abstraction level consideration for hardware virtual machine.

Fig. 4(a) shows a logic level abstract FPGA model. Corresponding to commercial FPGAs, the abstract logic level FPGA model also contains three blocks. They are abstract logic block, abstract routing architecture, and abstract I/O pads [6]. Applications are first mapped and pre-placed and routed onto this abstract FPGA architecture. Then on the client side, the pre-placed and routed bytecode will be converted into local bitstream.

Fig. 4(b) shows a register transfer level abstract FPGA model. It consists of two parts: datapath and controller. The datapath is composed of different RTL level cores, e.g. ALU, ACU, multiplier, adder. The controller is based on microcode. Architectural synthesis tools like Frontier A|RT Designer [15] will be used to generate the RTL level structural VHDL netlist from the high level specification. In this structural VHDL netlist, the datapath is described by a netlist of datapath cores, while the controller is described by microcode, allowing for a flexible RAM implementation.

By using the RTL-level abstract FPGA model instead of the logic level one, RTL-level HVM is better than logic level HVM from several different aspects. From the bytecode size point of view, the RTL HVM bytecode size is much smaller than that of the logic level HVM, since less design information is contained at the RTL-level. The logic level bytecodes size normally are in the magnitude of MBits, wheras the RTL-level bytecodes are of the order of KBits (as shown in the table. 1). Besides, the RTL HVM enables those architectural specific features like carry chain to be used in its library cores, while logic level HVM does not. Moreover, because there are less net connections in the RTL-level than in the logic level, the run time interpretation of RTL HVM is much faster than that of the logic level HVM.

Bitstream, logic and RTL level bytecodes have been obtained for 5 large MCNC benchmark circuits [10]. The bitstream sizes are calculated according to XC4000 series FPGAs. The logic and RLT level bytecodes are obtained using VPR tools [11].

Circuit	#Gates	#FF	Bitstream (bits)	logic HVM Bytecode (bytes)	RTL HVM Bytecode (bits)
bigkey	4675	224	95,008	324,638	46,418
clma	22136	33	422,176	1916,162	189,931
elliptic	9475	1266	178,144	712,704	86,317
s38417	16911	1463	329,312	112,296	144,280
spla	10182	0	247,968	880,228	81,700
Average			254,521	789,205	109,729

Table 1. Bytecodes vs bitstreams comparison

Of which, logic bytecodes are based on their routed netlists, while RTL bytecodes are based on the placed netlist. Since the placed netlist of those benchmark circuits have already been at the gate level, therefore the bytecode sizes of their RTL level floorplanned netlists will be even smaller.

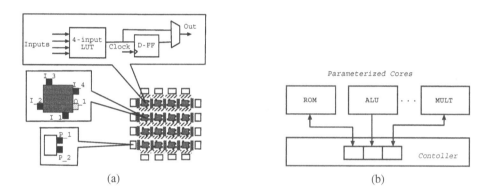

(a)   (b)

Fig. 4. Logic and register transfer level abstract FPGA. (a) logic level,   (b) register transfer level.

4.2   Implementation Flow for RTL HVM

In the hardware virtual machine implementation, JBits software [12] will be highly relied on. JBits software is a set of Java classes which provide an Application Programming Interface (API) to access the Xilinx FPGA bitstream. The interface can be used to construct complete circuits and to modify existing circuits. In addition, the object-oriented support in the Java programming language has permitted a small library of parameterizable, object oriented macro circuits or Cores to be implemented [13]. There is also a run-time router JRoute [14] to provide an API for run-time routing of FPGA devices.

Fig. 5 shows the implementation flow for the register transfer level hardware virtual machine. The circuit to be implemented is first processed to be described by a combination of datapaths and microcode-based controllers with architectural synthesis tools like Frontier A|RT Designer [15]. Both datapaths and controllers are considered as cores which can be abstractly described on the server side. The real implementations of those cores are provided in the core library on the client side.

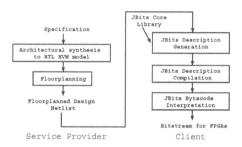

Fig. 5. Implementation flow for register transfer level hardware virtual machine.

On the client side, the hardware virtual machine maps each macro-netlist item into a JBits RTPCore module call. The floorplan and platform dependent information are used in the mapping process. After that, the platform independent macro-netlist is translated into a specific JBits Java program, which can finally create the FPGA specific bitstream.

4.3   JBits Description Generation

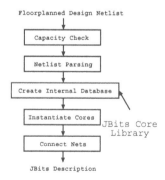

Fig. 6. JBits description generation.

The central task of the hardware virtual machine is to interprete the hardware bytecode and generate its corresponding JBits description. As shown in fig. 6, the JBits

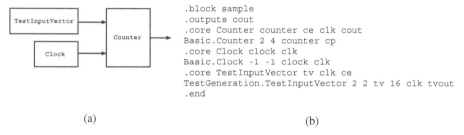

```
.block sample
.outputs cout
.core Counter counter ce clk cout
Basic.Counter 2 4 counter cp
.core Clock clock clk
Basic.Clock -1 -1 clock clk
.core TestInputVector tv clk ce
TestGeneration.TestInputVector 2 2 tv 16 clk tvout
.end
```

(a)   (b)

Fig. 7. Example for JBits description generation. (a) RTL level structural view of the counter to be implemented, (b) floorplanned netlist description obtained from its hardware bytecode.

program generation starts from the capacity check of the floorplanned design netlist, which checks that whether the local platform is big enough to accommodate to the application to be downloaded. The second step is to create the internal database by parsing the netlist. This database is based on the JBits core library, where the JBits description for each of the RTL-level cores is stored. From the information in the database, cores are instantiated, and nets between cores are specified. The outcome of those transformation steps is a full JBits description (program) that can be used to generate the final bitstream in seconds.

Fig. 7 gives an example of JBits program generation. To implement a small design as shown in fig. 7(a), a floorplanned netlist like in fig. 7 is first extracted from its bytecode. When this netlist is fed into hardware virtual machine, a JBits program will be generated. This program will be later compiled by the Java precompiler and executed by Java virtual machine to get the bitstream. In this counter example, it takes only 7 seconds to get the bitstream from its JBits bytecode.

5 Virtual Interface

To enable network application developers design their applications with only one interface in mind when considering the interfacing issues, a platform independent virtual interface as shown in fig. 8(a) has been previously worked out in [7]. The virtual interface has two functions: Firstly it provides platform independent API calls to prepare a configuration interface for the FPGAs to be configured. Secondly it provides platform independent API calls for communication (reading and writing) between the software implemented on CPU and the hardware implemented on FPGA.

The virtual interface consists of software and hardware parts. As you can see from fig.8(a), the local HW/SW interface has been isolated by the virtual software and hardware interface respectively. The software (Java program) only communicates with the virtual software interface, wheras the hardware (FPGA) only communicates with virtual hardware. Nevertheless the real communication is still done through the local SW/HW interface. This solution abstracts as much as possible platform specific details from the application designer, at the expense of some performance sacrifice for the interface. The measurments for reading and writing operations with and without virtual interface are

	time per write (us)	time per read (us)
without virtual interface	23	27
with virtual interface	214	381
penalty	191	354

Table 2. Performance measurement for virtual interface

given in table. 2. We saw around 10 times penality for the virtual interface with respect to specially designed interface. (The measurements are done by HPjmeter for reading and writing with virtual interface, and gprofiler for reading and writing without virtual interface).

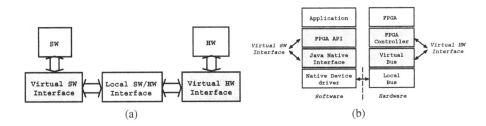

(a)   (b)

Fig. 8. (a) overview of the virtual software hardware interface,   (b) detailed diagram of the virtual Java FPGA interface.

A more detailed high-level overview of the FPGA API implementation is shown in fig. 8(b). On the software side, FPGA API and Java Native Interface constitute the virtual software interface. On the hardware side, virtual bus and FPGA controller constitute the virtual hardware interface.

6   Case Study

A web MPEG player demonstrator had been implemented on a APS-X208 board [16]. In the demonstrator, a co-designed MPEG player is designed and deployed in the framework. IDCT decoder of the player is partitioned to hardware, wheras all the other functions are partitioned to software. Bitstream of the IDCT and Java bytecodes for the rest of the MPEG player are put on the http server. On the client side, a client can visit the server page, and download the co-designed MPEG player and implement it on his own platform. On his platform, the virtual interface had been installed.

This web MPEG player is constructed to demonstrate the design flow of our framework. But in the current demonstrator, the HVM part of the design flow is bypassed, and only the bitstream for the IDCT block are transmitted with Java bytecode. Our final goal is to transmit hardware bytecode with Java bytecode, instead of bitstream in this demonstrator. For further details of the demonstrator, please refer to [7].

7   Current Status and Future Work

The framework structure as shown in fig.2 has been established and functions for each of the components in the framework have been identified. The virtual interface for the framework has been designed and a MPEG movie player demonstrator has been constructed to show the framework design flow [7]. Logic level HVM has been investigated, and its bytecode format and sizes have been obtained and reported in [6]. As for the RTL-level HVM design flow, the floorplanned netlist for high level specifications can be generated, and we are currently working on the JBits description generator. In the future, the JBits core library will be built for the core library of architectural synthesis tool Frontier A|RT Designer, and the RTL HVM implementation flow will be evaluated by using it to design a complete application.

8   Conclusions

A framework that enables networked reconfiguration of both software and hardware is presented. In the framework, networked reconfiguration users only need to develop a single service description targeted on a single abstract software and hardware platform. The SW/HW co-designed services developed in the framework allow a write once run everywhere scheme. The framework is a new Java platform with a hardware extension.

References

1. The source for Java technology.(http://java.sun.com)
2. G. Brebner: Circlets: Circuits as applets. Proceedings of FCCM. (1998)
3. G. Brebner: A virtual hardware operating system for the Xilinx XC6200. Proceedings of 6th FPL. Springer LNCS 1142 (1996) 327-336
4. B. Hutchings, and B. Nelson: Using general-purpose programming languages for FPGA design. Proceedings of DAC. (2000)
5. Y. Ha, S.Vernalde, P. Schaumont, M. Engels, and H. De Man: Building a virtual framework for networked reconfigurable hardware and software objects. Proceedings of PDPTA. 6 (2000) 3046–3052
6. Y. Ha, P. Schaumont, M. Engels, S.Vernalde,F. Potargent, L. Rijnders, and H. De Man: A hardware virtual machine to support networked reconfiguration. Proceedings of RSP (2000) 194–199
7. Y. Ha, G. Vanmeerbeeck, P. Schaumont, S.Vernalde, M. Engels, R. Lauwereins, and H. De Man: Virtual Java/FPGA Interface for Networked Reconfiguration. Proceedings of ASP-DAC. (2001) 558–563
8. R. Sevcik, Internet Reconfigurable Logic, white papers, Xilinx Inc, 1999.
9. CoWare Software. (www.coware.com)
10. S. Yang: Logic Synthesis and Optimization Benchmarks, Version 3.0. Technical Report, Microelectronics Center of North Carolina. 1991
11. V. Betz and J. Rose: VPR: A New Packing, Placement and Routing Tool for FPGA Research. Int. Workshop on Field-Programmable Logic and Applications. 1997 213–222
12. S. Guccione, D. Levi and P. Sundararajan: JBits: Java based interface for reconfigurable computing. Proceedings of 2nd Annual Military and Aerospace Applications of Programmable Devices and Technologies Conference

13. S. Guccione, D. Levi: Run-Time Parameterizable Cores. Proceedings of the 9th International Workshop on Field-Programmable Logic and Applications. (1999) 215–222
14. Eric Keller: JRoute: A Run-Time Routing API for FPGA. Proceedings of the Reconfigurable Architecture Workshop. (2000) 874–881
15. Frontier Design. (www.frontierd.com)
16. APS-X208 FPGA test board user's guide. Associated Professional Systems Inc. Dec 1998.

The MOLEN $\rho\mu$-Coded Processor

Stamatis Vassiliadis, Stephan Wong, and Sorin Coţofană

Computer Engineering Laboratory,
Electrical Engineering Department,
Faculty of Information Technology and Systems,
Delft University of Technology,
Delft, The Netherlands
{Stamatis, Stephan, Sorin}@CE.ET.TUDelft.NL

Abstract. In this paper, we introduce the MOLEN $\rho\mu$-coded processor which comprises hardwired and microcoded reconfigurable units. At the expense of three new instructions, the proposed mechanisms allow instructions, entire pieces of code, or their combination to execute in a reconfigurable manner. The reconfiguration of the hardware and the execution on the reconfigured hardware are performed by ρ-microcode (an extension of the classical microcode to allow reconfiguration capabilities). We include fixed and pageable microcode hardware features to extend the flexibility and improve the performance. The scheme allows partial reconfiguration and includes caching mechanisms for non-frequently used reconfiguration and execution microcode. Using simulations, we establish the performance potential of the proposed processor assuming the JPEG and MPEG-2 benchmarks, the ALTERA APEX20K boards for the implementation, and a hardwired superscalar processor. After implementation, cycle time estimations and normalization, our simulations indicate that the execution cycles of the superscalar machine can be reduced by 30% for the JPEG benchmark and by 32% for the MPEG-2 benchmark using the proposed processor organization.

1 Introduction

Reconfigurable hardware coexisting with a core processor can be considered as a good candidate for speeding up processor performance. Such an approach can be very promising. However, as indicated in [1], the organization of such a hybrid processor can be viewed mostly as an open topic. In most cases, the hybrid organization assumes the general-purpose paradigm. In such an organization, it is assumed that the processor operates in "ordinary processor environments" and is extended by reconfigurable unit(s) that speed-up the processing when possible. The execution and the reconfiguration are under the control of the "core" processor. Furthermore, due to the potential reprogrammability of the reconfigurable processor, a high flexibility is assumed in terms of programming resulting in tuning the reconfiguration for specific algorithms [2] or for the general-purpose paradigm [1].

In this paper, we introduce a machine organization where the hardware reconfiguration and the execution on the reconfigured hardware is performed by firmware via ρ-microcode (an extension of the classical microcode to include reconfiguration

G. Brebner and R. Woods (Eds.): FPL 2001, LNCS 2147, pp. 275–285, 2001.
© Springer-Verlag Berlin Heidelberg 2001

and execution for resident and non-resident microcode). Mechanisms within the extended microcode engine allow permanent and pageable reconfiguration and execution ρ-microcode to coexist. Furthermore, we provide partial reconfiguration capability for "off-line" configurations and prefetching of configurations. Assuming the proposed machine organization, realistic implementations for reconfigurable operations, and cycle time computations regarding the implementation of the reconfigurable part, we show via simulations that: we are able to reduce the superscalar machine cycles by 30% for the JPEG encoding benchmark. Furthermore, the superscalar machine cycles were reduced by 32% for the MPEG-2 encoding benchmark.

The organization of the paper is as follows. Section 2 discusses in detail the new custom computing processor and the required architectural extensions. Furthermore, it also introduces a number of mechanisms to enhance the performance of the reconfigurable unit. Section 3 introduces the framework we have used to evaluate the performance and the expected performance of our proposal. Section 4 discusses some related work. Section 5 presents some concluding remarks.

2   General Description

In its more general form, the proposed machine organization can be described as in Figure 1. In this organization, the I_BUFFER stores the instructions that are fetched from the memory. Subsequently, the ARBITER performs a partial decoding on these instructions in order to determine where they should be issued. Instructions that have been implemented in fixed hardware are issued to the core processing (CP) unit which further decodes them before sending them to their corresponding functional units. The needed data is fetched from the general-purpose registers (GPRs) and results are written back to the same GPRs. The control register (CR) stores other status information.

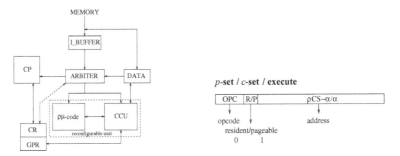

Fig. 1. *The proposed machine organization.*

Fig. 2. *The* p-set, c-set, *and* execute *instruction formats.*

The reconfigurable unit consists of a custom configured unit (CCU)[1] and the $\rho\mu$-code unit. An operation[2] performed by the reconfigurable unit is divided into two distinct process phases: **set** and **execute**. The **set** phase is responsible for configuring the

---

[1] Such a unit could be for example implemented by a Field-Programmable Gate Array (FPGA).

[2] An operation can be as simple as an instruction or as complex as a piece of code of a function.

CCU enabling it to perform the required operation(s). Such a phase may be subdivided into two sub-phases: partial **set** (*p*-**set**) and complete **set** (*c*-**set**). The *p*-**set** sub-phase is envisioned to cover common functions of an application or set of applications. More specifically, in the *p*-**set** sub-phase the CCU is *partially* configured to perform these common functions. While the *p*-**set** sub-phase can be possibly performed during the loading of a program or even at chip fabrication time, the *c*-**set** sub-phase is performed during program execution. In the *c*-**set** sub-phase, the remaining part of the CCU (not covered in the *p*-**set** sub-phase) is configured to perform other less common functions and thus *completing* the functionality of the CCU. The configuration of the CCU is performed by executing reconfiguration microcode[3] (either loaded from memory or resident) in the $\rho\mu$-code unit. In the case that partial reconfigurability is not possible or not convenient, the *c*-**set** sub-phase can perform the entire configuration. The **execute** phase is responsible for actually performing the operation(s) on the (now) configured CCU by executing (possibly resident) execution microcode stored in the $\rho\mu$-code unit.

In relation to these three phases, we introduce three new instructions: *c*-**set**, *p*-**set**, and **execute**. Their instruction format is given in Figure 2. We must note that these instructions do *not* specifically specify an operation and then load the corresponding reconfiguration and execution microcode. Instead, the *p*-**set**, *c*-**set**, and **execute** instructions directly point to the (memory) location where the reconfiguration or execution microcode is stored. In this way, different operations are performed by loading different reconfiguration and execution microcodes. That is, instead of specifying new instructions for the operations (requiring instruction opcode space), we simply point to (memory) addresses. The location of the microcode is indicated by the resident/pageable-bit (R/P-bit) which implicitly determines the interpretation of the the the address field, i.e., as a memory address α (R/P=1) or as a ρ-CONTROL STORE address ρCS-α (R/P=0) indicating a location within the $\rho\mu$-code unit. This location contains the first instruction of the microcode which must always be terminated by an *end_op* microinstruction.

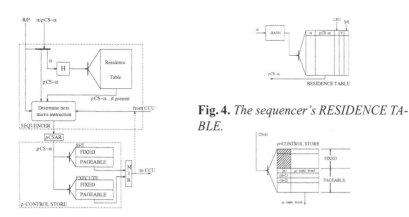

Fig. 3. *$\rho\mu$-code unit internal organization.*

Fig. 4. *The sequencer's RESIDENCE TABLE.*

Fig. 5. *Internal organization of one section of the ρ-CONTROL STORE.*

---

[3] Reconfiguration microcode is generated by translating a reconfiguration file into microcode.

The $\rho\mu$-code unit: The $\rho\mu$-code unit can be implemented in configurable hardware. Since this is only a performance issue and not a conceptual one, it is not considered further in detail. In this presentation, for simplicity, we assume that the $\rho\mu$-code unit is hardwired. The internal organization of the $\rho\mu$-code unit is given in Figure 3. In all phases, microcode is used to perform either reconfiguration of the CCU or control the execution on the CCU. Both types of microcode are conceptually the same and no distinction is made between them in the remainder of this section. The $\rho\mu$-code unit comprises two main parts: the SEQUENCER and the ρ-CONTROL STORE. The SEQUENCER mainly determines the microinstruction execution sequence and the ρ-CONTROL STORE is mainly used as a storage facility for microcodes. The execution of microcodes starts with the SEQUENCER receiving an address from the ARBITER and interpreting it according to the R/P-bit. When receiving a memory address, it must be determined whether the microcode is already cached in the ρ-CONTROL STORE or not. This is done by checking the RESIDENCE TABLE (see Figure 4) which stores the most frequently used translations of memory addresses into ρ-CONTROL STORE addresses and keeps track of the validity of these translations. It can also store other information: least recently used (LRU) and possibly additional information required for virtual addressing[4] support. In the cases that a ρCS-α is received or a valid translation into a ρCS-α is found, it is transferred to the 'determine next microinstruction'-block. This block determines which (next) microinstruction needs to be executed:

- When receiving address of first microinstruction: Depending on the R/P-bit, the correct ρCS-α is selected, i.e., from instruction field or from RESIDENCE TABLE.
- When already executing microcode: Depending on previous microinstruction(s) and/or results from the CCU, the next microinstruction address is determined.

The resulting ρCS-α is stored in the ρ-control store address register (ρCSAR) before entering the ρ-CONTROL STORE. Using the ρCS-α, a microinstruction is fetched from the ρ-CONTROL STORE and then stored in the microinstruction register (MIR) before it controls the CCU reconfiguration or before it is executed by the CCU.

The ρ-CONTROL STORE comprises two sections[5], namely a **set** section and an **execute** section. Both sections are further divided into a **fixed** part and **pageable** part. The fixed part stores the resident reconfiguration and execution microcode of the **set** and **execute** phases, respectively. Resident microcode is commonly used by several invocations (including reconfigurations) and it is stored in the fixed part so that the performance of the **set** and **execute** phases is possibly enhanced. Which microcode resides in the fixed part of the ρ-CONTROL STORE is determined by performance analysis of various applications and by taking into consideration various software and hardware parameters. Other microcodes are stored in memory and the pageable part of the ρ-CONTROL STORE acts like a cache to provide temporal storage. Cache mechanisms are incorporated into the design to ensure the proper substitution and access of the microcode present in the ρ-CONTROL STORE. This is exactly what is provided by the RESIDENCE TABLE which invalidates entries when microcode has been replaced (utilizing the valid (V) bit) or substitutes the least recently used (LRU) entries with new ones. Finally, the RESIDENCE can be common for both the **set** and **execute**

---

[4] For simplicity of discussion, we assume that the system only allows real addressing.

[5] Both sections can be identical, but are probably only differing in microinstruction wordsizes.

pageable ρ-CONTROL STORE sections or separate. In assuming a common table implementation, an additional bit needs to be added to determine which part of pageable ρ-CONTROL STORE is addressed (depicted as the S/E-bit in Figure 4).

3   Performance Evaluation

To evaluate the proposed scheme, we have performed various experiments. The framework of our evaluations and assumptions are described below. We use as benchmark multimedia applications comprising: $ijpeg$ benchmark from the Independent JPEG Group (release 6b) and $mpeg2enc$ benchmark from the MPEG Software Simulation Group (v1.2). As data sets for the benchmarks we used: for $ijpeg$, we have four pictures taken from the SPEC95 $ijpeg$ benchmark: $testimg$ (277×149), $specmun$ (1024×688), $penguin$ (1024×739), and $vigo$ (1024×768). For $mpeg2enc$, we have taken the three frames set which is part of the benchmark. Furthermore, the well-known shortcut before the IDCT operation has been removed in order to abtain a fair comparison.

We have used the *sim-outorder* simulator from the SimpleScalar Toolset (v2.0)[3]. This base machine we use for comparison comprises: 4 integer ALUs, 1 integer MULT/DIV-unit, 4 FP adders, 1 FP MULT/DIV-unit, and 2 memory ports (R/W). We are interested in a realistic possibly worse case scenario, not just maximum potential performance. In order to achieve a realistic comparison: We have assumed the ALTERA APEX20K[6] chip and used the following software: FPGA Express from Synopsis (build 3.4.0.5211) and MAX+PLUS II (version 9.23 baseline). We have implemented the configurations of reconfigurable operations in VHDL and compiled it to the Altera technology directly or we implemented sub-units and mapped an operation on these sub-units. For all implementations we estimated: total area in terms of LUTs, number of cycles to perform an operation, and cycle clock frequency.

Furthermore, we assumed that the base superscalar machine can be clocked at 1 GHz. Given that cycles in a reconfigurable machine are slower than a hardwired machine, we determine the cycles required for the reconfigurable part using a normalization. The assumed normalization can be explained via an example. Assume that an reconfigurable instruction requires 2 cycles and that the estimated frequency is 200 MHz. Comparing the number of cycles alone is not enough to evaluate the scheme. We normalize to the superscalar cycles by multiplying the 2 cycles by 5 as the machine cycle of the reconfigurable units is 5 times slower than the hardwired counterpart. That is in our evaluation, the reconfigurable instruction takes 10 machine cycles rather than 2 cycles to complete. Finally, we assume that no partial reconfiguration is possible (i.e., no p-**set** phase). This is the worst time assumption for our scheme providing a low bound for our schemes performance gains. Further, we have assumed that there is no resident microcode which also is a worse case scenario for the proposed scheme.

---

[6] We have to note that our FPGA technology assumption is a worse case scenario when compared to other more advanced FPGA structures with storage capabilities such as the Xilinx Virtex II family [4]. Therefore, it is expected that more improvements can be expected when our proposal is used in conjunction with such FPGA structures.

By considering the application domain, we have decided to consider for reconfigurable code the following operations: SAD, 2D DCT, 2D IDCT, and VLC operations. These operation can be found in multimedia standards like JPEG and MPEG-2.

Area and speed estimates: In the first stage of estimating the overall performance of our approach, we have estimated the area requirements and possible clock speeds of the four multimedia operations within the multimedia standards JPEG and MPEG-2. The results are presented in Table 1. Column one shows the operations performed. Column two presents the area that is required to implement the operation on an Altera APEX20K FPGA chip. Column three shows the number of clock cycles that the implemented operation needs to produce its results. The number in parentheses shows the maximum possible clock speed that was attainable as presented by the synthesis software. The normalized clock cycles are shown in the fourth column. By taking these normalized clock cycle numbers into our simulations, we can better estimate the performance increases when using our configurable unit inside a 1 GHz processor. We must note that the implementations used are not optimal and were only used to provide us with a good estimation of the number of clock cycles to use in the to be discussed simulations. Better implementations will yield higher performance increases. For the SAD operation, a complete VHDL model was written for the whole operation. For the DCT and IDCT cases, we did not write a complete VHDL model. Instead, we opted to estimate the area of the implementation based on the area and the performance of a 16x16 multiplier and a 32-bit adder and implemented the algorithm presented in [5].

operation	area	clock cycles (clock speed)	normalized cycles
16x16 SAD	1699 LUTs	39 (197 MHz)	234
16x16 multiply	1482 LUTs	12 (175 MHz)	69
32-bit adder	382 LUTs	5 (193 MHz)	21
DCT	using multiplier & adder		282
IDCT	using multiplier & adder		282
VLC	21408 RAM bits	variable	variable

Table 1. *Area and speed estimates.*

abbreviation	description
RLL (1000)	reconfiguration microcode load latency
RL (1000)	reconfiguration latency
MLL (100)	execution microcode load latency
ML	execution latency

Table 2. *Important latencies.*

Finally, the VLC case also requires special attention as also no VHDL model was written for it to estimate its area requirements. Instead, we obtained the higher bound on the area requirement by multiplying the total number of entries in the tables by the longest VLC code length. This resulted in an area requirement of 21408 RAM bits. Since the VLC operation greatly depends on the coarseness of the quantization step, it is not possible to use a single number of clock cycles that applies to all cases. Instead, we opted to simulate the VLC using a wide range of possible clock cycles in order to get an insight of the benefits of utilizing such an implementation in the CCU.

Simulation of the reconfigurable unit: Before we discuss the simulation results, we present the assumptions we have made prior to running the simulations. We have assumed that we extend a superscalar architecture with only two new instructions, namely the *c*-**set** and the **execute** instructions. Furthermore, we have assumed that we extend a superscalar processor with our reconfigurable unit to support the new instructions. Other assumptions are: the CCU can only contain one of the implementations as presented in the previous paragraphs. All microcode must be loaded at least once into the $\rho\mu$-code unit. Thus, we assume no microcode is present in the FIXED parts. The PAGE-ABLE part is only large enough to contain at most four microcode programs and we do not use the caching residence table. Furthermore, we have assumed a bandwidth of 32 bits per clockcycle between the processor and the caches. Finally, the loading of both the reconfiguration and execution microcode is handled by the existing memory units.

There are four latencies closely related to our processor that possibly affect the overall performance (see Table 2). In the discussion to follow, we fixed all the values (using number shown in brackets) except the ML value. By varying the ML value, we tried to gain more insight into potential performance gains when faster implementations were used (i.e., lower ML values). Our implementation is indicated in bold.

Simulation results of *ijpeg* **benchmark:** In Table 3, we show the results of the encoder within the *ijpeg* benchmark which utilizes both the DCT and VLC implementations. We have varied the ML values between different values. The default case does not utilizes the new $\rho\mu$-code unit.

	testimg	*specmun*	*penguin*	*vigo*
default	6512947	129706215	142284352	149363055
DCT ML				
100	4525549 (-30.51%)	91279280 (-29.63%)	100581306 (-29.31%)	106461146 (-28.72%)
200	4610649 (-29.21%)	92930480 (-28.35%)	102373306 (-28.04%)	108304346 (-27.49%)
282	**4680431 (-28.14%)**	**94284464 (-27.31%)**	**103842746 (-27.02%)**	**109815770 (-26.48%)**
400	4780849 (-26.59%)	96232880 (-25.81%)	105957306 (-25.53%)	111990746 (-25.02%)
VLC ML				
100	6004054 (-7.81%)	120259786 (-7.28%)	131813270 (-7.36%)	138643470 (-7.18%)
200	6094054 (-6.43%)	121910986 (-6.01%)	133618070 (-6.09%)	140486670 (-5.94%)
400	6274054 (-3.67%)	125213386 (-3.46%)	137227670 (-3.55%)	144173070 (-3.47%)
DCT & VLC	4505811 (-30.82%)	91167689 (-29.71%)	100294922 (-29.51%)	106157895 (-28.93%)

Table 3. *ijpeg encoder* cycle *results.*

Table 3 clearly shows that implementing the DCT and VLC operations in the CCU is able to reduce the total number of clock cycles to complete the *ijpeg* encoder. For the DCT implementation, varying the ML-value between 100 cycles and 400 cycles is able to reduce the total number of clock cycles by between 30% and 25%. Assuming our implementation (ML = 282) for the DCT results in a reduction of about 27%. For the VLC implementation, the reduction is between 8% and 3%. Allowing the CCU to be reconfigured to either the DCT and VLC implementations shows a decrease of about 30%. In this case, we have assumed an ML-value of 200 for the VLC implementation. We can clearly see that the reconfiguration latencies is having an effect on the performance. This can be seen by adding the reduction of the only using the DCT and only the VLC implementations which is higher than 30%. Besides looking at the total number of clock cycles, we have also taken a look at some other metrics. In the cases, that the CCU can be configured to both the DCT and the VLC implementation, the following results were also obtained from the simulations: the total number instructions was reduced by 40.16%, the total number of branches was reduced by 28.55%, the total number of loads was reduced by 44.70%, and the total number of stores was reduced by 33.83%.

Simulation results of *mpeg2enc* **benchmark:**   In the simulations we have intentionally left out the results of both the IDCT and VLC implementations as they did not provide much performance increases. The main reason is that they only constitute a small part of all the operations in the MPEG-2 encoding scheme. From the result presented in the left table in Figure 6, we can see that the biggest contributor to the overall performance gain is the SAD which is able to decrease the number of cycles by about 35% (in a more ideal case). Using our implementation (ML = 234) results in a reduction of the number of clock cycles by 20%. Allowing the CCU to be reconfigured to either the DCT or the SAD implementation shows a decrease of 32%. Here we observe that the result is additive suggesting that the reconfiguration and execution of both operations do not influence each other. Besides looking at the metric the total number of execution cycles, we have also taken a look at other metrics and they are also presented in the right two tables in Figure 6.

	# of cycles	difference (in %)		total number of		difference		total number of		difference
default	93245923	(0.00%)		*instructions*				*loads*		
DCT ML				default	137500555	0.0%		default	36191189	0.0%
100	81350756	(-12.76%)		DCT	118757904	-13.63%		DCT	33387057	-7.75%
200	81465956	(-12.63%)		SAD	66016988	-51.99%		SAD	22316745	-38.34%
282	**81560420**	**(-12.53%)**		DCT & SAD	46291842	-66.33%		DCT & SAD	19512613	-46.08%
400	81696356	(-12.39%)		*branches*				*stores*		
SAD ML				default	23233942	0.0%		default	2679153	0.0%
100	59803641	(-35.86%)		DCT	21242800	-8.57%		DCT	2450749	-8.53%
200	70797383	(-24.07%)		SAD	10137590	-56.37%		SAD	2679174	+0.00%
234	**74608673**	**(-19.99%)**		DCT & SAD	8146448	-64.94%		DCT & SAD	2450770	-8.52%
400	93528041	(+0.30%)								
DCT & SAD	**62928429**	**(-32.51%)**								

Fig. 6. *mpeg2enc* cycle *results (left table) and other metrics (right table).*

The big decrease in the total number of loads in the case SAD is due to the fact that previously the data elements (which are 8 bits) were loaded one by one. However, in our CCU implementation we fully utilized the available memory bandwidth and loaded 4 elements at the same time and thus tremendously diminishing the number of loads. The number of stores remains the same as the intermediate results in the original could be stored in registers and therefore not requiring stores. We must note, that the computation of the SAD was dependent on two variables, namely the height and the distance (in bytes in memory) between vertically adjacent pels. Four resulting possibilities emerge and for each of these possibilities a different microcode was needed.

4   Related Work

In this paper, we introduce a machine organization where the reconfiguration of the hardware and the execution on the reconfigured hardware is done in firmware via ρ-microcode (an extension of the classical microcode to include reconfiguration and execution for resident and non-resident microcode). The microcode engine is extended with mechanisms that allow for permanent and pageable reconfiguration and execution code to coexist. We provide partial reconfiguration possibilities for "off-line" configurations and prefetching of configurations. Regarding related work, we have considered over 40 proposals. We report here a number of them that somehow use some partial or total reconfiguration prefetching. It should be noted that our scheme is rather different in principle from all related work as we use microcode, pageable/fixed local memory, hardware assists for pageable reconfiguration, partial reconfigurations, etc.. As it will be clear from the short description of the related work, we differentiated from them in one or more mechanisms. The *Programmable Reduced Instruction Set Computer (PRISC)* [6] attaches a Programmable Functional Unit (PFU) to the register file of a processor for application specific instructions. Reconfiguration is performed via exceptions. In an attempt to reduce FPGA reconfiguration overheads, Hauck proposed a slight modification to the PRISC architecture in [7]: an instruction is explicitly provided to the user that behaves like a NOP if the required circuit is already configured on the array, or is in the process of being configured. By inserting the configuration instruction before it is actually required, a so-called *configuration prefetching* procedure is initiated. At this point the host processor is free to perform other computations, overlapping the reconfiguration of the PFU with other useful work. The *OneChip* introduced by Wittig and Chow [8] extends PRISC and allows PFU for implementing any combinational or sequential circuit, subject to its size and speed. The system proposed by Trimberger [9] consists of a host processor augmented with a PFU, *Reprogrammable Instruction Instruction Set Accelerator* (RISA), much like the PRISC mentioned above. *Garp* designed by Hauser and Wawrzynek [10] is another example of a MIPS derived Custom Computing Machine (CCM). The MIPS instruction set is augmented with several non-standard instructions dedicated to loading a new configuration, initiating the execution of the newly configured computing facilities, moving data between the array and the processor's own registers, saving/retriving the array states, branching on conditions provided by the array, etc. PRISM (*Processor Reconfiguration Through Instruction-Set Methamorphosis*) one of the earliest proposed CCM [11], was developed as a proof-of-concept system, in order to handle the loading of FPGA configurations, the compiler inserts library function calls into the program stream. From this description, we can conclude that explicit reconfiguration procedures are present. Gilson's [12] CCM architecture comprises a host processor and two or more FPGA-based *computing devices*. The host processor controls the reconfiguration of FPGAs by loading new configuration data through a Host Interface into the FPGA Configuration Memory. Schmit [13] proposes a partial run-time reconfiguration mechanism, called *pipeline reconfiguration* or *striping*, by which the FPGA is reconfigured at a granularity that corresponds to a pipeline stage of the application being implemented. The PipeRench coprocessor developed in Carnegie Mellon University [14] is focused on implementing linear (1-D) pipelines of arbitrary length. PipeRench is envisioned as a coprocessor in a general-purpose computer, and has direct access to the same memory space as the host processor. The *Reconfigurable Data Path Architecture* (rDPA) is also a self-steering autonomous reconfigurable architecture. It consists of a mesh of identical Data Path Units (DPU) [15]. The data-flow direction through the mesh is only from west and/or north to east and/or south and is also data-driven. A word entering rDPA contains a configuration bit which is used to distinguish the configuration information from data. Therefore, a word can specify either a SET or an EXECUTE instruction, the arguments of the instructions being the configuration information or data to be processed. A set of computing facilities can be configured on rDPA. The input/output data for these computing facilities can be written/read either by routing them through the mesh, or directly by means of a global I/O bus.

5   Conclusion

In this paper, we introduced the MOLEN $\rho\mu$-coded processor which contains a hardwired microcoded configurable unit. The proposed mechanisms allow, at the expenses of three new instructions to perform instructions, entire pieces of code or their combination to execute in a reconfigurable manner. The reconfiguration of the hardware and the execution on the reconfigured hardware are performed by ρ-microcode (an extension of the classical microcoded engines to allow reconfiguration capabilities). We include fixed and pageable microcode hardware features to extend the flexibility and improve the performance of reconfiguration. The scheme allows partial reconfiguration, partial set of the hardware and caching mechanisms for non-frequently used reconfiguration and execution microcode. As future research directions, we envision: establish additional performance benefits when the caching microcode mechanisms are added to the simulation. Finally, consider more applications, e.g.,: Galois Field multiplications used in error correction for CDs and DVDs, a wide variety of table lookup methods primarily used in IP-routing algorithms, support for random switching patterns of sub-fields within register words, identify graphics functions that can benefit from our reconfiguration scheme and determine the possible potential benefits our mechanism can provide.

References

[1] J. Hauser and J. Wawrzynek, "Garp: A MIPS Processor with a Reconfigurable Coprocessor," in *Proceedings of the IEEE Symposium of Field-Programmable Custom Computing Machines*, pp. 24–33, April 1997.

[2] J. M. Rabaey, "Reconfigurable Computing: The Solution to Low Power Programmable DSP," in *Proceedings 1997 ICASSP Conference*, (Munich), April 1997.

[3] D. C. Burger and T. M. Austin, "The SimpleScalar Tool Set, Version 2.0," Technical Report CS-TR-1997-1342, University of Wisconsin-Madison, 1997.

[4] "Virtex-II 1.5V FPGA Family: Detailed Functional Description ." http://www.xilinx.com/partinfo/databook.htm.

[5] C. Loeffler, A. Ligtenberg, and G. Moschytz, "Practical Fast 1-D DCT Algorithms With 11 Multiplications," in *Proceedings of the International Conference on Acoustics, Speech, and Signal Processing*, pp. 988–991, 1989.

[6] R. Razdan, *PRISC: Programmable Reduced Instruction Set Computers*. PhD thesis, Harvard University, Cambridge, Massachusetts, May 1994.

[7] S. A. Hauck, "Configuration Prefetch for Single Context Reconfigurable Coprocessors," in *6th Int. Symposium on Field Programmable Gate Arrays*, pp. 65–74, February 1998.

[8] R. D. Wittig and P. Chow, "OneChip: An FPGA Processor With Reconfigurable Logic," in *IEEE Symposium on FPGAs for Custom Computing Machines* (K. L. Pocek and J. M. Arnold, eds.), (Napa Valley, California), pp. 126–135, April 1996.

[9] S. M. Trimberger, "Reprogrammable Instruction Set Accelerator." U.S. Patent No. 5,737,631, April 1998.

[10] J. R. Hauser and J. Wawrzynek, "Garp: A MIPS Processor with a Reconfigurable Coprocessor," in *IEEE Symposium on FPGAs for Custom Computing Machines*, (Napa Valley, California), pp. 12–21, April 1997.

[11] P. M. Athanas and H. F. Silverman, "Processor Reconfiguration through Instruction-Set Metamorphosis," *IEEE Computer*, vol. 26, pp. 11–18, March 1993.

[12] K. L. Gilson, "Integrated Circuit Computing Device Comprising a Dynamically Configurable Gate Array Having a Reconfigurable Execution Means." WO Patent No. 94/14123, June 1994.

[13] H. Schmit, "Incremental Reconfiguration for Pipelined Applications," in *IEEE Symposium on FPGAs for Custom Computing Machines*, pp. 47–55, April 1997.

[14] S. C. Goldstein, H. Schmit, M. Moe, M. Budiu, S. Cadambi, R. R. Taylor, and R. Laufer, "PipeRench: A Coprocessor for Streaming Multimedia Acceleration," in *The 26th International Symposium on Computer Architecture*, (Atlanta, Georgia), pp. 28–39, May 1999.

[15] R. W. Hartenstein, R. Kress, and H. Reinig, "A New FPGA Architecture for Word-Oriented Datapaths," in *Proceeding of the 4th International Workshop on Field-Programmable Logic and Applications: Architectures, Synthesis and Applications.*, pp. 144–155, September 1994.

Run-Time Optimized Reconfiguration Using Instruction Forecasting

Marios Iliopoulos and Theodore Antonakopoulos

Computers Technology Institute (CTI), Riga Fereou 61, 26221 Patras, Greece
Department of Electrical Engineering and Computers Technology,
University of Patras, 26500 Patras Greece
Tel: +30-61-997346, e-mail: antonako@ee.upatras.gr

Abstract. The extensive use of reconfigurable computing devices has imposed a new category of processors, the dynamic instruction set processors (DISPs) that customize their instruction sets dynamically to the application needs. One of the major drawbacks of DISPs is the reconfiguration time needed to alter the instruction set, which is directly added to the program execution time discouraging the use of DISPs especially for time critical processing applications. This paper introduces a methodology for optimizing reconfiguration time through instruction forecasting and presents the results obtained when applying this method to Medium Access processing systems that execute time critical network tasks.

1. Introduction

Dynamic Instruction Set Processors (DISPs) can solve the usual trade-off between performance and flexibility by tailoring their instruction sets to application needs. Runtime reconfiguration allows DISPs to implement an arbitrary long and complex instruction set by loading instructions on demand.

There is a major drawback in using Run-Time Reconfiguration (RTR). The long reconfiguration time of current devices is in some cases unacceptable, especially when time critical tasks are executed, thus there has been extensive research on methods for reducing the reconfiguration time and to expand the use of DISP systems.

There are two approaches to the problem of RTR. The first approach is related to changes in FPGA structure that can lead to reduction of configuration time, such as, configuration bandwidth increase, use of partial reconfiguration or use of multiple contexts inside the FPGA [1]–[5]. The second approach is related to time optimization techniques in DISPs independently of FPGA structures, such as, exploiting temporal locality, compressing the configuration bit streams or partitioning the instructions into dynamic and static using code analysis [6]–[8].

The technique that directly reduces the reconfiguration time is the increase of configuration bandwidth. The time needed to configure a portion of reconfigurable logic is given by $T_{conf} = \dfrac{L}{r} + b$, where, L is the amount of data required for configuration, r is the configuration bandwidth and b is a system specific

G. Brebner and R. Woods (Eds.): FPL 2001, LNCS 2147, pp. 286–295, 2001.

configuration overhead [1]. Eventually, if we increase the configuration bandwidth the configuration time is decreased. The same effect is achieved by reducing the configuration data needed to reconfigure a portion of logic. Several devices (such as Xilinx Virtex family [2] and Atmel's AT40K family [3]) support partial reconfiguration of their resources.

The multiple context [4] or time-multiplexed FPGAs [5] are based on the idea of replicating the configuration memory within the reconfigurable device. According to this approach the multiple configurations can be stored in different internal memory planes and be selected by a global context select signal.

A general optimization technique that targets reconfiguration optimization in DISPs and is independent to the FPGA structure, is the exploitation of temporal locality [6]. According to this technique, the instructions are cached inside the DISP like in memory caches and are replaced only when there is a cache miss, otherwise the cached instruction is executed without requiring reconfiguration. Instruction caching exploits the temporal locality of instructions used in program execution. This technique is extended in [7] by partitioning the instructions into dynamic and static using code analysis, in order to achieve application specific RTR optimization. Finally, as proposed in [8], reconfiguration overhead can be reduced by applying configuration compression and thus reduce the amount of data required to reconfigure the device.

This paper proposes a new methodology for reducing the reconfiguration overhead by exploiting code analysis in DISP systems that use instruction caching, in order to pre-fetch instructions that are most likely to be used shortly. Section 2 introduces the problem of configuration bandwidth utilization in DISP processors and the basic idea of the proposed solution. Section 3 describes code analysis methodology used to extract the information needed for instruction forecasting. Section 4 outlines the scheduler implementation that exploits the instruction forecasting information while Section 5 demonstrates the experimental results obtained when applying the methodology to a MAC processing emulation system.

2.   The Problem of Configuration Bandwidth Utilization

In DISP systems that use caching of instructions, the reconfiguration process is initiated each time a new instruction that has to be executed, is not contained in the cache, i.e. when there is a cache-miss. Observing the configuration bus usage in DISP systems with caching, we noticed that when there is a cache-miss, the instruction scheduler initiates a reconfiguration process that loads the missed instruction into the reconfigurable logic. When this process finishes, the scheduler remains in idle state until a new instruction miss occurs. This is illustrated in Figure 1a.

The methodology presented in this paper is based on the exploitation of the idle states of the scheduler in order to transfer an instruction that will most likely be used in the future into the reconfigurable logic (Figure 1b). This instruction is called forecast instruction. This method decreases the possibility of a potential cache miss, since an instruction that has to be executed is more likely to be into the cache due to forecasting. Although, the instruction forecasting can dramatically reduce the cache-miss effect, it does not eliminate it, due to the fact that instruction forecasting is based on statistical analysis and occurrence probabilities.

As it is shown in Figure 1, the idea of instruction forecasting optimization is based on the fact that forecasted instructions do not stop normal program execution since there is no actual cache-miss that would put the DISP processor in a hold state. Based on this idea we introduced the code analysis methodology that produces the information for instructions forecasting using a parametric forecast window.

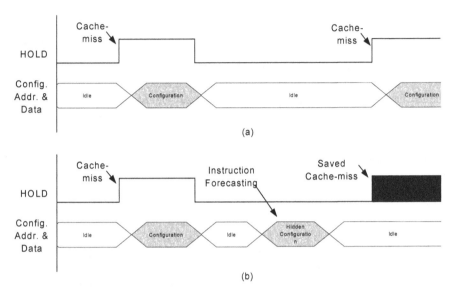

Fig. 1. (a) Normal Instruction fetching, (b) Instruction fetching with forecasting

3.   Code Analysis Method for Parametric Forecasting Window

The methodology for producing the forecast instruction information is based on code analysis. More specifically, the code that has to be executed in the DISP is compiled in order to produce the assembly program. The program is parsed in order to identify the execution paths based on the branches met in the code. The parser produces dataflow graphs such as the one illustrated in Figure 2. In this DFG there are two points of interest:

- Point A, which represents the instruction that has to be executed by the DISP processor at a specific time.
- Point B, which is the instruction that is going to be executed after n instructions, where n is the length of the forecasting window. Point B is not unique and depends on the number of branches that exist between point A and point B.

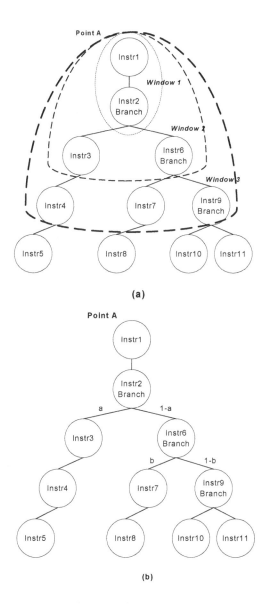

Fig. 2. Dataflow graphs (a) forecasting windows, (b) path probabilities

The instruction-forecasting algorithm uses the address space of the compiled program and initiates the forecasting field for each address. Then for each address, the algorithm checks for all possible instructions in the window with length n. For example, in Figure 2a the possible instructions in the window with length 3, starting from point A, are Instr4, Instr7 and Instr9.

In general, the probability for an instruction being executed after n instructions is the product of the probabilities of the intermediate paths. For example, in Figure 2b the forecasting for Instr1 and window length 3 is: Instr5 with probability a, Instr7 with probability $(1-a)b$ and Instr9 with probability $(1-a)(1-b)$. This probability depends on several factors such as the length of the window, the intermediate branches, and the external events that could affect the execution paths.

More specifically, the window size affects the maximum number of intermediate branches that are interleaved between point A (current time) and point B (future time). A longer-range window is more likely to achieve worse forecasting than a shorter-range window. Another factor that affects the probability of a future instruction is the kind of intermediate branches. For example, if a branch is part of a loop that is executed N times then the probability to follow the return path in the loop is N times higher than the probability to follow the path that leads outside the loop. Finally, the most important factor is the interaction of the processor with external events. In order to forecast branches that depend on external events we can emulate the system's dynamicbehavior. The results of emulation can be combined with static analysis to produce the information for forecast instructions as illustrated in Figure 3.

The outcome of the optimization method is the reconfiguration bitmaps and the reconfiguration timing information that contains the forecasting instructions used as input by the scheduler. The forecasting information is a table of addresses, each of them containing two fields, the current instruction field that is the instruction which is executed now, and the forecast instruction field, which is the instruction that is going to be executed after n instructions.

There are two approaches for integrating the forecasting information into the instruction set. The first approach embodies this information into the opcode of each instruction in order to be decoded from the instruction-decoding unit of the processor. The second approach extends the memory bus in order to directly pass forecasting instruction information to the scheduler. The second approach has the disadvantage of wasting memory for storing forecast instruction information, but since this approach is simpler, it is the one used in the presented system.

4.   Scheduler Implementation for Instruction Forecasting

The RTR optimization method is implemented by a scheduler that exploits the forecast information produced by the code analysis. When a scheduler is used in common DISP systems with instruction caching, it executes the following procedures:

1.   It checks the opcode of the decoded instruction and if the instruction is static or if it is already in the reconfigurable array (by checking the instruction cache), then the scheduler remains in idle state waiting for the next decoded opcode, otherwise proceeds to the next step.

2.   If the instruction is not contained in the reconfigurable array, the scheduler stops normal execution flow by issuing a HOLD signal to the processor. Then the scheduler checks if there are available reconfigurable resources. If there are

available resources, it loads the instruction and returns to idle state, otherwise it replaces an existing instruction according to a replacement algorithm (such as random, First-in-First-out, Least Recently Used - LRU). Loading a new instruction or replacing an existing one causes changes into the cache and modifies the system resources. When reconfiguration is completed, the scheduler deasserts the HOLD signal allowing normal code execution.

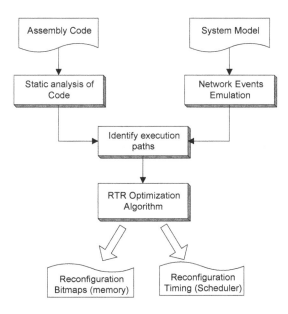

Fig. 3. Optimization of reconfiguration time

In order to exploit the forecast instruction information, the scheduler state machine has to be changed to the one shown in Figure 4. The new state machine uses the scheduler idle states for executing the following steps:

1. Each time the scheduler is in the idle state, which means that either the executed instruction is in the cache or is a static instruction, it looks for the next forecast instruction that corresponds to the current execution position. If the forecast instruction is in the instruction cache, then the scheduler rearranges the cache so that the instruction would not be replaced until it is executed (after n instructions). The rearrangement is done by using a LRU-like algorithm, i.e. the instruction that corresponds to the cache-hit position comes to the first position of the instruction queue.

2. If the forecast instruction is not in the cache, then the scheduler initiates a fetching cycle of the instruction by replacing the instruction that is at the end of the instruction queue. The whole process is transparent to the processor execution flow until there is a cache miss. In that case, the processor is in hold state until the forecast instruction is loaded.

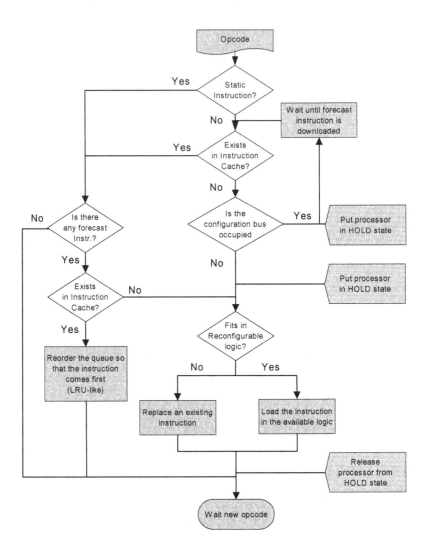

Fig. 4. State diagram of the scheduler that exploits forecast instructions

5.   Experimental Results

In order to evaluate the effectiveness of the method we emulated a dynamic version of the ARM processor and we constructed an emulation platform, which is illustrated in Figure 5. The dynamic ARM processor contains the same set of instructions with the static version but part of the instruction set is executed dynamically using the scheduler described in the previous section. Two MAC processing systems were tested using the emulation platform, the IEEE802.11 [9] and the IEEE802.3 MAC protocol [10] with the addition of the scheduler and a monitor module, which traced exchanged signals and recorded statistical information. The monitor module recognized instructions and different scheduler modes (cache-miss, cache-hit, static-instruction) and gathered statistical information for the size and the content of the instruction cache, the forecast instruction performance, like the number of cache-misses, the number of cycles that the processor is in HOLD state, etc.

The emulation platform contained also all the procedures that emulated real network events. For example, there were procedures for transmitting and receiving network packets for both protocols, procedures for host transaction emulation, like uploading or downloading data from the packet memory etc. Finally, there was the MAC implementation software, which was executed by the ARM and was used for the forecast instructions analysis.

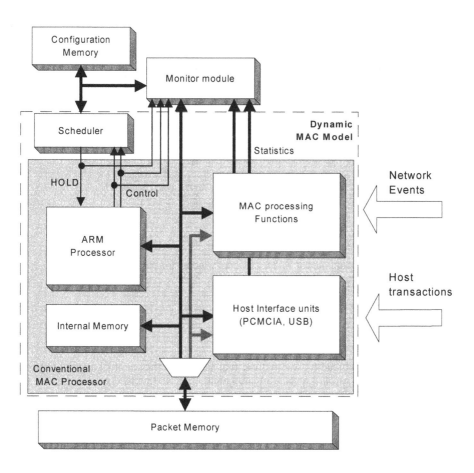

Fig. 5. Emulation platform for Dynamic MAC processing systems

The dynamic version of the MAC processing program was executed for 11 different partitions of dynamic and static instructions keeping the system resources constant (i.e. Half of the cache resources were used to implement the instructions statically). Five (5) different ranges for window forecasting were used. Each range was calculated in instruction downloading time units. The instruction downloading ranged from 2 to 12 time units, while the window sizes ranged from 8 to 20. Figure 6 shows the experimental results for different forecasting windows along with simple (no instruction forecasting) FIFO and LRU replacement algorithms. We observe that forecasting algorithm achieved an improvement in the range of 30 to 50% in cache-misses (and thus reconfiguration time). All forecasting window sizes have better performance than the simple algorithms. In our experiments the best forecasting window is equal to 16.

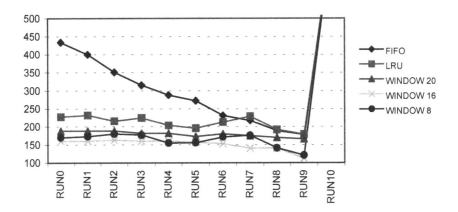

Fig. 6. Cache-misses for FIFO, LRU and window forecasting algorithm

6.   Conclusions

In this paper we introduced a new method that decreases the reconfiguration time in DISP systems with instruction caching independently of the FPGA architecture or instruction swap technology and uses instruction forecasting. We demonstrated the results obtained in a MAC processing emulation platform by analyzing the IEEE802.11 and IEEE802.3 MAC protocols. The new system flow that contains the method described in this paper uses the following steps: The assembly program generated by the compiler is analyzed by an optimizer in order to generate an instruction mix of dynamic and static instructions. The instruction mix is further analyzed by the reconfiguration optimizer to produce an extended instruction set that contains forecast instruction information for the scheduler.

References

1. Michael J. Wirthlin, Improving Functional Density Through Run-Time Circuit Reconfiguration, Ph.D. thesis, 1997.

2. Xilinx, Application Note: Virtex Series Configuration Architecture User Guide, Virtex Series, XAPP151, v1.3, February 2000.

3. Atmel, AT40K05/10/20/40 FPGAs with DSP Optimized Core Cell and Distributed FreeRam, Datasheet, rev. 0896B-01/99, January 1999.

4. E. Tau, I. Eslick, D. Chen, J. Brown, and A. DeHon. A first generation DPGA implementation, Proceedings of the Third Canadian Workshop on Field-Programmable Devices, pages 138-143, May 1995.

5. Steve Trimberger, Dean Carberry, Anders Johnson, and Jennifer Wong. A time-multiplexed FPGA. In J. Arnold and K. L. Pocek, editors, Proceedings of the 5th IEEE Symposium on FPGAs for Custom Computing Machines, pages 22-28, Napa, CA, April 1997.

6. M.J. Wirthlin, and B.L. Hutchings, A Dynamic Instruction Set Computer, Proceedings of the 3rd IEEE Symposium on FPGAs for Custom Computing Machines (FCCM), 1995, pp. 99-107.

7. Iliopoulos, M., Antonakopoulos, T., Optimized Reconfigurable MAC Processor Architecture, IEEE International Conference on Electronics and Computer Systems (ICECS), Malta, 2001.

8. S. Hauck, Z. Li, and E. J. Schwabe. Configuration Compression for the Xilinx XC6200 FPGA, Proceedings of the 6th IEEE Symposium on FPGAs for Custom Computing Machines (FCCM), April 1998.

9. Iliopoulos, M., Antonakopoulos, T., A Methodology of Implementing Medium Access Protocols Using a General Parameterized Architecture, 11th IEEE International Workshop on Rapid System Prototyping (RSP), June 2000, Paris, France

10. Iliopoulos, M., Antonakopoulos, T., Reconfigurable Network Processors based on Field Programmable System Level Integrated Circuits, 10th International Conference on Field Programmable Logic and Applications (FPL), Villach, Austria, August 2000.

CRISP: A Template for Reconfigurable Instruction Set Processors

Pieter Op de Beeck, Francisco Barat, Murali Jayapala and Rudy Lauwereins

KULeuven, Kasteelpark Arenberg 10,
Leuven-Heverlee 3001, Belgium
{Pieter.OpdeBeeck, Francisco.Barat, Murali.Jayapala,
Rudy.Lauwereins}@esat.kuleuven.ac.be

Abstract. A template for reconfigurable instruction set processors is described. This template defines a design space that enables the exploration of processors potentially suitable for flexible, power and cost efficient implementations of embedded multimedia applications, such as video compression in a hand held device. The template is based on a VLIW processor with a reconfigurable instruction set. In the future this template will be used for design space exploration, compiler retargeting and automatic hardware synthesis. Several existing reconfigurable- and non-reconfigurable processors were mapped onto the template to assess its expressiveness.

1   Introduction

Current and future multimedia applications such as 3D rendering, video compression or object recognition are characterized by computationally intensive algorithms with deep nested loop structures and hard real time constraints. It has been demonstrated that implementing this type of applications in embedded systems (e.g. multimedia terminals, notebook computers or cellular phones) leads to a power-optimizing problem with time and area constraints [1]. Although an application specific integrated circuit (ASIC) might give the best results in terms of power and speed, other cost factors have to be considered as well. One of them is design time, which for an ASIC is extremely high compared to writing software for a processor. Related to this are the higher non-recurring costs in ASIC designs (e.g. building prototypes) compared to software designs. Another cost is introduced when trying to cope with different applications, changing standards or different levels of quality of service as in MPEG-4 [2]. We can therefore conclude that embedded implementations of multimedia applications should be power efficient, meeting the area and time budget. Furthermore, they should be flexible and economically viable to design in the first place.

It is common practice that in order to meet the above stated design goals

- the embedded system should be processor based, and
- the processor should have many processing elements working simultaneously (temporally as in VLIW processors [3] and spatially as in FPGAs [4]).

Also, we believe that the instruction set should be modifiable at runtime by using a tightly coupled reconfigurable unit (i.e. a reconfigurable instruction set processor [6]).

G. Brebner and R. Woods (Eds.): FPL 2001, LNCS 2147, pp. 296–305, 2001.

However there exists no methodology yet to decide whether this is true or not for a given embedded application. In order to make this decision we need a description of the design space that covers both the reconfigurable and the non-reconfigurable processors suitable for embedded multimedia systems.

The goal of this paper is to describe a template processor architecture that covers this design space. We will call instances of this template *"(C)onfigurable, (R)econfigurable (I)nstruction (S)et (P)rocessors"* or CRISPs. Configuration is done at design time, while reconfiguration is done at runtime. Viewed as a configurable processor, CRISP is similar to parameterizable processors such as PlayDoh [14] and ARC Cores [15]. Its runtime reconfiguration capabilities are comparable to existing reconfigurable processors like Chimaera [11] and OneChip [5].

In the future this template will be used for design space exploration, compiler retargeting and automatic hardware synthesis. Indeed, to execute an application on a CRISP, three main steps will need to be done. First of all a processor should be instantiated from the CRISP template. This effectively gathers all information for the compiler/synthesis tool to map the source code to an executable, which is the second step. The final step is to synthesize the CRISP processor. Again, compiler/synthesis tools are used.

The reconfigurability of CRISP will be addressed in the next section. In section three we describe the CRISP template as a configurable processor architecture. In the next section, a number of case studies validate that CRISP covers these processor architectures in which we are interested. In the final section we present the conclusions of this paper and outline future work.

2   Reconfigurable Processor Architecture

A reconfigurable instruction set denotes a runtime modifiable instruction set. There are several academic and commercial reconfigurable instruction set architectures in existence with this characteristic [9, 10, 11]. The common thread among these is a RAM based memory that controls or even implements the instruction decoding. This memory is called decoder memory or configuration memory (as used in the FPGA community). A few examples are shown in Figure 1.

In the first example, the ARMThumb [9] architecture, two different instruction set decoders are implemented. A bit in a special register will decide which one is used (this bit is considered as decoder memory). The REAL DSP [10], as a second case, has a set of reconfigurable instructions. The decoder is not fixed for these, but is implemented as RAM memory (decoder memory) indexed by the opcode of the reconfigurable instruction. If the instruction is not a reconfigurable one, a standard hardwired decoder is used. Finally, Chimaera [11] has a totally reconfigurable decoder for one of its functional units. This decoder is implemented with a single RAM, addressed by the opcode.

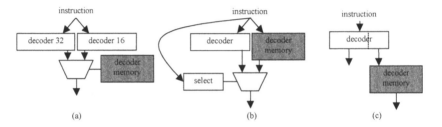

Fig. 1. Instruction decoding in
the ARM Thumb (a), the REAL DSP (b) and the Chimaera (c)

The sizes of the decoder memories in Figure 1 naturally differ. In fact, the decoder memory size of the ARM Thumb is only one bit, for the REAL DSP it is 256x96. The decoder memory of the Chimaera is actually the FPGA configuration memory and this contains 45056 bits (estimated). This example shows the continuum of decoder memory sizes for reconfigurable decoders.

There are power- and speed considerations when using (very) wide decoder memories. Indeed, each time a different configuration is needed, a fair amount of bits would have to be loaded from external memory, a time consuming process for sure. That is why most current FPGAs are not runtime reconfigurable. In order to reduce these loading times, the decoder memory could contain several contexts. These are implemented as the addressable RAM in the REAL and Chimaera processors. In the end the actual reconfigurable operation is an address pointing to the desired entry in this decoder memory, and as such selecting the required context. What actually happens is aggressive encoding/decoding of the instruction because from instruction memory an address is fetched, while only later on this address is 'decoded' into a context. In other words, the size of the Very Long Instruction Word (VLIW) grows proportional only to the number of contexts, instead of the number of configuration bits, which in itself is proportional to the number of processing elements. As a result, there is no need anymore to transfer a huge amount of configuration bits through the internal memory system. Instead, an external memory management unit, operating at a much lower bandwidth, can offload this transfer. However, to make it really work the decoder memory should be distributed over all processing elements, otherwise there would still be a power- and speed bottleneck located between decoder memory and processing elements. Nevertheless, we consider the decoder memory a part of the memory hierarchy as described in section 3.3.

Loading times are further amortized by grouping processing elements into segments. These are defined as the smallest unit of reconfiguration. Having several segments, then, leads to a scheme where some segments are being reconfigured while others are actually executing an operation. This effectively hides reloading times.

3   Configurable Processor Architecture

The CRISP template is organized in a hierarchical way, as depicted in Figure 2. Fixing all the associated parameters instantiates a particular CRISP processor. As was outlined in the introduction, this step is termed design time configuration.

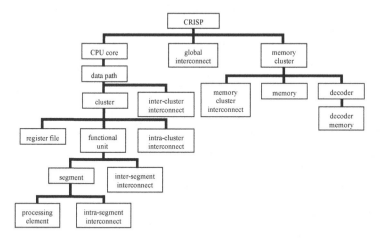

Fig. 2. CRISP hierarchy

3.1   CRISP

At the top level in Figure 2, a CRISP consists of CPU cores, memory clusters and global interconnect. The template covers both single and multiprocessor architectures.

Figure 3 shows such a CRISP multiprocessor with its memory hierarchy made out of a number of memory clusters, but for clarity only the complex one is indicated. Furthermore, no decoder memory is visible since it is distributed inside the CPU cores, as was motivated in section 2.

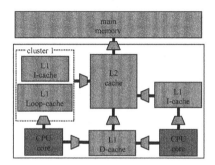

Fig. 3. A CRISP architecture at the highest level

3.2   CPU Core

At the level of the CPU core the characteristics of the instruction set are defined. In CRISP an instruction is a group of operations that will execute concurrently in a manner similar to VLIW processors [8], a powerful implementation to exploit this parallelism [3]. In the case of a reconfigurable instruction set, a specific amount of operations (not necessarily all of them) will change their behavior at runtime.

In order to reduce the effect of branch latencies, CRISP processors can include speculative execution, branch prediction and predication. For the latter this will affect the instruction format and introduce one or more predicate registers. Predication is a technique typically used in VLIW processors to collapse two or more control flows into a single one. This reduces the number of branches and allows powerful scheduling techniques such as software pipelining.

The execution pipeline has N stages which are grouped into fetch, decode, execute and write back phases, like in most processors. All instructions require a fixed number of pipeline stages for the fetch, decode and write back stages (assuming there are no instruction cache misses), but need a varying number of execute stages depending on the operation type.

3.2.1   Data Path and Clusters

The data path can be composed of one or more data path clusters. It contains one or more register files and one or more functional units. By clustering, the routing length and interconnect complexity inside a cluster are reduced (i.e. good for both power and speed), at the price of increased compilation complexity due to the additional cluster-to-cluster data transfers. Between clusters there is still communication possible by means of inter-cluster interconnect. This, and all other interconnect resources in the CRISP hierarchy, are modeled using an interconnect matrix, such as in Figure 4.

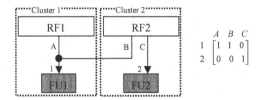

Fig. 4. Inter-cluster interconnect modeled as a matrix

In Figure 5 a functional unit is depicted. It is an element of the processor to which operations, generated by the compiler, are issued. Inside the functional unit this operation is further decoded and routed to the different resources it is composed of, namely, processing elements and interconnect. Processing elements are the subunits of the functional units. This description unifies all types of reconfigurable logic going from processing elements in fine-grained architectures, such as CLBs in an FPGA, to coarse-grained architectures build from ALUs. Furthermore it allows us to present the functional unit on different levels of abstraction. Which level is needed depends on where it is used. For instance, during instruction scheduling only the notion of a functional unit is required, whether it is a reconfigurable- or a fixed one. However, prior to that, some reconfigurable operations had to be mapped onto the reconfigurable functional unit, resulting in the configuration bits. This requires full knowledge of the internal processing elements.

As motivated in section 2, the functional unit should be divided into segments because this can hide the long reloading times associated with large amounts of configuration bits.

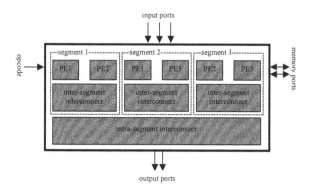

Fig. 5. Functional unit and segment model

The cycle-accurate timing of the functional unit is specified using a resource model. For each operation performed in the functional unit, this resource model indicates the processing elements used in each cycle of the operation. This information is of vital importance to the compiler/synthesis tools.

3.3 Memory Cluster and Decoder

A memory cluster is defined as a number of memory blocks with common input- and output ports. In Figure 3, for instance, CPU core 1 will receive instructions from either the loop cache or the L1 instruction cache. A memory selection unit decides which one to take. The memory blocks themselves could have a complex internal memory organization (e.g. interleaved memory banks) and local memory control (like loop control, cache replacement policy or FIFO control).

Each cluster has a set of ports connecting to other memory clusters. It also has an optional decoder that is used to reduce the instruction traffic on the memory bus (which is power consuming) and to reduce the size of the required program memories (which are expensive).

In most modern architectures, only the decoder closest to the data path is actually implemented (normally referred to as the instruction decoder). Having the possibility to place it at different levels of the instruction memory hierarchy extends the decoder concept. In theory, even the decoder memory could be clustered and hierarchical, but we will not focus on this aspect of the design space. Most work only focuses on placing the instruction decoders in the execution pipeline [17]. Some work has been done on placing them in the external memory interface to reduce external memory traffic by compressing the data stream [18].

Several decoder types exist, such as hardware (i.e. fixed) decoders, decoders with decoder memory or a mixture of these two. A decoder can even be software based [16] even though this is usually called instruction set translation or emulation. As indicated in section 2, RAM based decoders are the key point in the template where reconfigurability is accounted for.

4   Case Studies

In this section, several existing processors (both commercial and academic) are mapped onto the CRISP template. The goal behind this mapping is to show that the design space represented by the template covers most of the processor types we are interested in. This would validate CRISP as a design space, which will allow us to make a trade-off between non-reconfigurable (VLIW) and reconfigurable processors in an embedded context. The focus is on the data path of the processors and on the decoding characteristics of the instruction set. Table 1 summarizes the main characteristics of each of the processors.

4.1   MIPS32 4KP

The MIPS32 4Kp core from MIPS Technologies [7] is a 32-bit MIPS RISC core designed for custom system-on-a-chip applications. The four execution units (ALU, shifter, multiply/divide and branch) can be considered as a functional unit with four distinct processing elements. In this processor, decoding is only performed in the last stage of the program memory hierarchy and is not reconfigurable. This processor represents one of the simplest processors that can be instantiated from the CRISP template.

4.2   TMS320C64x

The TMS320C64x core [8] is a VLIW processor core specifically designed to maximize channel density in communications infrastructure equipment. It contains two identical clusters with four functional units each, and represents a typical clustered processor. The functional units are specialized in multiplication, arithmetic and logical operations, branching and load/store operations. In CRISP terminology, this is a clustered processor without a reconfigurable instruction set.

4.3   ARM7TDMI

The ARM7TDMI [9] is a RISC core designed for simple, low-cost applications. The differentiating characteristic of this processor is that it can use two different instructions sets, the standard ARM instruction set and the Thumb instruction set. Thumb instructions are a subset of the most commonly used 32-bit ARM instructions that have been compressed into 16-bit opcodes. On execution, these 16-bit instructions are decompressed to 32-bit ARM instructions in real time. Designers can use both 16-bit Thumb and 32-bit ARM instruction sets and therefore have complete flexibility to compile for maximum performance or minimum code size. Both instruction sets cannot be active at the same time however. The instruction set used is selected through a bit in a status register. This is our first case of a reconfigurable processor that can be instantiated from the CRISP template. It uses the simplest reconfigurable decoder you can place in a processor.

4.4   R.E.A.L. DSP

The R.E.A.L. DSP [10] is a traditional DSP with two 16-bit data bus pathways to its Data Computation Unit (DCU). The instruction set word length ranges from 16 to 32 bits. With the limited 32-bit instruction word length it is not possible to freely control all the available functional units (2 multipliers, 4 ALUs and 2 address generation units) inside the DCU. A reconfigurable decoder extends these 32 bits to 96 bits length (what is referred to as Application Specific Instructions or ASIs). In order to call these instructions from R.E.A.L. DSP's 16-bit program memory, selected ASIs are stored in a look-up table and pointed to by a special class of 16-bit opcodes. This look-up table is actually one of the reconfigurable decoders presented in section 2. Up to 256 ASIs can be concurrently stored in the R.E.A.L. DSP, which means that the depth of the decoder memory is 256.

4.5   Chimaera

The Chimaera [11] is a processor for high performance, general-purpose reconfigurable computing. It is based on a fine-grained logic functional unit connected to a MIPS R4000. The reconfigurable logic is organized in 32 rows of 32 logic blocks each (for a total of 1024 logic blocks or processing elements). The reconfigurable decoder is implemented inside one of the functional units, while other functional units have fixed decoding. This means that only one of the functional units is reconfigurable. It is clear that the Chimaera can be instantiated from the CRISP template.

4.6   Remarc

Remarc [12] is a reconfigurable coprocessor connected to a RISC processor. It consists of a global control unit and 64 programmable logic blocks called nano processors. These nano processors have a 16-bit data path that support arithmetic, logical and shift operations. Each nano processor contains a local instruction memory of 32 entries. The instruction address to be executed in the nano processors is selected by the global controller. This address is the same for all the nano processors.

It is possible to consider the Remarc coprocessor as a CRISP (without the controlling RISC). The processor now has one functional unit with 64 processing elements. The functional unit has a completely reconfigurable decoder. This case is the extreme, where all functional units are reconfigurable.

Table 1. CRISP parameters of some processors

	MIPS32 4KP	C64x	ARM7	REAL	Chimaera	Remarc
Clusters	1	2	1	1	1	2
Register files	1x32x32	2x32x32	1x32x32	1x8x16	1x32x32	
Instruction width	32	32 to 256	16 or 32	16 - 32	32	32
#Independent parallel ops	1	8	1	1	1	1
Number of units active in parallel	1	8	1	8	1024	64
Number of units	4	8	4	8	1024	64
Pre-execution stages	1	6	2		1	1
Execution stages	4	1 to 5	1		4	1
Predication	No	All units	No	No	No	No
Memory ports	1x32	2x64	1x32		1	
Decoder memory	0	0	1	256x96	45056	65536

5   Conclusions and Future Work

In this paper we have described a template processor architecture, named CRISP. CRISP covers the design space of reconfigurable and non-reconfigurable processors suitable for embedded multimedia systems. A CRISP instance is a VLIW processor with, optionally, reconfigurable functional units. It can be configured at design time and reconfigured at run-time.

Several existing processors have been mapped onto the CRISP template to test it. The results have shown that the most interesting processors can be represented. In fact the template defines a continuum of reconfigurability levels going from zero to fully reconfigurable.

We are currently working on a methodology for implementing multimedia applications on a custom CRISP. This will include design space exploration tools, retargetable compilation and automatic hardware synthesis. In the end it will allow that, given an application and a set of constraints, the best instance of CRISP will be found. The outcome could be a reconfigurable- or a totally fixed VLIW processor.

References

1. Catthoor F., et al, Custom Memory Management Methodology, Kluwer Academic Publishers (1998)
2. Overview of the MPEG-4 Standard, International Organization for Standardization, ISO/IEC JTC1/SC29/WG11 N4030 (march 2001)
3. Jacome M. F., de Veciana G., Design Challenges for New Application-Specific Processors, IEEE Design & Test of Computers (2000) 40-50
4. Seals R. C., Whapshott G. F., Programmable Logic: PLDs and FPGAs, Macmillan Press Ltd (1997)
5. Wittig R., Chow P., OneChip: An FPGA Processor With Reconfigurable Logic, Proc. IEEE Symp.FCCM (1996) 145-154
6. Barat F., Lauwereins, R., Reconfigurable Instruction Set Processors: A Survey, IEEE Workshop in Rapid System Prototyping (2000) 168-173
7. MIPS32 4Kp™ Processor Core Datasheet, MIPS Technologies Inc. (June 2000)
8. TMS320C6000 CPU and Instruction Set Reference Guide, SPRU189F, Texas Instruments, (October 2000)
9. ARM7TDMI Technical Reference Manual, Rev 3, ARM (2000)
10. Kievits P., Lambers E., Moerman C., Woudsma R., R.E.A.L. DSP Technology for Telecom Baseband Processing, ICSPAT (1998)
11. Hauck S., Fry T.W., Hosler M.M., and. Kao, J.P., The Chimaera Reconfigurable Functional Unit, IEEE Symposium on FPGAs for Custom Computing Machines (1997)
12. Miyamori T., Olukotun K., REMARC: Reconfigurable Multimedia Array Coprocessor, FPGA'98 (1998)
13. Jacob J. A., Chow P., Memory interfacing and instruction specification for reconfigurable processors, Proceedings of the 1999 ACM/SIGDA seventh international symposium on Field programmable gate arrays (1999) 145-154
14. Kathail V., Schlansker M. S., Rau, B. R., HPL-PD - Architecture Specification, Version 1.1, Hewlett-Packard Labs Technical Report HPL-98-128 (February 2000)
15. Technical Summary of the ARC Core, www.arccores.com (2001)
16. Klaiber A., The Technology Behind Crusoe Processors, Transmeta Corporation (January 2000)
17. TM1000 Data Book, Philips Electronics North America Corporation (1997)
18. Benini L., et al, Selective Instruction Compression for Memory Energy Reduction in Embedded Systems, ISLPED '99 (1999) 206-211

Evaluation of an FPGA Implementation of the Discrete Element Method

Benjamin Carrion Schafer[1], Steven F. Quigley[1], Andrew H.C. Chan[2]

[1]School of Electronic and Electrical Engineering, University of Birmingham
Edgbaston, Birmingham B15 2TT, United Kingdom
schaferb@eee.bham.ac.uk, s.f.quigley@bham.ac.uk
[2]School of Civil Engineering, University of Birmingham
Edgbaston, Birmingham B15 2TT, United Kingdom
a.h.chan@bham.ac.uk

Abstract. The Distinct Element Method (DEM) is a numerical method for the simulation of the behaviour of media consisting of discrete particles, and is widely used for process optimisation in the food and pharmaceutical industries. The DEM is very computationally expensive, but has properties that make it amenable to acceleration by reconfigurable computing. This paper presents the design of an implementation of the DEM in FPGA hardware. Its performance is about 5 times faster than that of a software implementation running on a 1 GHz Athlon processor. The paper discusses how improvements to the design, notably greater use of parallelism, can give a much greater speed advantage.

1 Introduction

Reconfigurable computing is based around the use of field programmable gate arrays (FPGAs) to form coprocessors that can be configured to provide custom hardware accelerators. The types of problem that can benefit from reconfigurable computing are established by the properties of the FPGA. In general, FPGAs are good at tasks that use short wordlength integer or fixed point data, and exhibit a high degree of parallelism.

Traditionally reconfigurable computing has been regarded as unsuitable for problems in computational mechanics, such as are used in civil, mechanical or chemical engineering, because these problems generally require floating point and high wordlength. A notable exception to this generalisation is the Distinct Element Method (DEM), a numerical method for simulating the flow of granular materials. The DEM is of great importance for the pharmaceutical and food processing industries, but its use is hampered by its extremely high computational demands. The DEM uses simple arithmetic operations in a massively parallel way on a large data set, and it *can* retain numerical stability using short wordlength fixed point data. It is therefore tempting to examine how well it can be accelerated using reconfigurable computing.

G. Brebner and R. Woods (Eds.): FPL 2001, LNCS 2147, pp. 306-314, 2001.

This paper presents preliminary results of an implementation of the DEM in a Xilinx V1000 FPGA, and estimates how these results can be extrapolated to future systems using larger, faster FPGAs. The paper is organised as follows:

Section 2 provides an overview of the formulation of the DEM that has been implemented. Section 3 explains how the method has been implemented in hardware, and summarises the hardware requirements and speed achieved. Section 4 estimates how the results will scale to larger, faster FPGAs, and contrasts this with how software implementations of the DEM are likely to scale on larger, faster parallel computers. Section 5 provides a summary, and indicates the direction of future work.

2 The Discrete Element Method (DEM)

The DEM models the behaviour of assemblies of granular materials. Granular materials can be defined as large conglomerations of discrete macroscopic particles [1]. They behave differently from any other familiar form of matter. Like liquids, they can flow and assume the shape of the container, and like a solid, they can support weight, but can not normally support a tensile stress [2]. They can therefore be considered as a state of matter in their own right. They can be found everywhere; sand, sugar, and beans are just some examples.

Many of the raw materials used in the food, chemical and pharmaceutical industries are granular media. With the advent of modern machinery, the speed at which granular raw materials are processed has increased dramatically. This increase in speed has greatly increased the chance of damage to the fine particles during processing. In order to optimise the speed of production, and to reduce the amount of damage caused to the particles, the effect of these mechanical interactions needs to be known. In many cases, for the purpose of processing speed-up, water and other fluid may be added which would alter the surface energy and adhesion between particles. All these require an understanding of the microscopic mechanical properties and the behaviour of their interactions so that the macroscopic behaviour of the bulk can be understood.

The DEM is an excellent method to provide such an understanding. A flow chart for the method is shown in fig. 1. The method is based on the assumption that particles only exert forces on one another when they are in contact. A simulation starts by assuming some initial configuration of particle positions, and then computing which of the particles are touching. The simulation then proceeds by stepping in time, applying the sequence of operations of fig. 1 at each step. The force between two particles can be calculated from the strength of the contact between them [3][4]. The resultant force on a particle is the vector sum of the forces exerted by each of its neighbours. Once the resultant force on each particle has been computed, it is simple to compute a velocity and position increment for each particle. Finally, the list of which particles are in contact must be re-computed.

Every particle's force interaction, acceleration and movement is calculated individually at each time step. The assumptions underlying the method are only correct if no disturbance can travel beyond the immediate neighbours of a particle within one time step. This generally means that the time step must be limited to a very small value, thus making the DEM extremely computationally expensive.

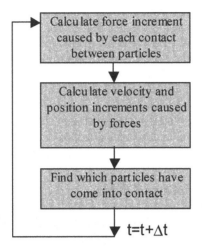

Fig. 1 Flow chart for operations performed in the DEM algorithm

Sections 2.1 and 2.2 provide more detail about the case that we have considered, namely the case of circular particles of identical radius moving in two dimensions.

2.1 Interparticle Force Update

For every contact identified between two particles, the resulting force is calculated. This is proportional to the distance between the balls. The resultant force on a particle is the vector sum of the forces caused by each contact with its neighbours.

The model that we have implemented considers a granular medium, all of whose particles are of identical radius R. This greatly simplifies the implementation of the algorithm, because it means that for a 2-D implementation, a particle can have a maximum of 6 other particles in contact with itself (see Fig. 2 and equations 1 and 2). This means that contact information can be represented by a simple data structure, in which each particle has six memory slots allocated to hold the identities of the particles in contact.

$$\alpha = \cos^{-1}\left(\frac{R}{2R}\right) = 30^{0} \tag{1}$$

$$2\alpha = 60 \Rightarrow \frac{360^{0}}{60^{0}} = 6 \tag{2}$$

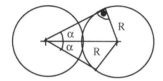

Fig. 2. Geometrical deduction of maximum number of contact balls

2.2 Contact Check

In order to update the interparticle forces and displacements each disc needs to know the discs with which it is in contact. Two discs are in contact if the following condition is satisfied:

$$D = \sqrt{(x_1 - x_2)^2 + (y_1 - y_2)^2} < R_1 + R_2 \tag{3}$$

with x_i y_i being the respective centre coordinates of the particles which are being checked for contact. (see Fig 3)

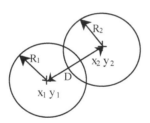

Fig. 3. Particles in contact

3 DEM Implementation on a FPGA

3.1 Parallel Implementation

The DEM was implemented on a Celoxica RC1000 board containing a single Xilinx Virtex V1000 FPGA. Fig 4 shows a block diagram of the hardware implementation. It consists of four main units. A *contact check unit* which identifies the particles in contact, a *force update unit* which updates the interparticle forces, a *movement update unit* which calculates the particles' new velocities and coordinates, and a *control unit*, which synchronizes all the units.

The block RAM of the FPGA is used to hold the data required to describe each particle (position, velocity, angular momentum, identity of neighbours, and the force that it is experiencing).

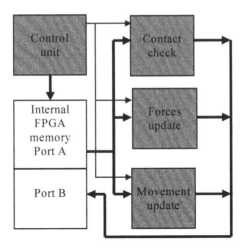

Fig. 4 FPGA hardware implementation

The units that compute the contacts, forces and movement are organized as three pipelines, each of which can produce one new result on each clock cycle. The block RAM is configured as a dual port memory, so that the update units' inputs can read data for one particle pair, whilst their outputs retire data for another particle pair. In order to keep the pipelines fully loaded with data, the RAM is clocked at a rate four times higher than the update computation units.

3.2 Hardware Requirements

The hardware required for one instance of each of the units is shown in fig. 5. The contact check unit is the simplest (it does not need to compute equation 3; instead it just checks the overlap of the bounding box of each particle in the pair, because particles of same radius are considered). The force update unit (which does need to compute the terms of equation 3) requires a large amount of hardware. The dividers and square rooters do not pipeline as well as the other operations, and impose the upper limit on clock speed of the update computation units. For our implementation, the clock speed used in the pipelines was 7.3 MHz, though we believe that optimisation of the square rooter circuit will at least double this figure in future.

Contact check	Force update	Movement update
2 adders	18 adders 10 multipliers 8 constant coefficient multipliers 2 dividers 1 square rooter	7 adders 15 constant coefficient multipliers

Fig. 5 Hardware requirements for the building blocks of fig. 4

The limitation to the size of simulation was established by the available block RAM. Using 16 bit data on an XCV1000 device, which has 131 kbits of block RAM, a maximum of 500 particles could be processed.

3.3 Performance Comparison of Hardware and Software DEM

A 2-dimensional DEM simulation using 500 particles was carried out using the hardware implementation. 80% of the FPGA resources were consumed using one instance each of the contact check unit, the coordinate update unit and the force update unit. For comparison, a corresponding simulation was carried out on an optimised software version on a PC with a 1GHz Athlon processor and 750 Mbytes of RAM. The DEM running in FPGA hardware was found to be 5.6 times faster.

The hardware version uses pipelining to obtain one new result (contact identification, force component update or movement update) on each clock cycle, but within the pipeline it uses a slow clock (about 7 MHz). By contrast, the software version runs on a processor of very high clock speed, but takes many hundreds of clock cycles to generate each result.

4 Scalability of Software and Hardware DEM

In this section we discuss the issues related to estimating the performance of the DEM in hardware and software as the problem size is increased.

4.1 Complexity of the Algorithm

In order to understand how this result is likely to scale to problems of a larger size, it is instructive to consider the asymptotic complexity of the DEM algorithm. For N particles, force update entails the computation of up to six components of the resultant force for each particle. This requires $O(N)$ operations. Movement update entails the solution of Newton's second law for each of the n particles. This requires $O(N)$ operations. Identification of which balls are in contact requires that each possible pairing of balls be examined. This requires $O(N^2)$ operations.

Thus, for large problem sizes, contact identification dominates the complexity of the problem.

4.2 Optimisation of Software DEM

For a software implementation on a single processor, performing all operations in serial, the execution time will grow as $O(N^2)$, due to the requirements of the contact check.

This can be alleviated by dividing the domain up into cells [5]. Each particle is tagged as belonging to a particular cell, and it will only be checked for contacts with particles within the same cell. If there are c particles per cell, the execution time is then proportional to $\dfrac{N}{c} O(c^2)$.

Occasionally a particle may transition from one cell to another, or may straddle the boundary between two cells. The ideal cell size is given by a balance between two conflicting requirements:

> The cells should be small in order to reduce the number of particles against which a contact check will be performed.

> The cells need to be reasonably coarse, otherwise the overhead associated with particles transitioning or overlapping between cells becomes large.

A near-optimal cell size was used for the software DEM used for the comparison in section 3.3.

4.3 Scope for Parallelisation of Software DEM

The DEM can be run on a parallel computer by farming out different cells onto different processors. However, particles transitioning from one cell to another create communication and synchronisation overheads [9] which limit the speed-up achieved by parallel processing. Also, if some cells become much more heavily populated than others, then there will be inefficiencies due to load imbalance between the processors.

How well these factors can be solved limits the degree of speed-up achieved by running the DEM on parallel computers [6,7,8]. For example, a parallel implementation on a 64 node Alta Technologies T805 achieved a rather modest 8-fold speed-up compared to the serial implementation [8]. Another implementation on a Cray T3D parallel computer achieved a speed up of 47 for 64 processing elements[7].

4.4 Performance Achievable by Hardware DEM

The hardware demonstrator that has been built and tested uses only one instance of each computational unit. For an N particle simulation, the number of clock cycles taken by the units to generate a result is

Velocity & position update	$t = N$ clock cycles
Force update:	$t = 6 N$ clock cycles
Contact check	$t = \frac{1}{2} N (N-1)$ clock cycles

Figure 6 shows of the number of clock cycles needed to perform 1 single DEM time step. It can readily be seen that as the problem size increases, the contact check becomes dominant.

Within the each of the pipelines there is no sequential data dependence. This means that multiple instances of each of the units can be used (provided that excessive congestion and conflict does not occur as results are written back to the RAM). As can be seen from fig. 5, the contact check unit has a very low hardware requirement, and it would be cheap to implement a large number of them. In this case, the number of clock cycles required for contact checks becomes

$$t = \tfrac{1}{2}\, N\, (N\text{-}1)\, /\, (\text{number of contact check units})$$

As the number of contact check units becomes large, the time required to implement the contact check is greatly improved. We are presently designing a circuit to allow multiple contact check units to share the same block RAM data without causing significant congestion overhead. We are also developing a method to allows the force update, movement update and contact checking to be done in parallel within a timestep, rather than in serial as is done in the present implementation.

It is also possible to increase the number of force and movement update units, though this is a lower priority. Fig. 6 shows that these units become a significant proportion of the execution time only for small problem sizes. Fig. 5 shows that it would be expensive to implement large numbers of these units.

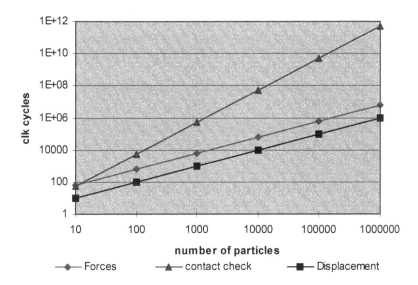

Fig. 6. Clock cycles needed by each unit to perform 1 DEM cycle

For large problems, it will be necessary to partition the problem into cells, as described in section 4.3. If the FPGA has sufficient capacity, this could be done by implementing multiple cells within one FPGA. Otherwise, the problem could be split across multiple FPGAs. Work is in progress to find methods to facilitate the communication between FPGAs as particles move over cell boundaries.

5 Conclusions

The results strongly suggest that reconfigurable computing is a viable alternative to large parallel computers to solve DEM problems. Our FPGA version has demonstrated superior speed to a software version running on a fast microprocessor. Increasing the level of fine-grained parallelism, by using a large number of computational pipelines, should give an even greater speed-up.

The number of particles within a cell is limited by the available embedded RAM within the FPGA. The Xilinx XCV1000, which represented the state of the art about two years ago, has only 1 million system gates, and 131kbits of embedded RAM, which limited our design to 500 particles. The state of the art moves very rapidly, and devices are becoming available that have 10 times more logic capacity, and 20 times more embedded RAM. A reconfigurable computer based on one of these devices could handle problems of up to 10,000 particles.

Further work is in progress on the following issues:

- Investigation of the required numerical precision within the pipelines.
- Optimisation of the throughput of the arithmetic circuits
- Methods to increase the number of pipelines that operate in parallel on the data set stored in the block RAM.
- Communications management for a problem that is partitioned into multiple cells.

References

1. Heinrich M. Jaeger, Sidney R. Nagel,, Robert P. Behringer. Physics Today, April 1996. *An introduction to granular physics, page 32.* Available at http://arnold.uchicago.edu:80/~jaeger/granular2/introduction
2. S.G. Bardenhagen, J.U. Brackbill, D. Sulsky. *The material-point method for granular materials.* Elsevier on Computer methods in applied mechanics and engineering 187 (2000) 529-541.
3. P.A. Cundall O.D.L. Strack, *A discrete numerical model for granular assemblies.* Geotechnique 29, pp. 1-8, 1979
4. C. Thornton & S.J.Antony, *Quasi-static deformation of particulate media*, Phil Trans R Soc Lond, A356: 2763-2782, 1998
5. P.A. Cundall, *BALL -A program to model granular media using the distinct element method.*, 1978 Appendix I pp. 5-6
6. Mario Antonioletti. *The DEM application demonstrator* pp.7. Available at http://www.epcc.ed.ac.uk/epcc-tec/JTAP/DEM.html
7. Jean-Albert Ferrez, Didier Mueller, Thomas M. Liebling. *Parallel Implementation of a distinct element method for granular media simulation on the Cray T3D.* Available at http://www.epfl.ch/SIC/SA/publications/SCR96/scr8-page4.html
8. Andrew I. Hustrulid. *Parallel implementation of the discrete element method.* Available at http://egweb.mines.edu/dem/
9. ML Sawley & PW Clearly. CSIRO Mathematical & Information Sciences, Clayton, Australia. *A Parallel discrete element method for industrial granular flow simulations*, EPLF Supercomputing review -SCR No 11, Nov. 99

Run-Time Performance Optimization of an FPGA-Based Deduction Engine for SAT Solvers*

Andreas Dandalis, Viktor K. Prasanna, and Bharani Thiruvengadam

University of Southern California, Los Angeles CA 90089, USA
{dandalis, prasanna, thiruven}@usc.edu

Abstract. FPGAs are a promising technology for accelerating SAT solvers. Besides their high density, fine granularity, and massive parallelism, FPGAs provide the opportunity for run-time customization of the hardware based on the given SAT instance. In this paper, a parallel deduction engine is proposed for backtrack search algorithms. The performance of the deduction engine is critical to the overall performance of the algorithm since, for any moderate SAT instance, millions of implications are derived. We propose a novel approach in which, p, the amount of parallelization of the engine is fine-tuned during problem solving in order to optimize performance. Not only the hardware is initially customized based on the input instance, but it is also dynamically modified in terms of p based on the knowledge gained during solving the SAT instance. Compared with conventional deduction engines that correspond to $p = 1$, we demonstrate speedups in the range of $2.87 - 5.44$ for several SAT instances.

1 Introduction

The Boolean Satisfiability Problem (SAT) is a central problem in artificial intelligence, combinatorial optimization, and mathematical logic. SAT is a well-known NP-complete problem and many problems can be proved NP-complete by reduction from SAT [3]. In this paper, the conjunctive normal form (CNF) formula is considered. A CNF formula on boolean variables is expressed as an AND of clauses, each of which is the OR of one or more literals. A literal is the occurrence of a variable or its negation. Given a CNF formula, the objective of a SAT solver is to identify an assignment to the variables that causes the formula to evaluate to logic 1 or verify that no such assignment exists.

Numerous FPGA-based SAT solvers have been proposed [1,2,7,11,14,15] that take advantage of the fine granularity and the spatial computing paradigm of FPGAs. Compared with software implementations, the main advantage of implementing SAT solvers in FPGAs is the hardware customization of the bit-level operations and the inherent parallelism in checking a truth variable assignment against the constraints imposed by the clauses (i.e., deduction process). Furthermore, reconfigurable hardware allows instance-specific customization and run-time modification of the hardware in order to achieve superior performance.

* This work is supported by the US DARPA Adaptive Computing Systems program under contract no. DABT63-99-1-0004 monitored by Fort Huachuca and in part by the US National Science Foundation under grant no. CCR-9900613.

G. Brebner and R. Woods (Eds.): FPL 2001, LNCS 2147, pp. 315–325, 2001.
© Springer-Verlag Berlin Heidelberg 2001

Our research focuses on FPGA-based implementations of the deduction process described in the Davis-Putnam procedure [5]. The deduction process described in [5] is the most widely used in backtrack search algorithms. Such algorithms have been proven to be superior for several classes of SAT instances compared with local search algorithms and algebraic manipulation techniques [10]. In general, backtrack search algorithms consist of iterative execution of decision, deduction, and backtrack processes. The performance of the deduction engine is critical to the overall performance of the algorithm since, for any moderate SAT instance, millions of implications are derived [13]. In [8], we have demonstrated that, for various SAT instances, a parallel deduction engine can lead to up to an order of magnitude speedup compared with "serial" implementations. In this paper, we develop a parallel deduction engine and introduce an heuristic based on which the engine is fine-tuned during problem solving in order to optimize performance. Not only the hardware is initially customized based on the input instance (a common feature of known FPGA-based SAT solvers), but it is also dynamically modified based on the knowledge gained during solving the SAT instance.

An overview of backtrack search algorithms and the deduction process is given in Section 2. In Section 3, the state of the art is briefly presented and the motivation for our research is described. The parallel deduction engine and the associated heuristic are described in Section 4. Experimental results are demonstrated in Section 5 and finally, in Section 6, conclusions are drawn and future work is described.

2   Backtrack Search Algorithms and Deduction Process

Backtrack search algorithms start from an empty truth variable assignment (TVA) and organize the search by maintaining a binary decision tree. Each tree level corresponds to a variable assignment. Thus, each tree node is associated with a truth partial assignment to the set of variables. Searching the decision tree starts from the root of the tree and consists of the following iterative processes [10]:

- Decision: at a tree level, the current assignment is extended by deciding a value to an unassigned variable.
- Deduction: the current assignment is extended by implication assignments to unassigned variables and possible conflicts are detected. If no conflict is detected, a new decision is made at one level below. Conflict occurs when a variable is assigned to different values.
- Backtrack: if a conflict is detected, the current assignment is not valid and the search process will continue by making a new assignment at the same level or at a level closer to the root of the tree.

The deduction process described in the Davis-Putnam procedure [5] is the most widely used by backtrack search algorithms (e.g., GRASP [10]). Various algorithms have been derived that incorporate different techniques for decision and backtrack. Deduction is based on the unit clause rule, that is, if a clause is not "true" and all but one literal in that clause have been assigned, then the unassigned literal is *implied* to logic 1 in order for the clause to be "true". Implications are derived using Binary Constraint

Propagation (BCP) of a TVA. For any moderate SAT instance, millions of implications are derived [13]. In the remainder of this paper, Unit Propagation Time (UPT) is the average time to resolve implications or detect a conflict for every TVA determined by decision or backtrack. As a result, UPT=$\frac{T}{d}$, where T is the total time spent by the deduction process during problem solving and d is the total number of decisions and backtracks.

There are two primary approaches to improve the performance of backtrack search algorithms: reducing the number of tree nodes visited and optimizing the deduction process. Incorporating decision assignment techniques can have a significant impact on the total number of decisions made. Furthermore, sophisticated backtracking techniques can significantly prune the search space. However, sophisticated decision assignment and backtrack techniques necessitate complex data structures that favor software over hardware implementations. On the other hand, the bit-level operations and the inherent parallelism of the deduction process matches extremely well with the hardware characteristics of FPGAs. *In this paper, we focus on instance-dependent implementations of the deduction process using FPGAs that can be optimized at runtime based on the knowledge gained during solving the SAT instance.*

3   State of the Art

In [14,15], FPGA-based SAT solvers have been presented based on the deduction process described in the Davis-Putnam procedure [5]. In [14], instance-dependent mapping was utilized to take advantage of the parallelism inherent in the deduction process. Given a SAT instance, the implication circuit for each variable was derived on the fly and was then hard-wired on the FPGA. An implication circuit corresponded to the conditions under which the considered variable would be *implied* by applying the unit clause rule to all the clauses that contain it. As a result, the deduction process was highly parallelized resulting in $O(1)$ UPT at the expense of slow clock rates ($1-2$ MHz). The proposed instance-dependent mapping led to irregular interconnect that required excessive compilation time (i.e., time to derive the configuration and map it onto hardware). This excessive compilation time degraded the effective execution time. For example, compared with software implementations, the observed speedup of $51\times$ for the *hole10* SAT instance [6] reduced to $8.3\times$ due to the compilation time overhead [14]. Intuitively, the compilation time would be more severe for hard SAT instances or, even worse, the resulting mapping may not be routable.

In [15], a new architecture was proposed to drastically reduce the compilation time. Instead of the irregular global interconnect used in [14], a ring-based interconnect was utilized to connect modules in a pipelined fashion. Each module corresponded to a clause and contained the implication circuits for each of its variables based on the unit clause rule. Given a SAT instance, the modules were adapted to the input clauses. As a result, compared with [14], the compilation time was drastically reduced. However, the resulting UPT was $O(n + e)$, where n is the number of the variables and e is the number of the clauses in the input instance. Compared with [14], higher clock speeds were achieved but a larger number of clock cycles was required for problem solving after mapping the solver onto the hardware.

While the performance of the design in [14] is limited by the compilation time, the performance of the design in [15] is critically affected by the increase in the UPT. In this paper, a parallel deduction engine is proposed with low compilation overhead which is similar to the compilation overhead in [15]. However, the UPT is $O(n + \frac{e}{p})$, where $1 < p < e$ is the amount of parallelization. The parameter p that leads to overall minimum execution time is closely related to intrinsic characteristics of the given instance. To the best of our knowledge, there is no published work related to the computation of the optimal value for p. Different values for p correspond to different implementations for the deduction engine (see Section 4) and lead to different time performance. In our approach, the deduction engine is initially adapted based on the instance and a value for p. Then, the architecture dynamically *evolves* in terms of p to optimize overall performance. On the contrary, in [14] and [15] (as well as in other FPGA-based SAT solvers), the deduction engine is initially adapted to the instance but remains *static* (i.e., fixed amount of parallelization) during problem solving. In [15], new clauses are added in the deduction engine to support conflict-directed dynamic learning. However, the amount of parallelization remains the same at $p = 1$.

4   An Adaptive Parallel Architecture for Deduction

In [8], we have evaluated the performance of a novel implementation of the deduction process. The key idea was to split the clauses of the input instance into p groups and perform the deduction process in each group in parallel. As a result, the deduction process consisted of the following steps:

1. The current variable assignment is fed to each group of clauses. Implications are resolved independently in each group. If a conflict is detected, the deduction process is terminated and backtrack is performed. If no implications occur, a new decision is made. Otherwise, *Step 2* is performed.
2. A merging process is performed to combine the distinct TVAs derived in each group. As a result, a single TVA is derived that contains all the assigned variables. If a variable has been implied to conflicting values in different groups, the deduction process is terminated and backtrack is performed. Otherwise, *Step 1* is repeated using the resulting TVA as input.

A simulator written in C++ was developed in [8] to evaluate the overall performance of a SAT solver that incorporates the above modified deduction process. Each group of clauses was implemented as a linear array of modules operated in a pipelined fashion. Hence, the deduction engine implemented in [14] corresponds to $p = 1$. The simulation results (cycle count) demonstrated that the speedup achieved compared with the baseline solution could be significant. The baseline solution corresponds to a deduction engine with $p = 1$. Speedup refers to the overall performance of the SAT solver. Static ordering of variables and chronological backtracking were considered. The observed speedups were up to an order of magnitude for the chosen instances [8]. However, given a SAT instance, the selection of a value for p that would optimize the performance of the SAT solver is a key research problem for realizing SAT solvers based on the parallel deduction process proposed in [8].

In Figure 1, the speedup for several values for p is shown for various SAT instances[1]. The graphs were obtained using our simulator. For any SAT instance and values for p close to 1, the amount of parallelization of the deduction process is small resulting in relatively poor speedup compared with the maximum speedup that can be achieved. On the other hand, for values for p close to the number of clauses e, the speedup degrades drastically since the second step of the modified deduction process is repeated a large number of times. Given a SAT instance, the problem is to find a value for p that leads to maximum speedup. This *optimal* value for p is intrinsic to the instance. In Section 4.3, a fast heuristic is described that leads to near-optimal speedup. This heuristic is applied on the fly during problem solving.

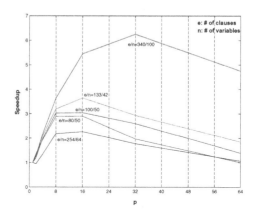

Fig. 1. Speedup compared with $p = 1$ for various SAT instances

4.1   Hardware Organization

A parameterized architecture for the deduction engine has been developed consisting of groups of clauses. The architecture is scalable with respect to the number of clauses in the input instance. Each group of clauses corresponds to a linear array of modules connected in a pipelined fashion. Each module is associated with one clause of the given instance. The parameters of the architecture are the number of clauses e, the number of group of modules p, the number of variables B that are moved per clock cycle to/from the architecture, and the maximum number of variables v that a module contains (i.e., every module can correspond to a clause with up to v variables). The engine extends an input TVA with implication assignments and detects conflicts. However, it can be modified to incorporate hardware implementations of decision and backtrack engines. The decision and backtrack processes are assumed to be executed by a host machine.

In Figure 2, an illustrative example of a parallel deduction architecture is shown for $p = 3$ and $e = 24$ along with the module architecture. The TVA is fed to the architecture by the host at a rate of B variables per clock cycle. The merged TVA is repeatedly fed back to the architecture until no more implications occur or a conflict is detected. The main difference compared with [8] is that the merging process occurs concurrently with implication resolution. The merging process is implemented as a linear array of

---

[1] The results shown in Figures 1 and 3 correspond to the following SAT instances from the DIMACS benchmark [6]: par8-1-c, hole6, aim-50-2_0-no-4, aim-50-1_6-yes1-1, and aim-100-3_4-yes1-4. Static ordering of variables and chronological backtracking were incorporated by the simulator.

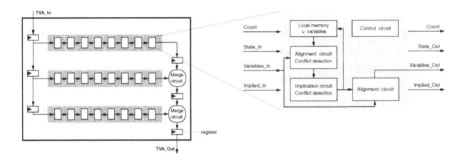

Fig. 2. Parallel deduction engine architecture and module details

simple OR structures that are located at the end of each group. As a result, the hardware organization is simplified leading to reduced compilation overhead and hardware area. For the proposed architecture, $UPT = t_p \times (\lceil \frac{n}{B} \rceil + \lceil \frac{e}{p} \rceil + p)$, where n is the number of variables in the given instance. The parameter t_p is intrinsic to the SAT instance and can be determined after actually solving the SAT instance. In the proposed architecture, t_p also depends on the parameter p, the way in which the clauses are split into groups, and the ordering of clauses within each group.

The architecture of a module is the same for all the clauses (see Figure 2). Modules are connected in a pipelined fashion and thus, the clock cycle of the engine is approximately equal to the latency through a module. The variables associated with a clause are stored in the local memory of the associated module. A standard 2-bit encoding is used for unassigned and assigned variables. Up to v variables can be stored locally. The implication and the control circuits are generic for any clause containing up to v literals. The implication circuit resolves implications and detects possible conflicts. The control circuit supervises the dataflow and the operation of the module based on the state of the engine (i.e., idle, implication, conflict). The state is propagated and updated through the modules by the *State_In* and *State_Out* signals. Similarly, the *Implied_In* and *Implied_Out* signals trace the occurrence of implications. The alignment circuits are specific for each clause and are used to update the variables in the local memory with the variables on the bus and vice versa. Both alignment circuits have been implemented using ROM-based lookup tables. As a result, a module can be customized with respect to a given clause by updating the ROM contents only. Finally, the global signal *Count* is used to identify which variables are fed to the module, and thus it controls the alignment of variables.

4.2 Run-Time Mapping

The time overhead to map the above deduction engine architecture onto reconfigurable hardware should be minimal since the mapping contributes to the overall time performance. The modularity and the simplicity of the proposed architecture lead to templates with fast compilation times. Templates can be developed off-line to facilitate run-time mapping. The major requirement for implementing a deduction engine is to adapt a template to the input instance for a given value for p.

The templates correspond to FPGA configurations. A configuration corresponds to a deduction engine with specific values for B, v, and e_p, where e_p is the number of modules per group. The parameter e_p determines the amount of parallelization p explored in the hardware for a given instance. The number of groups mapped onto an FPGA depends on the density of the FPGA. The parameter B depends on the I/O resources of the FPGA. A conservative estimate of the maximum value for B is 32 variables per clock cycle. The parameter v is associated with the clause that contains the largest number of literals in the given SAT instance. However, large clauses can be decomposed into smaller ones resulting in a smaller v at the expense of an increased e. Given a SAT instance, the number of clauses e determines the number of FPGAs needed to map the proposed deduction engine architecture.

For a given p and a SAT instance, the FPGA(s) is configured at runtime. The resources of the FPGA(s) are assumed to be sufficient for solving the SAT instance. Without loss of generality, we assume that p divides e and the deduction engine can be mapped onto one FPGA. Initially, the FPGA is loaded with a configuration corresponding to $v \geq v_{max}$ and $e_p = \frac{e}{p}$, where v_{max} is the number of literals in the largest clause of the given instance. Then, by altering the interconnect, only the first $\frac{e}{p}$ groups of modules remain connected to the merge circuits (Figure 2). This can be realized using partial reconfiguration in order to either disconnect the remaining groups of modules from the corresponding merge circuits or to bypass these merge circuits. As a result, e clauses are implemented in p groups. Finally, using partial reconfiguration, the contents of the local memory in the modules are updated based on the clauses of the given instance. A conservative estimate of the time for mapping a deduction engine is twice the time required to configure the entire FPGA. During problem solving, the above procedure can be repeated to implement a deduction engine with a different p. An alternate solution for modifying the parameter p of the engine would be to alter the interconnect. The advantage of this approach is that there is no need to update the contents of the local memory in the modules. However, further study is needed to understand the impact of such an approach on the reconfiguration cost and the clock speed.

4.3   Run-Time Performance Optimization

Given a SAT instance with e clauses and a set of available templates with different values for e_p, the objective of performance optimization is to determine the value for p that leads to maximum speedup compared with the baseline solution. Heuristics for splitting the clauses into groups and ordering the clauses inside a group are not considered in the proposed approach. In general, the time spent in the deduction process is a dominant factor for the performance of a backtrack search algorithm [10]. The total time spent for deduction during problem solving is $d \times$ UPT, where d is the total number of decisions and backtracks. Hence, intuitively, optimizing the deduction process can lead to maximizing the speedup. The behavior of UPT for various SAT instances and values for p is shown in Figure 3(a). The graphs were obtained using our simulator. For values for p close to 1 or to the number of clauses e, the UPT value degrades from the global minimum. In Figure 3(b), the product of UPT for each value for p (see Figure 3(a)) with the corresponding speedup (see Figure 1) is shown. Clearly, the product is nearly a constant. Therefore, the optimization problem of maximizing the speedup can be indeed approximated by the optimization problem of minimizing UPT.

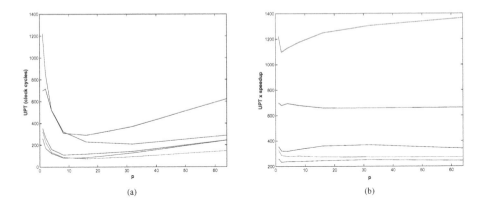

(a)   (b)

Fig. 3. (a) UPT and (b) product of UPT with the corresponding speedup

In the following, a greedy heuristic is described for optimizing performance at runtime. Given a set of templates and a SAT instance, the objective is to find the template with the minimum UPT while solving the SAT instance. The heuristic is executed by the host machine and decides the template based on which the FPGA(s) is configured. Initially, a sorted linked list is created. Each element in the list corresponds to a template. The list is sorted in ascending order of e_p. As a result, the head of the list corresponds to the template with the minimum e_p. Starting from the head of the list, the associated template is used to configure the FPGA(s) and the backtrack search algorithm begins execution. The implemented deduction engine is operated for $kp(e_p + n + p)$ clock cycles and is further continued until no more implications occur or a conflict is detected. The parameter k is an integer and $e_p = \lceil \frac{e}{p} \rceil$. Empirical results suggest that for $k \leq 5$, a good approximation of the UPT can be derived. The derived UPT is recorded as the minimum UPT. Then, the template associated with the subsequent element in the list is used to configure the FPGA(s). The backtrack search algorithm continues using the mapped deduction engine and the UPT is evaluated again. If the derived UPT is larger than the minimum UPT, the template corresponding to the minimum UPT is used to configure the FPGA(s) again and the backtrack search algorithm continues until it solves the SAT instance. Otherwise, the derived UPT becomes the minimum UPT, the template associated with the subsequent element in the list is used to configure the FPGA(s), and the same procedure is repeated.

An interesting feature of the above optimization process is that the backtrack search algorithm need not restart over again from an empty TVA at the root of the binary decision tree after switching templates but it continues with the current TVA at the current tree level. The convergence rate of the heuristic and the achieved speedup depend on the distance between consecutive e_p values of the templates and the minimum e_p. Different optimization heuristics or sets of templates can lead to higher speedup. Our idea of

UPT-based performance optimization during problem solving can incorporate various heuristics and sets of templates.

5   Experimental Results

The proposed deduction engine (Figure 2) was mapped onto the Virtex XCV1000 -6 -FG680 FPGA [12] for various values for e, p, v, and B. The Foundation Series 2.1i software development tool was used for synthesis and place-and-route. No placement or timing constraints were imposed. In Figure 4, for $e = 32$, the hardware area and the clock speed are shown for various values for v and B. The results are the average over implementations with $p = 1, 2, 4, 8$. For a given e, the hardware area and the clock speed are approximately the same for different values for p. Hardware area is proportional to e and is primarily determined by v and B. Approximately 100 modules with $v = 16$ and $B = 16$ can be mapped on the above FPGA. The clock speed of the engine is primarily determined by v and decreases by a factor of $2 - 3$ as v increases from 4 to 32. The sensitivity of the software tools used as well as the absence of placement constraints are the main reasons for the observed reduction of the clock speed with respect to different values for B.

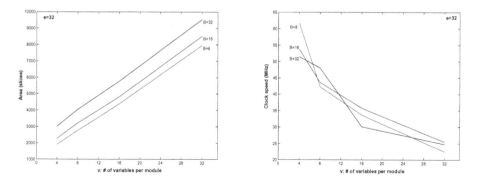

Fig. 4. Hardware area and clock speed in terms of v and B

Using our simulator [8], the heuristic proposed in Section 4.3 was applied to several SAT instances. The considered instances are shown in Figure 3. A set of templates with $e_p = \lceil \frac{e}{p} \rceil$ was assumed, where $p = \{4, 8, 16, 32, 64\}$. Compared with the baseline solution, the speedup achieved by applying our approach is shown in Table 1. The results correspond to $B = 16$. Furthermore, the optimization steps are shown in terms of the parameter p. In addition, the maximum speedup that can be achieved and the associated value for p are shown. The maximum speedup was determined by solving the SAT instance for each value for p without applying our heuristic.

For the SAT instance par8-1-c, the problem was solved before evaluation of UPT was completed for the template with minimum e_p. For hole6 and aim-50-20-no-4, the template that leads to maximum speedup was found and the achieved speedup was 3.12

and 3.03 respectively. Compared with the maximum speedup, the achieved speedup was 1-15% smaller depending on the time spent on templates with different values for p. Finally, for aim-50-16-yes1-1 and aim-100-34-yes1-4, the template that leads to maximum speedup was not found but the achieved speedup was only 1-13% smaller than the corresponding maximum speedup. The achieved speedup is indicative for classes of SAT instances of similar hardness and number of clauses and variables.

Table 1. Speedup compared with the baseline solution ($p=1$)

SAT Instance	Optimization Steps	Speedup	
		Achieved	Maximum
par8-1-c	64	1.06	2.26 @ 16
hole6	$64 \rightarrow 32 \rightarrow 16 \rightarrow 8 \rightarrow 16$	3.12	3.64 @ 16
aim-50-20-no-4	$64 \rightarrow 32 \rightarrow 16 \rightarrow 8 \rightarrow 16$	3.03	3.04 @ 16
aim-50-16-yes1-1	$64 \rightarrow 32 \rightarrow 16 \rightarrow 8 \rightarrow 16$	2.87	2.90 @ 8
aim-100-34-yes1-4	$64 \rightarrow 32 \rightarrow 16 \rightarrow 8 \rightarrow 16$	5.44	6.25 @ 32

The performance results shown in Table 1 do not include the time required to configure the FPGA(s). Considering the configuration overhead, the time performance of our approach becomes $l \times r_1 + t_1/s$, where l is the number of the optimization steps, s is the achieved speedup, and t_1 and r_1 are the time performance and the configuration overhead respectively of the baseline solution. Similarly, the time performance of the baseline solution becomes $r_1 + t_1$, where r_1 is usually in the order of seconds or minutes [15]. If r_1 and t_1 are of the same order of magnitude, then the baseline solution and our solution will both achieve similar overall performance. However, for larger values for t_1 (i.e., harder SAT instances), the overall speedup achieved by our solution will be equal to s.

6   Conclusions

In this paper, a novel FPGA-based deduction engine for backtrack search algorithms was proposed. An optimization heuristic was also developed based on which the engine *evolves* during problem solving with respect to the amount of parallelization p. Our objective was to find a value for p that results in maximum speedup compared with the baseline solution. This value for p depends on the input instance. To the best of our knowledge, there are no other published results related to performance optimization in terms of p. In the state-of-the-art FPGA-based SAT solvers [15], a deduction engine with $p = 1$ is used for any given instance; initially the engine is adapted to the input instance but $p = 1$ remains fixed during the entire problem solving. On the contrary, in our approach, not only the engine is initially adapted to a given SAT instance, but it is also dynamically reconfigured with respect to p based on the knowledge gained during solving the SAT instance. Using our approach, we demonstrate speedups in the range of $2.87 - 5.44$ for several SAT instances compared with the state of the art.

Intuitively, for harder instances, the achieved speedup is expected to be larger than an order of magnitude. The work reported here is part of the USC MAARCII project (http://maarcII.usc.edu).

We believe that the UPT-based optimization approach introduced in this paper could be the basis for parallel deduction engines for backtrack search algorithms. Future work includes further experimentation with instances from the DIMACS benchmark [6] and evaluation and enhancement of the proposed heuristic. Another interesting topic to study would be the effectiveness of parallel deduction engines with respect to various decision and backtrack techniques. Finally, further study is needed to understand the behavior of UPT in terms of different heuristics for splitting the clauses into groups and ordering the clauses inside a group. Related problems are addressed in [4].

References

1. M. Abramovici and D. Saab, "Satisfiability on Reconfigurable Hardware," International Conference on Field Programmable Logic and Applications, September 1997.
2. M. Abramovici, J. Sousa, and D. Saab,"A Massively-Parallel Easily-Scalable Satisfiability Solver using Reconfigurable Hardware," ACM/IEEE Design Automation Conference, 1999.
3. T. H. Cormen, C. E. Leiserson, and R. L. Rivest, "Introduction to Algorithms," The MIT Press, Cambridge Massachusetts, 1997.
4. A. Dandalis, "Dynamic Logic Synthesis for Reconfigurable Devices," PhD Thesis, Dept. of Electrical Engineering, University of Southern California. Under Preparation.
5. M. Davis and H. Putnam, "A Computing Procedure for Quantification Theory," Journal of ACM, 7:201-215, 1960.
6. DIMACS SAT benchmarks, ftp://dimacs.rutgers.edu/pub/challenge/satisfiability/
7. M. Platzner and G. De Micheli, "Acceleration of Satisfiability Algorithms by Reconfigurable Hardware," International Conference on Field Programmable Logic and Applications, September 1998.
8. M. Redekopp and A. Dandalis, "A Parallel Pipelined SAT Solver for FPGAs," International Conference on Field Programmable Logic and Applications, September 2000.
9. J. P. M. Silva, "An Overview of Backtrack Search Satisfiability Algorithms," International Symposium on Artificial Intelligence and Mathematics, January 1998.
10. J. P. M. Silva and K. A. Sakallah, "GRASP: A New Search Algorithm for Satisfiability," CSE-TR-292-96, Computer Science and Engineering Department, University of Michigan, Ann Arbor, April 1996.
11. T. Suyama, M. Yokoo, and H. Sawada, "Solving Satisfiability Problems on FPGAs," International Conference on Field Programmable Logic and Applications, September 1996.
12. Xilinx Inc., http://www.xilinx.com
13. H. Zhang and M. Stickel, "An Efficient Algorithm for Unit-Propagation," International Symposium on Artificial Intelligence and Mathematics, 1996.
14. P. Zhong, M. Martonosi, P. Ashar, and S. Malik, "Accelerating Boolean Satisfiability with Configurable Hardware," IEEE Symposium on FPGAs for Custom Computing Machines, April 1998.
15. P. Zhong, M. Martonosi, S. Malik, and P. Ashar, "Solving Boolean Satisfiability with Dynamic Hardware Configurations," International Workshop on Field Programmable Logic and Applications, September 1998.

A Reconfigurable Embedded Input Device for Kinetically Challenged Persons

Apostolos Dollas

Tom Kean

Kyprianos Papademetriou

Nikolaos Aslanides

Dept. of Electronic and Comp. Eng.
Technical University of Crete
Akrotiri Campus
73100 Chania, Crete
Greece

Dollas@mhl.tuc.gr

Algotronix Ltd.
P.O. Box 23116
Edinburgh EH8 8YB
Scotland
United Kingdom

Tom@Algotronix.com

Abstract. A new input device for kinetically challenged persons has been developed. This device is based on solid-state accelerometers to sense motion in space, a microcontroller to sample the data in real time, and an embedded FPGA to distinguish types of motion from programmable lists of motions. The FPGA computational model for the first version, presented in this paper, is an implementation of finite state machines (FSM) running in parallel, one for each type of motion which is detected by the system. The design is modular, allowing for different lists of motions and/or thresholds on input data to be incorporated with reconfiguration of the FPGA. A personal computer is used to determine the appropriate settings for each motion, which are then converted to FSM. The architecture of the system, types of motions it detects, and its performance characteristics are presented in this work.

1 Introduction - Motivation

Input devices in general are based on the translation of a stimulus to some action. With the pervasiveness of computers today, a large selection of input devices for computer I/O is available for kinetically challenged persons (large keyboards, eye-tracking devices, etc.)[1], [2], [3]. Essentially all research and associated products to date have focused on making computers more accessible to kinetically challenged persons [4], or, in using computers to perform tasks (e.g. turn lights on/off, etc.), whereas physical devices are controlled in traditional, mechanical ways (e.g. wheelchairs are still controlled by joysticks).

G. Brebner and R. Woods (Eds.): FPL 2001, LNCS 2147, pp. 326-335, 2001.
© Springer-Verlag Berlin Heidelberg 2001

The next logical step is to detach the input devices from the need to be connected to a personal computer, and, by making them embedded, to associate such devices directly with desired tasks, such as wheelchair motion, or direct device control (without the need of a general purpose computer). Furthermore, for kinetically challenged persons, it is desirable to decouple the input device functionality from the actual manipulation of physical entities (e.g. joysticks, trackballs, keyboards, mouse devices) and rather rely on free motion which may be more comfortable. Taking example from advances in virtual reality applications for scientific and entertainment purposes alike, which employ 3D input and manipulation devices, we consider that an input device which is based on free motion of kinetically challenged persons would be useful in real-world applications, if it is reliable in its results, robust in its operation, reasonable in its size and power consumption, and inexpensive. Furthermore, the device should be easily tunable to the specific motion characteristics of different persons. We thus needed to solve the problem in a different design space than that of the corresponding virtual reality input devices.

The work, which is presented in this paper, is a first generation full-scale embedded system. It is complete with:

- motion sampling and off-line preprocessing by a personal computer,
- mapping different motions on finite state machines (FSM) within an embedded FPGA,
- running the algorithms in real time from a standalone system which is based on accelerometers as sensors, a microcontroller for the sampling of sensor data, and a FPGA for real-time processing,
- small and inexpensive construction.

Section 2 of this paper presents related work on sensors and real-time processing using FPGA's. Section 3 has the architecture and applications of the new system, motivating also why the use of FPGA's is needed in the system. Section 4 presents the input subsystem, which also motivates why a microcontroller is needed. It is followed by Section 5 on how a personal computer was used to sample and pre-process input data. Section 6 has the FPGA real time FSM computation model and results including area and speed characteristics. Lastly, there is a section on conclusions and alternative computation models.

2   Related Work

There is no related work which involves motion sensing and reconfigurable logic for persons with kinetic disabilities, so related work on each aspect of this project will be presented separately in this section. Regarding persons with motor disabilities, a real-time system has been designed, such that electromyographic (EMG) biosignals from cranial muscles and electroencephalographic (EEG) biosignals from the cerebrum's occipital lobe, are transformed into controls for two-dimensional (2-D) cursor movement[4]. The above system is based on a Digital Signal Processor (DSP) for its computations, and it is used for computer I/O.

Dynamic Time Warping (DTW) has been used for real time motion sensing of similar motions in a different time frame, in the context of a mobile robot [6]. This algorithm measures similarity between multivariate time series, and although Hidden Markov Models (HMM) outperform in terms of results the DTW algorithms, the latter are still used due to lower computational requirements. Another motion sensing project, with accelerometers as sensors [7], is using HMM's for (non real-time) signature verification and falls in the general category of "smart pens". A project combining FPGA's, DSP's and accelerometers (and other sensors too) is the "Air Drummer" [8]. The goal of this project is to make a virtual drumset which will enable the generation of drum sounds through the process of "air drumming" or "virtual drumming". Air drumming is the process of mimicking the actions of a drummer through the syncopated motion of one's upper and lower limbs. A part of a project called "3D Eye Tracking Device" [9] combines accelerometers and reconfigurable logic in order to measure successive head and eye movements. An FPGA is used as the interface between sensors and the processor board. An FPGA/DSP combination is used for the online, real-time acquisition and preprocessing of sensor data for medical purposes, and the entire system is used in conjunction with a computer.

On a different type of a real-time reconfigurable application, a system that supports reconnaissance, surveillance and target acquisition operation [10] comprises of microsensors, a DSP module and a FPGA module. The purpose of the FPGA is for signal processing (FFT) and for the control of various subsystems towards low-power consumption. FPGA's have also been used for real time 3D volume visualization [11]. It should be noted that most of these projects use large FPGA's, e.g. in [10] a large Xilinx Virtex FPGA is used, whereas in [11] multiple FPGA's are used. In our system such approaches would not meet size, cost, and power consumption limits for an embedded application.

3   Architecture and Applications of the System

The general characteristics of the new system, defined functionally and not in terms of implementation are:

- low cost solid state (non-mechanical) sensors which are reliable and suitable for motion sensing,
- real-time sampling of the data,
- motion detection for a large number of motions (vocabulary), tunable to different persons needs, and,
- ability to directly control devices through a direct electronic interface which can be easily adapted to mechanical interface control.

The key decision for the system was the usage of solid state accelerometers. Although other sensors were considered (e.g. Hall effect sensors), accelerometers were deemed to be sufficiently small in size, reliable, and low cost. The choice of accelerometers as input devices opened a slew of design considerations, as described in Section 4. From the general characteristics of the architecture we developed a system-level block diagram, shown in Figure 1.

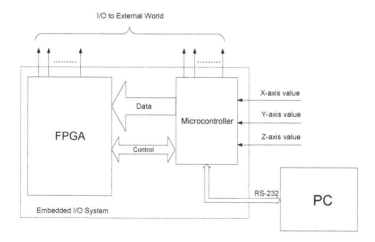

Fig. 1. A concept for the generic diagram of the system

The diagram in Figure 1 is generic, and as the project progressed there were considerations to leave out the FPGA if the microcontroller proved sufficiently powerful, or, to leave out the microcontroller if the FPGA was sufficient. The connectivity with the PC was envisioned as a rapid prototyping tool, so that several algorithms and their computational requirements could be assessed. In the standalone operation of the system the personal computer is not connected. In terms of applications, the original requirement for direct I/O was incorporated into the architecture with I/O lines, which can take any desirable logical values. Through optocouplers, direct interfacing to devices can then be accomplished (e.g. wheelchair Control). Moreover, these I/O lines can be easily converted to infrared (IR) ports, so that remote devices may be accessed (e.g. IR controlled door locks, IR controlled telephone device pick-up). Lastly, the I/O lines can be either decoded, leaving one line per device, or, encoded, allowing for larger numbers of devices to be accessed at the expense of more complex per-device decoding of multiple signals.

4   The Input Subsystem

Several generations of input subsystems were implemented and experiments were conducted in real-time input sampling. All versions were based on some kind of solid state accelerometer, a board with the ATMEL AVR 90S8515 microcontroller (but with different interfaces and software), and a personal computer to hold files of sampled data for post processing. The two most significant versions were

- the three-axes analog accelerometer system, with three Analog Devices ADXL05 accelerometers, and with a microcontroller system to sample and average input data, and,
- the two-axes digital (PWM) accelerometer based system, with a single two-axes Analog Devices ADXL210 integrated circuit.

We found that analog accelerometers have extensive noise, leading to the need for signal conditioning. Following extensive experimentation with the analog accelerometer system we determined that the inclusion of a third axis was not necessary for our purposes, as it complicated unnecessarily the computational requirements. Indeed, for a system which is attached during operation to a wrist, the degree of rotations is bounded in first place, and, limited partial rotations are permissible as long as the final system can detect the desired motion among a fixed list of motions.

The calculations to convert accelerometer output to fixed point digital data are performed by the microcontroller. Subsequently, in the development process the data is sent to the PC via RS232, whereas in the final embedded system the data is sent to the FPGA via an 8-bit port. Every X,Y acceleration value is interpreted as one 16-bit number. The first 8-bits transmitted to the FPGA represent the integer part of the acceleration value and the remaining 8-bits represent the fractional part. Thus, each sample comprises of four bytes of X,Y acceleration information, plus some control bits. This application takes roughly 2Kbytes, or 25% of the microcontroller on-chip program memory. It uses little of the CPU power, but most of the timers and counters. A system calibration process is done by the microcontroller and entails measurement of accelerometer output for zero acceleration. The calibration leads to a slightly different frequency of operation for each implementation; however, the standard frequency of sampled data (determined by worst case analysis) for the FPGA is 2.5 msec per set of samples, or, 400 samples/sec, where each sample is comprised of two 16-bit numbers. We note that a 50Hz sampling could detect all motion by a human hand, so the 400 samples afford an 8X oversampling with the associated robustness of data. The resolution of the system is 1.25 mg for the nominal, 2.5 msec sampling rate.

5   The Personal Computer Data Preprocessing System and Motion Detection Experiments

After sampling the input data, several strategies were considered, based on the processing of accelerometer data, or, results after one or two integrations (velocity and position, respectively). After considerable experimentation we concluded independently that previous results suggesting that these approaches led to excessive error [5], [12] were correct, and we abandoned such approaches in favor of processing the original data. The main reason for the excessive error is that since an integration is performed by multiplying the output of an accelerometer by t (velocity) and t^2 (position), any errors in the output of the accelerometer are also multiplied by these factors. Due to the inherent accumulation of absolute positional errors, inertial sensors (e.g. accelerometers) are much better suited for relative motion sensing or tracking.

Many experiments have been performed, and thirteen motions have been successfully sampled and processed. This "vocabulary" can be dynamic, and depending on the freedom of motion of a person it can be adjusted both in terms of sensitivity and in terms of range of motions. Eight of the thirteen motions detected by our present system are shown in Figure 2, whereas Figure 3 shows X-Y accelerometer data (in g) over time for two motions. Detection of each motion is independent of the detection of the remaining motions, and in terms of resources it is subject only to the availability of logic blocks (CLB's) on a FPGA, leading to a broad range of potential implementations with varying cost and performance.

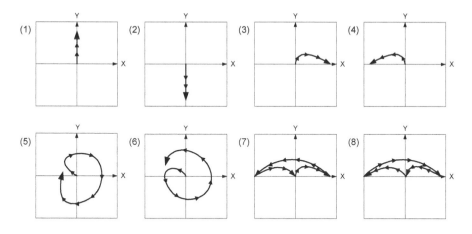

Fig. 2. Partial vocabulary of motions for the first generation of the system

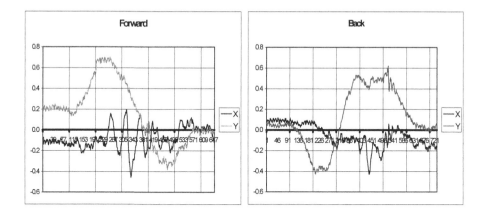

Fig. 3. Acceleration (in g) chart for motions (1) and (2) of Figure 2 (forward and back). The average duration of each motion is about 1.3 sec

Although a recent generation PC can perform a large range of computations, our experiments were computationally limited to reasonable models for final embedded implementation by microcontroller or FPGA. After consideration with several alternatives, we determined that a parallel implementation of finite state machines (FSM) on an FPGA gave a linear increase in the range of motions that could be detected with no performance loss. On the other hand, for a small number of motions

(2-4 motions) a microcontroller would be acceptable computationally. Especially in the case of a system that needs to be tuned to each individual's operational parameters and motion preferences with different FSM's, a microcontroller-based solution would be severely limited.

6   The Embedded FPGA Real Time Processing System - Results

We briefly motivated in the previous section why the FPGA turned out to be necessary for our application. We will now state why the microcontroller is also necessary. In the final version of the system, a standardized embedded system with broad usage will need to be "tuned" to each individual's motion preferences and abilities. This entails a process which is most conveniently performed by a personal computer. Whereas an FPGA could certainly perform the input sampling, it is tasks such as the calibration for each accelerometer, to which we referred in Section 4, and accurate timing of operations, in which a microcontroler is vastly superior due to timers, interrupts, RS 232 port, and other built-in resources. These make the cost-performance of a combined FPGA/microcontroller system superior to any FPGA-only or microcontroller-only approach. Whereas we could use any kind of FPGA or microcontroller, we opted for a Xilinx XC4010 low cost FPGA, and the ATMEL AVR 90S8515 microcontroller. Together with the accelerometers, such a system can be constructed for less than $50, which is consistent with our low-cost goal. The diagram of the final system is shown in Figure 4, and bears substantial resemblance to that of Figure 1, but comes after study to justify the role of each subsystem.

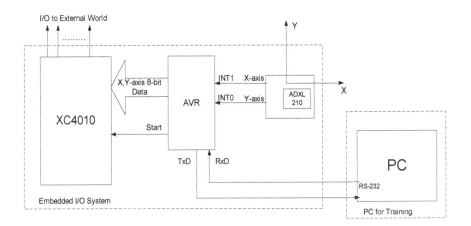

Fig. 4. Final diagram of the overall system

The computational model is that of parallel FSM's, each of which is comprised of stages for detection of values/ranges of X-Y data, followed by similar stages, or stages to wait for a predefined period of time. This way each motion is represented in terms of thresholds which need to be exceeded for the state to be active, followed by periods of "not examining the input", which are useful in avoiding local minima (from irregular motion or noise). These FSM's, one per motion that is desirable to be detected, are reset by a master FSM and operate in parallel. Once an FSM has detected a motion, its ID denotes which motion was detected, and the master FSM outputs the type of motion and resets the FSM's. The overall organization of the parallel detection of motions is shown in Figure 5.

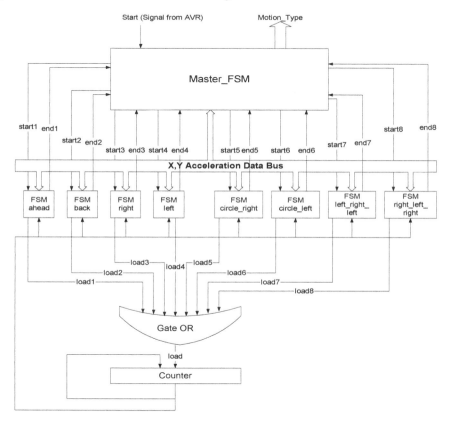

Fig. 5. Implementation of FSM's in hardware

In order to present quantitative results for the speed and the complexity of this scheme, Table 1 shows the usage of CLB's for the eight motions of Figure 2. Although usage of CLB's is not uniform per FSM, a good approximation is that a Xilinx XC4010 can hold the interface to the microcontroller, the master FSM, and all eight of these motion FSM's. Transferring the design to a larger (but still low cost) FPGA such as the Xilinx XC4044 allows for dozens of motions to be detected.

Motion	CLB's	Frequency
"Forward" (1)	30	59MHz
"Back" (2)	30	61MHz
"Right" (3)	34	53MHz
"Left" (4)	34	52MHz
"CircleRight" (5)	54	34MHz
"CircleLeft" (6)	54	34MHz
"Right-left-right" (7)	49	39MHz
"Left-right-left (8)	50	38Mhz

Table 1. CLB usage and speed operation while implementing 2 FSM's in XC4010XL.

The regular structure of the FSM's makes customization of the system through reconfiguration quite easy. Without a new synthesis process each time, once training has determined thresholds and delays for each FSM, a simple script can alter the configuration file, meaning that an application can be developed which customizes the system through reconfiguration, but without the usual synthesis process.

In terms of speed of the FPGA, the structure alone of the solution readily shows that it is a few orders of magnitude faster than what is needed. For example, typical speeds for the FPGA operation are in excess of 35 MHz, whereas we have a sample every 400Hz. Even if we transfer the 4-byte data from the AVR to the XC4010 at its nominal frequency of 8MHz bursts, the FPGA can still run at less than 10MHz and have most of its cycles unused (two cycles for each of the X-Y data set -four cycles total- are sufficient to determine the next state of each FSM). In practice the minimum allowable clock frequency is used to lower power requirements.

7   Conclusions and Alternative Computational Models

In conclusion, a low cost system has been developed to detect motions from an initial vocabulary range of thirteen motions (eight are shown in this paper). The system was implemented with an ATMEL AVR 90S8515 microcontroller, a Xilinx XC4010 FPGA, and Analog Devices ADXL 210 accelerometers. The prototype of the system comprises of several printed circuit boards and breadboards, connected with ribbon cable.In terms of computational models, the general architecture allows for much more sophisticated computations, including fuzzy logic algorithms, discrete Hidden Markov Models, and neural networks. Although we do have preliminary results with such models, we have found that these are much more intensive in resources, and to the extent that the simplistic FSM model that was presented here works adequately, it should be preferred for reasons of cost performance.

Subsequent steps of this work include clinical testing (which is underway), the development of training tools for the system to automatically determine thresholds for the FSM's and better integration of the subsystems in one or two printed circuit boards.

Acknowledgements

We wish to acknowledge funding for this work by the Greek Secretatiat of Research and Technology (GSRT) and the British Council, under the Britain Greece Joint Research Program, and, the EPET II European Union program under the Second Framework of Support to Greece. We also acknowledge generous donations to our educational and research activities by Xilinx Corporation, and electronics parts support by Analog Devices. We also thank University of Edinburgh Professors Gordon Brebner and John Gray for hosting at the Division of Informatics the Greek partners of the program during a week-long work visit to Edinburgh.

References

1. Lau C., O' Leary S. "Comparison of computer input devices for persons with severe physical disabilities", Am.J.Occup. Ther. Nov. 1993, 47:11.
2. Hawley M.S. et al. "Wheelchair mounted integrated control systems for multiply handicapped people", J. Biomed Eng. 1992 May, 14:3.
3. Luttgens K. et al Kinesiology-Scientific Basis of Human Motion" 8th Ed.,Brown and Benchmark Publishers, 1992, ISBN 0-697-11632-8.
4. Armando B. Barreto, Scott D. Scargle, Malek Adjouadi, "A practical EMG-based human-computer interface for users with motor disabilities", Journal of Rehabilitation Research and Development Vol. 37 No. 1, January/February 2000
5. C. Verplaetse "Inertial proprioceptive devices: Self-motion-sensing toys and tools", IBM Systems Journal, Vol 35, NOS 3&4, 1996.
6. T. Oates; M. D. Schmill and P. R. Cohen, "Identifying Qualitatively Different Outcomes of Actions: Gaining Autonomy Through Learning". In Proceedings of the Fourth International Conference on Autonomous Agents, pages 110-111, 2000.
7. Jim Broyles, Nicolas Karlsson, Rob Swanson, and Eduardo Velarde, "The Signature Verification System", January 1997, http://www.analog.com/publications/magazines/accel_news/issue6/2.html.
8. Jean-Louis, Racine Jeremy Risner, "Air Drummer", http://www.me.berkeley.edu/ME235/groups/psi
9. Kayser-Threde GMBH, 3D Eye Tracking Device, Technical Description, November 2000, Munchen.
10. S. Scalera, M. Falco, and B. Nelson, "A Reconfigurable Computing Architecture for Microsensors", In Proceedings of the FCCM April 2000, pages 59-67
11. A. Kaufman, F. Dachille, B. Chen, I. Bitter, K. Kreeger, N. Zhang, and Q. Tang, "Real-Time Volume Rendering", Special Issue on 3D Imaging of the International of Imaging Systems and Technology, 2000, pp.
12. C. Verplaetse, "Can A Pen Remember What It Has Written Using Inertial Navigation ?: AnEvaluation Of Current Accelerometer Technology", part of a class project for "Physics and Media" class, http://xenia.media.mit.edu/~verp/projects/smartpen/ruff_drapht.html.

Bubble Partitioning
for LUT-Based Sequential Circuits

Frank Wolz and Reiner Kolla

Universität Würzburg, Lehrstuhl für Technische Informatik
{wolz,kolla}@informatik.uni-wuerzburg.de

Abstract. In this paper, we present an incremental clustering technique for LUT-based sequential circuits targetting a delay-optimized partitioning of the LUT and latch blocks for FPGA placement. Our cost function considers a slack-based relative delay criticality of circuit nets. As partitions are being constructed simultaneously, the method is open also for further evaluation criteria, e.g. in respect of placeability or routability.

1 Introduction

Multiway partitioning of sequential circuits can be described as the art of dividing a circuit (which consists of combinatorial nodes, latch nodes and nets) such that specific requirements on the resulting parts are met. Already from a theoretical point of view, this problem is NP–complete [GJ79], so in real world, commonly heuristic methods minimizing some cost functions are used to get good solutions.

Previous Research. Much research has been performed on partitioning developing refined data structures and algorithms to cope with performance and local minima problems. Traditional bottom–up methods capturing single nodes into clusters or group swapping [KL70, FM82] have been extended for multiway partitioning [WC91] and integrated in top–down algorithms like ratiocut methods [WC89], for example. But also simulated annealing [KGV83], network flow [MS86] and eigenvector decomposition methods [AY95] have been studied. Additionally, there has been various research on circuit partitioning especially for FPGAs [KAS97, LZW98, MBR99]. However, FPGA partitioning methods oriented to cost functions, that take into account only the structure of a circuit, do not necessarily produce "good" solutions in the sense they probably should. Especially, if the architecture model is not restriced to a unique logic element type, it is difficult to estimate realizability during partitioning. Hence, an objective–optimal solution could also be discarded, if partitions could not be realized (efficiently) on architecture segments. As a consequence, some approaches lift the problem on the safe theoretical site by simply assuming a good cost function, and some other approaches are fixed to a special target architecture, where a few parameters seem to be sufficient for justifing a hope on an efficient realizability.

G. Brebner and R. Woods (Eds.): FPL 2001, LNCS 2147, pp. 336–345, 2001.
© Springer-Verlag Berlin Heidelberg 2001

Problems with Partitioning. Depending on the architecture model, without a real placement and routing, it truly can be rather difficult to get an exact estimation about the resulting delay, for example. Therefore, more abstract measures are used, like slack and connectivity informations of the circuit. Partitioning then simply assumes delay–efficient realizations of nets inside a partition (intra–cluster) and more expensive realizations of nets crossing partition borders (inter–cluster). However, also different possibilities of realizing a circuit node on the architecture provide different delays. Furthermore, the capacity of a partition is limited. But a limitation given in the number of assigned circuit nodes could easily be too rough. Again, the main reason is a possible non–realizability. The common solution is to give a theoretical capacity limit and change nodes, if the subcircuit is not placeable and routable. Instead of performing a circuit traversal and filling partition by partition, our bubble partitioning method grows up partitions simultaneously, such that evaluating interaction can be inserted. Our motivation was to develop a flexible circuit partitioning method, that can be interlocked with a retargetable incremental place and route tool.

Outline. The next section introduces some definitions about LUT-based sequential circuits and the circuit partitioning problem. Section 3 first explaines the used abstract partitioning criteria and presents our bubble partitioning algorithm. Partitioning results on 24 MCNC benchmark circuits will be shown in section 4. Finally, the last section comprises our experiences with bubble partitioning.

2 Partitioning on Sequential Circuits

A *LUT-based sequential circuit* C is described by a directed graph $C = (V, E)$, where V represents the set of nodes and E represents the set of edges. The set of nodes consists of four disjoint subsets $V = I \uplus O \uplus F \uplus L$, where I is the set of primary inputs, O is the set of primary outputs, F is the set of functional nodes (LUTs) and L is the set of latches of the circuit. The indegree $indeg(v) = 0$ of primary inputs $v \in I$ is zero, just like the outdegree of primary output blocks $v \in O$. We assume a global clock not contained in the circuit graph, so the indegree of latch nodes is one. We denote nodes from $I \cup L$ as *sources* and nodes from $O \cup L$ as *targets* of the circuit C. Given a node $v \in V$, let $pred(v)$ be the set of its predecessor nodes and let $succ(v)$ be the set of successor nodes of v. The set of outgoing edges $E_v \subseteq E$ of a node v is called a *net*. For a net N, we denote $driver(N)$ as the driver node of N and $targets(N)$ as the set of driven nodes by N. For a circuit C, let be $N_C = \{E_v \mid v \in V\}$ the set of all nets. Note, that a cycle in C must always contain at least one latch node. So, if we split each latch node into a source and a target node, then C separates into a (set of) combinational circuit(s). Let $C = (V, E)$ be a LUT-based sequential circuit with node set partitions (I, O, F, L). Then, a *partitioning* of C is described by an injective mapping $\chi : (F \cup L) \to \mathbb{N}$. The mapping assigns a partition number to each LUT node and each latch node. Let $P_n^\chi = \{v \in F \cup L \mid \chi(v) = n\}$ be the the set of all nodes of partition n. However, if context allows, for better readability we denote it by P_n.

3   Bubble Partitioning

3.1   Relative Delay Criticality

As mentioned before, the actual delay caused by a circuit LUT or latch block on a field-programmable architecture depends on its realization in a programmable cell. In strongly separated design stages, such a delay is not computable before a block has been placed and routed. However, because the main delay on field-programmable architectures is caused by routing, a practicable delay estimation in pre-placement stages is the slack-based relative delay criticality (RDC). Let again $\mathcal{C} = (V, E)$ be a LUT-based sequential circuit. Given a node $v \in F \cup L$, let $D_i(v)$ be the maximum number of edges on a path from any source of $\mathcal{C}$ to v and let $D_o(v)$ be the maximum number of edges on a path from v to any target node of $\mathcal{C}$. The D_i and D_o values can be easily computed by one forward and one backward breadth-first-traversal from source or target nodes of $\mathcal{C}$, respectively. Starting with $D_i(v) = D_o(v) = 0$ for all nodes $v \in V$, we only have to ensure, that both values are not propagated over latch nodes. We also calculate $D_{max} = \max_v\{D_i(v), D_o(v)\}$. The relative delay criticality of a net N now is:

$$RDC(N) = \frac{D_i(driver(N)) + \max_{w \in targets(N)} D_o(w) + 1}{D_{max}}$$

Obviously, $0 \leq RDC(N) \leq 1$, for all nets N. Furthermore, $RDC(N) = 1$, if and only if a critical path of $\mathcal{C}$ runs over net N.

3.2   Movement Costs

For a given partitioning χ of a circuit $\mathcal{C}$ and a net N, we denote the set of partitions, to which N is adjacent, by:

$$ADJ_\chi(N) = \{P_i^\chi \mid \exists_{u \in P_i^\chi} u = driver(N) \vee u \in targets(N)\}$$

We define the total cost of the partitioning χ as:

$$c(\chi) = \sum_{N \text{ net}} \#ADJ_\chi(N) \cdot RDC(N)$$

Consider a move of a circuit node u from partition P_i to partition P_j. Obviously, u must be either driver or target block of a net N with $P_j \in ADJ_\chi(N)$. Otherwise, the cardinality of $ADJ_\chi(N)$ would increase and hence, also the total partitioning costs would increase. Let χ' be the resulting partitioning of this move. However, we need not to calculate $c(\chi')$ completely in each step, because an update of $c(\chi)$ reduces only to an update of ADJ_χ. We have to consider four cases when updating the ADJ_χ sets:

Case 1: Let N be the net driven by node u. If there are no successor nodes of u in P_i, but in P_j, then cardinality of $ADJ_\chi(N)$ decreases, because P_i will be taken out. However, if there are no successor nodes of u in P_j, then cardinality of the set does not change, because P_i will be taken out, but P_j is taken into $ADJ_\chi(N)$.

Case 2: Let N be the net driven by node u. If there are successor nodes of u in P_i, but not in P_j, then cardinality of $ADJ_\chi(N)$ increases, because P_j will be taken in. However, if there are also successor nodes in P_j, the set does not change.

Case 3: Now, let N be a net driving node u. If u is the only node of net N in P_i and at least one other node of N is in P_j, then cardinality of $ADJ_\chi(N)$ decreases, because P_i will be taken out. However, if there is no other node of N in P_j, cardinality of the set does not change, because P_i will be taken out, but P_j will be taken into $ADJ_\chi(N)$.

Case 4: Let N be a net driving node u. If, besides u, at least one other node of net N is in P_i and there's no node of N is in P_j, then cardinality of $ADJ_\chi(N)$ increases, because P_j will be taken in. However, if there is already a node of N in P_j, then the set does not change.

The complexity of calculating the movement costs for a node v is $O(|pred(v) \cup succ(v)|)$.

3.3   Critical Path Reduction

While calculating movement costs for all blocks, there could be also a set of blocks with minimum costs. Therefore, we use a tie break decision, that takes into account, how many critical paths will be "shortened" by the move of a selected node. We say, moving a block u from partition P_i to partition P_j *shorts* a critical path, if a critical path runs over a net adjacent to u and the appropriate neighbour node of u is already in P_j.

In the initial step, we also calculate the following measures for each node $v \in (F \cup L)$ by a forward and a backward circuit traversal: $icp(v)$, the number of critical paths from any circuit source to v, and $ocp(v)$, the number of critical paths from v to any circuit targets. Now, while calculating the cost for moving a block u to partition P_j, we additionally compute the number of critical paths shortened by this move:

$$CPS(u) = icp(u) \cdot \sum_{v \in succ(u) \cap P_j} ocp(v) + ocp(u) \cdot \sum_{v \in pred(u) \cap P_j} icp(v)$$

The first addend expresses the number of critical paths running from node u to its successor nodes in P_j, the second addend expresses the number of critical paths running from predecessor nodes in P_j to node u.

3.4   Bubble Algorithm

The principle of Bubble Partitioning is rather simple: for each circuit node we initially generate a new partition. Then, we continue iteratively by calculating "cost relation-ships" between all nodes and all partitions using criteria explained in the previous sub-sections. Finally, we select the best node and move it to the appropriate destination partition. These steps are repeated, until there is no node with a negative cost update. If a partition gets empty, it is not longer considered at following iterations. Finally, partitions can be renumbered after last iteration.

The Bubble Partitioning Algorithm below consists only of an initialization routine *init_bubble*, that creates the start partitions and calls the pre-computation of the partitioning measures. Then, each call of the *bubble_step* routine yields a best node and its destination partition and performs the move, until the partitioning is stable.

We call a partitioning *stable*, if there is no node with movement costs less than zero. In this case, the method returns the boolean value *false*. Obviously, this bubble partitioning method always yields a stable partitioning after a finite number of steps, because each bubble step requires a negative cost update, that cannot get arbitrarily small. On the other hand, in all cases a strict lower bound of partitioning costs obviously is zero.

```
init_bubble()
{
    forall nodes v ∈ (F ∪ L) do
        create a new partition {v};
    calculate relative delay criticality RDC for all nets;
    calculate path reduction measures icp and ocp for all nodes;
}
bool bubble_step()
{
    best_block = nil;
    best_part = nil;
    best_cost = 0;
    best_cpath = −∞;
    forall pairs of partitions (Pᵢ, Pⱼ) with: i ≠ j, |Pᵢ| > 0, |Pⱼ| > 0 do
    {
        forall nodes v ∈ Pⱼ do
            if capacity_sufficient(v,i) then
            {
                current_cost = calc_move_cost(v,i);
                if (current_cost < best_cost)
                   || ((current_cost == best_cost) && (CPS(v) > best_cpath)) then
                {
                    best_cost = current_cost;
                    best_cpath = CPS(v);
                    best_node = v;
                    best_partition = i;
                }
            }
    }
    if best_cost < 0 then
    {
        move_node(best_node,best_part);
        return true;
    }
    else
        return false;
}
```

The method *calc_move_cost(v,i)* computes the cost change, if block v would be moved to partition P_i, as specified in section 3.2. The method *capacity_sufficient(v,i)* checks, whether the capacity of partition P_i allows a takeover of node v. As the abstract version of the algorithm does not have any exact criteria on capacities of partitions, it is quite obvious to define a maximum number of blocks as capacity limit. In our implementation, we distinguish between LUT and latch blocks and keep two appropriate block limits.

As partitions grow simultaneously, an evaluation of the last move can be performed, e.g. a check, whether the moved node can actually be placed and routed at its new partition. Then, the capacity decision method can be adjusted or a local repartitioning can be initialized.

4   Benchmarking

Table 1 shows a list of 24 selected MCNC'93 benchmark circuits. The selection was taken manually from circuits up to 1000 nets, where only the number of blocks (LUTs and latches) were considered to get a cross section in size. Although there are much larger benchmarks, we used this set of MCNC benchmarks because of two reasons. First, many of the larger partitioning benchmarks are just hypergraph benchmarks and so they are not suitable to our problem of dealing with more complex architecture models, like different types of logic elements, for example. Second, it has to be recognized, that our bubble partitioning method covers a much larger search space than straight methods, like those in the work of Marquardt et al. [MBR99], and hence it is not designed to be used on very large circuits. However, a comparison between straight and bubble algorithms is presented below. Our selected benchmarks were converted from

Circuit	raw		LUT2		XC4000	
	Blocks	Nets	Blocks	Nets	Blocks	Nets
5xp1	175	182	126	116	40	30
apex7	295	344	272	235	143	106
b12	778	793	97	88	47	38
c8	253	281	154	136	85	67
cm162a	87	101	48	43	31	26
comp	231	263	127	124	69	66
count	227	262	160	144	82	66
C432	362	398	209	202	100	93
C880	705	765	377	351	186	160
decod	43	48	49	33	37	21
ex6	132	138	100	92	43	35
inc	153	160	133	124	61	52
mult16a	274	292	211	210	77	76
pm1	104	120	70	57	47	34
s344	253	263	155	144	72	61
s510	202	222	264	257	118	111
s641	418	454	223	200	138	115
s820	259	278	278	259	131	112
s838	627	663	345	343	128	126
s953	690	707	424	401	207	159
styr	285	295	414	404	169	159
vg2	434	459	112	104	57	49
x1	451	502	346	311	192	157
x4	674	768	453	382	295	224
Avg.	338	364.92	213.46	198.33	106.46	90.33

Table 1. Selection of MCNC'93 Benchmarks

edif to *blif* format by *e2fmt* and then synthesized by SIS 1.3 [SIS92] for two architecture types: LUT2 and XC4000. While the XC4000 architecture is a well-known coarse-grain structure, the LUT2 architecture consists of programmable cells that contain only 2-input look-up-tables and latches, so it can be classified as a fine-grain architecture. At first, we synthesized all benchmarks by *script_rugged* and *script_algebraic*. Then, for XC4000, we used the recommended script from the SIS manual and for the LUT2 architecture, we only splitted big blocks for two inputs. The number of remaining blocks and nets after synthesis can also be seen in table 1.

Our bubble algorithm worked on this double set of benchmarks with partition capacities from 2, 4, 6 . . . 32 look-up-tables and latches, respectively. The partition costs have been calculated as described in section 3.2. The length of a critical path has been calculated by a hard measure: nets crossing partition borders have length 1, while partition-internal nets have length 0.

Generally, it is to observe, that increasing partition capacity limits cause an increase of internal (intra–cluster) nets and a decrease of external (inter–cluster) nets. Assuming, internal nets can be routed more delay–efficient than external nets, this clearly results in a circuit speedup. On the other hand, if partitions are very large, internal delays also could grow and the gain of local routing could be lost. But this depends mainly on the quality of placement and routing algorithms working on each partition.

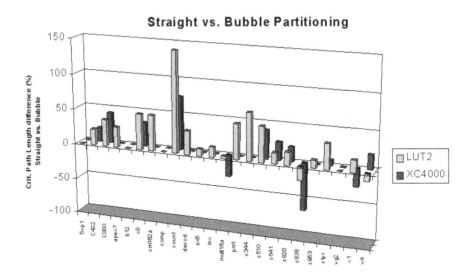

Fig. 1. Straight vs. Bubble Partitioning

We compared our bubble partitioning method to another greedy (straight) partitioning method, that sorts circuit nodes by ascending degree and performs a single circuit traversal filling partition by partition. Figure 1 shows results for all 24 benchmark circuits synthesized for LUT2 and XC4000 architecture, respectively. For these examples, the selected partition capacity was six LUTs and six latches. The figure illustrates the relative difference in critical path length between the two partitioning methods *straight* and *bubble*. Positive percentages are expressing a higher critical path length after straight partitioning in opposite to bubble partitioning. Negative percentages result from longer critical paths after bubble partitioning in opposite to the straight method. With respect to LUT2 blocks, bubble partitioning is outperformed only slightly for two circuits, but leads very significantly for at least half the circuits. With XC4000 blocks, the two partitioning methods produce equal results for half the circuits. The bubble method looses at three circuits and wins at the remaining nine circuits. In opposition to the compared straight algorithm, that performs a simple circuit traversal and, hence, is much faster, our bubble partitioning method provides multiple frontiers in search, when it calculates the move costs from the viewpoint of each growing partition. Hence, bubble partitioning results (in respect of critical path length) are mostly better than straight partitioning results. However, if simultaneous growth of partitions is not needed, bubble partitioning can also be used to improve a partitioning given by a previous straight partitioning sweep, for example. An implementation of such a hybrid partitioning method led to improved results in most cases and a significant reduction in runtime.

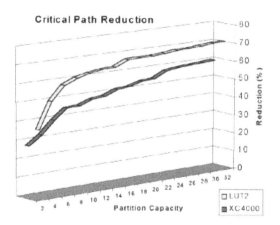

Fig. 2. Critical Path Reduction

A comparison of critical path reduction after bubble partitioning for fine-grain and coarse-grain blocks, respectively, is illustrated in figure 2. Partitionings have been computed for different partition capacities. Results of all 24 benchmark circuits have been averaged. For partition capacities greater than six, there is only small further gain. However, bubble partitioning generally yields better results for fine-grain than for coarse-grain blocks, which actually seems to draft the expected higher potential in optimization for fine-grain cells.

From section 3.2, it is clear, that only connected blocks can form a partition. On the other hand, a strongly delay-oriented partitioning algorithm tends to divide a circuit along depth. The connectivity of blocks represents only an implicit secondary criteria, in terms of packing all terminals of a critical net in its source node partition. Hence, by increasing partition capacity, partition usage decreases.

Figure 3 outlines partition usage for different capacities averaged over all 24 benchmark circuits, respectively. For low capacities, bubble partitioning works much better on

XC4000 blocks, than on LUT2 blocks, because lower number of blocks and lower connectivity does not lead to local minima so fast. However, for capacities greater than 10, there is only very slight difference between coarse- and fine-grain blocks. Obviously, higher capacities neutralize tight connectivity. As already mentioned in section 3.2, the definition of our movement criterion results in a connectivity of all blocks inside a partition. Hence, cluster utilization must get low along with higher capacities, but it could be increased subsequently by combining small clusters. However, this would only blur the results. Finally, we have to take into account, that block delays were not considered

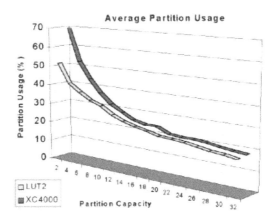

Fig. 3. Partition Usage

in our plain test version, because this depends on the actual realization of a block on the given target architecture. Along with greater delays, also the increased area consumption of coarse–grained programmable cells put apparently worse fine–grain results into perspective for competition.

5   Conclusion and Future Works

We presented a multiway partitioning method for LUT–based sequential circuits, that creates partitions simultaneously node by node. Given initial capacity bounds for LUT blocks and latches, a more sufficient evaluation of a current partitioning, e.g. in respect of effective placeability and routability, can be performed interactively and thus, it can be taken influence on the partitioning progress.

Furthermore, we proposed another application of bubble partitioning: the improvement of a given partitioning calculated by fast greedy algorithms, like the straight partitioning method mentioned in the previous section.

However, our application of bubble partitioning will be an interlocking with new incremental placement and routing algorithms targetting user–defined segmented architectures of periodic structures. In our research, bubble partitioning is a part of a macro generator concept, that will be embedded in an universal CAD tool for FPGA architectural research.

References

[AY95] C. J. Alpert and S. Z. Yao: *Spectral Partitioning: The More Eigenvectors, the Better*, Proceedings of the 32nd Design Automation Conference, pp. 195-200, 1995

[BR97] Vaughn Betz and Jonathan Rose: *VPR: A New Packing, Placement and Routing Tool for FPGA Research*, 7th Int'l Workshop for Field–Programmable Logic and Applications, LNCS 1304, pp. 213-222, 1997

[FM82] C. M. Fiduccia and R. M. Mattheyses: *A linear time heuristic for improving network partitions*, Proc. of the 19th Design Automation Conference, pp. 175-181, 1982

[GJ79] Michael R. Garey, David S. Johnson: *Computers and Intractability: A Guide to NP–Completeness*, Freeman, New York, p. 209, 1979

[KAS97] Helena Krupnova, Ali Abbara, Gabriele Saucier: *A Hierarchy–Driven FPGA Partitioning Method*, Proceedings of the 34th Design Automation Conference, pp. 522-525, 1997

[KGV83] S. Kirkpatrick, C. D. Gelatt Jr. and M. P. Vecchi: *Optimization by simulated annealing*, Science, 220(4598), pp. 671-680, 1983

[KL70] B. W. Kernighan and S. Lin: *An efficient heuristic procedure for partitioning graphs*, Bell Systems Technical Journal, pp. 291-307, Vol. 49, No. 2, 1970

[LZW98] Huiqun Liu, Kai Zhu, D.F. Wong: *Circuit Partitioning with Complex Resource Constraints in FPGAs*, International Symposium on Field–Programmable Gate Arrays, pp. 77-84, 1998

[MBR99] Alexander (Sandy) Marquardt, Vaughn Betz and Jonathan Rose: *Using Cluster-Based Logic Blocks and Timing-Driven Packing to Improve FPGA Speed and Density*, International Symposium on Field–Programmable Gate Arrays, pp. 37-46, 1999

[MS86] D. W. Matula and F. Shahrokhi: *Graph partitioning by sparse cuts and maximum concurrent flow*, Technical Report, Southern Methodist University, Dallas, TX, 1986

[SIS92] Ellen M. Sentovich, Kanwar Jit Singh, et al.: *SIS: A System for Sequential Circuit Synthesis*, http://www-cad.eecs.berkeley.edu/, 1992

[WC89] Yen-Chuen Wei and Chung-Kuan Cheng: *Towards Efficient Hierarchical Designs by Ratio Cut Partitioning*, Proceedings of the International Conference on Computer-Aided Design, pp. 298-301, 1989

[WC91] Yen-Chuen Wei and Chung-Kuan Cheng: *A General Purpose Multiple Way Partitioning Algorithm*, Proceedings of the 28th Design Automation Conference, pp. 421-426, 1991

Rapid Construction of Partial Configuration Datastreams from High-Level Constructs Using JBits

Satnam Singh and Philip James-Roxby

Xilinx, Inc
San Jose, CA 95124 USA
{Philip.James-Roxby, Satnam.Singh}@xilinx.com

Abstract. A technique for rapidly generating configuration datastreams from high-level HDL-like constructs is introduced. This new technique allows a wide variety of client applications to send a fully placed netlist to a sever which routes the netlist and then generates a configuration datastream (either full or partial). The configuration datastream can then be used by the client to reconfigure hardware. This new technology provides an experimental infrastructure that can realize many existing abstractions for reconfigurable computing. This paper considers an implementation of configuration data graphs.

1 Introduction

The objective of the work reported in this paper is to facilitate research into abstractions for describing dynamic reconfiguration by providing a flexible back-end infrastructure for experimental tools. We build on the JBits™ system which provides an interface for creating bitstreams via a Java language level interface. The JBits system also provides a fast router. However, it is not always convenient for research tools to interface directly with a Java-based system. This paper describes a client-server based architecture which allows flexible communication between a client (e.g. JHDL or Lava) and a back end server (i.e. JBits). When the client and server run on the same machine this results in a very fast flow from a high level HDL down to a bitstream which is significantly faster than the conventional flow. This makes possible the implementation of many kinds of custom computing applications that would otherwise have been infeasible.

In previous work [1], a method of rapidly constructing configuration datastreams from a high level language was described. A physical EDIF file was used as the hand-over point between the front end tools (Lava) and the back end flow (implemented using JBits). It was shown that much of the processing time was spent parsing the physical file. Also, there was no real support for partial configuration.

A method of rapidly generating partial configuration datastreams is introduced. The system is implemented using a client-server architecture, whereby a server

G. Brebner and R. Woods (Eds.): FPL 2001, LNCS 2147, pp. 346-356, 2001.

process accepts high-level logical constructs from a client process. The client process is responsible for generating constructs such as nets and instances, and can thus be based on a variety of implementation technologies such as Lava or JHDL. The server translates the high-level constructs into low-level configuration calls using the JBits API. Furthermore, in order to support partial configuration effectively, configuration data graphs are used, which allows the client at design-time to construct partial configuration frames to implement known transitions between configurations. These partial configurations can then be used to support fast run-time reconfiguration.

As in [1], it is worth re-iterating the limitations of this flow when compared to the mainstream flow offered by Xilinx. The logic accepted by the new flow must be fully mapped to the primitives found in the Virtex™ CLB. All logic must also be fully placed. This would prohibit the use of this flow for general logic implementation, where the mainstream tools excel. The new flow is specifically intended for rapidly moving between a HDL to partial configurations in the shortest length of time.

The current state of JBits has been described elsewhere [1]. In summary, with the addition of RTPcores and the run-time router, JBits can now be considered a high-level design language supporting partial configuration, with a number of debug capabilities. This work complements the role of JBits as a design language by adding new ways in which client tools can interface to JBits.

2   High-Level Support for Reconfiguration

2.1   Previous Work

A number of efforts exist to provide a high-level support for run-time reconfigurable designs. Brebner [2] has proposed a number of models, based on high-level abstractions called Swappable Logic Units (SLU). The main idea of this work is to provide operating system-like support for run-time reconfiguration, by allowing SLUs to be swapped into and out of an FPGA which is pre-loaded with a communications harness, allowing SLUs to interact if required.

Luk et al[3] have proposed an abstraction termed RC_Mux. In the RC_Mux flow, components that are changed at run-time are sandwiched between a fan-out block, and a multiplexor. If the value on the multiplexor's select line is known at compile time, then the appropriate component is instantiated, and the RC_Mux removed. If the value is not known until run-time, then separate EDIF files are produced for each of the possible components, and separately implemented. Each configuration can then be loaded onto the FPGA in turn. The advantage of the RC_Mux approach is that the circuit can be simulated without any modification, since the RC_Mux can be mapped to a real multiplexor. Furthermore, if space allows, the RC_Mux's can be implemented in silicon by real multiplexors.

Another approach is the combination of signal flow graphs (SFGs) and configuration data graphs (CDGs) proposed by Woods et al [4]. The aim of this work is to produce groups of circuits that are designed for reconfiguration. This is performed by describing algorithms using SFGs. These SFGs are then manipulated to produce similar graphs for different functions. By maximizing the amount of similarity between graphs, the amount of reconfiguration is reduced.

A configuration data graph (CDG) is generated which describes how the overall algorithm will be implemented, in terms of combinations of implementations of SFGs. In order to handle this system at run-time, a virtual hardware handler has been produced. The designs to be placed onto the FPGA are stored in a data structure called the reconfiguration state graph (RSG). The RSG is derived from the CDG, and is designed to be queried rapidly at run-time. At run-time, the hardware handler uses RDG to perform high-speed reconfiguration. Since the items stored in the RSG are explicitly designed to be friendly for reconfiguration, the time to perform this reconfiguration is reduced.

2.2   High-Level Support for Reconfiguration in Lava

Dynamic reconfiguration is an appealing concept allowing reuse of the limited resources on an FPGA. However current digital design methodologies are designed to support the description of static circuits due to their initial application to ASIC design. Several techniques have been proposed to bridge the gap between the theoretical possibilities of the technology and the limitations of the expressive power of HDLs.

One such abstraction is partial evaluation borrowed from extensive related work in functional programming. The hardware analog of this technqiue is run-time constant propagation. In this approach infrequently changing inputs are propagated as constants requiring rapid partial reconfiguration. This may occur when the weights for a filter change in a software radio application or some networking parameters are updated or in graphics when new control points are given for a curve. In many applications, the overhead of the dynamic specialization is more than compensated by the increased performance of the dynamic specialized design. However, significant technical hurdles prevent the mainstream adoption of such a methodology for describing and controlling this kind of dynamic reconfiguration. One of the main challenges is the timing analysis that needs to be performed to measure the increased speed of the specialized circuit. Another is the lack of support for performing dynamic reconfiguration from a very high level language. This paper introduces a simple mechanism that solves the latter problem allowing high-level reconfiguration constructs in Lava to be effected on actual device configurations via the JBits system.

The partial evaluation abstraction can itself be used to describe and implement other reconfiguration abstractions. For example, the RC_MUX abstraction proposed by Luk [3] can be described via partial evaluation on the control signal of the RC_MUX. Then will then effectively specialize the RC_MUX network into one of the two possible circuits that drive it and allow the possibility of both of these circuits sharing the same physical resource.

3   Construction of Configuration Datastreams

As mentioned previously, the current system uses a client-server architecture to remove the need for a physical file. The client and server processes can exist on the same machine, but they need not. The server could exist anywhere accessible via the network.

The main aim of the system is the same as the system described in [1], that is to move rapidly from a high-level language to configuration datastreams. Since support is added for RSGs, multiple configurations will now be produced. As shown in figure 1, once the configurations are received back from the server, the client can then use these configurations to configure either local or remote hardware via the XWHIF interface supplied as part of JBits.

3.1   Architecture

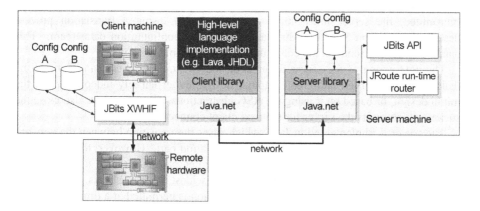

Figure 1 : Client-server architecture

3.2   Client Responsibilities

The client is responsible for making the link between the high-level language currently in use, and the high level constructs used by the client library functions. If Java is used as the high-level language (e.g. JHDL), then the same network commands used in the Java-based server can be used in the client.

In the example system under consideration, Java cannot be used directly. To overcome this problem, two solutions have been identified. Firstly, the Java Native Interface (JNI) could be used to interface the Java network part of the client to a DLL which deals with the HLL part of the client. The second alternative is to use the fact that the server doesn't care which language was used to produce the incoming packets. Hence, the network part of the client could be re-implemented using sockets in the appropriate language. This language-neutrality is the main advantage of basing the system on a network interface.

The Lava front-end is implemented in Haskell, which contains high-level support for network sockets. These sockets works seamlessly with the Java-based sockets, and this is the method of integration chosen. Previously, the Lava front-end has created an EDIF file, as described elsewhere [1]. This has now been modified, so the front-end can now establish two-way communications with the server, and then send the high-level constructs as the elaboration process determines they are needed, rather than producing the equivalent EDIF net or instance declaration.

3.3   Server Responsibilities

The server is responsible for controlling the dialog with the client. A very simple protocol is used. The server is initially set up to listen for connections on a port. When a connection is made, the client will send its IP address, which the server then uses to set up two further ports, one for textual acknowledgments, and one for the partial configuration datastreams. The server must then listen as the client begins to send the high-level constructs defined in section 4. Once the design has been entirely transmitted, the server must implement this design, using a translation process described in section 5, and produce a full or partial configuration datastream. This datastream is then send via the configuration port previously set up.

The next action of the server depends on the client. The client can continue the dialog with the server, and create another design, either entirely independent of the initial design, or based on it using the RSG abstractions. The client can also close the socket, which resets the server for the next client connection.

The server is implemented in Java, which eases the transition between the network part of the client, and the JBits-based implementation part. However, the server uses the generic byte-handling part of the java.lang.net package, rather than the more flexible object-based facilities. This enables the widest range of clients, since there is no reliance on Java. Currently, only one connection is permitted at a time. By careful threading of the code, it would be possible to remove this limitation.

4   API Description

The API consists of 10 instructions. Apart from instruction 10, none of these instructions return any arguments. Instruction 10 will return a partial configuration datastream.

Inst	Name	Arguments	Description
0	New design	designName deviceType	*Resets the server with the result that all previous design data is deleted. A new design is then initialised for the specified device type (e.g. XCV1000).*
1	New partial	partialName baseName	*Allows the construction of a new partial configuration datastream. The design will consist of all the configuration changes required to move from the configuration called baseName to the new design. If baseName is null, this corresponds to the power-up state*

2	New instance	name	Defines a new instance that is not locked to a physical location on
		type	the device. This is useful, for example, when specifying VCC or
			GND components. This instruction cannot be used for general
			logic instantiation, since no automatic placement is performed
3	New instance	name	Defines a new instance that is locked to a physical location on the
		type	device. The instance is given a symbolic name, which is used when
		row	specifying nets to interconnect instances. The type must be a legal
		col	primitive name taken from the unisim library. Currently, the
		slice	following primitives are supported: LUT1, LUT2, LUT3, LUT4,
			XORCY, MUXCY, all variants of RAM16X1, all variants of SRL16,
			and all variants of FD. The row, column and slice must be defined.
4	New instance	name, type	Defines a new instance with an initialisation value which is locked
		row, col	to a physical location on the device. Initialisation values are used
		slice, INIT	by components such as the look-up tables to define the contents.
5	New net	name	Constructs a new (initially empty) net. The net is populated with
			sources and sinks by instructions 6 and 7. The net is named, though
			this name is only used for debugging purposes.
6	Add source	name	Adds a source or sink to the current net. The system determines
	or sink	instanceRef	whether the symbolic name refers to an input or output port by
			doing a look-up on a library declaration of the instance reference.
			The port name is used to determine the direction of the library port,
			and hence whether this is a source or a sink on the net.
7	Add source	name	Adds a source or sink to the current net from a top-level input or
	or sink		output (i.e. a device pin) allowing the use of IOBs.
8	Add input	name	Constructs a new input resource, corresponding to an IOB. The
		padLoc	IOB is set up at a location defined by the padLoc argument. This is
			a textual name for a particular physical pin.
9	Add output	name	Constructs a new output resource, corresponding to an IOB. The
		padLoc	IOB is set up at a location defined by the padLoc argument. This is
			a textual name for a particular physical pin.
10	GetPartial	Returns	Instructs the server to return a new partial configuration
		bitstream	datastream, which consists of all the configuration frame changes
			required to move between the base configuration and the
			configuration corresponding to the current design.

Table 1 : API instructions

5   Translation Details

The translation from the high-level constructs to the low-level configuration datastream is a mechanistic task, consisting of four distinct phases: mapping, placement, routing and bistream generation. The translation is described briefly in [1]. In this section, we describe the more interesting aspects of this translation.

5.1   Component Instantiation

Component instantiation is a relatively straightforward task, consisting mainly of parameterization of the FPGA fabric through initialisation values. No explicit instantiation is required, as the components all exist already in the silicon. The complication arises for components which are not locked to a physical location, such as constant values and clock buffers. Clock buffers are simplified by using the global clock distribution network: buffers are allocated in the order in which they are found.

5.2   Constant Values

Constant values occur within the Virtex slice for a variety of reasons. For example, constant values are often injected into the bottom of carry chains.   The implementation of constant 1's and 0's depends on their ultimate use.

Constants can be generated without using any additional logic by means of the features of Virtex after the global set-reset (GSR) signal has been asserted. Inputs to the Virtex CLB that are not driven by any signal are pulled high. By using the configurable inverters on inputs such as BX and BY, it is possible to generate an essentially free 1 or 0. By examining the Virtex slice diagram in figure 2, it can be seen that these constants can drive a wide range of components, with further configuration settings. For instance, a constant can be injected into the CI input of a MUXCY component packed in the F LE, by leaving BX unconnected, inverting the pulled-high signal if required, and then setting the programmable multiplexor marked with an S in figure 2 to drive the DI input from the BX signal.

There are other locations within the Virtex slice where constants can be generated by means of configuration settings. For example, a 1 can be injected into the S port of a MUXCY component by setting a programmable multiplexor.   Similarly, 0's or 1's can be injected into the DI port of a MUXCY by a programmable multiplexor.

6   Support for Partial Configuration

As described previously, support for partial configuration is present by an implementation of reconfiguration state graphs (RSG). In the RSG paradigm, nodes of the graph correspond to actual configuration states of the FPGA. Arcs between the nodes represent partial configurations required to make a directed transition between two nodes. An example of a reconfiguration state graph is shown below in figure 3.

In addition to fully operative configuration states denoted by f_n in figure 3, there are a number of meta-states, which represent the common configuration of a series of configurations. Meta-states exist in order to speed up reconfiguration, but are not essential. For the purposes of this work, meta-states are not implemented.

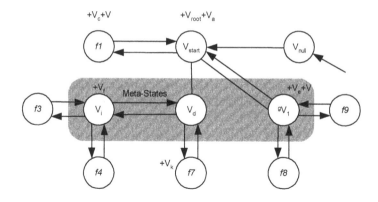

Figure 3 : Reconfiguration state graph from [4]

An API exists as part of the JBits environment, which is explicitly designed for handling partial reconfiguration of devices. JRTR [5] is an API using a combination of software and hardware techniques to enable very small changes to made to a device's configuration. In Virtex for example, the atomic unit of configuration is a frame, which varies in size across the device family. Configuration items will typically be spread across multiple frames [6]. JRTR assists by keeping track of which configuration frames become 'dirty' as a result of configuration changes. When all the required changes have been made, the dirty frames requiring reconfiguration are amalgamated into a single partial configuration packet for downloading.

The task is thus to construct the partial configuration frames required to move from one configuration (**current**) to another (**next**). The aim is to produce the minimum number of frames required, which is the same aim as the well-known ConfigDiff [3] program designed for the XC6200 series devices. Heron and Woods [7] presented a proposed modification to ConfigDiff, which allowed rapid configuration in both directions. In the modified version, parts of the logic which are in **current**, but not **next** are disconnected from the rest of the device, but are for the most part left intact. If reconfiguration is then required back from **next** to **current**, a smaller number of changes would be required overall that if the standard ConfigDiff algorithm were used. A system called JBitsDiff for constructing cores using a JBits based method of the modified ConfigDiff algorithm has previously been presented [8].

When the server is asked to produce a partial configuration, two parameters are given: the names of the base and target configurations. The first task that must be performed is the minimal disabling of the base configuration. The only thing that must be initially removed are any interactions with either BlockRAM or IOBs. Since the nets used in the base configuration are stored, it is straightforward to determine which of these deal with either the IOBs or the BlockRAM, and then the unroute() method in JRoute can be called to remove these routes. The IOBs are then configured as unused. All other logic is initially left intact.

The new system treats clashes between resources in **current** and **next** in a more robust way than the original JBitsDiff tool. In the case of shared logical resources, such as LUT primitives, a change if needed policy is used, which will only set a programmable resource, after it has been read, and found to be not the value required (reading does not affect the 'dirty' frames tracked by the JRTR API).

Routing is more complex. All routing from current is initially left intact, apart from any routes dealing with BlockRAMs or IOBs. When using JRoute, a net is defined as a single source, and a variable length number of sinks. When a new route is to be made which requires the JRoute API, the source and each of the sinks are first checked by the trace utility built into JBits to see if they are in use. If the existing source is the same as the new source, and all the sinks are identical, then the route can be left intact. If any variation is found, then the existing net is removed in its entirety, using the unroute() method in JRoute. The new net can then be routed.

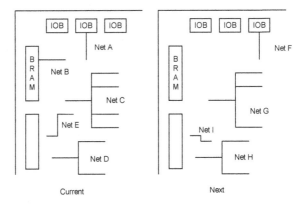

Figure 4 : Supporting routing in partial configurations

For example, consider the design shown in figure 4. Initially, the two nets A and B will be removed, since they affect an IOB and a BlockRAM respectively. All other nets will initially be left intact. When the system finds net G requiring routing, its source and three sinks are examined. Since this net does not correspond exactly to net C, net C will be unrouted, and net F routed. Similarly, when the system finds net H requiring routing, its source and two sinks will be examined. Since this net is identical to net D, net D will be left intact, and net H will not explicitly be routed. Finally, in the case of net I, whilst its sink is unused, the source is in use as part of net E. Therefore, net E will be unrouted, and net I routed.

7   Performance

The performance has been measured for a number of examples. To measure the performance of the system when using RSGs, a simple example of changing the functionality of one gate has been tested on an XCV300.

Operation	First circuit	Second circuit
Making data structures	140 ms	77 ms
Mapping	63 ms	32 ms
Instantiating logic	265 ms	0 ms
Routing	766 ms	63 ms
Total	1,234 ms	172 ms
Configuration bytes produced	218,980	1,464

A design which occupied all logic in an XCV300 had the following performance.

Operation	Time
Making data structures	1,750 ms
Mapping	969 ms
Instantiating logic	1,149 ms
Routing	4,875 ms
Total	8,734 ms
Configuration bytes produced	218,980

The final circuits used for the performance experiments are butterfly network sorters that have been fully placed in Lava. Lava calculates the location of every cell and this information can be exploited to perform dynamic reconfiguration by modifying LUTs contents to change functionality. The experimental circuits use a 2-sorter element circuit for the butterfly network.

Operation	Time
Transmission of constructs	422 ms
Making data structures	641 ms
Mapping	281 ms
Instantiating logic	250 ms
Routing	2,125 ms
Total implementation time	3,297 ms
Configuration bytes produced	218,980

8   Conclusions and Future Work

A method for remotely constructing configuration datastreams from high-level language like constructs has been described. By using a client-server architecture, it is possible to connect a wide range of front-end tools. Once the client has received the partial configurations from the server, these configurations can then be used to configure actual devices. By using the JBits XWHIF interface, it is possible to configure either local devices, or devices hosted on a remote machine. In this paper we presented a technique for interfacing to a lazy functional language which has a wildly different underlying execution model from the JBits system. Future work will add interfaces for other popular languages in the reconfigurable computing domain, as well as providing an improved interface for fully-mapped, fully-placed EDIF.

Acknowledgments

This work is supported under DARPA contract no. DABT63-99-3-004. "Virtex" and "JBits" are registered trademarks of Xilinx, Inc.

References

1. Singh, S and James-Roxby, P, "Lava and JBits: From HDL to Bitstream in Minutes", Proc. FCCM01, April, 2001, to be published
2. Brebner, G, "The Swappable Logic Unit: A Paradigm for Virtual Hardware", Proc. FCCM97, April, 1997, pp. 72-81
3. Luk, W, Shirazi, N and P. Cheung, "Compilation Tools for Run-Time Reconfigurable Designs", Proc. FCCM97, April 1997, pp 56-65
4. Sezer, S et al, "Fast Partial Reconfiguration for FCCMs", Proc. FCCM98, pp. 318-319
5. McMillan, S and Guccione, S, "Partial Run-Time Reconfiguration Using JRTR", Proc. FPL 2000, Sept. 2000
6. Xilinx, Inc : " Virtex Series Configuration Architecture User Guide", XAPP151, available on line at http://www.xilinx.com/xapp/xapp151.pdf, 2000
7. James-Roxby, P and Guccione, S, "Automated Extraction of Run-Time Parameterisable Cores from Programmable Device Configurations", Proc. FCCM00,
8. Heron, J-P and Woods, R, "Accelerating run-time reconfiguration on custom computing machines", Proc.SPIE International Symposium on Optical Science, Engineering and Instrumentation, San Diego, USA, 1998

Placing, Routing, and Editing Virtual FPGAs

Loïc Lagadec[1], Dominique Lavenier[2], Erwan Fabiani[2], and Bernard Pottier[1]

[1] Université de Bretagne Occidentale - Brest
{lagadec,pottier}@univ-brest.fr
[2] IRISA / CNRS - Rennes
France
{lavenier,efabiani}@irisa.fr

Abstract. This paper presents the benefits of using a generic FPGA tool set developed at the university of Brest for programming virtual FPGA. From a high level description of the FPGA architecture, the basic tools such a placer, a router or an editor are automatically generated. The description is not constrained by any model, so that abstract architectures, such as virtual FPGAs, can directly exploit the tool set as their basic programming tools.

1   Introduction

Reconfigurable Computing (RC) aims to use the flexibility of the configurable logic proposed by FPGA components to enhance computation performance. The common idea is that RC fills the gap between a general purpose Von Neumann architecture (microprocessor) and a highly specific full custom architecture (ASIC: Application Specific Integrated Circuit) by *programming* an appropriate architecture. Microprocessor performance is limited by the sequential behavior while ASICs suffer the definitive silicon implementation. FPGA components appear as a tradeoff between these two alternatives: the same physical support can be re-programmed (or reconfigured) to support any architecture. Hence, reconfigurable computing claims to add both the flexibility of programming machines and the speed of specific architectures.

The reality is not so obvious. First, an FPGA architecture is much slower than its ASIC counterpart. This is mainly due to its programmable nature, which requires signals to pass along many programmable electronic switches, compared to a direct silicon implementation. Second, the synthesis of a specific architecture onto a FPGA component is still a long and error-prone process that is far to be completely automated. The architecture to implement is often specified in VHDL, and requires a lot of simulation steps to be validated. In addition, a design targeted for a particular reconfigurable platform is usually impossible to re-use: the portability between different reconfigurable platforms is not ensured due to the absence of a *programming model*. Thus, if it is theoretically possible to implement any kind of architecture, the non-portability, the time and the efforts devoted to implement an architecture tend to weaken the notion of flexibility.

G. Brebner and R. Woods (Eds.): FPL 2001, LNCS 2147, pp. 357–366, 2001.

One way for increasing this flexibility is to define a **virtual FPGA architecture**. In that case, an architecture is not defined relative to a specific FPGA component, but relative to a virtual FPGA architecture which will be implemented across the different existing components and hopefully across future generations of FPGA components.

As with any virtual machine, such as the Java Virtual Machine, we must deal with the loss of performance introduced by the virtual layer. In our case a virtual architecture will have a limited amount of resources (virtual logic blocks) and the clock speed will be slowed down compared to a real FPGA component. To keep performance reasonable we propose to **specialize** the virtual architecture towards a specific field of applications. In that case, the slowness may be partially compensated by integrating into the virtual level fast specific functions inherent to the application domain.

If designing a range of specialized virtual FPGA architectures targeted to various application domains will guarantee a minimum of performance, one has to wonder how these architectures will be programmed. More precisely, the problem is to develop appropriate utility programming tools, such as the placer or the router, for each specialized FPGA. Of course, we cannot imagine rewriting such tools from scratch each time a new FPGA architecture is proposed.

This paper addresses this problem. It presents a generic FPGA tool set [1] which, from a high level specification of a FPGA architecture, automatically provides the basic tools required to configure it. This generic tool has not been developed especially for programming virtual specialized FPGA architectures. Any kind of FPGA architectures can take advantage of it. The purpose, here, is to focus on the benefit of using this approach in the context of virtual FPGAs.

The rest of the paper is organized as follows: Section 2 briefly describes the concept of specialized virtual FPGA architectures. Section 3 presents the generic FPGA programming tool set. Section 4 exemplifies a virtual FPGA architecture dedicated to linear systolic arrays and shows how the tool set works. Section 5 concludes this paper.

2   Specialized Virtual FPGA Architectures

The concept of virtual FPGA architecture is identical to the concept of virtual machine. Our view of a virtual FPGA is different from the definition given in [5] where it is seen as an extension of the physical FPGA device: the applications have a virtual view of the FPGA that is mapped on the available physical device by the operating system, in a way similar to virtual memory. In other words, the FPGA is virtualized by multiplexing its physical components. The same idea [9] has also been followed for increasing the number of FPGA I/O pins, leading to the concept of virtual wires. In both cases the goal is to extend the capabilities of the FPGA devices.

On the contrary, we see a virtual FPGA as a simplified version of a physical FPGA. The idea is not to enhance the FPGA features, in terms of a higher number of logic blocks or a better frequency, but to set a stable and portable

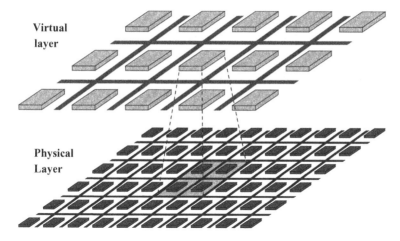

Fig. 1. Physical layer and Virtual layer: A virtual configurable logic block is made of several physical ones.

architecture like a virtual machine. Transposed to the hardware domain, a virtual FPGA is a regular pattern of virtual configurable logic blocks, each of them made up of several physical ones (cf figure 1). We assume that the blocks of the virtual layer are more complex than the physical ones. Nevertheless preserving portability over new technologies may lead the physical resources to be sub-exploited by letting some blocks to implement simple functions.

Compared to a virtual machine, it has nearly the same advantages and drawbacks. On the positive side it provides:

- A **portable** architecture: Architectures targeted to a virtual FPGA architecture can be implemented on any physical FPGA supporting the virtual layer.
- An **open** architecture: The details of the architecture are not constrained by confidentiality. They can be made freely available, allowing groups of people to develop and test their own tools.
- A way to investigate **new** FPGA architectures: Today, available FPGA components are not well suited for reconfigurable computing. They are mainly designed to meet the market requirement (ASIC substitution) and don't support advanced functionalities such as fast dynamic or partial reconfiguration.

On the negative side we can point out:

- the reduction of available resources: a virtual logic block will be made of several physical ones, leading probably to a reduction of an order of magnitude in terms of useful hardware. This is may be the price to pay for portability.
- the speed: the architectures mapped onto FPGA components are renowned to be slow compared to an ASIC implementation. Adding an intermediate layer will further slow them down!

– the absence of programming tools: the tools provided by the FPGA vendors are useless for mapping an architecture on the virtual layer. New tools are required and must be developed.

The solution we propose to remedy the speed problem is to specialize virtual FPGA architectures to target specific applications or well-defined models of architectures. In this case, the low speed may be partially compensated by integrating into the virtual level fast specific functions inherent to the architecture or the application domain. The idea of specialization is illustrated in section 4.

However, from our point of view, the absence of programming tools is a much more serious barrier to the concept of virtual FPGA. The main reason is that developing such tools is a long and complex task. There are no development tools, such as retargetable C compilers [7] available for microprocessors. Everything must be nearly redesigned from scratch. The next section presents the generic FPGA programming tool set developed at the University of Brest as a solution to suppress this stage.

3   The Generic FPGA Programming Tool Set

The software we have developed aims to provide very quickly a set of essential tools for programming a FPGA architecture (virtual or not). By *programming tool*, we mean the basic tools such as placer, router, editor, etc. We don't include synthesis tools which are supposed, here, to generate a comprehensive netlist for our tools.

The first step is to specify the FPGA architecture. It is then compiled and a tool set (placer-router, editor, estimator, ...) is immediately generated. This section focuses first on how a FPGA architecture is specified, then the different available tools are described. We end by giving a word about the implementation.

3.1   Specification of a FPGA Architecture

An FPGA architecture is always a hierarchical organization of patterns replicated in a regular way. A pattern is an assembly of cells and routing resources. Cells may contain one or several look-up tables (LUT), registers, and specific functions such as, for example, carry propagation logic. Routing includes wires and their interconnection mechanism (transistors, tri-states, multiplexers).

An FPGA architecture is specified using a grammar style as shown in the example of figure 2. This example specifies an array of 100 × 100 cells. A cell is composed of 2 wires (wireH and wireV), one switch and one 4-input logic function. All the possible connections are specified with the keyword connectTo.

A specification may contain different kinds of cells. In that case, the abutment of different cells is resolved using a specific mechanism, called *PortMapper*. It describes the signal interconnection at the cell borders and specifies how the routing is managed. Cells located on the borders of an array are managed by adding specific resources to the elements rather than by defining new kinds of elements.

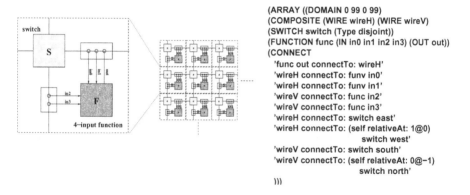

```
(ARRAY ((DOMAIN 0 99 0 99)
(COMPOSITE (WIRE wireH) (WIRE wireV)
(SWITCH switch (Type disjoint))
(FUNCTION func (IN in0 in1 in2 in3) (OUT out))
(CONNECT
    'func out connectTo: wireH'
    'wireH connectTo: funv in0'
    'wireH connectTo: funv in1'
    'wireV connectTo: func in2'
    'wireV connectTo: func in3'
    'wireH connectTo: switch east'
    'wireH connectTo: (self relativeAt: 1@0)
                            switch west'
    'wireV connectTo: switch south'
    'wireV connectTo: (self relativeAt: 0@-1)
                            switch north'
)))
```

Fig. 2. FPGA architecture example. It is a 2D array of identical cells. A cell is composed of one switch and one 4-input boolean function.

An important specification possibility is that an FPGA architecture can be totally or partially parameterized. It allows the designer of the reconfigurable architecture to tune elements such as the granularity of the logic functions, the number of routing resources, etc. This is particularly useful during the definition step for guiding the designer towards the best choices. In addition, custom parameters can be added to enlarge the tools functionalities (delays, reconfiguration power consumption, etc).

3.2   The Tool Set

Once the FPGA architecture has been specified, a basic set of tools is available for programming this architecture. The next subsections detail the different tools we provide.

Input Format   The logic to implement in the FPGA architecture must be described as a netlist of logic functions. There must be a direct relation between the available resources and the netlist. For instance, a 5-input function is not allowed in the netlist if the FPGA architecture accepts only 4-input functions. The LUT partitioning has to be done before. We currently accept the Berkeley Logic Interchange Format (BLIF) for working environment convenience, but the EDIF format will be the standard way to input the designs in a future version.

Place-and-route   The placer-router implements random logic, regarding some constraints (IOs, bounding box, etc). The placer relies on a simulated annealing algorithm. All nodes (logic functions) are placed randomly before the annealing starts. At each step, pairs of nodes are swapped. An approximation of the global interconnection cost is evaluated using a cost function. This function is strongly dependent of the architecture[1], and conforms to [2] when programming an island style FPGA. In case it is higher than the previous one, all the swapped nodes are

---

[1] In our case, dependent of the virtual layer

discarded even if local costs are lower. This new placement is considered for the next iteration. Bad moves can be accepted with a decreasing probability to prevent the algorithm from being trapped into a local minimum. The router starts once the placement is completed, so that any pre-placed solution or partially placed and routed circuit can be considered. The router is a PathFinder-like router [8], using a negotiated scheme for resolving congestion over the routing resources. The router iterates until no congestion remains. All resources have an associated cost depending on the congestion of the resource. Each iteration detects all the signals sharing a congested resource to be ripped up and rerouted. This mechanism forces the signals to use unnecessarily congested resources, as these resources make the cost of the route prohibitive relative to alternative routes.

Regular Editing The placer-router is not only well suited for random logic. When the objective is to achieve high performance, circuits must be architectured as a regular assembly of patterns (such as systolic arrays for example). To specify regular circuits, a higher level tool than a conventional placer-router is needed. Our regular editor provides a way to replicate modules within FPGA architectures, both for the logic and the routing.

Floorplanning The editor relies on geometric informations and processes no optimization over the assembly of modules. Acceptable results are restricted to an assembly of modules of comparable size. The placement of the modules is processed under some optimization criteria (global area, routing cost, etc.). Circuits can be partitioned, either at a logic level or at an application level and split into several sub-circuits. Then, these smaller circuits are placed and routed. The floorplanner rebuild the global circuit from the produced modules.

Estimators The quality of the place-and-route stage must be analyzed, with respect to several criteria. The technology mapping stage results in a set of nodes and nets to be implemented that depend on the logic granularity. The placer processes an annealing schedule over the location of the nodes based on a cost function and a bounding box. The algorithm is parameterized to enable different quality/cpu time trade-offs. A timing analyzer is being added. Frequency performance estimation of the circuits will be then possible. An important point is that every resource has a private set of parameters, so that the virtual layer can be *tuned* on demand by extracting useful information from the physical layer.

3.3   Implementation

The Generic FPGA Programming Tool Set is developed in the Visualworks object-oriented programming environment, using SmallTalk as programming language. An FPGA architecture is then represented as a composition of classes we can express at four distinct levels:

- The first level is called *the abstract model.* It represents all the different kinds of elements that can be found inside a FPGA architecture: routing, registers,

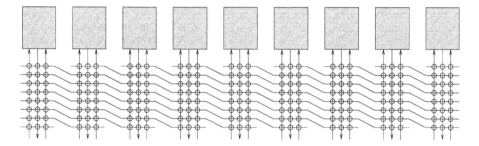

Fig. 3. Virtual Linear Systolic Array: it is composed of a linear array of 2-input N-bit virtual cells. The output of one virtual cell can reach the input of 14 adjacent operators (7 to its left and 7 to its right).

logic blocks, organization, etc. Each of these elements is represented by an abstract class[2] which describes its properties and its behavior.

- The second level relies on the abstract model to produce a concrete model. It is instantiated by compilation of the FPGA architecture specification. It permits fast architectural exploration as parameters (from the specification) can be quickly modified, allowing the concrete model to be rebuilt from new values.
- The third level is called *the concrete model*. It represents a given FPGA architecture and its specific elements: CLBs, patterns, etc. These elements are modeled through a set of concrete classes.
- The last level is produced by instantiation of the classes of the concrete model. This model, called *the architecture*, is a copy of the FPGA architecture that the concrete model describes. This level is manipulated by the tool set.

Each tool manipulates the elements of the FPGA architecture through its software interface (API). This API is described within the abstract model, so that any element of an *architecture* inherits from and conforms to it. As a consequence, the tools manipulate only the abstract level. They are differentiated from the model so that the model can be upgraded with few or no changes. Similarly, new tools can be added, and run over the existing models.

4   Example: Virtual Architecture for Linear Systolic Arrays

We illustrate the functionalities of the generic FPGA programming tool set by defining a virtual FPGA architecture well suited for implementing linear systolic arrays.

---

[2] An abstract class has no instances, and acts as a template for subclass production.

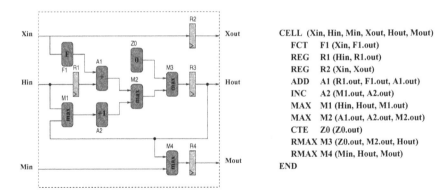

Fig. 4. Systolic processor for DNA comparison: schematic and netlist description

4.1 Architecture

Figure 3 represents the virtual FPGA architecture we want to implement. It is a linear array of 2-input N-bit cells. A cell can be configured as a logic or as an arithmetic function. The two inputs can be connected to neighboring cells ranging from 7 to the left or to the right. To program a systolic architecture on this virtual FPGA architecture, one has to place-and-route a systolic processor and to replicate it over the whole structure. Of course, the router must ensure that the routing of a single processor is suitable for replication.

A 8-bit virtual cell has been designed for experimentation purposes and synthesized for the Xilinx Virtex family. In addition to all the basic logic functions, a virtual cell can perform arithmetic operations such addition/subtraction or min/max operations. A virtual cell includes all the required configuration mechanism and fits into 65 Virtex slices. A Virtex-1000 component (filled at 80%) can then house 150 of such 8-bit element. By extension, the Virtex-II XCV2-10K, for example, will be able to fit 800 8-bit virtual cells.

4.2 Using the Tool Set

To highlight the tool set functionalities let us take a systolic architecture derived from a real application: the comparison of DNA sequences. The purpose, here, is not to describe how a systolic array can implement this task (details of implementation can be found in [6]) but to show how such an architecture can be easily implemented.

Figure 4 represents a systolic DNA processor and its associated netlist. It is composed of a 10 8-bit operators (virtual cells). Each line of the body of the cell represents a zero-, a one- or a 2-input function that a virtual cell can house. The process for implementing an array is first to place and route one processor, that is, in our case, to place-and-route 10 virtual cells, and to replicate this placement (and the routing) over the virtual structure.

A virtual architecture representing a linear array of 800 8-bit virtual cells has been specified. We run the place-and-route tool giving as input the BLIF netlist corresponding to one processor. It takes only 3 seconds on a standard PC to place-and-route one processor. Then we replicate it 80 times to fill up the virtual array. It just takes a fraction of second to perform this last task.

This first experiment highlights the possibilities of the FPGA tool set as a good candidate for virtual FPGA architectures. First it confirms that specifying a new FPGA architecture is fast. It takes less than a couple of hours to write down the specification and half a day for tuning the graphical editor parameter (cf figure 5). Although this FPGA architecture is quite simple, it gives an idea of the time one can expect to spend for getting the minimum basic set of tools. It is also worth mentioning that once the general architecture is set, further slight modifications can be performed very quickly.

Second, a high level specification of a FPGA architecture permits some abstraction. In our case, the data-path width of the cells is not stated. Neither is the connection width between the processors. We just specify that an operator connects its neighbors in an interval ranging from 7 operators to the left to 7 operators to the right. The place-and-route step is thus independent of the size of the virtual cell. It is also very fast since a set of wires (a bus) is routed as a single entity.

Third, the regularity can be fully exploited, both for placement and routing. The editor provides the possibility to replicate a regular pattern that has been previously placed-and-routed. These features usually don't exist, or are extremely limited in other tools, leading to a poor exploitation of the regularity [4]. In the context of automatic loop parallelization, for example, the synthesis step for deriving a hardware regular array from high level specifications can now be shrunk to a few minutes [3]. To keep the global synthesis time low, the mapping time onto a reconfigurable architecture needs to be very fast. Of course irregular circuits can be handle by the placer-router in the same way a regular architecture is flatten.

5   Conclusion

The tool set we have presented does not aim to challenge the today's best placers and routers (such as VPR [2]) in terms of speed. The objective is to offer a prospective tool that fits non conventional FPGA architecture and benefits from the absence of layers from the high level behavioral logic to the hardware execution management.

Our approach focuses on genericity, by separating the tools from the model. No assumption is made over the range of representable architectures. This means that an architecture is described as an arbitrary composition of resources (logic, routing, ...). The routing channels can start and end at any location on the architecture. The logic blocks can be LUTs, operators, potentially pieces of hardwired circuits, etc. These last features make this approach particularly well suited for designing non conventional FPGA architectures such as specialized virtual FPGAs.

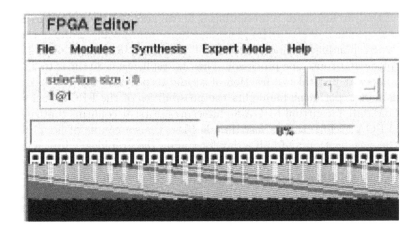

Fig. 5. FPGA editor: it shows a partial view of the DNA systolic array.

References

1. L. Lagadec, B. Pottier Object Oriented Meta tools for Reconfigurable Architecture, Conference on Reconfigurable Technology: FPGAs and Reconfigurable Processors for Computing and Applications, SPIE Proceedings 4212 in Photonics East 2000, Boston, 2000.
2. V. Betz, J. Rose, A. Marquardt, Architecture and CAD for Deep-Submicron FPGAs, Kluwer Academic Publishers, 1999.
3. D. Lavenier, P. Quinton, S. Rajopadhye, Advanced Systolic Design, in Digital Signal Processing for Multimedia Systems, Chapter 23, Parhi and Nishitani Eds, March 1999.
4. E. Fabiani, D. Lavenier, Placement of Linear Arrays, FPL 2000: 10th International Conference on Field Programmable Logic and Applications, Villach, Austria, Aug 2000
5. W. Fornaciari, V. Piuri, Virtual FPGAs: Some steps behind the physical barrier. In Parallel and Distributed Processing (IPPS/SPDP'98 Workshop Proceedings), LNCS 1388, 1998.
6. P. Guerdoux-Jamet, D. Lavenier Systolic Filter for fast DNA Similarity Search ASAP'95, Strasbourg, France, 1995.
7. C. Fraser, D. Hanson, A retargetable C compiler: design and implementation, The Benjamin/Cumming Publishing Company, Inc., 1995.
8. L. McMurchie, C.Ebeling, PathFinder: A Negotiation-Based Performances-Driven Router for FPGAs, in FPGA'95, Monterey, CA, 1995.
9. J. Babb, R. Tessier, A. Agarwal, Virtual Wires: Overcoming Pin Limitations in FPGA-based Logic Emulators, Proceedings of the IEEE Workshop on FPGAs for Custom Computing Machines'93, 1993.
10. V. Betz, J. Rose, Using architectural famillies to increase FPGA speed and density, in FPGA'95, Monterey, CA, 1995.

Virtex Implementation of Pipelined Adaptive LMS Predictor in Electronic Support Measures Receiver

Lok-Kee Ting, Roger Woods, Colin Cowan

School of Electrical and Electronic Engineering
The Queen's University of Belfast, Stranmillis Road, Belfast, N. Ireland
{l.ting, r.woods, cfn.cowan}@ee.qub.ac.uk

Abstract. This paper presents an FPGA solution for a high-speed front-end digital receiver of an Electronic Support Measures (ESM) system. An LMS-based adaptive predictor has been chosen to improve the signal-to-noise ratio (SNR) of the received radar signals. Two fine-grained pipelined architectures based on the Delay LMS (DLMS) algorithm have been developed for FPGA implementation. This paper also highlights the importance of choosing a suitable filter architecture in order to utilise FPGA resources resulting in a more efficient implementation. FPGA implementation results, including timing and area, are given and discussed.

1 Introduction

In electronic warfare [1], there is considerable interest in the detection of hostile radar pulses, particularly from a targeting radar, such as ESM receivers. ESM receiver systems require wide bandwidth to maximise probability of interception of signals. However, an increase in bandwidth results in increased noise thus reducing the receiver sensitivity. Detection of a radar pulse requires that the received radar signal energy is much larger than the background energy. Sensitivity to low power signals is currently achieved by channelisation, offering multiple narrowband signal measurement channels with the ensuing increase in SNR. However, such receivers are both large and expensive. In addition, pre-defined parameters in the channelisation require the designer to have foreseen all possible input conditions, at least statistically, which often results in poor filtering performance.

To date, advances in digital technology make digitisation of received signals as far forward as the Intermediate Frequency (IF) block possible in ESM receivers. This facilitates processing of received signals at the IF prior to demodulation, offering the possibility of correction for signal coloration in the front-end. Furthermore, SNR enhancement can be applied at this stage to increase ESM sensitivity.

Adaptive filters [2] have been proposed for increased radar ESM receiver sensitivity [3,4]. Adaptive filters allow filter parameters such as bandwidth and resonant frequency to change with time. This is done by allowing the coefficients of the adaptive filter to vary with time and to be adjusted automatically by an adaptive algorithm. This is the important effect of enabling adaptive filters to be applied in areas where the exact required filter operation is unknown. In ESM receivers, the

G. Brebner and R. Woods (Eds.): FPL 2001, LNCS 2147, pp. 367-376, 2001.

adaptive filter seeks to form a matched filter to the input signal, resulting in a frequency response with narrow passband which rejects the noise from a broadband channel. Therefore, the SNR of the received radar signal is enhanced.

In high-speed applications, such as radar, the base-band sampling rate is of the order of 100 MHz. Sequential implementations of the adaptive filters on microprocessors or DSP processors often prove unsatisfactory because they are unable to meet the sampling rate. FPGA implementations are preferable as they allow parallel implementation to be realised with high levels of pipelining. However, the long feedback loops in adaptive filter structures require a large area and long interconnect on the FPGA acts to limit the throughput rates achievable. Whilst pipelining has been proposed as a mechanism to reduce the longer connection paths and improve performance, pipelining of LMS (Least Mean Square) adaptive filters is difficult as it introduces delay into the error feedback loop. During the past two decades, many research groups have proposed algorithms in order to overcome this difficulty [5,6,7]. These involve modification of the adaptation algorithm to enable pipeline implementations, resulting in the development of look-ahead and Delay LMS (DLMS) based algorithms. These algorithms act to ensure stable convergence behaviour of filters that have been pipelined.

The performance achieved when implementing fast arithmetic functions on FPGA is not as fast as with ASIC technology. However, the programmability of FPGAs allows circuits to be optimised to specific system needs, whereas an ASIC implementation needs to be designed to be generic in order to justify its high development costs. In military applications, low volume production is often required, and in such cases, high performance systems using custom silicon are too expensive. FPGAs provide a perfect solution, as their set-up cost is much lower than ASICs. Furthermore, the non-recurring engineering cost for an ASIC implementation is too high. Therefore, this analysis leads ideally to an FPGA based solution.

2   Choice of Pipelined Adaptive Algorithm - Delayed LMS

The LMS predictor is well known for noise reduction filtering of noisy signals. Its configuration is schematically represented in Figure 1. The LMS algorithm [8] has been considered for high-speed DSP applications because of its simple structure, stable performance and great tolerance to errors caused by pipelining. The LMS algorithm is described by:

$$w(n) = w(n-1) + \mu e(n-1)x(n-1) \qquad (1)$$

where $w(n)$ is the filter tap weight vector at time n, $x(n)$ is the observed data vector at time n and μ is the constant step size that determines the convergence rate. The predictor error, which is given as $e(n)$, is the difference between the input $x(n)$ and output $y(n)$ of the system and the output of the predictor is given by:

$$y(n) = x^T(n-1)w(n) \qquad (2)$$

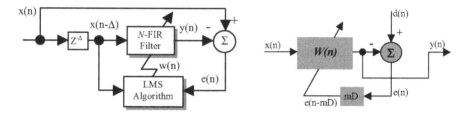

Fig. 1. Block diagram of LMS predictor system

Fig. 2. Equivalent structure of the DLMS algorithm

The DLMS is an extension of the LMS algorithm. It is implemented by inserting registers along the filter and error feedback path. There is no pipelining involved in the recursive loop of the coefficient update block, and its pipelined architecture has the simplest hardware complexity of its kind. The behaviour of the DLMS algorithm has been studied by Long et al [5]. It is known that the upper limit of step size guaranteeing convergence in Mean Square Error (MSE) is reduced. Therefore, by increasing the number of pipelining delays in the filter, it becomes possible to operate the LMS filter at a higher clock rate. At the same time, a slower convergence rate due to the smaller value of the step size used in the DLMS filter is expected. The DLMS algorithm is described by the following equations:

$$w(n)=w(n-1)+\mu e(n-mD)x(n-mD) \tag{3}$$

$$e(n-mD)=d(n-mD)-y(n-mD) \tag{4}$$

$$y(n-mD) =w^{T}(n-mD-1)x(n-mD) \tag{5}$$

where mD is the number of delays distributed along the filter and error feedback path. The structure is illustrated in Figure 2.

3   Choice of Design Architectures

In the context of fine-grained pipelined processing, the pipeline technique can be extended into the computational component. For instance, pipelining an individual multiplier into a few processing clock-cycles can reduce the critical path of the architectures, thus improving the processing rate. Pipelining is a natural mode of system optimisation on Virtex designs. The register rich architecture allows pipelining at the Logic Cell (LC) level i.e. fine-grained pipelining

The dedicated arithmetic logic in a Virtex Configurable Logic Block (CLB) provides fast arithmetic capability for high-speed arithmetic functions. The fast carry path of the Virtex CLB allows the implementation of fast Carry-Ripple Adders (CRAs) and it is organised such that it allows a highly regular structure to be realised at a small cost. Figure 3 shows a single bit CRA implemented on a single slice in a Virtex CLB with its output registered. In this context, the pipelining of each adder stage is essentially 'free' in the Virtex FPGA (as a flipflop exists in each LC) allowing for fast, pipelined multipliers to be achieved. For an adder-tree structure multiplier, $log_2(wordlength)$-level pipelining can be applied to obtain a throughput of close to that of a single adder performance. However, pipelining within the individual CRA is not possible due to physical reality imposed by the Virtex CLB layout. Thus, the throughput rate of both the 8-bit adder and 8-bit pipelined multiplier are 5.0 ns and 5.1 ns respectively for the Virtex device.

Routing in an FPGA chip contributes significantly to signal propagation delay in the circuit, making the net delay often up to 60% of the total delay in some FPGA designs. Hence, the highest achievable throughput of the filter design is $1/(T_a+T_d)$ for the Virtex FPGA, where T_a is the computation time required for an adder and T_d is the total delay associated with the adder involved in the critical path.

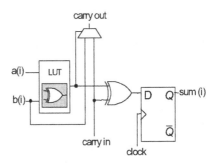

Fig. 3. 1-bit fast carry-ripple full adder with output registered in a single LC

Two different adaptive LMS predictor architectures based on the fine-grain pipelined DLMS algorithm are selected. The first is designed for ease of expansion whilst still maintaining the system sampling rate. The second is well optimised for filtering and speed/cost performance. There are the Transposed-Form Fine-grained Pipelined DLMS (TF-FPDLMS) architecture and Direct-Form Fine-grained Pipelined DLMS (DF-FPDLMS) architecture.

(a) Transposed-form fine-grained pipelined DLMS architecture: The transposed-form is popular due to its regular structure and ease of pipelining. The TF-FPDLMS has the advantage of increasing the filter order (N) by simply adding more Processing Module (PM) elements without increasing the system sampling rate. On the other hand, this cascaded PM structure poses a limitation on the number of pipeline-cuts allowed in a single PM, as the effect of every pipeline-cut is rippled through every PM. The output latency of the system, as a result of pipelining delay, is linearly dependent on the filter order.

A short TF-FPDLMS filter requires a significant number of pipelining registers to achieve a finer-grained pipelined architecture. This not only increases the output latency but also increases the delay between filter weights and incoming data. Hence, a much smaller step size has to be employed to stabilise the convergence, resulting in a slower convergence rate and poorer tracking capacity. Therefore, for a reasonable filtering performance, the finest-grained pipeline is constrained to a single multiplier. The TF-FPDLMS architecture with a critical path of T_m (computation time required for a multiplier) is shown in Figure 4(a).

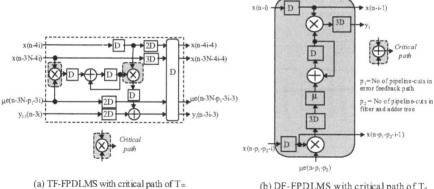

(a) TF-FPDLMS with critical path of T_m (b) DF-FPDLMS with critical path of T_a

Fig. 4. Processing module of the TF-FPDLMS and DF-FPDLMS architecture

(b) Direct-form fine-grained pipelined DLMS architecture: The direct-form implementation of the FIR filter has irregular circuitry due to the binary-tree adder structure in the accumulator of the adaptive filter. Apart from the accumulator, the DF-FPDLMS filter is implemented using regularly-connected processing modules. The multiply & accumulators (MAC) in the filter block and the associated coefficient update loop are organised into a single tap to represent a single PM, making a shorter interconnect between the components within the tap. This has been achieved by using the Relative LOCation (RLOC) information (Xilinx placement commands) to ensure efficient placement of components during the place and route process in FPGA implementation. The binary-tree adder structure reduces the latency of the pipelined filter and shortens the interconnect paths of the adders.

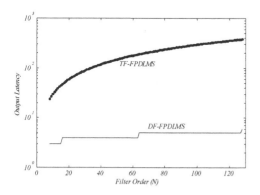

The principal advantage of using direct-form implementation compared to the transposed-form implementation is that the output latency of the DF-FPDLMS with respect to filter order is not linear. This is shown in Figure 5. Therefore, a finer-grain pipeline can be used to improve the system speed. In this case, the critical path of T_a is chosen for DF-FPDLMS architecture as shown in Figure 4(b).

Fig. 5. The output latency of TF-FPDLMS and DF-FPDLMS with regards to the filter order (N)

Figures 6 and 7 show the complete system of the TF-FPDLMS and DF-FPDLMS predictors respectively. In the DF-FPDLMS filter, the longest net delay path is found to be in the error feedback path. This signal delay propagation time can be decreased by inserting registers along the interconnect path to reduce the distance, giving a latency in the DF-FPDLMS filter of 12-clock cycles.

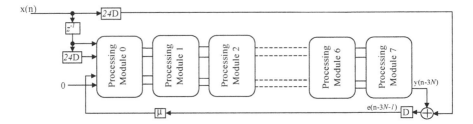

Fig. 6. 8-tap predictor system with TF-FPDLMS architecture (critical path = T_m) based on the PM architecture in Figure 4(a).

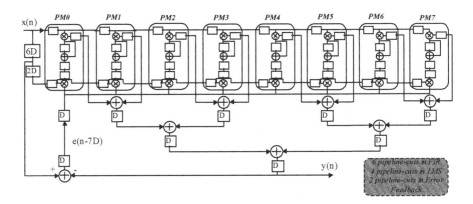

Fig. 7. 8-tap predictor system with DF-FPDLMS architecture (critical path = T_a) based on the PM architecture in Figure 4(b)

4   Theoretical Implementation Results

Table 1. Comparison of the characteristics of different architectures

Architecture	Critical path	Latency	Number of hardware elements		
			Adder	Multiplier	Delay Element
Standard LMS	$2T_m + \{\log_2(N)+1\}T_a$	1	2N	2N	2N
TF-FPDLMS	T_m	3N	2N+1	2N	21N
DF-FPDLMS	T_a	$\log_2(N)+8$	2N	2N	9N+8

Table 1 presents the theoretical implementation results of the proposed fine-grained pipelined LMS architectures: TF-FPDLMS and DF-FPDLMS. It shows that the only additional hardware overhead for fine-grained pipelined DLMS is the delay elements used for the pipelining. Whilst this has been listed as 21N, and 9N+8 for the TF-FPDLMS and DF-FPDLMS respectively, the actual area needed is much smaller in the Virtex FPGA implementation due to the availability of flipflops in the CLBs. If the flipflop in a CLB was originally unused and then utilised for pipelining, then the flipflop is essentially "free" as no area increase results.

For the general case, we estimate that around (2N+8) delay elements are needed in the unoccupied Virtex CLBs for DF-FPDLMS. This highlights that direct-form pipelined approaches are highly attractive in a Virtex FPGA implementation environment. However, the transposed-form implementation does not enjoy the same benefits provided by the Virtex FPGA layout, as most of the pipelining registers in the TF-FPDLMS architecture require a new unoccupied slice in a Virtex CLB. This inevitably increases the FPGA area, which may deteriorate the speed performance of the overall structure. This highlights the importance of choosing an appropriate architecture for a specific FPGA layout for area/speed optimisation.

4.1   Speedup

Table 2. Speedup for the proposed fine-grained pipelined LMS architectures, where $T_m=3T_a$ for 8-bit multiplier

Critical Path	Architecture	Speedup
T_m	TF-FPDLMS	$S = \{(log_2N\,)T_a+2T_m\}/\,T_m$ $S = (log_2N)/3 +2$
T_a	DF-FPDLMS	$S = \{(log_2N\,)T_a+2T_m\}/\,T_a$ $S = log_2N +6$

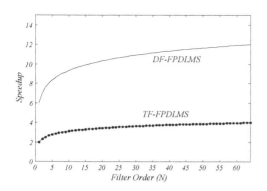

Fig. 8. Speedup of the pipelined filters over the standard LMS filter with regards to the filter order (N)

The theoretical implementation result of the speedup for the fine-grained pipelined LMS predictor over the conventional implementation of the standard LMS filter is shown in Table 2. The estimated theoretical speedup of the fine-grained pipelined LMS predictors compared to the standard LMS based on the binary adder tree structure is shown on Figure 8. For the DF-FPDLMS architecture, the speedup is a factor of 10 or more, and for the TF-FPDLMS is less than 5 times for most of the cases.

5   Virtex Implementation Results

To investigate if the theoretical savings on Virtex implementation could be achieved, the fine-grained pipelined designs were implemented and measurements taken. The fine-grained pipelined filters have been implemented using fixed-point arithmetic and all fixed-point implementation issues have been considered. This study includes: a detailed study of wordlength growth in order to achieve best wordlength; application of truncation/rounding circuitry; use of saturation and; exploitation of bit shifting for simple multiplication. An input/output wordlength of 8-bit and a maximum internal wordlength of 16-bit are determined for the FPDLMS filters. It is found that 8-bit input has a reasonable system noise level for guaranteeing the convergence in MSE of the FPDLMS adaptive filters. Input/output and internal wordlength can be increased to gain a more accurate adaptation and a lower system noise level but this is achieved at the expense of increased size and longer critical path. A step size of the power-of-2 is used in the filter to reduce the scaling multiplication in the filter to a simple shift operation. Details on the design of the circuitry can be found in the previous paper [9], which only considered the direct-form approach.

In Table 3, the results of the Virtex implementation of an 8-bit/8-tap LMS, TF-FPDLMS and DF-FPDLMS predictor system are presented with their post-layout timing information on a Virtex XCV300-6 chip. These results are generated by the *Xilinx Design Manager* software tools.

Table 3. Virtex implementation (post-layout) results for system clock rate and area

XCV300-6	*Standard LMS*	*TF-FPDLMS*	*DF-FPDLMS*
Area (slice)	845 slices	1285 slices	945 slices
Sampling Rate (MHz)	12	68	120
Max. Net Delay Associated with Critical Path	6.54 ns	4.96 ns	3.36 ns
Relative Area	1.00	1.52	1.12
Relative Speed	1.00	5.70	10.00

The implementation results obtained by the FPGA design tools show that the system performance can reach up to 120 MHz for an 8-bit input sample for the DF-FPDLMS architecture. In the FPGA design, the speedup for the pipelined design is nearly 10 times that of the standard LMS design due to the improvement in the critical path. This is very close to what we estimated in the previous section. The actual speedup is 5.7 times for the TF-FPDLMS predictor. This is slightly higher than the theoretical result we estimated, since the transposed-form approach has a more regular structure than the direct-form or standard LMS structure.

Pipelined designs also show a better routing net delay associated with the critical paths resided in the error feedback paths compared to their non-pipelined counterparts, as shown in Table 3. This is due to the fact that the pipelining delays are not only used for pipelining of the logic but also used for shortening the net delay in the critical to improve the overall speed performance. The limited area increase for the DF-FPDLMS architecture and 52% area increase for the TF-FPDLMS architecture indicate that pipelining on the Virtex, if only in some contexts, is essentially 'free' and very much dependent on the pipelined architecture.

5.1   Hardware Simulation

In this section, we present hardware test results to verify the performance of the DF-FPDLMS predictor. The system used for the simulation model is an 8-bit/8-tap predictor as shown in Figure 7. It is simulated with a noise-free sinusoidal input signal with sufficient sampling rate to ensure a stable prediction. We compare the DF-FPDLMS convergence performance with that of the LMS. Tests were performed in a Virtex XCV300-6 chip in the Ballynuey Virtex demonstration board. A number of real-time simulations were carried out and averaged to give the simulation plots in Figure 9.

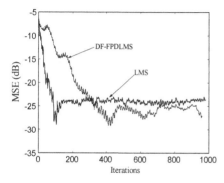
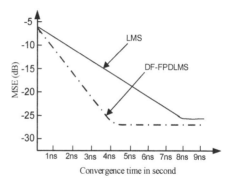

Fig. 9. Virtex hardware simulation plots for LMS and of DF-FPDLMS2 based 8-bit/8-tap predictor

Fig. 10. Simulations plots for LMS and DF-FPDLMS convergence in hardware to their steady-state values: The convergence times in second for DF-FPDLMS and LMS are 3.5 ns (420 iterations /120 MHz) and 8.3 ns (100 iterations/12 MHz) respectively

In Figure 9, the optimal step sizes were applied to the different architectures for the test. The pipelined design demonstrated a longer convergence time than the non-pipelined design thereby giving a larger error burst. This large error burst, which caused the overshooting of the system output, results in extra time being needed for the pipelined system to settle down to its steady-state value. After the initial period of overshooting, the pipelined systems experienced a lower MSE level than the LMS design. Despite a longer convergence time compared to the non-pipelined counterpart, the system clock rate for the pipelined design was found to be much higher than the non-pipelined type. Thus, the actual convergence time is still less than the LMS as shown in Figure 10.

6   Conclusion

In this paper, a high-speed FPGA implementation of the pipelined LMS filter is presented. An approach based on the DLMS filter is used which reduces the fine-grained pipelining delay to the time taken to perform a single addition. The DLMS-based algorithm without the pipelining of the coefficient update loop is preferred for its better convergence rate and simplicity when compared to other pipelined architectures. In terms of the high-speed architecture, the direct-form approach is preferred for a finer-grained pipelined design, otherwise, the transposed-form approach would have more regularity. Two new fine-grained pipelined architectures based on the DLMS algorithm have been successfully implemented into Virtex XCV300-6 chip in the Ballynuey Virtex demonstration board. A 120 MHz system clock rate performance is achieved for an 8-bit DF-FPDLMS predictor system. For a longer critical path, T_m, a system clock rate of 60-70 MHz is also obtained. The main advantage of using Virtex FPGAs for pipelined design is reflected in the DF-FPDLMS architecture, which results in only a limited area increase due to the pipelining. This is true, provided an appropriate pipelined architecture is chosen, otherwise a huge increase in the FPGA area as a result of pipelining is inevitable, such as in the TF-FPDLMS architecture.

References

1.   D.C. Schleher, *Electronic warfare in the information age*, Artech House INC., 1999.
2.   S. Haykin, *Adaptive filter theory*, Third Edition, Prentice-Hall Information and system science series, 1996.
3.   C.F.N. Cowan, R.F. Woods, LK. Ting, E. Key and P.R. Cork, "Preconditioning of radar data using adaptive predictors: algorithm and Implementation," EUREL meeting on 'Radar and sonar signal processing', pp. 21/1-21/2, Peebles Hotel Hydro, July 1998.
4.   P.R. Cork, C.J. Sprigings, R.F. Woods and LK. Ting, "An FPGA adaptive line enhancer for increased radar EW receiver sensitivity," HPEC'99 workshop, Boston (USA), Sept. 1999.
5.   G. Long, F. Ling, and J.G. Proakis, "The LMS algorithm with delayed coefficient adaptation," IEEE Trans. Accoust., Speech, Signal Processing, vol. 37, pp. 1397-1405, Sept. 1989.
6.   N.R. Shanbhag and K.K. Parhi, "Relaxed look-ahead pipelined LMS adaptive filters and their application to ADPCM coder," IEEE Trans., on Circuits and System-II: Analog and Digital Signal Proc., vol. 40, pp. 753-766, Dec. 1993.
7.   M.D. Meyer and D.P. Agrawal, "A high sampling rate delayed LMS filter architecture," IEEE Trans., on Circuits and System-II: Analog and Digital Signal Proc., vol. 40, pp. 727-729, Nov. 1993.
8.   B. Widrow, J. McCool, M. Larimore, and C. Johnson, "Stationary and nonstationary learning characteristics of the LMS adaptive filter," Proc. IEEE vol. 64, pp. 1151-1162, Aug. 1976.
9.   LK. Ting, R.F. Woods, C.F.N. Cowan, P.R. Cork, and C.J. Sprigings, "High-performance fine-grained pipelined LMS algorithm in Virtex FPGA," Advanced Signal Processing Algorithms, Architectures, and Implementations X: SPIE San Diego 2000, vol. 4116, pp. 288-299, Aug. 2000.

A Music Synthesizer on FPGA

Takashi Saito[1], Tsutomu Maruyama[1], Tsutomu Hoshino[1], and Saburo Hirano[2]

[1] Institute of Engineering Mechanics and Systems, University of Tsukuba
1-1-1 Ten-ou-dai Tsukuba Ibaraki 305-8573 JAPAN
saitou@darwin.esys.tsukuba.ac.jp
[2] School of Design, Faculty of Art, University of Kyoto Seika

Abstract. Software synthesizers have great flexibility in the connection of the basic components of many synthesis methods, and can generate any kinds of sounds of any synthesis methods. However, the performance of the current microprocessors are not still enough for generating many sounds at a time. Speedup of the computation by some simple hardwares is expected especially for real time performance. We are now developing hardware accelerators for the software synthesizers using off the shelf boards with Field Programmable Gate Arrays (FPGAs). With these hardware accelerators, we can realize any kinds of combinations of different sampling rates and data width of sounds not only generating many sounds (350 sounds on a desktop computer and 110 sounds on a note computer) at a time. This performance can be achieved by fully utilizing the flexibility of FPGAs, and outperforms DSPs.

1 Introduction

Hardware synthesizers which are widely used now generate sounds based on their own synthesis methods, which are fixed in their hardwares. Each synthesis method has its own characteristic, but the hardware synthesizers can not generate sounds by different methods. On the other hand, software synthesizers generated by software tools such as PureData [1,2], jMAX, MAX/MSP, CPS etc have great flexibility in the connection of the basic components of each synthesis method. In the software synthesizers, computations of all digital components are executed by microprocessors, and the synthesizers can generate any kinds of sounds of any kinds of synthesis methods by connecting components of each synthesis method freely using GUIs. However, the performance of current microprocessors are still not enough for generating many sounds at a time, which means software synthesizers can not be used for real time performance. Thus, speedup of the computation by some simple hardwares which can be easily obtained and put in computers in use is expected especially for real time performance.

We are now developing hardware accelerators for the software synthesizers using off the shelf boards with Field Programmable Gate Arrays (FPGAs). Almost all operations executed on the accelerators are multiply-and-accumulate (MAC) operations, which can be also accelerated by DSPs. However, because of the features of the computations of the synthesizers (which will be discussed

G. Brebner and R. Woods (Eds.): FPL 2001, LNCS 2147, pp. 377–387, 2001.
© Springer-Verlag Berlin Heidelberg 2001

in the section 3), we chose off the shelf boards with Xilinx FPGAs as our accelerators. Distributed RAMs in Xilinx FPGAs are very convenient to make up for the limited memory bandwidth of the off the shelf FPGA boards by overlapping the computation of MACs and loading/storing data for the MAC units from/to the memory banks on the boards. With these hardware accelerators, we can realize any kinds of combinations of different sampling rates and data width of sounds not only generating many sounds (350 sounds on a desktop computer with RC1000-PP (XCV1000), and 110 sounds on a note computer with Wildcard (PC card with XCV300)) at a time.

This paper is organized as follows. Section 2 describes the features of music synthesizers, and in section 3, we discuss why we chose FPGAs (not DSPs) as the hardware accelerators. Section 4 shows the overview of our system, and in section 5, the details of our system are described. In section 6, current status and future works are given.

2   Software Synthesizers

2.1   Overview of Software Synthesizers

When music synthesizer was first developed, it was constructed by analog components, and by connecting the components freely by wires, it could generate many kinds of sounds, although the number of sounds it could generate at at time was very limited. Analog synthesizers are still produced, but most of current commercial synthesizers generate sounds based on their own synthesis methods. In each synthesis method, the connections among the components are fixed and users control the sounds by changing only the parameters of the oscillators and filters.

Software tools for designing software synthesizers such as PureData, jMAX, MAX/MSP, CPS etc have been developed to realize flexibility of the analog synthesizers on current digital computers. With these tools, user can connect any kinds of components freely using GUIs, and can generate any kinds of sounds of any kinds of synthesis methods. Figure 1 shows an example of software synthesizers generated by PureData. Figure 2 and figure 3 show the basic structures of the oscillators and filters. In the figure 2, the output Y_i is delayed (Y_{i-1} and Y_{i-2}), multiplied ($Y_{i-1} \times j$ and $Y_{i-2} \times k$ respectively) and then added to its input X_i. By changing the parameters (j and k), the oscillator can generate sound of different frequency. In the filter shown in the figure 3, the input (X_i) is also delayed (X_{i-1} and X_{i-2}), multiplied and then added to its input, as well as its outputs as shown in the figure of the oscillator.

2.2   Features of the Computations in the Software Synthesizers

In the software synthesizers, almost all operations executed in the digital components such as oscillators and filters are multiply-and-accumulate (MAC) operations as shown in the figure 2 and 3, which are also main operations in digital

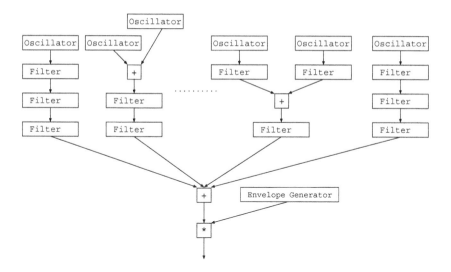

Fig. 1. An Example of Software Synthesizers

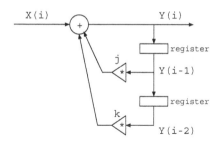

Fig. 2. Basic Structure of Oscillators

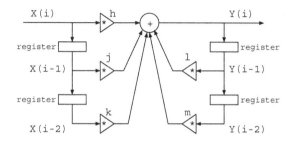

Fig. 3. Basic Structure of Filters

filters (such as FIR) for many other applications, and many approach for high speed computation with FPGAs and DSPs have been developed to date. However, the computations in the software synthesizers have features as follows.

1. All oscillators and filters for a sound (at most several taps) need to be processed only once in the fixed period (typically 1/44.1KHz for CD quality and 1/96KHz for DVD quality), which is very slow compared with operation frequency of FPGAs and DSPs.
2. As many as oscillators and filters have to be processed in the fixed period in order to generate many sounds. For example, in order to simulate a orchestra, we need to generate more than one hundred of sounds, which requires more than several thousands of oscillators and filters.
3. In real time performance (which is the main purpose of the acceleration by the hardwares), the length and the strength of sounds are not given in advance, which means that optimal scheduling of the computations of the components can not be obtained in advance.

3   FPGAs vs. DSPs and Related Works

In this section, we would like to discuss the performance of FPGAs and DSPs for music synthesizers. Because of the features described in the previous section, we need to process the oscillators and filters by time division processing. The time division processing requires

1. full multipliers (which are not specialized for multiplication with constant coefficients) and
2. high memory bandwidth to load and store data for the oscillators and filters.

3.1   Peak Performance

First, we compare the peak performance of FPGAs and DSPs for MACs operations with 16 bit width. Table 1 shows the performance of our current implementation on Xilinx FPGAs, and two DSP series which are one of the fastest DSPs. As shown in the table, peak performances are almost comparable, because the DSPs are designed for covering many applications, and are not specialized for MAC operations, while all hardware resources can be used for MAC operations in FPGAs.

Table 1. Peak performance of MACs by FPGAs and DSPs (Mega MACs)

FPGA (Xilinx Virtex)	1390 (XCV1000)	(5570 (XCV4000E))
DSP (TI TMS320C6000)	1200 (300MHz)	(4400 (1100MHz))
DSP (Motorola)	1200 (MSC8101)	(4800 (MSC8102))

3.2   Memory Bandwidth

Suppose that one filter is processed by one hardware unit for MAC operations (MAC unit). Then, the input to the unit (X_i in the figure 3) is just one word in each cycle of the computation of the filter, and the output from the unit (Y_i) is also one word, if the all constant coefficients and the intermediate results (X_{i-1}, X_{i-2}, Y_{i-1} and Y_{i-2}) can be held on the unit. However, when the unit has to process many filters by time division processing, the unit needs to store and restore the coefficients and the intermediate results of each filter in each computation of the filters.

In the latest FPGAs and DSPs, however, the performance for MACs and the memory bandwidth do not balance for the requirements above. In order to reduce memory access operations, we need to process each oscillator and filter for N times continuously (In our current implementation, N is 32. This means that the output from the accelerator delay about 0.7 msec, which is very short for human being and can not be recognized (actually the time delays in many MIDI systems are much longer than 1 msec)). Then, we can reduce the overhead for storing and restoring the coefficients and the intermediate results to $1/N$.

For example, the number of the coefficients and the intermediate results in the filter shown in the figure 3 is 9. Then, when N is 32, we need to store and restore 18 ($= 9 + 9$) words for each 180 (5×32) MACs. This overhead can be completely hidden in Xilinx FPGAs by overlapping the MAC operations and the storing/restoring using distributed RAMs and block RAMs (this approach requires very high memory bandwidth (for example, 2560 bits are necessary in total when the number of MAC units is 32)), though it is not possible on DSPs because the memory access paths are limited. Therefore, the performance of FPGAs is a bit better than DSPs. Furthermore, in the DSPs with very high operation frequency, size of the high speed memory on the DSPs is not large enough to hold all data of the oscillators and filters.

3.3   Scalability and Flexibility

Our system runs on FPGA boards with Xilinx FPGAs, at least two memory banks on the boards, and DMA functions for data transfer between the boards and the host computer. By using FPGAs, we need to develop only one software system for very wide range (performance and costs) of FPGA boards, because we can realize same architecture (only the number of MAC units is different) on the FPGAs. We only need to modify programs to control the FPGAs from the host computers according to the driver programs developed by the board makers. Furthermore, we can realize any kinds of data width efficiently with FPGAs (especially for overflows), though data width in DSPs is fixed to 16 or 32 bits.

3.4   Related Works

A dedicated FPGA board for sound synthesis has been developed[3]. On the board, 8 FPGAs (up to 4085) are used to achieve very high memory bandwidth, and sounds are generated mainly by reading out data from waveform look-up table stored in the DRAMs on the board.

Our goal is to accelerate software synthesizers using off the shelf boards which can be easily obtained by anyone. The memory bandwidth of the off the shelf boards are very limited, but it can be made up for by overlapping the computation and the memory access using distributed RAMs as described in the section 5. Furthermore, by using off the shelf FPGA boards, we can use larger size of FPGA easily. This is also important because we can implement any kinds of combinations of 16, 24 and 32 bit MAC units more efficiently on larger size FPGAs.

4   Overview of Our Synthesizer System

We use PureData as the user interface program of our synthesizer system. Figure 4 shows the overview of our approach. In our approach, first, data files of the synthesizers generated by PureData are translated to the data sequences for the FPGA, and then, one of the configuration data which are prepared on the host computer in advance is selected according to the data width and the sampling rates, and downloaded to the FPGA in order to realize the circuits to process the data sequences on the FPGA.

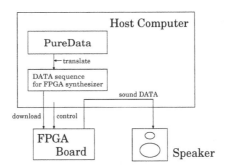

Fig. 4. Overview of the Synthesizer

When we need to generate sounds, parameters in the data sequences are modified according to the keys of the sounds and so on, and the data sequences are downloaded to the memory banks on the FPGA board from the host computer. Then, the FPGA processes the data sequences and makes data for the sounds. The data for the sounds are sent back to the host computer, and written to the sound board on the host computer. The FPGA continues to generate data for the sounds until the data sequences in the memory on the FPGA board are cleared by the host computer. As for the envelops, parameters (coefficients) of filters (amplifiers) can be automatically changed in our implementation as described in the next section, though the host computer also can change the parameters dynamically.

In our approach, the FPGA works as an accelerator just for computing oscillators, filters and amplifiers, and all other things including timings of the sounds are under control of the host computer.

5   Details of the Synthesizer System

5.1   Basic Filter Units

As shown in the figure 2 and 3, the right half part of the filter is exactly same with the structure of the oscillator, and some filters require only the left half part of the filter shown in the figure 3. Therefore, we decided to use basic filter units shown in figure 5 as basic components of the digital synthesizer on FPGAs. The structure of the two filter units are slightly different, but can be processed with one multiplier by only changing order of some operations. As shown in the figure 1, additions are also required, and the additions are also executed using the multiplier for the filter unit by changing its input sequence.

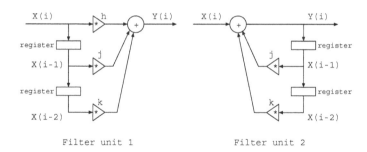

Fig. 5. Structure of Filter Units

5.2   Time Division Processing of the Filters

Figure 6 shows the basic strategy for the time division processing. In the figure, three memory banks are used for one MAC unit. In the *Data Buffer*, the control information and input data to each filter unit (X_{i-1} and X_{i-2}) are stored, and constant coefficients (i, j, k and *max*) are stored in the *Constant Table*. Data in the *Data Buffer* and the *Constant Table* are read out and processed by the MAC unit, and then, the intermediate results (X_{i-1} and X_{i-2}) are written back to the *Data Buffer*. At the same time, some variables in the *Control Info* are updated and the value of the *Const-Addr-L* may be changed according to the results (these values are also written back to the *Data Buffer*) in order to read out different set of constant coefficients in the next computation of each filter

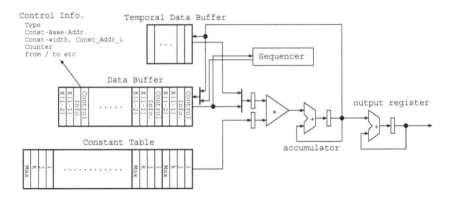

Fig. 6. Basic Strategy for Time Division Processing

unit. The output X_i is written in the *Temporal Data Buffer* in order to transfer data between basic filter units.

However, the memory bandwidth of off the shelf FPGA boards are not enough to realize this architecture as it is. Figure 7 shows the MAC units designed for RC1000-PP board which has one Virtex XCV1000 and four memory banks (32 bit width, and 2MB for each block (8MB in total)). The features of the implementation are as follows.

1. Two sets of input buffers which consist of distributed RAMs are prepared for each input to the MAC unit.
2. The *Data Buffers* and the *Constant Table* are placed on the memory banks on the FPGA board because the size of the internal memories of FPGAs is not large enough to store all of them, while the *Temporal Data Buffers* are placed on the FPGA using block RAMs. In other to achieve higher performance, we need to implement as many as MAC units on one FPGA. With one Virtex XCV1000, we could implement 32 MAC units when the data width is 16 bits. Therefore, eight MAC units are connected to each external memory bank.
3. Data for three basic filter units are held in each set of the input buffers in order to fill all the pipeline stages of the MAC unit (especially for the basic filter unit 2 in the figure 5).
4. Data in one set of the input buffers are processed 32 times continuously by the MAC unit (data in the *Temporal Data Buffer* are used for this computation when the unit processes filters), and the results are stored in the *Temporal Data Buffer*. The outputs from the FPGA are delayed for about 0.7 msec (44.1KHz × 32) by repeating the computation for 32 times, However, the period (0.7 msec) is very short for human beings and can not be recognized.
5. In parallel with the computation, data in another set of the input buffers (which are already processed by the MAC units) are written back to the

Data Buffer, and new data are loaded from the *Data Buffer* and the *Constant Table*.

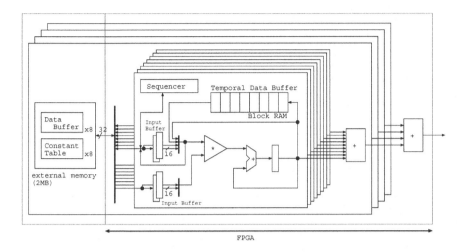

Fig. 7. Details of Multiplier units on RC1000

Figure 8 shows the processing timing for the three filter units. The MAC unit consists of seven stages, and the output of the previous cycle (Y_i) are directly transferred to the next cycle (as X_{i-1}).

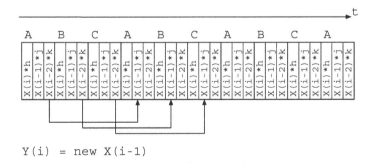

Y(i) = new X(i-1)

Fig. 8. Time Division Processing

The 32×3 (repetition $\times$ the number of filter units) results generated by processing the three filter units are stored in the *Temporal Data Buffer* which are placed on the block RAMs, and transferred to the following filter units. The size of each block RAM is 16 bit $\times$ 256 words. Therefore, each block RAM can store temporal data for eight filter units.

For processing three filter units for 32 times, 288 clock cycles ($=$ 3 filter units $\times$ 3 MAC operations for each unit $\times$ 32 repetition) are necessary. Therefore, 12 clock cycles ($=$ 288 clock cycles / 8 MAC units / 3 filter units) is available in order to load and store data for one filter unit. Figure 9 shows the details of the data format for each filter unit. The numbers in the parentheses show the data width. The first two words of the *Input Data* (X_{i-1}, X_{i-2}, *Counter* and *Const-Addr-L*) need to be written back after the filter is processed 32 times. Therefore, 5 read and 2 write operations have to be executed in the 12 clock cycles.

X(i-1) (16)		X(i-2) (16)		
Counter (16)		Const.Addr.Low (10)	From(3)	To(3)
Const.Addr.Base(18)		Const.Width(10)	Type(2)	Clear(2)

Format for Input data

h (16)	i (16)
j (16)	max (16)

Format for Constant Values

Fig. 9. Data Formats

6   Current Status and Future Works

We showed that a music digital synthesizer system which consists of a FPGA board and a microprocessor can outperform most of commercial products in the performance and in the flexibility.

In the current implementation, 32 multiply-and-accumulate units can be implemented on one Xilinx XCV1000, and the circuits run about at 43 MHz, Therefore, the system can process 10500 filter units at a time, which means that the system can generate about 350 different sounds at time. The same circuits can be implemented on PC card with Xilinx XCV300, and 110 sounds can be generated at a time.

The development has just started, and there are many parts which should be improved. For example, in the current implementation, the FPGA runs at the same speed with the SRAMs on the board. However, by making the pipeline deeper, we can double the FPGA internal clock speed, and can generate more sounds at a time. The software system also needs to be improved in order to achieve higher performance.

References

1. Puckette, M. "Pure Data" Proceedings, International Computer Music Conference. San Francisco, 1996, pp. 269-272.

2. Puckette, M. "Pure Data: recent progress" Proceedings, Third Inter-college Computer Music Festival, Tokyo, Japan, 1997. pp. 1-4.
3. Raczinski and Sladek, "The Modular Architecture of SYNTHUP, FPGA Based PCI Board for Real-Time Sound Synthesis and Digital Signal Processing", FPL 2000, pp.834-837.

Motivation from a Full-Rate Specific Design to a DSP Core Approach for GSM Vocoders

Shervin Sheidaei[1], Hamid Noori[2], Ahmad Akbari[1], Hosein Pedram[2]

[1] Iran University of Science and Technology, Computer Engineering Department
sh_sh2@hotmail.com, akbari@iust.ac.ir
[2] AmirKabir University of Technology, Computer Engineering Department
hamid_noori@yahoo.com, pedram@ce.aku.ac.ir

Abstract. The Global System for Mobile (GSM) communications uses a 13Kbps vocoder which expands to 22.8Kbps after channel coding. To increase the user capacity the half-rate channel has a gross transfer rate of 11.4Kbps. The vocoder for the half-rate channels operates at 5.6Kbps. To obtain better performance, GSM introduced enhanced full-rate vocoder which operates at 12.2Kbps. The computational requirements of these vocoders require the design of an entirely new digital signal processing architecture geared towards 1-D signal and speech processing. In this paper, at first the architecture of a specific design for full-rate vocoder is introduced, then according to the results of this architecture and common features available in all three vocoders, a DSP Core for implementing these vocoders is suggested. The architecture of the DSP Core is characterized by pipelining and parallel operation of functional units. This Core is a 16-bit fixed-point processor implemented on an FPGA and can be used as a real-time GSM vocoder.

1 Introduction

The GSM standard is a mobile telephony standard in Europe for cellular phones operating in the 900 MHz range. GSM permits encoded speech and user data to be carried over a mixture of full-rate, half-rate and enhanced full-rate channels. By using half-rate channels exclusively, the number of users on the network can be doubled.

Speech is encoded in the full-rate channel at 13Kbps, using RPE-LTP (Regular Pulse Excitation–Long Term Prediction) algorithm. Similarly, the half-rate encoder operates at 5.6Kbps, using VSELP (Vector Sum Excited Linear Prediction) algorithm. Enhanced full-rate transcoder operates at 12.2Kbps, using ACELP (Algebraic Code Excited Linear Prediction) algorithm. These speech coding algorithms process 20 ms frames. Each frame has 160 samples that each sample is 13-bits [1,2,3].

This paper firstly describes a specific design for GSM full-rate vocoder. Secondly a DSP Core as a substitution for the previous specific design to implement all three well-known GSM vocoders, has been introduced. This Core can do 16-bit and 32-bit fractions fixed-point operations. Pipelining and parallel operations of functional units, according to the specifications of GSM vocoders are main features of the DSP Core. To demonstrate how algorithm structures can be exploited by architectural enhancements, the VSELP algorithm has been chosen and implemented.

G. Brebner and R. Woods (Eds.): FPL 2001, LNCS 2147, pp. 388–397, 2001.
© Springer-Verlag Berlin Heidelberg 2001

2 Full-Rate Vocoder Specific Design

A full custom integrated circuit implementation can be designed for low power, but it does not have any flexibility. We follow this choice for full-rate vocoder as first step in our design.

2.1 Full-Rate Vocoder Computational Requirements

High data throughput and low power consumption can be achieved only by determining the required computational power according to algorithm. In order to achieve good specific design, the most important two factors are : firstly, the type of operations and secondly the average usage of each operation in every iteration of algorithm. For this reason, the fixed-point version of RPE-LTP speech coding algorithm has been reviewed. As shown in table 1, the algorithm uses some functions which are basis of its structure. There are both 16-bit and 32-bit (denoted by $L\_$) integer arithmetic and shift operations in specification. Table 2 shows the maximum usage of different operations in this algorithm. According to the table 2, frequency of multiplication is high and most attention must be paid to the design of its architecture. On the other hand, the frequency of division is low enough to be performed in software and no hardware block is dedicated to it. In this way the hardware complexity and power consumption have been reduced.

2.2 Architecture of Full-Rate Specific Design

Figure 1 shows the architecture.

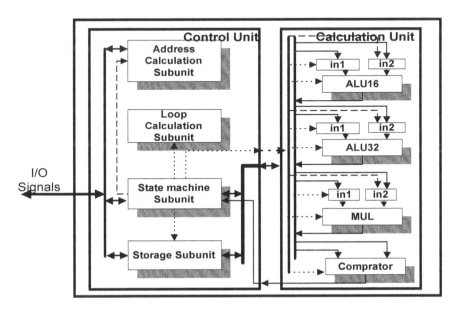

Fig 1 . Architecture of Full-Rate Specific design

Table 1. Primitive and macro functions in RPE-LTP[1], VSELP[2] and ACELP[3]

Name	Macro	Function	1	2	3
abs_s	negate + L_comp	Absolute 16 bits	✓	✓	✓
Add	L_add + saturate	Add 16 bits	✓	✓	✓
divide_s	L_sub+L_comp+shiftreg	Divide 16 bits	✓	✓	✓
Extract_h	✗	Extract 16 MS bits of 32 bits longword	✗	✓	✓
Extract_l	✗	Extract 16 LS bits of 32 bits longword	✓	✓	✓
L_abs	L_sub + L_comp	Absolute 32 bits	✗	✓	✓
L_add	✗	Add 32bit with saturation	✓	✓	✓
L_add_c	L_add	Add 32bit with carry	✗	✗	✓
L_deposit_h	✗	Put 16 bits into 16 MSB of longword	✗	✓	✓
L_deposit_l	✗	Put 16 bits into 16 LSB of longword	✓	✓	✓
L_mac	L_mult + L_add	Multiply accumulate	✗	✓	✓
L_macNs	L_mult + L_add	MAC with carry	✗	✗	✓
L_msu	L_mult + L_sub	Multiply subtract	✗	✓	✓
L_msuNs	L_mult + L_sub_c	Multiply subtract with borrow	✗	✗	✓
L_mult	✗	Multiply two 16 bits input ,32 bits output with saturation	✓	✓	✓
L_negate	L_sub + L_comp	Negate 32 bits	✗	✓	✓
L_sat	✗	Limiting 32bit according to carry & overflow	✗	✗	✓
L_shl	✗	Shift left 32 bits with saturation	✓	✓	✓
L_shr	✗	Arithmetic shift right 32 bits	✓	✓	✓
L_sub	✗	Subtract 32 bits with saturation	✓	✓	✓
L_sub_c	L_sub	Sub 32 bit with borrow	✗	✗	✓
mac_r	L_mac + round	MAC and round	✗	✓	✓
msu_r	L_msu + round	Multiply subtract and round	✗	✓	✓
mult	L_mult + extract_h	Multiply 16 bits , saturation and truncation	✓	✓	✓
mult_r	L_mult + round	Multiply 16 bits and round	✓	✓	✓
negate	✗	Negate 16 bits	✗	✓	✓
norm_l	✗	Normalize shift count(32bit)	✓	✓	✓
norm_s	L_deposit_h + norm_l	Normalize shift count(16bit)	✗	✓	✓
round	✗	Round 32 bits to 16 bits with saturation	✗	✓	✓
saturate	✗	Limit 32 bits to range of a 16b	✗	✓	✓
Shl	✗	Shift left 16 bits with saturation	✓	✓	✓
Shr	✗	Arithmetic shift right 16 bits	✓	✓	✓
sub	L_sub + saturate	Subtract 16 bits with saturation	✓	✓	✓
comp	L_comp	Compare 16 bits	✓	✓	✓
L_comp	✗	Compare 32 bits	✓	✓	✓
shift_r	(shl shr)+L_add+saturate	Shift and round (16 bits)	✗	✓	✓
L_shift_r	(L_shl L_shr)+L_add	Shift and round (32 bits)	✗	✓	✓
shr_r	shr + L_add + saturate	Shift right and round (16 bits)	✗	✗	✓
L_shr_r	L_shr + L_add	Shift right and round (32 bits)	✗	✗	✓

Table 2. Number of function calls for GSM vocoders in 20 ms (frame time)
RPE-LTP(No. of function calls in 20ms)[1], VSELP(No. of function calls in 20ms)[2],
ACELP(No. of function calls in 20ms)[3]

Function Name	1	2	3	Function Name	1	2	3
Abs_s	180	54	230	L_sub	175	405	1864
add	3155	1715	8671	L_sub_c	0	0	0
divide_s	9	135	48	mac_r	0	139	0
extract_h	0	17138	4819	msu_r	0	10	0
extract_l	489	2887	1569	mult	72	0	17290
L_abs	0	84	200	mult_r	3327	3886	480
L_add	17944	3098	474	negate	0	1576	261
L_add_c	0	0	0	norm_l	10	158	132
L_deposit_h	0	396	138	norm_s	0	232	20
L_deposit_l	320	168	4	round	0	1135	10616
L_mac	0	82798	77663	saturate	0	0	0
L_msu	0	37791	15800	shl	816	2152	86
L_macNs	0	0	160	shr	869	6485	1756
L_msuNs	0	0	0	shr_r	0	0	0
L_mult	16368	5759	12588	sub	617	5046	6274
L_negate	0	10	15	comp	575	9926	5962
L_sat	0	0	0	L_compare	465	2411	1863
L_shl	191	7668	6362	Logic16	0	9341	786
L_shr	660	2980	1799	Logic32	0	24310	0
L_shr_r	0	0	0	shiftr_r	0	44	0
				L_shiftr_r	0	0	0

The clock period (clk) is 59ns which is reasonable for low power. The architecture consists of two units. The control unit provides all control signals for other components in architecture and exactly follows the execution of algorithm. The calculation unit performs all arithmetic, comparison and shift operations according to control signals receiving from control unit.

Control unit consists of four sub-units:

- Address calculation sub-unit which provides proper direct addresses for accessing data RAM.
- Loop sub-unit which performs nested loops
- State machine generator sub-unit is the heart of the architecture. This sub-unit controls all of the algorithm operations. This sub-unit is designed on basis of a state machine.
- Storage sub-unit is used for fast storage of temporary values.

As most volume of operations are arithmetic type, so high consideration must be paid to the design of calculation unit components and their connectivity in order to have the most parallel operation with less dedicated hardware. MAX+PLUS II addition/subtraction operator gives the best result, according to implementing different architecture, in both of two aspects: lower delay and less area (Logic Cell).

Also a 16x16 modified booth multiplier is selected for this architecture through different tested architectures [13].

This architecture was implemented on FLEX10KA family of Altera FPGAs with EPF10K250A device number. 7100 LCs been dedicated to hardware implementation of specific design. Maximum execution time per frame for this vocoder is 7.22 ms. So it has the capability of real-time execution of full-rate GSM vocoder.

3 DSP Core for GSM Vocoders

To extend the full-rate specific design for half-rate and enhanced full-rate vocoders, the most optimal solution was to design an application oriented DSP Core which can have smaller power consumption than a general purpose DSP, but still preserving its flexibility.

3.1 Half-Rate and Enhanced Full-Rate Computational Requirements

These three algorithms use some basic functions for being implemented [4,5,6]. The basic functions can be divided into two categories: primitive functions and macro functions.The macro functions use a sequence of several primitive functions (table 1). Table 2 shows maximum number of basic function calls for each encoder algorithm in a frame processing time (20 ms).

In the Core, the primitive functions are implemented in hardware blocks called functional units. For this reason the computational power of the Core must be corresponding to the number of primitive function calls in table 2.

3.2 DSP Core Architecture

The Core is a 16-bit fixed-point processor i.e. the data is a 16-bit integer represented as a 2`s complement number. The datapath is 16-bit and 32-bit fractions. There is no instruction decoder unit. The Core can operate as a processor in conjunction with a controller.

Block diagram of Core architecture is shown in figure 2. The Core consists five main units: Processing unit, Memory unit, Address Generating unit, Loop unit and Register Bank unit.

Processing unit contains the functional units. According to table 2 L_mult and L_add dedicate most of the computational capacity to themselves and are the most effective functional units in determining the execution time of the algorithms.

Because about 92% of L_mac and 64% of L_msu in VSELP (about 82000 L_mac and 38000 L_msu calls per frame in VSELP), about 80% of L_add in RPE-LTP and 90% of L_mac in ACELP (about 78000 L_mac) are recursive ($a_n = a_{n-1} + b*c$, $a_n = a_{n-1} - b*c$), pipelining L_add and L_sub not only dose not increase the performance but also decreases it. However there is no data dependency in L_mult. So a two stages pipeline L_mult, with a delay almost equal to L_add delay for each stage can be considered. Also outputs of L_add and L_sub go directly to one of their inputs.

In this way a recursive L_add or L_sub can be done in one clock if clock period be equal to L_add delay.

Table 3. Number of logic cells and delay of DSP Core
hardware components and functional units
Hardwre component[1], Clock (27.5)[2], Number[3], Delay (ns)[4], Logic Cell[5]

1	2	3	4	5	1	2	3	4	5
reg 3bit	-	2	-	6	mux 20x16	1	4	20.8	208
reg 16bit	-	42	-	16	mux 16x16	1	5	15.4	160
reg 32bit	-	6	-	32	mux 12x16	1	5	15	128
counter 16bit	-	1	-	18	mux 10x16	1	3	14	112
L_add	1	1	26.6	68	mux 8x16	1	5	14.5	80
L_and	1	1	10.6	32	mux 4x16	1	14	13.6	32
L_comp	1	1	25.9	55	mux 3x32	1	1	13.5	64
L_mult	2	1	24(one stage)	581	mux16x1	1	1	12.7	10
L_or	1	1	10.6	32	adder 10bit	1	1	13.4	10
L_shl	2	1	36.4	202	counter 8bit	-	18	-	10
L_shr	1	1	21.6	147	counter 10bit	-	5	-	12
L_sub	1	1	27.2	97	mux 4x10	1	2	13.6	20
L_xor	1	1	10.6	32	mux 8x10	1	2	14.8	50
Left shiftreg 16bit	-	1	-	16	mux 4x8	1	2	13.5	16
Left shiftreg 32bit	-	1	-	32	mux 8x8	1	4	13.8	40
Negate	1	1	19.3	22	RAM (1K * 16bit)	-	1	-	16384 (mem. bit)
norm_l	2 to 34	1	12.9	53	RAM (256 * 16bit)	-	8	-	4096 (mem. bit)
round	1	1	20	19	counter 9bit	-	8	-	10
saturate	1	1	19.3	26	mux 4x9	1	2	13.6	18
Shl	1	1	24.5	86	mux 2x9	1	2	13.1	9
Shr	1	1	17	56	comparator 9bit	1	1	19.4	11

Implementation of other functional units shows that except L_shl, delays of other functional units are less than or alomost equal to L_add. Each functional unit has several input registers and one output register. The fastest way that functional units can use from each other outputs, is using multiplexers. Delay of the biggest multiplexer used in the Core is less than L_add. So if the clock period be equal to L_add delay, the Core will have a two stages pipeline: Selection stage and Processing stage. In the selection stage, input registers of functional units are loaded through multiplexers by selecting a proper value and in the processing stage, functional units process input data and store the result in their output registers.

L_mult function accepts two 16-bit inputs, multiplies them and after shifting the result left by one, produces a 32-bit result. So there is an exceptional case for L_mult, when both inputs are equal to 8000h. This exceptional case checking and overflow and underflow checking for L_add, L_sub, L_shl and shl is done by hardware.

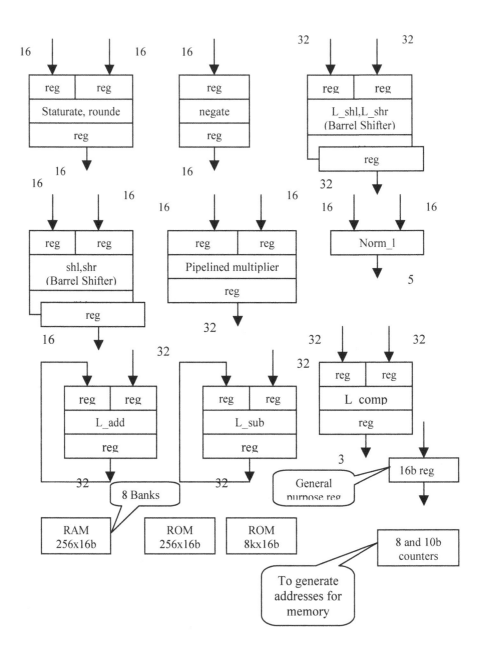

Fig.2. Block diagram of DSP Core

Memory unit has nine RAMs (eight banks have an 8-bit and one bank has a 10-bit addressing space of 16- bit words each) and two ROMs (one 8K and the other 256 words). In order to achieve higher memory bandwidth, instead of using one big RAM, number of small RAMs are used. The addressing of all banks are independent. All banks can be accessed simultaneously. The access can either be a single word or a double word (32 bits). Each memory uses an up/down counter with synchronous load ability for memory addressing. Input data of memories come from multiplexers and also the output data of memories go to the multiplexers.

Address generating unit uses a 10-bit adder and some 10-bit and 8-bit up/down counters with synchronous load ability for temporary storage and generating addresses for memories. Loop unit contains eight 9-bit counters and a 9-bit comparator. There are 36 16-bit registers in register bank unit (table 3). To increase throughput, parallel execution capability in the form of multiple functional units is introduced in the Core.

3.3. DSP Core Implementation

Different architectures of functional units were implemented on EPF10K200EGC599-1 (an Altera FPGA of FLEX10KE family) and the best architecture according to the delay and LC (logic cell) of implementations is selected for the functional units [14]. According to these tables the megafunctions are used for implementing the adder, subtractor and multiplier in the DSP Core.

6838 LCs , 49152 memory bits , 331 input pins and 9 output pins have been dedicated to hardware implementation of the DSP Core (except ROMs) on EPF10K200EGC599-1.The suggested clock period is 27.5 ns. With this selection, recursive L_mac and L_msu can be executed in one clock cycle.

Simulation of execution of several VSELP functions on the Core for a frame is done through state machines.   The results of execution time of these functions are shown in the table 4. Also estimation of execution time of other functions of VSELP on this Core is shown in table 5. Maximum estimated execution time per frame of this vocoder is maximally 8.1 ms (less than 20 ms), so it is capable of real time execution of GSM vocoders.

4 Conclusion

In this paper an FPGA implementation of a full-rate vocoder specific design has been suggested. That is capable of real time execution of GSM full-rate vocoder in 7.22ms. Also a DSP Core as a substitution for full-rate specific design to implement all of three well-known GSM vocoders (full-rate [RPE-LTP], half-rate [VSELP] and enhanced full-rate[ACELP]) has been introduced. Throughput of this Core is enhanced by pipeline and parallelism according to GSM vocoder algorithms. This Core has a two stages pipeline and operates at 36.36 MHz. Because of more complexity in half rate vocoder algorithm, it was selected and implemented on this Core. Execution time per frame for worst case is 8.1 ms. Some enhancements, according to other implementations, like using one multiplier, one adder, one subtractor and processing frames in a shorter time have been considered. The maximum MAC operation for this Core is 36.36 MOPS. This DSP Core can be considered as a data path for a VLIW processor too.

Using FPGA for implementing these designs is based on consideration of some important aspects. Firstly, FPGA implentation is fast and in some cases the easiest way to reach to a fairly real design, especially in educational enviroments. This helps us to see the results sooner and according to the results, if it be a proper architecture, the VLSI implementation can de done. Secondly, the reconfigurability feature of FPGA can be used in this design. In other words as our DSP Core can perform vocoder algorithm in less than 20 ms, after speech coding we can reconfigure the FPGA to perfom channel coding and encryption, which are necessary steps for completing GSM speech process, in the remaining time. This may results in low power and less area.

Table 4. Execution time of some implemented
VSELP functions on the DSP Core

Function	Execution time per frame (us)	16x16 L_mult per frame
filt4_2nd	176.87	2240
cov32	95.71	2270
Flat	299.19	2068
Aflat	1053.13	16373
RcToADp	11.48	100
GetNWCoefs	160.36	2222

Table 5. Estimate of execution time of other
non implemented VSELP functions on the DSP Core

Function	Execution time per frame (us)	16x16 L_mult per frame
getSfrmLpcTx	294.34	4446
weightSpeechFrame	157.94	3520
openLoopLagSearch	1018.81	26209
sfrmAnalysis		
(subframe 0)	1098.66	15724
(subframe 1)	1063.72	15224
(subframe 2)	1091.67	15624
(subframe 3)	1063.72	15224
All Functions	7585.6	121244

References

1. GSM 06.10: Digital Cellular telecommunications system:GSM full rate speech transcoding , Version 3.01.02, April 15,(1989).
2. GSM 06.20: Digital Cellular telecommunications system:GSM half rate speech transcoding,Version 8.0.0,(1999).
3. GSM 06.60,: Digital Cellular telecommunications system: Enhanced Full Rate (EFR) speech trancoding, Version 8.0.0, (1999).
4. http://www.kbs.cs.tu-berlin.de//jutta/gsm
5. GSM 06.06:Digital Cellular telecommunications system:ANSI-C code for GSM half rate speech codec,Version 8.0.0, (1999).
6. GSM 06.53: Digital Cellular telecommunications system: ANSI-C code for the GSM Enhanced Full Rate (EFR) speech codec , version 8.0.0 ; (1999).
7. J. Nurmi,V. Eerola , E. Ofiner and A. Gierlinger:A DSP core for speech coding applications , ICASSP 94, vol 2, pp.429-432,(1994).
8. M.K.Prasad , P. D.Arcy , A. Gupta , M. S. Diamondstein and H.R. Srinivas: Half-rate GSM vocoder implementation on a DUAL MAC digital signal processor,(1997) ICASSP 97,vol 1,pp.619-622.
9. R.E. Henning and C. Chakrabarti,: High-level design synthesis of a low power, VLIW processor for the IS-54 VSELP speech encoder, IEEE international conference on VLSI in computer and processor,pp.571-576,(1997).
10. Z. Gu , R. Sudhakar and K.B. Lee: Power efficient architectures for VSELP speech coders , IEEE, Vol 33, No 20, pp. 1682-1683,(Sep 1997).
11. M. Alidina, G. Burns, C. Holmqvist, E. Morgan, D. Rhodes, S. Simanapalli and M. Thierbach: DSP16000: A High Performance, Low Power Dual-MAC DSP Core for Communications Applications, IEEE Custom Integrated Circuits Conference , pp. 119-122 ; (1998).
12. J. Du, G. Warner, E. Vallow, P. Breyer and T. Hollenbach: GSM EFR IMPLEMENTATION FOR TRAU APPLICATION ON DSP16000 , IEEE, pp. 2207-2210;(1999).
13. Sh. Sheidaei: Hardware implementation of GSM base station full rate vocoder, M.Sc. Thesis, Iran University of Science and Technology, (June 1999).
14. H. Noori, An architecture to implement GSM Half-Rate vocoder, M.Sc. Thesis, AmirKabir University of Technology, (June 2000).
15. H. Noori, H. Pedram, A. Akbari and Sh. Shedaei: FPGA implementation of a DSP Core for Full Rate and Half Rate GSM Vocoders, IEEE, Twelfth International Conference on Microelectronics, pp. 273-276, (2000).
16. TMS320C6000 CPU and Instruction Set Reference Guide, Texas Instrument, (March 1999).

Loop Tiling for Reconfigurable Accelerators[*]

Steven Derrien and Sanjay Rajopadhye

IRISA, Campus de Beaulieu, 35042 Rennes Cedex, FRANCE
[sderrien|rajopadh]@irisa.fr

Abstract In this paper, we focus on system level-optimizations for automatic parallelization of nested loop on Reconfigurable Accelerators. Specifically, as off-chip bandwidth plays a major role in total performances for such implementations, we propose some partitioning techniques based on loop tiling which can take advantage of the hierarchically structured RA memory systems.

1 Introduction

Although FPGAs are slower and take more area than an equivalent ASIC, Reconfigurable Accelerators (RA's) have demonstrated their ability to significantly outperform software implementations for several applications [9]. Most of these applications are compute-bound and have large number of simple and regular computations which exhibit potentially massive parallelism.

Although many prototype tools (both academic/research & commercial) are now able to perform a large part of this parallelization automatically, we may question whether this performance will scale well with technology. Specifically, it is well known that the gap between available on-chip computational power and off-chip memory bandwidth grows exponentially. Since most target applications usually involve large data-sets, I/O bandwidth is likely to become the limiting factor in the performance of RAs. Automatic parallelization tools must hence take these evolutions into consideration and and provide adequate system level optimizations.

In this paper, we focus on the parallelization of doubly nested loops onto unidirectional linear regular arrays. Such architectures can reach very high performance, but are not very well suited to take advantage of hierarchically structured memory systems. In most cases, data is only seen as a stream read from a source device, processed within the array, and then flushed out to an output device. Besides, data is processed at each clock cycle, and performance is dramatically affected by insufficient bandwidth.

We propose a novel processor array partitioning technique based on loop tiling, that overcomes limitations of traditional methods (LSGP, LPGS, co-partitioning) when dealing with size constrained or highly hierarchical memory systems. We also develop an analytical performance model for the execution

---

[*] Supported in part by IFCPAR project 1802-1: CORCoP Compilation and Optimization for Reconfigurable Co-Processors

G. Brebner and R. Woods (Eds.): FPL 2001, LNCS 2147, pp. 398–408, 2001.
© Springer-Verlag Berlin Heidelberg 2001

of nested loops on a generic RA with a two-level memory hierarchy, and obtain closed form solutions for the optimal tiling parameters. We are currently validating the method on a number of applications.

The paper is organized as follows. Section 2 recapitulates array synthesis techniques and introduces out target architectural model. Section 3 reviews existing partitioning techniques and points out their weakness when it comes to size/bandwidth constrained memory hierarchy. The next few sections describe points enumerated above (partitioning through tiling, the analytic performance model, optimal tiling parameters and preliminary experimental validation). Section 7 presents our conclusions and future work.

2   Background

We consider the parallelization of a restricted class of loop nests: we assume a $W \times H$ perfectly nested rectangular loop with uniform dependences represented by m dependence vectors with positive integer components (this is a prerequisite for tiling), viewed as the columns of a matrix $D = [\vec{d_1} \ldots \vec{d_m}]$. Using well established space-time transformation methods [13] we derive an array of processors (PE) executing the loop in parallel (see Fig. 1). In addition, we choose the mapping and scheduling functions such that the interconnections are (i) unidirectional, and (ii) nearest-neighbor (details and justifications are given elsewhere [5], suffice to say that in practice, they do not impose a significant limitation).

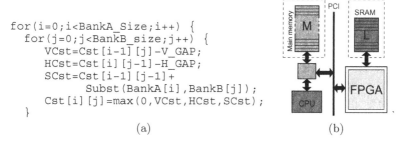

```
for(i=0;i<BankA_Size;i++) {
    for(j=0;j<BankB_size;j++) {
        VCst=Cst[i-1][j]-V_GAP;
        HCst=Cst[i][j-1]-H_GAP;
        SCst=Cst[i-1][j-1]+
            Subst(BankA[i],BankB[j]);
        Cst[i][j]=max(0,VCst,HCst,SCst);
    }
}
```

(a)   (b)

Fig. 1. (a) A common two dimensional loop nest (sequence comparison); (b) the typical target architecture on which it is to be implemented.

For the example of Fig. 1.a we may obtain a linear array of BankB_Size processors operating on a stream of BankA_Size data using $\vec{\tau} = [1\ 1]$ as the schedule vector and $\pi = [0\ 1]$ as the processor allocation.

We seek to implement this array on a target RA (see, eg. Fig. 1) which has a distinct memory hierarchy consisting of a main memory M (assumed to have unlimited capacity), on board memory L, and on chip memory/registers, comprising logic cells (LCs) which may be configured to emulate small grain memories[1]. Input data is present in (M) and results computed by the RA must be written back to (M) to be used by the host CPU application. M is generally accessed through a PCI type bus, offering relatively low bandwidth, often as low as 15MBytes/sec [11].

When implementing processors arrays on such a target architecture, one difficulty is that the derived array has application dependent characteristics in terms of parallelism level and communication volume with the host. Hence a straightforward implementation, if even possible, is likely to give poor performance. A post-processing step is then required to transform it to a form more suitable for the RA architecture at hand.

3   Array Partitioning

The problem of the efficient implementation of processor arrays on resource constrained architectures has been widely studied, and many approaches have been proposed [12, 3, 5, 14, 8].

The *serialization* transformation consists of clustering several PEs into a single one, and executing the iterations within this cluster sequentially. For linear arrays, if we *serialize* the array by a factor σ, a *virtual* array containing n PEs will be transformed into a $\lceil \frac{n}{\sigma} \rceil$ PE array. In addition to the array size, *serialization* also affects bandwidth: external I/O accesses (an also the array throughput) are slowed down by a factor σ. Finally *serialization* induces extra area requirements since it duplicates all the *internal registers*[2] by σ and creates a feed-back loop for each input port (see [5] for more details and formal proofs).

An alternative to *serialization* is to use multiple-pass (or LPGS) partitioning. In this approach, the space time domain is split into identical slices, each of size p, and implemented on a p-processor array. The whole loop domain is then computed by a succession of passes, each of them executing iterations from one slice. The number of passes is thus $\lceil \frac{n}{p} \rceil$. Note that this transformation is only valid for arrays with unidirectional connections [12]. Although this approach avoids the area overhead of serialization, it significantly increases (by a factor p) the overall number of I/O accesses, and does not reduce the array throughput requirements. Besides, since each pass reuses results from previous passes, an external FIFO memory (whose size is equal to the entire array output data volume) is required to store all inter-pass temporary data.

Since *serialization* induces an area overhead proportional to σ, it alone is obviously not suited to arrays with a large number of PEs: the larger the array size the larger the will be the σ factor, and hence, each PE will require much more area. Since we are resource constrained by the FPGA area, fewer PEs can be implemented, and the thus the available parallelism decreases.

Eckhardt et al. [8] showed how to combine serialization with a multi-pass approach. The array is then partitioned into p sub-arrays, in which the $\lceil \frac{n}{p} \rceil$

---

[1] In this paper we do not try to exploit embedded memory blocks available in most recent FPGA architectures.

[2] i.e., registers not connected to a neighboring PE.

PEs are serialized by a factor σ. Such an approach allows a trade-off between local memory cost and bandwidth adaptation: the *serialization* factor is usually chosen so that the array throughput matches external I/O bandwidth (since the σ needed for this is not too large, the area overhead of *serialization* is not too high). Its most severe limitation is the required FIFO size which is directly dependent on the loop bounds: hence it does not scale well.

This limitation is even more stringent in the scope of an RA architecture: since on-board memory size is fixed, this forces us to use memory M as FIFO memory despite its poor bandwidth. The only cure is then to serialize the array to match this low bandwidth, resulting in a severe loss of parallelism due to the local memory area overhead.

4   Loop Tiling

In this section we propose an adaptation of a well known loop transformation called tiling. Contrary to traditional array partitioning where the n dimensional space-time domain is partitioned using $n-1$ hyper-planes, a complete loop tiling will perform the partitioning using n hyper-planes resulting in a sub-domain basic block (or tile) for which all dimensions can be scaled down.

Tiling was initially introduced as a means to improve the performance of nested loop parallelization on (i) hierarchically structured memory systems and (ii) distributed memory machines [10, 2, 4]. The basic idea is to partition the loop-domain into tiles which are then executed atomically. The tiling problem is then to determine: (i) the tile shape and (ii) the tile dimensions which will give the best performance. Several criteria can be used to influence the choice of the tile, one can choose the tile volume to (i) balance communication and computation volume (ii) adapt the data accesses locality to some hierarchical memory level (from registers to main memory).

4.1   Application to Processor Arrays

Our goal here is to adapt the tiling approach to processor arrays, so that we can tune the data access locality to the the RA memory hierarchy. We will not broach the tiling problem in the general case, instead we will only consider a restrictive (but practical) case : 2D orthogonal tiling [2]. Here, the tile shape is chosen to have its boundaries parallel to the loop domain (see Fig. 2.a). Each of the resulting tiles is then parallelized on a (virtual) linear array of processors. The tile height H_T will correspond to the size of the derived virtual PE array, and the tile width W_T to the size of the data stream processed by the array.

The transformation yields two types of data dependences: dependences with both vertices within the tile correspond to *intra-tile* dependences (leading to local communications in the array), whereas dependences with vertices in different tiles correspond to *inter-tile* dependences and necessitate data to be stored in some external memory and reused when the corresponding tile is executed.

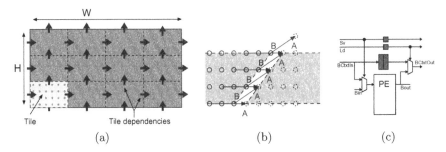

Fig. 2. (a) Tiled loop domain. The area within the dash-dotted bound is a tile. Dark grey arrows represents the data dependences at the tile level. (b) example of inter-tile horizontal (or temporal) dependences in the space-time domain. The array context data corresponds to data dependences whose source is in previous tile column. (c) context Load/Shift mechanism.

Hence, by changing the tile dimensions it is possible to tune the amount of *inter-tile* communication and also the number of external data accesses of a tile.

Contrary to classic array partitioning, tiling requires that between each tile execution, all the array internal variable are *saved* and *restored*. This is intuitively explained as follows. Tiling *breaks* the computation "pipeline" in the temporal dimension, and we need to save (and restore) this pipeline's *temporal context* in order to finish/restart the computation when subsequent tiles are executed. This of course induces an execution overhead since during these steps, the array can not perform any useful computation.

We also need additional control circuitry to save/restore the *array context*. This additional control mechanism (omitted here for brevity, but illustrated in Fig. 2.c, is required for every *variable* of the loop nest, be it local or spatial, and is independent of σ. It is important to note that the *context switching* phases can be overlapped (a tile context can be saved while another context is restored), resulting in an efficient array utilization.

4.2 Tiling Strategies

The added degree of freedom provided by tiling gives a larger design space, notably in selecting the "tile-level" schedule, namely the order in which the tiles are executed. Now, row-major scheduling of tiles is nothing but increasing the tile width, but in addition to the column major order, other schedules (e.g. wavefront) are possible. However, the control logic becomes complicated and it is not clear that the yield better performance. Also note that it is possible tile at multiple levels corresponding to the levels of the memory hierarchy [4] and this holds even more so for our target architecture. This opens up different possibilities related to where the data is stored. In the rest of this paper, we consider only (full or partial) column major schedules, and explore two tiling strategies: *vertical tiling* and *horizontal tiling*.

Vertical Tiling is a two level tiling where we call the inner level of tiling as a pass (of size $W_p \times H_p$) and the outer tiling as a band ($W_b \times H_b$). We study the case where $H_b = H$ and $W_p = W_b$ (Fig. 3.a). All data accesses from or to the *band* are made through the PCI bus to the host system main memory M. Internal data access (i.e: between *tiles* of a same *band*) are made through the local on board memory L. Since the tile schedule is column major order, computations associated with a given *band* cannot start before all its preceding *bands* are done. Finally, note that only data associated to vertical dependences are saved in L memory, to be immediately reused in the following pass execution.

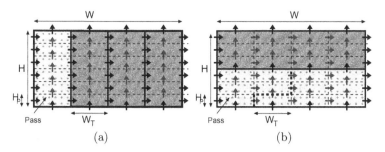

(a)   (b)

Fig. 3. (a) Vertical and (b) horizontal tiling. Arrows represents (inter) tile dependences, their color indicate which memory level is used to save intermediate results: black for main memory (L), light grey for local memory (L). The dashed line (in b) represents the maximum data volume that must be saved in L memory.

Horizontal tiling is also a two-level tiling strategy (we call the outer level *tiles* as ($W_s \times H_s$) *stripes*). We set $W_s = W$, and $H_s = kH_p$, for some positive integer k (see Fig. 3.b). All data accesses inside or outside a *stripe* are made through the PCI bus to memory M, and internal data access (i.e., between *tiles* of a same *stripe*) are made through L memory. As noted above, the *pass* schedule within a *stripe* is column major. As opposed to vertical tiling, here we use L memory to save data associated with both vertical and horizontal tile dependences.

5   Performance Modeling

We now develop an analytical model for our two tiling strategies. This will enable us to predict performance early in the design flow, and also explore the trade-offs involved with the choice of the tile dimension.

Our first step is to model the execution of a *pass* (or inner level tile). We decompose this into two phases (see Fig. 4). Let α and β respectively denote the number of words per-iteration that are used/produced as (i) context data (ii) input data. The pass execution hence consists of: (i) an overlapped *context loading/saving* phase during which βH_p data are loaded from (saved to) the internal registers of the array; (ii) a *computation* phase during which the stream of αW_p data words flows through the array pipeline.

Note that the RA performance is increasingly dictated by I/O bandwidth rather than by effective clock-speed [11]. We have shown that by using *serialization*, the effective array trough-put can be reduced at the price of a certain loss of parallelism [7]. It was also predicted that the best compromise would consist of finding the *serialization* factor which allows the closest match to the one of the external memory bandwidth (either M or L depending on which accesses have the stronger influence on overall execution time). In the scope of this work, we assume large loop domains and seek as much as possible to use the faster L rather than M. We hence make the choice to always *serialize* the array to match L bandwidth (let σ_L denote this serialization factor). The duration of the computational phase of a tile can then be approximated by the duration of its associated I/O operations (this is a crucial point and allows us to considerably simplify the analytical model).

Knowing this serialization factor, we can now estimate the number of PEs that are likely to fit on our FPGA. Let A_f be the available FPGA real estate (in slices), A_d be the combinational datapath area cost (in slices) of all operators involved in the loop body computation, S_m be the size (in bits) of the original PE local memory, and A_m the average area cost (in slices) of a memory bit for serialization. The number of *physical* PEs n_p is given by (a), and thus the pass height H_p which corresponds to the virtual array size $n_p\sigma_L$ is given by (b):

$$(a) n_p \approx \frac{A_f}{A_d + \sigma_L A_m S_m} \qquad (b) H_p \approx \frac{A_f \sigma_L}{A_d + \sigma_L A_m S_m}$$

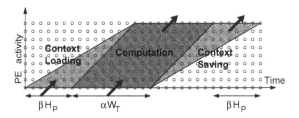

Fig. 4. Execution time for a $W_p \times H_p$ tile. Context loading and saving each require βH_p I/O accesses, computations requires $2\alpha W_p$ accesses (αW_p read operation and αW_p write operation).

6   Performance Optimization

Our goal of optimal performance, is equivalent to minimizing the time spent per iteration. Let ρ denote this average iteration execution time, T the whole loop execution time, and $T_{i,j}$ the inner tile (i,j) (or pass) execution time. We then have $\rho = \frac{T}{WH}$, $T = \Sigma_{i=1}^{n_h}\Sigma_{j=1}^{n_w} T_{i,j}$ where n_h and n_w represent the number of passes along vertical and horizontal axis. We can hence provide a general closed form for the performance optimization problem (see below), and use it to determine the optimal tile size for our two strategies.

$$\arg_{W_p, H_p} \max \frac{WH}{\sum_{i=1}^{n_h} \sum_{j=1}^{n_w} T_{i,j}}$$

6.1   Vertical Tiling

We first need to express the pass execution time as a function of its index i, j. Remember that we equate the pass execution time to that of its I/O. We see from Fig. 3.a, that there are three types of pass (in regard of their I/O access scheme). All passes access their context data from M, and only top and bottom passes access their computation stream from M, all other access being performed through L. If t_M and t_L denote the access time respectively for M and L, we obtain

$$T_{i,j} = \begin{cases} (\alpha W_P + 2\beta H_P) t_M + \alpha W_P t_L & \text{for a } top \text{ or } bottom \text{ pass} \\ 2\beta H_P t_M + 2\alpha W_P t_L & \text{otherwise} \end{cases}$$

Using this expression we can formulate our performance metric ρ as shown in (a). We see that H_p is set to a fixed value dependent upon (i) the loop body area requirements (ii) the available FPGA real estate (iii) L memory bandwidth and (iv) array throughput requirements. Additionally in this tile schedule, W_p is constrained by the size of L since the whole pass computation results must fit within the on-board memory. Let W_L denote L memory capacity, this translate as $\alpha W_p \leq W_L$. Since ρ decreases when W_p grows, it is clear that the optimal inner tile width is $W_p^* = \frac{W_L}{\alpha}$, and thus optimal tile dimension are given by (b).

$$\text{(a) } \rho \approx \frac{2\alpha t_L}{H_P} + \frac{2\alpha(t_M - t_L)}{H} + \frac{2\beta}{W_P} t_M \qquad \text{(b) } \begin{cases} W_P^* = \frac{W_L}{\alpha} \\ H_P^* = \frac{\sigma_L A_f}{A_d + A_m \sigma_L} \end{cases}$$

6.2   Horizontal Tiling

Again, let us express the pass execution time. Here, we can have (see Fig. 3.b) four different type of passes: (i) *corner passes* which access half their context and computation data from M and the rest from L, (ii) *internal passes* access all their data from L, (iii) *horizontal boundary passes* access all their context data from L and half of their computation data from M and (iv) *vertical boundary passes* access half their context data from M, the rest being accessed from L. We can then write $T_{i,j}$ as below:

$$T_{i,j} = \begin{cases} (\alpha W_P + \beta H_P)(t_M + t_L) & \text{for a corner boundary tile} \\ (\alpha W_P + 2\beta H_P) t_L + \alpha W_P t_M & \text{for a horizontal boundary tile} \\ (2\alpha W_P + \beta H_P) t_L + \beta H_P t_M & \text{for a vertical boundary tile} \\ 2\beta H_P t_M + 2\alpha W_P t_L & \text{for an internal tile} \end{cases}$$

The average iteration execution time is then given by the following expression:

$$\rho \approx t_L \left(\frac{2\beta}{W_P} + \frac{2\alpha}{H_P} \right) + \left(\frac{2\alpha}{kH_P} + \frac{2\beta}{W} \right) (t_M - t_L)$$

Contrary to vertical tiling, both W_p and $H_b = kH_p$ (with k positive integer) are variables of the optimization problem, and are coupled together by the constraint on W_L, the size of L memory (where both computation and context data need to be stored). Specifically we have $\alpha W_p + \beta k H_p \leq W_L$. To solve the equivalent continuous constrained optimization problem, we use the well known Lagrange multipliers. Due to space limitations, mathematical details are omitted, and we only provide the closed form solution for the optimal tile dimension:

$$\begin{cases} k^* &= \frac{\gamma - \sqrt{\gamma}}{\gamma - 1} \frac{W_L}{\beta H_p} \text{ with } \gamma = \frac{t_M}{t_L} - 1 \\ W_p^* &= \frac{1}{\alpha} \left(W_L - \beta k^* H_p \right) \end{cases}$$

7   Experimental Validation

To validate our model an its predictions, we used a Spyder X2 board [1]. It consists of a Xilinx XCV800-4 and two 256kx32 SRAM memory banks (we currently use only one of the) connected to a PIII-600Mhz through a PCI bus.

Observed PCI bandwidth is approximately 12MBytes/sec while our current SRAM interface allows 110 MBytes/sec. In our implementation, approximately 1300 slices are used to implement the overall system control logic (host interface, memory controller, array control, etc ...), the rest of the resources (8000 slices) being used to implement the PE array.

The target application is a modified version of the loop nest of Fig. 1.a. with a loop domain size of $10^7 \times 10^7$. By integrating a bubble sort mechanism to the PE architecture, we compute a more useful result, namely for each sequence, its K best matches (along with their similarity score) in the other data base (with $K \approx 300$). Due to the lack of space, the architecture is not presented in its details, we will only give an overview of its characteristics in terms of speed, through-put and resource usage (more details should be available in the extended version of this work [6]):

The PE maximum achievable clock speed of $68MHz$ (estimated after place and route), the array being effectively clocked to $f_c = 66Mhz$. Note that to reach this frequency, we went through a post-optimization step as described in [5]. The PE datapath is 7 byte wide during the computational phase and 9 bytes wide during context switching phase, leading to the parameters $\alpha = 7$ and $\beta = 9$.

From these figures, we can determine the initial through-put requirements: $\alpha f_c = 912$MBytes/sec during computational phase and $\alpha f_c = 1188$MBytes/sec during context switching phase. Hence, since neither M or L can sustain such a through-put, we are clearly in a case where our implementation performance is I/O bounded.

Let us now exploit the *serialization* transformation to perform bandwidth adaptation. Using the PE array characteristics, it is easy to determine the *serialization* factor σ_M matching M bandwidth: we have $\sigma_M = \lceil \frac{912}{12} \rceil \approx 76$. Using expression 5.b, we can, from the observed PE area cost $A_{p_m} \approx 510$ slices (after mapping) estimate: (i) the number of PEs $n_{p_m} \approx \frac{8000}{510} \approx 15$ and the pass height $H_p = 1140$ (note that this case is a standard co-partitioning scheme, where the pass width w_p is equal to the loop domain width W). Total execution time is thus $T \approx 2t_M \frac{H}{H_p}(\alpha W + \beta H_p)$ leading to an average iteration execution time of $\rho = 2t_M \left(\frac{\alpha}{H_p} + \frac{\beta}{W} \right) \approx 1.0$ ns per iteration.

Our goal is now to quantify the benefit of tiling: as seen previously, although it yields a more efficient utilization of L memory bandwidth, loop tiling induces an execution overhead due to context switching. We must hence understand how severe is the impact of this overhead on overall performance for each of the presented strategies. As seen previously, we make the choice of serializing the array to match L bandwidth, and then use the tiling transformation to minimize the number of M memory I/O accesses. Following previous paragraph, we obtain for $\sigma_L = \lceil \frac{924}{110} \rceil \approx 8$, leading to an observed PE area cost of $A_{p_l} = 301$ slices, an achievable number of processor of $n_{p_l} \approx \frac{8000}{301} \approx 26$, and a pass height $H_p \approx \sigma_L n_{p_l} \approx 208$.

From there, we can determine the (optimal) passes and tile dimensions for both tiling strategies: (i) for vertical tiling, we obtain $W_p^* \approx 146 \times 10^3$ and $H_p \approx \sigma_L n_{p_l} \approx 208$. Using our performance model, we then obtain for the average iteration execution time $\rho \approx 0.6$ns per iteration (ii) for horizontal tiling, we have $k^* \approx 166$ and $W_p^* = 98 \times 10^3$, leading to a value of $\rho \approx 0.6$ns practically identical to the one obtained for vertical tiling. In both case, the improvement over the co-partitioned solution is noticeable (around 40%), even for a target architecture in which the local memory size requirement are small. Hence for applications with higher local memory needs [11], we can expect even better results.

Besides, this improvement corresponds almost exactly to the gain in parallelism due to the smaller *serialization* factor: this means that, in our case, the impact of context switching over global performance is neglectable compared to the area overhead caused by a bandwidth adaptation to M.

8   Conclusion

In this paper we have presented a new partitioning methodology for processors array implementation based on the loop tiling transformation. As opposed to traditional partitioning techniques, this one allow to scale the off-chip memory requirements to suit the target system characteristics. We also provided a performance model which allow (i) to estimate the achievable performance (ii) to obtain a closed from solution for the optimal tile size problem. Since our current model is limited to the 2D orthogonal case, we would like to extend it to higher dimension loop nests and to non orthogonal tiling solutions.

References

[1] Spyder Board x2 Manual Rev 1.1. FZI Website and http://www.x2e.de/.

[2] R. Andonov, H. Bourzoufi, and S. Rajopadhye. Two-dimensional orthogonal tiling: from theory to practice. In *International Conference on High Performance Computing (HiPC)*, 1996.

[3] J. Bu and E.F. Depreterre P. Dewilde. A Design Methodology for Partitioning Systolic Arrays. In *IEEE conference on Application Specific Array Processor*, 1990.

[4] L. Carter, J. Ferrante, S. Hummel, B. Alpern, and K. Gatlin. Hierarchical tiling: a methodology for high performance. In *Technical Report CS-96-508 and University of California at San Diego*, 1996.

[5] S. Derrien, S. Rajopadhye, and S. Sur-Kolay. Combining Instruction and Loop Level Parrallelism for FPGAs. IRISA Research report N°1376 and February 2001.

[6] S. Derrien, S. Rajopadhye, and S. Sur-Kolay. Loop Tiling for Reconfigurable Accelerators. IRISA Research report.

[7] S. Derrien, S. Rajopadhye, and S. Sur-Kolay. Optimal partitionning for FPGA based regular array implementations. In *IEEE PARELEC'00*, August 2000.

[8] Uwe Eckhardt and Renate Merker. Co-Partitionning - A Method for Hardware/Software design for scalable Systolic Arrays. In *Reconfigurable Architectures and ITPress*, 1997.

[9] J. Vuillemin et al. Programmable active memories: Reconfigurable systems comes of age. In *IEEE Transaction on VLSI Systems*, 1991.

[10] K. Hogsted, L. Carter, and J. Ferrante. Selecting tile shape for minimal execution time. In *ACM Symposium on Parallel Algorithms and Architectures*, 1999.

[11] D. Lavenier. FPGA Implementation of the k-means Clustering Algorithm for Hyper-Spectral Images. Los Alamos Unclassified Report 00-3079 and July 2000.

[12] D. I. Moldovan and J. A.N. Forbes. Partitioning and Mapping Algorithms into Fixed Size Systolic Arrays. In *IEEE Transactions on Computers*, January 1986.

[13] P. Quinton. Automatic Synthesis of Systolic arrays from Recurrent Uniform Equations. In *International Conference on Computer Architecture*, pages 208–214, 1984.

[14] L. Thiele J. Teich and L. Zhang. Scheduling of Partitioned Regular Algorithms on Processor Arrays with Contrained Resources. In *International Conference on Application Specific Processor Arrays (ASAP)*, 1996.

The Systolic Ring : A Dynamically Reconfigurable Architecture for Embedded Systems

Gilles Sassatelli[1], Lionel Torres[1], Jerome Galy[1], Gaston Cambon[1], Camille Diou[1]

[1] University of Montpellier II, UMR5506, LIRMM
161 Rue ADA 34392 Montpellier France
{Sassate, Cambon, Torres, Galy}@lirmm.fr
http://www.lirmm.fr

Abstract. Internet is becoming one of the key features of tomorrow's communication world. The evolution of mobile phones networks, such as UMTS will soon allow everyone to be connected, everywhere. These new network technologies bring the ability to deal not only with classical voice or text messages, but also with improved content: multimedia. At the mobile level, this kind of data oriented content requires highly efficient architectures; and nowadays mobile system-on-chip solutions will no longer be able to manage the critical constraints like area, power and data computing efficiency. In this paper we will propose a new dynamically reconfigurable network, dedicated to data oriented applications such as the one allowed on third generation networks. Principles, realizations and comparative results will be exposed for some classical applications targeted on different architectures.

1 Introduction

Tomorrow's mobile phone networks will definitely be Internet oriented. They will not only be phones, but will also provide numerous functions today considered as pertinent to desktop computers or PDA (Personal Data Assistants). Agenda, Walkman (MP3), memo and portable drives are only a few of these new items that nowadays mobile phones are just beginning to provide.

The actual circuit based commutation technology, used in the second generation networks will soon evolve to packet mode, and more precisely IP (Internet Protocol). Its efficiency in physical resource sharing, joint to the new data width brought by third generation networks technologies such as CDMA (Code Division Multiple Access) will allow mobile phone users to have direct internet access. There are several and even new commercial services, such as trading, shopping, but also multimedia file transfer such as audio (MP3), video (MPEGx) and even videoconferencing which will become reality in the next years.

Figure 1 shows schematically the network architecture of a possible future third generation mobile phone network. There are two main different streams, the data stream and the voice stream. Second generation networks are circuit-commutation based, as the third generation ones will mainly be packet-commutation based. Each mobile will send and receive data through a base station, which will be connected to a

G. Brebner and R. Woods (Eds.): FPL 2001, LNCS 2147, pp. 409–419, 2001.

packet data network. According to the content type (voice or data), the data will pass through a circuit gateway directly to a classical telephone network (Public Switched Telephone Network) or will be sent over the internet through a packet gateway.

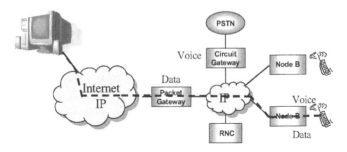

Fig. 1. A third generation mobile phone architecture

All these newly allowed high-demand applications, joint to the network-relative technologies management (CDMA for the channel access, TCP/IP for the network protocol stack) are bringing a new challenge in mobile phones design:

Designers have now to deal with computing intensive applications in a mobile context, as to say, with the strong power and cost constraints.

Nowadays mobile phones are mostly based on a SoC (System on Chip) approach (figure 2). On the same silicon die are grouped heterogeneous IP (Intellectual Property) modules.

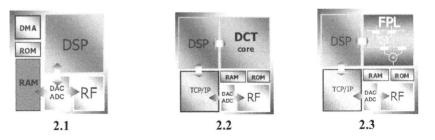

Fig. 2. The three main SoC approaches

A second generation mobile phone SoC (figure 2.1) consists in the following parts: the radio frequency core (this one however takes often place on a different chip) can be assimilated to the physical layer of a network stack. Its function is essentially to amplify, filter and demodulate the incoming RF signal. It transmits the baseband signal to the ADC (Analog Digital Converter) and the resulting digital signal is then sent to a DSP or μP which manages at the software level all digital functions of the phone, including the ones which are still relative to the channel, like data compression, encoding and logical channels multiplexing/demultiplexing.

There are different ways to face these new problems:

- The easiest and actual way to deal with this increasing computing power is naturally to use a bigger, more powerful DSP/μP than the ones used today (figure 2.1); but it will probably not be feasible for the most demanding applications, as the resulting processor will grow until the size of a Pentium (such as the ones which take place in the most powerful PDA or pocket PCs) with the corresponding area, cost and consumption problems.

- Another way is to try to identify the future application field and to use a dedicated core to compute the common parts of the algorithms (figure 2.2). For example, if we target JPEG and MPEG based applications, we will make the choice of implementing a wired IDCT (Inverse Discrete Cosine Transform) core, which is known to be the common most demanding part of both algorithms [7][8]. An interesting, but restrictive solution as the application field is thus not extensible.

- Yet another way is the reconfigurable computing [3][4][10] by the way of integration of field programmable logic (FPL). For example, integrate a FPGA core [1][2], where, depending on the target application, different algorithm/architecture solutions could be synthesized (figure 2.3). Here if we target JPEG applications, we will choose to synthesize the IDCT core in the FPGA and also an application dependant part of the algorithm, like Huffman coding or quantization. But in the other way if we target MPEG [9] applications, we will still make the choice of a wired IDCT, but this time we will also select the motion estimation [6], which is one of the most demanding part of the MPEG. A closer look to the kind of tomorrow's mobile applications shows a very data oriented, data intensive trend: the multimedia content needs a very high count of arithmetic operations; which would naturally imply to synthesise numbers of arithmetic operators in case of using fine grained reconfigurable logic (FPGA for example).

In a LUT-based FPGA [1][11], two main layers are used:

- The operative layer, in which take place all the CLB, IO blocks and switch matrix. This kind of CLB-based architecture is designed to manage bit-level data.
- The configuration layer, which can simply be seen as a big SRAM. The configuration is downloaded before the operating phase in this RAM, this is therefore a statically configurable architecture

In our context the granularity has to be quite different, as we have to compute arithmetic-level data. This 'mismatch' of granularity implies a majored total cost, mostly due to arithmetic operators synthesis.

This kind of approach seems to be quite interesting; we can thus imagine, depending on a given application, a video streaming one for example, that the mobile could directly connect to the vendor's site to download the corresponding applet, which is nothing else than the configuration file of the considered reconfigurable network.

2 System Overview

Dataflow oriented applications require the use of coarse grained reconfigurable network. In this way, our architecture follows a original concept:

1. The operative layer is no longer CLB based, but use a coarse-grained granularity component: The Dnode (Data node). It is a datapath component, with an ALU and a few registers, as shown in figure 4. This component is configured by a microinstruction code.
2. The configuration layer follows the same principle as FPGAs, it's a RAM which contains the configuration of all the component of the operative layer.
3. We also use a custom RISC core [5] with a dedicated instruction set; its task is to manage dynamically the configuration of the network and also to control the data injection and data recuperation in the operative layer.

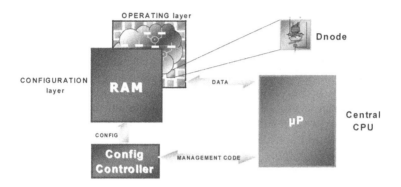

Fig. 3. System overview

This architecture is thus not intended to be a stand-alone solution, rather an IP core for data oriented intensive computing, which would take place in a SoC. Figure 3 shows schematically our system in a SoC context. The μP can thus confide the most demanding part of a given application to our IP core. So it downloads to the RISC memory the corresponding configuration program (manages the dynamic reconfiguration).

From a functional point of view:
- The host processor first sends the management code to the configuration controller memory (the custom RISC has its own program memory). This is a object code, ready to be executed, and specially designed to manage dynamically the configuration of the network (the content of the RAM thus changes from one cycle to another), as to say, the functionality of the operating layer. Each clock cycle, the configuration controller is able to change up to the entire content of the RAM thanks to its dedicated instruction set,.
- Once done, our core is ready to compute. The host processor sends the data to the operating layer via a specific scheme and then get back the computed data. As the configuration is dynamically managed, it is possible to multiplex the sent data, and to compute them by several sequential (hardware multiplexing) or concurrent(static) synthesised datapaths.

3 Operating Layer Architecture

In this section we will give more emphasis on the operating layer architecture.

3.1 D-Node Architecture

It essentially consists in an ALU-Multiplier, able to make all the classical arithmetic and logic operations : addition, multiplication, subtraction, roll, shift and so on. As shown in figure 4, there is also a register file and two multiplexers. This optimised architecture is able, in the same clock cycle, to make all possible operations, even between two different registers. Its corresponding microinstruction code, the configuration code, comes from a memory location in the configuration layer. As previously said, this code evolves during the computing phase, the functionality can thus be changed from one clock cycle to another, from an addition to a multiplication, load to register. Each Dnode has in fact two execution modes :

- Global mode (normal mode), already exposed : the Dnode executes the microinstruction code which comes from the configuration layer, managed by the RISC configuration controller.

- Local mode : The stand-alone mode : Each Dnode has 7 registers, a up to 6-states counter and a 6 to 1 multiplexer which forms a small controller. Each one of the 6 first registers can contain a Dnode microinstruction code, and each clock cycle the counter increases the value on the multiplexer address input, thus sending the content of a register to the datapath part of the Dnode.

In this mode the Dnode is able to compute various algorithms like MAC or serial digital filters. This scheme, joint to a specific input/output Data controller (exposed later) allows very efficient, high bandwidth data oriented computation.

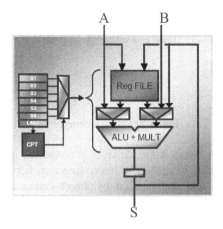

Fig. 4. The Dnode architecture

3.2   The Ring Architecture

A regular array implies interconnection and data transfer problems, as a dataflow often, nearly all the time needs data feedback (figure 5).

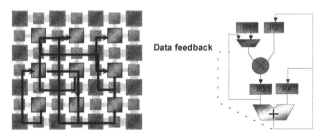

Fig. 5. The Data routing problem

These operations require important routing capabilities (figure 5), which limit the size, or the performance of the array (latency cycles). Our approach to solve this problem takes place in the use of a curled structure:

3.2.1   Forward : The Main Dataflow

We use a curled, pipelined systolic structure as shown in figure 6. All the D-nodes form a ring, which length (D-nodes layers number) and width (Dnodes per-layer number) can easily be scaled.

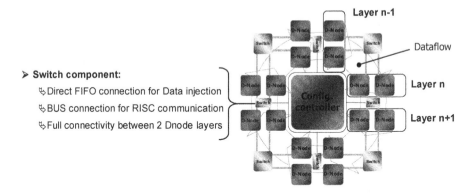

Fig. 6. The Ring architecture

Dnodes are organised in layers; a Dnode layer is connected to the two adjacent ones by switch components able to make any interconnection between two stages. It also manages data injection and recuperation by direct dedicated FIFOs, and optional RISC communications via a shared bus. In normal mode, each Dnode can be seen as an arithmetic operator of a datapath which computes a data each clock cycle. In stand-alone mode each Dnode can be seen as a autonomous CPU. The structure is also flexible in the way that all Dnodes have not to run in the same mode, allowing to compute either in global mode (normal mode) or local mode (stand-alone).

3.2.2   Reverse: The Secondary Dataflow

The data feedback problem is addressed by this one : we use special feedback pipe-lines (figure 7), forming a reverse Dataflow to avoid complex routing structures. The last task that accomplishes each switch is to write unconditionally (no control needed) the computed result of the previous D-node layer in a dedicated pipeline (each switch owns its pipeline), which allows the feedback of each data to the previous stages (fig-ure 9). These ones can then choose to get these data through the switches, which have direct access to all the pipelines. This technique ensures a good scalability of the ar-chitecture, as the routing problem is thus removed.

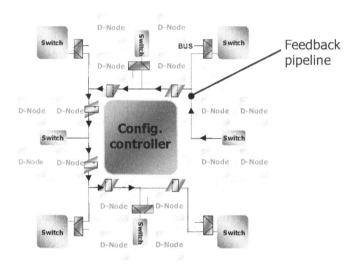

Fig. 7. The feedback network architecture

4   Comparisons & Realisations

4.1 Comparative Results

This version has a maximal computing power of 1600 MIPS at the typical 200 MHz evaluated functional frequency, quite impressive compared to the 400 MIPS of a Pentium II 450 MHz processor. The theoretical maximum bandwidth of this version of the structure is about 3 Gbytes/s, limited to 250 Mbytes/s in our implemented commu-nication protocol (a PCI based bus) between the host CPU and the core.

To program this structure we wrote an assembler, which parse both RISC level (for the control) and Ring level primitives. It generates the machine code, ready to be executed in the architecture. In the application field targeted by third generation sys-tems we can find lots of video-relative techniques. One of these well known comput-ing intensive algorithm is the motion estimation. Widely used in video compression techniques for broadcasting, storing, and videoconferencing, his task is to remove the temporal redundancy in video streams, as the DCT's is to remove the spatial redundancy. Block matching and specially Full Search Block Matching (FSBM) algorithm is the most popular implementation, also recommended by several standard committees (MPEG (video) and H.261 (videoconferencing) standards).

The Mean Absolute Difference (MAD) criterion, used to estimate the matching of the current block can be formulated as follows:

$$MAD(m,n) = \sum_{i=1}^{N} \sum_{j=1}^{N} |R(i,j) - S(i+m, j+n)|$$

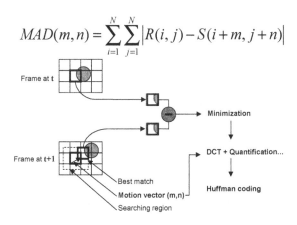

Fig. 8. The motion estimation algorithm

R(i,j) is the reference block (figure 8) of size N x N and S(i+m,j+n) the candidate block within the search area determined by p and q which are the maximum horizontal and vertical displacements. The size of this area is (N+p)(N+q) pixels; and the displacement vector represented by (m,n) is determined by the least MAD(m,n) among all the (p+1)(q+1) possible displacement within the search area. Let's consider the following common specifications: An image size of 352 x 240 pixels at 15 frames/s with a block size of 8 x 8 pixels and a maximum displacement of 8 pixels in horizontal and vertical directions. For each candidate block the first summation (j=1 to 8) requires N operations and the accumulation N-1 operations, thus a total of 2N-1 operations. The second summation requires to compute N times the previous one account of operations and again N-1 operations for the accumulation of the partials sums. The total amount of arithmetic operations to compute is so $2N^2 - 1$. The (2N-1).N first operations can be achieved within (2N-1).N / (0,75.Nx) clock cycles in a Nx Nodes version of our structure, as there are no dependencies on these data and one node over four is in wait state (layer n: 2 nodes computing two R()-S() operations; layer n+1: 1 node accumulating of the two previous computed results).The last N-1 operations (accumulation) are achieved in int(ln(N))+1 clock cycles for N <= Nx. In a 16 Nodes version of our structure, and with the previous specified codec (N=8) the computation of the MAD for a candidate block requires 13 clock cycles. Each reference block requires the computation of 289 candidate blocks and there are 1320 reference blocks in each frame. The total processing time of an image frame is 1320x289x13=4959240 cycles. At the 200MHz estimated frequency the computation time would be 24ms, which is two times smaller than the frame period (1/15s). Table 1 shows the performances of the Systolic Ring compared with the ASIC architecture implemented in [12] and Intel MMX instructions [13] using the criterion of the number of cycles needed for matching a 8x8 reference block against its search area of 8 pixels displacement.

Systolic Ring	ASIC[12]	MMX[13]
3757	581	28900

Table 1. Motion Estimation performance comparison (cycles)

Our structure shows again its efficiency in a such computing intensive context. The ASIC implementation is much faster than our solution at the price of flexibility: The Systolic Ring provides the advantage of hardware reuse and is also almost 8 times faster than a MMX solution.

Another example treated is the 2D-Wavelet transform using the approach presented in [14]. A 16 Dnodes version of the systolic ring was used in this case (Ring 16). We are able to decompose a full image (a 16-bits coded image 1024x768 pixels) in wawelet coefficient in 3 ms, each coefficient are treated in one clock cycle which allow to obtain an output data rate about 400 Mb/S, which is comparable to an ASIC implementation [14]. In this way, more than 300 transformed frames could be reached in one second.

4.2   Synthesis Results & Future Work

The entire architecture has been described in both behavioural and structural VHDL. A 8 D-nodes, 16 bits data width version has been fully simulated, and synthesised in both HCMOS7 and HCMOS8, respectively 0.25μm and 0.18μm ST technology.Table 2 shows the comparative synthesis results in both technologies.

	0.25μm	0.18μm
D-node area	0.06 mm^2	0.04 mm^2
Core area	0.9 mm^2	0.7 mm^2
Estimated Frequency	180 MHz	200 MHz

Table 2. Table of synthesis results

The low area of each D-node, joint to the exposed specific architecture shows that this one could easily be scaled to larger realizations. Figure 9 shows a foreseeable .18μm technology, 12 mm^2 die area SoC for high constrained embedded solution. Our specific architecture allows the integration of powerful 64 Dnodes version of our Ring (3.4 mm^2 on-die area) with a widely used ARM7 CPU, able to run various operating systems like windows CE, Linux. This kind of solution could provide a great computation power/cost ratio, which combines the flexibility of a CPU / reconfigurable architecture couple with the efficiency of dedicated core.

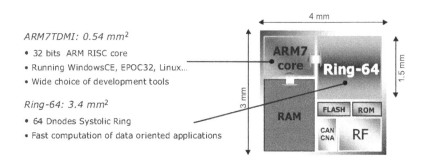

ARM7TDMI: 0.54 mm²
* 32 bits ARM RISC core
* Running WindowsCE, EPOC32, Linux...
* Wide choice of development tools

Ring-64: 3.4 mm²
* 64 Dnodes Systolic Ring
* Fast computation of data oriented applications

Fig. 9. A foreseeable SoC

5   Conclusion

We have proposed a new coarse grained arithmetic block based dynamically recon-figurable architecture which proves its efficiency in data oriented processing. His scalability shows that its field of applications can not only be limited to embedded high-constrained applications, but can also make be worth its faculties in other con-texts, where data oriented high data bandwidth processing remains critical. A small 8-Dnodes version of this structure already provides up to 1600 MIPS of raw power for data dominated application with a sustained data rate of 300 Mbytes/s at 20 MHz, either in global or local mode. Our future work takes place in the translation of the structure to floating point and also in the writing of an efficient compiling/profiling tool which harder task would be to maximize the computation density (the objective is no D-node in wait state) in the architecture.

References

1. Stephen Brown and J. Rose, "Architecture of FPGAs and CPLDs: A Tutorial," IEEE Design and Test of Computers, Vol. 13, No. 2, pp. 42-57, 1996
2. M. Gokhale et al, "Building and Using a Highly Parallel Programmable Logic Array," IEEE Computer, pp. 81-89, Jan. 1991
3. W. H. Mangione-Smith et al, "Seeking Solutions in Configurable Computing," IEEE Com-puter, pp. 38-43, December 1997
4. J. R. Hauser and J. Wawrzynek, "Garp: A MIPS Processor with a Re-configurable Co-processor," Proc. of the IEEE Symposium on FPGAs for Custom Computing Machines, 1997
5. A. Abnous, C. Christensen, J. Gray, J. Lenell, A. Naylor and N. Bagherzadeh, " Design and Implementation of the Tiny RISC microprocessor," Microprocessors and Microsystems, Vol. 16, No. 4, pp. 187-94, 1992
6. C. Hsieh and T. Lin, " VLSI Architecture For Block-Matching Motion Estimation Algo-rithm," IEEE Trans. on Circuits and Systems for Video Technology, vol. 2, pp. 169-175, June 1992.
7. N. Ahmed, T. Natarajan, and K.R. Rao, "Discrete cosine transform," IEEE Trans. On Computers, vol. C-23, pp. 90-93, Jan 1974

8. ISO/IEC JTC1 CD 10918. Digital compression and coding of continuous-tone still images – part 1, requirements and guidelines, ISO, 1993 (JPEG)
9. ISO/IEC JTC1 CD 13818. Generic coding of moving pictures and associated audio: video, ISO, 1994 (MPEG-2 standard)
10. Challenges for Adaptive Computing Systems, Defense and Advanced Research Projects Agency, at www.darpa.mil/ito/research/acs/challenges.html
11. Xilinx, the Programmable Logic Data Book, 1994
12. A.Bugeja and W. Yang, "A Re-configurable VLSI Coprocessing System for the Block Matching Algorithm", IEEE Trans. On VLSI systems, vol. 5, September 1997.
13. .Intel Application Notes for Pentium MMX, http://developer.intel.com/
14. C.Diou, M. Robert, L. Torres , "A Wavelet Core for Video Processing", ICIP2000, IEEE Signal Processing Society 2000 International Conference on Image Processing, Vancouver, September 10 - 13, 2000, pp 35-40.

A n-Bit Reconfigurable Scalar Quantiser

Oswaldo Cadenas* and Graham Megson

University of Reading, Department of Computer Science
PO Box 225 Whitenights, RG6 6AY, Reading, UK
{sir98joc,g.m.megson}@reading.ac.uk

Abstract. A reconfigurable scalar quantiser capable of accepting n-bit input data is presented. The data length n can be varied in the range $1 \ldots N - 1$ under partial-run time reconfiguration, p-RTR. Issues as improvement in throughput using this reconfigurable quantiser of p-RTR against RTR for data of variable length are considered. The quantiser design referred to as the priority quantiser PQ is then compared against a direct design of the quantiser DIQ. It is then evaluated that for practical quantiser sizes, PQ shows better area usage when both are targeted onto the same FPGA. Other benefits are also identified.

1   Introduction

Quantisation is one of the simplest lossy compression techniques, it is used for applications such as PCM modulation and analog-to-digital conversion [1]. The use of a quantiser has become an integral part of the JPEG standard for image compression algorithms [2]. A look-up table reference scheme is a common solution for the quantiser. Although simple, a basic systolic cell proposed in [3] is claimed to be faster than a memory reference and hence a systolic solution could be suitable for high throughput demanding applications such as data streaming where there is time to prime the pipeline. RTR exploits the possibility of allocating and reallocating hardware during the run time of an application. We refer to RTR when all the FPGA resources are allocated at once and p-RTR when a selective part of the FPGA is changed. This allocation of resources can be managed by downloading complete or portions of configuration bitstreams to the FPGA. Reconfigurable architectures based on FPGAs have demonstrated supercomputer-class performance [4] for some applications. In [5] reduction in size of specialist circuits to compute vector products resulted in a way to optimise the use of reconfigurable hardware. A metric to evaluate quantitatively the benefits of circuit specialisations is proposed as a combination of area and time in [6]. In [7] RTR and p-RTR were used to evaluate area-time to encode variable bits-per-pixel images. However, the direct systolic implementation quantiser design DIQ used there has given low FPGA usage of the total resources for regular placement and routing and more hardware resources where subject to partial reconfiguration to quantise scalars of different n. Here, a new systolic design PQ

---

* Supported by a grant from ULA-CONICIT, Venezuela

G. Brebner and R. Woods (Eds.): FPL 2001, LNCS 2147, pp. 420–429, 2001.

is proposed based on an internal priority scheme. This new PQ design requires partial reconfiguration on two gates to adapt the quantiser to any n-bit scalar. The PQ design not also takes less FPGA cells but also shows better area usage for the same FPGA compared to DIQ and both offer better performance to quantise variable length data under p-RTR than dedicated solutions under RTR. The saving can be used to incorporate more levels in the quantisation process on the same VLSI device.

2   Scalar Quantisation

Quantisation is the process of representing a large set of values with a much smaller set [2]. If the mapping done by *quantisers* acts on scalar inputs, the process is called *scalar quantisation* and produces a finite set of short codewords as outputs. The quantisation process involves both encoding and decoding functions. The *encoder* sets a number of intervals and simply classifies the input with the codeword assigned to the interval where it belongs. If just one interval size is used for the process, quantisation is said to be *uniform*. A *non-uniform* method uses different interval sizes. A set of boundary values b_j for $j = 0, \ldots, m$ establish m intervals with $b_j < b_{j+1}$. Normally, each interval is assigned with an integer l_j in the range of $0, \ldots, m + 1$ encoded in $log_2(m + 1)$ bits which is the codeword for the final output. From here, it is clear that some compression is obtained. For each input, say x_i the coding is done by assigning a corresponding l_i value for each x_i or $l_i(x_i) = l_j$ where

$$l_j = \begin{cases} 0, & if\ x_i \leq b_0 \\ j+1, & if\ b_j < x_i \leq b_{j+1} \\ m+1, & if\ b_m < x_i \end{cases} \tag{1}$$

The job of the decoding process is to extract the corresponding x_i which generated each l_j. As a unique l_j is assigned for a whole interval it is only possible to extract a representative value for each interval and hence the compression is lossy. If r_j is the representative value for each interval, the decoding is then trivial since a reconstructed value $\hat{x}_i$ becomes $r_j(l_i)$. As decoding is simpler in operation with less intensive computations, the focus of attention will be on the encoder.

3   A n-Bit Comparator

For a pipelined operation based on the above description for a quantiser it is clear that a module to compute comparisons has to be implemented. Based on comparison results derived from the input data x_i and boundary values b_j the appropriate actions to complete the quantisation process can be taken. A quantiser to operate on a n-bit scalar for $n = 1 \ldots N$ demands a comparator design to manage N-bit operands. Traditional approaches to design comparators are based on boolean equations derived for the problem. Magnitude comparators of small size s, usually $s = 4$, can be cascaded to any word length N to compare words whose actual length are $p * s \leq N$ and the results are taken on the same physical outputs. However, the most significant bits MSBs of operands at bit positions $p * s + 1 \ldots N - 1$ has to be set to zero [8]. Another approach is to use subtracter modules which is for example the approach used for hardware implementation of decision making instructions of the MIPS datapath processor [9]. It can be also argued that the compiler interprets small values as a N-bit quantity. In this section a comparator design based on a subtractor is presented. The design will be able to accept n-bit operands with don't care values at MSB $n + 1 \ldots N - 1$ and still get the result at the same physical position. It will be explained how partial run-time reconfiguration can be used to make appropriate modification on circuits to dynamically vary n to any value on its range.

3.1   Comparator Design

A comparator design based on 1-bit subtracter modules is shown in Fig. 1 for $N = 5$. The circuit can be pipelined if registers are inserted at the positions marked by the dotted lines. For the shown values all the data selectors take the upper input to form a plain subtracter and the comparison result is obtained according to the MSB of the subtraction result in two's complement form. Suppose that 2-bit operands have to be compared. If $T_2 = 1$ is forced the result at $a < b$ is the sign bit produced at stage 2 in the circuit independent of the values a, b at positions 3,4, and 5. If for example a new size of 4 is desired for the operands, the values $T_2 = 0, T_4 = 1$ have to be set and $a < b$ is a copy from stage 4 output independent of a, b values at stage 5. Similarly, for any n-operand two T_i values have to be set at most for any circuit of size N.

3.2   Partial Reconfiguration

Partial run-time reconfiguration p-RTR allows the possibility to modify selective subsets of the hardware executing a task at run-time [10]. Changes on values of T_i are perfectly possible to be partial reconfigured for a circuit similar to Fig. 1 if appropriate hardware supporting p-RTR is used. In [6] total time for a reconfigurable system is computed as $T = T_e + T_c$, where T_e and T_c are execution and configuration time respectively. Suppose k sets of M n-bit data are to be compared with each set with different n, the total time to compare all the sets with p-RTR can be decomposed in: $T_e = MT_{clk}$ which is M times the cycle time to process one data. T_c is the one time to download the original configuration file plus the partial reconfiguration time to change the two values for each k set, $T_{cf} + 2kT_r$ where T_r is the time to reconfigure one particular value and T_{cf} is the time to download a reconfiguration file. The total p-RTR time is $T_{prt} = MT_{clk} + T_{cf} + 2kT_r$. With run-time reconfiguration a complete new reconfiguration file is needed for each n-bit set and the total reconfiguration time is then $T_{rt} = kT_{cf} + MT_{clk}$. These equations will be used later with figures obtained from FPGA scalar quantiser circuit implementations using the comparator presented here.

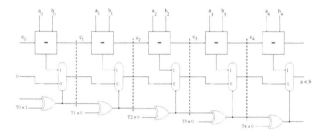

Fig. 1. A comparator with subtracter modules for $N = 5$.

4   Designs

In this section the DIQ and PQ designs are explained. The two designs share a great deal of the solution as a systolic array proposed in [3] and both can be implemented with the reconfigurable comparator design. The main difference between them is basically in the way the compressed codeword is generated for the scheme. The DIQ design will be explained first since it will facilitate the understanding of the PQ design.

4.1   DIQ Design

The DIQ design for uniform quantisation is straightforward based on the formulation given by Equation (1). The idea is to develop a PE for each interval by unrolling and pipelining the loop defined by the index j. Then, a one dimensional array of PEs act as the consecutive intervals for the process. Each PE generates its own b_{j+1} based on the previous value b_j from the PE to the left. A distance d is then needed for each PE in order to compute $b_{j+1} = b_j + d$ which requires an adder. The initial b_0 is given as an external source to the first PE in the array. The l_j values ranging from $0, \ldots, m+1$ suggest the use of an incrementer in the PE. The processing can be directly executed by a comparison between the data x_i and the b_j value while a data selector chooses either the incoming l_j value or the computed $l_j + 1$. The l_j value for each x_i is taken directly from the last PE in the array. The basic encoder PE of DIQ is shown in Fig. 2. For non-uniform operation the d data stream has to run twice as fast as the other data.

Compared with a sequential quantiser based on table look-up, this design can start new quantisations after the cost of operating one cell in the design compared with several memory probes to a quantisation table. The speed difference between the array and the memory reference approaches is offset against the latency and length of pipelining. For large data sets the array is a better choice.

4.2   PQ Design

An alternative design for the quantiser removes the adder to generate the internal b_j boundary values by assuming they are initially pumped through the x_i input

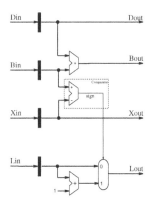

Fig. 2. An Encoder PE of a DIQ quantiser.

and then internally retained under external control. This control is a simple bit and is pipelined to the internal circuitry. The basic idea is to compare the x_i input with all the boundary values in a systolic way to generate the auxiliary signals m_i. A priority solver takes m_i to generate the priority information ep_i. The highest priority is given to the comparison result of x_i with the greater boundary value b_{m+1}, placed as the first PE in the array. This idea is depicted in Fig. 3 for the case of 5 boundary values. From the encoded priority information ep_i the final codeword for the quantiser can be designed in several different ways. The priority solver and codeword generation choices are briefly explained below. One advantage of PQ over DIQ is that it can be used as a non-uniform encoder since the actual values for b_i do not have to be generated.

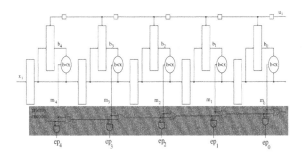

Fig. 3. Priority resolution for a quantiser.

Priority Resolution To clarify the idea with numbers, suppose a set of five boundary values $b = \{50, 40, 30, 20, 10\}$ and an input x of say 23 is set. The auxiliaries are then $m_i = \{0,0,0,1,1\}$ since 23 is greater than 20 and 10. From this, a priority resolution signal, say $ep = \{0,0,0,1,0\}$ is required. It is clear that highest priority is given to leftmost PEs in the array. Table 1 summarises, the binary values for ep needed in an array of 5 PEs. The priority resolution ep_i

Table 1. Priority comparator for a 5 PEs array.

Input	ep_4	ep_3	ep_2	ep_1	ep_0	code
$x_i > b_4$	1	0	0	0	0	101
$x_i > b_3$	0	1	0	0	0	100
$x_i > b_2$	0	0	1	0	0	011
$x_i > b_1$	0	0	0	1	0	010
$x_i > b_0$	0	0	0	0	1	001
other	0	0	0	0	0	000

is solved very easily according to Equation (2) [11]. The highlighted shade logic in Fig. 3 generates a priority recursive using the equation.

$$ep_i = m_i.\overline{m}_{i-1}.\overline{m}_{i-2}\ldots\overline{m}_0 \tag{2}$$

Codeword Generation The final codeword generation for the encoder quantiser, also shown in Table 1, can be solved in several ways. A very simple method is to allow the m_i to travel as tags with the data, and at the very end to apply a high-speed combinational priority encoder to the tags. An alternative idea is to distribute the code generation among the PEs. The ep_i values can be used to move a hardwired code systolically alongside the array. Any code for any PE can be hardwired but the logic grows with the size of the codeword although is fairly compact for quantisers of practical sizes. The area required with this scheme compared to the rest of the quantiser hardware of Fig. 3 is very small. The codeword can be also be produced in other ways. In Fig. 4 the codeword is held in the lower internal registers (which were initially input under hardware control at the same time as the b_i). The code stored at the activated priority encoded signal filters through to the output. If, for instance, $ep_1 = 1$ the value stored as l_2 is selected and moved to the output. If none ep_i signals is active, a default value (usually zero) is taken directly form the l_i input in the figure. This design takes more area but could be convenient if a large bit-quantiser has to be used.

5   Implementation

Both designs were implemented on an XC6216 FPGA (see [12]) embedded in a PCI board (and [13]) using Velab ([14]) as entry point to the XACT6000 software implementation tool from Xilinx (see [15]). As the development tools does not

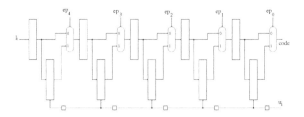

Fig. 4. Codeword generator based on registers.

allow simulation early in the design, a standard VHDL simulator was used both for functional and structural simulation. Verification was then carried out from the VHDL simulator. Actual results from the implementation running on the FPGA were verified from a C++ test program controlling the PCI board and the design. Circuits for both designs for each section of the PEs were created as bit-parallel pipelined circuits acting on skewed data. This way the limited routing resources of the XC6216 are used more effectively and local connections were obtained for each section of the PEs. Two different implementations of a quantiser for a 3-bit output codeword were done for each design. A dedicated quantiser for 8-bit scalars (D-prefix and subscript 8) and a generic reconfigurable quantiser PE to manage a greater lenght scalars using the reconfigurable comparator (referred with R-prefix and subscript n) . Details of both area and time are given for both designs below.

5.1   Implementation of DIQ

The circuit implementation in FPGA for the DIQ was naturally divided into the sections: adder, comparator, incrementer, and registers. FPGA area and cycle time for the reconfigurable and dedicated quantiser is presented in Tab. 2a. The figures shown in the table for the PQ were produced using a XC6264 (an internal array of 128×128 cells instead of 64×64 for the XC6216) in order to preserve the regularity of placement and routing for the design. A 24-bit version was not possible to route keeping regularity, it was possible however with a 16-bit version.

Table 2. FPGA area and time for a) DIQ PE and b) PQ PE

a) DIQ Quantiser PE			b) PQ Quantiser PE		
DIQ PE	**Area**	**t** (ns)	**PQ PE**	**Area**	**t** (ns)
D-DIQ$_8$	79	8.52	D-PQ$_8$	57	11.76
R-DIQ$_{16}$	191	11.37	R-PQ$_{24}$	210	19.04

5.2   Implementation of PQ

The only processing unit preserved was the comparator, and the rest of the implementation are merely registers and gates. FPGA area and cycle time for the reconfigurable and for the dedicated quantiser is presented in Tab. 2b. Real simulations for the reconfigurable design were run for 8-bit scalars.

6   Results

Using the equations presented in Section 3.2 for our case, and the data obtained from circuit tests, an evaluation on reconfigurable quantisers against dedicated quantisers for variable data length can be conducted. T_{cf} was measured in 1.5 ms while T_r for one gate reconfiguration is given by $10/f_{pci}$ [16] and corroborated by our experiments. M can be fixed to a representative number as 65536 which is the size of an image of 256×256 pixels. The following table shows the total reconfiguration time for the four options using these values. Clearly the

Table 3. Reconfiguration time for DIQ and PQ for k sets of 65536 scalars each.

	RTR time (ms)	p-RTR time (ms)
D-DIQ$_8$	$1.5k + 4.47$	-
D-PQ$_8$	$1.5k + 6.17$	-
R-DIQ$_{16}$	-	$0.6 \times 10^{-3}k + 7.46$
R-PQ$_{24}$	-	$0.6 \times 10^{-3}k + 11.48$

dedicated DIQ is superior to PQ in time for a 8-bit scalar circuit. Partial-RTR using the DIQ design would be advantegeous to RTR when at least $k = 2$. If two different scalar data lengths have to be quantised p-RTR is definitely better choice. Using the PQ design $k = 4$ or greater is necessary to justify p-RTR over RTR. The reconfigurable DIQ looks apparently better than the reconfigurable PQ. The superiority of DIQ over PQ lies on better placement regularity at the bit level if the design is organised vertically. This is true up to a scalar length of 8 bits. For 16 bits, the larger FPGA XC6264 was used and for 24 it was not possible to route without deterioration in the cycle time. The PQ design is easily accommodated onto the XC6216 even for scalar length of 24 bits. As seen in Tables. 2 and ?? 24% area saving is obtained using PQ rather than DIQ (DIQ$_{24}$ would have take 279 cells). R-PQ is preferred rather than R-DIQ from a practical point of view.

7   Discussion

The design and implementation issues for two different approaches to the problem of a reconfigurable encoder PE section of a systolic scalar quantiser has been presented. An array of any number of PEs can be easily arranged. However, the following discussion is based solely on one PE.

The improvement in throughput of p-RTR over RTR depends on technology factors as T_r and T_{cf} as well as application factors, M and k and on both, the cycle time, T_{clk}. If the cycle time for both could be kept similar, in general the term kT_{cf} grows faster than the term MT_{clk} and the maximum obtainable speedup for large k would be the ratio $T_{rt}/T_{prt} \cong T_{cf}/2T_r$. The limiting factor 2 in our case is the number of entities subject for partial reconfiguration, which is intuitive. This maximum speedup is mainly technology dependent and for the XC6216 was measured in 2500 (5000/2).

Savings in area were based on counting the number of FPGA cells of the PQ PE against the DIQ PE number. The main saving is due to not having to compute the boundary values for each interval in the quantisation. That is, an array of DIQ PEs uses an initial boundary value b_0 and a distance d_i to compute b_i. Additional saving is allowed by not computing the codeword in each interval as an incremented value but by filtering a preloaded value to the output. A little price is paid for this in the form of some external control and latency for the array. In Fig. 3 the u signal value has to be set to the sequence $u = \{1010\ldots10\}$ for a length of m followed by zeros traveling from right to left while the actual values for b_i are being sent through the x_i input. This way an extra latency of $2^{m+1} - 1$ is required to start collecting the results. Keeping this control signal is equivalent to keeping d_i in the DIQ design but it takes less bits. The increase in cycle time for PQ against DIQ is explained basically by more processing by unit area. For an 8-bit data and a codeword of 3-bits the number of input pins is reduced from 27 for the DIQ PE to 9 for the PQ PE and in general 3:1 for any size. In Tab. 4 the main results for both designs are outlined. The area usage and number of PEs was based on the design physical layouts. Although the area-time of both dedicated designs are similar and affected by FPGA routing in the same amount (roughly 40% logic delay and 60% routing delay), the PQ design makes a more efficient use of the FPGA resources due to more compact layout.

Table 4. Outline of DIQ_8 and PQ_8 PEs in XC6216.

	DIQ	PQ
FPGA cells	79	57
Freq. MHz	117	85
No. of PEs	21	63
Area usage	54%	80%
No. of inputs	1	1/3
Latency	0	$2^{m+1} - 1$
Operation	uniform	uniform
		non-uniform

8   Conclusions

Reconfigurable encoder quantisers PEs presented here show better performance to quantise variable n-bit scalars under partial-RTR. It is better choice than having dedicated circuits tailored for different bit-length of data even when just two different n-bit lengths need to be used. A quantiser based on priority PQ, makes better use of FPGA area resources to accommodate quantisers of practical sizes keeping similar area-time figures when compared to a direct systolic implementation DIQ. A clear advantage of the PQ design over DIQ is to quantise data with non-uniform intervals without any data speed constraint and shows one third saving in external pin-out.

References

1. Gray, R. M. and Neuhoff D. L. "Quantisation," in *IEEE Transactions on Information Theory*, 1998, Vol. 44, No. 6, pp. 2325-2327.
2. K. Sayood. *Introduction to data compression*. San Francisco, CA: Morgan Kaufmann Publishers, 1996.
3. Megson, G.M. and Diemoz E., 1997. "Scalar Quantisation Using a Fast Systolic Array," in *Electronics Letters*, 1997, Vol. 33, No. 17, pp.1435-1437.
4. Bolotski M., DeHon A. and Knight T. "Unifying FPGAs and SIMD Arrays," in *2nd Int. ACM/SIGDA Workshop on FPGAs*, Berkeley, USA, Feb. 13-15, 1994.
5. Benyamin D., Luk W. and Villasenor J. "Optimizing FPGA-based vector product design," in *IEEE Symp. on FPGAs for Custom Computing Machines*, Napa Valley, USA, Apr. 21-23, 1999.
6. Wirthlin M. J. and Hutchings B. L. "Improving functional density through runtime constant propagation," in *ACM/SIGDA Int. Symp. Field Programmable Gate Arrays*, Monterey, USA, pp. 86-92, Feb. 1997.
7. O. Cadenas, G. Megson and T. Plaks, "Quantitative evaluation of three reconfiguration strategies on FPGAs: A case study," in *Proc. of the HPC-Asia 2000* Beijing, China, May 14-17 2000, pp. 337-342.
8. J. F. Wakerly. *Digital Design Principles and Practices*. Englewood Cliffs, NJ: Prentice Hall, 1994.
9. D. A. Patterson and J. L. Hennessy. *Computer Organization and Design. The hardware/software interface*. Morgan Kaufmann Publishers, 1994.
10. Hutchings B. L. and M. J. Wirthlin "Implementation approaches for reconfigurable logic applications" in *Field Programmable Logic and Applications LNCS 975* pp. 419-428. Springer, 1995.
11. Delgado-Frias J. G. and Nyathi J. "A quantitative analysis of reconfiguration coprocessors for multimedia applications," in *IEEE Eigth Great Symp. on VLSI* Lafayette, Louisiana, Feb. 1998, pp. 59-64.
12. Xilinx: *XC6000 Field Programmable Gate Array*, 1996.
13. http://www.vcc.com/Hotworks.html
14. http://www.xilinx.com/apps/velabrel.htm
15. Xilinx: *Xact Step, Series 6000, User Guide*, 1997.
16. Xilinx :*32 × 16 reconfigurable correlator for the XC6200*, July 1997, Application Note XAPP 084.

Real Time Morphological Image Contrast Enhancement in Virtex FPGA

Jerzy Kasperek

Institute of Electronics, AGH Technical University Krakow
al. Mickiewicza 30, 30-059 Krakow, Poland
kasperek@uci.agh.edu.pl

Abstract. This paper describes the implementation of the real time local image contrast enhancement method. The system is based on Virtex FPGA chip and enhances the angiocardiographic data using the modified mathematical morphology multiscale TopHat transform. The morphological TopHat transform proved its effectiveness but the direct real time pipeline implementation of the multiscale version requires too many memory blocks. The author proposes a slight modification of the algorithm and presents satisfactory image contrast enhancement results and an efficient FPGA implementation. Proposed pipeline architecture uses the structural element decomposition and employs the Virtex *BlockRam* modules effectively. The processing kernel realises the contrast enhancement for the 512 x 512 image data with 8 bits/pixel representation in the real time in one XCV-800 Virtex chip.

1. Introduction

Mathematical morphology, hereafter referred to as MM, is a well-known and effective image processing environment. MM is successfully used in image filtering, segmentation, classification and measurements, pattern recognition or texture analysis, and synthesis. Yet MM algorithms generally require a significant computation power and usually in the real time image processing tasks the dedicated hardware is used. The new high capacity FPGA devices with on-chip RAM allows effective implementation even of complex morphological operations on reconfigurable hardware, which can effectively change its architecture to suit the processed task.

The paper describes the implementation of the real time local image contrast enhancement method based on MM TopHat transform. The proposed method was verified on human heart angiographic data DICOM records. During the clinical examination the patient's heart is irradiated by X-rays 25 (or 12.5) times a second with concurrent injection of a radiopaque substance to the examined vessels. Image data are digitally recorded, processed, and made available over the LAN for the medical inspection on CRT. They are also compressed and stored in DICOM standard for further inspection and analysis. Single frames have resolution of 512 x 512 with 8 bits/pixel representation, and generally show poor contrast, which inspired the work presented here. To enhance the image contrast the MM multiscale TopHat transform

G. Brebner and R. Woods (Eds.): FPL 2001, LNCS 2147, pp. 430–440, 2001.
© Springer-Verlag Berlin Heidelberg 2001

was evaluated. Unfortunately, the direct implementation of the classic approach was not satisfied, assuming FPGA resources requirements. After slight modification, the author noticed satisfactory image contrast enhancement results and an efficient Virtex FPGA implementation.

Presented angiographic data are used with kind permission of the medical staff of the Collegium Medicum of the Jagiellonian University in Krakow.

2. Fundamental Morphological Operations

Mathematical morphology is a theory devised for the shape analysis of objects and functions. MM operators treat the processed image as the set and are made of two parts: a reference shape – called the structuring element (SE) or function that is translated and compared to the original function all over the plane and a mechanism that details how to carry out the comparison. The set studied here represents either the objects of a binary image or the subgraph of the gray tone image.

The fundamental morphological operations are called the erosion and the dilation. Erosion of a set X by a structuring element B is denoted as $\varepsilon_B(X)$ and defined as the locus of points, x, such that B is included in X when its origin is placed at x.

$$\varepsilon_B(X) = \{x | B_x \subseteq X\} \tag{1}$$

Hence, the eroded value at a given pixel is the minimum value of the image in the window defined by the structuring element when its origin is at x.

$$[\varepsilon_B(f)](x) = \min_{b \in B} f(x+b) \tag{2}$$

Dilation is the dual operator of the erosion. The dilation of a set X by a structuring element B is denoted as $\delta_B(X)$ and defined as the locus of points, x, such that B hits X when its origin coincides with x.

$$\delta_B(X) = \{x | B_x \cap X \neq 0\} \tag{3}$$

Thus, the dilated value at a given pixel is the maximum value of the image in the window defined by the structuring element when its origin is at x.

$$[\delta_B(f)](x) = \max_{b \in B} f(x+b) \tag{4}$$

Hardware implementation of the dilation and the erosion for a small SE is usually the direct interpretation of the (2), and the (4). For larger SE its decomposition property (5) is frequently used.

$$\delta_{B_2}\delta_{B_1} = \delta_{\left(\delta_{B_2} B_1\right)} \quad \text{and} \quad \varepsilon_{B_2}\varepsilon_{B_1} = \varepsilon_{\left(\varepsilon_{B_2} B_1\right)} \tag{5}$$

Hence, the eroding or dilating with a large SE (figure 1 – B) could be replaced by sequences of operations with smaller SE (B_1 and B_2).

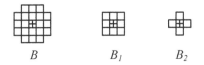

$$B \qquad B_1 \qquad B_2$$

Fig.1 Structuring element decomposition

Erosions and dilations could be combined to create more complex morphological transforms. To present the used TopHat transform we introduce the opening and the closing. The opening γ of an image f by a structuring element B is denoted by $\gamma_B(f)$ and it is defined as the erosion of f by B followed by the dilation with the transposed SE $\hat{B}$:

$$\gamma_B(f) = \delta_{\hat{B}}[\varepsilon_B(f)] \tag{6}$$

The closing ϕ of an image f by a structuring element B is denoted by $\phi_B(f)$ and it is defined as the dilation of f by B followed by the erosion with the transposed SE $\hat{B}$:

$$\phi_B(f) = \varepsilon_{\hat{B}}[\delta_B(f)] \tag{7}$$

Usually the symmetric SE ($\hat{B} = B$) is used and the opening and the closing are just the combination of the erosion and the dilation.

Openings are the anti-extensive transformations are and closings are extensive transformations. Therefore, they are always satisfy the following ordering relationship (I is the identity transform).

$$\gamma \leq I \leq \phi \tag{8}$$

3.   The TopHat Transform

The TopHat transform is a very useful tool for extracting features less the structuring element chosen from the processed image. There are two versions of the TopHat transform: the White TopHat (or TopHat by opening) denoted *WTH* and the Black TopHat (or TopHat by closing) denoted *BTH*. The *WTH* transform extracts the bright details from the background and is defined as the difference between the original image f and its opening γ.

$$WTH(f) = f - \gamma(f) \tag{9}$$

The dual transform of the *WTH* with respect to set complementation is Black TopHat transform. In practice it is defined as the difference between closing $\phi(f)$ of the image f and the original image.

$$BTH(f) = \phi(f) - f \tag{10}$$

The *BTH* transform extracts dark features from the image background. These remarks suggest that applying a combination of the *WTH* and the *BTH* we can achieve the contrast enhancement in the processed image. Figure 2a presents the original signal *f* and its erosion (in gray) by *B*. The figure 2c presents the construction of the *WTH* and the figures 2d, 2e, and 2f – the construction of the *BTH*. Finally, the figure 2g presents the corrected signal (the bold line) and its origin. It may be noticed that every peak and trough covered by *SE* has been enhanced. What is important, this correction has not changed the relations between particular signal samples and at the same it works independently from sample values.

The fact that the signal correction depends on the SE size was used by Mukhopadhyay and Chanda [9]. They propose to compute the new pixel value as the sum of original signal and *WTH* & *BTH* pyramids resulting from processing a successively enlarged *SE* sample. The new value $\tilde{g}$ (r,c) for the pixel with the (r,c) coordinates is calculated from:

$$\tilde{g}(r,c)= g(r,c)+0.5\sum_{i=n}^{m} WTH_{iB}(r,c)-0.5\sum_{i=n}^{m} BTH_{iB}(r,c) \qquad (11)$$

The selected 3x3 SE is enlarged in every pyramid level. Constant (e.q. 0.5) values were chosen to avoid saturation effect and to enhance both bright and dark features uniformly. In [9] result on the MR human brain image enhancement was presented for n=1 and m=6.

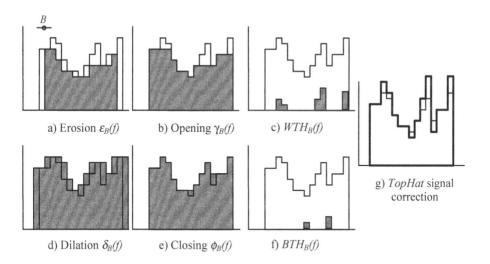

a) Erosion $\varepsilon_B(f)$ b) Opening $\gamma_B(f)$ c) $WTH_B(f)$

g) *TopHat* signal correction

d) Dilation $\delta_B(f)$ e) Closing $\phi_B(f)$ f) $BTH_B(f)$

Fig.2 *TopHat* transform contrast correction

4.   The Multiscale TopHat Transform Hardware Implementation in Virtex

Figure 3 presents direct implementation of the algorithm (11). The SE decomposition property (5) allows pipelining the multiscale TopHat computing. For clarity's sake, delay blocks for WTH_{iB} and BTH_{iB} products as well as for the original image are omitted. The erosion and the dilation are made with 3x3 SE. To achieve full pixel neighbourhood, the standard method utilising two delay lines is applied. Virtex *BlockRAM* module with two counters as the address pointers fulfils this FIFO task. Each XCV *BlockRAM* module is capable to store a single image line (512 pixels x 8bits). The main disadvantage of this implementation is the number of *BlockRAM* required. The number R_n of *BlockRAM* required only for the erosion /dilation modules of the n-stage multiscale TopHat realisation is given by (12).

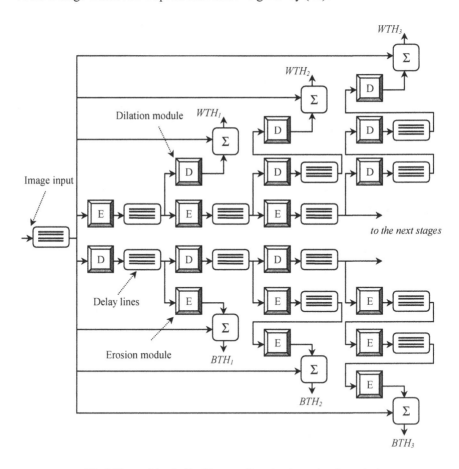

Fig.3 The multiscale TopHat transform hardware implementation

$$R_n = 2 + \sum_{i=1}^{n} 4 * i \tag{12}$$

These constraints on available *BlockRAM* modules encouraged the author to study how to simplify the algorithm and decrease the number of required delay lines. Simulation with MATLAB with specialised *SDC Morphology Toolbox* [13] proved that some kind of the TopHat transform degradation gives interesting results on image enhancement and much less hardware resources are required to implement it.

5.   The TopHat Transform Modification

Analysis of the block diagram from figure 3 suggests that the most *BlockRAM* consuming branch is the supplementation of the main processing stream for the larger SE. At this point, it is worth checking what the consequences of the degrading the TopHat transform are. Figure 4 shows the TopHat second stage case. In figure 4a an original signal and its double erosion is shown, yet instead of the double dilation known from the classic approach, we dilate only once – as in figure 4b. Next, we compute WTH_M (figure 4c). In the same way we construct BTH_M (figures 4d, 4e, and 4f). The final result is given in figure 4g. Despite small artefacts, we can notice much greater contrast enhancement than in the classic approach. After the MATLAB simulation, the desired number of stages for the proposed method was set to five.

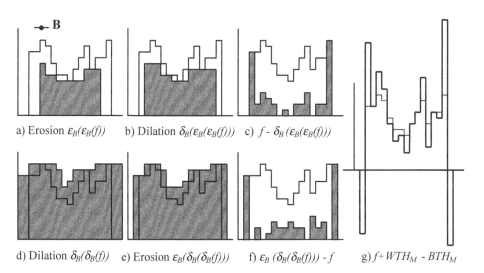

a) Erosion $\varepsilon_B(\varepsilon_B(f))$ b) Dilation $\delta_B(\varepsilon_B(\varepsilon_B(f)))$ c) $f - \delta_B(\varepsilon_B(\varepsilon_B(f)))$

d) Dilation $\delta_B(\delta_B(f))$ e) Erosion $\varepsilon_B(\delta_B(\delta_B(f)))$ f) $\varepsilon_B(\delta_B(\delta_B(f))) - f$ g) $f + WTH_M - BTH_M$

Fig.4 The modified *TopHat* transform results

6.   Architecture for Modified Multiscale TopHat Hardware Implementation in Virtex FPGA

Implementation of the proposed algorithm was tested on XESS XSV-800 prototype board [17]. Besides the Virtex 2.5V XCV-800 device, two independent blocks of SRAM were used as the video buffers, as well as SVGA and RS232 periphery devices. In the future work, the Media Access Controller project is planned to allow work with real cardioangiographic data over the LAN. So far, the simple 115 kbps UART was used to test the processing kernel. A video controller has been developed to visualise the enhanced image in the RS-343A standard. SVGA 800x600 mode was used with 60Hz vertical refresh rate and 40 MHz pixel clock.

Simulation framework is presented in figure 5. VHDL possibilities to integrate text files with the actual data were intensively used. The cardioangiographic DICOM CDROM data were read by the *Osiris* medical imaging software package [10]. Then single image frames were exported into the TIFF format. Further, the TIFF image was converted into the PGM text file format which clear for the behavioural SRAM video buffer VHDL model. After processing, the output video memory buffer, the VHDL behavioural SRAM model, stored the processed data in the output file. Finally, the comparison with the MATLAB data was made.

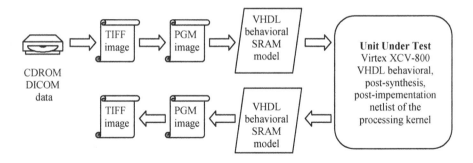

Fig.5 The simulation framework

The proposed architecture of the processing kernel is presented in figure 6.

To use logic resources and *BlockRAM* modules efficiently, the time multiplexing scheme in the computing path was designed. The processed image is divided into two half-planes: left and right. First, the left one is processed and the first delay lines unit is uploaded with 256 pixels from the left half-plane. Then the first erode/dilate stage performs its operation and the MUX0 unit uploads the main processing path (the lower) in such a way that the eroded and dilated pixels are mixed on time domain. Please, note that the pixel flow is doubled from this point. Then the second erode/dilate stage performs their job. The main processing path is now filled with double eroded/dilated pixels. Please, note also that when the dilation/erosion unit processes pixels for the main path to the next stage, the other one computes the Black/White TopHats to the upper path.

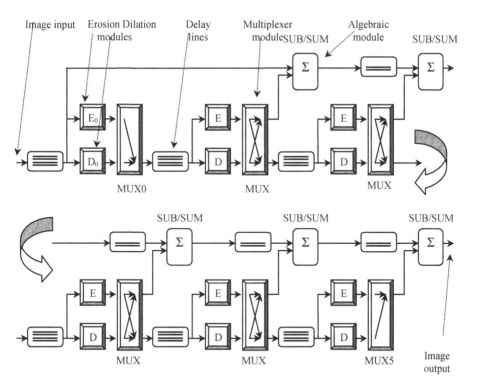

Fig.6 The modified multiscale TopHat transform kernel pipeline implementation

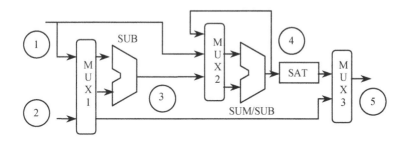

Fig.7 Algebraic module architecture

The algebraic module architecture is presented in figure 7. Presenting the signals in the circuit nodes explains its operation most efficiently. The point '1' is the original image multiplexed with calculated TopHat from the previous stage, whereas the point '2' corresponds to the input data from upper path from figure 6. The MUX1 module prepares the data for the WTH_{MOD} & BTH_{MOD} calculation according to (9) and (10). The point '3' is WTH_{MOD} & BTH_{MOD}. Please, note that due to (8) there is no need for saturation correction at this point. MUX2 together with SUM/SUB module performs addition $f + WTH_{MOD}$ and in the next cycle subtraction $(f + WTH_{MOD}) - BTH_{MOD}$ (point '4'). The SAT block corrects the optional pixel range correction. Finally, the

MUX3 mixes again the original image with just calculated TopHat for the next processing stage (point '5').

Processing image using half planes avoids extravagance in the application of Virtex *BlockRAM* modules and allows efficient logic resources utilisation. Also this way allows one data pass algorithm, which simplifying the memory management. The only additional cost is the requirement to process middle image columns twice due to the border effect.

Figure 8 presents a frame of the source data with its histogram and figure 9 presents the enhanced contrast image and its smoothed histogram by proposed modified TopHat transform. The vessels edge enhancement and overall visibility is noticeable and there is no "the block effect" like in the convolutional edge detection technique on the DICOM compressed image data.

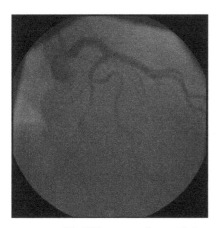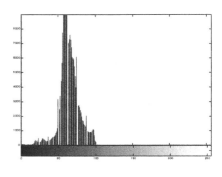

Fig.8 The source frame of the cardioangiography data with its histogram

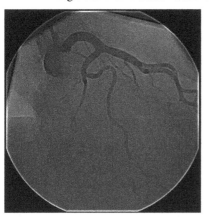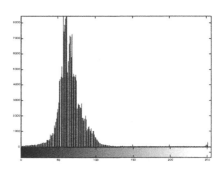

Fig.9 The processed frame and its histogram

7.   Conclusions and Future Work

The proposed architecture was successfully implemented on XESS XSV-800 prototype board. The processing kernel uses only 16 *BlockRAM* modules and 18% available slices from the XCV-800 chip which makes room for additional processing units. So far, the proposed algorithm was tested with the auxiliary serial 115kbits UART. In the future planned LAN interface will allow work with the full speed. Also, an integration a small microcontroller (Xilinx KCPSM is considered) will add the flexibility to the whole system.

The main data stream currently works well with 50 MHz clock. The processing time for one frame is about 11 ms, which is 25% the time allowed. This gives time for additional processing tasks which are also planned.

JBits tool suite is also considered as a very promising for adding the computational power to the reconfigurable hardware image processing platform.

Acknowledgements

This work was supported by Polish Committee of Scientifical Research (KBN) project number: 8 T11B 066 18. The author would also like to thank Aldec, Inc. for the AHDL Package donation, which made work possible.

References

[1]   Chaudhiri A.S., Cheung P.Y.K., Luk W., *A Reconfirable Data-Localised Array for Morphological Algorithms.* Proceedings of the International Workshop on Field-Programmable Logic and Applications, (FPL), Springer-Verlag 1997.

[2]   Coltuc.D, Pitas I., *Fast Runnig Max/Min Filters. .* Proceedings of the IEEE Workshop on Nonlinear Signal and Image Processing NSIP-95 Neos Marmaras, Greece

[3]   Dougherty E.R., Astola J. T., *Nonlinear Filters for Image Processing*, SPIE Optical Engineering Press, USA, 1999.

[4]   Gasteratos A., Andreadis I., *Non-linear image processing in hardware,* Pattern Recognition Vol. 33, 2000 pages 1013-1021.

[5]   Giardina Ch. R., Dougherty E.R., *Morphological Methods in Image and Signal Processing*, Prentice-Hall, Englewood Cliffs NJ, USA 1988.

[6]   Goren S., Balkir S., Dundar G., Anarim E., *Novel VLSI Architectures for Morphological Filtering. .* Proceedings of the IEEE Workshop on Nonlinear Signal and Image Processing NSIP-95 Neos Marmaras, Greece.

[7]   Haralick R. M., Shapiro L. G., *Computer and Robot Vision*, Addison Wesley Publishing Company, USA, 1992.

[8]   Jonker P. P., *Morphological Image Processing: Architecture and VLSI design*, Kluwer Technische Boeken B.V., Holland 1992.

[9]   Mukhopadhyay S., Chanda B., *A multiscale morphological approach to local contrast enhancement,* Signal Processing, Vol.80, 2000, pages 685-696.

[10] *Osiris ver* 3.6, University Hospital of Geneva. www.expasy.ch/UIN

[11] Pitas I., Venetsanopoulos A.N., *Nonlinear Digital Filters Principles and Applications,* Kluwer Academic Publishers, USA 1990.

[12] Schavemaker J.G.M., Reinders M.J.T., Gerbrands J.J., Backer E., *Image sharpeninig by morphological filtering,* Pattern Recognition Vol. 33, 2000, pages 997-1012.

[13] SDC Information Systems, *SDC Morphology Toolbox for Matlab 5 User's Guide, 2000.* www.morph.com

[14] Serra J., *Image analysis and mathematical morphology* Academic Press 1988

[15] Soille P., *Morphological Image Analysis Principles and Applications*, Springer-Verlag, Berlin Heidelberg, 1998.

[16] Woolfries N., Lysaght P., Marshall S., McGregor G., Robinson D., *Fast Adaptive Image Processing in FPGAs Using Stack Filters.* Proceedings of the International Workshop on Field-Programmable Logic and Applications, (FPL), Springer-Verlag 1998.

[17] X Engineering Software System Corporation. www.xess.com

[18] Xilinx *Data Book 2000.* www.xilinx.com

Demonstrating Real-time JPEG Image Compression-Decompression using Standard Component IP Cores on a Programmable Logic based Platform for DSP and Image Processing

Albert Simpson, Jill Hunter, Moira Wylie, Yi Hu, David Mann

Amphion Semiconductor Ltd., 50 Malone Road, Belfast, BT9 5BS, Northern Ireland, UK

http://www.amphion.com

Abstract. This paper describes the successful implementation of a hardware demonstrator for real-time JPEG standard colour image compression and decompression at picture refresh rates up to 25 frames per second using an FPGA-centric processing platform and design-reusable application-specific IP cores. The FPL device programming netlists for both JPEG encode and decode are directly derived from commercially available semiconductor Intellectual Property (IP Core) designs for Motion-JPEG applications; the target FPL devices form the core processing element in a commercial off-the-shelf recon-figurable module-based hardware platform for DSP and image processing applications. Performance metrics are presented for Xilinx Virtex and Altera APEX devices, and compared with semicustom ASIC implementations.

1 Introduction

The on-going deployment of multimedia-enabled communications systems for con-sumer, commercial, medical, aerospace and industrial applications has greatly facili-tated the opportunity to store, manipulate and render still images over local and wide area networks comprising imaging devices, personal computers, printers, worksta-tions, Internet appliances and mobile telephones. However, for optimised system per-formance these single images (or streams of images) must be compressed for storage and transmission. To date the most pervasive and successful compression standard is that developed by the Joint Photographics Experts Group (JPEG) in 1992 [1]. JPEG sets out the requirements and implementation guidelines for the encoding and decod-ing of continuous-tone still images, and for the coded representation of compressed image data for interchange between applications. (Note: the original JPEG standard has now been joined by the JPEG2000 standard, a wavelet-based image compression algorithm which addresses certain limitations of older JPEG standard and extends its applicability to newer forms of document and image manipulation).

The design of cost-effective JPEG systems for applications which demand high performance (for example, those capable of compressing full-frame colour input data at rates up to 25 frames per second) is normally a resource-consuming exercise across various engineering disciplines, including image processing theory, software engi-neering and integrated circuit systems design. For the JPEG ASIC designer, smaller

G. Brebner and R. Woods (Eds.): FPL 2001, LNCS 2147, pp. 441-450, 2001.

and smaller feature geometries (120nm and below) enable higher performance and very large scale designs capable of integrating whole systems (System-on-a-Chip or SoC technology). Developments in so-called System-level Integration [2] have also made a huge impact on the number of variables that need to be considered to make right-first-time design a commercially viable proposition.

It is becoming apparent that traditional design methodologies and conventional electronic design automation (EDA) systems in widespread use today are not quite capable of coping with the complexity silicon systems that wafer foundries are increasingly capable of fabricating. Additionally, the growth in chip complexity is coinciding with increasingly frantic pressures to reduce the time involved in developing new semiconductor based products. Accordingly, new methodologies are being sought that allow designers to fill the enormous capacity of new deep-submicron technologies and to reduce the time-to-market. These methodologies must cope with the migration of circuit designs from one implementation or fabrication technology to another.

The advent of so-called "Platform FPGA" technology and "System-on-a-Programmable-Chip" devices presents similar challenges to semiconductor and systems design engineers. However, as this paper goes on to suggest, the implementation of certain systems-on-silicon using high-density field programmable logic and third party application-specific Intellectual Property (IP cores) offers an attractive alternative to the semicustom ASIC approach.

The work presented in this paper is concerned with the development of a Motion-JPEG Encoder-Decoder (Codec) demonstrator system using IP Core based programmable System-on-a-Chip design technologies. This has been achieved through use of a hierarchical design methodology that combines custom-generated and off-the-shelf image processing Intellectual Property (IP Cores). The ease and rapidity at which the methodology is applicable to VLSI circuit design of this order complexity has been investigated; the design also involves the interfacing of pre-developed Verilog blocks with those purposely designed. The effort required to mix and match complex high-level blocks developed by different designers has been an important challenge. This is a key issue in the use of IP cores for SoC design.

To begin with, the underlying hierarchical design methodology for the system-level solution is introduced in Section 2. The overall architecture of the demonstration system follows in Section 3. A description of the structure and operation of the JPEG Encoder is then introduced. The performance of the demonstration system is discussed in Section 5 and contrasted with a range of JPEG IC solutions reported in published literature.

Finally Section 6 draws some conclusions about the merits of this demonstrator as a test vehicle for the evaluation of IP Cores using field programmable logic.

2   Design Methodology for System Level Solutions

It is becoming apparent that the design of complete video, image, speech and signal processing systems on a single chip will only become effective if complex building blocks are employed. This is generally known as the "IP-based approach to SoC design". One of the ways in which this can be achieved is through the use of more structured design methodologies that allow for the reuse of existing components and subsystems. It has been quantified that 70% of new designs correspond to existing components that cannot be reused because of a lack of methodologies and tools [4]. Accordingly, application-specific IP cores of the kind appropriate to image compression system implementation (MPEG-4, MPEG-2, JPEG, JPEG2000, etc) [5] must be designed for reuse in a modular design methodology. In such a methodology, hierarchies are used for decomposing a complex design into sub-parts that are more manageable. Regularity is also used to maximise the reuse of already designed components and subsystems.

Once a complex system has been decomposed into sub-parts, a design approach, based on reusable silicon IP cores, can be applied. This uses pre-designed, standardised and reusable IP cores that have been captured in various HDLs (VHDL, Verilog, etc). These are then combined to integrate circuitry from various sources on a single chip. Use of pre-designed IP functions and algorithms shortens the overall design cycle by many months, potentially reducing a two-year design cycle to six months or less [6]. Additionally their use minimises design risk as the designs have already been "taped-out", that is, proven in silicon.

Critical to the effective and sustained use of IP cores is their inherent deep reusability, that is their ability to migrate from one company's design environment to another, and from one process generation to another. The quality of the "intellectual property" encapsulated within the cores is also crucial. In order to facilitate high-level system design it is necessary to use architectures that can be optimised for specific applications. This is not simply a case of writing a high-level VHDL description of an algorithm. The IP cores must be designed for reuse at all levels in their design flow. Research has established that architectures that provide the best apparent implementations for specific designs are often not necessarily suitable for the broad levels of modularity and parameterisation required for automated synthesis and design reuse.

The underpinning process of directly mapping an algorithm such as JPEG into a VLSI architecture for later silicon implementation in ASIC or FPGA is still crucial in determining the overall system performance. This process of choosing an algorithm mapping for a particular application is often complex. Regularity, data interconnection and I/O requirements must all be considered to reach an optimal approach for a particular application. Additionally, the high-level design descriptions must also match exactly the required specification and be synthesisable. The code must also be structured and modular to enable reuse with minimal effort.

3   JPEG Demonstration System

3.1   Introduction

The complete system described in this paper is capable of demonstrating the operation and capabilities, when implemented in high-density field programmable logic device technology, of two complimentary IP cores for ISO standard Baseline JPEG image compression: the Amphion CS6100 JPEG Encoder core, and the Amphion CS6150 JPEG Decoder core. Both of these standard products are available in targeted-netlist formats as commercial off-the-shelf (COTS) application-specific virtual components (ASVCs) for a variety of commercial high-density FPGA devices and submicron semi-custom ASIC processes using industry-standard cell libraries.

The JPEG demonstration system is based on a PC plug-in card and is capable of displaying the decompressed images on a window on the PC. The real-time image input is supplied by television images in PAL format from a DVD player. The FPGA devices form the basis of a commercial off-the-shelf (COTS) reconfigurable computing platform for video processing developed and supplied by Nallatech [7]. This particular configuration of Nallatech's signal processing computing solutions is comprised of two PC cards, known as the Ballyvision and the Ballynuey, each with a single Xilinx Virtex device on board.

3.2   System Specification

The Nallatech DIME system (DIME = DSP and Image Processing Module for Enhanced FPGAs) choosen for the pupose of JPEG demonstration (Figure 1) comprises two standard boards: a Ballynuey board (Xilinx Virtex based single-slot PCI-based PC add-in board), and a Ballyvision DIME Module (add-on card for Ballynuey board), plus the requisite IP Cores for Motion-JPEG designed by Amphion.

- Ballynuey - Virtex based PCI card for DSP and Image Processing: The PCI add-in card embeds a single Xilinx Virtex XCV800 (BG432A, Speed Grade 6). A data processing interface card to the PC, also containing the Amphion JPEG CS6150 Decoder core and a Block-to-Raster (RTB) Convertor core.

- Ballyvision - Analog Video I/O DIME Module: This add-on (97mm x 59.5mm) module card for the Ballynuey Virtex based PCI board comprises: a single Xilinx Virtex device; Brooktree Bt829A Video Decoder ASSP converting composite PAL video to YCrCb data; a bank of Fujitsu SDRAM. The Ballyvision was programmed with Amphion's Raster-to-Block Convertor core and CS6150 Encoder core. The Xilinx device is Virtex XCV800 (BG432A, Speed Grade 6). The clock speed for JPEG encoding is set to 25-MHz.

- PC with PCI card slot for the above.

3.3   Architecture Overview

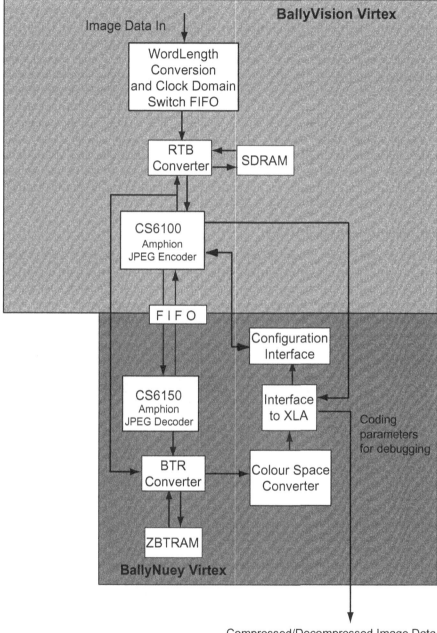

Fig.1. Amphion JPEG demonstrator system block diagram

3.4 System Operation

In operation, image data in the form of PAL video output from a consumer DVD player source arrives through a Brooktree Video Decoder ASSP on the Ballyvision FPGA in 8-bit YcrCb format as Cb,Y,Cr,Y. This data is collected as a 32-bit word and stored in an asynchronous FIFO. The Raster-to-Block (RTB) convertor reads this data and stores it in SDRAM. The RTB stores two fields of the image in separate locations in the SDRAM. When requested by the CS6100 the RTB supplies blocks of image data to the CS6100. The CS6100 compresses the image and stores the compressed data in a fifo. The Xilinx Virtex on the Ballynuey PCI board reads the compressed image data to the JPEG Decoder. This is then block-to-raster converted and colour-space converted and read back to the PC through the PCI interface. The original image data is also read by the Ballynuey board and displayed on the PC for comparison. The GUI used to display the compressed/decompressed image allows manipulation of quantisation table scaling and bit rate control parameters.

3.5 Data Ordering and MCUs

The image processing system will process the data in 4:2:2 block order, where a block is a group of 64 samples from a colour plane. Each PAL image will have dimensions of 768*288 and in 4:2:2 format the Y plane will consist of 96*36 blocks and each of the Cb and Cr planes will consist of 48*36 blocks. The data will be input to the CS6100 and output from the CS6150 in a series of MCUs, where an MCU consists of a 4 blocks of samples as show below:

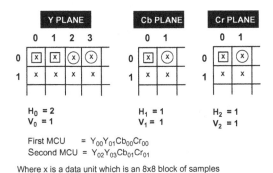

Fig.2. 4:4:4 Interleaved Format Image

3.6 Raster-to-Block Convertor and Colour-Space Convertor

The Raster-to-Block Convertor reads the image data from the Asynchronous FIFO and stores it in the SDRAM. The data is stored in dual Ping-Pong buffers with each buffer holding a field of the image. It then supplies the data to the CS6100 as requested. For decoding, the data is block-to-raster converted using ZBT RAM, and colour-space converted on the Ballynuey PCI board.

3.7 PCI Interface

The PCI interface provides the main interface between the application and the image processing system. It provides three functions:

- It allows the image data to be read back to the PC for display.
- It allows configuration data to be passed down to CS6100.
- It provides a general register interface, allowing reading from and writing to the various control registers in the design for control and debugging purposes.

The configuration data is downloaded from the PC through the PCI interface on the Ballynuey's Xilinx Virtex device.

4 JPEG Circuits

4.1 JPEG Encoder Architecture

The Amphion-designed JPEG Encoder core circuit (Figure 3) combines the JPEG encoder functions - Run-Length Coder (RLC), Huffman Encoder, and Data Packer - and those specifically designed (DCT and quantization).

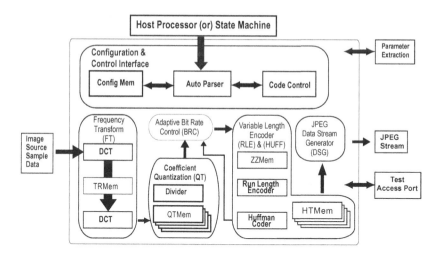

Fig.3. Amphion CS6100 JPEG Encoder system block diagram

The encoding starts by partitioning the input image into non-overlapping blocks of 8x8 pixels. These input pixel values are then converted from unsigned integer format to signed integer and the transform is achieved by applying a 2D 8-point DCT [8] to each 8x8 tile. For each image the algorithm is performed from left to right and from top to bottom.

The next stage is to quantize each frequency component emerging from the transform using a 64-element quantization matrix. This reduces the amplitude of the coefficients and increases the number of zero-value coefficients. After quantization, the values are further compressed through a run-length encoder (RLE) using a special zig-zag pattern designed to optimise compression of like regions within the image. Final compression is achieved within the Huffman encoder.

The circuit configuration is performed via the configuration data port using a standard JPEG data stream, without the entropy coded data or restart marker included. After reset, the configuration stream containing the Huffman tables, quantization tables, restart interval definition and frame header is fed to the port byte by byte. Upon receiving the last byte of the header, the circuit enters the entropy-coding state. The input image data is then fed in via the input data port. The circuit automatically performs bit and byte stuffing and restart maker insertion for entropy coded data, and combines it with the configuration JPEG data to form a complete JPEG data stream. After completion of the encoding of a scan, the table and frame definitions remain and by sending in another scan header, the core can start to encode the new scan.

4.2 JPEG Decoder Architecture

The JPEG Decoder architecture mirrors that of the encoder:

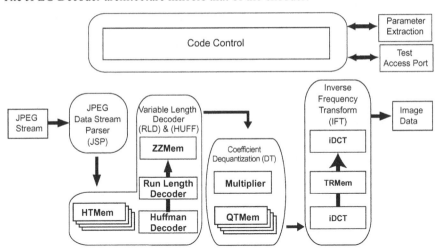

Fig.4. Amphion CS6150 JPEG Decoder block diagram

5   JPEG Encoder Performance Comparisons

Table 1 compares the performance obtained for the Nallatech-supplied on-board Xilinx Virtex FPGA against those expected for other Xilinx Virtex-E and Virtex-II devices, plus a comparison for a similar implementation using an alternative programmable logic device architecture from Altera. In performance terms, both the JPEG Encoder and JPEG Decoder core are capable of processing full-colour frames at PAL or NTSC rates. The JPEG Encoder is also within the tolerance limits laid down in the Encoder Test Compliance Procedures [1]. Additionally, each of the constituent blocks has been functionally verified using specified ISO reference data.

Table 1. Amphion CS6100 JPEG Encoder implementations in Xilinx and Altera.

Vendor Part No.	Performance MSa/sec	Logic	Memory	Clock Rate MHz
Demo System: Xilinx Virtex XCV800	25	4460 Slices	8 BlockRAM	25 (37 possible)
Xilinx Virtex-E XCV600e-8	46	4461 Slices	8 BlockRAM	46
Xilinx Virtex-II XCV	70	3413 Slices	5 BlockRAM	70
Altera EP20K300E-1X	40	9246 LEs	17 ESBs	40

Table 2. JPEG Encoder IC designs reported in past literature

Author [Reference]	Area mm^2	Gate Count + Memory	Clock Rate MHz	Power mW
Amphion [Xilinx]	n/a	4500 Slices 8 BlockRAM	25	Not reported
Asada et. al. [Asad 97]	125 (0.5 µm)	200 kgates + 38k RAM	17.5	500 mW
Okada et. al. [Okad 97]	54 (0.6 µm)	70 kgates 17 k RAM	18	400 mW
Kovac and Ranganathan [Kova 95]	168 (1.0 µm)	n/a	100	Not reported

Table 2 shows that Amphion's JPEG implementation in FPGA compares favorably against JPEG IC designs reported in past literature. A team from Hitachi [9] has developed a low-power JPEG Codec that is also capable of performing MPEG compression and decompression; despite its physical area it has impressive processing rates for the area/power characteristics. A single 70-kgate Motion-JPEG Codec chip has been developed by Okada et al [10] at Sanyo; this chip can compress and decompress VGA-size (640x480) JPEG images at a rate of 30 frames/second - again with low power dissipation. Kovac and Ranganathan [11] have also presented a single-chip VLSI IC design for implementing the Baseline JPEG image compression standard; they developed a highly efficient pipelined architecture which permits a fast system clock rates and allows for data processing rates up to that specified for HDTV.

6   Conclusion

The aim of this development project was to demonstrate the attainable performance, design flexibility, and ease of system integration of reusable IP cores for a demanding real-time image processing applications when targeted at high-density FPL devices. The use of a set of this complex user-parameterisable IP cores for Motion-JPEG aptly demonstrates the feasibility, scope and power of design reuse at the system level. In summary then, an approach to FPL design was evaluated which allows for the timely implementation of systems-on-silicon efficiently, predictably and rapidly to meet performance, cost and time-to-market requirements. The project helped to validate the following:

- real-time Motion-JPEG image processing using FPL technology
- applicability of IP Cores to rapid "System-on-a-Programmable-Chip" design
- FPL technology as a platform for reconfigurable computing

The authors wish to thank Malachy Devlin of Nallatech Limited for his assistance during the course of this project.

References

1. ISO 10918 (ISO/IEC) "Digital Compression and Coding of Continuous Tone Still Images (JPEG)"
2. Institute for System Level Integration (ISLI), Livingston, Scotland, UK. URL http://www.sli-institute.ac.uk
3. J.McCanny, D.Ridge, Y.Hu, J.Hunter "Hierarchical VHDL Libraries for DSP ASIC Design" ICASSP 1997, pp 675 -678
4. A.Jerraya, H.Ding, P.Kission, M.Rahmouni "Behavioural Synthesis and Component Reuse with VHDL" Kluwer Academic Publishers, 1997
5. V.Bhaskaran, K.Konstantinides "Image and Video Compression Standards" Kluwer Academic Publishers, 1997
6. D.Bursky, "Accelerating system designs by leveraging Intellectual Property", Microelectronics Design, Vol. 2, No. 1, Feb 1998
7. Nallatech Limited: "DIME - The Module Standard for FPGAs" URL http://www.nallatech.com
8. J.Hunter, J.McCanny "Rapid Design of Discrete Cosine Transform Cores" IEE Colloquium (Digest), 1998, No.197, pp.5/1-5/6
9. SK.Asada, H.Ohtsubo, T.Fujihira and T.Imaide, "Development of a low-power MPEG1/JPEG Encode/Decode IC" IEEE Transactions on Consumer Electronics, Vol.43, No.3, August 1997, pp. 639-644
10. S.Okada, Y.Matsuda, T.Wantanabe and K.Kondo "A single chip motion JPEG codes LSI" IEEE Transactions on Consumer Electronics, Vol.43, No.3, August 1997, pp. 418-422
11. M. Kovac and N.Ranganathan "JAGUAR: A fully pipelined VLSI architecture for JPEG image compression standard" Proc. IEEE, Vol.83, No.2, Feb 1995, pp.247-258

Design and Implementation of an Accelerated Gabor Filter Bank Using Parallel Hardware

Nikolaus Voß and Bärbel Mertsching

University of Hamburg, Department of Computer Science, IMA Lab
Vogt-Kölln-Straße 30, 22527 Hamburg, Germany
{voss,mertsching}@informatik.uni-hamburg.de
http://ima-www.informatik.uni-hamburg.de

Abstract. In computer vision, images are often preprocessed by the so-called Gabor transform. Using a Gabor filter bank, an image can be decomposed into orientational components lying in a specified frequency range. This biologically motivated decomposition simplifies higher level image processing like extraction of contours or pattern recognition. However, the IEEE floating-point implementation of this filter is too slow for real-time image-processing, especially if mobile applications with limited resources are targeted. This paper describes how this can be overcome by a hardware-implementation of the filter algorithm.
The actual implementation is preceded by an analysis of the algorithm analyzing the effects of reduced-accuracy calculus and the possibility of parallelizing the process. The target device is a Xilinx Virtex FPGA which resides on a PCI rapid-prototyping board.

1 Introduction

1.1 Convolution Filters

Gabor filters are a subtype of convolution filters. This means that the filter results are obtained by a discrete cyclic convolution. Using quadratic images with N pixels per axis the filter-response is obtained by

$$P'_{mn} = \sum_{m',n'=0}^{N} W_{m'n'} \, P_{m-\frac{N}{2}+m',n-\frac{N}{2}+n'}, \tag{1}$$

where $W_{m',n'}$ is the amplitude of the two-dimensional filter-mask at (m',n') and the dimension of the filter is the dimension of the image. The indices $(m-\frac{N}{2}+m', n-\frac{N}{2}+n')$ of the original image are defined modulo N. This operation with N^2 multiplications and additions has to be carried out for each pixel P'_{mn} in the filtered image, so it has a time-complexity of M^2, where $M = N^2$ is the total amount of pixels of the image. For a typical image of 256×256 pixels, this yields $4.3 \cdot 10^9$ additions and multiplications. Even a 1 GHz microprocessor capable of doing one multiplication or addition per clock-cycle would need almost 10 seconds to perform such an operation, which is far from real-time.

G. Brebner and R. Woods (Eds.): FPL 2001, LNCS 2147, pp. 451–460, 2001.
© Springer-Verlag Berlin Heidelberg 2001

1.2 Fourier Space Convolution

The common method of reducing the computational cost of the above operation (1) is to perform the convolution in Fourier space where it boils down to a simple, element-wise multiplication with linear time-complexity:

$$p * w = \mathcal{F}^{-1}\{\mathcal{F}\{p * w\}\} = \mathcal{F}^{-1}\{\mathcal{F}(p)\,\mathcal{F}(w)\} \tag{2}$$

The transformation into Fourier space and back is done with a COOLEY-TUKEY-type algorithm which has a complexity of $O(n \log_2 n)$. Using a radix-4 algorithm, the number of operations for the above convolution can be reduced to $7.1 \cdot 10^6$ operations. This already is a reduction by three orders of magnitude. It is important to say that only 20% of the operations are cost-intensive multiplications, compared to 50% in (1). By defining a filter bank consisting of multiple filters in frequency space, the overall number of operations can be further reduced significantly as only one forward transformation has to be done.

1.3 Gabor Filters

In 1946, D. GABOR published a paper [4] in which he shows that the effective width of a function in direct space multiplied with the effective width of the same function transformed into Fourier space has a lower limit:

$$\Delta x \Delta k \geqslant a \tag{3}$$

This is a consequence of the mathematical relation of a function and its Fourier transform (cf. Heisenberg's uncertainty relation in physics).

Gabor further proved that a family of functions ("Gabor functions") satisfy the above time-bandwidth uncertainty relation at the lower limit. These functions consist of a Gaussian distribution multiplied with a complex oscillation:

$$g(x) := \frac{1}{\sqrt{2\pi}\sigma}\, e^{-\frac{x^2}{2\sigma^2}}\, e^{jk_0 x} \qquad \text{(one-dimensional)} \tag{4}$$

These functions are usable in digital image processing because if features of an image lying in a specific frequency range and orientation shall be extracted, using a Gabor filter as two-dimensional band-pass will yield an optimal resolution in both time and frequency domain. Further, biological research suggests that the primary visual cortex performs a similar orientational and Fourier space decomposition [5], so this approach seems to be sensible for a technical vision-system.

In our lab, a Gabor filter bank developed by R. TRAPP is used [8] for preprocessing camera images. The used two-dimensional Gabor function is defined as follows:

$$g(\boldsymbol{x}) := \frac{1}{2\pi\sigma_x\sigma_y} \exp\left(\frac{1}{2}\,{}^t\boldsymbol{x}\mathbf{A}\boldsymbol{x} + j\,{}^t\boldsymbol{k}_0\boldsymbol{x} \right), \tag{5}$$

The matrix $\mathbf{A}$ contains the orientation ϕ of the filter relative to one image-axis in form of the rotational matrix $\mathbf{R}$ and the variance-parameters σ_i of the two-dimensional Gaussian distribution in the positional matrix $\mathbf{P}$:

$$\mathbf{A} = \mathbf{R}\mathbf{P}^t\mathbf{R} = \underbrace{\begin{pmatrix} \cos\phi & -\sin\phi \\ \sin\phi & \cos\phi \end{pmatrix}}_{\mathbf{R}} \underbrace{\begin{pmatrix} \sigma_x^{-2} & 0 \\ 0 & \sigma_y^{-2} \end{pmatrix}}_{\mathbf{P}} \underbrace{\begin{pmatrix} \cos\phi & \sin\phi \\ -\sin\phi & \cos\phi \end{pmatrix}}_{{}^t\mathbf{R}} \qquad (6)$$

k_0 is the modulation-frequency which, analogous to the biological model [5], is oriented parallel to the longer axis of the Gaussian function.

The transfer function is obtained by Fourier transformation:

$$G(k) = \exp\left\{ -\frac{1}{2}{}^t(k - k_0)\,{}^t(\mathbf{A}^{-1})(k - k_0) \right\} \qquad (7)$$

It is only real-valued, what saves computational effort concerning multiplications in frequency space. Figure 1 shows two filter sets generated with the above equation (7).

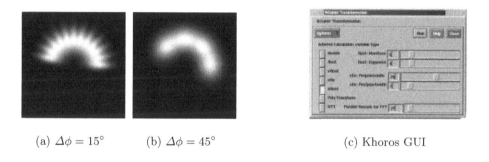

(a) $\Delta\phi = 15°$ (b) $\Delta\phi = 45°$ (c) Khoros GUI

Fig. 1. (a) and **(b)** show example filter sets. Gabor filter sets in Fourier space generated with equation (7). **(a)** has an angular resolution of 15 degrees. This gives 12 filters to cover all orientations. The matrix $\mathbf{P}$ in equation (6) is chosen in such way that the Gaussian distributions in (5) overlap at $\frac{1}{2}$. **(b)** shows a filter set with an angular resolution of 45 degrees resulting in 4 filters. Again, we have chosen an overlap of $\frac{1}{2}$, which results in a much broader distribution. **(c)** is part of the "Khoros" GUI for C++-implementation. The I/O-specific part present in every Khoros-"Glyph" and some other controls are not shown. The visible controls specify the used bit-width and the transform-method. Additionally, the number of parallel execution-threads can be specified.

2   Algorithm Analysis

For efficient hardware-coding, the algorithm had to be carefully analyzed. It was especially necessary to determine a minimal bit-width for the internal calculation variable-type and to find a suitable numerical representation.

Due to the large number of additions, two-dimensional filtering requires a rather big dynamic range; so the question was, if it was better to use a floating-point representation for the variables as opposed to a less complex fixed-point representation.

To answer these questions, a quality measure, which allows the comparison of the filter responses calculated with different accuracies, was developed. A Gabor algorithm prototype was implemented in C++ in such way that classes with different number representations could be plugged in at runtime to compare the different configurations. This way, in addition to the number representations, various algorithms for two-dimensional Fourier transform were evaluated for an efficient hardware implementation. The whole test-bench was embedded into the "Khoros"-System for image processing [6] (Fig. 1).

2.1   Quality Measure

To compare images filtered with different accuracies, a formula derived from a stereoscopic similarity-measure [8] was taken as base and then adapted to our needs:

$$\rho_{mn}(\boldsymbol{x}) = \frac{w_{mn}(\boldsymbol{x}) * [h_{mn}(\boldsymbol{x})l_{mn}^*(\boldsymbol{x})]}{\sqrt{w_{mn}(\boldsymbol{x}) * |h_{mn}(\boldsymbol{x})|}\sqrt{w_{mn}(\boldsymbol{x}) * |l_{mn}(\boldsymbol{x})|}} \tag{8}$$

h and l represent the two images to be compared. w is a two-dimensional symmetric Gaussian distribution; by doing a convolution with this function, a local environment is taken into account, which is necessary because of the quantization noise of the images. The denominator scales the result to a range between zero and one. Thus the resulting image is a 2D local correlation giving a measure for the similarity of the images. To obtain a scalar value for comparison, the median of all pixels is calculated (denoted with G in all figures).

2.2   Floating-Point Number Representation

Experiments were done using a floating-point C++-class ($xfloat$) which has the bit-widths of the fraction and exponent as parameters. Figure 2 shows the results. It turned out that for acceptable results at least a 5 bit fraction and a 6 bit exponent was needed. The high number of bits for the exponent shows the need for a high dynamic range due to the great number of arithmetic operations. However, the complexity of a hardware-implementation of floating-point arithmetic is much higher than for fixed-point arithmetic.

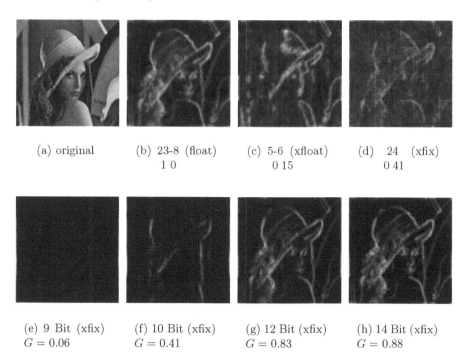

(a) original

(b) 23-8 (float)
1 0

(c) 5-6 (xfloat)
0 15

(d) 24 (xfix)
0 41

(e) 9 Bit (xfix)
$G = 0.06$

(f) 10 Bit (xfix)
$G = 0.41$

(g) 12 Bit (xfix)
$G = 0.83$

(h) 14 Bit (xfix)
$G = 0.88$

Fig. 2. Filtering results. The filtering was done using 12 filters with $\Delta\phi = 15°$. All bands are added and the real-part of the filter-response is shown. Image (**b**) was computed using 32 bit IEEE floating-point numbers. In a float number representation 6 exponent- and 5 fraction-bits are necessary for acceptable results (**c**), the not-rescaled fixed number representation needs 24 bits (**d**). Images (**e**)-(**h**) are results of the rescaling ("block-float") algorithm. The images were generated using a rescaling fixed-point radix-4 FFT. After each of the four stages for a 256-point transform, the two least significant bits were truncated off the intermediate result.

2.3 Fixed-Point Number Representation

First, a simple fixed-point number representation with variable bit-width was tested. As expected, due to the high dynamic range of the 2D Fourier transform, as high a bit-width as 24 bits was needed to obtain acceptable results (see Fig. 2).

To reduce this number, we experimented with rescaling the intermediate results within the transform algorithm. This method is commonly referred to as "block-float"-calculation. We tested different algorithms and rescaling points and factors. The best compromise for an FPGA implementation turned out to be a row-column algorithm based on a radix-4 decimation-in-frequency FFT. After each of the four stages for a 256-point radix-4 FFT the intermediate result was rescaled by a factor of four, i.e. the two least significant bits were cut off.

We got usable results already with 10 bits; using 14 bits the resulting image was hardly distinguishable from the IEEE float filtered image (see Fig. 2). Figure 3 shows the quality measure dependent on the bit-width. It saturates to a value of about 0.9 instead of 1. This is because of value-overflows in the algorithm as the value range is $]-1;1[$, independent of the bit-width. Due to the high number of additions, there might be absolute values above unity which then are set to the maximal representable value.

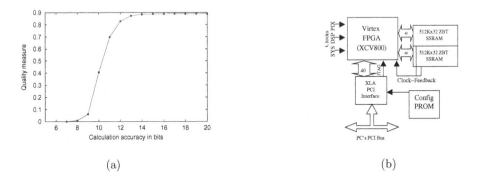

(a) (b)

Fig. 3. (a) Quality vs. computational effort. The diagram shows the results of the quality measure dependent on the bit-width of the variables using a "block-float" number representation. As it can be seen, the quality saturates to a value of about 0.9 for more than 13 bits. This is due to the occurrence of overflows in the algorithm. **(b)** FPGA environment. This is the part of the Ballynuey2 rapid-prototyping system used for the implementation of the Gabor filter bank.

2.4 Fourier Transform Algorithms

For a fast hardware-implementation it is necessary to use an algorithm which can be partitioned into concurrent execution threads. As the routing resources on a FPGA are limited, it is especially useful to have a straightforward structure of the algorithm, as with complex structures, the possible clock for the chip will dramatically decrease. For the Gabor filter implementation, we had to find an algorithm which is a good compromise between scalability, a simplicity of structure and its overall computational complexity.

Considering 2D Fourier transform algorithms, the simplest and at the same time best parallelizable algorithm is the simple row-column method, which reduces the 2D problem to a conventional 1D problem:

$$F_{kl} = \sum_{n=0,m=0}^{N-1} f_{nm}\, \omega_N^{nk}\, \omega_N^{ml} = \sum_{n=0}^{N-1} \left[\sum_{m=0}^{N-1} f_{nm}\, \omega_N^{ml} \right] \omega_N^{nk} \tag{9}$$

Although there are methods with much lower computational complexity (see e.g. [3] for a good overview), this algorithm is very easy to implement on a FPGA. The 1D FFT can be implemented using one of the commercially or non-commercially available cores.

Even in 1D, there are a lot of algorithms available. The most popular with respect to a good complexity/performance ratio is the so called split-radix FFT which is a combination of the well-known radix-2 and radix-4 FFTs [7]. A commercially available FFT-core using this method is the Jaguar-core from Drey Inc. [2]. It is capable of doing a 256-point FFT in 256 clock-cycles and has a block float number representation with up to 32 bits.

However, studies implementing this core with a a word-width of 16 bits on the Virtex FPGA show that its structure is too complex for an FPGA implementation as the resulting clock is disappointingly low (about 16 MHz on our lowest speed-grade device). Another drawback is the high resource consumption (about 60% of our XCV800).

Compared to this, the 16 bit fixed-point FFT from the Xilinx Core-generator consumes only 17% of the device and runs at 55 Mhz. It is based on a single radix-4 dragonfly and does a 256-point FFT in 768 clock-cycles but uses much less memory than the Jaguar core. This makes it possible to use two of these cores and thus double the throughput.

Compared to the Jaguar core we have an overall throughput that is more than two times greater with less resources usage although the core uses a less efficient algorithm (about 8% more multiplications).

3 Implementation

3.1 Target Hardware

The filter was implemented using the rapid-prototyping PCI FPGA interface-card Ballynuey2 of Nallatech Inc.. It is equipped with a Xilinx Virtex XCV 800 FPGA and 4 MB fast on-board ZBT-RAM organized in two 32 bit wide memory-banks. The Virtex is linked to the host's PCI bus using an additional FPGA as glue-logic (Fig. 3).

The design was implemented using the VHDL hardware description language on a register-transfer level. Synthesis was done with the FPGA Compiler II from Synopsys.

The software front-end was implemented in C++ and does the format conversion from float to fixed-point and controls the chip through a simple instruction set (see below).

3.2 Block-Scheme of the Design

Figure 4 shows the block-scheme of the design. For an efficient and fast implementation, we used the 16 bit fixed-point FFT provided by Xilinx via the Core-generator, which runs at 55 Mhz. A problem was that the Xilinx FFT is

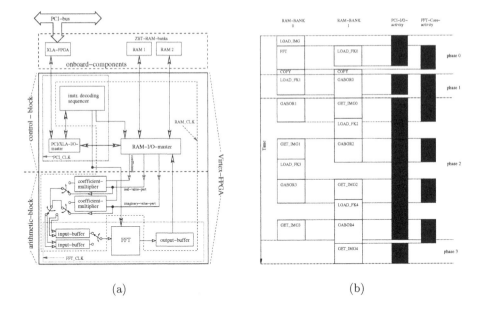

(a)   (b)

Fig. 4. (a) Block-scheme of the hardware implementation. The upper part shows components external to the Virtex FPGA. The upper block (control-block) decodes the instructions from the host and controls the arithmetic block below. The number of arithmetic blocks is scalable; in our design, two such blocks were used. The dashed lines limit different clock domains; to maximize the performance, the design uses three different clocks. **(b)** Timing-scheme of the design. The first two columns show the activity of the RAM banks. Column three shows transfer activity on the PCI bus, column four activity of the arithmetic units. In continuous operation (phase 2) the throughput of the filter bank is limited by the PCI bus transfer-rate.

based on a radix-4 unit, but it rescales with a factor of 2^4 rather than 2^2. To implement the proper rescaling, the EDIF-file delivered by the Core-generator had to be patched accordingly. To maximize the performance, two FFT-Cores were used, which were operated in an interleaved mode (Fig. 4).

Like the FFTs, the coefficient-multipliers were also implemented using the Core-generator. It is a high throughput pipelined type, in our design running at 80 Mhz.

3.3   Application Flow

The host controls the Gabor core using a simple instruction set. Instructions can be transfered to the chip via the host's PCI bus and are decoded in the controller unit of the chip. We have defined instructions to load the image/coefficients into the RAM, to read back the result to the host and to reset the core.

As can be seen from Fig. 4, in continuous mode (phase 2) Gabor coefficient matrices are loaded into the prototyping board and results are transfered into the host's RAM in turn without wait-states, so the throughput of the system is limited only by the PCI transfer-rate (which is assumed to be 80 MB/s net-data). This is achieved through the interleaved operation mode of the two RAM banks of the system; in the start- and stop-phase, when only one bank is used, there are some idle times of the PCI bus.

3.4   Resource Usage

Table 1b shows the resource usage of the components on the Virtex XCV800 FPGA. The whole design including the I/O-master for the data-transfer takes up about 60% of the available slices. It could be reduced to 40% if only one arithmetic unit was used.

3.5   Comparison with Other Chips

Although we have not found any direct hardware-implementations of Gabor filters, there are some chips which can do two-dimensional convolutions. For comparison we also list Chips that can only do one-dimensional FFTs. Additionally, one multi-purpose (ADSP-21061 from Analog Devices) and one FFT-accelerated DSP (DSP-24 from DSP Architectures Inc.) is listed. The DSP-24 is a hybrid chip, it contains a dedicated FFT-processor; that is why it performs much better than the general-purpose DSP (Tab. 1a).

3.6   Conclusion

The comparison shows than only the DoubleBW FFT-chip is faster than our Gabor-core but its design is far more resource-intensive. Additionally, it needs an external controller FPGA. The general design of the other ASICs, i.e. the high bit-width of the FFT, results in a rather slow operation compared to our core, which has the smallest bit-width. Our device is fast enough for real-time applications as it delivers 20 frames/s for 12-band and up to 130 frames/s for single-band filtering.

4   Summary

Beginning with the classification of the algorithm, a complete hardware implementation cycle for an important image-processing operation has been described. Considering different algorithms and number representations, a minimal data-word length has been determined.

An interesting result is that with appropriate rescaling, fixed-point arithmetic with a surprisingly small word-length could be used to obtain very good results. This justifies the development of a specialized system for mobile and low-power

Processor	Bit	Type	Clock (MHz)	1D FFT (μs)	2D conv. (ms)	12 bd. (ms)
Programmable DSPs						
ADSP 21061	24	float	50	115	120.6	768
DSP-24	24	block	100	5.2	7.4	59.1
ASICs						
Spiffee [1]	20	fix	173	7.5	—	—
DoubleBW	24	float	128	2.6	3.5	27.15
Spitfire [9]	32	block	66	20	13	156
Gabor-Core	16	block	55/80	7.0	7.2	46.8

(a)

Component	Clock (MHz)	Slices
Controller	40	840
RAM I/O-master	80	280
PCI I/O-master	40	691
2 Xilinx FFT cores	55	3286
4 multipliers	80	672

Overall slice usage: 5769 of 9408

(b)

Table 1. Comparison with other chips and resource usage of design subcomponents

applications as a significant resource-reduction in comparison with standard-components can be achieved. On the other hand, this fact also enabled us to use highly optimized off-the-shelf components for some hardware design-components (the 16 bit fixed-point FFT-Core and the high-speed pipelined multipliers from the Xilinx Core-generator) what led to a very time- and performance-efficient FPGA-implementation of the filter-operation.

References

1. B.M. Baas. A 9.5 mw 330 μs 1024-point fft processor. Technical report, Department of Electrical Engineering, Stanford University, 1995.
2. Drey Inc. *Jaguar 256 Interface Specification.*
3. P. Duhamel and M. Vetterli. Fast fourier transforms: A tutorial review and a state of the art. *Signal Processing*, (19):259–299, 1990.
4. D. Gabor. Theory of communication. *Journal of the Institute for Electrical Engineers*, 93:429–439, 1946.
5. J.P. Jones and L.A. Palmer. The two-dimensional spectral structure of simple receptive fields in cat striate cortex. *Journal of Neurophysiology*, 58(6):1187–1211, December 1987.
6. K. Konstantinides and J. R. Rasure. The khoros software development environment for image and signal processing. *IEEE Transactions on Image Processing*, 3(3):243–52, 1994.
7. H. J. Nussbaumer. *Fast Fourier Transform and Convolution Algorithms.* Springer Verlag, Berlin, 1981.
8. Ralph Trapp. *Stereoskopische Korrespondenzbestimmung mit impliziter Detektion von Okklusionen.* Ph.d. thesis, Universität-GH Paderborn, 1998.
9. Matthias Wosnitza. A high precision 1024-point fft processor for 2d convolution. In *International Solid-State Circuits Conference (ISSCC)*, San Francisco (CA), feb 1998.

The Evolution of Programmable Logic: Past, Present, and Future Predictions

Bill Carter

Xilinx Inc.
2100 Logic Drive
San Jose
CA 95124
U.S.A.

Abstract. Programmable logic is one of the fastest growing segments of the total digital logic market, and it is forecast to be one of the fastest growing segments going forward. This paper traces the history of programmable logic from its surprising roots in memory circuits, where small PROMs were used to implement simple combinatorial logic functions, to the multi-million gate FPGAs that are available today. It will also make some predictions about the future of programmable logic and the role it will play in the complex digital systems that will appear in the next five to ten years.

G. Brebner and R. Woods (Eds.): FPL 2001, LNCS 2147, pp. 461–461, 2001.

Dynamically Reconfigurable Cores

John MacBeth and Patrick Lysaght

Dept. Electronic and Electrical Engineering
University of Strathclyde
204 George Street
Glasgow, G1 1XW
United Kingdom
Fax: +44 (0) 141 552 4968
j.macbeth@eee.strath.ac.uk

Abstract. Dynamic reconfiguration of digital circuits on FPGAs has been an area of active research for the past decade. The identification of generic classes of circuits that would benefit from being dynamically reconfigured remains a key, open problem. We report on an investigation of the application of dynamic reconfiguration to programmable, multi-function cores (PMCs). An abstract analysis of the technique is included to emphasise the generality of the methodology. Empirical results for a case study involving a universal asynchronous receiver and transmitter (UART) are presented. We show that significant improvements in area efficiency and the operating speeds of the circuits are achieved. Furthermore, the results indicate the potential for reducing the power consumption of the circuits.

1.   Introduction

Dynamic reconfiguration of FPGAs has been actively researched for the last decade. During this time several interesting applications of dynamic reconfiguration have been reported [1 - 8]. Despite this progress, the identification of generic classes of circuits that would benefit from being dynamically reconfigured remains a key, open problem. This paper reports on an investigation to establish a class of circuits whose performance can be improved by the use of dynamic reconfiguration. We refer to the class of circuits as programmable, multi-function cores (PMCs). This is a broad category of circuits that includes devices such as UARTs, PCI controllers, CRT controllers and USB controllers. Each PMC is, in effect, capable of implementing a whole set of circuits. The control registers of the PMC are programmed at run-time to select the particular circuit that is required by the application. At any given time the PMC implements one particular element of its set of circuits. Consequently the PMC architecture is highly redundant.

When the target technology for the PMC is a mask programmed ASIC, we have one level of redundancy. However, when the target technology for the PMC is an FPGA, then two levels of redundancy are apparent: the inherent redundancy of the FPGA and the redundancy of the PMC. In effect, we configure the PMC onto the FPGA at compile-time and we configure the function of the PMC on the FPGA at run-time.

G. Brebner and R. Woods (Eds.): FPL 2001, LNCS 2147, pp. 462-472, 2001.
© Springer-Verlag Berlin Heidelberg 2001

The essence of the technique adopted in this work is to remove one level of redundancy by implementing only one element of the set of PMC circuits on the FPGA at any time. When a change in function is required, a new element of the set is dynamically reconfigured on to the FPGA. This approach is viable because changes in function occur infrequently. Moreover, relatively long reconfiguration latencies can be tolerated because changes are typically initiated by human intervention. For example in the case of the UART adopted as a case study in this work, a user may select to change the parity of the transmission protocol from even to odd. This would typically happen infrequently when connecting to a new service and the user would be tolerant of delays of several hundred milliseconds.

The benefits of the dynamically reconfigurable designs are that they are considerably smaller than the PMCs of which they are elements and can operate at higher speeds. They also have the potential to consume less power. The area advantage may not initially seem important given the increasing size of FPGAs. However, for high-volume applications it is essential to use the smallest possible FPGA to be able to compete effectively against mask-programmable ASICs. In a system-on-chip (SoC) application, several PMCs can potentially be replaced, thus multiplying the area advantage. Moreover, in SoC designs, we expect that an embedded host CPU will be responsible for reconfiguring the dynamic circuits. Thus the need for a separate controller is obviated. The trend toward such systems is already established with products available from several vendors [9-11].

The dynamically reconfigurable design approach is not without its disadvantages. Clearly the configuration of each of the circuits that the PMC can implement must be stored elsewhere in the system. The most obvious trade-off is between external non-volatile memory and FPGA size. In terms of silicon area, and hence ultimately cost, it is preferable to store inactive designs in cheaper non-volatile memory. In the future it may be that for some networked applications, the external configurations can be stored on a remote server, in the way that printer drivers are often managed today.

The remainder of this paper is organised into five sections. In section 2 we present an abstract analysis of our approach using set theory. This serves to define the terminology that has been adopted in later sections and to emphasise the generality of the approach. Section 3 introduces the UART. It describes the approach adopted in creating the fully programmable UART and the dynamically reconfigurable circuits. The results of implementing the fully programmable UART and the most complex of the dynamically reconfigurable designs are presented. In section 4, the results are analysed. The results of further work to determine the precise sources of the area reductions are also reported. The opportunities for future work are outlined in section 5. Section 6 concludes the paper.

2.   PMC Analysis

We said previously that the PMC implements a set of circuits. We instantiate an element of this set by programming the control registers of the PMC at run-time. We refer to the PMC set (that is the programmable multi-function core set) as simply the core set and denote it by C. The set C can be partitioned into two subsets. The first subset is the set of circuits controlling PMC programmability, denoted by P. The second is the set of circuits that realise the application functionality, denoted by A. Instead of implementing the PMC directly we will implement each element of A individually. If there are n distinct permutations of the application functionality that can be programmed at run-time in the original PMC, we obtain n distinct circuits. Each of these n circuits can be dynamically reconfigured on to the FPGA but cannot in itself be programmed via control registers at run-time. If we denote each individual circuit by c_i, the application set A is equal to the union of all n circuits, that is:

$$A = \bigcup_1^n c_i \qquad (1)$$

The union of circuits needs to be interpreted carefully. Each individual circuit c_i realises a subset of the functionality of the core set C. Any pair of arbitrary circuits c_i and c_j can be distinguished from each other because they implement different subsets of C. We interpret the union of the pair of circuits c_i and c_j as the combination of the functionality implemented by circuits c_i and c_j, with common functions and their associated circuitry included only once. Note that this interpretation implies the ability to identify and compare the particular circuitry within circuits that corresponds to specific functionality. This operation is significantly more complex than the traditional comparison of netlists.

We assume that there is a function *sizeof* which takes a circuit c_i as its argument and returns the area of that circuit. The *sizeof* function imposes a total ordering on the set A. We are especially interested in the circuit that has the largest area, that is c_{max}, which is defined by the following property:

$$sizeof(c_{max}) = \max(sizeof(c_i)), \quad i = 1 \cdots n \qquad (2)$$

Note that for the purposes of this discussion c_{max} need not be unique. Figure 1 summarises the relationship between the sets C, P, A, and the element c_{max}.

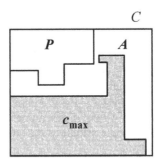

Fig. 1. PMC Components

The area reductions that are achieved with the dynamically reconfigurable designs derive from the removal of the programmable circuits and the simplification of the application circuits. The latter component has an upper bound, which corresponds to the difference between the application set A and the element of A with the greatest area, that is c_{max}. The area reduction, R, can therefore be expressed as:

$$R \geq sizeof\left(P+\left(A-c_{\max}\right)\right) \tag{3}$$

This reduction is guaranteed for all application circuits. For the simpler circuits it is routinely exceeded. The circuits that form the elements of the application set A, are sets in their own right since they correspond to netlists of logic components and their associated nets. The intersection of all the circuit elements is called the static circuitry, and denoted S:

$$S = \bigcap_{1}^{n} c_i \tag{4}$$

The static circuitry corresponds to that circuitry which is present in all of the elements of the application set. If we assume that PMCs are typically deployed with a host CPU, then all PCMs and every dynamically reconfigurable circuit associated with set A will use a common bus interface to communicate with the host CPU. Hence S is typically a non-empty set. The largest area that has to be reconfigured is given by:

$$\max(reconfig.\ area) = sizeof\left(c_{\max} - S\right) \tag{5}$$

When reconfiguring one circuit instance c_i to become c_j, the common static circuitry need not be reconfigured. This approach has the potential to reduce reconfiguration latency and to decrease the amount of external storage required for reconfiguration bitstreams. At the logical design level, we are proposing that the static circuitry will be designed once and subsequently instantiated structurally during the design of the sets of which it is a common component. At the physical level, it implies that the footprint of the static circuitry is fixed.

3. UART Case Study

The block diagram of the UART is shown in Figure 2. The architecture is based on the 16550 UART that became the *de facto* standard with PCs [12].

The processor interface on the left of the diagram shows separate write and read busses because multiplexed buses are used to implement the interface on the FPGA. Modem status registers are coloured grey and unused bits in the control and status registers are shown in black. Figure 2 corresponds to the full PMC or equivalently the set C introduced in section 2.

Our goal now is to identify and remove the elements of the set P. Then the circuit that has the largest area $c_{\max}$ must be identified and the set of application circuits, A, must be simplified to $c_{\max}$. Completing these transformations will allow us to determine the extent of the area reduction with the dynamically reconfigurable design. For the UART, $c_{\max}$ corresponds to the circuit required to implement simultaneous transmission and reception with full buffering on both channels. In addition interrupts and full modem control must be enabled. Figure 3 depicts $c_{\max}$. All of the unnecessary circuits associated with programmability are also removed in this diagram.

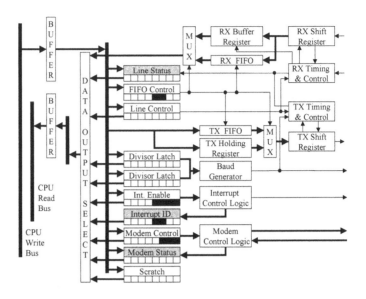

Fig. 2. UART Block Diagram

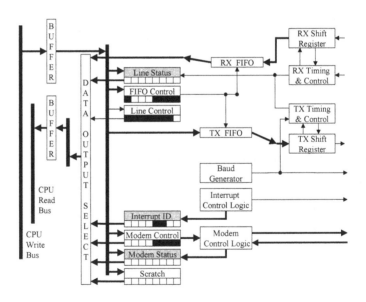

Fig. 3. The circuit with largest area, c_{max}

The UART was designed as a parameterised VHDL program. The code parameters can be adjusted to generate the fully programmable UART or any of the non-programmable circuits corresponding to individual modes of operation of the fully programmable core. The benefit of this approach is that the synthesis tools are used to automatically optimise each of the many individual circuits. We synthesised, placed, and routed the UART and c_{max}, the circuit with largest area, for both the Xilinx Spartan II and Xilinx Virtex II FPGA families. The Spartan device family is not dynamically reconfigurable while there is some uncertainty about the exact support for dynamic reconfiguration in the Virtex II family. For this study, we decided to ignore these issues and proceed as though both were dynamically reconfigurable. The goal was to use state-of-the-art FPGAs to report the most meaningful results and comparisons to the design community. The floorplans for the fully programmable UART and c_{max} on the Spartan II are shown in Figure 4.

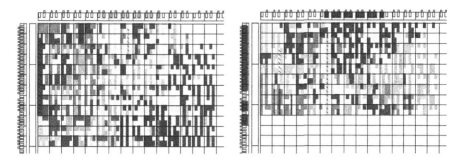

Fig. 4. UART (left) and c_{max} (right) on the Xilinx Spartan II

Each square in the floorplans in Figure 4 represents a single configurable logic block (CLB) comprising four, four-input look-up tables (LUTs) and four flip-flops. The floorplans for the same circuits on the Virtex II are shown in Figure 5. The larger squares consisting of two-by-two, smaller squares represent a single Virtex II CLB. These CLBs consist of eight, four-input (LUTs) and eight flip-flops. The vertical stripe in the floorplans corresponds to the Virtex II's block select RAM which is not used in either of the circuits.

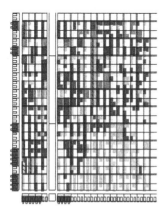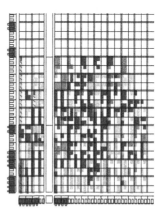

Fig. 5. UART (left) and c_{max} (right) on the Xilinx Virtex II

The floorplans clearly show the anticipated reductions in area. Note that c_{max} is the circuit with largest area, so the results for c_{max} correspond to the worst-case results. All the non-programmable circuits corresponding to other UART modes offer larger area reductions. Table 1 compares the performance of the four circuits in terms of CLBs, LUTs, flip-flops, nets and connections. These figures were produced by the Xilinx place and route tools. For ease of comparison the entries for c_{max} include an extra column that shows the percentage reduction relative to the figures for the fully programmable UART.

Table 1. Comparison of resource utilisation and maximum operating speeds of the four circuit implementations

	SPARTAN II FPGA			VIRTEX II FPGA		
	PMC UART	c_{max}		PMC UART	c_{max}	
Flip-flops	300	241	19.67%	300	241	19.67%
Nets	642	482	24.92%	864	650	24.77%
Connections	2,559	1,856	27.47%	2,930	2,153	26.52%
CLBs	175	133	24%	89	70	21.35%
Slices	346	264	23.7%	349	263	24.64%
LUTs	564	395	29.96%	549	377	31.33%
Max. Speed MHz	30.8	42.1	36.7%	51.4	58.6	14.05%

4.   Interpretation and Analysis of Results

The number of flip-flops used by the UART and c_{max} are independent of target FPGA as one would expect and show a reduction of almost 20%. The numbers of nets and hence connections are clearly more dependent on the architecture of the target FPGA and the CAD tool algorithms. The consistency of the percentage reductions of 24.92% and 24.77% for nets and 27.47% and 26.52% for connections, for the Spartan II and Virtex II respectively, is noteworthy. The reduction in the number of CLBs is greater for the Spartan II case. Remember however that the Virtex II CLB is approximately twice the size of that of the Spartan II CLB. The discrepancy can be accounted for by noting that the finer granularity of the latter results in fewer CLBs being partially used and hence included in the count. To support this argument a row showing the usage of Virtex II "slices", where these are defined as one quarter of a Virtex II CLB is also included. This produces a percentage reduction of 24.64%, which is much closer to the figure, obtained for the Spartan II. Finally, the Virtex II architecture requires slightly fewer LUTs than the Spartan II for both the fully programmable UART and c_{max}. The reverse is true for nets, leading us to suggest that improved routing in the Virtex II architecture allows more efficient use of LUTs under certain circumstances. The percentage reductions are the highest figures yet at

29.96% and 31.33%. Of all the six metrics, the figure for CLBs is used as the estimate of area, that is for the Xilinx devices the function *sizeof* returns the number of CLBs used. Hence the worst-case reduction with the worst-case circuit is 21.35%.

From the last row of Table 1, we note that the Virtex II implementation is much faster. We assume that the main reason for the speed improvement is that it is implemented with smaller silicon process geometries and has more layers of metal than the Spartan II. The relative speed improvements for the Spartan II and Virtex II are 36.7% and 14.05% respectively.

To increase our understanding of the results, we repeatedly synthesised c_{max} for the Spartan II architecture, but for each synthesis run we enabled one distinct programmable feature. For example as Figs. 3 and 4 show the transmit and receive datapaths in c_{max} have replaced a programmable option that allows the user to select between a single data register and a FIFO with a hardwired FIFO. The first of our synthesis re-runs reinstates the programmable FIFO/register option in the design. We then proceeded to measure the cost of this programmable option by recording the increase in the number of LUTs and flip-flops. Table 2 lists the results for the six most significant options ordered according to cost.

Table 2. Effects of programmable options on Spartan II implementation

UART Feature	Number of LUTs	Number of Flip-flops
Programmable FIFO/Register	40	23
Programmable speed	34	20
Programmable wordlength	42	3
Programmable parity	18	4
Programmable interrupts	13	5
Programmable loopback	5	1
Total:	152	56

We have also calculated the sum of the costs of turning all the individual options on. When these figures are added to the cost in LUTs and flip-flops of c_{max} implemented on the Spartan II (395 and 241 respectively) we get 547 and 297 respectively. These figures correlate well with the cost in LUTs and flip-flops for the fully programmable UART, namely 562 and 300 respectively.

So far our discussions have concentrated on the relationships between c_{max} and the fully programmable UART. The UART has several hundred modes of operation, even millions, if each transmission speed is treated as a separate mode. A clear disadvantage of our method is that we need a separate circuit for each mode, that is we need a distinct circuit and corresponding bitstream for each element of the PMC set. One proposal for combating this weakness is to change the strategy of implementing every element individually to one of selectively implementing subsets of circuits. Note that we are obliged to delimit an area equal to $sizeof(c_{max})$ of the floorplan irrespective of what circuit we are actually implementing, since the user may request c_{max} to be loaded at any time. This area is often large enough to permit us to implement a subset of the PMC set, in effect a programmable UART of restricted functionality. We will denote such a subset by C_i and observe that provided the following inequality holds

$$sizeof(c_{max}) \geq sizeof(C_i) \qquad (6)$$

we can implement any appropriate subset of the PMC set. For example, we can configure the UART with the programmable FIFO/register option disabled so that the transmit and receive channels each have a single buffer register in their datapaths. We then define a subset of circuits, C_{alpha}, with respect to this configuration by making all the other UART features, such as speed and wordlength, programmable. After synthesising C_{alpha} we find $sizeof(C_{alpha})$ equals 194 flip-flops and 356 LUTs which is comfortably within the constraints of 241 flip-flops and 395 LUTs imposed by $sizeof(c_{max})$. This technique of identifying an arbitrary subset, C_i, of the PMC whose area is less than that of the largest single element can be applied repeatedly to reduce the total number of circuits and bitstreams while preserving the area reductions.

5.   Future Work

Our results have proven that even under worst-case conditions the dynamically reconfigurable UART core has 21% fewer CLBs than the fully programmable UART. Future work will extend these results to other cores. The first candidate will be an IrDA controller [13]. The IrDA PMC has been selected because it is a superset of the UART core with greater redundancy. This arises because the UART output is modulated to produce one of a number of possible IrDA protocols. The effect of the increase in the number of mutually exclusive protocols is to increase the size of the P set and the size of the set difference $A-c_{max}$. Consequently, we expect that the dynamically reconfigurable IrDA controller will exhibit even greater reductions than those reported for the UART case study.

In [14], IBM engineers report some of their experiences of deploying hard, soft and firm cores in SoC ASIC design. In one example, they replace a single large hard core for a PCI controller with a smaller hard core and several soft cores. In addition to reducing floorplan congestion, the change allowed them to optimally select at compile-time the exact PCI functionality to include for particular applications. This reduced the area of the PCI core by approximately 35%. We anticipate that these reductions can be replicated and extended with a dynamically reconfigurable PCI core.

With 25% fewer LUTs, flip-flops, interconnections and ports the dynamically reconfigurable UART should consume less power. We need to correlate these reductions with the relevant levels of switching activity to estimate accurately the power reductions. We also need to consider the software running on the host CPU and the effect of the increased activity on the reconfiguration port. The latter has the potential to offset any improvements unless reconfiguration is infrequent. Finally, we defined the static set S and noted that it is a non-empty set for all PMCs with internal bus interfaces. We have not yet exploited this property to reduce the size of the reconfiguration bitstreams.

6. Conclusions

The principal contribution of this paper has been to establish that programmable multi-function cores constitute a generic class of applications that benefit from dynamic reconfiguration under certain conditions. The nature of these conditions has been described and an abstract analysis of the general technique has been presented. The results of the UART case study quantify the reductions in area at greater that 21% for all modes. Meanwhile, a simultaneous increase of 14% in maximum operating speed has also been recorded.

Directions for future work include extending the number of case studies, quantifying the potential for low power operation, and exploiting the non-empty static set to reduce the size of configuration bitstreams.

7. Acknowledgement

The authors would like to thank the reviewers for their generous help in improving the paper. This work was funded in part by the SHEFC RDG grant 850 "Design Cluster for System Level Integration", with the support of the UK Engineering and Physical Sciences Research Council (Award number 98316997) gratefully acknowledged.

8. References

[1] P. W. Foulk, "Data-folding in SRAM Configurable FPGAs", in IEEE Symposium on Field Programmable Custom Computing Machines, K.L. Pocek and J. Arnold (Eds.), pp 163 - 171, Los Alamitos, California, April 1993

[2] P. Lysaght, J. Stockwood, J. Law and D. Girma, "Artificial Neural Network Implementations on a Fine-Grained FPGA", in Field Programmable Logic and Applications, R. Hartenstein, M. Z. Servit (Eds.), pp 421 - 431, Prague, Czech Republic, Sept. 1994

[3] G. Brebner and J. Gray, "Use of Reconfigurability in Variable-length Code Detection at Video Rates", in Field Programmable Logic and Applications, W. Moore and W. Luk (Eds.), pp 429 - 438, Oxford, England, Sept. 1995

[4] M. J. Wirthlin and B. L. Hutchings, "DISC: The Dynamic Instruction Set Computer", in Field Programmable Gate Arrays (FPGAs) for Fast Board Development and Reconfigurable Computing, J. Schewel (Ed.), Proc. SPIE 2607, pp 92 - 103, Philadephia, PA, USA, Oct. 1995

[5] H. Eggers, P. Lysaght, H. Dick and G. McGregor, "Fast Reconfigurable Crossbar Switching in FPGAs", in Field Programmable Logic and Applications, R. Hartenstein and M. Glesner (Eds.), pp 297 - 306, Darmstad, Germany, Sept. 1996

[6] W. Luk, N. Shirazi, S. Guo and P.Y.K. Cheung, "Pipeling Morphing and Virtual Pipelines", in Field Programmable Logic and Applications, W. Luk, P. Cheung and M. Glesner (Eds.), pp 111 - 120, London, England, Sept. 1997

[7] A. Donlin, "Self-modifying Circuitry – A Platform for Tractable Virtual Circuitry", in Field Programmable Logic and Applications, R. Hartenstein and A. Keevallik (Eds.), pp 199 - 208, Tallinn, Estonia, Sept. 1998

[8] G. McGregor and P. Lysaght, "Self Controlling Dynamic Reconfiguration: A Case Study", in Field Programmable Logic and Applications, P. Lysaght, J. Irvine and R. Hartenstein (Eds.), pp 144 - 154, Glasgow, Scotland, Aug. 1999

[9] Triscend Corporation, "Triscend A7 Configurable System-on-Chip Family", Datasheet, www.triscend.com, Aug. 2000

[10] Altera Corporation, "ARM-Based Embedded Processor Device Overview Data Sheet", www.altera.com, Sept. 2000

[11] Xilinx Inc., "IBM and XILINX to Create New Generation of Integrated Circuits", Press Release, www.xilinx.com/prs_rls/ibmpartner.htm, July 2000

[12] National Semiconductor Corporation, "PC16550D UART with FIFOs", Datasheet, www.national.com/pf/PC/PC16550D.html, June 1995

[13] Texas Instruments Inc., "TIR2000 Data Manual: High-Speed Serial Infrared Controller With 64-Byte FIFO", Data Manual, June 1998

[14] A. M. Rincon, C. Cherichetti, J. A. Monzel, D. R. Stauffer and M. T. Trick, "Core Design and System-on-a-Chip Integration", in IEEE Design & Test of Computers, Volume: 14 Issue: 4, pp 26 - 35, Oct. - Dec. 1997

Reconfigurable Breakpoints for Co-debug

Tim Price[1] and Cameron Patterson[2]

[1] Xilinx Inc., 720 Spadina Ave. Suite 509, Toronto, Ontario M5S 2T9, Canada
Tim.Price@xilinx.com
[2] Xilinx Inc., 2300 55th Street, Boulder, CO 80301, USA
Cameron.Patterson@xilinx.com

Abstract. Over the last decade, a large effort has gone into researching the use of FPGA devices for co-processing. Much of the emphasis of this work has been in the area of design entry tools. As FPGA co-processing moves into the mainstream, tools to support the complete design and implementation process are being more actively investigated. In particular, the ability to perform integrated hardware / software co-debug in these environments is of interest. One key element of FPGA co-processing is system synchronization and clock control. Today, some commercially available FPGA co-processing systems contain simple clock control such as single- and multi-stepping. Others have no clock control whatsoever, offering only a free-running system clock. In this paper a set of Reconfigurable Hardware Breakpoint cores is described. These cores are used to provide the control necessary for co-debug in FPGA co-processing systems and can be used to trace the flow of a circuit at run-time or control its operation. Reconfigurable hardware breakpoint cores are independent of circuit board clock implementation and are shipped as part of the JBits^{TM} Software Development Kit as Run-Time Parameterizable (RTP) Cores.

1 Introduction

A considerable amount of research has been done in debug of reconfigurable systems [1,2], yet little has been done on debugging hardware/software co-designs [3,4,5] (co-debugging). Hardware/software co-debug is difficult because they are inherently separate tasks. Once the hardware portions have been sectioned, the circuits are described with an HDL and then verified using hardware simulators. Meanwhile the original application is written with a high level language and debugged with another system. Work has been done so that both the circuit and the application are written in one common language [8,6,7] yet debug tools are still lagging. Many FPGA hardware board manufacturers [9] have tried to keep debugging features—such as readback and programmable clocks with single-multistep capability—in mind. However, in some cases, there is no standard for how the clock stepping features are implemented.

This paper presents reconfigurable breakpoint cores and their usefulness in co-debug of hardware/software co-designs, verification of IP cores and tracing circuits. The cores do not rely on implementation of clock support by board makers and were built using the JBits tool suite from Xilinx. It takes only a few extra lines in a JBits Java application to implement these cores into a design.

G. Brebner and R. Woods (Eds.): FPL 2001, LNCS 2147, pp. 473–482, 2001.
© Springer-Verlag Berlin Heidelberg 2001

2   Background

Debugging hardware and software is currently done on many levels. Both have breakpoints, or the ability to control program/design flow. When a program is compiled in a certain way, debug support can be added or turned on. There are also tools that simulate and emulate hardware. This section provides a background for debugging techniques and how they, and some new ones, are applied to FPGA devices.

2.1   Reconfigurable Computing Systems

Reconfigurable computing systems use FPGA devices as data co-processors. Typical reconfigurable computing systems are as shown in Figure 1. Reconfigurable computing applications are represented in a high-level language and once validated, partitioned into sections that will run on a standard microprocessor or FPGA co-processor.

Verification of the reconfigurable computing application can simply be done with simulators and standard high level language debuggers. Once the application has been split into its hardware (FPGA co-processor) and software (standard microprocessor), the debugging environment changes. In this combined hardware/software co-design domain, tools are lacking as far as co-debugging is concerned.

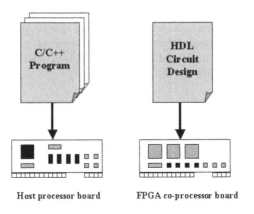

Fig. 1. Typical reconfigurable computing system model.

2.2   Debugging

In software, an invaluable tool for debuggers is the ability to insert breakpoints to control the flow of a target program. The target program executable is usually required to be compiled with special compiler options to enable debugging. There are many commercial-off-the-shelf debuggers and IDEs available.

Table 1. Virtex Hardware Manufacturers and Type of Hardware Debug Supported

Virtex Board Maker	Board	Readback	Clock Step	XHWIF
Alpha Data Parallel Systems, Ltd.	ADCRC1000^{TM}	X	X	
Annapolis Micro Systems Inc.	Wild^{TM}			
Celoxica	RC1000PP^{TM}	X	X	X
Compaq	Pamette^{TM}	X	X	X
Mirotech	Black Magic^{TM}	X	X	
Nallatech, Ltd.	BallyNuey^{TM}	X		
SEVITS Technology	FatBaby-XL^{TM}	X	X	
SLAAC	SLAAC1V^{TM}	X	X	X
The Dini Group	DN2000K10^{TM}	X		
Virtual Computer Company	Virtual Workbench^{TM}			
XESS Corp.	XSV^{TM}	X	X	X

This technique exists in the hardware domain and many microprocessors come with debug circuitry included. For example, the debug unit of the Intel XScale^{TM} Architecture [10] uses hardware breakpoints and a trace history buffer for output to debug programs. When this unit is activated, device operation can be traced and controlled.

Hardware A key part of debugging reconfigurable computing systems is the ability to get circuit state information. It is paramount to have the capability to readback circuit state and configuration information from the FPGA device. Circuit state information can also be used by simulators such as the Modelsim HDL Simulator [11] to *fast forward* the hardware simulation. This cuts down the simulation time by limiting simulation to a subcircuit of the original design and a small range of clock cycles. The state data is obtained by readback of the FPGA device. Circuit simulation is a useful tool but it is not able to deal with real-time events.

Debugging of FPGA devices is system board dependent. It is in the best interest of FPGA board manufacturers to implement a thorough debugging environment complete with readback and full clock control, but the reality is quite different. Table 1 surveys some Xilinx Virtex^{TM} FPGA board manufacturers (obtained from Optimagic) and the availability of debug features (including implementation of the JBits XHWIF^{TM} hardware interface). A debugging solution that does not rely on hardware clock control would be most beneficial.

ChipScope The ChipScope ILA^{TM} tool [12] inserts debug cores into Verilog or HDL code and connects them to the internal buses and signals to be traced. The design is synthesized, placed and routed using the Xilinx implementation tools. The bitstream is downloaded, and can be analyzed through the ChipScope software, with or without a system level logic analyzer. If FPGA designs are thought of as software programs, this is very similar to the way software debugging is done. When a design is compiled in a certain way, debug units can be added.

JHDL JHDL [13,7] is a set of Java class libraries with circuit simulation and configurable computing machine (CCM) runtime support. Its design browser serves both as a simulation and execution debugging tool. Hardware control is provided through a hardware application program interface (API) from the board vendor. This API performs such runtime operations as setting the clock frequency, stepping the clock, loading configurations, etc.

2.3   JBits

The JBits tool suite is a set of Java classes that provide an API into the configuration bitstream for the Xilinx Virtex family of FPGA devices. All configurable resources in these devices can be individually programmed using this interface. RTP Cores are logic cores that are constructed and instantiated with parameters that are defined at run-time [14]. These circuits can be configured and reconfigured based on information supplied in real-time by user software, user input or sensor data. All of the tools in JBits interface to hardware and hardware simulators via the XHWIF interface. This interface provides portable access to Virtex hardware and simulation environments. Typically, applications can be moved to different platforms without recompilation.

With the JBits API, the typical reconfigurable computing system (see Figure 1) is reduced to the environment in Figure 2. The key difference here is that one program, written in Java, can both run on the host microprocessor and control FPGA resources. This program can modify entire or partial bitstreams out of the FPGA board in response to real-time data.

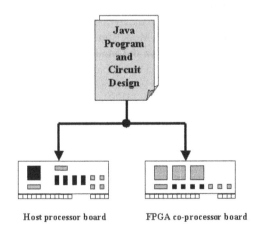

Fig. 2. JBits reconfigurable computing system model.

Verification of JBits applications is still in development, and not much research has been done on co-debug of hardware/software designs. The BoardScope^{TM} graphical debugger supports the single- and multiple-stepping of the system clock and interactive probing of FPGA resources. It also displays RTP Core layout information as well as graphical and waveform state data.

3   Reconfigurable Hardware Breakpoints

During development of an image processing application, it became obvious that more control over the FPGA clock was necessary. Single-stepping the system clock was intolerably slow. It was thought that circuit processing could be sped up by controlling the clock on the chip. This section will describe the types of reconfigurable breakpoint cores that have been implemented.

3.1   Operation

The goal was to control the system clock of the FPGA device and have it turn on and off as required. A resettable one-shot clock breakpoint core was implemented with a parameter that tells it how many clocks cycles to let through. Figure 3 shows the desired result with a parameter of n after a system reset. *Clk In* represents the system clock of the FPGA. It can be free-running or single-stepped and is therefore independent of the board vendor. *Clk Out* pulses for exactly n cycles and then deasserts. *Enable Out* is a signal that can be used to enable another circuit. It remains high for n signals and then deasserts. Upon a reset, the circuit starts controlling the clock once more.

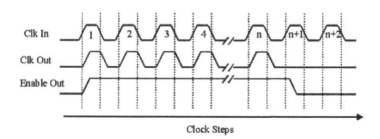

Fig. 3. Timing diagram showing the operation of a clock gate (n cycles).

3.2   Design

The programmable one-shot clock breakpoint core is an RTP Core with a run-time parameter of n, the number of clock cycles to pass. Figure 4 shows the basic blocks of the core. Each block is itself an RTP Core. The constant core has a value equal to the number of clock cycles. The counter simply counts the number of system clocks that have occurred. The outputs of these two cores are fed into the subtracter whose output is in turn fed into a wide OR gate. The output of the wide OR gate will be zero only when the constant and counter match up, otherwise it is a one. Note that a wide AND circuit could have been used just as effectively. The control of the output signals is done by a finite state machine. This FSM will let the output clock pulse for exactly *n* cycles and then disable it. Only upon a reset will the output clock be enabled again.

The state machine that controls the output is composed of three smaller FSMs, two of which are transition detectors. The transition detectors spot passages from zero-to-one and one-to-zero. They are comprised of a flip flop for state and a LUT for the detection functionality. The third FSM present simply inspects the transition detector states and decides to enable or disable clock gating.

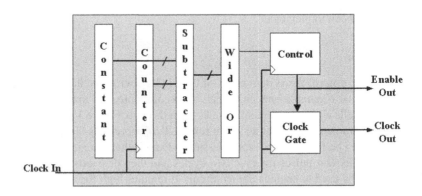

Fig. 4. Schematic diagram of a one-shot programmable clock breakpoint core

This core is three Configurable Logic Blocks (CLBs) wide and has a height in CLBs commensurate with the number of clock cycles to pass (*n*). Equation 1 shows how the height varies with *n*.

$$Height(CLBs) = (ceil(log_2(n+1)))/2 . \tag{1}$$

The global clock converter core produces, on regular routing lines, a clock signal output with the same frequency as the source clock from a global clock line (see Figure 5). It uses two flip flops and three LUTs. The flops are controlled by the global clock and are each triggered by a different clock edge. The outputs of the flops, once inverted, are fed back to the inputs. The new clock is the XOR function of the flop outputs.

4   Debugging Examples

There are many uses of a programmable clock breakpoint core. Like ChipScope ILA, circuits can be reconfigured with debug units. The time required using the JBits tool flow is of the order of seconds as opposed to minutes. Using Run-Time Reconfiguration (RTR), the number of clock pulses allowed may be changed dynamically. This permits for flexible debugging environments. Hardware breakpoints and the BoardScope debugger provide an effective debug environment for IP verification.

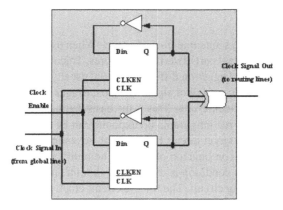

Fig. 5. Schematic diagram of a global clock to regular routing core

4.1 Co-debug

Debugging is done separately in most reconfigurable computing systems (see Figure 1). Software can be verified and hardware can be simulated. However, a dynamic recon-figurable computing platform (see Figure 2) poses a different situation. Here the re-configurable application and the hardware description are both written in Java. The application runs on a standard microprocessor yet it has direct control over the FPGA hardware and may reconfigure circuits dynamically. Systems may include soft micro-processors running on the FPGA hardware. Co-debugging this combined hardware and software design is largely unexplored. A framework that supports co-debugging exists in the JBits tool suite. JBits applications have distinct advantages to current co-debug methods:

- RTP Cores are parameterizable at run-time.
- RTP Cores can be inserted to a design with a minimum of overhead (as opposed to synthesizing, mapping, placing and routing designs).
- Partial and full run-time reconfiguration of devices is supported.
- The XHWIF interface supplies control over system resources (loading configura-tion bitstreams, clock control, etc.).
- All of the above capabilities are driven from one executable.

This begs the question, how does one debug a JBits application? Or better yet, how does one co-debug a JBits application? One might be tempted to use a standard Java debugger. This approach however does not take into consideration the hardware aspect. Combining the use of a standard Java debugger with a hardware debugger is better but does not account for the reconfigurability of hardware. The goal is to be able to control software and the hardware circuit. The control of hardware can be done with reconfigurable hardware breakpoints. Reconfigurable breakpoints and tracers can be inserted into the design with a minimum of overhead.

4.2   Tracing

Tracing circuits capture a sequential flow of events. When used to track the operation of a core, they are an important part of verifying IP cores. Tracing circuits are non-intrusive and can be configured to trigger on different criteria, usually some combination of output signal states or the rise of fall of signals. Once a trigger is hit, outputs are recorded for a certain number of clock cycles. This is the basis behind ChipScope ILA.

Figure 6 shows how reconfigurable breakpoints can be used in tracing circuits. In such a system there is a target circuit to be traced. A comparator or trace enabler circuit takes as input some combination of the target circuit's input or output signals (not shown). Once the trigger condition is met, the breakpoint circuit is enabled and tracing begins through the tracing circuit. The tracing circuit clock is driven by the breakpoint gate. Certain output or input signals (not shown) of the target circuit are latched every clock gate cycle and stored in memory.

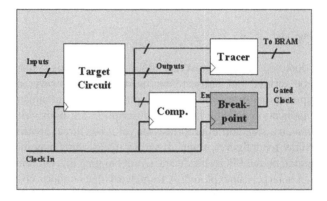

Fig. 6. Tracing using reconfigurable breakpoints.

While a tracing circuit is not innovative in and of itself, the fact that the debug circuitry can be reconfigured at run-time is novel. JBits cores are run-time parameterizable and JBits applications provide an entry way to the hardware. It would be quite simple to build a tool to perform logic analysis based on these cores. In fact, the basic FSM cores have been implemented as part of the clock gating circuit, a zero-to-one and a one-to-zero transition detector (see Section 3.2).

5   Conclusions and Future Work

Reconfigurable hardware breakpoint cores provide an effective way to debug FPGA circuits. These cores are independent of board vendor implementation of debug support. The verification of IP, possibly using of tracing circuitry, and co-debug of hardware/software designs is greatly assisted.

During the testing of the clock breakpoint core, a few limitations were encountered. The first limitation was the lack of clock tile support in the JBits API. This meant that the global clock lines could not serve as a source to the clock breakpoint core. A work-around was developed and discussed in Section 3.2. Fan-out of secondary clock networks is an issue when using regular routing lines. Unlike global clock lines, single wires are not built to handle high fan-out conditions. When a large image processing circuit was driven from the output of the core, it failed to be clocked properly yet a simpler circuit, with only a counter, register and BlockRAM^{TM} memory, worked successfully. One can use Xilinx M3^{TM} constraint *USELOWSKEWLINES* for high fan-out lines but a suitable approximation will take some time to develop with the JBits tool. Some experiments are underway to buffering the clock output. The most logical solution is to drive the global clock lines directly from the clock breakpoint core. In order to do this, one has to hand wire signals with Xilinx FPGA Editor^{TM}. While these cores are reconfigurable at run-time, the time necessary to reconfigure them, even with partial reconfiguration, limits their use to non-real-time environments.

As efforts continue to build soft microprocessors on an FPGA fabric, so too will the effort to build soft debug units. Future work includes further exploration into true hardware/software co-debugging and expanding the cores to include multiple clock support. Other work will include developing a logic analysis tool based on the reconfigurable aspects of these cores. Additional work is planned to add clock tile and multiple clock support to the JBits API.

6   Acknowledgements

This work was partially funded by DARPA under contract DABT63-99-3-0004 in the Adaptive Computing Systems (ACS) program.

References

1. D. Levi and S. A. Guccione, "BoardScope: A debug tool for reconfigurable systems," in *Configurable Computing Technology and its use in High Performance Computing, DSP and Systems Engineering, Proc. SPIE Photonics East*, J. Schewel, ed., SPIE – The International Society for Optical Engineering, (Bellingham, WA), November 1998.
2. T. Price, D. Levi and S. A. Guccione, "Debug of reconfigurable systems," in *Reconfigurable Technology: FPGAs for Computing and Applications II, Proc. SPIE Photonics East*, J. Schewel, P. Athanas, C. Dick, J. McHenry eds., SPIE – The International Society for Optical Engineering, (Bellingham, WA), November 2000.
3. T. P. Carpenter, S. Kumar and F. Rose, "Hardware/software co-development: differentiating between co-design and co-debug," in *VHDL Times*, Volume 6, Number 1, First Quarter 1997.
4. K. A. Tomko and A. Tiwari, "Hardware/software co-debugging for reconfigurable computing," in *IEEE International High Level Design Validation and Test Workshop*, R. Gupta and J. Hayes, eds., pp. 59–63, IEEE Computer Society Press, (Berkeley, CA), November 2000.
5. D. A. Clark and B. L. Hutchings, "Supporting FPGA microprocessors through retargetable software tools," in *IEEE Symposium on FPGAs for Custom Computing Machines*, K. L. Pocek and J. Arnold, eds., pp. 195–203, IEEE Computer Society Press, (Los Alamitos, CA), April 1996.

6. P. Bellows and B. L. Hutchings, "JHDL - An HDL for reconfigurable systems," in *IEEE Symposium on FPGAs for Custom Computing Machines*, K. Pocek and J. Arnold, eds., pp. 175–184, IEEE Computer Society Press, (Napa, CA), April 1998.

7. B. L. Hutchings and B. Nelson, "Using general-purpose programming languages for FPGA design," in *IEEE Proceedings of the 37th Conference on Design Automation*, pp. 561–566, IEEE Computer Society Press, (Los Angeles, CA), June 2000.

8. S. A. Guccione and D. Levi, "XBI: A Java-based interface to FPGA hardware," in *Configurable Computing: Technology and Applications, Proc. SPIE 3526*, J. Schewel, ed., pp. 97–102, SPIE – The International Society for Optical Engineering, (Bellingham, WA), November 1998.

9. http://www.optimagic.com.

10. http://www.intel.com.

11. http://www.model.com.

12. http://www.xilinx.com/products/software/chipscope/index.html.

13. B. L. Hutchings, P. Bellows, J. Hawkins, S. Hemmert, B. Nelson and M. Rytting, "A CAD suite for high performance FPGA design," in *IEEE Symposium on FPGAs for Custom Computing Machines*, K. Pocek and J. Arnold, eds., IEEE Computer Society Press, (Napa, CA), April 1999.

14. S. A. Guccione and D. Levi, "Run-time parameterizable cores," in *Field-Programmable Logic and Applications*, P. Lysaght, J. Irvine, and R. W. Hartenstein, eds., pp. 215–222, Springer-Verlag, Berlin, August/September 1999. Proceedings of the 9th International Workshop on Field-Programmable Logic and Applications, FPL 1999. Lecture Notes in Computer Science 1673.

Using Design-Level Scan to Improve FPGA Design Observability and Controllability for Functional Verification*

Timothy Wheeler, Paul Graham, Brent Nelson, and Brad Hutchings

Department of Electrical and Computer Engineering
Brigham Young University
Provo, UT 84602, USA
{wheelert,grahamp,nelson,hutch}@ee.byu.edu

Abstract. This paper describes a structured technique for providing full observability and controllability for functionally debugging FPGA designs in hardware, capabilities which are currently not available otherwise. Similar in concept to flip-flop scan chains for VLSI, our design-level scan technique includes all FPGA flip-flops and RAMs in a serial scan chain using FPGA logic rather than transistor logic. This paper describes the general procedure for modifying designs with design-level scan chains and provides the results of adding scan to several designs, both large and small. We observed an average FPGA resource overhead of 84% for full scan and only 60% when we augmented existing FPGA capabilities with scan to provide complete observability and controllability in hardware.

1 Introduction

With time to market being a chief concern for many hardware designers, shortening the debug and validation time for FPGA-based designs is critical. Software simulation is a common approach for validating hardware designs since it provides complete design observability and controllability. Observability refers to the ability to access all internal state of the circuit, similar to the ability of a software debugger to view the values of variables, etc. Controllability is the ability to modify the run-time state of the circuit, similar to changing the values of program variables in a software debugger. Unfortunately, software simulation is extremely slow and can take hours or days to reach some of the more interesting points in a system's execution, thus lengthening the design's validation time.

Another debug approach is to perform design validation on the existing FPGA hardware itself. Direct hardware execution is thousands of times faster

---

* Effort sponsored by the Defense Advanced Research Projects Agency (DARPA) and Wright-Patterson Air Force Base, Air Force Materiel Command, USAF, under agreement number F33615-99-C-1502. The U.S. Government is authorized to reproduce and distribute reprints for Governmental purposes notwithstanding any copyright annotation thereon.

G. Brebner and R. Woods (Eds.): FPL 2001, LNCS 2147, pp. 483–492, 2001.

than software simulation, and the reconfigurability of FPGAs allows design modifications to be reprogrammed directly onto the FPGA. To be the most effective, hardware execution should provide the same level of observability and controllability as a software simulator to enable designers to quickly locate and remove bugs from the design. These capabilities should be provided automatically, without having to generate new configuration bitstreams every time a designer chooses to view different signals.

Unfortunately, no existing hardware debugging technologies for FPGA designs currently provide software-like observability or controllability for functional verification of FPGA designs. Despite being built-in features for some FPGAs, configuration readback[6, 9, 15] and partial configuration[16] only are available for a few families of FPGAs and even those which support these capabilities do not provide complete observability or controllability, the Virtex II family of FPGAs being a *possible* exception. While providing design visibility at hardware execution speeds, the embedded logic analyzer technologies from Xilinx [14] and Altera [1] provide limited internal visibility into FPGA designs, require time-consuming modifications to the designs if their parameters need to be modified, and provide no design controllability. In some senses, using logic analyzers for functional debugging is analogous to using print statements to debug software.

As we mentioned, what is desired is a mechanism which provides full hardware observability and controllability into the user design at all times without recompilation—such a mechanism would provide the foundation for a hardware debugging environment having similar functionality to that of simulators or software debuggers. Design-level scan is a structured technique that has been investigated at BYU as a means of providing these capabilities. It is implemented with user circuitry in a manner similar to the way flip-flop scan chains are employed for VLSI testing [12]. The rest of this paper explores the use of scan to overcome the limitations of the debug methods mentioned above to provide *complete* observability and controllability for functional verification of FPGA-based designs.

2   Design-Level Scan Implementation

Design-level scan involves wiring up the memory elements, such as flip-flops and embedded RAMs, so that the state bits contained in these elements exit the circuit serially through a *ScanOut* pin whenever the *ScanEnable* control signal is asserted. New state data for the FPGA concurrently enters the circuit serially on the *ScanIn* pin. When *ScanEnable* is deasserted, the circuit returns to normal operation. Design-level scan is different from normal VLSI scan since its purpose is to obtain or modify the circuit state in order to validate the circuit logic rather than to find defects in the silicon after the logic has already been verified extensively in software.

The benefits of scan are many. First, an FPGA does not require any special capabilities to implement design-level scan—it can be added to any user design on any FPGA. Second, the amount of data scanned out of the circuit is much smaller and easier to manipulate than for configuration readback bitstreams, since scan bitstreams contain only the desired circuit state information. Third, determining the positions of signal values in the scan bitstream is straightforward since it is easy to determine the order in which the memory elements are arranged in the scan chain. Fourth, the state of the entire circuit can be retrieved by scan, whereas this is not always the case for *ad hoc* and readback methods. Fifth, due to the reprogrammable nature of FPGAs, the scan chain can be removed from the design after verification, thus eliminating the overhead of the scan logic. Sixth, scan allows the state of the circuit to be set to known values for full circuit controllability. Lastly, methods like scan can be instrumented systematically and are not design specific, so the instrumentation processes can be automated. The biggest downside to scan is the large area and speed penalty it causes, which will be discussed in greater depth in Section 3. Fortunately, the FPGA can be configured without scan after the design has been validated, so the overhead is only temporary.

2.1   Instrumenting Design Primitives

When implementing scan, only memory elements are inserted into the scan chain[1]. This section explains how the primitive memory elements in the Xilinx XC4000 and Virtex libraries are instrumented for scan. Similar techniques can be applied to other FPGA vendor libraries.

Instrumenting Flip-Flops FPGA flip-flops (FFs) can be inserted into a scan chain by simply attaching a multiplexor (mux) before the data input of the FF and logic gates in front of the enables and set pins, as shown in Figure 1.

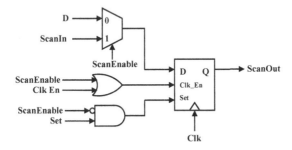

Fig. 1. Instrumenting a Flip-Flop for Scan

The *ScanIn* signal in the figure is the *ScanOut* from the previous memory in the scan chain, and the *ScanOut* signal becomes the *ScanIn* for the next

---

[1]   Once the state of the memory elements is known, the values for any combinational portions of the circuit are easy to infer.

memory in the scan chain. Thus, when *ScanEnable* is asserted, the memories in the circuit form a single-bit-wide shift register; when *ScanEnable* is deasserted the circuit resumes normal operation. While *ScanEnable* is asserted, the FF must be enabled and allow its state bit to be shifted out. The two extra gates in front of the clock enable and set pins in this example serve this purpose.

The worst-case area overhead for a scannable FF is 300% to add the mux and two logic gates, but this price is rarely paid. In many instances, clock enables, sets, and resets in a design are either tied to a constant voltage or shared by multiple FFs. In the former case, the two gates in Figure 1 are not required; in the latter case, the gates can be shared by multiple FFs. Also, sometimes the LUT in front of a FF is empty or has unused inputs, and can thus be used for either the mux or one of the gates.

Instrumenting ARSW RAMs Inserting asynchronously-read, synchronously-written (ARSW) RAMs into scan chains is a bit more complicated than FFs. Examples of ARSW RAMs include the synchronous LUT RAMs in the Xilinx XC4000 and Virtex libraries. A RAM has multiple internal values to scan out, so it is wired up so that it operates like a single-bit-wide FIFO when *ScanEnable* is asserted. It outputs its contents one bit per cycle while upstream *ScanIn* values are concurrently scanned in at one bit per cycle. Similar to the FF shown in Figure 1, the data input to the RAM is connected to a mux and the write enable is connected to an OR gate so that scan data is written to the RAM each clock cycle. The address input to the RAM is also connected to a mux which selects the output of an address generator whenever *ScanEnable* is asserted. The address generator is basically an up-counter that continuously cycles through all of the RAM addresses. It starts at an address of zero during the first cycle of scanning out so that the RAM bits are retrieved in a predictable order. The address generator must also ensure that the RAM contents are scanned back in at their correct addresses.

The overhead required to instrument an m-bit deep by n-bit wide RAM is $2 \times log_2(m) + 1$ LUTs for the address generator and $log_2(m) + n + 1$ LUTs for the muxes and OR gate to the RAM for a total overhead of $3 \times log_2(m) + n + 2$ LUTs. If there are multiple RAMs in the circuit, the address generator logic is shared by all of the RAMs so each additional RAM costs only $log_2(m) + n + 1$ LUTs to instrument.

Instrumenting Fully Synchronous Embedded RAMs Another type of RAM to be instrumented for scan is the fully synchronous RAM, such as the dual-ported Block SelectRAM found in the Xilinx Virtex library. Since both the reads and writes are synchronous, if the read and write addresses are ever the same during a given clock cycle, the data at that location will be overwritten before it is read. Thus, the approach for scan is to inhibit writing to the RAM during the first cycle of scan to allow the first bit of data to exit the RAM. After this, writes occur one address behind the reads during scan so as to not overwrite unread data. Reading and writing to different addresses on the same cycle requires the BlockRAM to be multi-ported; if the BlockRAM is single-ported, it is simply replaced with its multi-ported counterpart at the time of scan instrumentation. In addition, if the width of the data ports on the BlockRAM is greater than one bit, serial-to-parallel and parallel-to-serial converters can be placed at the inputs and outputs to cause the RAM to receive and produce one bit per cycle in the scan chain. Also, since the contents of a BlockRAM's output registers cannot be reloaded, shadow registers must be used to capture their contents during scan. Instrumenting BlockRAMs for scan is very expensive; depending on the configuration of the BlockRAM, it costs between 80-150 additional LUTs and 20-80 additional FFs per BlockRAM.

2.2   Instrumenting the Design Hierarchy

Numerous methods can be used to actually instrument a design with scan. A few methods include making modifications to a placed and routed design, an EDIF netlist, or a circuit database prior to netlisting in the original CAD tool. The latter option is the approach of choice within the JHDL design environment since it is relatively simple to implement and can easily be automated.

In this approach, the user design is placed inside a design "wrapper" that adds the wires for controlling the scan chain—*ScanEnable*, *ScanIn*, and *ScanOut*—and connects these and the user wires to I/O pins on the FPGA. In addition, a *ScanMode* wire is also added if BlockRAMs are present in the circuit. The behavior for scanning the data out of a BlockRAM is slightly different than the behavior for scanning data back in; *ScanMode* thus indicates whether we are scanning data in or out of the circuit. The instrumentation tool then traverses the circuit hierarchy in a depth-first fashion, visiting all design submodules and inserting all primitive memory elements into the scan chain. This is done by adding the four scan signals as ports to each hierarchical cell, and adding scan logic to each flip-flop and embedded RAM, as described previously. Finally, an address generator is added as needed for controlling the memories. Once the design is instrumented, an EDIF netlist is generated and run through the FPGA vendor's back-end tools.

2.3   FPGA System-Level Issues

The AND gate shown in Figure 1 is to disable the set/reset input to the FF during scan to prevent the FPGA state from being inadvertently modified while scan is taking place. This same principle must be applied to the entire FPGA system so that the state of the system is not inadvertently affected and the system itself is not damaged. For instance, writes to external memories can be disabled during scan by tri-stating the I/O pins of the write enables and connecting them to weak pull-ups (write enables are active low). Further, reads and writes to external memories that have begun, but have not yet completed when scan first begins must be handled. An easy solution is to buffer the data being read so that it can be used after scan and to buffer the data being written to ensure the correct state is still written to the memories. Additionally, logic must be added to tri-state buffer enables so they are deasserted during scan to eliminate any possibility of bus contention at the FPGA or system level.

3   The Costs of Design-Level Scan

This section discusses the costs of instrumenting user circuits with scan chains. Some of scan's costs include the extra I/O pins used for the *ScanIn*, *ScanOut*, *ScanEnable*, and *ScanMode* control signals mentioned in Section 2 as well as the storage of the scan bitstream when operating in scan mode. The main concern to a designer, however, is the circuit area and speed overhead of scan. Full scan in VLSI has been reported to require area overheads of 5–30% [4, 7, 11]. As will be seen shortly, the area overhead of full scan in FPGAs is much greater than this. In addition, we found that adding scan logic on average reduces the speed of the circuit by 20%.

Table 1. Full Scan Costs of User Designs

Design	Original					With Full Scan			
	FF Count	LUT RAM Count	BlockRAM Count	LUT Count	LE Count	LUT Count	LUT Ratio	LE Count	LE Ratio
cnt	4	0	0	4	4	9	2.25	9	2.25
mult	615	0	0	270	630	871	3.23	871	1.38
cordic	768	0	0	780	812	1596	2.05	1596	1.97
EBF	2216	67	0	1775	2658	3413	1.92	3445	1.30
LPBF	738	1935	30	14559	14719	24245	1.67	24391	1.66
CDI	4478	40	18	5738	6675	12812	2.23	13434	2.01
SQ	4890	3658	0	11806	14087	32192	2.73	32192	2.29
averages							**2.30**		**1.84**

3.1   Scan Costs for Sample Designs

Consider the scan overheads of several JHDL[2, 8] designs, as shown in Table 1. The first three designs are basic JHDL library modules—a 4-bit up-counter; a 16-bit-by-16-bit, fully-pipelined array multiplier for which only the upper 16 bits of the product are used; and a 16-bit, fully-pipelined rotational CORDIC unit. The other four circuits are large designs created at BYU and consist of *EBF*, which is a heavily pipelined sonar beamformer that does matched field processing; *LPBF* [10], which consists of a 1024-point FFT unit and an acoustic beamformer, but is unpipelined due to power constraints; *CDI* [13], an automatic target recognition (ATR) unit which performs histogramming and peak finding; and *SQ*, which performs adaptive image quantization to optimally segment images for target recognition. The beamformers have significant datapaths including multipliers and CORDICs; the other two large designs are control intensive. We should also mention that *EBF* is an XC4000 design while the others are Virtex designs.

Both the original design sizes and their sizes when instrumented with full scan are shown in Table 1. The LUT count is the number of 4-LUTs contained in the design, and the logic element (LE) count shows the number of basic logic blocks, which consist of a single 4-input LUT, carry logic, and a FF. LE counts are useful for showing the true overhead of scan, for if the FF in a particular LE is being used, but the corresponding 4-LUT is empty, that 4-LUT can be used for some of the scan logic without increasing the number of LEs in the design.

As the table shows, both *cnt* and *cordic* have roughly the same number of 4-LUTs as they do FFs in the original design; thus, adding a scan mux and other scan logic to each FF effectively doubles the number of 4-LUTs in the designs. In addition, since most of the LEs in their original designs used up both the FF and the LUT, little scan logic could be placed into partially filled LEs, so the LE growth for these two designs is roughly the same as the LUT growth. Contrast this with *mult*, where the design area is dominated mostly by pipeline and skew registers. Thus, while the LUT count increased by a factor of 3.23 when instrumented for scan, much of the scan logic could be placed in LEs where only the FF was being used, so the LE count only increased by a factor of 1.38.

The other four designs in the table have the additional cost of instrumenting LUT RAMs and BlockRAMs for scan. *EBF* can place much of its scan logic into partially filled LEs, so the LE ratio is significantly lower than the LUT ratio. *LPBF* has relatively few FFs, so the large number of LUT RAMs and the high cost of instrumenting BlockRAMs give it most of its 66% increase in LE area. *CDI* has many FFs, so the FFs and high cost of instrumenting BlockRAMs contribute to most of its 101% LE overhead. Lastly, *SQ* has a high number of both FFs and LUT RAMs, so it has a high overhead of 129%.

3.2   Scan Overhead in FPGAs vs. VLSI

This section has shown the costs for implementing full scan in FPGA systems is much greater than the 5–30% overheads for VLSI mentioned earlier in this section. So why does scan cost so much more in FPGAs than it does in VLSI? The answer lies in the granularity of the devices used for implementing scan logic—transistor logic costs much less than FPGA LUT logic [5]. For example, [11] claims that a D flip-flop instrumented for scan is only 10% larger in area. In an FPGA design, however, instrumenting a FF for scan effectively doubles its size, since the FF and the scan mux are each half of an LE. The size may even triple or quadruple by using additional LUTs for the clock enable and set/reset scan logic. In addition, using an entire 4-LUT for the scan mux costs at least 167 transistors [3], whereas the same logic could be implemented in VLSI for about 16 transistors.

4   Supplementing Existing Observability and Controllability

We have proposed full scan as a method for providing complete observability and controllability for functional verification of FPGA-based designs. Full scan is often necessary for providing this capability since FPGAs from many vendors, such as Altera and Cypress, have neither built-in observability nor controllability features. However, many FPGAs, such as those produced by Xilinx, Lucent, and Atmel, are equipped with limited capability to read or modify the state of a circuit. Readback and configuration bitstream modification are examples of such capabilities in Xilinx XC4000 and Virtex FPGAs. Variations of scan instrumentation can be applied at a fraction of the cost of full scan to supplement these existing features to provide complete observability and controllability of the user circuit. This section will show how scan can supplement readback and bitstream modification on Xilinx XC4000 and Virtex FPGAs to provide complete observability and controllability of user designs at a lower cost than full scan.

4.1   Supplementing Readback for Observability

The built-in Virtex readback capability provides almost complete observability. The problems are twofold: BlockRAM output registers cannot be readback and performing a readback corrupts their contents. As a fix, shadow registers, which are visible via readback, can be added to the circuit to capture the BlockRAMs' output registers and preserve their state for use immediately after readback. This eliminates the need for full scan for observability. Thus, full observability via readback can be achieved for very low cost as will be shown later.

4.2   Supplementing Bitstream Modification for Controllability

Xilinx FPGAs provide the ability to externally modify the state of their LUT RAMs and BlockRAMs through configuration bitstream modification; however, the state of the FFs cannot be encoded in the bitstream independent of their set/reset logic. Thus, one option to provide full controllability of Xilinx FPGAs is to use bitstream modification techniques to control the state of the LUT RAMs and BlockRAMs, and to use scan to control just the FFs. The area overhead for this method consists of the cost of instrumenting the FFs for scan and a minimal amount of extra logic required to disable all other memories to preserve their state during scan.

4.3   Best-Case Results

Table 2 shows the results of supplementing Xilinx's built-in observability and controllability features with variations of full scan. The left section provides the overhead required if the designer is only interested in obtaining complete observability of the circuit. The overhead is in the form of shadow registers as

Table 2. Best-Case Results for Xilinx Designs

Design	Full Observability				Full Controllability				Both			
	LUT Count	LUT Ratio	LE Count	LE Ratio	LUT Count	LUT Ratio	LE Count	LE Ratio	LUT Count	LUT Ratio	LE Count	LE Ratio
cnt	4	1.00	4	1.00	9	2.25	9	2.25	9	2.25	9	2.25
mult	270	1.00	630	1.00	871	3.23	871	1.38	871	3.23	871	1.38
cordic	780	1.00	812	1.00	1596	2.05	1596	1.97	1596	2.05	1596	1.97
EBF	1775	1.00	2658	1.00	3306	1.86	3427	1.29	3306	1.86	3427	1.29
LPBF	14809	1.01	15231	1.03	16035	1.10	16035	1.09	16362	1.12	16584	1.13
CDI	6065	1.06	7368	1.10	10945	1.91	10945	1.64	11371	1.98	11679	1.75
SQ	11806	1.00	14087	1.00	20342	1.72	20342	1.44	20342	1.72	20342	1.44
ave.		**1.01**		**1.02**		**2.02**		**1.58**		**2.03**		**1.60**

discussed in Section 4.1 which fix the readback limitations in Virtex BlockRAMs. Since only *LPBF* and *CDI* use BlockRAMs, they are the only designs affected by the extra logic.

The middle section shows the overhead required if the designer only desires full controllability. In this case, only the FFs are instrumented for scan, while the the the state of the embedded RAMs are controlled via bitstream modification, as described in Section 4.2. This approach is particularly useful for designs that either have relatively few FFs or that were paying a huge price to instrument their RAMs with full scan, such as *LPBF*, *CDI* and *SQ*. However, the state of the other designs in the table consist mostly of FFs, so for them this approach results in about the same circuitry as instrumenting the design with full scan.

Finally, the right section of Table 2 shows the cost of supplementing existing Xilinx debug features with a combination of the readback shadow registers and scanning only the FFs to provide complete observability and controllability of user designs. It shows a 60% LE overhead, as opposed to the 84% overhead associated with full scan. Although this is certainly an improvement, it shows that since FPGA vendors currently do not provide full observability and controllability features on their FPGAs, the cost of obtaining such capabilities for debug is very high.

5   Conclusions

None of the currently available methods for debugging FPGA-based circuits provide the full ability to view and modify the circuit state. This work has shown how full scan can be used to overcome their limitations to provide complete observability and controllability of user designs. It comes at a high price, though, with full scan costing an additional 84% in area overhead on average. When scan techniques are used to supplement readback and configuration bitstream modification for Xilinx XC4000 and Virtex designs, the overhead is reduced to 60%. Although the costs in either case are still high, they may be justified if the designer can take advantage of fast hardware execution rather than be forced to use software simulation to validate the design, thus, reducing its overall "time-to-market". In addition, design-level scan costs are temporary since the scan logic can be removed for the final production design.

References

[1] Altera Corporation, San Jose, CA. *SignalTap User's Guide*, 1999.10 (revision 2) edition, November 1999.

[2] P. Bellows and B. L. Hutchings. JHDL—an HDL for reconfigurable systems. In J. M. Arnold and K. L. Pocek, editors, *Proceedings of IEEE Workshop on FPGAs for Custom Computing Machines*, pages 175–184, Napa, CA, Apr. 1998.

[3] V. Betz, J. Rose, and A. Marquardt. *Architecture and CAD for Deep-Submicron FPGAs*, chapter Appendix B, page 216. The Kluwer International Series in Engineering and Computer Science. Kluwer Academic Publishers, Boston, 1999.

[4] A. L. Crouch. *Design for Test for Digital IC's and Embedded Core Systems*, chapter 3, page 97. Prentice Hall PTR, Upper Saddle River, NJ, 1999.

[5] A. DeHon. *Reconfigurable Architectures for General-Purpose Computing*. PhD thesis, Massachusetts Institute of Technology, September 1996.

[6] W. Hölfich. Using the XC4000 readback capability. Application Note XAPP 015, Xilinx, XC4000, San Jose, CA, 1994.

[7] S. L. Hurst. *VLSI Testing: Digital and Mixed Analogue/Digital Techniques*, chapter 5, page 218. Number 9 in IEE Circuits, Devices and Systems Series. Institution of Electrical Engineers, London, 1998.

[8] B. Hutchings, P. Bellows, J. Hawkins, S. Hemmert, B. Nelson, and M. Rytting. A CAD suite for high-performance FPGA design. In K. L. Pocek and J. M. Arnold, editors, *Proceedings of the IEEE Workshop on FPGAs for Custom Computing Machines*, pages 12–24, Napa, CA, April 1999. IEEE Computer Society, IEEE.

[9] Lucent Technologies, Allentown, PA. *ORCA Series 4 Field-Programmable Gate Arrays*, December 2000.

[10] S. Scalera, M. Falco, and B. Nelson. A reconfigurable computing architecture for microsensors. In K. L. Pocek and J. M. Arnold, editors, *Proceedings of the IEEE Symposium on Field-Programmable Custom Computing Machines*, pages 59–67, Napa, CA, April 2000. IEEE Computer Society, IEEE Computer Society Press.

[11] M. J. S. Smith. *Application Specific Integrated Circuits*, chapter 14, page 764. Addison-Wesley, Reading, Mass., 1997.

[12] T. W. Williams and K. P. Parker. Design for testability - a survey. *IEEE Transactions on Computers*, C-31(1):2–15, January 1982.

[13] M. J. Wirthlin, S. Morrison, P. Graham, and B. Bray. Improving performance and efficiency of an adaptive amplification operation using configurable hardware. In K. L. Pocek and J. M. Arnold, editors, *Proceedings of the IEEE Workshop on FPGAs for Custom Computing Machines*, pages 267–275, Napa, CA, April 2000. IEEE Computer Society, IEEE.

[14] Xilinx, San Jose, CA. *ChipScope Software and ILA Cores User Manual*, v. 1.1 edition, June 2000.

[15] Xilinx. Virtex FPGA series configuration and readback. Application Note XAPP138, Xilinx, San Jose, CA, October 2000.

[16] Xilinx. Virtex series configuration architecture user guide. Application Note XAPP151, Xilinx, San Jose, CA, February 2000.

FPGA-Based Fault Injection Techniques for Fast Evaluation of Fault Tolerance in VLSI Circuits[1]

Pierluigi Civera, Luca Macchiarulo, Maurizio Rebaudengo, Matteo Sonza Reorda, Massimo Violante

Politecnico di Torino - Dipartimento di Automatica e Informatica / Elettronica
Torino, Italy
http://www.cad.polito.it

Abstract. Designers of safety-critical VLSI systems are asking for effective tools for evaluating and validating their designs. Fault Injection is commonly adopted for this task, and its effectiveness is therefore a key factor. In this paper we propose to exploit FPGAs to speed-up Fault Injection for fault tolerance evaluation of VLSI circuits. A complete Fault Injection environment is described, relying on FPGA-based emulation of the circuit for fault effect analysis. The proposed approach allows combining the efficiency of hardware-based techniques, and the flexibility of simulation-based techniques. Experimental results are provided to support the feasibility and effectiveness of the approach.

1. Introduction

In recent years, there has been a rapid increase in the use of computer-based systems in areas where failures can cost lives and/or money, such as railway traffic control, aircraft flight, telecommunications, and others. This trend has led to a growing interest in the techniques for the validation of the fault tolerance properties of these systems and for the evaluation of their reliability.

On the other side, the continuous increase in the integration level of electronic systems is making increasingly difficult to guarantee an acceptable degree of reliability, due to the occurrence of transient faults (often modeled as soft errors) that can dramatically affect the behavior of a system. As an example, the decrease in the magnitude of the electric charges used to carry and store information is seriously raising the probability that alpha particles and neutrons hitting the circuit could introduce transient errors in its behavior (often modeled as Single Error Upsets, or SEUs) [1].

To face the above issues, mechanisms are required to increase the robustness of electronic devices and systems with respect to possible errors occurring during their

---

[1] The work is partially funded by the Italian Ministry for University through the project "Sistemi di elaborazione reattivi ed affidabili per applicazioni industriali", the Italian Space Agency through the basic research project "Definizione e valutazione di tecniche software per la realizzazione di sistemi di elaborazione tolleranti ai guasti a basso costo", and by Politecnico di Torino through the Giovani Ricercatori project.

G. Brebner and R. Woods (Eds.): FPL 2001, LNCS 2147, pp. 493-502, 2001.

normal function. At the same time, designers strongly need effective techniques and methods to debug and verify their correct design and implementation.

Fault Injection [2] imposed itself as a viable solution to the above problems. Several Fault Injection techniques have been proposed and practically experimented; they can basically be grouped into *simulation-based* techniques (e.g., [3]), *software-implemented* techniques (e.g., [4]), and *hardware-based* techniques (e.g., [5]).

As pointed out in [2], physical Fault Injection (hardware- and software-implemented Fault Injection approaches) is well suited when a prototype of the system is already available, or when the system itself is too large to be modeled and simulated at an acceptable cost. Conversely, simulation-based Fault Injection is very effective in allowing early and detailed analysis of designed systems, since it can be exploited when a prototype is not yet available, and allows the analysis of practically any faulty behavior, but requires very high CPU time to simulate the model of the system (provided that it is available).

An intermediate solution, providing most of the benefits of both physical and simulation-based techniques, while avoiding most of their disadvantages, has recently become viable, thanks to the latest advancements in the FPGA technology. Modern FPGA-devices can be fruitfully exploited to emulate systems composed of hundred of thousands gates at a reasonable cost. The FPGA technology can be effectively exploited not only for rapid prototyping and for small-volume productions, but even to perform Fault Injection experiments. This allows performing the evaluation of the fault tolerance properties of a circuit when only a model is available and its prototypical implementation is not ready, yet. By resorting to FPGAs we can perform Fault Injection campaigns at the same speed of hardware prototypes but at a negligible fraction of their costs. Moreover, FPGA-based Fault Injection techniques generally support a more accurate fault behavior analysis than hardware-based ones, since they may allow the injection of a wider set of faults (e.g., specific faults inside the circuit).

Several works already explored the usage of FPGAs for speeding-up Fault Simulation [6] [7]. In [8], the extension of their usage to Fault Injection is proposed, but the approach is based on reprogramming the FPGA once for each fault, which results in large requirements in terms of required time for Fault Injection campaigns. In this paper we describe a new approach for performing Fault Injection exploiting FPGA devices, and outline the architecture of an FPGA-based Fault Injection environment we set up. Our solution does not require FPGA reconfiguration for each fault experiment, thus attaining a much greater efficiency in terms of required time. Moreover, our solution allows not only to efficiently perform Fault Injection, but also to effectively support the observation of faulty behavior. Experimental results are provided on some benchmark circuits, which allow a preliminary evaluation of the advantages of the approach.

When compared with state-of-the-art Fault Injection environments based on gate-level fault simulation techniques [9], experimental results show that our method is faster by a factor ranging from 30 to 60. On the other side, if Fault Injection is performed using commercial VHDL simulation tools (such as in [10]), this factor becomes greater than 4 orders of magnitude.

The paper is organized as follows: Section 2 describes the proposed Fault Injection system, describing its whole architecture, the circuit transformations required to support Fault Injection once the circuit is mapped on an FPGA, and the process for performing a Fault Injection campaign. Section 3 outlines the prototype we implemented for evaluating the approach; Section 4 reports some experimental results and evaluates the cost of the approach in terms of FPGA area overhead and time requirements. Section 5 draws some conclusions.

2.   The Fault Injection System

2.1.   Background

A typical Fault Injection environment is composed of three modules:
- *Fault List Manager*: it is in charge of analyzing the system and generating the list of faults to be injected.
- *Fault Injection Manager*: it in charge of orchestrating the selection of a new fault, its injection in the system, and the observation of the resulting behavior.
- *Result Analyzer*: it analyzes the data produced by the previous module, categorizes faults according to their effect, and produces statistical information.

For the purpose of this paper (but without any loss of generality) we assume that the system to be considered is a VLSI circuit (or part of it). Therefore, we assume that a gate-level description of the system itself is available, possibly including some fault tolerance mechanism. We also assume that the input stimuli to be used during the Fault Injection campaign are already available, and we do not deal with their generation or evaluation. Moreover, the fault model adopted for the experiments reported in Section 4 is the single transient bit flip in the circuit storage elements; however, the method can be immediately be extended to support multiple bit-flips. The bit flip fault model perfectly matches the characteristics of SEUs, whose effects are increasingly important not only for systems targeted to space, but even for ground applications.

Finally, we assume that fault effects are classified according to the following categories:
- *Silent*: the output trace of the faulty circuit and its state at the end of the simulation correspond to the ones of the fault-free circuit.
- *Latent*: the output trace of the faulty circuit corresponds to the one of the fault-free one, but their states at the end of the simulation do not match. As a consequence, the fault is still active in the circuit and may produce wrong outputs in the following clock cycles.
- *Failure*: the output trace of the faulty circuit does not match the one of the fault-free circuit
- *Detected*: any Error Detection Mechanism (EDM) existing in the circuit detects the fault.

The assumptions described above closely match the specifications coming from some of the European car and space industries designing safety-critical VLSI circuits.

2.2. FPGA-Based Fault Injection Manager

The Fault Injection Manager we propose exploits a FPGA board that emulates the gate-level system with and without faults. A host computer drives the FPGA board and it also executes the other modules composing the Fault Injection system. To efficiently determine the behavior of the circuit when a fault appears, the FPGA board emulates an instrumented version of the circuit, which allows both the injection of each fault, and the observation of the corresponding faulty behavior.

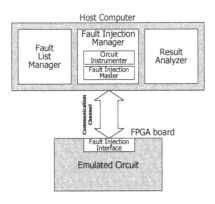

Figure 1: Fault Injection environment architecture

More in details, the Fault Injection Manager is composed of the following parts:
- *Circuit Instrumenter*: it is in charge of generating an instrumented version of the circuit description, to be downloaded on the FPGA board for performing Fault Injection; it is a software module running on the host computer. Details about the circuit transformations implemented by this module can be found in Section 2.3.
- *Fault Injection Master*: it is in charge of:
    - Downloading to the FPGA board the instrumented circuit description.
    - Setting up the environment for the Fault Injection campaign.
    - Repeatedly accessing the fault list, selecting a fault, and sending to the FPGA board the information for its injection (in terms of fault location).
    - Launching the circuit emulation, by providing the input stimuli and the triggering signal for the injection of the fault.
    - Retrieving from the board the information about the faulty system behavior.
    The Fault Injection Master corresponds to a software module running on the host computer.
- *Fault Injection Interface*: it is implemented as a hardware module on the FPGA board, and it is in charge of receiving and executing the commands issued by the Fault Injection Master.

In the following Subsection we will describe the transformations we introduce in the circuit description in order to support Fault Injection; moreover, details on the implementation of the resulting Fault Injection, whose architecture is reported in Figure 1, system are reported.

2.3. Circuit Transformations for Fault Injection

We developed a method for easily modifying the value in the circuit memory elements; moreover, the method implements an effective way to trigger the occurrence of faults at the injection time and for supporting the observation of the faulty behavior.

The architecture we devised, reported in Figure **2**, is based on adding to the original circuit a register (named **Mask Chain**) storing the binary information about which flip-flop(s) should be affected by the fault, and an ad-hoc logic for performing the Fault Injection. The signal inject controls the Fault Injection: the Fault Injection Master asserts it to force the occurrence of the selected bit-flip(s).

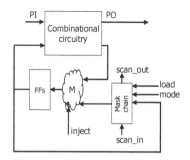

Figure 2: Instrumented circuit   **Figure 3:** instrumented flip flop

The modules added to the circuit are the following:

- Mask Chain: each bit in FFs is associated to a bit in Mask Chain, which is a parallel- and serial-load register (the load and mode signals control its operations). The register operates as follows:
  - During the experiment initialization phase, it works as a shift-register, and loads a bit stream coming over the scan_in signal. The bit stream contains a 1 in the positions corresponding to the flip flop(s) where the fault must be injected, 0s elsewhere.
  - At the injection time (i.e., when the inject signal is activated), each bit in Mask Chain set to 1 produces a bit-flip, i.e., the corresponding FFs module loads the complement of the value coming from the Combinational Circuitry.
  - The Mask Chain may load the content of the FFs module. The state of the circuit can then be read through the scan_out signal by operating the module as a shift register. This feature may be exploited at the end of each experiment to better classify fault effects.
- M: it is the combinational logic in charge of complementing the output of the Combinational Circuitry that is loaded into the FFs module. The behavior of M depends on the contents of the Mask Chain module and on the inject signal.

Figure **3** reports a detailed description of how each flip flop in the original circuit is modified; the figure includes one element of **FFs**, the corresponding element in the **Mask Chain**, and the logic **M**.

2.4. The FI Process

The Fault Injection process is composed of the following steps:
- The circuit description is instrumented according to the previously described transformations.
- The FPGA board is loaded with the instrumented circuit description.
- The circuit description is simulated and the output values at each clock cycle are recorded. During this phase faults are not injected; the obtained output trace is the reference trace we use to classify fault effects.
- The Fault Injection Manager executes the procedure described in Figure **4**, which is in charge of initializing the FPGA, feeding the emulated circuit with the input vectors, activating the injection, and observing the system response.

```
for every fault F_i {
        reset the circuit
        load Mask Chain
        for every input vector V_i {
                apply vector V_i at time T_i
                if( T_i == Injection Time (F_i) )
                        inject = 1
                else
                        inject = 0

                emulate the circuit for one clock cycle
                observe output
                classify fault effects
                i = i+1
        }
        read circuit FFs
}
```

Figure 4: Fault Injection procedure

The following phases are executed during each Fault Injection experiment:
1. *Initialization*: the mask defining the fault to be injected is loaded in the **Mask Chain** module.
2. *Simulation and Injection*: the emulated circuit is fed with a stream of input vectors, and the fault is injected.
3. *Latent fault analysis*: after all the input vectors have been applied, the content of the **FFs** module is loaded in the **Mask chain** module and then sent to the Fault Injection Master through the **scan_out** signal.

The method we propose guarantees the accessibility of every memory element in the circuit during Fault Injection and allows a detailed result analysis. Moreover, it allows a time resolution of one clock cycle: the Fault Injection Master can inject faults at any clock cycle by triggering the inject signal at that cycle, and observing the system behavior at any clock cycle.

3. Prototypical Implementation

We developed a prototype of the Fault Injection system described in the previous Section using the ADM-XRC development board [11], equipped with a Xilinx Virtex V1000E FPGA. The development board owns a PCI connector and it is inserted in a standard Pentium-class PC, which manages the board as a memory-mapped device.

In order to modify the circuit description to support Fault Injection, we developed a tool that, starting from the original circuit, automatically synthesizes all the required modules. In particular, for each flip-flop in the circuit the tool inserts the cell outlined in Fig. 3. Then, the new cells are connected to form a parallel-load/serial-load register and the required control signals are added.

The hardware/software Fault Injector Manager is composed of the following modules:

- The *Fault Injection Master*, which amounts to 500 lines of C++ code; it is in charge of implementing the software module (running on the host) implementing the procedure described in Figure 4.
- The *Fault Injection Interface*, which has been implemented by the Xilinx FPGA along with the circuit under evaluation; it is a simple finite state machine that recognizes and executes the commands issued by the Fault Injection Master. We used a memory-mapped protocol to control the operations of the Xilinx, providing a series of addresses to remotely guide from the host PC all steps of the Fault Injection experiments. In particular, the Fault Injection Interface captures the PCI bus cycles directed toward the ADM-XRC board, and it executes one of the following commands depending on the requested operation (read or write) and the specified address:
    - *Reset*: the instrumented circuit clock is disabled and all the registers are set to the start state
    - *Load Mask Chain*: the scan chain is loaded with the values specifying the fault to be injected. This phase takes a number of clock periods to complete which depends on the number of the circuit flip-flops.
    - *Apply vector*: the circuit Primary Inputs (PIs) are fed with a given vector.
    - *Step*: the circuit executes one step and computes the output values and the next state, depending on the given input vectors and the current state.
    - *Fault Injection*: the enable signal is activated, while the circuit clock is disabled. Since the activation of the signal the circuit outputs and state will possibly exhibit a faulty behavior.
    - *Output read*: the values on the circuit Primary Outputs (POs) are read.
    - *State read*: the content of the circuit flip-flops are loaded in the Mask Chain and sent to the Fault Injection Master.

The instrumented circuit, together with the Fault Injection Interface, is described in an automatically generated synthesizable VHDL code. We then used typical development tools to obtain the stream needed to program the Xilinx device. Synplicity™ is used to map the description to the Xilinx device, while the proprietary tool Alliance^{TM} is then employed to perform place, route and timing analysis of the implemented design. The final result is a valid Xilinx configuration bit stream, which can be used to program the device.

After programming has taken place, the behavior of the system is completely controlled by the Fault Injection Master, which uses the basic functionality offered by the aforementioned addressing scheme to flexibly direct all phases of the Fault Injection experiments.

The entire procedure can be modified according to different Fault Injection schemes; for example it is easy to sample the simulation output on given periods only (instead of comparing the entire output trace), or repeat the experiments multiple times with different injection times.

4.   Experimental Results

To evaluate the time performance of our approach, we considered some circuits coming from the ITC'99 benchmark suite [12]. The circuits characteristics are reported in Table 1.

Name	Gates	PIs	POs	FFs	Virtex occupation		
					Normal Circuit [%]	Instrumented Circuit [%]	Overhead [%]
b14	4,787	33	54	245	7	10	42.8
b15	8,922	37	70	449	15	18	20.0
b17	24,195	38	97	1,415	40	44	10.0

Table 1: Benchmarks characteristics

Table 1 also reports the area of the benchmarks in terms of percentage of occupation of the Xilinx V1000E device, and the overhead of the instrumented circuit with respect to the original circuit. These figures indicate that the proposed transformations introduce a limited hardware overhead that decreases with the size of the considered circuits. This is mainly due to the fact that the area overhead depends on two factors: the cost of the Fault Injection Interface, which is independent on the circuit size, and the one for instrumenting the circuit by inserting the **Mask Chain**, which depends on the number of flip flops.

As far as the timing is concerned, in the current version we still did not stress the optimization process and used for the Synplicity-Alliance tool chain an operation frequency equal to 20 MHz.

We performed a first set of experiments feeding the circuits with 1,000 functional vectors and injecting 100,000 randomly selected faults. Results of this set of experiments are reported in Table 2. Columns F, S and L report the percentage of Failure, Silent, and Latent faults we recorded, respectively; since no Error Detection Mechanism was implemented in the considered circuits, no faults were classified as Detected. The remaining columns report the time spent for performing the experiments by two different tools and the computed speed-up figures.

In these experiments we compared our FPGA-based approach with an efficient in-house developed simulation-based Fault Injection tool based on the approach proposed in [9]. Table 2 reports the results we attained on a Sun UltraSparc 5 running at 300 MHz and equipped with 256MB of RAM. We observed that the FPGA-based approach attains speed-up figures ranging between 31 and 42.

Bench.	F [%]	S [%]	L [%]	FPGA-based Fault Injection [sec]	Gate-level Fault Injection [sec]	Speed-up
b14	57.1	0.0	42.9	83	2,556	31
b15	20.6	0.0	79.4	123	3,883	32
b17	10.9	1.2	87.9	125	5,259	42

Table 2: FPGA-based vs gate-level simulation-based Fault Injection

We then performed a second set of experiments, aimed at evaluating how the performance of the proposed approach scales with the number of simulated vectors. We considered the benchmark b17 and performed 4 sets of experiments where the number of randomly selected vectors ranges between 100 and 100,000 and the number of faults is 1,000. Results are reported in Table 3 and demonstrate that the attained speed-up grows with the number of simulated vectors.

Num. of Vectors [#]	FPGA-based Fault Injection	Simulation-based Fault Injection	Speed-up
100	0.69	5	7
1,000	1.75	74	42
10,000	13.33	776	58
100,000	117.70	7,062	60

Table 3: Results of the Fault Injection campaigns on b17

Finally, the reader should note that no commercial tool is currently able to perform Fault Injection of temporary faults on gate level descriptions. Therefore, the common practice within several companies is to exploit VHDL or Verilog simulators. Even if optimized techniques are exploited such as those proposed in [10], the time required to perform Fault Injection with this approach is about 4 order of magnitude grater than the ones reported in Table 2.

5. Conclusions

This paper presented an environment for performing Fault Injection campaigns that is based on the adoption of an FPGA device for emulating the system under analysis. A major novelty in the proposed approach lies in the circuit transformations adopted to inject faults in the circuit emulated through the FPGA. These transformations introduce an area overhead that ranges from 8% to 42% for the considered benchmark circuits, but allow a significant reduction in the time required to perform the Fault

Injection experiments even with respect to the most effective simulation-based techniques. By exploiting a prototypical version of the described Fault Injection environment, we were able to evaluate its effectiveness with respect to state-of-the-art alternative approaches. Speed-up figures up to 60 have been recorded when our technique is compared with a state-of-the-art gate-level approach.

6. References

[1]   M. Nikoladis, *Time Redundancy Based Soft-Error Tolerance to Rescue Nanometer Technologies*, IEEE 17th VLSI Test Symposium, April 1999, pp. 86-94

[2]   R. K. Iyer and D. Tang, *Experimental Analysis of Computer System Dependability*, Chapter 5 of Fault-Tolerant Computer System Design, D. K. Pradhan (ed.), Prentice Hall, 1996

[3]   E. Jenn, J. Arlat, M. Rimen, J. Ohlsson, J. Karlsson, *Fault Injection into VHDL Models: the MEFISTO Tool*, Proc. FTCS-24, 1994, pp. 66-75

[4]   G.A. Kanawati, N.A. Kanawati, J.A. Abraham, *FERRARI: A Flexible Software-Based Fault and Error Injection System*, IEEE Trans. on Computers, Vol 44, N. 2, February 1995, pp. 248-260

[5]   J. Arlat, M. Aguera, L. Amat, Y. Crouzet, J.C. Fabre, J.-C. Laprie, E. Martins, D. Powell, *Fault Injection for Dependability Validation: A Methodology and some Applications*, IEEE Transactions on Software Engineering, Vol. 16, No. 2, February 1990

[6]   S. A. Hwang, J. H. Hong, C. W. Wu, *Sequential circuit fault simulation using logic emulation*, IEEE Transactions on Computer-Aided Design of Integrated Circuits and Systems, Volume: Vol. 17, No. 8, Aug. 1998, pp. 724 -736

[7]   K. T. Cheng, S. Y. Huang, W. J. Dai, *Fault emulation: A new methodology for fault grading*, IEEE Transactions on Computer-Aided Design of Integrated Circuits and Systems, Vol. 18, No. 10, Oct. 1999, pp. 1487 -1495

[8]   L. Antoni, R. Leveugle, B. Fehér, *Using Run-time Reconfiguration for Fault Injection in Hardware Prototypes*, IEEE International Symposium on Defect and Fault Tolerance in VLSI Systems, 2000, pp. 405-413

[9]   C. Hungse, E.M. Rudnick, J.H. Patel, R.K. Iyer, G.S. Choi, *A gate-level simulation environment for alpha-particle-induced transient faults*, IEEE Transactions on Computers, Vol. 45, No. 11, Nov. 1996 , pp. 1248-1256

[10] B. Parrotta, M. Rebaudengo, M. Sonza Reorda, M. Violante, *New Techniques for Accelerating Fault Injection in VHDL descriptions*, IOLTW2000: International On-Line Test Workshop, July 2000

[11] *ADM-XRC PCI Mezzanine card User Guide Version 1.2*, ALPHA DATA parallel systems ltd, http://www.alphadata.co.uk/

[12] F. Corno, M. Sonza Reorda, G. Squillero, *RT-Level ITC 99 Benchmarks and First ATPG Results*, IEEE Design & Test of Computers, July-August 2000

A Generic Library for Adaptive Computing Environments

Tilman Neumann and Andreas Koch

Tech. Univ. Braunschweig (E.I.S.), Gaußstr. 11, D-38106 Braunschweig, Germany
neumann,koch@eis.cs.tu-bs.de

Abstract. The Generic Library for Adaptive Computing Environments (GLACE) consists of a comprehensive set of module generators currently targeting Xilinx XC4000 and Virtex devices. In contrast to other research efforts in this area, it provides detailed meta-data *about* the generated circuits (behavior, area, timing, topology etc.) using the active FLAME interface. All of the modules adhere to a common layout scheme which allows the efficient automatic composition of high-performance data paths.

1 Introduction

While well known for decades, the use of module generators in VLSI design flows has recently been exploited with renewed interest. In the ASIC field, commercial products such as ModuleCompiler [1] are achieving good results in terms of design time and quality. For FPGAs with their limited interconnect resources and coarse-grain logic blocks, module generators have traditionally been the tool of choice to quickly provide fast and dense circuits [2] [3] [4] [5] [6].

However, most of the existing generator systems for FPGAs generate only structural circuit descriptions (e.g., netlists or pre-placed layouts). What they sorely lack is meta-data *about* the generated instance: Main design flow tools (such as compilers and synthesis) rely on accurate area and timing data for making optimization decisions. More advanced flows including automatic floorplanning steps [9] additionally require topological information (layout shape, port placement and pitch) as the base of their operation.

This work introduces the Generic Library for Adaptive Computing Environments (GLACE). It offers a comprehensive suite of parameterized module generators suitable for automatically composing data paths on adaptive computers. In addition to placed layouts and simulation models, it also makes a broad spectrum of meta-data available to the client tools.

2 GLACE Architecture

The GLACE architecture (Figure 1) is not monolithic. Instead, it encompasses a number of other technologies which remain hidden from clients in the main design flow. These are being presented with a single consistent tool- and device-independent interface.

G. Brebner and R. Woods (Eds.): FPL 2001, LNCS 2147, pp. 503–512, 2001.

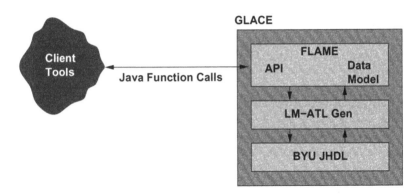

Figure 1. GLACE Architecture

2.1   JHDL

The BYU JHDL package [6] is used as the foundation for actually creating circuits. JHDL consists of a Java class library that allows the composition of primitives to describe designs at the structural level. These circuit elements may then be annotated with device-specific mapping and placement directives. The environment, which also allows for seamless simulation of the design, currently supports the Xilinx XC4000 [7] and Virtex FPGA [8] families.

Since the full expressive power of Java including features such as inheritance and polymorphism is available to the designer, very powerful and flexible module generators can be implemented and verified with relative ease.

Unfortunately, JHDL does not exploit the structural, placement, and device data of a design to automatically derive timing, area and topology information from the circuit description. Instead, these characteristics have to be calculated manually in explicitly coded sections of the generators (Section 3.2).

2.2   Gen

The Gen package was implemented by Lockheed-Martin Advanced Technology Laboratories as part of DARPA ACS project "A Nimble Compiler for Agile Hardware" [10]. It uses JHDL to provide a complete set of parameterized basic operators suitable for use by automatic hardware compilation. The behaviors and interfaces of the functions follow the FLAME Library Specification (Section 2.3). Thus, instead of offering just basic gates, Gen also includes higher-level operations such as absolute value, arithmetic negation, signed and unsigned shifters, etc. Parameters now extend beyond simple bit widths to data types, optional registering of outputs, and architectural choices (e.g., pipelining depth for a multiplier).

In addition to the specific cells, Gen adds some area and timing estimation capabilities to JHDL. However, even though Gen can create circuits for both XC4000 and Virtex, the estimation is only supported for the XC4000 series.

2.3   FLAME

The very flexibility of modern module generators can cause significant difficulties when they are to be integrated with the main design flow. Since cell characteristics vary with the actual parameter values used (such as bit widths, data types, absence or presence of optional inputs), the standard approach of static "library files" simply enumerating all alternatives is doomed to fail.

The Flexible API for Module-based Environments (FLAME) [11] solves these problems. It consists of three major components: The API itself, the design data model, and the library specification. Currently, GLACE uses a Java-based FLAME implementation. However, using the Java Native Interface (JNI), its services can be accessed from languages other than Java.

API The API and communications infrastructure provided by the FLAME Manager (Figure 2) replace static library files with an active function call-based interface. Clients in the main design flow can thus enter into a dialog with the module libraries and retrieve data specific to the actual parameter values of the current instance. In GLACE, the client queries accepted by the FLAME Manager will be forwarded down the chain of Gen and JHDL to result in the computation of estimated characteristics or the creation of actual circuits (netlists, placed layouts).

Data Model The information exchanged in this manner is represented using the FLAME design data model. This model is partitioned into a number of task-specific views: A front-end compiler might request a "behavior" view to determine which functions are available for a given target technology. Later on, it could query for a "synthesis" view to

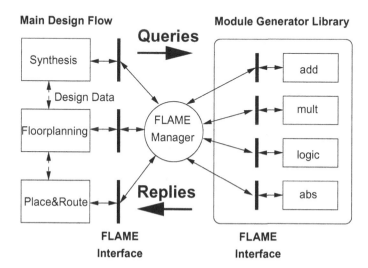

Figure 2. FLAME Architecture Overview

retrieve area and timing characteristics for a specific module instance. Additional views include, e.g., "topology" for layout shapes and port pitch (crucial for efficiently laying out regular data paths). "netlist", "placed", and "mapped" views contain the circuit itself. Instead of defining yet another netlist format, FLAME seamlessly encapsulates existing formats such as EDIF [12] or XNF.

Library Specification The FLAME Library Specification describes a set of behaviors and interfaces. One or more of these can be attached to a hardware cell to precisely define its function for automatic use by a main flow tool. For example, the cell of a switchable adder/subtracter might have both the addition and subtraction behaviors attached. The interface carefully distinguishes between the logical (e.g., the operands of the adder) and the physical perspective (e.g., clock ports and clock enable signals). Furthermore, in FLAME, an interface extends beyond port specifications, such as width and data type, to the control characteristics of the cell. This could cover "start" and "done" signals as well as mode switches (e.g., alternating between addition and subtraction). By considering all of these aspects, a main flow tool can choose the cell most applicable to a given task and automatically drive it correctly from the central data path controller.

3   Cell Library

The following sections deal with the capabilities of the current version of GLACE and their implementation.

3.1   Behaviors

Table 1 shows a selection of FLAME behaviors including their logical interfaces. Optional ports are marked by square brackets. For example, a simple addition behavior without carry ports is expressed as add(sum,a,b). Optional input ports have well-defined default values (e.g., 0 for a carry-in cin). Unused output ports may result in more compact circuits when their driving logic can be completely suppressed during module generation.

Individual logical ports in the behaviors are constrained further in a FLAME query to parameterize the specific module instance. E.g., the logical inputs a,b in the behavior lt(lt,a,b) can be annotated with the constraints (WIDTH 7) (SIGNED_2) to create a 7-Bit Less-Than comparator using two's complement signed arithmetic.

With these behaviors, all data flow graphs resulting from high-level synthesis (such as compilation from C using the Nimble Compiler) can be mapped to their corresponding hardware operators.

3.2   Implementation

The behaviors described in the previous section are decoupled from their actual implementation. For that, we have to consider both technology-specific features as well as a general module architecture. Often, these two issues are closely related.

Technology-Specific Features Many FPGA architectures support registering the outputs of combinational logic within the same block. Since this is an extremely useful capability for RTL-style circuits and efficient pipelining, the FLAME data model has dedicated constructs for expressing the capabilities of the device registers (flip-flops, latches, clock enables) and to actually request their use. The tri-state buffers available on certain devices are handled in a similar manner. In the current implementation, the Gen package is able to create registered versions of all combinational behaviors when a client tool sends the appropriate FLAME query.

General Module Architecture The module architecture is heavily influenced by the underlying device architecture. For the Xilinx XC4000 and Virtex chips, the orientation of the on-chip carry chains (vertical) determines the direction of data flow (horizontal). Furthermore, efficient datapath layout relies on aligning busses with matched pitch and avoiding corner-turns in the routing. To this end, all of the GLACE modules targeting Virtex are laid-out as shown in Figure 3, which depicts a very simple 32-bit instance that has only one operand a and one result y. Modules consist of one or more columns of CLBs, with each vertical CLB processing two bits of each operand word (thus having a data path pitch of two). In order to balance logic outputs (2 per Virtex *slice*) with available tri-state buffers (2 per Virtex *CLB*), only slice S1 of the column containing the module outputs is used. This approach guarantees the availability of nearby buffers when a client requests the outputs to be tri-stateable. Again, note that this waste of area only occurs in the output columns. Inside of a module, all slices may be used.

Description	Behavior Name and Logical Interface
Addition	add(sum, [cout,] [ovfl,] a, b [, cin])
Subtraction	sub(diff, [bout,] [ovfl,] a, b [, bin])
Multiplication	mul(prod, [ovfl,] a, b)
Division	div(quot, [zerodiv,] a, b)
Modulus	mod(rem, [zerodiv,] a, b)
Negation	neg(neg, [cout,] a [,cin])
Absolute	abs(abs, [cout,] a)
Logical Shift Left	lsl(lsl, din, bits)
Logical Shift Right	lsr(lsr, din, bits)
Arithmetical Shift Right	asr(asr, din, bits)
Less-Than	lt(lt, a, b)
Less-Than-Equal	le(le, a, b)
Equal	eq(eq, a, b)
Not-Equal	ne(ne, a, b)
Greater-Than-Equal	ge(ge, a, b)
Greater-Than	gt(gt, a, b)
Logic	logic(y, a, b, c, d, [e,] [f,] [g,] ttable)
Multiplexing	mux(mux, a, b, [c,] [d,] [e,] ..., sel)
Register	reg(q, d [,clk, en] [,lt])

Table 1. Sample FLAME behavior names and interfaces

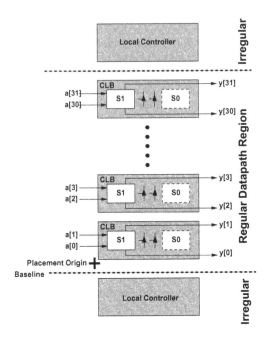

Figure 3. GLACE module architecture for Virtex devices

3.3 Module Characteristics

Figure 4 shows the layout and an excerpt from the FLAME timing and area data for an 8-bit adder on a Xilinx Virtex XCV50 device (speed grade -4). Note that only the left (S1) column of the CLB slices has been used in the generated circuit. The DPEXTENT attribute specifies the maximal area for the data path in CLBs. TIMESCALE sets the time unit to 10^{-10}s $= 0.1$ns. This is used in the TIMING attribute: The addition result on the output port sum will be valid 2.4ns after the operand inputs stabilize. The circuit can process one datum per clock cycle. Finally, the description states that the adder will use 4 of the 384 CLBs available.

The topology information for an unsigned 8-bit multiplier is shown in Figure 5. The instance has been pipelined to have a register for every two shift/add stages. First, note that the density within the module is higher than for separate modules: In many cases, both slices of a CLB are used. Furthermore, this module has two irregular components which are placed below and above the regular data path region. All busses are spaced so 2 bits of each word are processed per CLB of module height.

The meta-data is defined by equations or (in some cases) more complex algorithmic descriptions. These are then evaluated using the instance-specific values for width, data types, etc., as actual parameters. In the current version of GLACE, this knowledge had to be explicitly coded by someone familiar with the internal composition of the module. However, it could also be calculated automatically from the module structure and the accompanying partitioning and placement directives (see Section 4).

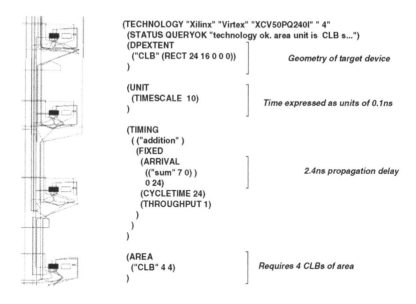

```
(TECHNOLOGY "Xilinx" "Virtex" "XCV50PQ240I" " 4"
  (STATUS QUERYOK "technology ok. area unit is  CLB s...")
  (DPEXTENT                                                    ⎤
    ("CLB" (RECT 24 16 0 0 0))                                 ⎥ Geometry of target device
  )                                                            ⎦

  (UNIT                                                        ⎤
    (TIMESCALE  10)                                            ⎥ Time expressed as units of 0.1ns
  )                                                            ⎦

  (TIMING
    ( ("addition" )
      (FIXED
        (ARRIVAL                                               ⎤
          (("sum" 7 0) )                                       ⎥
          0 24)                                                ⎥ 2.4ns propagation delay
        (CYCLETIME 24)                                         ⎦
        (THROUGHPUT 1)
      )
    )
  )

  (AREA                                                        ⎤
    ("CLB" 4 4)                                                ⎥ Requires 4 CLBs of area
  )                                                            ⎦
```

Figure 4. Timing/area characteristics of an 8-bit adder

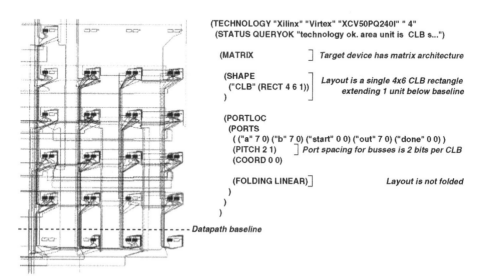

```
(TECHNOLOGY "Xilinx" "Virtex" "XCV50PQ240I" " 4"
  (STATUS QUERYOK "technology ok. area unit is  CLB s...")

  (MATRIX                     ⎤ Target device has matrix architecture

  (SHAPE                      ⎤ Layout is a single 4x6 CLB rectangle
    ("CLB" (RECT 4 6 1))      ⎥ extending 1 unit below baseline
  )                           ⎦

  (PORTLOC
    (PORTS
      ( ("a" 7 0) ("b" 7 0) ("start" 0 0) ("out" 7 0) ("done" 0 0) )
      (PITCH 2 1)             ⎤ Port spacing for busses is 2 bits per CLB
      (COORD 0 0)

      (FOLDING LINEAR)⎤                     Layout is not folded
    )
  )
)
```
- Datapath baseline

Figure 5. Topology data for an 8-bit unsigned multiplier

Function	Area in CLBs	Max. Clock in MHz
Abs	1x16	116.9
Add	1x16	128.3
Eq	1x16	128.3
Gt	1x16	128.3
Div	4x18	34.9
Logic	1x16	167.5
Mod	4x18	39.1
Mul1	3x18	79.1
Mul2	4x18	62.9
Mul3	5x18	53.4
Mul4	6x18	45.4
Mux	1x16	173.2
Neg	1x16	135.5
Reg	1x16	200.6
Shift	1x16	72.4
Sub	1x16	128.3

Table 2. Area and performance data for 32-Bit functions

3.4   Performance Evaluation

Table 2 lists area and performance data for a number of GLACE cells on a Virtex device with speed grade -4 (the slowest). The instances have been created with 32 bits of width, unsigned operands and registered outputs. The topology data is expressed as a CLB rectangle (rows x columns). Furthermore, note that the speed in MHz is the *system* speed measured when instantiating a single module and includes the delay for routing all of its ports to the chip pads.

For some of the cells, additional comments are in order: Mul1 to Mul4 differ in their degree of pipelining. Mul1 has a register inserted after each shift/add stage, Mul2 only after every second one etc. While more stages lead to a slower clock rate, the latency in clock cycles to compute the result drops. In this manner, the area/performance of the multiplier can be matched to the clock rate of the rest of the data path. The current divider implements a very simple iterative add/subtract scheme. Later GLACE versions will replace it with a faster circuit. The shifter can perform any left shift in the range of 0 to 31 bits.

Figure 6 shows a complete data path composed from 14 GLACE operators. This example (created by the Nimble Compiler [10]) realizes the first loop in the `block-quantize` function of the Versatility benchmark from Honeywell's ACS benchmark suite [13]. The loop searches an integer array for its minimum and maximum elements. The circuit consists mainly of 32-Bit comparators, registers, muxes and adders. In the non-pipelined version shown here, it runs at 54.8 MHz on the -4 speed grade. Note the very regular placement and routing resulting from exploiting the module architecture described in Section 3.2.

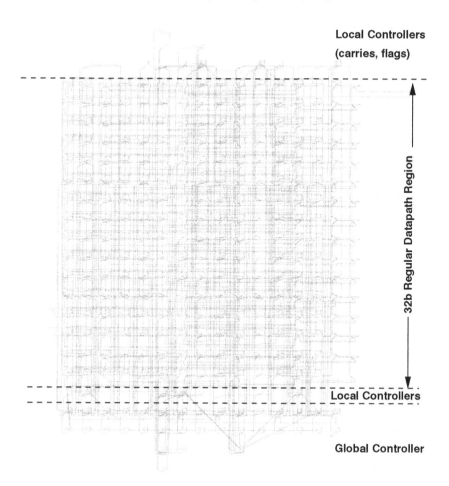

Figure 6. Sample GLACE datapath

4 Future Work

While already in a practically usable state, the current GLACE version has much potential for improvement and expansion. Providing a greater number of generators with different time/area trade-offs is just one route of advance. Additionally, the productivity of a module implementor would be considerably improved if JHDL could be extended to evaluate the structural, mapping, and placement data it has available anyway to automatically generate the FLAME meta-data views. Realizing this functionality is the major item on our mid-term agenda.

5 Summary

With GLACE, we have introduced a module generator system for adaptive computing systems that goes beyond simple macro-cell creation. Instead, it also offers a comprehensive set of meta-data views that present the front-end tools with sufficient instance-specific characteristics to base optimization decisions on.

Cell layouts created by GLACE have a consistent layout style which allows their efficient composition to form entire data paths. By using the general FLAME interface for all interactions and data representations, the internals of the system are abstracted. The resulting infrastructure is thus easily extended by adding other generator cores without affecting the client-tools. Furthermore, by relying on a programmatic API instead of a command-line or graphical user interface, GLACE supports the completely transparent use of module generators in fully automatic compile flows.

References

1. Synopsys Inc., "Module Compiler User Guide", *EDA software documentation*, Mountain View (CA) 1997
2. Xilinx Inc., "X-BLOX Reference", *EDA software documentation*, San Jose (CA) 1995
3. Dittmer, J., Sadewasser, H., "Parametrisierbare Modulgeneratoren für die FPGA-Familie Xilinx XC4000", *Diploma thesis*, Tech. Univ. Braunschweig (Germany), 1995
4. Chu, M., Weaver, N., Sulimma, K., DeHon, A., Wawrzynek, J., "Object Oriented Circuit Generators in Java", *Proc. IEEE Symp. on FCCM*, Napa Valley (CA) 1998
5. Mencer, O., Morf, M., Flynn, M.J., "PAM-Blox: High Performance FPGA Design for Adaptive Computing", *Proc. IEEE Symp. on FCCM*, Napa Valley (CA), 1998
6. Hutchings, B., Bellows, P., Hawkins, J., Hemmert, S., "A CAD Suite for High-Performance FPGA Design", *Proc. IEEE Symp. on FCCM*, Napa Valley (CA), 1999
7. Xilinx, Inc., "XC4000E and XC4000X FPGA Series", *device datasheet*, http://www.xilinx.com/partinfo/4000.pdf, 2000
8. Xilinx, Inc., "Virtex 2.5V FPGAs", *device datasheet*, http://www.xilinx.com/partinfo/ds003.pdf, 2000
9. Koch, A., "Regular Datapaths on Field-Programmable Gate Arrays", *Ph.D. thesis*, Tech. Univ. Braunschweig (Germany), 1997
10. Li, Y.B., Harr, R., et al. "Hardware-Software Co-Design of Embedded Reconfigurable Architectures", *Proc. Design Automation Conference*, 2000
11. Koch, A., "Enabling Automatic Module Generation for FCCM Compilers", *Proc. IEEE Symp. on Field-Programmable Custom Computing Machines*, 1999
12. Electronics Industry Association, "EDIF Version 4 0 0", *ANSI/EIA 682-1996 Standard*, Washington (DC) 1996
13. Kumar, S. et al, "A Benchmark Suite for Evaluating Configurable Computing Systems" *Proc. Intl. Symp. on FPGAs*, Monterey (CA), 2000

Generative Development System for FPGA Processors with *Active Components*

Stephan Rühl, Peter Dillinger, Stefan Hezel, and Reinhard Männer

Universität Mannheim, Informatik V, B6, 26, 68131 Mannheim, GERMANY
{ruehl,dillinger,hezel,maenner}@ti.uni-mannheim.de

Abstract. A development environment for FPGAs has been created, which allows to build a data-flow system easily by assembling pre-designed components. To get a high-level, platform independent description we introduce *Active Components*. They contain several implementations for several hardware platforms and ensure correct usage of the communication interface. This offers an improved portability and reusability compared to standard FPGA modules. A comparison with a hand-crafted implementation shows its applicability without any serious drawback in resource utilization and performance.

1 Introduction

In the last years, field programmable gate arrays (FPGA) became very popular. They are powerful instruments for enhancing performance in industrial and scientific applications. Unfortunately programming of such logic devices is a very complicated process and takes a long time for learning and understanding the hardware and their description languages. For PC-based systems it is also possible to use the FPGA as an extra processor implemented on standard PCI cards. But such hybrid systems need an extra amount of time for understanding the system and the communication model, and also require the knowledge of two different programming languages.

Many hardware modules can only be used in a new design after doing some serious modifications of fundamental parameters, e.g. the number of pins, or the type of handshaking. The same holds true if the module should be implemented on different hardware.

There are a number of development systems targeting the programming of heterogeneous systems. Yet they have serious drawbacks concerning the need for portable system descriptions, widely reusable modules and supported target platforms.

Development systems like LYCOS [6] and VULCAN [7] merely support systems consisting of a single CPU and a single ASIC or FPGA. Other approaches like Handel-C [5] support the usage of other resources like RAMs and off-chip interfaces in addition to FPGAs, but much manual work is needed to port this description to other target platforms. All systems have in common that they only allow the definition of modules with fixed implementations and communication interfaces, resulting in low reusability.

G. Brebner and R. Woods (Eds.): FPL 2001, LNCS 2147, pp. 513–522, 2001.

To avoid such time-consuming developer work there is a need for intelligent modules capable of implementing themselves on a selected platform (a processing unit like an FPGA or CPU) and of negotiating a communication protocol with other connected modules. Such intelligent modules are called here *Active Components*. They are provided with a set of various implementations for different platforms and functions to establish context based interfaces to communicate with each other. Since *Active Components* are independent of any processing unit, the application can be used on any other hardware platform by changing the platform description, which holds the types and structures of the processing units.

We are about to create a development system on the highest abstraction level, the domain specific level that uses *Active Components*. At this level, there are problem dependent function blocks and the algorithm is described by connecting the different blocks. The problem description gives you a possible data flow solution, so that only critical parameters, such as running time and available processing units (CPU, DSP boards, FPGA coprocessors, etc.) need to be specified. After evaluating which of the available platforms are most suitable for the specified restrictions (like running time), a compiler-like instance can translate the given problem description into executable programs, DSP codes, hardware designs etc.

2   Main Parts of the Development System

2.1   Active Components

Active Components are the basic building blocks that are used for describing the problem to be solved. Each component supplies a function and interfaces to access the function. Figure 1 shows the structure of an *Active Component*.

Each component can either be a data source, which produces only output data (e.g. camera modules, sensor signals), it can be a data terminal, which receives only input data (e.g. display image data, store sensor data), or it can be a functional unit, which uses its input data to generate appropriate output data.

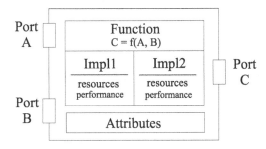

Fig. 1. Structure of an *Active Component*.

Therefore the interface must supply means to handle incoming and outgoing data as well as information for controlling the execution of the corresponding function.

This is achieved by using ports. Each port is assigned a port type, which specifies the kind of information to handle and the type of communication methods to use. The transferred information can range from simple boolean control information to complete images including line and frame synchronization information. It is also possible to leave the communication mechanism unspecified and merely specify the required communication properties like data throughput or maximum latency. Therefore interfaces are independent of a concrete implementation. This provides a high level of abstraction for the user of the component and leaves room for a wide range of optimizations concerning the communication mechanisms and for choosing a suitable implementation for the component.

In addition *Active Components* offer attributes to influence the properties of the realized functions. This includes parameters like size and coefficients of the convolution mask for a convolution function, or performance requirements like the necessary data throughput.

Another property of *Active Components* is the ability to choose an implementation that is tailored to the context in which they are used. To translate a problem description into an executable implementation, the types of the used ports must be fixed, and an implementation for the used components must be created. The selection of a port type affects the performance and resource requirements for the resulting implementation code of the component and the whole system. For this reason additional information is attached to the parameters which signifies which effect the selection of the given port type will have on the performance and on the implementation cost (resources) of the resulting system.

Therefore each component has a set of different implementation alternatives out of which the most appropriate one for the given context is chosen automatically. The designer of an *Active Component* not only supplies the various possible implementations, but also a criterion to select the most suitable one for the context in which the component is used. Thus, not only the implementation itself but also the decisions for choosing a given implementation are reusable.

2.2   Extending *Active Components*

An approach to improve the usability and portability of components is the use of port adapters. Port adapters are *Active Components* which can adapt different communication mechanisms and data types. They are automatically inserted between the ports and the implementation of a component. They are fully transparent to the component itself. This increases the range of implementation possibilities without having to change the implementation of the component. In many cases there is not even a significant trade-off in performance, especially if the conversion takes place between port types with equal communication properties but different implementations. Simple port adapters can e.g. convert active low boolean signals into active high boolean signals and vice versa. Other more complex ones can synchronize synchronous data transfers using different clocks, or change parallel data to serial data and backward to reduce the number of used pins. This process is completely transparent to the components, because the port adapters are automatically placed behind the sender and in front of the receiver. The port adapters may even choose a higher transfer rate for the serial data parts to reduce the performance impact.

Some other properties of *Active Components* are used to simplify the generation of the components itself. Instead of describing the various implementations of a component using standard implementation languages like VHDL, CHDL [1] or C++, it is possible to generate new, more complex components by using a hierarchic structure. The implementation of a new component can therefore be described by chaining up other more simple components, inheriting the optimization features of the underlying components.

2.3   Platform Description

Active Components are implemented on the platform they support by providing several implementation variations.

To define the target platform, which is chosen or available to solve the problem, an additional platform description is needed. Included in this description are the available processing units (FPGAs, DSPs, PCs etc.), the communication mechanism between them, routing resources and additional resources like memory units and clock generators.

A target platform can be an array of connected FPGA processors running stand-alone, or the same configuration linked to a PC, or a PC with or without any special hardware boards, such as PCI FPGA boards.

A special kind of routing resource is needed to bridge the gap between different processing units using incompatible communication mechanisms. If, e.g. an FPGA processor is connected to a PC via a PCI interface, there is no simple way of establishing a connection between their components. The FPGA based component uses most likely a simple channel orientated communication mechanism which is completely incompatible with the PCI bus protocol needed to utilize the PC. To overcome this restriction, active routing resources are introduced into the platform description. In addition to the specification of the locations that can be connected by a routing resource, they also provide a mechanism to adapt the communication mechanisms used by the components and the ones provided by the target platform. In the example given above, the active routing resource, that connects FPGA processor and PC, would automatically create implementations on both processing units that use the PCI protocol to enable communication between the components. Active routing resources enhance the portability of the problem description.

2.4   Base System

Even though *Active Components* are smart function blocks, an overlaying module is still needed to control the process to check each component, negotiate the communication method between them, and instruct each component to provide the appropriate implementation code for the chosen target platform and communication mechanism. This module is called the base system.

It is implemented in Java and each component is an extra class with the described properties and implementation code provided by the module function developers. The class knows all about the ports and implementation criteria to participate in the complete system solution.

3   Implementing the Problem Description

In order to describe an algorithm to solve a given problem, suitable components have to be selected and connected in a way to specify the functionality intended.

After finishing the problem description, it has to be transformed into an implementation on the target platform. This process can be divided into four steps:

1. Choose a target platform
2. Map each component on the target platform
3. Map the connections on the target platform
4. Implement the *Active Components* and generate a description file for each processing unit (e.g. FPGA, PLD, CPU)

It is the task of the base system to control these steps. It uses the problem description as a starting point and the data supplied by the *Active Components* and the target platform description to make the implementation decisions that are not local to a single *Active Component* or are related the target platform. Only the implementation of each *Active Component* is done by the components themselves.

Choice of a target platform This is the only remaining step that still has to be done by the developer.

Mapping of the components During this step of the implementing process, each *Active Component* is mapped on a processing unit of the target platform - or if specified by the component - on other resources like RAM banks, fixed function chips like clock generators and I/O controllers.

Mapping of the connections During the next step, the connections given in the problem description are realized on the target platform. Every component participating by its port in a connection is asked which communication methods are supported for this port. The port types that are supported by all connected ports and that fulfill the user defined communication requirements are extracted and sorted in such a way, that the port type providing the best trade-off between performance and implementation cost is selected first. If by choosing this port type, the connections cannot be mapped to the target platform, the next port

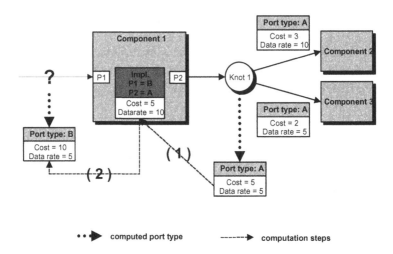

Fig. 2. Knots and port types.

type is selected and the mapping process is restarted. If no port type is available that can be mapped, an error is asserted.

The necessary steps for computing the port types available for a port are shown in Figure 2. In this example the port types and resulting performance data for port P1 of Component 1 have to be calculated. The types that can be selected for P1 depend on the implementations that can be chosen for Component 1. This decision has to take the port types into consideration that are feasible for Knot 1. Only an implementation providing port types for P2, which are compatible with the port types of Knot 1, ensures that an implementation for the whole system can be generated. As both components connected to Knot 1 support the port type A, this type is supported by Knot 1. Each port type is supplemented by attributes that specify the transmission rate (Data rate) and the implementation cost (Cost) caused by selecting the port type which is given for the corresponding port. These values are used to calculate the port types supported for Knot 1. Usually all ports connected to a knot are used in this calculation. In the case stated above, a component only needs to know the restrictions caused by the ports of the other components that are connected to the knot. It can therefore request to exclude its own port from this computation. Component 1 can now use the port types available for Knot 1 to calculate the port types supported for P2. The implementations compatible with the port types of Knot 1 are selected and used to determine the port types for port P1. The attributes of the port type are calculated to reflect the impact the port type and the implementation chosen for the component have on the performance and the implementation cost. This approach ensures that each port type available for a knot indicates the impact its usage has on the properties of the whole system.

Implementation of the Active Components When all communications between all components have been realized as they are given in the problem description, the *Active Components* will be implemented on the chosen processing unit. Each component chooses the implementation for the function it supplies, which fulfills the requirements as defined by the attributes set by the user, the type and amount of implementation resources, and the port types fixed in the previous step.

When all components have been implemented, a description file for each processing unit is assembled and a function to initialize the target system is created.

Finally the whole system, which now consists of the implementation description of all *Active Components*, can be compiled with the compiler provided by the implementation language (C++, VHDL, etc.).

4   Example

To illustrate the use of the generative development system an example is taken from the field of image processing originated by the OpenEye project[1]. In this project many modules for image processing applications were implemented for an FPGA in CHDL, a special hardware description language also developed for this purpose. This C++ based hardware description language is described in [1].

The target platform used for the following examples is composed by a PC and an FPGA coprocessor (a microEnable board as described in [4]) connected via a PCI bus. In addition a digital CMOS camera is connected to the FPGA processor.

4.1   Local Orientation

A local orientation is a gradient image, where each pixel has an individual vector representing the direction and the amount of the change of its gray value. For a better visualization this gray-scaled gradient image can be colorized by assigning different directions to different colors. The intensity of the colors is defined by the gradient value. The gradient image and its colorization can easily be calculated in three steps:

1. Generate two edge images using a DoG (Derivation of Gaussian) [3] convolution mask each in x and y direction

$$g(x,y) \mapsto (dx, dy) = (\frac{\partial g}{\partial x}, \frac{\partial g}{\partial y})$$

2. Calculate the direction and the absolute value of the two dimensional vector image

$$\varphi = \arctan \frac{dy}{dx}$$
$$l = \sqrt{dx^2 + dy^2}$$

[1] Grant No. 4-4332.62-IMS/4 by industry and the Ministry of Commerce Baden-Württemberg.

3. Represent this vector image in the HSV (Hue, Saturation, Value) color domain

$$H = \varphi, \; S = \infty, \; V = l$$

The DoG is a Sobel mask and gives an appropriate result even for a 3×3 size. The calculation of the absolute value can be approximated by the sum of both absolute values, which is sufficiently precise for this visualization context.

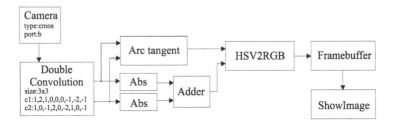

Fig. 3. Local Orientation.

Figure 3 not only represents the function diagram of a local orientation, it is the actual input of the generative system. The description is created by a CAD tool which provides the needed components from a library.

The *Camera* component is used to gain access to the pictures taken by the camera. Its implementation consists of two *Active Components* not shown in the figure: the camera controller and the interface to the digital camera. The controller component is needed to support different kinds of cameras. Access to the camera signals is possible by using the interface component to control its operation and to retrieve the picture information. This component can only be mapped on resources of the target system that are connected to the required signals, e.g. to the pins of the FPGA processor to which the camera is connected. Components like these are needed to specify I/O connections in a platform independent way.

The *Double Convolution* component is a special development for FPGA processors. It can calculate two different convolution masks by sharing a set of registers and FPGA internal RAM. Details on the operation of this enhanced FPGA processing unit are given in [2]. A convolution component needs at least two additional parameters to describe its function: the size, which is the same for both masks, and its coefficients, which may differ.

The *Arc tangent* component consists of a LUT (Look Up Table), which stores all result values of the function. The input values are used as indexes for the table. To avoid a division by zero error, the *Arc tangent* component uses two input values to look up the appropriate angle of the tangent. The *Abs* function supplies the absolute value of a signed input value, and the *Adder* function adds two values on its input.

Although it is possible at this point to transfer an HSV image to the PC, the image is transformed into the RGB color domain by using the *HSV2RGB* component. The conversion can be accelerated by performing this step through the FPGA instead through the PC.

It must be guaranteed that both images, that are sent to the input ports of the *HSV2RGB* component, arrive at the same time. This is necessary because the color domain conversion operates on corresponding pixels of both pictures. Many other components like *Adder* and *Arc tangent* component face the same problem. To achieve a reusable solution, the port adapters for ports transporting image data are extended. They allow computing the amount of time a picture generated by the camera needs to arrive at the given port, and to adjust the latency if necessary. To support this calculation each component indicates the latency it causes between one of its input and output ports. A component like the *HSV2RGB* component only has to specify, which ports have to be latency-adjusted. In the example above the latency value given from the *Arc tangent* is greater than the added values from the chained *Abs* and *Adder* components. Therefore the port adapter for the input port of the *HSV2RGB* connected to the *Adder* adds a delay unit to adjust the different latencies.

The RGB image data is stored in the *Framebuffer* component, from where it is transferred to the *ShowImage* component, which is designed to visualize the image data. The *Framebuffer* component signals the availability of a new picture to the *ShowImage* resource, which in turn updates its display with the new picture.

Whereas the *Camera* and the *Framebuffer* component provide implementations suitable for FPGAs, the *ShowImage* component needs to be implemented on a PC. Therefore the connection between *Framebuffer* and *ShowImage* must utilize the PCI bus connection between FPGA processor and PC. The target platform description provides the active routing resources which are needed to implement this connection. The communication model used for this connection is the DMA (direct memory access) transfer, which is very fast for large blocks such as whole images. All this is invisible to the developer.

5 Results

A crucial part in programming FPGA processors is the performance of the resulting implementation, indicated by the implementation cost and the processing speed. Table 1 shows the values obtained for the example mentioned above[2]. Hand-crafted designs have been created by using C++ and CHDL as description languages. Performance data for the part of the system that is implemented on the PC is omitted, because the values are identical for both approaches.

As shown in this figure, the usage of *Active Components* leads to implementations that have increased resource requirements, but offer the same processing speed as hand-crafted designs. As the increase of resource requirements is less than 8%, this does not impose any serious drawback.

---

[2] To evaluate these values, Version 1.52 of the Place&Route Software provided by Xilinx has been used.

Active Components		Hand-crafted	
Cost	Frequency	Cost	Frequency
2841 CLBS	39 MHz	2679 CLBS	39 MHz

Table 1. Comparison of system performance

The results show, that *Active Components* offer a high level approach for developing FPGA processor applications which leads to an increased programming productivity without any serious impact on the performance of the implementations.

6   Future Work

As for today, each *Active Component* requires considerable programming work before it can be used in the described development system. Several implementations on different processing units must be developed to use the generative feature to choose the best method for a given system. For each module written in CHDL, VHDL or in C++ a complete port description must be given in order to give the base system the information, which communication methods it can choose from. A user friendly interface is necessary to simplify these steps and to enhance the applicability of the system.

System improvements can be achieved by involving a backtracking algorithm to discard implementation decisions already made, or communication paths already routed. Thereby an iterative mapping process is possible and drifting into a local minimum is avoided.

References

1. K. Kornmesser et al.: Simulating FPGA-Coprocessors using the FPGA Development System CHDL. Proceedings of PACT '98 Workshop on Reconfigurable Computing (1998).
2. P. Dillinger, S. Hezel, H. Lauer: FPGAs zur Echtzeit-Bildverarbeitung mit 1D/2D-FIR-Filteroperationen. Image Processing and Machine Vision, 213–218, VDI Berichte 1572, (2000), Düsseldorf
3. B. Jähne: Practical Handbook on image processing for scientific applications, CRC Press LLC, Boca Raton, FL, (1997)
4. O. Brosch, P. Dillinger, K. Kornmesser, A. Kugel, R. Männer, M. Sessler, H. Simmler, H. Singpiel, S. Rühl, R. Lay and K.-H. Noffz, L. Levinson: MicroEnable - A Reconfigurable FPGA Coprocessor. 4th Worksh. on Electronics for LHC Experimentsi, Rome, Italy, (1998), 402–406
5. Embedded Solutions Ltd.: Handel-C Language Reference Manual (Version 2.1)
6. J. Madsen: LYCOS: The Lyngby Co-Systhesis System. Design Automation for Embedded Systems, vol.2, nr.2 (1997)
7. R. K. Gupta, G. De Micheli: System Synthesis Via Hardware-Software Co-Design. Computer system Labority, Stanford University (1992)

Compilation Increasing the Scheduling Scope for Multi-memory-FPGA-Based Custom Computing Machines[*]

João M P Cardoso[1] and Horácio C Neto[2]

INESC-ID, Lisboa
[1]Faculty of Sciences and Technology/University of Algarve
Campus de Gambelas, 8000 117 – Faro, Portugal, email: jmpc@acm.org
[2]IST, Lisboa, email: hcn@inesc.pt

Abstract. This paper presents new achievements on the automatic mapping of abstract algorithms, written in imperative software programming languages, to custom computing machines. The reconfigurable hardware element of the target architecture consists of one field-programmable gate array coupled with one or more memories. The compilation flow exposes operation- and functional-level parallelism, and speculative execution. Such expositions are efficiently represented in a hierarchical model. In order to take full advantage of such representation, the scheduling scope is significantly improved by merging basic blocks at loop boundaries and by considering the parallel execution of exposed concurrent loops. The paper describes the scheduling technique, shows a study on the impact of the merge operation, and reveals the improvements achieved when the exposed parallelism is fully satisfied.

1. Introduction

One of the most challenging issues for reconfigurable computing systems is the development of mapping methods able to reduce the growing gap between design capacity and technology REF[1]. New field-programmable gate arrays (FPGAs) with millions of logic gates are becoming available, but high-level methods still lack.

The goal of our work is to provide a compilation framework to automatically map abstract algorithms written in software programming languages, such as Java, to a reconfigurable hardware (*reconfigware*) system [2, 3]. REFREFWe believe, as other authors doREF [4], that efforts on mapping from high-level programs are fundamental for the success of reconfigurable computing systems, because typical users do not have the design expertise required today for developing the *reconfigware* part. Furthermore, software languages are more apt than hardware specific languages to describe applications with huge complexity [5] REFand their use permits the migration to *reconfigware* of already developed algorithms - mostly programmed in C/C++ and/or Java.

---

[*] Research partially supported by the Portuguese PRAXIS XXI Program under the scope of the AXEL Project PRAXIS/2/2.1/TIT/1643/95.

G. Brebner and R. Woods (Eds.): FPL 2001, LNCS 2147, pp. 523-533, 2001.

This article addresses some hardware compilation issues of our approach and particularly presents a new technique to enlarge the scheduling scope when generating the control unit model. The approach resorts to compilation techniques to expose inherent parallelism in an abstract algorithm represented in an imperative software programming language. Such parallelism is embodied in intermediate formats. Multiple flows of control and loop-hierarchies are exposed and exhibited in those formats as well. An appropriate choice of the representation is essential for achieving high-performance results (inefficient representations may significantly hamper the results achieved by the scheduler). The goal is to take full advantage of using a specific architecture that can implement multiple-flows of control, high degrees of operation- and functional-level parallelism. Promoting, whenever possible, variables to wires (by means of variable renaming) permits that speculative execution implementations do not need to recover, unless when dealing with operations with side-effects (memory stores), and so creates a natural mode for speculative execution.

One of the mostly used representations is the traditional control-data flow graph (CDFG) [6]REF. It explicitly represents the control-flow structure of the input algorithm and groups operations in basic blocks (BBs). The low number of instructions in a BB in control-flow intensive applications [7] REFlimits the performance achieved by using the CDFG. The hyperblock [8] REFis one of the graph representations, which prioritizes regions of the control-flow graph (CFG) to be considered as a whole. The hyperblock has been used in [9] REFfor considering, among other goals, the mostly executed paths (or the paths possible to be implemented in the reconfigurable coprocessor) in a loop. Those paths are considered as a whole by a fine-grain scheduler. The approach is tailored to mixed *reconfigware*/software solutions and neither considers functional parallelism nor global reordering of the input programming structure. We propose the use of a hierarchical program dependence graph (HPDG), which is a representation based on the hierarchical task graph (HTG) [10] REFand on the Program Dependence Graph (PDG) [11]REF. It is constructed from the data-dependence (DDG) and merge-dependence (MDG) graphs [2, 3] REFREFand so BBs of the initial CFG emerge reordered only based on the dependences exposed. Loops are represented in hierarchical levels. REFAlthough with a different purpose, the HTG has been already used by *state-of-the-art* high-level synthesis approaches targeting ASICs [12]REF. This approach uses the HTG for moving operations beyond BBs but does not enable functional parallelism.

This paper is structured in the following sections. Section 2 describes briefly the GALADRIEL and NENYA compilers. Section 3 describes the intermediate representations and explains the scheduling by regions. Experimental results are shown in Section 4. Section 5 resumes the related work. Finally, in section 6, conclusions, future and ongoing work are enumerated.

2. Summary of the GALADRIEL & NENYA Compilers

GALADRIEL is a front-end compiler that receives the Java™ bytecodes of a given method and exposes various levels of parallelism. Such parallelism is represented in graph models (constructed using extensions to standard compilation techniques

[13]REF) that are input to the NENYA *reconfigware* compilerREF [2]. NENYA is customized to reconfigurable computing systems whose architecture consists of one FPGA connected to one or more memories (RAMs). The compilation steps performed by NENYA are illustrated in Fig. 1.

NENYA already integrates a number of dataflow optimizations suitable to improve the overall results: bit-width reductions, bit-constant-patterns propagation, tree-height reduction, operator strength reduction on multiplications by constants, etc. It considers the use of speculative execution for all operations (except for memory stores). The arrays in the input algorithm are mapped to memories connected to the FPGA. The base address assignment scheme used, for each array, permits to save area and reduce the delay of the address generation mechanism. Resource sharing is only considered when a bus is accessed by multiple sources (such as units interfacing to memories). When FPGA resources are insufficient to accommodate the architecture, temporal partitioning is performed [14] REFand multiple *reconfigware* instances are generated.

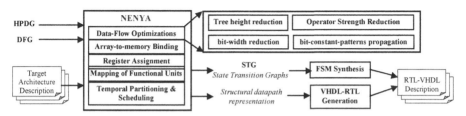

Fig. 1. Steps of the compilation flow performed by NENYA.

NENYA generates a behavioral VHDL-RTL description of each state transition graph (STG) and a structural VHDL-RTL description of each datapath. A logic synthesis tool is currently used for synthesizing the control unit circuit from the STG representations. Each datapath is entirely produced by using circuit generators. The use of circuit generators permits to have much more accurate area/performance estimations than those that are usually available by using logic synthesis (difficult to predict), and provides better results in some arithmetic operators with almost close-to-zero compilation overhead.

3. Region-Based Scheduling

The representation models used are an HPDG and a global dataflow graph (DFG). The HPDG explicitly exhibits the reordering of BBs and loops based on its dependencies, previously exposed from the initial sequential program. Loop bodies are represented in hierarchical levels. Loop blocks that appear side-by-side in the same level of the HPDG can be simultaneously executed (see Loop.1 and Loop.4 in Fig.2b). Such loop blocks contain BBs or/and another loop blocks. At the bottom level, the HPDG contains only BBs. A global DFG represents the original code at the operation level and so exhibits operation-level parallelism. The DFG uses multiplexer nodes in merge-dependence points, selection logic on the select signals of the multiplexers, and predicated logic on store operations existent in conditional paths, among other operations. The control unit manages execution of such store operations based on predicate's evaluation.

Each block in the HPDG is linked to the related set of nodes in the DFG. Each DFG node is annotated with the execution delay of the component in the library that implements the correspondent operation, considering the bit-width of operands and results. From the HPDG and the global DFG the scheduling phase outputs STGs responsible for the orchestration of the datapaths (see the block diagram in Fig. 2c).

Although the scheduler does not consider resource sharing, a temporal partitioning scheme is done, whenever needed, at the top level of the HPDGREF [3].

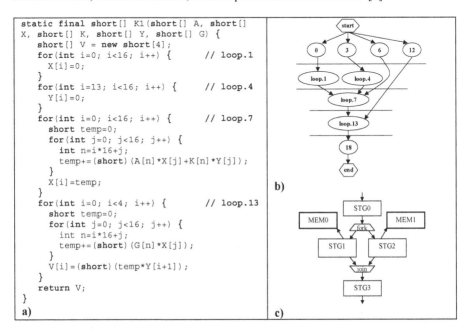

```
static final short[] K1(short[] A, short[]
X, short[] K, short[] Y, short[] G) {
  short[] V = new short[4];
  for(int i=0; i<16; i++) {        // loop.1
    X[i]=0;
  }
  for(int i=13; i<16; i++) {       // loop.4
    Y[i]=0;
  }
  for(int i=0; i<16; i++) {        // loop.7
    short temp=0;
    for(int j=0; j<16; j++) {
      int n=i*16+j;
      temp+=(short)(A[n]*X[j]+K[n]*Y[j]);
    }
    X[i]=temp;
  }
  for(int i=0; i<4; i++) {         // loop.13
    short temp=0;
    for(int j=0; j<16; j++) {
      int n=i*16+j;
      temp+=(short)(G[n]*X[j]);
    }
    V[i]=(short)(temp*Y[i+1]);
  }
  return V;
}
a)
```

Fig. 2. Kalman example: a) Java code; b) Top level of the HPDG; c) Block diagram of STGs.

Usual scheduling schemes consider, at each time, only operations in the same BB of the CDFG. Therefore, they produce a schedule that, although might consider the parallel execution of operations inside BBs, serializes the states according to the original sequence of BBs in the CDFG/CFG. Such schemes are unable to take advantage of all the inherent parallelism exposed.

As has been already explained, in our approach operation-, BB-, and functional-level parallelism are all exposed and explicitly exhibited in the HPDG. A scheduler should consider, whenever possible, the image of a whole group of BBs (herein, designated by region) in the global DFG to generate datapath solutions with high-performance. The capacity to deal with regions is an important scheme to improve scheduling results. Fig.3 shows a simple example illustrating the effect of considering a region during scheduling. Considering three clock cycles for the latency of each multiplier and one clock cycle for the other operations, the region reduces the schedule length by one clock step. Region based scheduling may have even more impact when two or more BBs and/or loop blocks in a region can be executed in parallel.

Regions are created hierarchically among loop boundaries (i.e., when a loop node is found in the HPDG all the region up to that point is scheduled) using an ASAP (as soon as possible) scheme. In Fig.2b the existent loops define the boundaries of the regions. The scheduler uses, for each region on the HPDG, the related section on the global DFG. The core of the scheduler, when scheduling each region, is based on a static-list scheduling algorithm [6]REF. The role of the scheduler is to generate STGs that model a control unit for orchestrating memory accesses and for executing loops (see Fig.2c). Currently, the scheduling scheme does not consider the parallel execution of two or more concurrent loops when they have accesses to the same single-port memory (an arbitration scheme needs to be addressed). When two or more loops can be simultaneously executed[1], independent STGs are created and a fork-join scheme is used to activate and synchronize them.

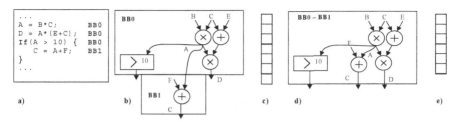

Fig. 3. Source code; b) BBs and each DFG; c) Scheduling at the BB level (7 steps); d) Creation of a region by merging BBs, and the global DFG; e) Scheduling the region (6 steps).

4. Experimental Results

In order to show the effectiveness of the approach, a number of test examples was considered and some of the results are reported here. All the results report estimations obtained by NENYA, from a description of each operation existent in the source code considering the implementation on the XC6000 family of FPGAs [15] (not considering interconnection costs).

The examples considered have low to medium complexity (maximum of 6 arrays and 6 loops) and all of them were automatically compiled from Java without any modification of the original code (except in the 5 examples where loops have been manually unrolled).

SQRT is a sqrt function (input of 12-bits/output of 6-bits), USQRT is another sqrt function (32/16-bits). CRC-32 is the **C**yclic **R**edundancy **C**heck of 32-bits using the

---

[1] Research in high-level synthesis has considered the scheduling of two concurrent loops whose bodies share functional units [16]. The approach does not use an arbitration scheme (maybe because it is unviable when sharing many functional units). It forms all the possibilities that could occur when scheduling two loops with different schedule lengths and furnishes a control unit with a single control flow to coordinate the parallel execution of such loops.

polynomial of the Ethernet protocol. QRS refers to the loop body of the benchmark from [17]. HAMMING is an hamming decoder (input of 7-bits and output of 4-bits). MASKBITS is an image processing algorithm that masks an input image (512×512) with a mask of equal dimension. CCW and INTERSECT are two geometric functions [18]. BPIC is a binary pattern image encoder [19]. FPBI is a low pass image filter with a window of 3×3 pixels. IDEA is a submodule of the International Data Encryption Algorithm (accepts 8 input bytes, a 52 element sub-key of 16-bit words and returns 8-bytes). SOBEL is the sobel operator over an image and performs horizontal and vertical convolutions. K1 refers to the Kalman filter [20]. DCT is the Discrete Cosine Transform and is performed on blocks of 8×8 elements (*short* type). DCT1, BPIC1-3, and FPBI1-2 are versions of the above examples with some loops unrolled. We group the examples in two sets: the 1st set has more *if-then-else* structures [SQRT to INTERSECT] and the 2nd set is more general [BPIC to K1].

Results represent the estimated schedule length (esl) of the longest path. Fig.4 shows the effect on the esl using the HPDG versus the CDFG approaches.

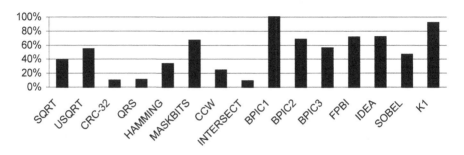

Fig. 4. Schedule lengths estimated from the HPDG normalized to lengths estimated from the CDFG.

Considering the estimated scheduling lengths with the first set of examples:
- For three examples (CRC-32, QRS and INTERSECT) the esl with the HPDG is less than 10% of the esl with the CDFG. For all the other examples, the esl with the HPDG is less than 70% of the esl with the CDFG.
- As far as the increase on the number of operations executed in parallel during a state of the control unit is concerned: for USQRT an increase from 12 to 54 is obtained, and for INTERSECT from 5 to 65. For the other examples the increase was lower but never insignificant.

Considering the estimated scheduling lengths with the second set of examples:
- For BPIC1 there is no improvement. For K1 the esl with the HPDG is about 90% of the esl with the CDFG. For all the other examples the esl with the HPDG is less than 70% of the esl with the CDFG.
- The most significant increases on the number of operations executed in a state of the control unit are obtained for BPIC2: from 37 to 53, BPIC3: from 120 to 134, and SOBEL: from 10 to 16.

The results summarized above show important performance gains when using the HPDG with increase of the scheduling scope. Next, the memory access bottleneck is quantified in some examples. We compare the esl when considering only one single-port external memory attached to the FPGA with the esl when considering no constraints about the number of ports of such memory. Fig.5 shows the resultant decrease in performance when considering only a single-port. When unrolling is used (e.g., BPIC1-2, FPBI1-3, and DCT1) the decrease in performance is even more accentuated.

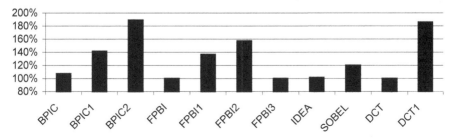

Fig. 5. Increase on the estimated schedule lengths (values larger than 100%) with a single-port memory compared with the use of a multiport memory.

For evaluation of the impact of the number of memories attached to the FPGA the following versions of the Kalman example (the example uses 6 arrays) are considered (see the main characteristics in Fig.6a): original version (K1); with the two inner loops unrolled (K2); with the first two loops and the two inner loops unrolled (K3); with the first two loops, the inner loop of the third loop and the last two loops unrolled (K4). Fig. 6b shows the esl for each version when increasing the number of memories attached to the FPGA. The best schedules need 2 memories for K1, 3 memories for K3 and 4 memories for K2 and K4. The figure also shows the improvement when considering loop unrolling. It can be seen that, for this example, speed-ups of almost 7 are achieved by the unrolling versions, considering various single-port memories, over the original version (K1) with a single-port memory.

Version	K1	K2	K3	K4
# Lo Java	30	96	135	239
# JVM Inst.	118	694	770	1,417
# BBs	19	13	77	4
# DFG Nodes	108	438	443	656
# loops	6	4	2	1
# memory accesses	1,191	1,191	853	853

a)

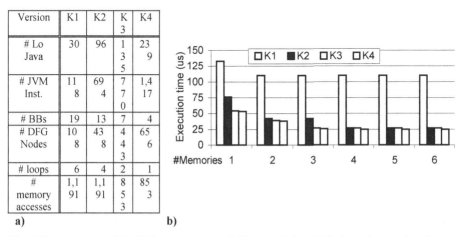

b)

Fig. 6. Four versions of the Kalman example: a) Characteristics; b) Estimated execution times.

5. Related Work

In this section we resume some research on compilation techniques for reconfigurable computing systems. Work on compilers targeting commercial FPGAs from abstract algorithms written in imperative software programming languages is emphasized since it is closer to the work described in this paper. Work on mapping methods using software programming languages enabled for describing hardware-like semantics and structures are not considered.

PRISM-IREF [21], II [22] REFand the Transmogrifier C [23] REFcompilers are some of the first compilation approaches for FPGA-based reconfigurable computing systems. Such approaches have identified important issues on compiling for reconfigurable computing but simple representation models have been used. Some authors adapted traditional high-level synthesis approaches to architectural synthesis for reconfigurable computing systems [24].REF

CAMERON [25]REF, CHAMPION [REF26] and MATCH [27] REFare recent approaches that resort to a commercial logic synthesis tool for generating the hardware structure to be implemented in FPGA-based systems. Both CAMERON and CHAMPION are tailored for image processing applications. CAMERON starts from a single-assignment C language (SA-C). CHAMPION starts from the Cantata graphical programming environment. MATCH accepts MATLAB™ descriptions and focuses on important aspects of mapping tasks to system resources (FPGAs, microprocessors, DSPs, etc.), but uses rudimentary approaches to compile to FPGAs (uses a direct translation of the abstract syntax tree to behavioral RTL-VHDL).

Important aspects of pipelining in applications with regular loops (constant loop bounds) and array indexing (using affine index access functions) have been studied in [28] REFand [29] iREFn the context of compilation from C to FPGA-based systems.REF

Many research efforts are being tailored to architectures of processing elements grouping a microprocessor with *reconfigware* in the same chip. Most of them research compilation techniques targeting their own architectures. The most remarkable are Garp-C [9] and NAPA-C [30] compilers, just to name a few.

The efforts of high-level synthesis from software programming languages have been mostly tailored to C. However, the low level used in the C language to manipulate memory contents, such as the use of pointers to fine-grain physical locations, can hinder static resolution and incapacitate a significant number of optimizations. Furthermore, the research targeting ASICs differs mainly from the research targeting FPGA-based systems on both the fixed architecture layer of the FPGAs and its programmable facility.

Our work differs from all the above approaches on several points. The one emphasized in this paper, proposes the use of intermediate representations that explicitly expose high levels of parallelism and multiple-flows of control. By increasing the scope of the scheduler, the compiler is able to satisfy all the exposed parallelism.

6. Conclusions and Future Work

This paper presents methods for reconfigurable hardware compilation from a high-level imperative software programming language. The mapping methods target systems with one FPGA coupled with one or more memories. The approach uses an intermediate representation model, which allows the full exploitation of the exposed parallelism from an input abstract algorithm. The representations proposed explicitly exhibit multiple flows of control, speculative execution, and parallelism at the operation and functional levels. A region-based scheduling scheme is described that tries to satisfy such levels of parallelism.

The results show the importance of the approach as far as performance is concerned. Performance increases are shown to be provided by the new scheduling technique when comparing it to basic block based schedulers.

Future work will address software pipelining, efficient algorithms to bind arrays to memories (including distributed on-chip memory banks), and arbitration schemes to allow the parallel execution of loops when the same memory port is shared among concurrent loops. Work on the backend for retargeting other FPGA devices will be also conducted, since this is an important issue from a compilation point of view. Another important aspect that needs to be improved is the capability to share large hardware resources (e.g. multipliers) and to consider specific treatments on the presence of mutually exclusive paths.

References

1. J. Becker, R. Hartenstein, M. Herz, U. Nageldinger , "Parallelization in Co-Compilation for Configurable Accelerators," In *Proc. of the Asia South Pacific Design Automation Conference (ASP-DAC'98)*, Yokohama, Japan, February 10-13.
2. João M. P. Cardoso, and Horácio C. Neto, "Macro-Based Hardware Compilation of Java™ Bytecodes into a Dynamic Reconfigurable Computing System," In *Proc. of the IEEE 7th Symposium on Field-Programmable Custom Computing Machines (FCCM'99)*, Napa Valley, CA, USA, April 21 - 23, 1999, pp. 2-11.
3. João M. P. Cardoso, *Compilation of Java™ Algorithms for Reconfigurable Computing Systems with Exploitation of Operation-Level Parallelism*, Ph.D. thesis (in portuguese), IST (*Instituto Superior Técnico*), Lisbon, Portugal, October 2000.
4. Scott Hauck, "The Future of Reconfigurable Systems," *Keynote Address, 5th Canadian Conference on Field Programmable Devices*, Montreal, June 1998.
5. J. Babb et al, "Parallelizing Applications into Silicon," In *Proc. of the 7th IEEE Symposium on Field-Programmable Custom Computing Machines (FCCM'99)*, Napa Valley, CA, USA, April 21-23, 1999, pp. 70-80.
6. D. Gajski, et al., High-Level Synthesis, Introduction to Chip and System Design, Kluwer Academic Publishers, 1992.
7. J. A. Fisher, and B. R. Rau, "Instruction-Level Parallel Processing," In H. C. Torng and S.Vassiliadis, editors, *Instruction-Level Parallel Processors*, IEEE Computer Society Press, 1995, pp. 41-49.
8. Scott A. Mahlke, David C. Lin, William Y. Chen, Richard E. Hank, Roger A. Bringmann, "Effective Compiler Support for Predicated Execution Using the Hyperblock," In *Proc. of the 25th International Symposium on Microarchitecture*, Dec. 1992, pp. 45-54.

9. Timothy J. Callahan, John Hauser, and John Wawrzynek, "The Garp Architecture and C Compiler," *IEEE Computer*, Vol.33, No. 4, April 2000, pp. 62-69.

10. M. Girkar, and C. D. Polychronopoulos, "Automatic Extraction of Functional Parallelism from ordinary Programs," In *IEEE Transactions on Parallel and Distributed Systems*, Vol. 3, No. 2, March 1992, pp. 166-178.

11. J. Ferrante, K. J. Ottenstein, and J. D. Warren, "The Program Dependence Graph and its uses in optimization," *ACM Transactions on Programming Languages and Systems*, vol. 9, no. 3, July 1987, pp. 319-349.

12. S. Gupta, N. Savoiu, S. Kim, N.D. Dutt, R.K. Gupta, A. Nicolau, "Speculation Techniques for High Level synthesis of Control Intensive Designs," in *Proc. of the 38th Design Automation Conference (DAC'01)*, Las Vegas, Nevada, USA, June 18-22, 2001.

13. S. S. Muchnick, *Advanced Compiler Design and Implementation*. Morgan Kaufmann Publishers, Inc., San Francisco, CA, USA, 1997.

14. João M. P. Cardoso, and Horácio C. Neto, "An Enhanced Static-List Scheduling Algorithm for Temporal Partitioning onto RPUs," In *Proc. of the IFIP X Intl. Conference on Very Large Scale Integration (VLSI'99)*, Lisbon, December 1-3, 1999, pp. 485-496.

15. Xilinx Inc., *XC6000 Field Programmable Gate Arrays*, v.1.10, April 24, 1997.

16. G. Lakshminarayana, K. S. Khouri, and N. K. Jha, "Wavesched: A Novel Scheduling Technique for Control-Flow Intensive Designs," In *IEEE Transactions on Computer-Aided Design of Integrated Circuits and Systems*, vol. 18, no. 5, May 1999, pp. 505-523.

17. ___, Benchmarks repository, Workshop on High-Level Synthesis, 1995, ftp://ftp.ics.uci.edu/pub/hlsynth/HLSynth95

18. R. Sedgewick, *Algorithms in C++*, Addison-Wesley, Publishing Company, Inc., 1992.

19. Morse Rodriguez, "Evaluating Video Codecs," In *IEEE Multimedia*, Fall 1994, pp. 25-33.

20. Cleland. O. Newton, "A Synthesis Process applied to the Kalman Filter Benchmark," In *Proc. of the Workshop on High-Level Synthesis*, DRA Malvern, UK. ftp://ftp.ics.uci.edu/pub/hlsynth/ HLSynth92/kalman

21. P. Athanas, H. Silverman, "Processor Reconfiguration through Instruction-Set Metamorphosis: Architecture and Compiler," IEEE Computer, vol. 26, n. 3, March 1993.

22. L. Agarwal, et al, "An Asynchronous Approach to Efficient Execution of Programs on Adaptive Architectures Utilizing FPGAs," In *Proc. of the 2nd IEEE Workshop on FPGAs for Custom Computing Machines (FCCM'94)*, Napa Valley, CA, USA, April 1994.

23. D. Galloway, "The Transmogrifier C Hardware Description Language and Compiler for FPGAs," In *Proc. of the 3rd IEEE Workshop on FPGAs for Custom Computing Machines(FCCM'95)*, Napa Valley, CA, USA, April 1995.

24. Ouaiss, et al., "An Integrated Partioning and Synthesis System for Dynamically Reconfigurable Multi-FPGA Architectures," In *Proc. of the Reconfigurable Architectures Workshop (RAW'98)*, Orlando, Florida, USA, March 30, 1998.

25. J. Hammes, R. Rinker, W. Böhm, W. Najjar, B. Draper, R. Beveridge, "Cameron: High Level Language Compilation for Reconfigurable Systems," In *Proc. of the Int. Conference on Parallel Architectures and Compilation Techniques (PACT'99)*, Newport Beach, CA, USA, Oct. 12-16, 1999.

26. Sze-Wei Ong, et al.,"Automatic Mapping of Multiple Applications to Multiple Adaptive Computing Systems," In *IEEE 9th Symposium on Field-Programmable Custom Computing Machines (FCCM'01)*, Rohnert Park, California, USA, April 30 – May 2, 2001.

27. P. Banerjee, et al., "A MATLAB Compiler For Distributed, Heterogeneous, Reconfigurable Computing Systems," In *Proc. of the IEEE Symposium on Field-Programmable Custom Computing Machines (FCCM'00)*, Napa Valley, CA, USA, Apr. 17-19, 2000, pp. 39-48.

28. M. Weinhardt, and W. Luk, "Pipeline Vectorization," In *IEEE Transactions on Computer-Aided Design of Integrated Circuits and Systems*, vol. 20, no. 2. Feb. 2001, pp. 234-233.

29. Pedro Diniz, and Joonseok Park, "Automatic Synthesis of Data Storage and Control Structures for FPGA-based Computing Engines," In *Proc. of the IEEE Symposium on*

Field-Programmable Custom Computing Machines (FCCM'00), Napa Valley, CA, USA, Apr. 17-19, 2000, pp. 91-100.

30. Maya Gokhale, and Janice M. Stone, "Napa C: Compiling for a Hybrid/FPGA Architecture," In *Proc. of the IEEE 6th Symposium on Field-Programmable Custom Computing Machines (FCCM'98)*, Napa Valley, CA, USA, April 1998, pp. 126-135.

System Level Tools for DSP in FPGAs

James Hwang, Brent Milne, Nabeel Shirazi, and Jeffrey D. Stroomer

Xilinx Inc, 2100 Logic Drive, San Jose, CA 95124, USA

Abstract. Visual data flow environments are ideally suited for modeling digital signal processing (DSP) systems, as many DSP algorithms are most naturally specified by signal flow graphs. Although several academic and commercial frameworks provide a high level of abstraction for modeling DSP systems, they have drawbacks as design tools for FPGAs. They do not provide efficient implementations, and their system behavior only approximates the hardware implementation. In this paper, we describe a software system that employs a visual data flow environment for system modeling and algorithm exploration. In this environment, the bit and cycle behavior of the FPGA implementation are manifest. By observing circuit behavior in the system environment, one obtains significant speed improvement over hardware simulation, while gaining substantial flexibility afforded by functional abstraction. In addition, the software automatically generates a faithful hardware implementation from the system model. Specific issues addressed include the mapping of system parameters into implementation (e.g., sample rates, enables), and implications of system modeling for testing (e.g., testbench generation).

1 Introduction

In recent years, field-programmable gate arrays (FPGAs) have become key components in implementing high performance digital signal processing (DSP) systems, especially in the areas of digital communications, networking, video, and imaging[1]. The logic fabric of today's FPGAs consists not only of look-up tables, registers, multiplexers, distributed and block memory, but also dedicated circuitry for fast adders, multipliers, and I/O processing (e.g., giga-bit I/O)[3]. The memory bandwidth of a modern FPGA far exceeds that of a microprocessor or DSP processor running at clock rates two to ten times that of the FPGA. Coupled with a capability for implementing highly parallel arithmetic architectures, this makes the FPGA ideally suited for creating high-performance custom data path processors for tasks such as digital filtering, fast Fourier transforms, and error correcting codes.

All major telecommunication providers have out of necessity adopted FPGAs for high-performance DSP. A third-generation (3G) wireless base station typically contains FPGAs and ASICs in addition to microprocessors and digital signal processors (DSPs). The processors and DSPs, even when running at GHz clock rates, are increasingly used for relatively low MIPs packet level processing, with the chip and symbol rate processing being implemented in the FPGAs and

G. Brebner and R. Woods (Eds.): FPL 2001, LNCS 2147, pp. 534–543, 2001.

ASICs [2]. The fluidity of emerging standards often makes FPGAs, which can be reprogrammed in the field, better suited than ASICs.

Despite these characteristics, broad acceptance of FPGAs in the DSP community has been hampered by several factors. First, there is a general lack of familiarity with hardware design and especially, FPGAs. DSP engineers conversant with programming in C or assembly language are often unfamiliar with digital design using hardware description languages (HDLs) such as VHDL or Verilog. Furthermore, although VHDL provides many high level abstractions and language constructs for simulation, its synthesizable subset is far too restrictive for system design.

Fundamentally, there is a lack of high-level tools and flows for DSP design in FPGAs. In this paper we describe a new software tool called System Generator for modeling and designing DSP systems in a visual data flow environment. In addition to providing a great deal of functional abstraction, the tool automatically maps the system model to a faithful hardware implementation. What is most significant is that the software provides these services without substantially compromising the quality of either the functional representation or the performance of the hardware implementation.

2   System Level Modeling

Two major trends have emerged in tools and techniques for system level design: the use of high-level languages and visual data flow. Language based approaches [4,5] have proven effective for system modeling, specification, and algorithm verification, but remain unsuitable for implementation in any target other than microprocessors. For targeting state-of-the-art DSPs, today's compilers often do not provide sufficiently good code for high-performance applications. Consequently, DSP programmers frequently resort to writing either in assembly or low level, highly stylized C [6].

Visual data flow environments[7,8,9,10] are ideally suited for modeling DSP systems, as many algorithms are most naturally specified by signal flow graphs. Data flow tools are similar to traditional schematic capture tools in that they provide libraries of functional blocks that can be composed graphically to model a system. In contrast to schematic tools, however, the library blocks and the simulation environment in a data flow tool provide a high level of functional abstraction, with polymorphic data types and operators to model arithmetic on integer, fixed-point, and floating point data. Time evolution is specified by sample rates rather than by wiring explicit clocks. Although previous environments support system modeling and in some cases derived implementations, their costs of abstraction include inefficient FPGA implementations, and inexact modeling of the hardware in the system simulation.

2.1   Related Work

The Ptolemy Project at U.C. Berkeley has developed a powerful visual environment for system modeling, with an emphasis on embedded system design [8].

It is an academic framework that does not support FPGA design. The Signal Processing Worksystem (SPW) from Cadence Design Systems is widely used for ASIC design in digital communications[7]. For the most part, SPW requires the user to provide an HDL implementation for the FPGA portion of a system. Although SPW provides libraries with high level functional abstractions (timed and untimed), it does not readily support bit and cycle accurate modeling of user and third-party intellectual property (IP) blocks except through HDL co-simulation. SPW is a powerful system, but its cost is many times that of a full suite of commercial FPGA implementation tools.

Another commercial tool of particular interest is Simulink, which runs within MATLAB, a popular mathematical modeling environment from The MathWorks, Inc. Simulink supports simulation of continuous-time and space as well as discrete-time and space dynamical systems. The latter makes it a suitable platform to model the evolution of hardware over time. Coupled with numerous libraries for modeling DSP and communications systems, as well as MATLAB's capabilities for data analysis and visualization, Simulink is an excellent platform upon which a system design tool for FPGAs can be built.

2.2   System Generator

System Generator is a new system level tool built on top of Simulink. It facilitates DSP design for FPGAs. Simulink provides a convenient high level modeling environment for DSP systems, and consequently is widely used for algorithm development and verification. System Generator maintains an abstraction level very much in keeping with the traditional Simulink blocksets, but at the same time automatically translates designs into hardware implementations that are faithful, synthesizable, and efficient.

The implementation is faithful in that the system model and hardware implementation are bit-identical and cycle-identical at sample times defined in Simulink. The implementation is made efficient through the use of Intellectual Property (IP) cores that provide a range of functionality from arithmetic operations to complex DSP algorithms. These cores have been carefully designed to run at high speed and be area efficient. In System Generator, the capabilities of IP cores are transparently extended to fit gracefully into a system level framework. For example, although most underlying IP cores operate on unsigned integers, System Generator allows signed fixed point numbers to be used as well, including saturation arithmetic and rounding. User-defined IP blocks can also be incorporated into a System Generator model as black boxes.

3   System Level Design with System Generator

The creation of a DSP design begins with a mathematical description of the operations needed and concludes with a hardware realization of the algorithm. The hardware implementation is rarely faithful to the original functional description;

instead it is "faithful enough". The challenge is to make the hardware area and speed efficient while still producing acceptable results.

In a typical design flow, also supported by System Generator, the designer is faced with the following steps:

1. Describe the algorithm in mathematical terms;
2. Realize the algorithm in the design environment using double precision;
3. Trim double precision arithmetic down to fixed point;
4. Translate the design into efficient hardware.

Step 4 is time consuming and error prone because it can be difficult to guarantee the hardware implements the design faithfully. System Generator eliminates this concern by automatically generating a faithful hardware implementation.

Step 3 is error prone because an efficient hardware implementation uses just enough fixed point precision to give correct results. System Generator does not automate this step, which typically involves subtle trade off analysis, but it does provide tools to make the process tractable. The reader might wonder why it is not possible to eliminate Step 3 and simply use floating point operations in hardware. The answer is that most operations have a sufficiently small dynamic range that a fixed point representation is acceptable, and the hardware realization of fixed point is considerably smaller and faster.

In the remainder of this section, we describe the capabilities of System Generator that simply the design process and contrast these capabilities with those of other tools.

3.1   Arithmetic Data Types

System Generator provides the three arithmetic data types that are of greatest use in DSP: double precision floating point, and signed and unsigned fixed point numbers. It does not provide mechanisms to convert floating point algorithms into hardware, but it does support them for simulation and modeling.

The set of arbitrary precision, fixed-point numbers has nice mathematical properties, with several advantages over familiar floating point representations. Operations on floating point numbers entail implicit rounding on the result, and consequently, desirable algebraic characteristics such as associativity and distributivity are lost. Both are retained for arbitrary precision, fixed-point numbers.

System Generator allows the quantization of the design to be addressed as an issue separate from the implementation of the mathematical algorithm. The transition from double precision to fixed point can be done selectively. In practice this means the designer gets the design working using double precision, then converts to fixed point incrementally. At all times, these three representations can be freely intermingled without any changes to the signal flow graph. This mixing is possible because library building blocks change their internal behavior based on the types of their inputs.

There is another benefit from this scheme in which quantization events are broken out as separate design parameters. At every point of the design, the designer can specify how both overflow and rounding are to be addressed. For overflow, the designer can choose whether saturation should be applied and do so in consideration of the hardware cost versus the benefit to the system design. Saturation is a more faithful reflection of the underlying mathematics, but more expensive in hardware; wrapping is inexpensive but less faithful. It is also possible to trap overflow events in the system level simulation. This is useful when debugging a subsystem that should never overflow.

Likewise, when quantizing at the least significant bit, the designer can choose whether the value should be truncated (with no hardware cost) or rounded under some particular rule (possibly improving the system design but with added cost in hardware).

In System Generator, many operators support "full precision" outputs, which means that the output precision is always sufficient to carry out the operation without loss of information. Combined with the data type propagation rules supported in Simulink, this can reduce the clerical burden in algorithm design.

The designer specifies the translation to fixed precision at key points in the model, namely, at gateways from non-System Generator blocks and in feedback loops. (Clearly, any operator whose output width exceeds that of its input cannot feed back on itself with full precision.) System Generator then propagates signal types and precisions as appropriate. The automatically chosen type is the least expensive that preserves full precision. Translations from signed to unsigned and vice versa are automatic as well .

3.2   Hardware Handshaking

In Simulink, time evolution is defined by sample rates for each block in the system. Sample rates propogate along signals and through blocks automatically, so in most cases it is not necessary for the designer to assign explicit rates to blocks. This is extremely flexible, but has implications for modeling hardware. A bit and cycle true simulation must provide mechanisms for defining and controlling clocked behavior in the system model. System Generator attempts to provide control mechanisms that do not compromise the abstract view afforded by Simulink.

In one such mechanism, every signal carries an implicit boolean "valid bit" that can be used to achieve hardware handshaking between blocks. For example, upon startup a pipeline may define its output "invalid" until it has flushed its pipe. By inspecting the valid bits of its inputs, a block can determine how to process its input data.

3.3   Multirate Systems

Multirate systems can be implemented in System Generator by using sample rate conversion blocks for up-sampling and down-sampling. The necessary control logic is automatically generated when the design is netlisted. Before netlisting, the sample rates in the system are normalized to integer values; in hardware, the system clock period corresponds to the greatest commond divisor of the integer sample periods. Clock enables are used to activate the hardware blocks at the appropriate moment in time relative to the system clock.

Consider for example, the multirate system model shown in Fig. 1. This system consists of I/O registers, an up-sampler, an anti-aliasing filter, and a down-sampler. The input signal is up-sampled by a factor of two, and subsequently down-sampled by a factor of three, giving an overall sample rate conversion by a factor of $\frac{2}{3}$. The ST blocks in the system model extract sample periods from Simulink signals. In the example, the input sample period is one. In the generated hardware implementation, as shown in the same figure, each element is driven by the system clock, with its respective clock enable driven according to its sample period in the original system model.

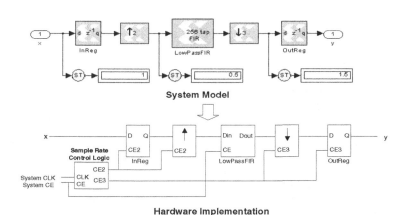

System Model

Hardware Implementation

Fig. 1   Sample rate conversion by a factor of $\frac{2}{3}$.

3.4   Bit-True and Cycle-True Modeling

System Generator produces a hardware implementation that is bit and cycle true to the system level simulation. We define the term "bit and cycle true" at the boundaries of the design. The boundaries of a design in System Generator are specified by Gateway In and Gateway Out blocks. These form interfaces between data representations within System Generator and data types standard to the Simulink environment. When hardware is generated, Gateway In blocks become input ports and Gateway Out blocks become output ports.

In the Simulink simulation, gateway blocks have data samples flowing in or out at regular sample periods. The values flowing in provide the stimuli, and those flowing out represent the response. In the generated hardware, if an identical stimulus sequence is presented at the input ports (at clock events corresponding to the input sample periods), then identical output sequences will be observed (at clock events corresponding to Simulink output events). The values presented to the hardware input ports and produced by the output ports are bit vectors interpreted as representing the fixed point values of the Simulink simulation. This correspondence between Simulink and hardware results is guaranteed to hold regardless of the particular input stimulus to the design or the positioning or number of Gateway Out blocks.

3.5   Automatic Testbench Generation

For a black box instantiation, the designer must provide both a Simulink model and an implementation. System Generator cannot automatically provide the verification that the two representations of the black box match. To assist the designer in verifying that the system model simulated in Simulink mirrors the generated hardware circuit, a VHDL testbench is automatically created during HDL code generation.

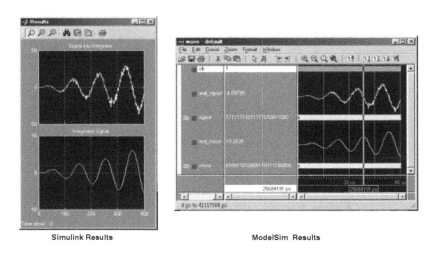

Simulink Results   ModelSim Results

Fig. 2   Simulation results from Simulink and ModelSim VHDL simulator.

Testbench input stimuli are recorded by Gateway In blocks during Simulink simulation. These blocks quantize double precision input data into a fixed point representation. The fixed point values are saved to a file and then used as input stimuli during VHDL simulation.

During HDL code generation, each Gateway In block is translated to a VHDL component which reads the input stimuli. Gateway Out blocks are translated to components that compare the VHDL results to the expected results. The comparisons are performed at the block sample rates. Only values which are tagged as valid by the valid bit are compared. The fixed point data type in Simulink is represented using a std_logic_vector in VHDL. The position of the binary point, size of the container, and treatment of sign are supplied to the VHDL as generic parameters. To ease the interpretation of fixed point types in VHDL, the gateway blocks convert the std_logic_vector into a VHDL real number by using the generic parameter information. A sequence of real numbers can be viewed as an analog waveform in an HDL simulator such as ModelSim from Model Technology Inc. This enables the user to view data in the same manner as a Simulink Scope. An example of this shown in Fig. 2.

3.6   Simulation Results

The automatically generated testbench was used to compare simulation times in Simulink to a behavioral VHDL simulation as well as a simulation of a back-annotated netlist. Table 1 shows the simulation results for a 1024-point FFT, a fully serial implementation of a distributed arithmetic FIR filter, and a fully parallel implementation of the same filter. Simulations were performed using ModelSim SE 5.5a on a 650 MHz Pentium III with 500 MBytes of RAM.

It can be seen that system level modeling not only increases design flexibility, it also provides much faster simulation than traditional HDL simulators. At the same time, the bit and cycle true simulation in Simulink gives an accurate idea of detailed system behavior.

Table 1   Simulation Times for DSP Designs.

Simulation Phase	1024 point FFT (15 transforms)	256 tap Parallel FIR (2K samples)	256 tap Serial FIR (2K samples)
Simulink	30 sec.	16 sec.	16 sec.
Behavioral VHDL	2.5 min.	2 min.	2 min.
Back-annotated VHDL w/o Timing Info.	36 min.	21 min.	24 min.
Back-annotated VHDL w/ Timing Info.	59 min.	40 min.	46 min.

4   Design Example

To demonstrate some of the significant features discussed in the previous section, we revisit the system model for the audio application depicted in Fig. 1. This system converts a single channel audio signal from a digital audio tape format, sampled at 48kHz, to a format for digital audio broadcast, sampled at 32 kHz [11]. This is accomplished by up-sampling by a factor of two and down-sampling by a factor of three. The Nyquist sampling rate of the digital output is 16kHz, and the up-sampler has an output rate of 96kHz, so we require an anti-aliasing filter with a stop band having a normalized frequency of $\pi/3$.

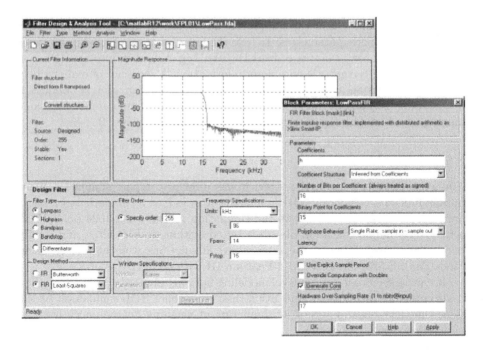

Fig. 3 Using FDATool and System Generator FIR parameterization GUI used to design a 256-tap anti-aliasing FIR filter. Coefficient vector h in the parameterization GUI is a vector exported from FDATool.

Designing a 256-tap FIR filter with a -100dB response over the stop band is straightforward using `FDATool`, a tool which runs in MATLAB (see Fig. 3). The filter coefficients were exported to the MATLAB workspace as the variable h. The System Generator GUI for the filter block, shown in Fig. 3, allows the user to choose from several implementation options.

System Generator detects that the filter coefficients are symmetric, and exploits this in the elaboration of the IP core to reduce the area required. The IP core employs distributed arithmetic [12] to compute the dot product. The number of input bits at a time used to index into the distributed memory is a user-selectable design parameter. For example, using a 16-bit input width yields a fully parallel (PDA) implementation, whereas using a single bit yields the most compact serial distributed arithmetic (SDA) implementation. In hardware, the IP core is over-clocked accordingly to ensure the system sample rate is seen at the filter output.

The SDA FIR filter can run well in excess of 102MHz in a Xilinx XCV50E-8 device, which for 16-bit data implies a sample rate of $102/17 = 6$MHz. Consequently, a single filter can in principle service $\lfloor \frac{6 \times 10^6}{9.6 \times 10^4} \rfloor = 62$ channels.

5   Conclusion

Modern FPGAs are powerful DSP devices, and with the availability of system level tools like System Generator, are poised to gain broad acceptance in the DSP community. System Generator supports bit and cycle true modeling, and automatically generates an FPGA implementation from a system model. In addition, it provides access to auxiliary tools for filter design, data analysis, visualization, and testbench creation. System Generator targets an increasingly broad IP library of DSP functions to take advantage of dedicated features in the FPGA to achieve high system performance. The combination of tools and IP libraries helps the system designer manage design complexity, provides a flexible modeling framework, and facilitates migration from algorithms into silicon.

Acknowledgements

The authors would like to thank their colleagues at Xilinx, Inc. and The MathWorks, Inc. for many fruitful discussions. In particular, they would like to acknowledge the contributions of D. Parlour, R. Turney, and C. Dick

References

1. C. H. Dick and f. j. harris,"Configurable Logic for Digital Communications: Some Signal Processing Perspectives", *IEEE Comm. Magazine*, vol. 2, Aug. 1999, pp. 107–111.
2. C. H. Dick and H. M. Pedersen, "Design and Implementation of High-Performance FPGA Signal Processing Datapaths for Software Defined Radios",*Embedded Systems Conference* Apr. 2001.
3. *Virtex-II Platform FPGA Handbook*, Xilinx, Inc., 2001.
4. http://www.systemc.org, SystemC.
5. M. Gokhale, J. Stone, and J. Arnold, "Stream-Oriented FPGA Computing in the Streams-C High Level Language", in *Proc. FCCM00*, B. Hutchings (ed.), IEEE Computer Society Press, 2000, pp. 49–56.
6. J. Eyre, "The Digital Signal Processor Derby", *IEEE Spectrum*, June 2001, pp. 62–68.
7. M. R. Sturgill et. al., "Design and Verification of Third Generation Wireless Communication Systems", White Paper, Cadence Design Systems, Inc.
8. E. Lee, "What's Ahead for Embedded Software", *IEEE Computer*, vol. 33, no. 9, September 2000, pp. 18–26.
9. B. Levine et. al., "Mapping of an Automated Target Recognition Application from a Graphical Software Environment to FPGA-based Reconfigurable Hardware", in *Proc. FCCM99*, K.L. Pocek and J.M. Arnold (eds.), IEEE Computer Society Press, 1999, pp. 292–293.
10. M. Schiff, "Baseband Simulation of Communications System", Application Note AN133, Elanix, Inc., April 2000.
11. R.Lagadec, D.Pellooni, and D. Weiss, "A 2-channel, 16-bit Digital Sampling Rate Converter for Professional Digital Audio", *Proc. IEEE Intl. Conf. ASSP*, April 1982, pp. 93–96.
12. S. A. White, "Applications of Distributed Arithmetic to Digital Signal Processing", *IEEE ASSP Magazine*, Vol. 6(3), July 1989, pp. 4-19.

Parameterized Function Evaluation for FPGAs

Oskar Mencer[1], Nicolas Boullis[2], Wayne Luk[3], and Henry Styles[3]

[1] Computing Sciences Research Center, Lucent, Bell Labs, Murray Hill, NJ 07974, USA
[2] Ecole Normale Superieure de Lyon, 69364 Lyon, France
[3] Department of Computing, Imperial College, 180 Queen's Gate, London SW7 2BZ, UK

Abstract. This paper presents parameterized module-generators for pipelined function evaluation using lookup tables, adders, shifters and multipliers. We discuss trade-offs involved between (1) full-lookup tables, (2) bipartite (lookup-add) units, (3) lookup-multiply units, and (4) shift-and-add based CORDIC units. For lookup-multiply units we provide equations estimating approximation errors and rounding errors which are used to parameterize the hardware units. The resources and performance of the resulting design can be estimated given the input parameters. The method is implemented as part of the PAM-Blox module generation environment. An example shows that the lookup-multiply unit produces competitive designs with data widths up to 20 bits when compared with shift-and-add based CORDIC units. Additionally, the lookup-multiply method can be used for larger data widths when evaluating functions not supported by CORDIC.

1 Introduction

The evaluation of differentiable functions can often be the performance bottleneck of many compute-bound applications. Examples of these functions include elementary functions such as $\log(x)$ or $\sqrt{x}$, and compound functions such as $(1 - \sin^2(x))^{1/2}$ or $\tan^2(x) + 1$. Hardware implementation of elementary functions are studied by Wong and Goto [16]. Advanced FPGAs enable the development of low-cost and high-speed function evaluation units, customizable to particular applications. Such customization can take place at run time by reconfiguring the FPGA, so that different functions or precisions can be introduced according to run-time conditions.

This paper presents parameterizable designs for evaluating a differentiable function using lookup tables, adders and multipliers, which can be implemented very efficiently using FPGAs and other stream-based architectures [4], [5], [7], [11]. We describe architectures based on full-lookup units, lookup-add units and lookup-multiply units, and compare their size and performance for different input data widths. These architectures are often highly pipelined for high throughput. Such parallelism provides an edge over general-purpose microprocessors.

Module generators are implemented in the PAM-Blox environment [8], so that instances of particular architectures can be generated rapidly and automatically from a parameterized description. The key problem addressed in this paper is the automatic generation of parameterized function evaluation units. The challenge is to find the required intermediate precisions given an input and output precision requirement. For example, if we require a 15-bit sine function from a 13-bit input, the module-generators have to create the function evaluation unit while optimizing speed and area of the unit.

G. Brebner and R. Woods (Eds.): FPL 2001, LNCS 2147, pp. 544–554, 2001.

Preliminary results suggest that there is a tradeoff between the various table lookup methods and shift-and-add based (e.g. CORDIC) units based on the number of required bits [2], [9], [14]. This paper sheds some light into the details of this tradeoff, and the applicability of the various methods to a module generation environment, which is the heart of computing with FPGAs.

2   Function Evaluation Methods

Our objective is to provide efficient circuits for differentiable function evaluation. In general, function evaluation consists of three stages. The first stage, range reduction (see for example Muller [10], Chapter 8), reduces the argument x to a small interval $[a, b]$, resulting in a new argument $\overline{x}$. The second stage evaluates the function $F(\overline{x})$. The third stage extrapolates $F(x)$ from $F(\overline{x})$. In this paper, we are only concerned with the second stage: evaluating a function $F(x)$ where x is in a small evaluation interval $[a, b]$. For any given function, area and timing restrictions, there exist many different architectures with different evaluation intervals [a,b].

For reconfigurable datapaths, we are mainly concerned with high throughput architectures. We therefore limit ourselves to fully-pipelined FPGA implementations of function evaluation units. In the following, we describe three architectures for evaluating a given function based on lookup tables.

2.1   Three Lookup-Table Based Units

The first architecture, a full-lookup unit, consists of a single lookup table. While a full-lookup table is straightforward to implement, its size and latency grows very rapidly with the required precision or range.

The second architecture, a lookup-add unit (Figure 1), is based on bipartite tables involving an addition of the results of two parallel lookups. The use of symmetric tables further reduces the required memory while improving the error bound [12]. However, in contrast to the full lookup, we now have to find the precision required for each of the tables and the precision for the final addition. Current techniques use simulation to find the appropriate internal bitwidths.

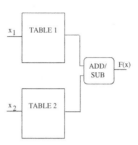

Fig. 1. Bipartite (lookup-add) tables computing the function $F(x)$. x_1 and x_2 are substrings of the original binary input x.

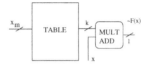

Fig. 2. A lookup-multiply unit evaluating $F(x)$. x_m are m bits of the binary input x.

The third architecture, which is the most promising, is a lookup-multiply unit (Figure 2) based on affine polynomial approximation of a differentiable function. The coefficients for a polynomial approximation can be computed to minimize the average error of the approximation over the desired interval. The m most-significant bits of the input x are used to lookup the intermediate value in the lookup table, and the product of this value and x is then produced.

2.2   Shift-and-Add Based CORDIC Units

CORDIC units are one of a family of shift-and-add based function evaluation methods. The basic CORDIC unit computes up to two functions simultaneously using only constant shifts and additions. Details of the CORDIC architecture can be found in the literature (e.g. [2], [9], [14]). In summary, CORDICs converge approximately at around 1 bit per shift-add. Thus, a 10-bit CORDIC unit requires about 10 stages of shifts and adds. CORDICs lend themselves naturally to high throughput pipelining. One of the disadvantages is that CORDICs are limited to a relatively small set of elementary functions.

3   The Lookup-Multiply Method

3.1   Parameterizing the Lookup-Multiply Unit

This section contains an exact mathematical description of the relationships between the external and internal precisions for a lookup-multiply unit. The availability of such a description is the main advantage of the lookup-multiply method over bipartite (lookup-add) methods and shift-and-add based CORDICs.

To construct a module generator for a lookup-multiply unit, we need to compute all internal parameters (precisions) given a particular function, and the required precision/range of the output, denoted by the width l of the result. Internal parameters consist of the width and height of the lookup tables and the number of bits for the multiplication and addition.

Assume we require a unit to compute a function $F(x)$. We first compute a continuous piecewise affine approximation of the function $F(x)$, as shown in Figure 3. This approximating function is called f. We compute the function F on an interval $[a, b)$. Then, we cut this interval into $n = 2^m$ intervals $[i/n, (i+1)/n)$ ($i \in [0, n]$). The value, m, is also the number of most-significant bits that are used to lookup the intermediate value in the lookup table. All the values are computed with k bits, and the result is

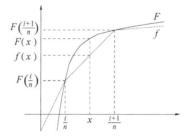

Fig. 3. $f(x)$ is the piecewise linear approximation of $F(x)$.

rounded to l bits ($l < k$). $\widetilde{f}$ is the function in hardware which approximates f, and it may contain rounding errors.

To provide a method for estimating the bitwidths required for a given precision, we have to deal with two sources of error: approximation error and rounding error.

$$\text{Error}_{\text{total}} = \text{Error}_{\text{approx}} \pm \text{Error}_{\text{round}} \tag{1}$$

The first error E_{approx} comes from the approximation of the function f:

$$\text{Error}_{\text{approx}} = |F(x) - f(x)| \leq (2^{-(2m+3)}) \cdot \max_{z \in [0,1]} (|F''(z)|) \tag{2}$$

The approximation error $\text{Error}_{\text{approx}}$ is a function of the number of intervals stored in the lookup table for f and the maximum deviation of $F(x)$ from its linearization $f(x)$. This maximal deviation is controlled by the second derivative $F''(x)$.

The second error $\text{Error}_{\text{round}}$ comes from rounding errors inside the evaluation unit:

$$\text{Error}_{\text{round}} = \left| f(x) - \widetilde{f}(x) \right| < 0.75 \cdot 2^{-(k-1)} + 2^{-(l+1)} \tag{3}$$

In this case, $\text{Error}_{\text{round}}$ is a function of the internal precision k and the final precision l. Given a piecewise differentiable function $F(x)$ and a target precision l, we can easily find values for m and k to guarantee the precision of the final result up to one unit in the last place.

More details on the derivation of the equations above can be found in a report available from the authors [3]. Similar error analysis techniques can be found elsewhere [13]. Using these equations, lookup table area can be minimized with respect to valid values of m and k for a target precision l.

For F to be approximated to l bit range and domain accuracy, ($l < k$) must hold. Under this condition there is no benefit in replacing the lookup table with a bipartite table, as its minimal area is bounded by the target function output width, k. A full lookup table is the most efficient approximator for functions with a small number of input bits (B) since the full-lookup grows with 2^B. Our experience shows that there is no benefit in cascading bipartite and lookup multiply function approximation methods.

3.2   Resources and Performance of Lookup-Multiply Units

Equation (2) and Equation (3) shown above provide a way of determining bitwidths for the multiply-lookup unit to meet accuracy requirements. This section suggests a generic layout for the hardware implementation, in order to develop parametric estimates of the required resources and the achievable performance.

We start by deriving an estimate for the resources. $\widetilde{f}(x)$ is encoded with l bits, whereas all the other numbers are encoded with k fractional bits. Let p be the number of bits of the input. Generally, we have $p > m$ and $p \simeq l$.

The goal is to place the unit into a rectangle. Our design contains two lookup tables, so that the two lookups for $F((i+1)/n)$ and $F(i/n)$ can be carried out in parallel (Figure 2). One lookup table (LUT1) contains 2^m numbers of $k+1$ bits, while the other lookup table (LUT2) has 2^m numbers of k bits. There are also one $(k+1)$-bit by $(p-m)$-bit multiplier, one $(k+1)$-bit adder, and an l-bit rounding unit.

If $m \geq 4$, then the two lookup tables fit into rectangles:

$$\texttt{size}_{\texttt{LUT1}} = \frac{2^{m-3} + 1 - 2 \cdot (m \bmod 2)}{3} \times (k+1) \qquad (4)$$

and

$$\texttt{size}_{\texttt{LUT2}} = \frac{2^{m-3} + 1 - 2 \cdot (m \bmod 2)}{3} \times k \qquad (5)$$

If $m < 4$, the rectangles are $\texttt{size}_{\texttt{LUT1}} = 1 \times (k+1)$ and $\texttt{size}_{\texttt{LUT2}} = 1 \times k$. The multiplier fits into a $(p-m) \times (k+1)$ rectangle, the adder in a $1 \times (k+1)$ rectangle, and the rounding unit in a $1 \times l$ rectangle. Hence the whole lookup-multiply design fits into a rectangle

$$\texttt{size}_{\texttt{total}} = \left(2 \cdot \frac{2^{m-3} + 1 - 2 \cdot (m \bmod 2)}{3} + (p - m) + 2 \right) \times (k+1) \qquad (6)$$

as shown in Figure 4, assuming that $m \geq 4$.

We now consider the performance of our design. The delay of both lookup tables is $1 + \max(0, \lceil (m-5)/6 \rceil)$ cycles. Both lookups can be performed in parallel. The delay of the multiplier is $1 + \lfloor (p - m + \lceil (8(k-2))/35 \rceil)/5 \rfloor$ cycles. The delay of the adder is 1 cycle; as is the delay of the rounding unit. Hence, the total delay of the fully pipelined approximator is:

$$\texttt{delay}_{\texttt{total}} = \max\left(0, \left\lceil \frac{m-5}{6} \right\rceil \right) + \left\lfloor \frac{p - m + \lceil 8(k-2)/35 \rceil}{5} \right\rfloor + 4 \qquad (7)$$

3.3   Example: $\ln(x)$

Consider the hardware unit for computing the natural logarithm which is a representative elementary function. We compute $\ln(x)$ in the interval $[1, 2)$: $F(x) = \ln(1+x)$.

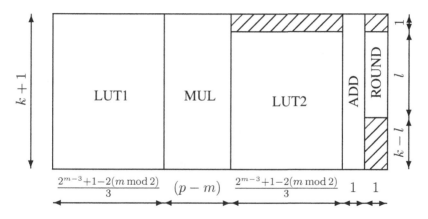

Fig. 4. Proposed layout of the lookup-multiply unit.

This function fulfills all the requirements outlined above. We know $F'(x) = 1/(1+x)$ and $F''(x) = -1/(1+x)^2$. Hence for Equation (2) with $F(x) = \ln(x)$:

$$\max_{x \in [0,1]} |F''(x)| = 1. \tag{8}$$

Assuming that the input and the output are both q bits wide, we have $l = q$ and $p = q-1$. We now have to choose m and k.

Because of the term 2^m in the space needed by the design, we choose the smallest possible m. Thus, we choose $m = \lfloor l/2 \rfloor$ so that

$$2^{-(2m+3)} \cdot \max_{x \in [0,1]} |F''(x)| < 2^{-(l+1)} \tag{9}$$

Consider the case that l is even, such that $m = l/2$. We choose $k = l + 2$ such that

$$\left(1 - \frac{1}{4}\right) 2^{-(k-1)} \le 2^{-(l+1)} - 2^{-(l+3)} \tag{10}$$

If l is odd, then $m = (l-1)/2$. We choose $k = l + 3$ such that

$$\left(1 - \frac{1}{4}\right) 2^{-(k-1)} \le 2^{-(l+1)} - 2^{-(l+2)} \tag{11}$$

Moreover, since the logarithm is an increasing function, we can adopt a rounding method so that all the values involved in the computation are positive. This means that there is no need to store or compute sign bits.

Hence the design for a lookup-multiply $\ln(x)$ unit fits into a rectangle:

$$\texttt{size}_{\ln(x)} = \left(2 \cdot \frac{2^{m-3} + 1 - 2(m \bmod 2)}{3} + (p - m) + 2 \right) \times k \tag{12}$$

4   Implementing the Module Generators in PAM-Blox

The function evaluation units are implemented as classes in C++ within PAM-Blox [8]. The input parameters set the precision of the input and output values. Inheritance is used throughout the implementation to optimize code efficiency. The top class evaluates polynomial functions. The first subclass inherits all the functionality of the top class and specializes the evaluation to, for instance, piecewise polynomial functions. The subclass of the piecewise polynomial evaluation class evaluates a given function using the lookup-multiply unit. Hence, we can reuse some parts of the code to build, for example, high degree polynomial approximations in the future.

The example in Figure 5 shows how to utilize the lookup-multiply class to build a hardware unit for the logarithm function. The code example shows the Lookup_Multiply_Log class, which generates $\ln(x)$ evaluation units that can guarantee a particular output precision given input and output precisions. The value of INTERNAL_WIDTH, which corresponds to the precision inside the unit, follows from Equation (2) and Equation (3).

```
// hardware unit for the logarithm function

const int INTERNAL_WIDTH = OUTPUT_WIDTH+2+(OUTPUT_WIDTH%2);

template<int INPUT_WIDTH, int OUTPUT_WIDTH>
class Lookup_Multiply_Log:
  public Lookup_Multiply<INPUT_WIDTH,
                         OUTPUT_WIDTH,
                         INTERNAL_WIDTH,
                         OUTPUT_WIDTH/2> {
  public:

  // constructor
  Lookup_Multiply_Log(WireVector<Bool, INPUT_WIDTH> &input_in,
                      Bool *clock=NULL,
                      const char *name=NULL):
        Lookup_Multiply<INPUT_WIDTH,
                        OUTPUT_WIDTH,
                        INTERNAL_WIDTH,
                        OUTPUT_WIDTH/2>(input_in, clock, name){}

  double Eval_Function(double x){
    return log(1.0+x);
  }

};
```

Fig. 5. The lookup-multiply method described in PAM-Blox.

5   Results

This section compares the results of implementing a given function using the full-lookup method, the lookup-add method, the lookup-multiply method, and a shift-and-add based CORDIC design.

In a full-lookup unit, the precision/range (l) determines width (l) and height (2^l) of the lookup table. The procedure for implementing lookup-add units can be found elsewhere [12], while that for implementing lookup-multiply units has been outlined in Section 3.1.

In contrast, parallel, pipelined CORDIC designs require two parameters: the number of bits per iteration stage, and the number of stages. Determining the minimal precision of each stage inside CORDIC units is complex. We can, however, give an upper bound on the required bits of precision inside the CORDIC unit: ($l + \ln(\#$ *of shift-and-add stages*$)$). The total number of required stages depends on the approximated function, the internal scaling method [1], [10], the precision of each stage, and of course the precision required at the output. In general, CORDIC units converge at the approximate rate of one bit per stage, which we use for our estimates. A more precise determination of the needed number of stages requires extensive simulations for each function, internal precision, scaling method, and for each output precision.

Figure 6 shows the results for the area of a function evaluation unit, in our case $F(x) = \ln(x)$ for Xilinx XC4000 FPGAs. Xilinx XC4000 FPGAs consist of a 2D array of Configurable Logic Blocks (CLBs). Each CLB contains two 4-input lookup tables and two flip-flops. In lookup-based function evaluation, the proportion of CLBs used as lookup table ROM grows as precision is increased. If implemented on a modern FPGA architecture such as Xilinx Virtex devices, CLB count could be significantly reduced by storing lookup table entries in available block RAMs.

Table 1 shows the latency of the fully-pipelined units in number of clock cycles. We assume that the cycle times for the different units are similar, because they are all fully-pipelined, possibly including a carry chain, between any two registers.

data width	full-lookup	lookup-add	lookup-multiply	CORDIC
4	1	2	4	5
8	2	2	5	9
12	2	3	6	13
16	3	3	7	17
20	4	4	7	21
24	4	4	9	25

Table 1. Speed comparison, in number of clock cycles, for designs with varying data width.

To summarize, for data width up to around 10 bits, a full-lookup unit provides the best trade-off in size and performance. For data width between 10 and 12 bits, the lookup-add design is appropriate. For data width between 12 and 20 bits, the lookup-multiply design should be considered. For data width more than 20 bits, CORDIC provides efficient solutions within its limitations.

The area results show that for data widths up to about 20 bits, a lookup-multiply strategy results in similar or smaller area than a shift-and-add CORDIC unit. However, while the lookup-multiply unit can be automatically designed to compute any differentiable function, the CORDIC unit is limited to a small set of elementary functions and

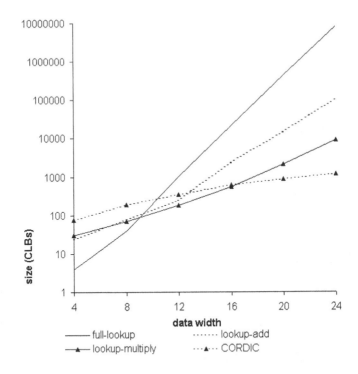

Fig. 6. Size comparison, in width $\times$ height $=$ CLBs, of designs with varying data width. Note that values for bipartite tables are estimated based on computational resources per CLB.

has a less regular architecture across all possible function evaluations than a lookup-multiply unit.

6   Conclusion

The paper presents an approach to parameterize pipelined designs for differentiable function evaluation using lookup tables, adders, shifters and multipliers. This approach can be used to develop efficient implementations of function evaluators based on lookup tables, the size and performance of which can be estimated parametrically.

Our approach is implemented in C++ as part of the PAM-Blox module generation environment. We demonstrate that, depending on the data width, different lookup-based implementations for function evaluation should be used to improve efficiency. Examples confirm that the lookup-multiply approach produces competitive designs for data widths up to 20 bits when compared with shift-and-add based CORDIC units, without suffering from the limitations of CORDIC. Additionally, the lookup-multiply method is applicable to designs with larger data widths when evaluating functions not supported by CORDIC.

Current and future work includes assessing the effectiveness of the lookup-multiply approach for various differentiable functions, relating our tools to other pipeline synthesis techniques [15], retargeting our module generators to cover the latest FPGAs, and extending the development framework to support run-time reconfigurable designs.

Acknowledgments

We thank Mike Flynn and Martin Morf for support and encouragement during this work, and Lorenz Huelsbergen for discussions and helpful suggestions. The support of UK Engineering and Physical Sciences Research Council (Grant number GRN/66599), Celoxica Limited and Xilinx, Inc. is gratefully acknowledged.

References

1. H.M. Ahmed, *Signal Processing Algorithms and Architectures*, PhD Thesis, E.E. Department, Stanford University, June 1982.
2. R. Andraka, "A Survey of CORDIC Algorithms for FPGAs," *Proc. ACM/SIGDA Int. symp. Field Programmable Gate Arrays*, ACM Press, pp. 191–200, 1998.
3. N. Boullis, *Designing Arithmetic Units for Adaptive Computing with PAM-Blox*, MIM Internship Report, ENS-Lyon, France, Sept. 2000.
4. C. Ebeling, D.C. Cronquist, P. Franklin, J. Secosky and S.G. Berg, "Mapping Applications to the RaPiD Configurable Architecture," *Proc. IEEE Symp. on FPGAs for Custom Computing Machines*, IEEE Computer Society Press, pp. 106–115, 1997.
5. R. Laufer, R.R. Taylor and H. Schmit, "PCI-PipeRench and SWORD API: A System for Stream-based Reconfigurable Computing," *Proc. IEEE Symp. on FPGAs for Custom Computing Machines*, IEEE Computer Society Press, pp. 200–208, 1999.
6. O. Mencer, *Rational Arithmetic Units in Computer Systems*, PhD Thesis (with M.J. Flynn), E.E. Dept., Stanford University, Jan. 2000.
7. O. Mencer, H. Huebert, M. Morf and M.J. Flynn, "StReAm: Object-Oriented Programming of Stream Architectures using PAM-Blox", *Field-Programmable Logic and Applications*, LNCS 1896, Springer, pp. 595–604, 2000.
8. O. Mencer, M. Morf and M.J. Flynn, "PAM-Blox: High Performance FPGA Design for Adaptive Computing," *Proc. IEEE Symp. on FPGAs for Custom Computing Machines*, IEEE Computer Society Press, pp. 167–174, 1998.
9. O. Mencer, L. Séméria, M. Morf and J.M. Delosme, "Application of Reconfigurable CORDIC Architectures," *Journal of VLSI Signal Processing*, Vol. 24, No. 2–3, pp. 211-221, March 2000.
10. J.M. Muller, *Elementary Functions, Algorithms and Implementation*, Birkhaeuser, Boston, 1997.
11. S. Rixner et al., "A Bandwidth-Efficient Architecture for Media Processing," *Proc. ACM/IEEE Int'l Symposium on Microarchitecture*, IEEE Computer Society Press, pp. 3–13, 1998.
12. M.J. Schulte and J.E. Stine, "Approximating Elementary Functions with Symmetric Bipartite Tables", *IEEE Trans. Comput.*, Vol. 48, No. 8, pp. 842–847, August 1999.
13. P.T.P. Tang, "Table Lookup Algorithms for Elementary Functions and Their Error Analysis," *Proc. 10th IEEE Symp. Computer Arithmetic*, IEEE Press, pp. 232–236, 1991.
14. J.E. Volder, "The CORDIC Trigonometric Computing Technique," *IRE Trans. on Electronic Computers*, Vol. EC-8, No. 3, Sept. 1959.

15. M. Weinhardt and W. Luk, "Pipeline Vectorization," *IEEE Trans. Comput. Aided Design*, Vol. 20, No. 2, pp. 234–248, February 2001.
16. W.F. Wong and E. Goto, "Fast Hardware-Based Algorithms for Elementary Function Computations Using Rectangular Multipliers," *IEEE Trans. Comput.*, Vol. 43, pp. 278-294, March 1994.

Efficient Constant Coefficient Multiplication Using Advanced FPGA Architectures

Michael J. Wirthlin and Brian McMurtrey

Brigham Young University, Provo UT 84602, USA
wirthlin@ee.byu.edu, mcmurtre@ee.byu.edu

Abstract. Constant coefficient multiplication using look-up tables is a popular form of multiplication in FPGAs. The ample look-up table resources found within the FPGA match well to the architecture of a look-up table based multiplier. While this form of multiplication maps well to FPGAs, it isn't particularly efficient. This paper presents an efficient variant of this multiplier using the advanced features of the Xilinx Virtex FPGA. Specifically, this approach combines the look-up and add operations required by this multiplier architecture.

1 Introduction

Constant coefficient multiplication using look-up tables is a popular method of performing multiplication within FPGAs. These multipliers perform multiplication by a constant by determining partial-products using table look-up and summing their results with a network of adders. Multiplication based on this technique is frequently referred as KCM multiplication. The extensive array of small look-up tables (LUT) within an FPGA make this implementation style an attractive and efficient alternative for constant multiplication. Several FPGA vendors and users have reported the use of these multipliers in FPGA designs [1, 2].

Although there are several styles of performing constant coefficient multiplication in FPGAs, this approach offers a number of specific advantages. First, the structure of this multiplier is regular and maps nicely to the tile-based FPGA architectures. Second, this multiplier is easy to configure for any constant of interest. Since the structure of the multiplier does not depend on the constant of interest, any arbitrary constant can be performed in the multiplier by modifying the contents of the look-up tables.

While this style of multiplication is popular, recent results suggest that other styles of constant coefficient multiplication may be more efficient than the KCM multiplier[3, 4]. There are two disadvantages of this multiplier: first, this multiplier offers little or no constant specific optimizations. All constant multipliers of similar bit-size are the same size and do not exploit constant-specific optimizations. Second, this multiplier requires separate resources for both the constant-look up and the adder network. This separation of resources makes the multiplier relatively larger than other constant multiplication approaches.

G. Brebner and R. Woods (Eds.): FPL 2001, LNCS 2147, pp. 555–564, 2001.

This paper introduces an efficient look-up table based constant multiplier that exploits advanced properties of the Xilinx Virtex FPGA[5]. Using advanced features of this device, this KCM multiplier is able to merge both the look-up and adder network of this operation. Such merging reduces the overall size of the multiplier by an average of 33%. In addition, the Virtex FPGA simplifies the process of modifying the constant at run-time by providing built-in shift registers for the look-up tables. This paper will begin by reviewing the KCM constant coefficient multiplier and tabulating its area for a variety of multiplier sizes. Next, the inefficiencies of this multiplier on conventional FPGA architectures will be described. The optimized KCM multiplier for the Virtex architecture will be introduced and demonstrated with an example. The paper will conclude by contrasting the optimized multiplier with the conventional approach of constant coefficient multiplication.

2   Constant Coefficient Multiplication

Like any boolean function, a multiplication can be performed using a look-up table or memory. However, multiplication is an extremely expensive operation to perform with look-up tables since the size of memory needed for the multiplication grows exponentially with the size of the multiplier operands. The size of the memory can be reduced by performing a multiplication by a constant. The multiplication of an arbitrary m-bit multiplicand (M) by some c-bit constant (C) can be performed with a 2^m word memory. This memory is pre-loaded with the product of the constant and *every* possible value of the multiplicand. The result is obtained by addressing the memory with the m-bit multiplicand value.

A more efficient approach for multiplication by a constant (with respect to memory size) is to use the look-up tables for computing the *partial products* of the constant multiplication operation. The m-bit multiplicand is decomposed into digits that are each 4 bits in size. Each 4-bit digit of the multiplicand is used to address a partial-product look-up table [1]. This look-up table contains the product of the constant multiplied by all possible 4-bit digit values (i.e. 16 entries). One look-up table is needed for each of the $\lceil \frac{m}{4} \rceil$ digits of the multiplicand. The final result is obtained by summing the results of all partial products as follows:

$$M \times C = \sum_{i=0}^{\lceil \frac{m}{4} \rceil - 1} m_i C \cdot 2^{4i}, \tag{1}$$

where m_i represents bits $4 * (i+1) - 1$ through $4i$ of the multiplicand.

An architecture that implements this method of constant multiplication requires multiple look-up tables to compute each of the partial products and adder circuits to sum their results. Figure 1 demonstrates this approach for multiplication between an 8-bit constant and a 12-bit multiplicand. This multiplier requires three 4x12 look-up tables to perform the partial-product look-up and two 12-bit

---

[1] 4 bits are used since the common size of most FPGA look-up tables is 2^4 words deep.

adders. The contents of all three ROM blocks are the same, with location i of each ROM containing the value $i \times C$.

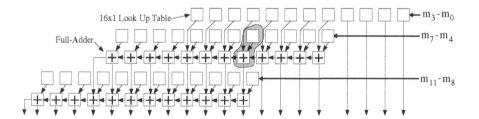

Fig. 1. Architecture of a Constant 8x12 Bit Multiplier.

3   Implementing KCM Multiplier on Conventional FPGA Architectures

Building the KCM multiplier on an FPGA requires two distinct pieces: a set of look-up tables to determine the partial products and an adder network to sum the results. Each look-up table performs a $c \times 4$ bit multiplication resulting in a $c + 4$ bit partial product. One 16×1 LUT is required for each bit of the partial-product for a total of $c + 4$ LUTs for each ROM. Since one ROM is needed for each four-bit digit of the multiplicand, the total LUT count for the ROMS is $\lceil \frac{m}{4} \rceil \times (c + 4)$.

To sum the partial-product results, $\lceil \frac{m}{4} \rceil - 1$ adders are necessary (one fewer adder stage than the number of look-up tables). If an array of adders is used to sum the results, each adder stage will produce a $c + 5$ bit result[2]. Assuming each full-adder requires a look-up table and the carry logic is included within the logic cell, $\left(\lceil \frac{m}{4} \rceil - 1 \right) \times (c + 4)$ logic cells are required for the adder network. The total logic cell count for this constant multiplier is as follows:

$$\#\text{LogicCells} = (c + 4) \cdot \left(2 \cdot \left\lceil \frac{m}{4} \right\rceil - 1 \right) \qquad (2)$$

4   Merging Look-Up Tables with Adders

The use of separate resources for both the look-up tables and adders is not particularly efficient. Specifically, the use of look-up tables to perform the addition wastes valuable look-up table resources. To perform a sum, only three inputs of a four-input look-up table are used (A, B, and Carry In). Since one input

---

[2] Alternative adder networks such as a tree network may be used instead.

is unused, *half* of the look-up table is wasted. One possible method for improving the efficiency of this multiplier is to use the wasted LUT resources to assist with the table look-up operation. If part of the table look-up operation could be combined with the summation, significant logic resources may be saved.

Consider the detailed arrangement of adders and look-up tables in Figure 1. The multiplier is composed of an initial look-up stage followed by a series of look-up/adder pairs. If the look-up and adder pair can be combined into a single row of logic blocks, significant FPGA resources can be saved. For example, consider the combined look-up table, full-adder cell of Figure 2. This combined cell includes both a look-up table to perform a single-bit partial-product as well as a full-adder. The full-adder sums the result of the look-up with the sum of the previous stage. Further, the full-adder produces a carry to support chaining of cells. This cell is represented by the shaded cells in Figure 1.

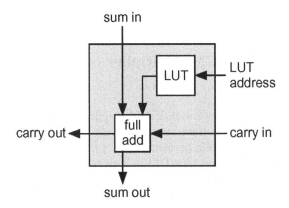

Fig. 2. Combined Look-Up/Adder Cell.

While the arrangement of Figure 2 appears to be straightforward, it does not map well to most FPGA architectures. For most architectures, the high-speed carry chain appears *before* the look-up table as shown in Figure 3-a. Because the carry chain logic occurs before the table look-up, the logic cells cannot perform a full-adder operation (including carry) using the results of the table look-up. Instead, the carry logic has access only to the cell inputs and is limited to performing a single full-add operation.

5   Virtex Architecture

Unlike most FPGAs, the Xilinx Virtex carry logic exits *after* the look-up table as shown in Figure 3-b. This arrangement of the carry chain allows the combined look-up and full-adder operation of Figure 2 to fit within a single logic cell of the FPGA. The LUT within the logic cell performs a partial-product look-up

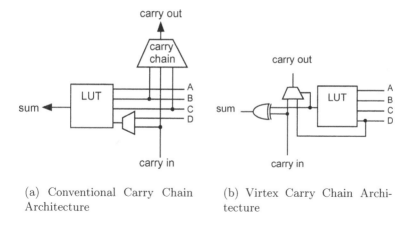

(a) Conventional Carry Chain Architecture

(b) Virtex Carry Chain Architecture

Fig. 3. FPGA Carry Chain Architectures

operation *and* a summation (sum the results of the look-up with the previous sum). By merging the partial-product look-up with the full-adder, the multiplier can be built with fewer resources.

5.1 Combined Cell

The key feature of the Virtex CLB architecture that enables the combining of the look-up with the add is the additional logic provided at the *output* of the LUT. As shown in Figure 3-b, an exclusive OR (XOR) and multiplexer are available to the designer *after* the results of the look-up table are computed[3]. Both the output XOR and Carry Chain multiplexer are used to combine the look-up and full adder.

Although the look-up table within the Virtex logic cell provides 4 inputs (i.e. a $2^4 \times 1$ ROM), only three of the four input wires are used for table look-up. The fourth LUT input is used for the previous sum input as shown in Figure 4. Internally, the LUT is programmed to add the three-bit table lookup with the previous sum input. This half-add is performed by an exclusive OR operation between the 3-bit look-up and previous sum as shown in the LUT of Figure 4. This look-up and XOR operation are all performed within a single 4-input LUT.

The actual sum value is determined by the taking the LUT output (half-add) and performing an exclusive OR with the carry-in. This XOR is performed in the output XOR gate that is provided within all Virtex slices. Using this XOR gate, no additional LUT resources are needed.

Computing the carry is slightly more complicated than the sum. As shown in Figure 4, the carry out is driven by a multiplexer. The select line of the

---

[3] This CLB architecture contains additional logic that is not used for this operation.

multiplexer is driven by the output of the LUT or, in this case, the result of the half-add operation. The carry out is computed for two different cases based on the value of the LUT output.

When the output of the LUT is 0, the multiplexer selects the previous sum for the carry out (note that the previous sum must be mapped to the D input of the LUT for this to occur). Under these conditions, the inputs to the half-add (previous sum and the 3-input LUT) are the same value. A carry out will only be generated when they are both 1 (See Figure 4-a). Since the carry out is driven by the previous sum, the proper carry value will be generated.

When the output of the LUT is 1, the multiplexer selects the the carry in for the carry out signal. Under this condition, the result of the XOR between the previous sum and the 3-input LUT is 1. As shown in Figure 4-a, the carry out under this condition is simply the carry in.

$Prev$ Sum	$3bit$ LUT	$Carry$ In	LUT Out	SUM Out	$Carry$ Out
0	0	0	0	0	0
0	0	1	0	1	0
0	1	0	1	1	0
0	1	1	1	0	1
1	0	0	1	1	0
1	0	1	1	0	1
1	1	0	0	0	1
1	1	1	0	1	1

(a) Truth Table for a single bit of the ROM/Adder stage

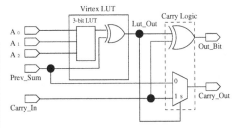

(b) The Virtex Cell with LUT and Carry Logic

Fig. 4. One bit of the ROM/Adder stage

As described above, the additional logic at the output of the CLB allows a look-up and add operation to be combined within a single logic cell of the CLB. Although the look-up operation is only three bits, this combined cell uses 33% less area than a separate four bit look-up table and separate sum operator.

5.2   Organization of Combined Cells

The combined ROM/Adder cell of Figure 4 are tiled together to form a multi-bit ROM/Adder stage. Each stage requires $c + 3$ cells to perform a multiplication between three bits of the multiplicand and the c bit constant.

To form a complete multiplier, this approach requires an initial 4-bit ROM stage followed by as many combined 3-bit ROM/adder stages as necessary. An initial ROM stage is needed to provide the "previous sum" for the following combined ROM/Adder pair (there is no previous sum for the first stage). Since the first stage is not a combined stage and does not take the previous sum input, a full 4-bit LUT can be used. Figure 5 shows the stages of this modified 16 × 16 KCM.

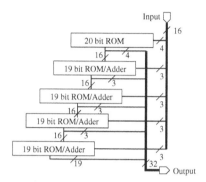

Fig. 5. 16x16 KCM with Combined ROM/Adder Stages

A module generator has been designed to create this Virtex KCM for any arbitrary constant. Written in JHDL [6], this module generator computes the contents of each LUT ROM, insures proper mapping of FPGA logic within the FPGA slice and performs relative placement of the design. Placement decisions are made to optimize its area and timing. An example layout of this multiplier is shown in Figure 6.

5.3   Reprogramming the Multiplier

Most constant coefficient multipliers perform multiplication by optimizing the *structure* of the logic. While such approaches are efficient, they are difficult to modify at run-time. Modification of the constant involves modification of the circuit structure. Although recent approaches suggest that the structure of the multiplier can be changed at run-time using novel architectural techniques and bit-stream manipulation, modification of the constant is still slow and cumbersome [4].

Unlike these constant multipliers, the structure of the KCM does *not* need to be modified to support additional constants. KCM multipliers can support arbitrary constants by modifying the contents of its look-up tables. In conventional KCMs, support for constant modification occurs by replacing the ROM look-up table with a RAM. The use of a RAM allows the designer to update the constant by writing new values into the RAM. Although this requires some

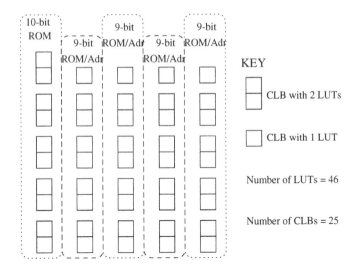

Fig. 6. The Layout of the Modified KCM on an Virtex FPGA

additional logic for RAM addressing and data formatting, updating the constant is relatively straightforward and fast.

The Virtex FPGA contains an additional architectural feature to ease the process of updating the constant. In the Virtex FPGA, the 16×1 LUT can be organized as a 16-bit shift register. Acting as a shift register, the contents of the LUT can be loaded serially with little external logic. Further, the individual look-up tables can be cascaded serially to form a single, long shift register containing the contents of all LUTs in a stage of the multiplier. While taking longer to update the constant, this approach allows the multiplier to be updated with little external logic and only two additional inputs (serial data in and serial data enable). The enhanced FPGA features allow the constant to be modified quickly, easily and with little external logic.

6   Comparison

By combining the ROM with the full-adder, this combined KCM multiplier is smaller than the conventional look-up table approach for constant coefficient multiplication. As described above, this modified multiplier requires an initial ROM stage followed by a series of combined ROM/Full-adder stages. The first ROM stage of the multiplier consumes $c + 4$ logic cells (the result of a $4 \times c$ bit multiply). This pure ROM stage is followed by $\lceil \frac{m-4}{3} \rceil - 1$ ROM/adder stages with each stage taking $c + 3$ logic cells (each stage performs a $3 \times c$ bit multiply). The total size of this multiplier is:

$$\#\text{LUTs} = c + 4 + \left\lceil \frac{n-4}{3} \right\rceil \cdot (c + 3) \qquad (3)$$

$$\approx \frac{(m-1)c}{3} + m \tag{4}$$

The area of this multiplier is plotted in Figure 7 for various sizes of the constant and along with that of the conventional multiplier approach. Clearly, the merged multiplier is smaller than the conventional approach. On average, merging the look-up tables and the full-adder reduces the size of the multiplier by 33%. The actual reduction in area of a specific multiplier will vary based on the size of the multiplier. Note in the graph the distinct steps of both multipliers. For the conventional multiplier, the addition of every fourth bit requires an additional look-up and adder stage. For the merged multiplier, the addition of every third bit requires an additional look-up/adder stage.

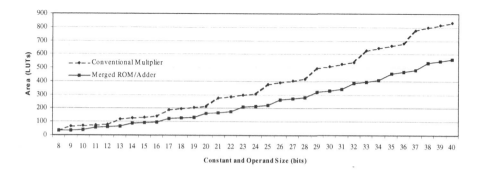

Fig. 7. Size of Conventional and Merged KCM Multiplier.

7   Conclusion

The efficiency of the KCM constant multiplier can be improved by merging the look-up table operation with the summation operation. This merging of look-up table and adder has been mapped to the Xilinx Virtex FPGA. Using the additional logic resources found within the Virtex slice, the look-up and add can be combined for a 33% reduction in logic resources. A module generator has been written to synthesize arbitrary constant multipliers on the Virtex architecture.

Additional optimizations can be made to further reduce the size of the KCM multiplier. Currently, the KCM multiplier is a fixed area for all constants and multiplicands of a specific size. Further improvements to the area can be made by taking advantage of constant-specific optimizations. While such multipliers cannot be reprogrammed to support other constants, they are extremely efficient and a viable alternative for constant multiplication.

References

[1] Ken Chapman, "Constant coefficient multipliers for the XC4000E," Tech. Rep. XAPP 054, Xilinx Corporation, December 11 1996, Version 1.1.

[2] Kenneth David Chapman, "Fast integer multipliers fit in FPGA's," *EDN*, pp. 79–80, May 12 1994.

[3] Florent de Dinchin and Vincent Lefèvre, "Constant multipliers for FPGAs," in *Proceedings of the International Conference on Parallel and Distributed Processing Techniques and Applications*, H.R. Arabnia, Ed. June 2000, vol. I, pp. 167–173, CSREA Press.

[4] Tim Courtney, Richard Turner, and Roger Woods, "Multiplexer based reconfiguration for Virtex multipliers," in *Field-Programmable Logic and Applications. Proceedings of the 9th International Workshop, FPL 2000*, 2000, pp. 749–758.

[5] Xilinx Corporation, *Virtex-II 1.5V Field-Programmable Gate Arrays*, January 2001, DS031-2 (v1.3).

[6] B. Hutchings, P. Bellows, J. Hawkins, S. Hemmert, B. Nelson, and M. Rytting, "A cad suite for high-performance fpga design," in *Proceedings of the IEEE Workshop on FPGAs for Custom Computing Machines*, K. L. Pocek and J. M. Arnold, Eds., Napa, CA, April 1999, IEEE Computer Society, pp. 12–24, IEEE.

A Digit-Serial Structure for Reconfigurable Multipliers

Chakkapas Visavakul, Peter Y.K. Cheung, and Wayne Luk

Department of EEE, Imperial College of Science Technology and Medicine
Exhibition Road, London SW7 2BT, UK
c.visavakul@ic.ac.uk, p.cheung@ic.ac.uk, wl@doc.ic.ac.uk

Abstract. This paper presents a design for combining a reconfigurable multiplier array known as Flexible Array Blocks (FABs) and digit-serial techniques to produce arbitrary size multipliers with limited resources. Any $4M{\times}4N$ bit multipliers can be implemented. In-depth evaluation of the tradeoff between resources and performance is presented. The resulting design is suitable for embedding in heterogeneous FPGA structures for fixed point DSP applications.

1 Introduction

FPGAs are commonly used in many DSP and video processing applications where multiplication forms one of the most common operations. Whilst existing FPGA architectures are optimised for binary addition, configuring FPGAs for binary multiplication is much less efficient. Haynes and Cheung reported the design of a reconfigurable multiplier array (known as Flexible Array Blocks or FAB) that can improve area efficiency by more than one order of magnitude [1]. A FAB is a 4×4 bit reconfigurable building block formed from a regular adder array structure that supports both signed and unsigned number representations. Any $4M{\times}4N$ bit parallel multiplier can be implemented by cascading together $M{\times}N$ FABs as a two dimensional array.

Although the proposed design improves area and time efficiency, it suffers from a major limitation on flexibility. If a required multiplier cannot be fitted into the available on-chip FAB resources, it cannot be implemented. There are no possibility for trading off resources with multiplication time. This paper proposes a solution to this problem by exploiting digit-serial techniques to provide the necessary tradeoff between the number of clock cycles needed to perform a multiplication and the number of FAB resources used. In addition, digit-serial technique reduces the minimum cycle time of the circuit. The resulting structure, known as DigiFAB, can be configured to implement any $4M{\times}4N$ multiplier with any amount of FAB resources. An in-depth quantitative study of the tradeoff between hardware and performance is also made.

This paper is organised as follows. In Section 2 a slight modification to the original FAB structure is introduced. In Section 3, the detailed design of Digi-FAB, a digit-serial version of the FAB structure, is described. An in-depth eval-

G. Brebner and R. Woods (Eds.): FPL 2001, LNCS 2147, pp. 565–573, 2001.
© Springer-Verlag Berlin Heidelberg 2001

uation of the area-time tradeoff of DigiFAB is presented in Section 4. Section 5 concludes the paper.

2   Reduced Flexible Array Block

The original FAB structure [1] was designed as a 4×4 bit multiplier array that can be configured to form larger signed 2's complement or unsigned multipliers. The block uses a modification of the array developed by Baugh-Wooley for two's complement multiplication [4]. The original FAB consists of two parts: (i) a multiplier array which reduces the four bit multiplication to two 5 bit numbers, and (ii) an adder to produce the final output. This architecture can be simplified to a Reduced Flexible Array Block, or RFAB (Figure 1), by removing the partial product adder which is only used if the FAB is located on the right-most column of the 2-dimensional array.

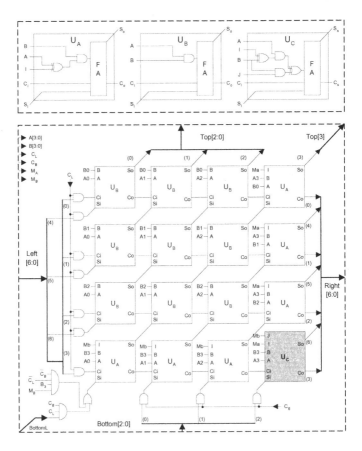

Fig. 1. Reduced Flexible Array Block (RFAB)

The configuration of the FAB is achieved via the signals M_A, M_B, C_L and C_B according to Table 1. A $4M{\times}4N$ multiplier can be constructed by simply connecting $M{\times}N$ reduced FABs together in a 2-dimensional array as shown in Figure 2.[1]

Config Bit	Meaning
M_A	High if A_3 is the MSB of a signed number
M_B	High if B_3 is the MSB of a signed number
C_L	High if A_0 is not the LSB of the multiplicand A
C_B	High if B_3 is not the MSB of the multiplicand B

Table 1. Configuration setting for FAB

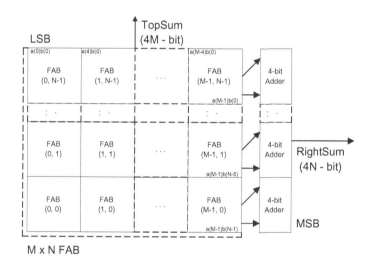

Fig. 2. $4M{\times}4N$ bit multiplier implemented with $M{\times}N$ FABs

3   Digit-Serial Multiplier Using FABs

Consider the case where instead of having the resource of $M{\times}N$ FABs on-chip, only $K{\times}L$ FABs are available.[2] To implement a $4M{\times}4N$ multiplier, the 2-dimensional FAB array can be divided into tiles of $K{\times}L$ FABs as shown in

---

[1] Hereafter the reduced form of FAB (RFAB) is used whenever FAB is mentioned.
[2] To simplify the discussion, we assume for the moment M/K and N/L are integers.

Figure 3. A digit-serial implementation can then be realised by mapping a single $K{\times}L$ FAB cluster to each tile on successive clock cycles. This can either be done row first or column first. In this way, tradeoff is made between area and performance (i.e. the number of clock cycles to complete each multiplication and the cycle time).

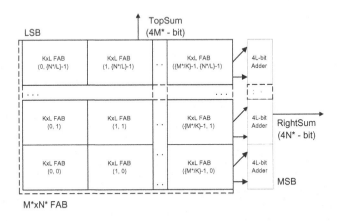

Fig. 3. $4M{\times}4N$ bit multiplier implemented with tiles of $K{\times}L$ FABs

Unfortunately this tradeoff is not direct, nor is it simple. Additional registers, multiplexers and control logic have to be added to the $K{\times}L$ FAB cluster in order to store the partial results. Figure 4 shows the basic structure of DigiFAB, a DIGIt-serial implementation of multiplier using FABs. All the peripheral circuits surrounding the $K{\times}L$ FAB cluster are overheads due to the digit-serial implementation These are additional components, such as serial-parallel converters and control circuits, which are not shown in Figure 4.

This situation is complicated further when M and N are not divisible by K and L respectively. In which case, the DigiFAB is configured to implement a $4M^*{\times}4N^*$ multiplier where

$$M^* = \lceil M/K \rceil {\times} K$$
$$N^* = \lceil N/L \rceil {\times} L$$

The number of additional registers needed to implement DigiFAB is given in Table 2. These registers are used to implement serial-parallel conversion and control circuits.

Given the hardware resource of W FABs, there are many ways to factorize it such that $W = K{\times}L$. For example 10 FABs can be employed to implement 4 different DigiFAB cluster configurations: 1×10, 2×5, 5×2 and 10×1. Table 3 shows the possible clustering arrangement for $W= 9$ to 12.

FAB	Top Registers		Right Registers		Mux Registers	
	width	level	width	level	width	level
1×1	4	1	7	N	1	N
$K×L$	$4K$	1	$8L-1$	N^*/L	1	N^*/L

Table 2. Summary of registers usage in DigiFAB

FABs (X)	Factors	Possible Configurations ($K×L$)
12	1 2 2 3	1×12, 2×6, 3×4, 4×3, 6×2, 12×1
11	1 11	1×11, 11×1
10	1 2 5	1×10, 2×5, 5×2, 10×1
9	1 3 3	1×9, 3×3, 9×1

Table 3. Examples of possible clustering of 9 to 12 FABs

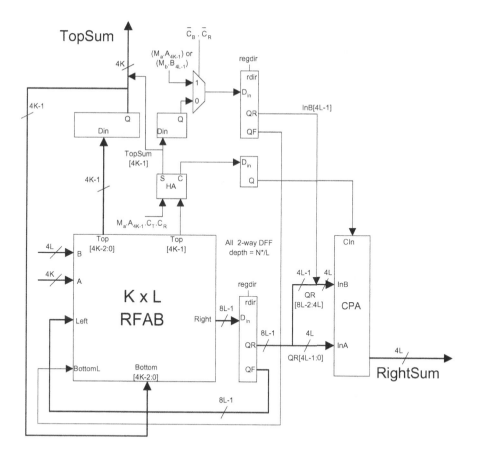

Fig. 4. DigiFAB structure

4   Evaluations and Results

In this section, the tradeoff between area and speed of DigiFAB is presented in two ways. Firstly DigiFAB using only a 4×4 FAB cluster (i.e. 16 FABs arranged in a 4×4 configuration) is compared with a fully parallel FAB-only implementation. Secondly the effect of using different cluster configurations on area and multiplication speed is investigated for a range of FAB resources.

4.1   Area and Speed Tradeoff for 4×4 Cluster

In order to evaluate the area-speed tradeoff of the digit-serial FAB proposed in this paper, both the FAB-only and the DigiFAB implementations were mapped to the Alliance standard cell library [2]. The area utilization is measured in terms of number of transistors used. Parametric models for the hardware complexity (i.e. transistor count) of the FAB-only implementation is found to be:

$$Tr_{FAB} = 836MN$$

Since the transistor count for DigiFAB includes estimates for all the control and serial-parallel conversion circuitry necessary for its proper function, its parametric model contains many more parameters and is found to be:

$$
\begin{aligned}
Tr_{DigiFAB} &= 654KL + 88K + 96L + 272N + 118 \\
Tr_{Controller} &= 29M^*/K + 21N^*/L + 138 \\
Tr_{DigiFAB\_Total} &= Tr_{DigiFAB} + Tr_{Controller} \\
&= 654KL + 88K + 96L + 272N + 29M^{*}\!/K + 21N^{*}\!/L + 256
\end{aligned}
$$

The number of interconnects used by the FAB-only and the DigiFAB implementations are shown in Table 4. Although the parametric model assumes that $4bit\times4bit$ FABs are used, the method presented here can easily be extended to cover different sizes of FABs (e.g. 8×8 FABs [5]).

Scheme	Number of Interconnects
FAB	$15M + 24N + 6MN - 1$
DigiFAB with controller	$8M^* + 8N^* + 5$

Table 4. Number of Interconnects in FAB and DigiFAB

Figure 5 shows the transistor counts for implementing a $4N\times4N$ multiplier using DigiFAB with a single 4×4 cluster, and compares it to a FAB-only implementation. As expected the transistor count for the FAB-only implementation increases as N^2 while the DigiFAB size remains substantially constant. This is in spite of the extra registers required to store partial results and the additional overhead due to the control circuitry.

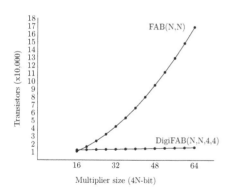

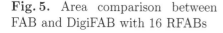

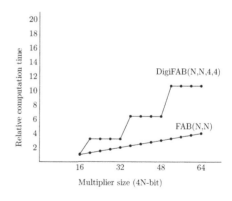

Fig. 5. Area comparison between FAB and DigiFAB with 16 RFABs

Fig. 6. Computation time comparison between FAB and DigiFAB with 16 RFABs

The timing model is also based on the Alliance CMOS cell library [2]. The multiplication time is dependent on two factors: the worst-case time delay on the combinatorial circuit, and the number of clock cycles required to complete a multiplication. The FAB-only implementation requires only a single clock cycle to compute the product, but it contains long delay paths through both sum and carry chains. The DigiFAB, as with all digital-serial approaches [3], allows much shorter clock period to be used. However it also requires $(\lceil M/K \rceil + 1) \times \lceil N/L \rceil$ cycles to complete a computation. The total computation time used for the evaluation is obtained by multiplying the shortest clock period with the number of clock cycles required.

Figure 6 shows the relative computation time versus the size of the multiplier for both implementations. The computation time is normalized to the delay of a 4×4 cluster. It can be seen that the computation time of the FAB-only design increases linearly with N, while the DigiFAB implementation has a step-like computation time due to the quantized nature of the circuit. This is because in the case of DigiFAB, a 4×4 FAB cluster will compute 17×17 to 32×32 multiplications in two digit-serial cycles with identical computation time.

4.2 Effects of Different Clustering Arrangements

So far only DigiFAB using 4×4 cluster of FAB cells has been considered. The same resource ($W = 16$) could also have been configured as 1×16, 16×1, 8×2, and 2×8. Which configuration would give the best area-speed tradeoff?

Figures 7 and 8 show respectively the relative area and compute time of all possible configurations for different values of W when compared with a FAB-only implementation of a 32×32 bit multiplier. For example, if 16 FABs are used in a DigiFAB structure, only around 30% of hardware resources is required, but the compute time would increase by a factor between 4 to 26, depending on the cluster arrangement. In other words, how W is factored into $K \times L$ affects the amount of area saving slightly, but it can have a significant effect on compute time. It can also be seen that having a cluster configuration that is essentially square provides the best arrangement (i.e. K and L are as close as possible). In contrast the long-and-thin, and the short-and-fat configuration are worst (i.e. $W{\times}1$ and $1{\times}W$).

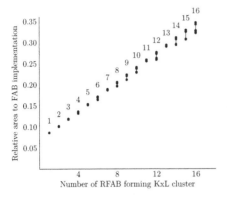
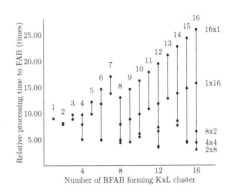

Fig. 7. Relative area to FAB-only implementation for building 32×32 bit multiplier using DigiFAB with 16 or less RFABs

Fig. 8. Relative calculation time to FAB-only implementation for building 32×32 bit multiplier using Digi-FAB with 16 or less RFABs

These two graphs can be combined to give a direct resource vs area vs compute time tradeoff for the different cluster configurations as shown in Figure 9. Each line represents a fixed amount of FAB resource. Every point on this graph is a possible solution to the problem of implementing a 32×32 bit unsigned/signed multiplier. Figure 10 shows a related tradeoff characteristic. Instead of showing the total compute time on the x-axis, this uses the maximum operating clock frequency relative to a FAB-only implementation. It can be seen that if DigiFAB is to be used in an embedded array with fast clocking, one would choose a small value for W.

5   Conclusion

In this paper, a digit-serial version of the original FAB reconfigurable multiplier is presented. It has been shown that by exploiting digit-serial techniques, a flexible tradeoff between array resource, area and compute time is available. It has also been demonstrated that although a given resource could be configured in many different ways, the optimum clustering configuration is one which is essentially as square as possible. The DigiFAB design also allows any size of multiplier to be implemented with any fixed amount of FAB resource.

Many questions remain unanswered. What is the appropriate mixture of FAB cells and conventional LUT-based logic cells? How should the routing to FABs

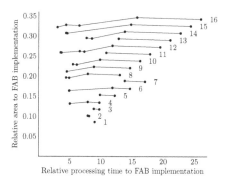

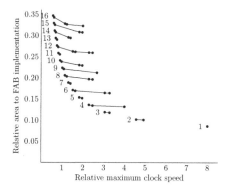

Fig. 9. Relative area vs relative computational time for different DigiFAB configurations

Fig. 10. Relative area vs maximum clock speed for different DigiFAB configurations

be organised and how much? However, results from this paper suggest that digit-serial FABs may provide sufficient advantages to warrant efforts to be devoted to answering these questions.

6   Acknowledgement

This work is partly supported by a scholarship awarded to the first author from Mahanakorn University of Technology, Thailand.

References

1. Simon D. Haynes and Peter Y. K. Cheung, "A Reconfigurable Multiplier Array For Video Image Processing Tasks, Suitable For Embedding In An FPGA Structure", in *Proceedings IEEE Symposium on FPGAs for Custom Computing Machines*, pp. 226-234, 1998.
2. A. Greiner and F. Pêcheux, "ALLIANCE: A complete set of CAD tools for teaching VLSI design", 3rd *Eurochip Workshop on VLSI Design Training*, Grenoble, pp. 230–237, 1992.
3. Yun-Nan Chang, Janardhan H. Satyanarayanan, Keshap K. Parhi, "Systematic Design of High-Speed and Low-Power Digit-Serial Multipliers", *IEEE Trans. Circuits and Systems-II Analog and Digital Signal Processing*, vol. 45, no. 12, December 1998.
4. A.R. Baugh and B.A. Wooley, "A two's complement parallel array multiplication algorithm", *IEEE Trans. Comput.*, C-22, (1-2), pp. 1045-1047, 1973.
5. S.D. Haynes, A.B. Ferrari, P.Y.K. Cheung, "Algorithms and Structures for Reconfigurable Multiplication Units", *The XI Brazilian Symposium on Integrated Circuit Design*, October 1998.

FPGA Resource Reduction Through Truncated Multiplication

Kent E. Wires[1], Michael J. Schulte[2], and Don McCarley[3]

[1] Agere Systems, Allentown PA 18103, USA
[2] EECS Department, Lehigh University, Bethlehem PA 18015, USA
[3] Agere Systems, Austin TX 78758, USA

Abstract. Significant reductions in FPGA resources, delay, and power can be achieved using truncated multipliers instead of standard parallel multipliers when the full precision of the standard multiplier is not required. With truncated multiplication, the less significant columns of the multiplication matrix are eliminated and correction terms are added to keep the total error to less than one unit in the last place. The truncated multiplication techniques presented in this paper are applied to FPGA parallel multipliers, and can be used in conjunction with a number of other performance enhancing techniques, such as pipelining, Booth encoding, and device specific optimizations to increase the effectiveness of device mapping, placing, and routing.

1 Introduction

Traditionally, digital signal processing (DSP) tasks have been handled by application specific integrated circuits (ASICs) or multimedia accelerated general purpose processors (GPPs) [1, 2, 3, 4, 5, 6, 7]. Recently, advances in field programmable gate array (FPGA) technology have allowed the logic density, speed, and power consumption of FPGAs to reach levels that are competitive with those of existing DSPs [8, 9, 10]. FPGA technology offers a customizable solution without the lengthy development time associated with the design and fabrication of ASICs and GPPs. This combination of time-to-market advantage and general feasibility has many developers investigating the possibility of executing DSP applications on FPGAs.

Many DSP algorithms, such as convolution, correlation, filtering, and finite Fourier transform computation are multiplication intensive [11]. Efficient multipliers are therefore important for FPGAs intended to execute DSP applications [8, 9, 10]. Truncated multipliers, which eliminate the less significant columns of the multiplication matrix, can be used when the full precision of the multiplication is not required. When this is the case, truncated multipliers provide a significant savings in area, delay, and power compared to non-truncated multipliers of the same operand size [12, 13, 14].

This paper investigates FPGA resource, delay, and power savings of two types of truncated parallel multipliers with various operand sizes, as compared to non-truncated parallel multipliers with the same operand sizes. These multipliers

G. Brebner and R. Woods (Eds.): FPL 2001, LNCS 2147, pp. 574–583, 2001.
© Springer-Verlag Berlin Heidelberg 2001

are based on ASIC designs presented in [12] and [13], however, modifications are made to optimize the designs for mapping onto a particular FPGA device. Section 2 gives an overview of constant correction and data dependent truncated multipliers. Section 3 describes the details of the design specification and device mapping optimization process. Section 4 compares the area, delay, and power dissipation of the truncated multipliers to standard parallel multipliers. Our conclusions are given in Section 5.

2 Truncated Multipliers

Truncated multiplication is a technique used to conserve multiplier area when the full precision of the multiplication is not required [12, 13, 14]. Using this technique, several of the less significant columns of the original multiplier are eliminated and correction terms are added to the more significant columns to reduce the overall error. By properly selecting the number of columns and the correction terms, the error can be made small enough to meet the requirements of a given application or system.

In the following discussion, it is assumed that an unsigned n-bit multiplicand A is multiplied by an unsigned n-bit multiplier B to produce an unsigned $2n$-bit product P. With minor modifications, the techniques for truncated multiplication discussed in this section can be extended to handle two's complement multipliers, multiply-add and multiply-complement units, Booth-encoded multipliers, and multipliers for which A, B, and P are different sizes.

For fractional numbers, the values for A, B, and P are

$$A = \sum_{i=0}^{n-1} a_i 2^{-n+i} \qquad B = \sum_{i=0}^{n-1} b_i 2^{-n+i} \qquad P = \sum_{i=0}^{2n-1} p_i 2^{-2n+i} \qquad (1)$$

In many DSP systems, P is rounded to n bits to avoid growth in word size. The multiplication matrix for a standard n-bit multiply is shown in Figure 1.

2.1 Constant Correction Truncated Multipliers

Constant correction truncated multiplication is performed by adding a constant to the more significant columns based on the number of truncated columns in the multiplication matrix, as shown in Figure 2 [12]. The correction constant is introduced to offset the error from eliminating the less significant columns and truncating the product to n bits. If the input operands are of length n bits and the $n-k$ least significant columns of the multiplication matrix are removed, the maximum absolute error due to removing columns 0 to $n-k-1$ is

$$E_{reduct} = \sum_{i=0}^{n-k-1} (i+1) \cdot 2^{-2n+i} \qquad (2)$$

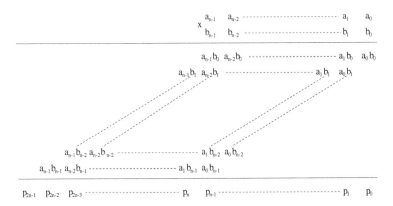

Fig. 1. Standard Multiplication Matrix

The maximum absolute error introduced by truncating the product bits in columns $n - k$ to $n - 1$ is

$$E_{round} = \sum_{i=n-k}^{n-1} 2^{-2n+i} = 2^{-n}(1 - 2^{-k}) \tag{3}$$

The total maximum error is

$$E_{total} = \sum_{i=0}^{n-k-1} (i+1) \cdot 2^{-2n+i} + 2^{-n}(1 - 2^{-k}) \tag{4}$$

or equivalently,

$$E_{total} = \sum_{i=0}^{n-k-1} (i+1) \cdot 2^{-n+i} + (1 - 2^{-k}) \tag{5}$$

units in the last place (ulps), where 1 ulp $= 2^{-n}$. The maximum absolute error is minimized by choosing the correction constant

$$C = \frac{round(2^{n+k-1} \cdot E_{total})}{2^{n+k}} \tag{6}$$

which corresponds to half the total maximum absolute error, E_{total}, rounded to $n + k$ fractional bits. This gives the new maximum absolute error

$$E_{trunc} = max(C, E_{total} - C) \tag{7}$$

An absolute error of C occurs when all of the truncated bits are zero, while an absolute error of $E_{total} - C$ occurs when all of the truncated bits are one.

Table 1 shows values for k that limit the maximum absolute error to less than one ulp for given ranges of n. For example, with a 32-bit multiplier, $k = 5$

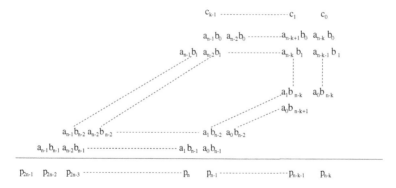

Fig. 2. Constant Correction Truncated Multiplication Matrix

Table 1. Values of k for Less than One Ulp Error for Constant Correction Multiplication

k	range of n
0	$1 \leq n \leq 1$
1	$2 \leq n \leq 3$
2	$4 \leq n \leq 6$
3	$7 \leq n \leq 11$
4	$12 \leq n \leq 20$
5	$21 \leq n \leq 37$
6	$38 \leq n \leq 70$
7	$71 \leq n \leq 135$

and the 27 least significant columns of the multiplication matrix are completely eliminated.

Figure 3a shows the dot diagram of a conventional 8-bit Dadda tree multiplier [15], which requires 64 AND gates, 35 full adders, 7 half adders, and a 14-bit carry-lookahead adder. In comparison, Figure 3b shows a constant correction truncated 8-bit Dadda tree multiplier with $k = 3$, which requires 49 AND gates, 29 full adders, 7 half adders, and a 10-bit carry-lookahead adder. As n increases, the hardware savings from using truncated multiplication also increases.

2.2   Data Dependent Truncated Multipliers

Data dependent truncated multiplication is performed by adding the partial product bits in the most significant column that is to be removed to the least significant remaining column of the multiplication matrix [14]. A sequence of $k - 1$ ones is also added to the multiplication matrix, where k is the number of columns kept after the rounding point. Figure 4 shows the partial product matrix for data dependent truncated multiplication. Only the $n + k$ most significant columns of the multiplication matrix are used to compute the product, which is

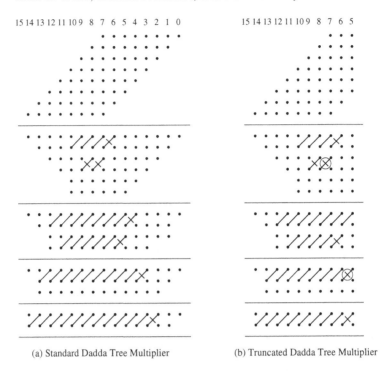

(a) Standard Dadda Tree Multiplier   (b) Truncated Dadda Tree Multiplier

Fig. 3. 8-bit Dadda Tree Multipliers

then truncated to n bits. Using a method similar to the one presented in [13], the partial product bits in column $n-k-1$ are added to column $n-k$ to compensate for the error that occurs by eliminating columns 0 to $n-k-2$. Adding partial product bits from column $n-k-1$ to column $n-k$ is equivalent to rounding these partial products to $n+k$ fractional bits, using round-to-nearest.

The maximum absolute error for data dependent truncated multiplication is bounded by

$$E_{trunc} \leq 0.5 + \sum_{i=1}^{\lfloor (n-k)/2 \rfloor} (n-k+2-2i)2^{-k-2i-1} \qquad (8)$$

ulps [14]. Table 2 shows values of k that limit the maximum absolute error due to truncated multiplication to less than one ulp for different ranges of n [14]. Compared to constant correction truncated multiplication, the data dependent method allows more columns to be removed while maintaining a maximum absolute error of one ulp for a given value of n. For given values of n and k, data dependent truncated multipliers require slightly more hardware to add the partial products in column $n-k-1$ to column $n-k$.

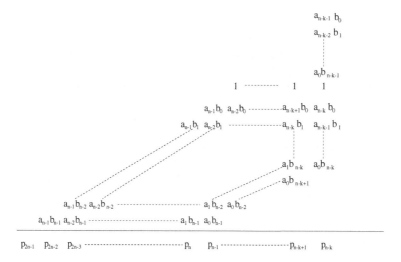

Fig. 4. Data Dependent Truncated Multiplication Matrix

Table 2. Values of k for Less than One Ulp Error for Data Dependent Multiplication

k	range of n
0	$1 \leq n \leq 3$
1	$4 \leq n \leq 7$
2	$8 \leq n \leq 14$
3	$15 \leq n \leq 27$
4	$28 \leq n \leq 52$
5	$53 \leq n \leq 101$
6	$102 \leq n \leq 198$

3 Implementation

The implementation process consists of two steps, design specification and device mapping. In the design specification phase, Verilog HDL descriptions of the designs are generated, and design decisions are made considering the target architecture. In the device mapping phase, the compilation results are examined and manually altered to make full use of the particular FPGA device resources before being passed to the place and route tools.

3.1 Design Specification

Structural level Verilog HDL descriptions of data dependent truncated, constant correction truncated, and standard parallel multipliers of various operand lengths are generated and passed to Synplicity's Synplify logic synthesis tool for compilation. The HDL descriptions are implemented as described in the previous section, and considerations are made to facilitate the optimization of the designs for FPGA architectures. In each case, an array of AND gates is used to generate the necessary partial product bits. The partial product bits are reduced according to the Dadda reduction method [15], using a combination of (3-2) and (2-2) counters.

The resulting designs lend themselves to FPGA-style architectures, because they can take advantage of the numerous multiplexors and simple arithmetic logic blocks within the functional units. In fact, the simple arithmetic components inherent to the designs can be easily arranged by the place and route tools amongst the numerous functional units of an FPGA. An exception to this is the final adder, which adds the sum and carry vectors. The method of optimizing this adder is specific to the target device, and is considered in the following section. Each multiplier is unpipelined to facilitate the comparison of the general FPGA resources, delay, and power characteristics of each type of n-bit multiplier, but pipelining the designs is a natural extension, due to the numerous latches found in each functional unit.

3.2   Mapping to ORCA Series 3 FPGAs

The target device is a Lucent Technologies ORCA OR3LxxxB series FPGA, which has a process technology of 0.25 μm/5 LM, 166K to 340K system gates, a speed grade of -7 or -8, and an internal operating voltage of 2.5 V [16]. Device specific libraries are used to link against the Verilog design file during compilation, and the result is modified manually to insure that the FPGA resources are efficiently utilized by the multiplier. The adder that performs the final addition was not considered in the design specification stage, but is instead addressed in the mapping stage. It is implemented using an appropriate configuration of ORCA-specific FADD4 and FADD8 fast adder macrocells. FADDm fast adder macrocells are simple m-bit fast adders that take advantage of the FPGA target technology. The result of the mapping is a flattened electronic data interchange format (EDIF) netlist, which is used by the ORCA Foundry place and route tools to place, route, and generate the bitstream file for the multiplier on the specified device.

The ORCA Series 3 FPGAs consist of two basic elements: programmable logic cells (PLCs) and programmable input/output cells (PICs). An array of PLCs is surrounded by the PICs. The PLCs consist of a programmable function unit (PFU) and a supplemental logic and interconnect cell (SLIC), along with all the routing for the PFU and SLICs. The logic for the multipliers discussed in this paper is implemented in the PFUs. Each PFU consists of eight 4-input look-up tables (LUTs), nine 1-bit registers, and 36 programmable muxes. Each PFU can implement up to 108 logic gates [16]. When used to implement non-pipelined multipliers, the registers are not used.

4   Area, Delay, and Power Estimates

Standard parallel, constant correction truncated, and data dependent truncated multipliers with 8, 16, 24, and 32-bit operands were synthesized, as described in the previous section. Area and delay estimates were obtained directly from the ORCA Foundry tools, and power estimates were obtained using [17], which estimates total operating power dissipation as

$$P = 0.045 + 0.053 \cdot n_{br} + 0.086 \cdot n_{PFU} + 0.002 \cdot n_{PIC} \tag{9}$$

where n_{br} is the number of clock branches, n_{PFU} is the number of PFUs, n_{PIC} is the number of PICs, and P is given in units of mW/MHz. The estimates pertain to the design after it has been mapped, placed, and routed. Power, area, and delay contributions from I/O ports are ignored, as these ports are included for simulation purposes and are not considered part of the design. Area is measured as the number of utilized PFUs, delay refers to worst-case critical path delay, and power is average power dissipation per MHz. The area, critical path delay, and power dissipation of each unit is found in Table 3.

Table 3. Area, Delay, and Power Estimates

Unit	Area (n_{PFU})	Delay (ns)	Power (mW/MHz)
8-bit multipliers			
standard parallel	28	19.87	2.453
constant correction	22	17.73	1.937
data dependent	24	21.86	2.109
16-bit multipliers			
standard parallel	143	38.36	12.341
constant correction	93	34.54	8.043
data dependent	102	34.59	8.817
24-bit multipliers			
standard parallel	317	125.51	27.307
constant correction	212	53.09	18.275
data dependent	194	49.53	16.729
32-bit multipliers			
standard parallel	619	214.55	53.279
constant correction	387	124.85	33.327
data dependent	325	101.99	27.995

Compared to the standard parallel 8-bit multiplier, the 8-bit constant correction truncated multiplier has an area that is 21% less, has a 12% shorter worst-case delay, and dissipates roughly 21% less power. The 8-bit data dependent truncated multiplier has an area that is 14% less, a worst-case delay that is 10% longer, and dissipates about 14% less power than the 8-bit standard parallel multiplier. The 16-bit constant correction truncated multiplier has an area that is 35% less, a worst-case delay that is 10% less, and dissipates 35% less power than the 16-bit parallel multiplier. Compared to the standard parallel 16-bit multiplier, the 16-bit data dependent truncated multiplier has a 29% smaller area, a 10% smaller delay, and dissipates 29% less power.

As routing becomes more complex with larger operand sizes, the FPGA resource, delay, and power savings from using truncated multiplication become more substantial. The 24-bit constant correction truncated multiplier has a 33% smaller area than the standard parallel multiplier, a 58% shorter delay, and consumes about 33% less power. The 24-bit data dependent truncated multiplier has a 39% smaller area, a 60% shorter worst-case delay, and dissipates 39% less power, compared to the 24-bit standard parallel multiplier. The 32-bit constant correction multiplier has a 37% smaller area, a 42% shorter delay, and dissipates 37% less power than the 32-bit standard parallel multiplier. Compared to the same multiplier, the 32-bit data dependent truncated multiplier has a 47% smaller area, a 52% shorter delay, and dissipates 47% less power.

5   Conclusions

When the full precision of an FPGA multiplier is not required, significant reductions in area, delay, and power can be achieved using truncated multipliers. When compared to standard parallel multipliers, constant correction truncated multipliers provide more efficient results than data dependent truncated multipliers for smaller values of n, but this trend reverses as n increases. Both techniques provide significant savings in area, delay, and power for values of n greater than eight. The techniques presented in this paper can be used in conjunction with other performance enhancing techniques, such as pipelining, Booth encoding, and device specific optimizations to increase the effectiveness of device mapping, placing, and routing.

Acknowledgments

This material is based upon work supported by the National Science Foundation under Grant No. CCR-9703421. This research is also supported by a grant from Agere Systems and the Pennsylvania Infrastructure Technology Alliance under Project No. IST-001.

References

[1] S. Oberman, F. Weber, N. Juffa, and G. Favor, "AMD 3DNow! Technology and the K6-2 Microprocessor," in *Proceedings of Hot Chips 10*, pp. 245–254, 1998.

[2] S. Thakkur and T. Huff, "Internet Streaming SIMD Extensions," *Computer*, vol. 32, no. 12, pp. 26–34, 1999.

[3] *AltiVec Technology Programming Environments Manual*. Motorola, Inc., 1998.

[4] K. Diefendorff, P. Dubey, R. Hochsprung, and H. Scale, "AltiVec Extension to PowerPC Accelerates Media Processing," *IEEE Micro*, vol. 20, no. 2, pp. 85–95, 2000.

[5] J. R. Boddie *et al.*, "A 32-Bit Floating-Point DSP with C Compiler," in *Conference Record of the Twenty-Second Asilomar Conference on Signals, Systems and Computers*, vol. 2, pp. 880–884, 1989.

[6] N. Vasseghi, K. Yeager, E. Sarto, and M. Seddighnezhad, "A 200-MHz Super-scalar RISC Microprocessor," *IEEE Journal of Solid-State Circuits*, vol. 31, no. 11, pp. 1675–1686, 1996.

[7] R. Weiss, "32-Bit Floating-Point DSP Processors," *EDN*, vol. 36, no. 23, pp. 127–146, 1991.

[8] M. Thornton, J. Gaiche, and J. Lemieux, "Tradeoff Analysis of Integer Multiplier Circuits Implemented in FPGAs," in *IEEE Pacific Rim Conference on Communications, Computers and Signal Processing*, pp. 301–304, 1999.

[9] Lucent Technologies, "Implementing and Optimizing Multipliers in ORCA FP-GAs," *Technical Application Note*, 1997.

[10] D. McCarley, S. Megeed, and J. Fried, "Module Generated Multipliers in Field Programmable Gate Arrays," *Lehigh University Technical Report*, 1999.

[11] A. V. Oppenheim and R. W. Schafer, *Digital Signal Processing*. Prentice-Hall, Inc., 1975.

[12] M. J. Schulte and E. E. Swartzlander, Jr., "Truncated Multiplication with Correction Constant," in *VLSI Signal Processing, VI*, pp. 388–396, 1993.

[13] E. J. King and E. E. Swartzlander, Jr., "Data-Dependent Truncated Scheme for Parallel Multiplication," in *Proceedings of the Thirty First Asilomar Conference on Signals, Circuits and Systems*, pp. 1178–1182, 1998.

[14] M. J. Schulte, J. G. Jansen, and J. E. Stine., "Reduced Power Dissipation Through Truncated Multiplication," in *IEEE Alessandro Volta Memorial International Workshop on Low Power Design*, pp. 61–69, 1999.

[15] L. Dadda, "Some Schemes for Parallel Multipliers," *Alta Frequenza*, vol. 34, pp. 349–356, 1965.

[16] Lucent Technologies, "ORCA OR3LxxxB Series Field-Programmable Gate Arrays," *Product Brief*, 1999.

[17] Lucent Technologies, "ORCA OR3LxxxB Series Field-Programmable Gate Arrays," *Data Addendum*, 1999.

Efficient Mapping of Pre-synthesized IP-Cores onto Dynamically Reconfigurable Array Architectures

Jürgen Becker, Nicolas Liebau, Thilo Pionteck, Manfred Glesner

Darmstadt University of Technology
Institute of Microelectronic Systems
Karlstr. 15, D-64283 Darmstadt, Germany
e-mail: {becker, liebau, pionteck, glesner}@mes.tu-darmstadt.de

Abstract. *Application-specific Systems-on-Chip (SoCs) introduce a set of various challenges for their interdisciplinary microelectronic implementation, from system theory (application) level over efficient CAD methods to suitable technologies, e. g. considering also reconfigurable hardware parts on different granularities. The paper sketches first major perspectives in architecture, design and application of Configurable Systems-on-Chip (CSoCs). The focus is the description of new CAD-algorithms for mapping automatized pre-synthesized IP-cores onto coarse-grain dynamically reconfigurable array architectures. Here, combinatorial optimization methods are combined with physical chip design algorithms, whereas dynamic reconfiguration of allocated hardware resources is considered.*

1. Introduction

In the last years, the fast technological development in VLSI possibilities has brought to the notion of single *System-on-Chip* (SoC) solutions [1]. Trends in microelectronic systems design point to higher integration levels, smaller form factor, lower power consumption and cost-effective implementations. The achievement of this goal has to be efficiently supported by the concurrent development of new design methods including such aspects as flexibility, mixed-signal system-level exploration, re-usability and top-down SoC design. Today SoCs are often mixed-technology designs, including such diverse combinations as embedded DRAM, high-performance or low-power logic, analog, RF, and even more unusual technologies like Micro-ElectroMechanical Systems (MEMS) and optical input/output. But this development also raises its problems, e. g. it takes an enormous amount of time and effort to design complex chips. So, new design methodologies are needed to improve the design process to keep up with the technology improvements. The concept of using already existing parts from previous designs incl. parts designed by third parties is called IP- or Core-based design [2], [8], [9]. Dependent on application areas and constraints, important aspects for microlectronic SoC candidates are:
- *time-to-market* and SoC *flexibility*, e.g. *risk minimization* for late spec. changes,
- long product life cycles, for multi-standard / multi-product perspectives, and due to multi-purpose usage, high SoC fabrication volumes (-> cost decrease per chip).

Microelectronic system designers have two alternatives for digital SoC integration [2]:
- ASIC-based SoCs, consisting mainly of processor-, memory-, and ASIC-cores, or
- *Configurable SoCs* (CSoCs), consisting of processor-, memory-, ASIC-cores, and reconfigurable hardware parts [3] [4] [5] [9] [10] for application customization.

CSoCs combine the advantages of both: ASIC-SoCs and multichip development using standard components, e. g. they require only minimal NRE costs, due inexpensive ASIC-

G. Brebner and R. Woods (Eds.): FPL 2001, LNCS 2147, pp. 584–589, 2001.
© Springer-Verlag Berlin Heidelberg 2001

tools and mask sets. Selected computation-intensive signal processing tasks have to be migrated from software to hardware implementation, e. g. to ASIC or (application-specific) reconfigurable hardware SoC parts. Based on this situation and future market demands, now many industrial and academic CSoC products and approaches arise [9] [10] [11] [12] [13] [16] [17] [18]. Here, new emerging technologies like reconfigurable hardware architectures of different granularity are considered as alternatives for DSP- and/or ASIC-technologies, dependent on implementation constraint trade-offs. Crucial for the success of CSoCs are efficient (IP-based) CAD-tools for application mapping and dynamic functional adaptation to different situations, compatible to specification approaches like SystemC [8]. First, underlying dynamically reconfigurable hardware is sketched, followed by new developed IP-based CAD-algorithms for coarse-grain arrays. In section 4 a RAKE-receiver for flexible CDMA-based mobile terminals is analyzed.

2.   DReAM: A New Dynamic Reconfigurable Hardware Array

An example for a CSoC with integrated coarse-grain dynamically reconfigurable hardware is the DReAM (Dynamically Reconfigurable Architecture for Mobile Communication), which is currently synthesized at Darmstadt University of Technology. The DReAM architecture is designed for the requirements of future mobile communications systems, e.g. third generation (3G) systems [6]. Especially in the application area of mobile communication, standards are often changed or extended, which requires an adaptable SoC solution. A typical SoC integrating DReAM array structures contains additionally memory-, DSP-, and microcontroler-core(s), currently interconnected with an AMBA-based AHB bus [6]. Reconfigurable Processing Units (RPUs) can both execute necessary arithmetic data manipulation for data-flow oriented protocol parts and execute FSM-type operations for control-flow oriented parts. The RPUs operate in parallel and have a 16-bit fast direct local connection to their direct neighbours and a 16-bit connection to the programable global communication network. In each RPU there is a small local memory in order to reduce the access of the main memory. Based on DReAM datapaths synthesized with an 0.35 m CMOS process promising performance results are obtained for computation-intensive tasks of future CDMA-based communication systems, e. g. for implementing flexible RAKE-receiver architectures with 1.5 Mb/s data throughput [6].

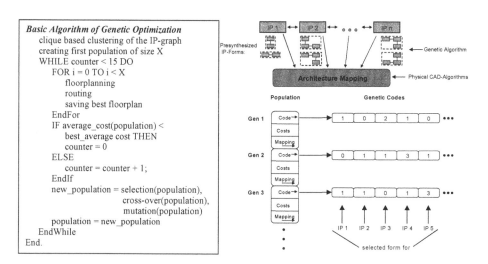

Fig. 1.   Genetic Optimization for Architecture Mapping of IP-Topologies

3.   IP-Based Mapping for Reconfigurable Hardware Arrays

For developing new and promising IP-based methods the corresponding CAD tools also have to operate on the higher abstraction levels. Automatized hardware synthesis from the behavioural and system level is still not sufficiently possible for ASICs and FPGAs, e.g. actual universal HDLs and their correpsonding synthesis environments are not suitable to support efficiently the application mapping of complex algorithms onto dynamically reconfigurable hardware arrays like DReAM. Here, for each IP-core used within the possible complex application scenarios several alternatives of pre-synthesized IP-shapes are available in a characterized library, similar to standard cell synthesis. Such pre-synthesized IP-shapes consist of a variable number of RPUs and are realized by considering the special hardware attributes and topology of the DReAM array (see Fig. 1). In addition, information about data dependencies and data rates is included. Global combinatoric optimization methods (genetic algorithms) are applied to find optimized IP-form combinations, resulting in mappings with minimized hardware resources. The genetic optimization examines efficiently the whole design space. The result is the selection and generation of several IP-topology combinations that are to be used in each actual architecture mapping step. Every chosen combination of IP-forms is mapped onto DReAM using extended macrocell floorplanning / placement methods based on *shape functions* [20].

At each step of the genetic algorithm so called individuals are created, whereas each of them is representing a particular combination of IP-forms or IP-topologies. The overall genetic optimization process is given in the basic genetic algorithm in Fig. 1), whereas the optimization proceeds until 15 times the average fitness of the population has not improved. The *fitness function* represents the quality metric for the genetic optimization process, which takes into account the needed number of RPUs (c_1 * $cost_{area}$), an virtual exceed of the allowed number of RPUs (c_2 * $cost_{vio}$), and the (global) communication costs between IP-cores (c_3 * $cost_{com}$). For every possible combination of the different IP-forms an optimal mapping onto DReAM will be determined using *extended shape functions,* for mapping rectangular shapes. The unused RPU will be marked in free-lists in order to be allocated

a)   Hadlock´s Algorithm Principle

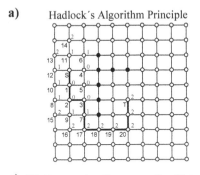

b)   Determination of Net Priorities
for DReAM Routing Sequence

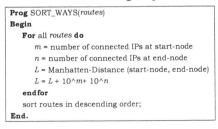

c) I/O Connection Resource Conflict

d)   Global Input Resource Conflict

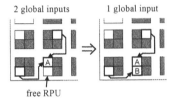

Fig. 2.   Extended Hadlock´s Routing Algorithm with determined Net Priorities

first by new IP-blocks. In addition to free-lists, the *shape function* based architecture mapping step is extended by PARETO-Point considerations. In theory there are 4^{n-1} mapping alternatives, where n is the number of IP-blocks to be mapped. To avoid combinatorical explosions during the mapping process, PARETO-Points are not dominated by another design space point and are used for excluding low quality mappings in advance. But with increasing number of IPs to be mapped the number of alternative mappings still grows exponentially. To reduce this effect an communication based clustering is performed before the genetic optimization starts. An adapted clique partitioning algorithm identifies clusters of IPs based on the their communication dependencies, corresponding to (global) DReAM interconnect resource allocation. Thus, an order for mapping the IPs is determined, which results in a drastical decrease in number of alternative mappings and corresponding run times.

DReAM supports either local or global communication to connect IPs with each other. For global communication between none-adjacent RPUs, a global bus system of 2 independent busses is used (Fig. 2 c). During the global routing process allocation conflicts are possible due to already routed connections,e. g. to connect all global signals to the bus system. Thus, a prioity order for routing the inter-IP nets is determined (Fig. 2 b). Further resource conflicts may result, because an RPU can concurrently handle only one global input (see Fig. 2 d). Based on a topologic routing graph an extended *Hadlock's Algorithm* [20] routes the global connections to minimize the necessary wiring hardware (Fig. 2 a). At connection boxes up to two signals can be put or taken from the global bus system. Except for the start point and end point of a global connection, it is always possible to plan detours, if resources are blocked. The adapted *Hadlock's Algorithm* is used now to route the connection on the gobal routing graph, which is an variant of Lee's maze routing algorithm with the advantage that it search for a way from the start node directly to the target node by expanding always from the node with the lowest detour number (see Fig. 2 a).

4.   Application Mapping Example: Complex RAKE-Receiver

As an example of an complex application for future mobile communication systems we examined a Rake receiver algorithm for CDMA-based transmission technology. It consists of 10 communicationgs IP-cores (see IP-graph in Fig. 3). For each of them several alternative IP-topologies were created in a library to use them in the optimization. The data tranfers between the IP-cores can be devided into 4 separat time steps. Therefore, for this example it is possible to optimize the necessary routing resources using dynamic reconfiguration. Fig. 4 shows a a resulting floorplan in all 4 time steps. The table in Fig. 3 shows the runtime measureements for different population sizes. The inclusion of communication based clustering improved the found results and reduced the runtime significantly. Further

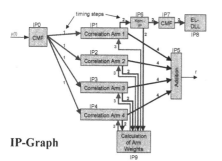

IP-Graph

Running Times and Cost Values for Different Population Sizes

Population Size	Total Running Time (min)	Time Floor-planning (min)	Time Routing (min)	Time Genetic Opt. (min)	Analyzed Solutions	Best Solution (Costs)
20	43,4	14,0	24,8	1,4	962	255
40	45,5	15,7	29,3	1,3	1446	245
60	89,5	29,9	53,2	5,0	2358	240
80	73,1	26,1	40,1	4,5	1992	216

Best Solution without Clustering: 260

Fitness Function (Mapping) =
$$c_1 * cost_{area} + c_2 * cost_{vio} + c_3 * cost_{com}$$

Fig. 3.   Architecture Mapping Analysis of RAKE-Receiver algorithm

details to this example and promising performance results regarding the manual mapping of this RAKE-specification for a data rate of 1.5 Mb/s based on already sythesized data paths of DReAM (0.35 μm CMOS-process) can be found in [6].

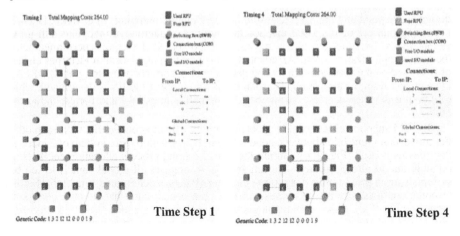

Fig. 4.   RAKE-Receiver Architecture Mapping Results for independent Time Steps 1 & 4

5.   Conclusions

The paper introduced first briefly the perspectives of *Configurable Systems-on-Chip* (CSoCs) with interdisciplinary microelectronic implementation, from system theory (application) level over CAD methods to suitable technologies, whereas for the industry the adaptivity of CSoCs is essential. Also major players like Hitachi and Lucent Technologies are in this market, proofing their great potential, especially with short *time-to-market* (risk minimization), *flexibility* (adaptivity) and *cost* (multi-purpose -> volume increase) constraints. The focus of this contribution was the introduction of efficient *Intellectual Property* (IP) based mapping techniques for coarse-grained dynamically reconfigurable array architectures, because they are crucial for the industrial acceptance of CSoCs. The approach introduced here combines combinatorial optimization methods, e. g. genetic algorithms, with CAD-algorithms from physical chip design, e. g. extended floorplanning methods for macrocell placement. Thus, pre-synthesized IP-cores of multiple granularity and complexity can be mapped efficiently, considering also dynamic reconfiguration, demonstrated by a complex RAKE-receiver example from future wireless terminals.

References

[1] "ASIC Sstem-on-a-Chip", Integrated Circuit Engineering (ICE), http:www.ice-corp.com
[2] M. Glesner, J. Becker, T. Pionteck: Future Research, Application and Education Perspectives of Complex Systems-on-Chip (SoC); in: Proc. of Baltic Electronic Conference (BEC 2000), October 2000, Tallinn, Estonia
[3] P. Athanas, A. Abbot: Real-Time Image Processing on a Custom Computing Platform, IEEE Computer, vol. 28, no. 2, Feb. 1995.
[4] R. W. Hartenstein, J. Becker et al.: A Novel Machine Paradigm to Accelerate Scientific Computing; Special issue on Scientific Computing of Computer Science and Informatics Journal, Computer Society of India, 1996.
[5] J. Rabaey, "Reconfigurable Processing: The Solution to Low-Power Programmable DSP", Proceedings ICASSP 1997, Munich, pp. , April 1997.

[6] J. Becker, et al.: DReAM: A Dynamically Reconfigurable Architecture for Future Mobile Communication Applications; in: 10th Int'l. Conf. on Field Programmable Logic and Applications, Villach, Österreich, 2000.

[7] J. Becker, M. Glesner: IP-based Application Mapping Techniques for Dynamically Reconfigurable Hardware Architectures; Proc. Int'l. WS on Eng. of Reconf. HW/SW Objects (ENREGLE´00), June 2000, Las Vegas, USA.

[8] Y. Zorian, R. K. Gupta: Design and Test of Core-Based Systems on Chips; in IEEE Design & Test of Computers, pp. 14-25, Oct. - Dec. 1997.

[9] Xilinx Corp.: http://www.xilinx.com/products/virtex.htm.

[10] Altera Corp.: http://www.altera.com

[11] Triscend Inc.: http://www.triscend.com

[12] LucentWeb] http://www.lucent.com/micro/fpga/

[13] Hitachi Semiconductor: http://semiconductor.hitachi.com/news/triscend.html

[14] Peter Jung, Joerg Plechinger., "M-GOLD: a multimode basband platform for future mobile terminals",CTMC'99, IEEE International Conference on Communications, Vancouver, June 1999.

[15] Jan M. Rabaey: System Design at Universities: Experiences and Challenges; IEEE Computer Society International Conference on Microelectronic Systems Education (MSE´99), July 19-21, Arlington VA, USA

[16] Pleiades Group: http://bwrc.eecs.berkeley.edu/Research/Configurable_Architectures/

[17] S. Copen Goldstein, H. Schmit, et al.:"PipeRench: a Coprocessor for Streaming Multimedia Acceleration" in ISCA 1999. http://www.ece.cmu.edu/research/piperench/

[18] MIT Reinventing Computing: http://www.ai.mit.edu/projects/transit dpga_prototype_documents.html

[19] S. M. Sait, H. Youssef: Iterative Computer Algorithms with Applications in Engineering, IEEE CS Press, USA, 1999

[20] T. Lengauer: Combinatorical Algorithms for Integrated Circuit Layout, Wiley - Teibner, 1990

An FPGA-Based Syntactic Parser for Real-Life Almost Unrestricted Context-Free Grammars

Cristian Ciressan[1], Eduardo Sanchez[2], Martin Rajman[1], and
Jean-Cédric Chappelier[1]

[1] Computer Science Dept., LIA, CH-1015 Lausanne, Switzerland
[2] Computer Science Dept., LSL, CH-1015 Lausanne, Switzerland
Swiss Federal Institute of Technology

Abstract. This paper presents an FPGA-based implementation of a syntactic parser that can process languages generated by almost unrestricted real-life context-free grammars (CFGs). More precisely, we study the advantages offered by a hardware implementation of a parallel version of an item-based tabular parsing algorithm adapted for word lattice parsing. A description of the parsing algorithm and of the associated hardware design is provided. A method called *tiling*, that allows a better processor and I/O bandwidth exploitation is introduced. Finally, an evaluation of the design performance on real-life data is given and the measured 244 speed-up factor makes our design a promising solution for Natural Language Processing applications, for which parsing speed is an important issue.

1 Introduction

Efficient parsing is an important element in most NLP applications, especially for those with strong real-time and/or data-size constraints. Typical examples of such applications include advanced Information Retrieval [7,8], Text Mining [5,6], and the design of vocal interfaces. In such cases parsing can either enhance performance by integrating more syntactic knowledge about the language or allow a better integration of syntactic processing with speech recognition.

As far as context-free languages are concerned, VLSI implementations, based on 2D-array of processors have been proposed, both for the CYK [2] and the Earley [3] parsing algorithms. Although these designs meet the usual VLSI requirements (constant-time processor operations, regular communication geometry, uniform data movement), the hardware resources they require do not allow them to accommodate unrestricted real-life context-free grammars used in large-scale NLP applications[1]. In previous contributions [11,12], we have proposed two FPGA-based implementations of the CYK algorithm [4] that can process real-life CFG. We choose the FPGA technology because it provides hardware designers with flexible and rapid system prototyping tools and also because, in the near future, it is expected to find FPGA components in general-purpose processors.

---

[1] for instance, the CFG extracted from the SUSANNE corpus [1] used in our experiments contains 1,912 non-terminals and 66,123 grammar rules.

G. Brebner and R. Woods (Eds.): FPL 2001, LNCS 2147, pp. 590–594, 2001.

The main advantages of our previous designs were: (1) their ability to parse word lattices, which makes them better adapted for integration within speech-recognition systems, (2) their scalability, and (3) a 30 speed-up factor [12] when compared against a software implementation of the CYK algorithm. On the other hand, the weak points of the these designs were: (1) the fact they require CFGs written in Chomsky Normal Form (CNF), (2) a low average processor load and (3) a low average I/O bandwidth exploitation. These different drawbacks are addressed in this paper, and a new implementation is proposed. The new design is based on a general item-based chart parsing algorithm (an enhanced version of the CYK algorithm [10,13]) that allows the processing of almost unrestricted CFGs. A better load of the processors and exploitation of the I/O bandwidth is obtained with a method called tiling. Among other improvements on the previous designs, we mention a simpler initialization procedure, and a faster processor implementation.

2   The General Item-Based Chart Parsing Algorithm for Word Lattice Parsing

The implemented parsing algorithm is designed to process *non partially lexicalized* CFGs, a subclass of CFGs (henceforth denoted as nplCFG) in which terminal symbols, i.e. words, only occur in rules of the form $X \rightarrow w_1 w_2 ... w_n$, (called lexical rules). For our design, the restriction to nplCFGs is very useful as it allows to restrict the processing of lexical rules to the initialization step only, which takes place outside the FPGA chip in the on-board general-purpose processor. In addition, to further increase the efficiency of the hardware implementation, we restrict to nplCFGs without chain rules (though this is not a restriction of the general item-based chart parsing algorithm, it strongly simplifies the FPGA design).

As the implemented algorithm is a tabular item-based parsing algorithm, the syntactic trees associated with an input sequence $w_1 \ldots w_n$ are represented in the form of sets of elements called items stored in a table (henceforth called the chart). More precisely, if $w_{ij} = w_i w_{i+1} \ldots w_{i+j-1}$ denotes the subsequence of $w_1 \ldots w_n$, of length j and starting with w_i, the cell at row j and column i in the chart, contains the following two sets of items:

- a set $N1_{i,j}$ of all non-terminals X that can derive w_{ij}, defined as:
  $N1_{i,j} = \{X \in N : X \Rightarrow^{\star} w_{ij}\}$[2]
- a set $N2_{i,j}$ defined as:
  $N2_{i,j} = \{\alpha\bullet : \exists\beta \in N^+, \exists(Z \rightarrow \alpha\beta) \in R, \text{ s.t. } (\alpha \Rightarrow^{\star} w_{ij})\}$[3] which is the set of all sequences of non-terminals that can derive w_{ij}.

---

[2] Where N is the set of non-terminals of the grammar and $\alpha \Rightarrow^{\star} \beta$ indicates that the sequence β can be obtained from the sequence α by applying a finite number of rewriting rules.

[3] Where R is the set of the rewriting rules contained in the grammar and N^+ stands for the set of all non-empty, finite, sequences of elements from N.

The implemented parsing algorithm is then defined as follows:

1: **for** $j = 1$ to n **do**
2:   **for** $i = 1$ to $n - j + 1$ **do**
3:     $N1_{i,j} = \{X : X \in N, (X \to w_{ij}) \in R\}$
4:     $N2_{i,j} = \{X\bullet : X \in N, \exists \beta \in N^+, \exists(Z \to X\beta) \in R, \text{ s.t. } X \to w_{ij}\}$
5: **for** $j = 2$ to n **do**
6:   **for** $i = 1$ to $n - j + 1$ **do**
7:     **for** $k = 1$ to $j - 1$ **do**
8:       $N1_{i,j} = N1_{i,j} \bigcup$
         $\{X : X \in N, \exists(\alpha\bullet \in N2_{i,k}), \exists(Y \in N1_{i+k,j-k}) \text{ s.t. } (X \to \alpha Y) \in R\}$
9:       $N2_{i,j} = N2_{i,j} \bigcup$
         $\{\alpha X\bullet : \exists(\alpha\bullet \in N2_{i,k}), \exists(X \in N1_{i+k,j-k}), \exists(\beta \in N^+) \text{ s.t.}$
         $\exists(Z \to \alpha X\beta) \in R)\} \bigcup$
         $\{X\bullet : X \in N1_{i,j}, \exists \beta \in N^+ \text{ s.t. } (Z \to X\beta) \in R\}$

The lines 1-4 correspond to the initialization step and the lines 5-9 correspond to the subsequent filling-up of the chart. When processing word lattices the initialization step is adapted in the same way as discussed in [11,12].

3   The FPGA Design

Our new design is similar as interface to the external world with our previous designs [11,12]. Basically, around the FPGA we have a memory that stores the chart and several memories storing identical copies of the CFG for processor lookup. Around each grammar memory we can cluster several processors in order to ensure optimal grammar memory utilisation. Indeed the utilisation of the grammar memories depends on the grammar characteristics and for this reason the possibility to configure the number of processors is an important feature of our design. The number of processors can be adjusted by "profiling" the grammar.

The main differences with the previous designs are (1) we can deal with nplCFG (see section 2) not only CNF CFGs and (2) a more efficient task distribution on the processors.

As in the previous designs, the low average processor load and I/O bandwidth exploitation were a direct consequence of the data-dependencies imposed by the CYK algorithm, we solved this problem by splitting big chunks of data to be processed in smaller parts, called tiles. In the new design, the tiles are distributed over the processors leading to a much more efficient load distribution. Thus, almost all processors are kept busy almost all the time and I/O bandwidth exploitation is also improved due to the continuous reading and writing of the processing results.

4   Design Performance

The performance measurements presented in this section were based on a grammar extracted from the SUSANNE corpus. The FPGA used for synthesis is a

Xilinx Virtex 2000efg1156 that allowed us to connect 16 grammar memories (databus of 16 bits) for grammar lookup. A number of 16 processors were used for this benchmark (one processor per grammar memory).

In order to determine the maximal clock frequency at which the system works, the design was synthesized (with LeonardoSpectrum v2000.1a2) and Placed&-Routed (with Design Manager (Xilinx Alliance) Series 2.1i) in the FPGA. The resulting system uses about 60% of the FPGA and was benchmarked (with ModelSim SE-EE 5.4c) at a clock frequency of 60 MHz.

The software used for comparison is a C implementation of the same parsing algorithm run on a SUN station (ultra-sparc 60) with 1 processor at 360 MHz. For comparison, 2,022 sentences were parsed and validated (the hardware output

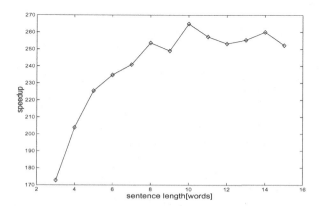

Fig. 1. Hardware speedup. Average over at least 100 sentences for each sentence length.

was compared against the software output to detect mismatches). The sentences had a length ranging from 3 to 15 words and were all taken from the SUSANNE corpus. The average speedup factor was of 244 and figure 1 shows its evolution as a function of the sentence length.

As the produced parse forest was dynamically made available at the output of the hardware, it was also important to determine the data-rate at which an external interface should collect the data in order not to create a bottleneck in the system at this point. The tests showed that the required transmission rate was less than 132 Mbyte/s, which can be achieved with a PCI interface.

5 Conclusions

A design implementing an enhanced version of the CYK algorithm for the parsing of word lattices with almost unrestricted CFG has been presented.

The main conclusions of this work are: (1) in the CYK framework, data-dependencies are the main reason for low processor load; (2) task distribution, as implemented through the tiling mechanism in our design, strongly contributes to the improvement of the overall processors load; (3) when tiling is used, I/O bandwidth and processor load are directly dependent.

In its current version, our design allows an promising speed-up factor of 244, when compared with a pure software implementation. Additional investigations will be carried out in order to determine the critical parameters that should be further optimized to increase the efficiency and integrability of our hardware parser.

References

1. G. Sampson (1994) The Susanne Corpus Release 3. School of Cognitive & Computing Sciences, University of Sussex, Falmer, Brighton, England.
2. K.H. Chu and K.S. Fu (1982) VLSI architectures for high speed recognition of context-free languages and finite-state languages. Proc. 9th Annu. Int. Symp. Comput. Arch., 43–49.
3. Y. T. Chiang and K.S. Fu (1984) Parallel Parsing Algorithms and VLSI Implementations for Syntactic Pattern Recognition. IEEE Transactions on PAMI.
4. A. V. Aho and J. D. Ullman (1972) The Theory of Parsing, Translation and Compiling. Prentice-Hall.
5. R. Feldman, et al. (1998) Text Mining at the Term Level. Proc. of the 2nd European Symposium on Principles of Data Mining and Knowledge Discovery (PKDD'98). Nantes, France
6. Feldman,R. et al. (1996). Efficient Algorithm for Mining and Manipulating Associations in Texts. *13th* European Meeting on Cybernetics and Research.
7. Schaüble,P. (1997) Mutlimedia Information Retrieval - Content-Based Information Retrieval from Large Text and Audio Databases. Kluwer Academic Publishers.
8. Hull,D., et al. (1996) Xerox TREC-5 Sire Report: Routing, Filtering, NLP and Spanish Tracks. NIST Special Publication 500-238: The Fifth Text REtrieval Conference (TREC-5). Gaithersburg, Maryland.
9. Fu K.S. (1974) Syntactic methods in pattern recognition. Academic Press.
10. J.-C. Chappelier and M. Rajman (1998). A Generalized CYK Algorithm for Parsing Stochastic CFG. TAPD'98 Workshop, 133–137. Paris, France.
11. C. Ciressan, et al. (2000). An FPGA-based coprocessor for the parsing of context-free grammars. 2000 IEEE Symp. on FCCM, Computer Society Press., 236-245.
12. C. Ciressan, et al. (2000). Towards NLP co-processing : An FPGA implementation of a context-free parser. TALN 2000, 99-100, Lausanne, Switzerland.
13. J.-C. Chappelier, M. Rajman (1998). A generalized CYK algorithm for parsing stochastic CFG (TR 98/284). DI-LIA, EPFL

Hardware-Software Partitioning: A Reconfigurable and Evolutionary Computing Approach

Jim Harkin, Thomas M. McGinnity, Liam P. Maguire

Intelligent Systems Engineering Laboratory,
Faculty of Engineering, Magee College, University of Ulster,
Northland Rd, Derry, N. Ireland, BT48 7JL, UK.
Email: jg.harkin@ulst.ac.uk

Abstract. The need for inexpensive, compact and adaptive systems has seen accelerated interest in the codesign of embedded systems. The ability to estimate the acceleration obtainable is highly desirable, as time to market deadlines are being ever shortened. The performance of such systems is fundamentally dependent on the hardware-software (HW-SW) partition. In this paper a genetic algorithm-based hardware-software partitioning method is presented. Demonstrative applications are used to show the effectiveness of the genetic algorithm at exploiting the reconfigurable nature of such systems.

1   Introduction

Embedded systems are designed to implement specific applications as efficiently and effectively as possible. Once a system is efficiently designed and implemented modification of the architecture can only be achieved in the reconfiguration of the system's software as the hardware is fixed. Hardware flexibility is now obtainable through the use of FPGAs. Embedded systems containing FPGAs exploit the ability to reconfigure the hardware during runtime execution. The disadvantage is the introduction of a reconfiguration latency for the hardware. As a result there is a need to optimise the allocation of the systems resources to meet application constraints, while trying to reduce the amount of time spent reconfiguring the system's hardware.

The partitioning problem can be viewed as making the decision as to what should be realised in hardware to increase the performance of the application while meeting any architectural constraints. In this paper the model of the hardware architecture is a host processor and a single dynamically reconfigurable device, as shown in Fig.1. In this study the Xilinx XC6216 FPGA has been used, but the approach is general and can be targeted at other devices.

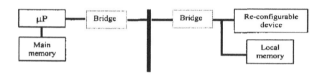

Fig.1 Architectural model of embedded system

G. Brebner and R. Woods (Eds.): FPL 2001, LNCS 2147, pp. 595-600, 2001.

2   Hardware-Software Partitioning Approaches

Several HW-SW partitioning approaches have investigated the partitioning of embedded applications when reprogrammable devices are utilised [1-5]. However, only a few approaches consider using the true re-programmability of the device through dynamic reconfiguration of the resources [3-5]. In these approaches, RTR and partial reconfiguration of new tasks in hardware is considered although none of the methods consider reducing the RTR further through the exploitation of commonality between sequences of scheduled hardware partitions [6].

The authors propose the use of a genetic algorithm (GA) with the partitioning methodology previously presented in [7] to optimally partition applications on Dynamically Reconfigurable Embedded Systems. A novel GA representation scheme of the partitioning problem and its fitness evaluation are presented. The work in this paper examines the effects of area-constrained scheduling when dynamic reconfiguration and functional commonality are exploited between the hardware partitions. Section 3 of this paper discusses the application of GAs to this partitioning problem and section 4 presents the results for two HW-SW partitioning examples.

3   Genetic Algorithm Problem Representation

The genetic algorithm is a stochastic optimisation algorithm loosely based on the concepts of biological evolutionary theory [8]. Using GAs requires the development of representation schemes and fitness evaluation techniques to reflect the problem. In this problem the GA is attempting to optimise the application's speedup by implementing the computation in reconfigurable hardware while reducing the communication and reconfiguration latency introduced through the RTR of the FPGA. In attempting to reduce the RTR the GA looks at scheduled candidates that exhibit functional commonality and the possibility of concurrent computation-reconfiguration overlap. Functional commonality reduces the reconfiguration by reducing the amount of circuitry being implemented on the device. Considering the overlap of a candidate's computation and the reconfiguration of a different candidate means that part of the reconfiguration time can be performed in parallel with the processor. These methods of reducing the reconfiguration time are dependent on the area available. This necessitates the development of such novel area-constrained and reconfiguration scheduling techniques as those presented by the authors in other work [9].

3.1   Representation

The employed representation scheme defines solutions at both the chromosome and the phenotype levels. At the chromosome level the candidates that are partitioned to software and hardware and those candidates that are to be examined for functional commonality are detailed. The chromosome represents these candidates as binary cells, accumulating the cells to make a binary string. The decoded phenotype solution details the scheduled sequence of reconfiguration and execution of candidates partitioned to hardware. To illustrate consider the composition of an example chromosome string shown in Fig 2. Here P_i - defines the partitioning status of the ith candidate and m is the number of eligible hardware candidates. A value of 1(0) for P_i indicates the partition of the ith candidate to hardware (software). The group of bits ci_1 $ci_2....ci_n$ – defines the candidate which is to have commonality with the ith candidate, where n is the number of bits (resolution) in a conventional binary coding scheme required to represent a candidate, i.e. representing 7 candidates only requires 3 bits.

$$\text{Chromosome cell} \rightarrow \{P_i, ci_1\ ci_2....ci_n\}$$

$$\text{Chromosome} \rightarrow [\{P_1, c1_1\ c1_2...c1_n\}, \{P_2, c2_1\ c2_2...c2_n\},... \{P_m, cm_1\ cm_2...cm_n\}]$$

Fig.2 String composition

The length of each chromosome is defined as $N = m \cdot (n+1)$. To illustrate the relationship between chromosome and phenotype solutions and the method of decoding chromosomes consider the example chromosome {1011, 1100, 1110, 1000, 1000, 1000}, where m=6 and each candidate is represented by 3 bits (n=3), e.g. candidate 1 = 001, 2 = 010, 3 = 011 etc. In this example the chromosome is represented as a fixed binary string of length N (=24) and contains the partition of candidates to hardware. The chromosome solution is comprised of 4-bit genes. They represent the information for each of the possible 6 candidates. In the example all eligible candidates are partitioned to hardware, as indicated by the presence of a value of 1 at the beginning of each gene. The decoding procedure details the candidates that are to be implemented through partial reconfiguration. This is realised by examining the 3-bit representation for each candidate. For example, the first cell {1011, ...} indicates that candidate 1 is to be examined for functional commonality with candidate 3. Candidates 4, 5 and 6 contain the value 000 signifying that they do not seek commonality with any future candidate.

3.2   Fitness Evaluation

Equation 1 expresses the fitness metric as the inverse of the speedup as the GA converges to a minimum fitness value. This expression is taken from previous work by the authors [7]. SWc and HWc denote the partitioned candidate's hardware execution time in software and hardware, respectively. The symbol η specifies the number of candidates that are scheduled to hardware, where η is less than or equal to the total number of candidates in the hardware schedule. Tr and Tm are the reconfiguration and memory latencies of the candidates in hardware. SWp is the execution time entirely in software. The fitness measure clearly evaluates the speedup from partitions and reflects the quality of solutions.

$$\text{Fitness} = \left((\text{SWp} - \sum_{i=1}^{\eta} \text{SWc}_i) + \text{Tr} + \text{Tm} + \sum_{i=1}^{\eta} \text{HWc}_i \right) \Big/ \text{SWp} \qquad (1)$$

The GA solves the problem by initially passing the application program to the profiler [7]. Identified hardware candidates constitute the GA's alphabet set. Once the population has been decoded to its phenotype the area-constrained scheduling algorithm is applied and the reduction in memory requirements of the partition, candidate functional commonality and scheduled dynamic reconfiguration are examined. The scheduled reconfiguration algorithm and the memory requirements stage, provide a reconfiguration time and memory latency for each member of the phenotype population. This information is passed to the fitness evaluation stage where each member of the population has its fitness calculated. When the GA performs a pre-defined N_{GEN} number of generations it exits the partition's evolution. Otherwise, its continues the evolution process.

4   Genetic Algorithm Partitioning Results

The tasks of speech and image processing demonstrate the hardware partitioning approach [7]. These applications perform the tasks of speech recognition and Shen-Castan (ISEF) edge detection. The speech and image applications were profiled using the approach detailed in [7]. For the two applications, the profiler highlighted between 9 and 14 potential hardware candidates, respectively. Representing both applications resulted in speech and image chromosome lengths of 45 and 70-bits respectively. The control parameter settings for the GA were as follows: population size (20), selection (0.8), crossover (0.7), mutation (0.038), max area (3276 CLBs).

For both applications the GA was executed a number of times. In each case the optimal speedup was detected within 30 generations of the population. The graphs in Fig. 3 show the convergence rate for the speech (a) and image (b) applications.

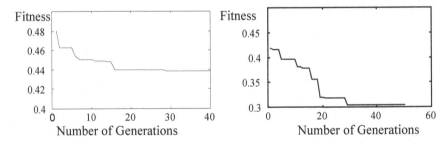

Fig 3a Convergence rate: speech application   **Fig 3b** Image application

In examination, the optimal HW-SW partition for the speech application exhibited functional commonality between 4 candidates and 4 instances of dynamic reconfiguration. The partition for the image application provides functional commonality between 4 candidates and 10 instances of dynamic reconfiguration.

Table 1 shows the resultant functional commonality (Wr) and dynamic reconfiguration weighting (Wd) for the two applications with their respective schedules. The two applications exhibit different levels of commonality and dynamic reconfiguration capabilities. The optimal speedup was found to be 2.28 for the speech application and 3.27 for the image application respectively. From previous work in [10], the theoretical maximum speedup for these applications was calculated as 2.47 and 3.34, respectively. Table 2 shows the optimal speedup when the area-constraint is set to the XC6216's limit [11]. It is clear from Table 2 that by physically increasing the available hardware resources the speedup of both applications can be increased.

5   Summary

The GA has shown that reconfigurable hardware can be exploited through RTR to provide increased hardware resources "on the fly". Table 1 shows the benefits in exploring functional commonality and dynamic reconfiguration capabilities. Table 2 also shows that the use of the novel scheduling algorithms aids the GA representation in the exploration of HW-SW partitions which can reduce the overheads resulting from runtime reconfiguration.

	Speech Application			Image Application	
Schedule	W_d	W_r	*Schedule*	W_d	W_r
4	N/A	N/A	1	N/A	N/A
1	0.9813	1	2	0.6525	1
2	1	0.1475 ($W_{r1,2}$)	3	0.9928	1
3	1	1	4	0.1507	0.2049 ($W_{r1,4}$)
5	1	1	5	0	0 ($W_{r2,5}$)
6	1	1	6	0.9928	0.257 ($W_{r4,6}$)
5	1	0.9141 ($W_{r6,5}$)	7	1	0 ($W_{r6,7}$)
6	1	1	8	0	1
5	1	0.9141 ($W_{r6,5}$)	9	0.3615	1
6	1	1	10	1	1
5	1	0.9141 ($W_{r6,5}$)	11	1	1
6	1	1	12	0.7169	1
7	0.8386	1	13	0.9522	1
8	0.9949	1	14	0.8619	1
9	0.9927	1	-	-	-

Table 1: Functional commonality and dynamic reconfiguration weights for the optimally partitioned speech and image applications

Application	GA XC6216 area	GA Relaxed area	Theoretical Relaxed area
Speech	2.28	2.39	2.47
Image	3.27	3.31	3.34

Table 2: Embedded application speedup

References

[1]   Chichkov, AV; Almieda, CB: An HW-SW Partitioning Algorithm for Custom Computing Machines, International Workshop on FPL, (1997) 274-283

[2]   Edwards, M; Forrest, J: A Practical Hardware Architecture to Support Software Acceleration, Microprocessor & Microsystems, Vol. 20 No 3, (1996), 167-174

[3]   Chatha, KS; Vemuri, R: HW-SWCodesign for Dynamically Reconfigurable Architectures, International Workshop on FPL, (1999) 175-184

[4]   Dave, BP: CRUSADE: Hardware/Software Co-synthesis of Dynamically Reconfigurable Heterogeneous Real-time Distributed Embedded Systems, Proc of the Design, Automation & Test in Europe (DATE) Conference (1999), 97-104

[5]   Fleischmann, J; Buchenrieder, K; Kress, R: Codesign of Embedded Systems Based on Java and Reconfigurable Hardware Components, DATE Conference, (1999), 768-769

[6]   Hutchings, BL, Wirthlin, MJ: Implementation Approaches for Reconfigurable Logic Applications, Field Programmable Logic & Applications, (1995), 419-428

[7]   Harkin, J; McGinnity, TM; Maguire, LP: A partitioning methodology for dynamically reconfigurable embedded systems, IEE Computers and Digital Techniques, Vol. 147 No 6, (2000) 391-396

[8]   Goldberg, GE Genetic and Evolutionary Algorithms Come of Age, ACM Communications, Vol. 37 No 3, (1993), 113-119

[9]   Harkin, J; McGinnity, TM; Maguire, LP: Genetic Algorithm driven Hardware-Software Partitioning", accepted to Microprocessors & Microsystems, (2001)

[10]   Harkin, J; McGinnity, TM; Maguire, LP: Accelerating embedded applications using dynamically reconfigurable hardware and evolutionary algorithms, IEEE FCCM, (2000) 321-322

[11]   Xilinx XC6216 Data Sheet, Ver. 1.10, Xilinx Corporation, USA, (1996)

An Approach to Real-Time Visualization of PIV Method with FPGA

Tsutomu Maruyama, Yoshiki Yamaguchi, and Atsushi Kawase

Institute of Engineering Mechanics and Systems, University of Tsukuba
1-1-1 Ten-ou-dai Tsukuba Ibaraki 305-8573 JAPAN
maruyama@darwin.esys.tsukuba.ac.jp

Abstract. Particle image velocimetry (PIV) is a method of imaging and analyzing field of flows. In the PIV method, small windows in an image of the field (time t) are compared with areas around the windows in the another image of the field (time $t + \Delta t$), and the most similar part to the windows are searched using two dimensional cross-correlation function. The amount of computations in the function is very large, and furthermore, parallel processing of the function requires complex shift operations. In this paper, we show that we can achieve real-time visualization of PIV method with one PCI board with one latest Xilinx FPGA. By combining shift register array and distributed RAM array, we can realize parallel processing of the two dimensional cross-correlation function very efficiently.

1 Particle Image Velocimetry (PIV) Method

Particle image velocimetry (PIV) is a method of imaging and analyzing field of flows. In the PIV method, many small particles are added into the liquid or air in field of flows, and the speed and direction of movement of the particles are measured by comparing two images (time t and $t + \Delta t$) of the field. In the figure 1, the left part and right part show the image of the field of t and $t + \Delta t$ respectively. Suppose that we want to know where particles in a window in time t (a gray square in the figure 1(A)) are moving to, and how fast the particles are moving. Then, the data of the window are compared with all sub-areas (same size of the window) in a target area (light gray square in the figure 1(B)), and the most similar sub-area (dark gray square in the figure 1(B)) is searched using cross-correlation function, and the direction of movement and the speed of the particles are obtained. The start positions of windows are shifted by $n/2$ and $m/2$ along x and y axis respectively (windows are overlapped in general).

Our goal is real-time visualization of flows measured using two dimensional cross-correlation function R shown below. In this function, I_1 and I_2 show values of pixels of images of time t and $t + \Delta t$ respectively.

G. Brebner and R. Woods (Eds.): FPL 2001, LNCS 2147, pp. 601–606, 2001.
© Springer-Verlag Berlin Heidelberg 2001

$$R(x,y,\xi,\eta)=\frac{\sum_0^{n-1}\sum_0^{m-1}\{I_1(x+i,y+j)-\overline{I}_1\}\{I_2(x+i+\xi,y+j+\eta)-\overline{I}_2\}}{\sqrt{\sum_0^{n-1}\sum_0^{m-1}\{I_1(x+i,y+j)-\overline{I}_1\}^2}\sqrt{\sum_0^{n-1}\sum_0^{m-1}\{I_2(x+i+\xi,y+j+\eta)-\overline{I}_2\}^2}}$$

$$=\frac{\sum_0^{n-1}\sum_0^{m-1}\{I_1(x+i,y+j)\times I_2(x+i+\xi,y+j+\eta)\}-\overline{I}_1\times\overline{I}_2\times nm}{\sqrt{\sum_0^{n-1}\sum_0^{m-1}I_2(x+i+\xi,y+j+\eta)^2-\overline{I}_2\times\overline{I}_2\times nm}}$$

where $\quad \overline{I}_1=\sum_0^{n-1}\sum_0^{m-1}I_1(x+i,y+j)/nm$

$\qquad\quad \overline{I}_2=\sum_0^{n-1}\sum_0^{m-1}I_2(x+i+\xi,y+j+\eta)/nm$

Most of the computation time of the function is exhausted for multiply-and-accumulate operations, which can be accelerated by FPGAs and DSPs. However, power of latest DSPs is still not enough for real-time visualization, and furthermore, parallel processing of the two dimensional cross-correlation function requires very complex shift operations or accesses to word data on word-boundaries, which will drastically reduce the performance. This cross-correlation function is widely used in image processing, and dedicated hardware systems have been developed for real-time stereo visualizations (the first system was [2]). However, in those systems, windows on a image are moved and compared only one-dimensionally (ξ or η is always zero in the cross-correlation function described above). In this case, the amount of the computation is much smaller, and we need no shift operations, nor access to words on word-boundaries.

2   Computation Method

In our approach, the comparison of each window is divided to comparison of four sub-windows (the size of sub-windows is $n/2 \times m/2$) in order to reduce the amount of computation. As shown in figure 2, data of pixels in the sub-window are placed on a shift register array, and the data of pixels in the target area are placed on a distributed RAM array. In the figure 2, the size of arrays is reduced to 4×4 (actual size is up to 16×16) in order to simplify the figure. The target area is divided into smaller sub-areas according to the size of the sub-window (these sub-areas must be smaller than the size of the sub-window), and the data

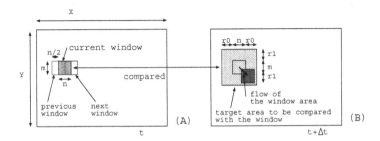

Fig. 1. Particle Image Velocimetry (PIV) Method

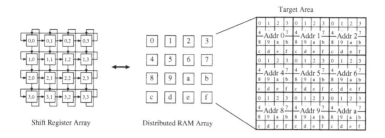

Fig. 2. Arrays of Shift Registers and Distributed RAMs

on the same positions in the sub-areas are stored in same distributed RAM as shown in the figure. The maximum number of the sub-areas is 16, because a distributed RAM can store up to 16 bits (this is enough because Δt is very small in PIV method).

Figure 3 and 4 show how values in the shift register array and the distributed RAM array are compared. In order to give addresses to distributed RAMs, four sets of lower two address lines run vertically, and four distributed RAMs on same column are connected to same address lines. On the other hand, four sets of upper two address lines run horizontally, and four distributed RAMs on same row are connected to same address lines. In the figures, numbers on each distributed RAM show position of data read out from the distributed RAM, and address given to the distributed RAM.

First, data of the sub-window are compared with data of a sub-area in the target area (gray square in the figure 3(A)). In the figure, values of all address lines are zero, and data on the register array are at initial position. Then, data in next sub-area (gray square in figure 3(B)) are compared with the data of the sub-window. In this case,

1. data on the shift register array are shifted from left to right, and
2. Addr(0) to first column of the distributed RAM array becomes 1 (which means addresses to the distributed RAMs on the first column becomes 1).

Figure 4(C) shows the comparison of the sub-window and the last sub-area of upper edge. In the figure, the data on the shift register array are at initial position again, and all Addr(1) to distributed RAMs are 1 (which means addresses to all distributed RAMs are 2). The next sub-area to be compared with the sub-window is shown in the figure 4(D). In this case,

1. data on the shift register array are shifted from top to bottom, and
2. Addr(1) to all columns are reset, and Addr(2) to first low of the distributed RAM array becomes 1 (which means that addresses to the first low becomes 4, while addresses to other rows are 0).

Then, data in next sub-area in figure 4(E) are compared with the data of the sub-window. For this comparison, data on the shift register array are shifted from left to right, and Addr(0) to the first column become 1 as described above.

As the results, the address to the left-upper distributed RAM becomes 5, while addresses to other three distributed RAMs on the first column and the first low become 1 and 4 respectively.

By repeating this simple shift operations, and address control to the distributed RAM array, we can compare the sub-window with all sub-areas in the target area.

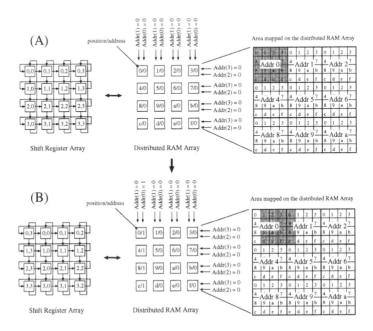

Fig. 3. Computation on the Two Arrays (1)

3   Implementation of the Circuit

Our current platform is RC1000-PP board with Xilinx XCV2000E by Celoxica. Figure 5 shows a block diagram of our circuit. The images obtained by our target PIV system [1] are sequences of pairs of images such as $(t_1, t_1 + \Delta t)$, $(t_2, t_2 + \Delta t)$ and so on. Therefore, two of the memory banks on the board are used to store images of time t_i, while other two banks are used for images of time $t_i + \Delta t$, and data in one pair of memory banks are updated while data in another pair are processed by the FPGA. FIFOs are prepared in each input from the external memory banks to convert data width, and to hide memory access overhead. The FIFOs are always filled with new data. The minimum operation frequency to realize real-time visualization is 40 MHz, which can be easily realized with latest FPGAs, because all parts of the circuit are pipelined.

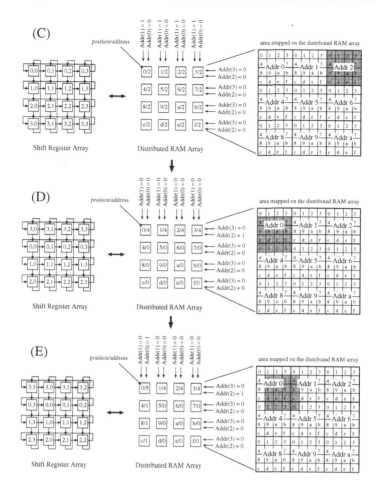

Fig. 4. Computation on the Two Arrays (2)

4   Current Status and Future Work

In this paper, we described that it is possible to realize real-time visualization of PIV method with one PCI board with one latest FPGA. However, our current implementation have several problems which should be improved. First, images obtained by camera are once sent to host computer, and then downloaded to the FPGA board. Therefore, we need to transfer 80MB data per second. We should connect the camera directly to FPGA board. Second, we simply reduce the data width by discarding lower bits, but because of this reduction, about 4% (this value depends on data in images) of results becomes different from the results obtained by computing with 8 bit width. We need to find out more sophisticated method to reduce the data width.

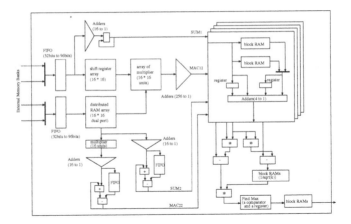

Fig. 5. Block Diagram of the Circuit

References

1. J. Sakakibara and T. Anzai, "Chain-link-fence structures produced in a plane jet", to appear in Physics of Fluids 2001
2. T. Kanade, et al, "Development of a Video-Rate Stereo Machine", IROS'95

FPGA-Based Discrete Wavelet Transforms System

Mokhtar Nibouche, Ahmed Bouridane, Fionn Murtagh, and Omar Nibouche

School of Computer Science, The Queen's University of Belfast.
18, Malone Road - Belfast BT7 1NN - UK
{m.nibouche, a.bouridane, o.nibouche, f.murtagh}@qub.ac.uk

Abstract. Although FPGA technology offers the potential of designing high performance systems at low cost, its programming model is prohibitively low level. To allow a novice signal/image processing end-user to benefit from this kind of devices, the level of design abstraction needs to be raised. This approach will help the application developer to focus on signal/image processing algorithms rather than on low-level designs and implementations. This paper presents a framework for an FPGA-based Discrete Wavelet Transform system. The approach helps the end-user to generate FPGA configurations for DWT at a high level without any knowledge of the low-level design styles and architectures.

1 Introduction

The Discrete Wavelet Transform (DWT) is an efficient and useful tool for signal and image processing applications and will be adopted in many emerging standards, starting with the new compression standard JPEG2000 [1]. This growing "success" is due to the achievements reached in the field of mathematics, to its multiresolution processing capabilities, and also to the wide range of filters that can be provided. These features allow the DWT to be tailored to suit a wide range of applications [2][3].

In the early 80s, in the quest for more flexibility and rapid prototyping at low cost, custom logic based re-configurable hardware in the form of Field Programmable Gate Arrays (FPGAs) has been introduced into the IC market. However, although the fact FPGA devices offer an attractive combination of low cost, high performance, and apparent flexibility, their programming model is at the gate level. To allow an FPGA novice signal/image processing developer to benefit from the advantages offered by such devices, high level solutions are desired. It is the aim of this paper to present a framework and the preliminary results of an FPGA-based Discrete Wavelet Transforms system. The proposed environment is a Java-based Graphical User Interface (GUI) combined with both a wavelet database and a parameterised VHDL code generator.

2 The System

Initially, the architecture designer provides the library with a suite of primitive building blocks covering the various indivisible components necessary for building

G. Brebner and R. Woods (Eds.): FPL 2001, LNCS 2147, pp. 607–612, 2001.

any new wavelet filter. The architecture designer is also responsible for updating the library with new blocks and providing the generator with efficient filter templates corresponding to a particular architecture. Due to the fact that DWT, unlike the Discrete Cosine Transform, is not unique, the filter template needs to be provided for each application with the parameters of the DWT (type, number of coefficients, 2's complement values..). The System is illustrated in Figure 1.

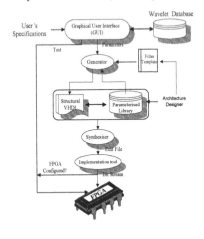

Fig.1. The FPGA-based System

For instance the user can choose between two architecture schemes: an area efficient structure and a high throughput structure. Each structure can be derived from the other either by folding or unfolding. The architectures have been derived from the architectures presented in [4][5] and partitioned adequately to ensure a maximum of hardware-macros reusability [6][7]. Even if the original architectures are VLSI-oriented (dedicated to VLSI implementations), it has been shown in [8] that efficient FPGA implementation of such regular structures can lead to good area/speed performances. Alongside, the system supports two multiplication schemes based on Baugh and Wooley algorithm. The first scheme is suitable for implementing systems with moderate throughput rate. The second one allows the implementation of high throughput rate systems through the use of a pipelined version of the first multiplication scheme. In this second case, the multiplier can be pipelined at the bit level when extended to a particular digit size [9]. More details about the multiplication and the supported wavelet structures are given in section 3 and section 4.

3 Architectures

To perform a 1-D wavelet analysis operation, a chain of processing elements combined with some delay elements, necessary for synchronisation purposes, are assembled together. The architectures used in the proposed framework for both orthonormal and biorthogonal bases are based on a time-interleaved filter's coefficient allocation approach in combination with two lines of adder [4][5]. In addition to the regularity feature, the architectures are scalable and are able to generate any wavelet filter from both families.

3.1 Architecturesfor Orthonormal DWT

Due to the fact that the high pass and low pass filters belonging to the orthonormal family are of the same length, the delay elements present a regular structure leading to a simple connection strategy between the low pass and the high pass filter [6].

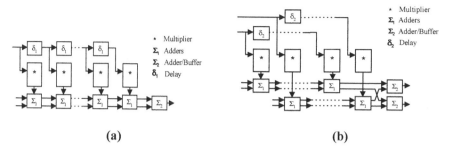

(a)   (b)

Fig.2. Generic Architecture for Orthonormal Filters
(a) Area Efficient   (b) High Throughput

Figure 2 shows the generic architectures of an area efficient and a high throughput 1-D wavelet filters, respectively. The elements constituting the filters are shown on the right hand side of each structure. The delay elements δ_1 and δ_2 are related by $\delta_1 = 2\delta_2$. $\sum_1$ is a combination of a demultiplexer and two bit-adders and $\sum_2$ is a combination of buffer and an bit-adder. The multiplier operators, represented by the asterisk, are similar. An orthonormal DWT is generated easily by adopting the approach proposed in [6].

3.2 Architectures for Bi-orthogonal DWT

Unlike the orthonormal basis, the high pass and the low pass filters belonging to the biorthogonal family are of different lengths. This fact leads to different connection strategies between the low pass and the high pass filters [4][7]. When designing the low level-programming model, this feature has been taken into account. Figure 3 shows the generic architectures of an area efficient and a high throughput 1-D wavelet filters, respectively. The modified delays δ_{m1} and δ_{m2} are combinations of δ_1, δ_2 and simple adders. This choice is motivated by the fact to keep the same PE for the two supported architectures and for both bases. A biorthogonal DWT is generated easily by adopting the approach proposed in [7]. The remaining elements are similar to those involved in the orthonormal architectures.

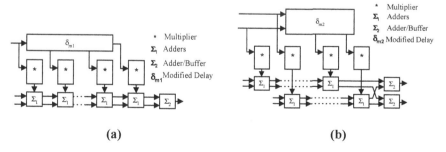

(a)   (b)

Fig.3. Generic Architecture for Biorthogonal Filters
(a) Area Efficient   (b) High Throughput

4 Low Level Components

The components involved generally in any signal/image processing operation include adders, substracters, shift registers, multiplexers, demultiplexers..etc. These components are then used to generate more complicated combinations depending on the application.

4.1 Bit-Level Multiplication Scheme

The most important device when building a filter-based architecture is the multiplier. To efficiently overcome the problem of handling the sign bits of the multiplier and the multiplicand of a two's complement multiplication, Baugh and Wooley algorithm is used [10]. Different structures can be envisaged to implement Baugh and wooley algorithm [10]. The structure illustrated in Figure 4 has been adopted. The structure is regular and only a single signal is used to control the required bit inversion and bit correction.

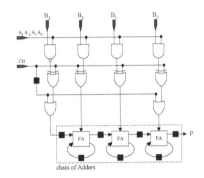

Fig.4. A Baugh and Wooley 4x4-bit 2's complement serial-parallel multiplier.

Serial-Parallel versus Digit-Parallel. In recent years, the concept of digit-serial arithmetic has been proposed as a compromise between the bit serial and the bit parallel arithmetic [11]. The systems based on this arithmetic give the DSP designers more flexibility in finding the appropriate trade-off between hardware cost and sample rate. However, due to the feedback loop associated, the multiplier obtained using traditional approach can only be pipelined at a digit level. To overcome this problem, a new algorithm that allows different level of pipelining has been developed [9]. To benefit from this approach, the chain of adders of Figure 4 needs to be adjusted to suit the algorithm [9]. In the other hand, since the filtering is based on a multiply and accumulate process, digit adders that can be pipelined at a bit level when extended to a digit size are also required. Details about pipelined digit adders can be found in [12].

4.2 Processing Element

The Processing Element (PE) is invariable through either the wavelet bases or the wavelet supported architectures. It is composed of a bit-multiplier, a demultiplexer and two 1-bit adders ($\sum_1$).

4.3 "Terminating" Element

The structure of a Terminating Element (TE) is identical for both bases and both architectures. It is composed of a bit-adder and a buffer ($\sum_2$).

4.4 Delay Elements

To handle the peculiarities of the biorthogonal and the orthonormal basis, it was decided to design two different delay modules. In the case of the orthonormal bases, the generation is easily achieved by connecting side by side either N-1 delay elements δ_1 or 2(N-1) delay elements δ_2. Unfortunately, the generation process in the case of the bi-orthogonal family is more complicated. More details can be found in [7].

5 Implementation Performances

To assess the effectiveness of the approach, a stage of 1-D 8 taps Daubechies wavelet pair has been generated and then implemented on the Xilinx XC4036 FPGA (speed grade-2). The XC4036 consists of 36x36 arrays of Configurable Logic Blocks (CLB) [13]. The input data and the multiplier are both 8-bits lengths. The delays δ_{m1}, δ_{m2}, δ_1, δ_2 and the buffers have been implemented efficiently by using the dedicated select-RAM distributed along each CLB. The implementation performances are resumed in Table 1.

Table 1: Implementation Performances

	Frequency	No of CLBs
Area Efficient (Bit Serial)	103 MHz	99
High Throughput (Bit Serial)	100 MHz	167
Area Efficient (Digit 4)	75 MHz	308
High Throughput (Digit 4)	73 MHz	615

The functionality of the bit-serial implementations has been verified using the functional and timing simulation tools of the Xilinx Foundation Software 2.1i. As it is apparent from Table 1, the FPGA area occupied by the high throughput architecture is almost double of the area efficient architecture, especially when the architecture is extended to digit size. However, the system speed remains almost unchanged for both architectures. The fact is that the critical path remains the same and the difference in speed is a consequence of routing and interconnection delays within the device.

6 Summary and Future Work

A framework for an FPGA-based Discrete Wavelet Transforms system has been presented. The methodology allows a signal/image processing application developer to generate FPGA configurations for DWT at a high level rather than spending a considerable time learning and designing at a gate and routing level. Thus, the end-user will benefit from the high performances of FPGA devices while designing at a high level with tools he is familiar with. The preliminary results are very promising; however, extensive further work needs to be done towards the extension of the system to handle different arithmetic representation, different wavelet analysis and synthesis schemes along with different architectures.

References

1. *"JPEG2000 Image Coding System"*, JPEG 2000 final committee draft version 1.0, March 2000 (available from http://www.jpeg.org/FCD15444-1.htm)
2. C. S. Burrus, R. A. Gopinath and H.Guo, *"Introduction to Wavelets and Wavelet Transforms - A Primer "*, Prentice Hall, New Jersey, USA, 1998.
3. G.Strang and T.Nguyen, *"Wavelets and Filter Banks"*, Wellesley-Cambridge Press, 1996.
4. S.Masud *"VLSI system for discrete wavelet transforms"*, PhD Thesis, Dept. of electrical engineering, The Queen's University of Belfast, 1999.
5. F.Marino, *"A'Double-Face' Bit-Serial Architecture for 1-D Discrete Wavelet Transform"* IEEE Trans. Circuit Syst.II , Vol. 47, NO.1, pp 65-71, Jan 2000.
6. M.Nibouche, A.Bouridane, O.Nibouche, D.Crookes, *"Rapid Prototyping of Orthonormal Discrete Wavelet Transforms on FPGAs"* IEEE International Symposium on Circuit and Systems, Sydney, Australia, May 2001.
7. M.Nibouche, A.Bouridane and O.Nibouche *"Rapid Prototyping Of Biorthogonal Discrete Wavelet Transforms on FPGAs"* To appear in IEEE International Conference on Electronics, Circuits and Systems, Malta, Sep 2001.
8. R F Woods, A Cassidy and J Gray, *"VLSI architectures for Field Programmable Gate Arrays: A case study"*, IEEE Symposium on FPGAs for Custom Computing Machines (FCCM'96), Napa, USA, April 1996, pp 1-8.
9. O.Nibouche, A.Bouridane, M.Nibouche and D.Crookes, *" New digit serial-parallel multiplier "* IEEE International Symposium on Circuit and Systems, Geneva, 2000.
10. K. K. Parhi, *"VLSI Digital Signal Processing Systems - Design and Implementation"*, John Wiley, USA, 1999.
11. R.I.Hartley and K.K.Parhi, *"Digit-Serial Computation"*, Kluwer Academic 1995.
12. O.Nibouche, A.Bouridane and M.Nibouche, *" A new pipelined digit serial computation"*, In preparation.
13. "XC4000E and XC4000X Series Field Programmable Gate Arrays", Xilinx 1999.

X-MatchPRO: A ProASIC-Based 200 Mbytes/s Full-Duplex Lossless Data Compressor

José Luis Núñez, Claudia Feregrino, Simon Jones, Stephen Bateman*

Electronic Systems Design Group, Loughborough University,
Loughborough, Leicestershire LE11 3TU. England.
*BridgeWave Communications, Inc.3350 Thomas Rd, Santa Clara, CA 95954, USA.

J.L.Nunez-Yanez@lboro.ac.uk, C.Feregrino-uribe@lboro.ac.uk,
S.R.Jones@lboro.ac.uk, SBateman@Bridgewave.com

Abstract. This paper presents the full-duplex architecture of the X-MatchPRO lossless data compressor and its highly integrated implementation in a non-volatile reprogrammable ProASIC FPGA. The X-MatchPRO architecture offers a data independent throughput of 100 Mbytes/s and simultaneous compression/decompression for a combine full-duplex performance of 200 Mbytes/s clocking at 25 MHz. Both compression and decompression channels fit into a single A500K130 ProASIC FPGA with a typical compression ratio that halves the original uncompressed data. The device is specially targeted to enhance the performance of Gbit/s data networks and storage applications where it can double the performance of the original system.

1 Introduction

Lossless data compression [1], where the original data is reconstructed exactly after decompression is accepted as a tool that can bring important benefits to an electronic system. Its applications have been increasing over the past years thanks to the arrival of compression standards and a combination of pressure for more bandwidth and storage capacity while still reducing power consumption. Lossless data compression has been successfully applied to storage systems (tapes, hard disk drives, solid state storage, file servers) and communication networks (LAN, WAN, wireless).

The remainder of this paper is organized as follows. Section 2 describes the basic characteristics of the X-MatchPRO algorithm. Section 3 depicts the X-MatchPRO full-duplex architecture. Section 4 compares our device with other high-performance lossless data compressors. Finally section 5 concludes this paper.

2 The X-MatchPRO Algorithm

The X-MatchPRO algorithm [2-4] uses a dictionary of previously seen data and attempts to match or partially match the current data element with an entry in the dictionary. Each entry is 4 bytes wide and several types of matches are possible where all or some of the bytes at different positions inside the tuple match. Those

G. Brebner and R. Woods (Eds.): FPL 2001, LNCS 2147, pp. 613-617, 2001.

bytes that do not match are transmitted literally. This partial match concept gives the name to the procedure- the X referring to 'don't care'. At least 2 bytes have to match and when no valid match is generated a miss is codified adding a single bit to the literal. The dictionary is maintained using a move to front   (MTF) strategy [5] whereby a new tuple is placed at the front of the dictionary while the rest move down one position. When the dictionary becomes full the tuple placed in the last position is discarded leaving space for a new one. X-MatchPRO reserves one location in the dictionary to code internal runs of full matches at location zero. This Run-Length-Internal (RLI) technique is used to efficiently code any 32-bit repeating pattern. Additionally an Out-of-Date-Adaptation (ODA) policy is used in X-MatchPRO for throughput purposes. This means that adaptation at time t+2 takes place using the adaptation vector generated at time t.

3 The X-MatchPRO Hardware

The architecture is depicted in Fig. 1. The full-duplex architecture has 5 major components, namely: the Model, the Coder, the Decoder, the Packer and the Unpacker.

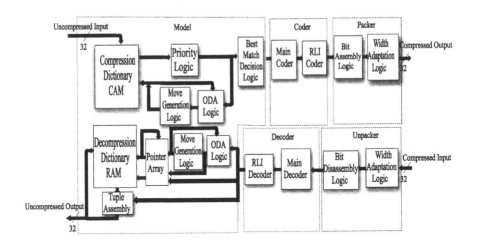

Fig. 1. X-MatchPRO full-duplex architecture.

The model is the section of the compressor whose function is to identify where the redundancy is located in a block of data and signal repetitive data sequences to the coder. The coder function is to use the information provided by the model to produce a minimum output of bits and obtain compression. The decoder function is to decode the compressed input stream and provided the model with a combination of dictionary address plus literal data so the model can reproduce the original uncompressed data. The packer function is to pack the variable length codewords output from the coder into fixed-length codewords of 32 bits. Finally, the unpacker function is to break the fixed-length codewords input from the compressed bus into variable length codewords to be processed in the decoder. The initialization of the compression CAM sets all words to zero. This means that a possible input word formed by zeros will generate multiple full matches in different locations but in this case the algorithm simply selects the full match closer to the top. This operational model initializes the dictionary to a state where all the words with location address bigger than zero are declared invalid without the need for extra logic because location x can not generate a match until location x-1 has been updated. X-MatchPRO uses a simple coprocessor style interface to communicate with the rest of the system. Compression and decompression commands are issued through a common 16 bit control data port. A 3-bit address is used to access the internal registers that store the commands plus information related to compressed and uncompressed block sizes for reading or writing. A total of 6 registers form the register bank. 3 registers are used to control the compression channel and the other 3 for the decompression channel. The first bit in the address line indicates if the read/write operation accesses compression or decompression registers. The chip is designed to compress any block size ranging from 8 bytes to 32 Kbytes. A decompression operation can be requested in the middle of a compression operation and vice versa. The full-duplex architecture using a 16-word dictionary has been implemented in a A500K130 ProASIC FPGA [6].

4 Results

Table 1 shows a comparison of the FPGA-Based X-MatchPRO implementation against several popular high-performance ASIC compressors. The selection includes:
1. The the ALDC1-40S [7] (IBM) and the AHA3521 [8] (AHA) that implement the ALDC [9] (Adaptive Lossless Data Compression) algorithm. This algorithm is a LZ1 derivative developed by IBM.
2. The AHA3211 [10] that implements the DCLZ [11] (Data Compression Lempel Ziv) algorithm. This algorithm is a LZ2 derivative developed by Hewlett/packer and AHA.
3. The Hi/fn 9600 [12] that implements the LZS [13] (Lempel-Ziv Stac) algorithm . This algorithm is another LZ1 derivative developed by STAC/Hifn.

Table 1 reports the complexity of the X-MatchPRO design in ProASIC tile's. Tile is the basic logic unit in the architecture of the ProASIC technology. Actel ProASIC tiles are simple blocks that can implement a logic function with 3 inputs and 1 output such as an AND gate or a flip-flop. Each tile can be configured to implement one of these simple functions using the internal non-volatile FLASH-based switches. Actel ProASIC architecture is fine-granularity and flat so the simple tiles are repeated across the device forming a matrix of identical logic elements. Dedicated memory blocks are group in the north side of the device. There are a total of 20 memory blocks in a A500K130 and each of them can implement 2304 bits of fully-synchronous dual port RAM. The design uses 70% of the device logic that is approximately equivalent to 30 Kgates and the 20 blocks of embedded RAM available (5 Kbytes). The total gate count equivalent of logic plus memory is 210 K gates. Table 1 shows that X-MatchPRO can achieve higher performance throughput than the ASIC compressors with a lower clock ratio and this is due to its optimal parallel architecture. The compression ratio figure in the last row is a ratio of output bits to input bits (output_bits/input_bits) and it is based on a data set formed by 100 Mbytes of data found in the main memory of a UNIX workstation compressing data in 4 Kbytes blocks. The FPGA-based X-MatchPRO uses a very small dictionary of only 16 locations and that limits its compression performance. The ASIC compressors use dictionary sizes from 512 to 2048 positions.

DEVELOPERS		IBM	Advance Hardware Architectures (AHA)		STAC Electronics	System Design Group Loughborough University
CHIP*		ALDC1-40S	AHA3521	AHA3231	Hi/fn 9600	X-MatchPRO
TECHNOLOGY DETAILS	PROCESS	IBM CMOS 0.8 micron triple-level gate array/std cell	0.5 micron CMOS	0.5 micron CMOS	0.35 micron gate array/std cell	0.25 micron FLASH-CMOS FPGA Actel A500K ProASIC
	COMPLEXITY	70 Kgates	Not Stated	Not Stated	100 Kgates	9039 TILE's 70% of a A500K130-BG456
	CLOCK SPEED	40 MHZ	40 MHZ	40 MHZ	80 MHZ	25 MHz
THROUGHPUT		40 Mbytes/s	20 Mbytes/s	20 Mbytes/s	80 Mbytes/s	100 Mbytes/s
FULL-DUPLEX PERFORMANCE		N/A	N/A	N/A	160 Mbytes/s	200 Mbytes/s
ALGORITHM		ALDC	ALDC	DCZL	LZS	X-MatchPRO
EXTERNAL RAM REQUIRED		NO	NO	NO	NO	NO
COMPRESSION RATIO		0.44	0.44	0.52	0.44	0.58

Table 1. X-MatchPRO comparison.

5 Conclusions

X-MatchPRO offers unprecedented level of compression/decompression throughput in a FPGA implementation of a lossless data compression algorithm for general application. The full-duplex implementation effectively uses the resources available in the FPGA to simultaneously handle a compressed and uncompressed data stream. The use of a fine granularity device like the ProASIC where each block defines a very simple logic function, has proven to be well suited to implement the CAM-based dictionary that represents most of the logic present in the device. Other FPGA architectures where the building blocks implement mixed combinatorial and sequential functions offer poorer utilization ratios

Acknowledgements: We acknowledge with gratitude the support donated by Actel/Gatefield corporation.

References

[1] M. Nelson, 'The Data Compression Book' , Prentice Hall, 1991.

[2] M.Kjelso, M.Gooch, S.Jones, 'Design & Performance of a Main Memory Hardware Data Compressor', Proceedings 22nd EuroMicro Conference, pp. 423-430, September 1996, Prague, Czech Republic.

[3] J.Nuñez, C. Feregrino, S.Bateman, S.Jones, 'The X-MatchLITE FPGA-based Data Compressor', Proceedings 25th EuroMicro Conference, pp126-133, September 1999.

[4] José Luis Núñez,, Simon Jones,'The X-MatchPRO 100 Mbytes/second FPGA-Based Lossless Data Compressor', proceedings of Design, Automation and Test in Europe, DATE Conference 2000, pp. 139-142, March, 2000.

[5] J. L. Bentley, D. D. Sleator, R. E. Tarjan, V. K. Wei, 'A Locally Adaptive Data Compression Scheme', Communications of the ACM, Vol. 29, No. 4, pp. 320-330, April 1986.

[6] 'ProASIC™ 500K Family', Data sheet, Actel corporation, 955 East Arques Avenue, Sunnyvale, CA, 2000.

[7] 'ALDC1-40S-M', Data sheet, IBM Microelectronics Division, 15080 Route 52, Bldg 504 Hopewell Junction, NY, 1994.

[8] 'AHA3521 40 Mbytes/s ALDC Data Compression Coprocessor IC', Product Brief, Advanced Hardware Architectures Inc, 2635 Hopkins Court, Pullman, WA, 1997.

[9] J.M.Cheng and L.M.Duyanovich, 'Fast and Highly Reliable IBMLZ1 Compression Chip and Algorithm for Storage',Hot Chips VII Symposium, August 14-15, pp. 155-165, 1995.

[10] 'AHA3211 20 Mbytes/s DCLZ Data Compression Coprocessor IC', Product Brief, Advanced Hardware Architectures Inc, 2635 Hopkins Court, Pullman, WA, 1997.

[11] 'Primer: Data Compression (DCLZ)', Application Note, Advanced Hardware Architectures Inc, 2635 Hopkins Court, Pullman, WA, 1996.

[12] '9600 Data Compression Processor', Data Sheet, Hi/fn Inc, 750 University Avenue, Los Gatos, CA, 1999.

[13] 'How LZS Data Compression Works', Application Note, Hi/fn Inc, 750 University Avenue, Los Gatos, CA, 1996.

Arithmetic Operation Oriented Reconfigurable Chip: RHW

Tsukasa Yamauchi, Shogo Nakaya, Takeshi Inuo, and Nobuki Kajihara

RWCP Adaptive Devices NEC Laboratory
1-1, Miyazaki 4-Chome, Miyamae-ku, Kawasaki, Kanagawa 216-8555, Japan
t-yamauchi@ap.jp.nec.com

Abstract. We have developed an ALU based reconfigurable device called RHW (Reconfigurable HardWare) that is designed to work with the CPU to accelerate the computation-intensive part of the application by reconfiguring its data paths and ALUs optimized for the algorithm. It is also important to develop high performance operation unit library to utilize function cells of RHW efficiently. This paper describes the basic architecture of the RHW, high performance operation unit library and evaluation results.

1 Introduction

The RHW works with the CPU to accelerate the computation intensive part of the application by reconfiguring its data paths and ALUs optimized for the algorithm, while FPGAs are mainly used for implementing general purpose logic circuits. Hence the RHW was designed to implement multi-bit data paths and ALUs efficiently. In this paper, we present a novel reconfigurable chip called RHW (Reconfigurable HardWare) with various new features including: 1) Two-dimensional array of multi-bit ALUs with high speed carry logic, 2) Full-adder based original ALU with multi-functional pre-logics that has capability of implementing logic functions that would require two conventional ALUs in general-purpose processors and 3) Diagonal routing resources for efficient multiplier mapping.

2 Reconfigurable Device

There are several reconfigurable architectures that use multi-bit data path elements. PipeRench [4] at CMU is designed to efficiently handle stream data computations by pipeline virtualization. Compared with their architecture, RHW does not equip any dynamic reconfiguration mechanism because we focus on mapping high speed multiplier efficiently and eliminate any mechanisms that sacrifice the performance. Routing resource of RHW chip is designed to have more flexibility compared with that of PipeRench, to be applied not only to stream data applications but also scientific calculations.

G. Brebner and R. Woods (Eds.): FPL 2001, LNCS 2147, pp. 618–622, 2001.
© Springer-Verlag Berlin Heidelberg 2001

3   Reconfigurable Chip RHW

Figure 1 (a) shows the overall architecture of the device. The bulk of the RHW chip is assigned to the main portion suited for mapping data paths. Surrounding it is a peripheral portion suitable for mapping control circuits or random logic. The I/O portion consists of an interface circuit. The main portion is composed of a regular two-dimensional array of 9-bit main ALUs (See Figure 1). The ALU is composed of eight bits of arithmetic cells (A-Cells) and one rich-function cell (R-Cell)(See Figure 1 (c)). The A-Cells share many common configuration data for efficient implementation of multi-bit operators, although each A-Cell has small individual configuration data keeping sufficient flexibility. The R-Cell in main ALU is located at the MSB of each main ALU and can be configured fully independent of the other cells. The R-Cell is used for simple logic operations such as various flag generations, absorbing irregularity in the boundary of regular multi-bit operators. The R-Cells in peripheral portion are individually configurable and is used for mapping various random logics. Figure 2 (a) shows the core logic circuit of each cell. A-Cell and R-Cell consist of almost same circuit except for the reconfiguration flexibility and dedicated carry logic. The inputs A0, A1, A2, A3, B0, B1, B2, B3 and the outputs CARRY, SUM are connected with a programmable interconnect network. The terminals G, P and B4 are connected to the dedicated fast ripple carry logic. The core logic has two modes (See Figure 2 (b),(c)). In the arithmetic mode, the core logic acts as a full-adder with pre-logic that is important to map multiplier efficiently (only one unit of proposed core logic is needed, although two units are required with the conventional core logic). In the logic mode, our core logic can implement any kind of tree shaped 4-input logic functions. Figure 3 shows programmable routing resources around a single A-Cell/R-Cell. We excluded excessive routing flexibility that brings too much load capacitance. Therefore we defined primary data-flow direction (horizontal direction) and enriched the horizontal routing resources. The most distinctive feature is the diagonal routing resources for efficient multiplier mapping. We developed a prototype LSI chip, RHW2 (0.35μm cell-based IC), that contains 6x63 main ALUs and the die size is 14.9mm^2. We are presently developing a high density and high speed version of the chip, RHW3 (0.25μm custom design IC), with largely improved architecture such as floating operation capability.

4   Mapping Tools

We have developed mapping tools that analyze an application program described in high level language and generate configuration data for the reconfigurable device RHW through behavioral synthesis, logic synthesis and layout process. We introduce *Cyber* [2] as a behavioral synthesis tool. Then the mapping flow is divided into two flows: 1) one for the control path and 2) the other for the data path. Following logic synthesis, the technology mapping and placement/routing processes are applied separately. We also have developed a fast technology mapping algorithm, data-flow oriented placement algorithm and an efficient routing algorithm for nets with multiple terminals[1].

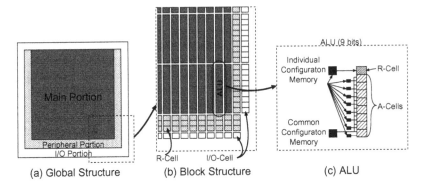

(a) Global Structure   (b) Block Structure   (c) ALU

Fig. 1. RHW Chip Architecture

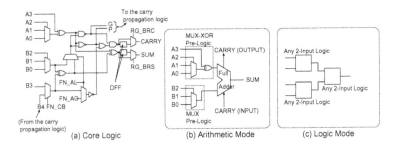

(a) Core Logic   (b) Arithmetic Mode   (c) Logic Mode

Fig. 2. Core Logic and Equivalent Circuits

5   Pipelined Multiplier Implementation

Multiplier is the most complicated operation unit and difficult to map efficiently on a reconfigurable device. Figure 4 shows pipelined multiplication algorithm and its implementation on RHW. Straight forward implementation consumes a diamond shaped area of A-Cells on RHW and that causes low cell utilization efficiency. However multiplier can be mapped in rectangular shape on RHW chip because of the diagonal routing resource (See Figure 3). The diagonal routing resource also decreases signal propagation delay by taking a shortcut. Furthermore, using the diagonal route, occupation of the horizontal/vertical routing resource decreases and layout flexibility increases. Since each A-Cell has MUX-XOR pre-logic with adder, each A-Cell can perform 'logical AND' and 'ADD' operation (primitive operation of multiplier) simultaneously and this feature of A-Cell contributes to mapping efficiency and performance of the multiplier. Shift registers to keep past value of input and output data are necessary for pipelined multiplier. In this implementation, n-bit multiplier runs at 1-clock throughput and n-clock latency, and consumes $n(n-1)/2$ extra A-Cells as shift-registers compared with non-pipelined multiplier. This means pipelined multiplier is about 1.5 times larger than non-pipelined multiplier.

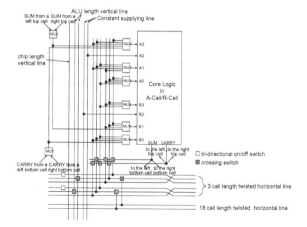

Fig. 3. Routing Resources of RHW

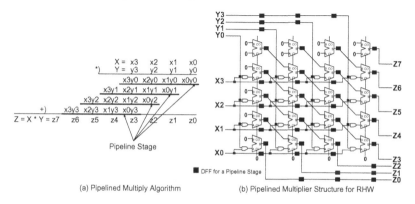

(a) Pipelined Multiply Algorithm

(b) Pipelined Multiplier Structure for RHW

Fig. 4. Pipelined Multiply Algorithm and Pipelined Multiplier Structure for RHW

6   Evaluation Result

Table 1 shows evaluation result of pipelined multiplier using real RHW2 chip. Introducing pipelining, calculation throughput becomes 57.7 [MHz] in 8-bit multiplier case. This result seems appropriate because this performance is almost near to the running frequency limit of RHW2 chip (about 70 [MHz]). The frequency limitation of 16-bit pipelined multiplier is caused by propagation delay of 'input Y' signal since the signal path length becomes longer according to the bit width (See Figure 4 (b)). Table 2 shows the evaluation result of the diagonal routing resource effect. In the case of 8-bit pipelined multiplier, total wire length reduces from 672 into 528 (27 percent reduction) and SUM output signal propagation path length reduces by half. Therefore the diagonal routing resource of RHW is extremely effective to reduce both signal propagation delay and routing resource consumption to map multiplier efficiently. Comparing 16-bit pipelined multiplier mapping efficiency with a commercial FPGA, Virtex of Xilinx, RHW consumes only 288 cells while Virtex consumes 336 LUTs (assuming the function of the cell of RHW is almost equal to a LUT). This means the RHW cell architecture is efficient to map multiplier compared with the LUT based cell architecture, although the full-adder based RHW cell is smaller than memory based LUT.

Table 1. Evaluation Result of Pipelined Multiplier

sample name	mulu8p	mulu16p
bit width	8	16
number of nets	200	815
number of cells	100	288
total wire length (number of switches)	528	2080
Frequency [MHz]	57.7	46.7

Table 2. Evaluation Result of the Diagonal Routing Resource

sample name	mulu8p (diagonal)	mulu8pnd (no diagonal)	mulu16p (diagonal)	mulu16pnd (no diagonal)
bit width	8	8	16	16
total wire length (number of switches)	528	672	2080	2656
wire length (SUM output)	2	4	2	4

7   Conclusion

We proposed the novel reconfigurable device RHW that is suitable for implementing multi-bit arithmetic/logic functions and high performance operation unit focusing multipliers. The evaluation results shows that the diagonal routing resource of RHW is extremely effective to reduce both signal propagation delay and routing resource consumption to map multiplier efficiently. Furthermore, the RHW cell architecture shows higher efficiency of multiplier mapping compared with the LUT based conventional cell architecture.

References

1. Yamauchi, T., *et al.*, 'Mapping Algorithms for a Multi-Bit Data Path Processing Reconfigurable Chip RHW', IEEE Workshop on FPGAs for Custom Computing Machines (FCCM'00), pp.281-282, April (2000)
2. Wakabayashi, K. and Tanaka, H., 'Global Scheduling Independent of Control Dependencies Based on Condition Vectors', 29th DAC, pp.112-115 (1992)
3. Yamauchi, T., *et al.*, 'SOP: A Reconfigurable Massively Parallel System and Its Control-Data-Flow based Compiling Method', IEEE Workshop on FPGAs for Custom Computing Machines (FCCM-96), pp.148-156, April (1996)
4. Goldstein, S.C., *et al.*, 'PipeRench: A Reconfigurable Architecture and Compiler', Computer, April, pp.70-77 (2000)

Initial Analysis of the Proteus Architecture

Michael Dales

Department of Computing Science, University of Glasgow,
17 Lilybank Gardens, Glasgow, G12 8RZ, Scotland.
`michael@dcs.gla.ac.uk`

Abstract. The Proteus Architecture proposed a general purpose microprocessor with reconfigurable function units. The ProteanARM represents an ARM-based realisation of this concept. This paper describes the initial details of the Protea-nARM architecture and demonstrates some performance benefits gained through the use of custom function units. Our examples show a promising performance increase compared to a standard ARM processor, with reconfiguration costs being quickly amortised.

1 Introduction

Field Programmable Logic (FPL) is an attractive solution to numerous problems, combining the flexibility of software with the performance of hardware. However, FPL has failed to enter the modern microcomputer arena, computation on desktop machines and workstations being the domain of either software or application specific expansion cards (e.g., graphics accelerators).

In an attempt to bring the benefits of FPL to the desktop machine we have proposed placing the FPL in the heart of the machine: the microprocessor itself. Our architecture, called the Proteus Architecture [2], has a Reconfigurable ALU (RALU) consisting of multiple Reconfigurable Function Units (RFUs) in the core of the processor. It allows applications to load custom instructions at run time. In this paper we describe an initial ARM-based implementation of the Proteus Architecture and examine its performance using a software simulator.

1.1 Motivation

Whilst combining FPL with microprocessors is certainly possible (see Section 1.2 for examples), building a processor that needs to work inside a desktop computer, with the workloads that entails, poses some interesting design challenges. A desktop processor that includes FPL must be designed with such use in mind and it must provide a rich enough set of mechanisms that the Operating System (OS) can efficiently manage the FPL resource, allowing many applications to make use of it.

The Protean Architecture takes into consideration OS issues such as resource contention, virtualisation, and overheads of state management. For example, having a single large array of FPL may lead to several applications trying to gain access to it at once, giving poor performance. Large amounts of state could lead to high context switch overheads. Our approach is to conduct a top–down design that addresses these issues, including appropriate architectural support.

G. Brebner and R. Woods (Eds.): FPL 2001, LNCS 2147, pp. 623–627, 2001.

1.2 Related Work

Here we only describe work directly relevant to the sections that follow. A wider discussion of related work can be found in [2]. The PRISC [6] architecture proposed having a Reduced Instruction Set Computing (RISC) processor augmented with multiple reconfigurable function units, though the authors only produced results for an implementation with a single reconfigurable unit. These function units are stateless, which avoids additional context switch overheads.

GARP [3] takes a MIPS core and extends it with a single large FPL array. A single large array is a point of resource contention, and so the authors have allowed configuration caching and have only minimal state to reduce the context switching overheads. The CoMPARE [7] processor links a traditional ALU and a Configurable Array Unit (CAU) that can be wired to operate individually, in parallel, or sequentially. To reduce reconfiguration times, the CAU supports partial reconfiguration, allowing only the necessary parts of the CAU to change, which is useful for keeping down circuit switching overheads. Like PRISC, the CoMPARE architecture has no state in its array.

Triscend produce a commercial combination of an ARM core and a Configurable Logic Unit (CLU) called the Triscend A7 [10]. The A7 is aimed at the Configurable System–on–Chip (CSoC) market; the CLU can be programmed only at start–up, and the processor core and CLU are individual entities. In the same vein there is the FIP-SOC (Field Programmable System–on–Chip) from SIDSA [9]. The FIPSOC has a 8051 microcontroller core and a reconfigurable array on a single chip, but again both as distinct entities. The Infineon Carmel 20xx architecture [4] offers tighter integration. The 20xx is a Digital Signal Processing (DSP) processor with four configurable Execution Units (EUs), similar to the RFU of the Proteus Architecture. Infineon claim this gives the 20xx twice the performance of its predecessor. Like the A7, the 20xx cannot be reconfigured at run time.

2 ProteanARM Architecture

The general ideas behind the Proteus Architecture were initially outlined in [2]. In order to realise the Proteus Architecture an existing processor architecture was taken and modified. Although the ideas could be applied to high–power processors, such as the Alpha, a simple architecture suffices to demonstrate the initial concepts and enables faster implementation and testing. For this reason the popular ARM processor was chosen. The ARM has a simple pipelined core and, through the use of internal coprocessors, has a well–defined way to expand the instruction set. We based our model on an ARMv4 core [1]. This platform is designed to be a starting point for our work, and will change as the project progresses and experimental work provides us with a better set of requirements for the archtiecture and highlights problem areas.

The ProteanARM extends the traditional ARM datapath with an RALU connected to a second register file. These are joined to the datapath using the standard internal coprocessor model. The Protean coprocessor cannot generate addresses in this model, so it must utilise the main core when loading and storing data, but data operations execute completely separately and may potentially run in parallel.

The RALU consists of a group of RFUs, meaning that multiple custom instructions can be present on the processor at the same time. We have chosen to have eight RFUs, which would allow several applications to have multiple instructions loaded at once. Currently the fabric for the RFUs is based on the Configurable Logic Blocks (CLBs) used in the Xilinx Virtex device [11]. Based on the die size of a Xilinx XCV1000, and subtracting area for the ARM core, we estimate having 6000 CLBs to divide between the RFUs, giving 750 CLBs per RFU. Each RFU will take in two 32 bit words and return a single 32 bit word result. The register file in the Protean coprocessor has sixteen 32 bit registers. The internal coprocessors access main memory through the same interface as the main processor core, and so gain all the benefits of the caches present.

The operation of the Protean coprocessor is quite simple. There are four types of instruction, all of which fit into the coprocessor instruction space. These use existing instruction mnemonics, allowing current compilers to work without modification. The first three types of instruction cover the usual operations of moving a value between the Protean coprocessor's register file and memory, moving a value between the main register file and the Protean coprocessor's register file, and executing an instruction loaded in an RFU. The only new type of instruction is that used to load a bitstream into an RFU. This is currently done as a long atomic operation to simplify the initial processor design.

Custom instructions can potentially last many cycles. An instruction is fed a start signal by the processor on its first cycle. When the instruction is finished it will send a completion signal to the processor, which will then store the result in the destination register. State in RFUs is not reset between calls, allowing for pipelined instructions.

The clock speed for the ProteanARM depends upon the speed that the ARM core can run at and the speed at which we expect instructions in RFUs to run. To guess the performance of the ARM core produced using the same technology as the RFU fabric would require detailed knowledge of how the ARM processor is implemented, which we do not have available. But, we can safely say that it should run at least as fast as the ARM core on a lesser technology. Thus, as a starting point, we have assumed that we can run the ProteanARM at the same speed as an ARM720T, which is 40 MHz.

3   Initial Experiments

Using a software simulation of the ProteanARM we have obtained some initial data to assess the performance of such a processor. In this section we describe two experiments that compare the performance of the ProteanARM with that of a conventional ARM.

3.1   Audio Processing

The first example is an echo filter algorithm taken from an Intel MMX technical note [5]. The aim is to show that the ProteanARM can handle MMX type instructions in its RFUs. But, thanks to the flexibility of reconfigurable logic, we are also able to perform optimisations not possible in MMX.

The algorithm processes a WAVE–format audio file, which uses 8 bits per sample at an 8 kHz sampling rate. The samples are stored as unsigned values, but must be normalised to be between -128 and 127 for processing. This is done by xoring each sample with 80_{16}. To add e echos of delay d to sample s we look back in the file's history and add attenuated values. The attenuation factor, G, is greater the further back in time we go. This is expressed as follows:

$$s'[n] = s[n] + \sum_{1 \le i \le e} (G^i \times s[n - i \times d])$$

The aim of the implementation is to use Single Instruction/Multiple Data (SIMD) techniques to work on four octets per instruction. The key operations of the MMX example are a SIMD signed add, a variable SIMD arithmetic shift left, and an xor operation to normalise the samples. We improve on this by building the normalisation into the add and shift instructions, by partially evaluating the xor with constant operation into the circuits' inputs and outputs where necessary. This level of customisation was only possible with reconfigurable logic.

3.2   Alpha Blending

Alpha blending is the process of superimposing images that contain a level of transparency (their alpha value). Images are made up using 32 bits per pixel, an octet for each of the Red, Green, Blue, and Alpha channels (referred to as RGBA format). Without the alpha channel, summing images fits nicely into the SIMD add with saturation instructions found in MMX. But summing RGBA is more complex. The equation for summing the alpha channel is different to that for summing the colour channels, and summing the colour channels depends on the result of summing the alpha channel. The equations for the alpha and colour addition can be seen below, with f and b referring to the front and back images:

$$A_n = \frac{A_f \times A_b}{255} \qquad C_n = \frac{((255 - A_f) \times C_f) + \left(\frac{A_f \times C_b \times (255 - A_b)}{255}\right)}{255 - A_n}$$

The aim of this example is to experiment with a circuit that adds two pixels in a single instruction, fitting nicely into the 32 bit datapath. The alpha blending circuit is both larger and more complicated than the circuits used in the previous example. It implements numerous Booth's multipliers and naive dividers, requiring the circuit to include state and take multiple cycles to complete.

3.3   Results and Discussion

For the echo example, the shift instruction required 75 CLBs and the adder instruction 20 CLBs. Both take less than a single cycle to complete at 40 MHz. Using the new instructions reduces processing a single sample from 570 cycles (in optimised C code) to 98 cycles. The alpha blending instruction uses 436 CLBs and takes 27 cycles to generate a result, substantially less than the corresponding 377 cycles required by software.

The test applications were run on a plain ARM simulator and a ProteanARM simulator. The echo example was run with a 2 second sample and alpha blending on two images of 350x194 pixels (the size of a dialog box). The cycle counts can be seen in Table 1.

Application	Conventional ARM	ProteanARM
Echo DSP	1,643,550	319,903
Alpha blending	28,409,137	3,180,453

Table 1. Cycle count results from experiments

Both examples demonstrate a significant reduction in cycle counts, despite the overhead of reconfiguration. The echo example amortised the reconfiguration costs in processing 35 samples, and the alpha blending example after 124 pixels. Both thresholds are likely to be easily achieved in most practical examples. Despite the costs of reconfiguration being easily amortised, the experiments have highlighted that atomic loads of circuits (notably the alpha blending circuit, which was 50k) is unreasonable.

4   Conclusion

This paper has demonstrated the validity of the Proteus Architecture as a platform for further work in the field of hybrid FPL processors. The experiments showed a favourable performance for our base architecture. In other work not reported here, we have achieved positive results with the Twofish encryption algorithm [8] and are currently working on a data retrieval example.

This work was in part supported by SHEFC RDG Project 85, Design Cluster for System Level Integration.

References

[1] ARM Ltd. *ARM Architecture Reference Manual*, DDI 0100D edition, 2000.
[2] Michael Dales. The Proteus Processor — A Conventional CPU with Reconfigurable Functionality. In *9th International Workshop on Field Programmable Logic and Applications*, pages 431–437. Springer–Verlag, September 1999.
[3] John R. Hauser and John Wawrzynek. GARP: A MIPS processor with a reconfigurable coprocessor. In J. Arnold and K. L. Pocek, editors, *Proceedings of IEEE Workshop on FPGAs for Custom Computing Machines*, pages 12–21, Napa, CA, April 1997.
[4] Infineon. Infineon introduces configurable CARMEL DSP Core for 3G wireless and broadband communication applications. Infineon Press Release, March 2000.
[5] Intel. Using MMX Instructions to Implement Audio Echo Sound Effects. Unpublished Technical Report, 2001.
[6] Rahul Razdan and Michael D. Smith. High–Performance Microarchitectures with Hardware–Programmable Functional Units. In *Proc. 27th Annual IEEE/ACM International Symposium on Microarchitecture*, pages 172–180, November 1994.
[7] S. Sawitzki, A. Gratz, and R. G. Spallek. CoMPARE: A Simple Reconfigurable Processor Architecture Exploiting Instruction Level Parallelism. In *Proceedings of the 5th Australasian Conference on Parallel and Real-Time Systems*, 1998.
[8] Bruce Schneier, John Kelsey, Doug Whiting, David Wagner, Chris Hall, and Niels Ferguson. *Twofish: A 128–Bit Block Cipher*, June 1998. AES Proposal.
[9] Sidsa. *FIPSOC Mixed Signal System–on–Chip*. SIDSA Semiconductor Design Solutions, 2000.
[10] Triscend. *Triscend A7 Configurable System–on–Chip Family*. Triscend Corporation, 2000.
[11] Xilinx. *The Programmable Logic Data Book 1999*. Xilinx, 1999.

Building Asynchronous Circuits with JBits

Eric Keller

Xilinx Inc.
2300 55th Street
Boulder, CO 80301
Eric.Keller@xilinx.com

Abstract. Asynchronous logic design has been around for decades. However, only recently has it gained any commercial success. Research has focused on a wide variety of uses, from microprocessor design to low power circuits. The fact that design tools and designer experience are geared more towards synchronous circuit design has limited the acceptance and popularity of asynchronous design. The JBits™ API provides low level access to the configuration of resources in a Xilinx® FPGA. Because of the control given to the user, the JBits API is an ideal design environment for implementing asynchronous circuits on mainstream FPGAs. An asynchronous full adder was implemented on a Virtex® FPGA. The design of the circuit is described as well as modifications to the design tools to simplify asynchronous circuit specification.

1 Introduction

As ASICs increase in size, asynchronous circuits are often cited as a possible alternative to standard synchronous circuit designs. Clock distribution can be a problem in larger ASICs, whereas with an asynchronous circuit there is no clock. While synchronous circuits currently are the main design technique, asynchronous circuits have been designed that are either faster or consume less power. The main problem with asynchronous design is the fact that commercial design tools are geared towards synchronous circuits.

The JBits API provides direct access into the configuration bitstream of a Xilinx FPGA. It provides abstraction layers that provides a design environment similar to a structural HDL while concurrently affording low-level control. The level of control is ideal for asynchronous circuits. Using the JBits API, an asynchronous full adder was implemented in a Virtex device.

2 Asynchronous Logic

Asynchronous logic has been actively researched for several decades [6] [8] [9]. However it has yet to reach mainstream use. Recently there has been a renewal of interest among the research community. Commercial products are slowly coming to market [5] [3] [7]. The advantages afforded by asynchronous logic are making it an increasingly viable alternative to synchronous design as ASICs continue to grow in size. The advantages generally cited are modularity, average-case performance, low power consumption, and no clock distribution.

G. Brebner and R. Woods (Eds.): FPL 2001, LNCS 2147, pp. 628–632, 2001.
© Springer-Verlag Berlin Heidelberg 2001

3   Asynchronous Design with JBits

The JBits API provides access into a Xilinx FPGA configuration bitstream. There is access to every resource, such as routing programmable interconnect points (PIPs), LUT values, and CLB configurations. Because of the level of control, the JBits tool kit provides an ideal environment to design asynchronous circuits in mainstream FPGAs. Research has either focused on implementing asynchronous circuits on mainstream FP-GAs [10] or on creating architectures better suited for asynchronous designs [11] [4]. Payne [4], for example, suggests an architecture that has a programmable delay element. However, with the JBits API, a programmable delay element can be implemented by directly controlling the routing. Althouse [13] created a programmable delay in the XC4000™ devices with a 50 ps resolution using the JBits API.

3.1   NCL Full-Adder

NULL Convention Logic™ [3] (NCL™) is a technique similar to Delay Insensitive Minterm Synthesis (DIMS) [12]. It uses four-phase signaling with a dual-rail communication protocol. While DIMS uses C-elements and OR gates, NCL provides for optimizations by allowing M-of-N gates. Using M-of-N gates results in smaller circuits than what would be created with DIMS. The M-of-N gate works by transitioning to a high value when M of the inputs are high. The transition to a low value does not occur until all of the inputs are low. Figure 1 shows the implementation of a 2-of-3 gate in a Virtex LUT. While it may appear that using feedback by going through general purpose routing may cause a problem, it does not. Because of the signaling protocol, the feedback only needs to have a shorter delay than the output going through circuitry that requests the NULL or DATA phase, and through the circuitry of the previous stage that sends the DATA or NULL signal. Also, hazards do not cause a problem because the transitions that can occur on the LUT and the LUT configuration do not result in any situations that cause hazards.

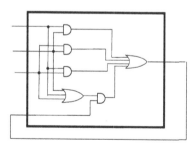

Fig. 1. Diagram showing the implementation of a 2-of-3 NCL gate in a Virtex LUT.

NCL is a case of a Quasi Delay Insensitive circuit. The delay sensitivity lies in the orphan of a circuit [2]. However, the timing constraints are a lot less stringent than an isochronic fork. In most cases the circuit can be considered delay insensitive. To analyze the timing constraints, only partial circuits must be analyzed.

Pipelined circuits can be created using asynchronous registers. In NCL this involves a circuit checking that the input has a complete data set. The register will pass the data through once an acknowledge signal is sent from the circuit that will receive the data. Once the data is passed through, the register will send a signal to the previous circuit requesting a return-to-zero (or NULL) transition. Figure 2, shows an example of an NCL register.

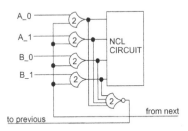

Fig. 2. Diagram showing an 2 bit asynchronous register in NCL.

Using the JBits design tool, an NCL full adder was created. The full adder is parameterizable by allowing variable width inputs and requires three Virtex slices per bit. The M-of-N gates were each made into cores and required a LUT with feedback. Interconnection between the M-of-N gates was done through the use of JRoute [1]. While JRoute does not support the ability to specify a delay for a given net, this control is not necessary when using NCL. Only a subset of the circuit needs to be analyzed for timing, and if a problem is found it is handled in a special case, such as a programmable delay element core. The special case would modify the net routed by JRoute with the use of templates to add delay. Shown in Figure 3 is a single stage of an NCL full adder circuit.

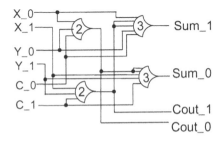

Fig. 3. Diagram showing the implementation of a full adder using NCL.

3.2   Modification to RTP Core Specification

The JBits run-time parameterizable (RTP) core specification provides a means for abstracting away the low level configuration calls, thereby creating an environment similar to traditional hardware design languages (HDLs), while concurrently affording the ability to make bitstream level modifications. However, the RTP Core specification did not provide clean support for dual-rail asynchronous circuits. The problem occurred when connecting high level cores; the Net and Bus classes were meant for single signals. However, in dual-rail logic a net is equivalent to a bus with two nets. For this a DualRailNet was created. It extends the Bus class and can only be of width two. A DualRailBus was also created and is similar to the Bus class, except that DualRailNet was used in place of Net. A method to traverse the hierarchy of cores to the physical pins was created. JRoute is then used to make the physical connections.

4   Results

One characteristic of asynchronous circuits is that they exhibit average case performance. Shown in Figure 4 is a graph of the delay, in nanoseconds, through a 4-bit NCL full adder for each combination of inputs. A Virtex device was used with a -6 speed grade and the circuit requires 6 CLBs. The graph looks nearly identical with a carry in of one as opposed to a carry in of zero. For a carry in of zero, the delay values range from 3.0463 ns to 10.0507 ns with an average delay of 6.0356 ns. For a carry in value of one, the delays range from 3.0537 ns to 10.0507 ns with an average of 6.2257 ns. The variation in the delays comes from the degree to which the carry bit propagates. If it must propagate through each stage then the delay will be longer than the case when no stages produce a carry out and therefore the output will be equal to the delay of a single stage. The average performance is worse than a synchronous full adder implemented on a Virtex device because Virtex devices are designed for synchronous circuits and contain such optimizations for common circuits as the fast carry chain. However, the graph does show that average case performance is exhibited.

5   Conclusions and Future Work

An asynchronous full adder was created along with a synchronous interface. The JBits design suite is believed to be an ideal environment for asynchronous circuitry because of the level of control provided. Research in the field has been ongoing for several decades. As more commercial applications find success with asynchronous design, CAD tools will become more supportive. Further research into a combination of asynchronous design and run-time reconfiguration is being explored. Run-time reconfiguration has shown many advantages in synchronous systems that are possibly applicable to asynchronous systems. The JBits API is an important tool to enable the design of run-time reconfigurable systems.

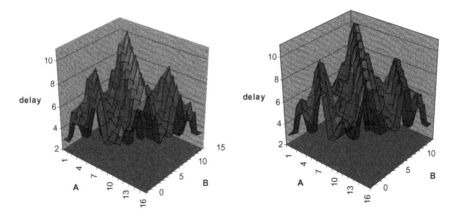

Fig. 4. Graph showing the delay, in nanoseconds, through the full adder circuit for each combination of inputs. The left graph has a carry in of 0, and right graph has a carry in of 1.

Acknowledgements

This work was supported by DARPA in the Adaptive Computing Systems (ACS) program under contract DABT63-99-3-0004.

NCL and NULL Convention Logic are trademarks of Theseus Logic, Inc.

References

1. E. Keller, "JRoute: A Run-Time Routing API for FPGA Hardware," Proc. RAW2000, pp 874-881.
2. K. Fant, R. Stephani, R. Smith, and R. Jorgenson. "The Orphan in 2 value NULL Convention Logic," Technical document, http://www.theseus.com/PDF/orph_paper.pdf.
3. K. Fant and S. Brandt, "NULL Convention Logic," Technical document, http://www.theseus.com/PDF/ncl_paper.pdf.
4. R. Payne, "Self-Timed FPGA Systems," Proc. FPL95.
5. A. Martin *et al,* "The design of an asynchronous MIPS R3000 microprocessor," *Advanced Research in VLSI*, September 1997.
6. I. Sutherland, "Micropipelines," *CACM*, 32(6):720-738, June 1989.
7. H. van Gageldonk *et al,* "An asynchronous low-power 80C51 microcontroller," *IEEE Symposium on Advanced Research in Asynchronous Circuits and Systems*, April 1998.
8. S. Unger, *Asynchronous Switching Circuits*, New York, NY: Wiley-Interscience 1969.
9. J. Udding, "A Formal Model for Defining and Classifying Delay-Insensitive Circuits and Systems," *Distributed Computing*, vol 1, no. 4, pp 197-204, 1986.
10. E. Brunvand, "Implementing Self-Timed Systems with FPGAs," Proc. FPL91.
11. S. Hauck, G. Borriello, S. Burns and C. Ebeling, "Montage: An FPGA for Synchronous and Asynchronous Circuits", Proc. FPL92.
12. H. Hulgaard and P. Christensen, "Automated Synthesis of Delay Insensitive Circuits," M.Sc. thesis (IDE 511), Dept. of Computer Science, Tec. University of Denmark, Lyngby, 1990.
13. C. Althouse, Technical Document, http://www.xilinx.com/xilinxonline/jbits_appexam.htm

Case Study of Integration of Reconfigurable Logic as a Coprocessor into a SCI-Cluster under RT-Linux

Thomas Lehmann and Andreas Schreckenberg

Heinz Nixdorf Institute, Paderborn University
D-33102 Paderborn, Germany
{torkin,schrecky}@upb.de

Abstract. Reconfigurable Logic is often integrated into a computer system as a combination of one CPU and one or more FPGAs. Here we investigated in the integration of FPGAs as coprocessors into a parallel computer system, respective a cluster computer system. The nodes of the cluster are coupled by the Scaleable Coherent Interface (SCI) and operate under RT-Linux. In this paper we describe how we integrated FPGAs into the system and show the first results of performance and latency measurement.

1 Introduction

The size of FPGAs grows rapidly and so the complexity of implementable algorithms. Hence it becomes more and more feasible to use FPGAs as specialized coprocessors for special algorithms. Nowadays FPGAs are most the time directly coupled with a single CPU over special busses or the system memory bus.

We are more interested in the integration of FPGAs into a cluster computer system. The FPGAs behave within the cluster as specialized processing nodes. In this case study we investigated in the integration of common available FPGA-boards into a SCI-cluster system operating under RT-Linux. Our main objective was the performance evaluation and the measurement of the system latencies.

2 Scalable Coherent Interface

The Scalable Coherent Interface is a network system specified in IEEE 1956-1992. It provides a distributed shared memory with optional cache coherence. Parts of the local main memory (chunks) can be offered as global shared memory to other computer nodes in the SCI-network. On the other machines the chunk is visible as remote memory respectively remote chunk.

The latency for write operations on a remote chunk within one SCI ring with the use of PCI-SCI adapter cards is approximately $5\,\mu s$ (read $15\,\mu s$)[1]. The bandwidth is between 64-104 Mbyte/s, depending on the data size and transaction form on the PCI bus[6].

---

[1] NUMA-non uniform memory access

G. Brebner and R. Woods (Eds.): FPL 2001, LNCS 2147, pp. 633–637, 2001.

The device driver for SCI network adapter provides API-calls for establishing the connection by means of creating and offering chunks and connecting to remote chunks. A memory access to the remote chunk is translated in hardware by the SCI network adaptors. Hence all data transfers are transparent to the CPU and to other systems on the PCI bus[3].

The system is able to send interrupt requests to other nodes which are translated to signals on the target node. Still the RT-SCI spcification is not finished, so SCI is only very fast but still not realy predictable for hard real-time sytems.

Due to the high bandwidth and hardware support the SCI system is interessting for distributed real-time systems and other distributed systems which like to use a shared memory.

3   RT-SCI-Cluster

At the Paderborn Center for Parallel Computing (PC^2) different clusters are operating. One is a SCI-Linux cluster with 96 SMP-nodes. All are interconnected by a SCI-ring in x- and y-direction (torus). One smaller cluster for experiments is running under Linux 2.2.17 with the real-time Linux extension RTAI 1.4 [1]. The Linux SCI device driver provides a kernel interface[7] which is accessible by the RT tasks. So with the use of RT tasks as sender and receiver of messages in the SCI network instead of user applications the latency of the complete system can be reduced. The cluster nodes are equiped with Spyder Virtex boards (XCV300) and RAPTOR[5] boards (XC4062XLA). With this system parallism on tree different levels can be explored: gate level, processor level and cluster level.

4   Test Design

If algorithms are implemented on a CPU and on a FPGA they behave as two asynchronous processes. So next to the data transfer duration the latency for synchronization is of interrest. Because of the different levels of parallism we are most interessted in the resulting synchronization latencies at the top level of the system. The data throughput is most the time limited by the different interconnection systems.

As a test design we used a word recognizer algorithm[2]. The algorithm processes 4 streams of text data and can be used as a filter for indexing in search engines. The main CPU of the system does the pre- and postprocessing of the indexing process. The design is implemented on a XC4062XLA on a RAPTOR board. The design act as a filter in the data bus to the on board dual port SRAM (128 Kbyte).

We enhanced the design to work in burst mode with PCI-clockrate of 33 MHz to process the data packages in burst mode. For the burst transfer we used the DMA controller of the on board PCI bridge PLX9080. The FPGA board driver can set up the parameter of the channels and starts the DMA transfer by a separate command. The DMA controller sends an IRQ on transfer completion to the device driver.

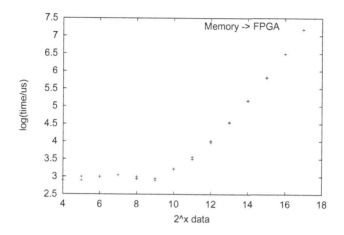

Fig. 1. Duration of DMA transfer over payload $\rightarrow$ $t_{x>8} \cong 24\mu s +$ $2^x/95\frac{\text{Mbyte}}{s}$.

For a performance evaluation we messured the duration between the DMA-start command (toggle of a flag in DMA controller) and the start of the interrupt service routine on an RT-Linux Pentium II/300 system. In figure 1 the duration over the package size is depict. The latency between DMA start and capture of the IRQ at low package size is more or less the task switching time to the hard real-time ISR of approximately $T_{L,ISR} \cong 24\mu s$.

Thus for one $4 \cdot 32$ Kbyte data package we reached a one way throughput of $\cong$ 93 Mbyte/s. The turnaround throughput main memory$\rightarrow$FPGA$\rightarrow$main memory is approximately 40 Mbyte/s.

5   Test System

In a cluster computer system the former described algorithm is used in the way that one node does the preprocessing and another node in the system does the postprocessing of the word recognizing algorithm. So we have a pipelined algorithm spanned over computer nodes.

The test environment consists of two computers, one Pentium II/400 SMP PC (named system 'A') and one Pentium II/300 PC with the FPGA-board (named system 'B'), coupled in one SCI ring (see figure 2). Both are operating under Linux 2.2.17 with RT-Linux extension RTAI 1.4. For all data transfers

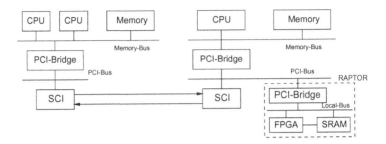

Fig. 2. Test environment of two PCs coupled by SCI.

write transactions on the SCI net are used because they have the lower latency and are burstable.

In the test system A sets up the data package in the main memory of system B by write transactions over SCI. After completion a IRQ is send to system B over SCI (SCI remote interrupt mechanism).

On reception of the IRQ system B starts the DMA transfer of the data package from main memory to the FPGA. The DMA controller sends an IRQ on DMA completion. Typically the ISR of the device driver receives the IRQ, acknowledges the IRQ and then sends a signal to a listening process. Here the hardware abstraction layer of the RT-system allows us to intercepted the IRQ. Our RT-ISR catches the IRQ and starts the second DMA transfer from FPGA-board SRAM to the SCI network board. So it is a direct burst from PCI board to PCI board and over the SCI network to the main memory of the postprocessing computer. Then the RT-ISR hands over the IRQ to the device driver ISR which acknowledges the DMA-IRQ. After the completion of the second DMA transfer an IRQ is send to the receiving system A over the SCI net.

Our main objective is the turnaround latency because the PCI bus is the main bottleneck for data transfers over SCI and the duration for bursts is known by the former tests (see above and in [6]). So we used a small data package of 128 byte, so only the latencies of the DMA-transfers and the SCI-network are measured. Between the send of the IRQ from system A to system B and the reception of the IRQ from system B at system A we measured a turnaround time of 220 μs. Thus for the two interrupt transfers on SCI approximately 75 μs are needed. The time of 220 μs (plus time for data transfer) can be interpreted as the time system B is blocked for the internal procssing, because each transfer is performed over the PCI bus.

The total time for processing 128Kbyte is approximately 4.2 ms wherein the latency is 5 %. The resulting throughput is 29 Mbyte/s. Hence the total throughput on a cluster system is nearly as high as on a single processor system if large packages are processed in burst mode. Depending on the cluster structure more parallel working pipelines can be established which can enhance the total throughput of the complete system.

6   Conclusion

In this paper it is shown a case study of how to integrate a FPGA system into a SCI cluster computer system. We showed a test environment and the first results of the perfomace messurements. Depending on the throughput and the latency results statements about expected performance of the complete cluster system are possible. Due to the fact that data packages are exchanged over the fast SCI network the system is transparent to other nodes. They do not recognize if there is a reconfigurable system processing the data or an algorithm on a CPU. Thus even local combinations of processing on local CPU and FPGA in one node is easy applicable.

7   Future Work

Still the FPGA-boards are not directly visible in the cluster system and a repeater task on the node is required for the data transfers. Hence we like to modify the SCI-driver in that way, that the FPGA-memory space is used as local memory for the chunk offer in the SCI network, like the interconnection of I/O subsystems in [4]. Than the FPGAs are directly visible and can be transparently mapped into memory space.

8   Aknowledgements

We like to thank Andreas Krawinkel and the other people of the Paderborn Center for Parallel Computing (PC^2) at the University of Paderborn for thier technical support.

References

[1] RTAI - Real Time Application Interface. http://www.aero.polimi.it/projects/rtai/.

[2] Christophe Bobda and Thomas Lehmann. Efficient Building of Word Recognizer in FPGAs for Term-Document Matrices Construction. In *10th International Conference on Field-Programmable Logic and Applications*, pages 759–768. Springer, August 27-30 2000.

[3] Roger Buthenuth. *Kommunikation in Parallelrechnern*. PhD thesis, Universität Paderborn, 1999.

[4] Hermann Hellwagner and Alexander Reinefeld, editors. *SCI: Scalable Coherent Interface*. Springer, 1999.

[5] Heiko Kalte, Mario Pormann, and Ulrich Rückert. Rapid Prototyping System für dynamisch rekonfigurierbare Hardwarestrukturen. In *AES 2000*, pages 149–157, Karlsruhe, 2000.

[6] Marius Christian Liaaen and Hugo Kohmann. Dolphin sci adapter cards. In Hermann Hellwagner and Alexander Reinefeld, editors, *SCI: Scalable Coherent Interface*. Springer, 1999.

[7] Stein Jorgen Ryan. The design and implementation of a portable driver for shared memory cluster adapters. Technical report, Universitz of Oslo, Department of Informatics, 1997.

A Reconfigurable Approach to Packet Filtering

Raymond Sinnappan and Scott Hazelhurst

School of Computer Science, University of the Witwatersrand,
Johannesburg, Private Bag 3, 2050 Wits, South Africa

Abstract. Network packet classification is an important function for firewalls and filters. Packet classification based on transport-layer headers is widely used, and is specified by providing the filter with a list of rules. The cost of lookup may become a bottleneck in network performance. We present a novel technique for packet classification using FPGAs that exploits the reprogrammable nature of FPGAs. The rules are converted into a boolean expression which is directly implemented as a circuit on an FPGA. This approach is cheaper and simpler than previous hardware implementations, and we have had good experimental results.

1 Introduction

The growth of network and internet communication creates challenges including security and performance. Network routers and firewalls can play an important role in improving performance and security by filtering out irrelevant or unauthorised packets.

Routers and firewalls ('filters') typically have a set of rules (the 'rule set') to determine whether packets should be accepted. When a packet arrives, the filter compares the packet (commonly only the packet header) against the filter rules and then either accepts or rejects the packet. However, this classification can become a bottleneck [1].

The paper presents a novel technique for representing the rule set and implementing it on FPGAs. The rule set is converted into a boolean expression. Each bit in the packet header corresponds to one variable in the expression. When a packet is to be filtered, the variables are instantiated with the corresponding value of the bit. If the expression is satisfied the packet is accepted; otherwise it is rejected. Using standard tools, the boolean expression representing the rule base is implemented as a circuit on an FPGA, which can then perform the lookup, using the full parallelism of hardware.

Content and structure of paper: Section 2 gives a brief overview of TCP/IP packet filtering and related work. Section 3 presents our proposed approach of performing packet filtering. Section 4 presents the experimental results. Section 5 discusses the results and suggests future research.

2 Background

Background on packet filtering: The rules of the packet filter determine its behaviour. Different filters have different specification languages, but the semantics

G. Brebner and R. Woods (Eds.): FPL 2001, LNCS 2147, pp. 638–642, 2001.

are broadly similar. Packet filter rules consist of two parts: an action and an associated condition [1]. The *action* specifies whether to deny or permit the packet. The *condition* specifies the selection criteria that the packet should meet in order for the action to be taken on it. Typical key components of the condition are the source and destination addresses (IP addresses); masks for the addresses (which act as wild cards); the protocol to which the rules apply; and a range of port addresses which are affected by the rule.

The list of packet filter rules is searched *sequentially* to determine one that applies to a given packet. Hence, the ordering of the rules is *critical* since in general many rules may apply to one packet, but it is the first rule in the list that matches which is applied.

Related work: Software and specialised hardware approaches have been used for rule lookup. Lookup takes longer in software because software is slower and because of overhead such as interrupt processing.

Hardware approaches are more expensive due to their specialised nature. They mainly involve embedding the lookup algorithms in application specific integrated circuits (ASICs) for faster performance [3,8].

FPGAs have also been used in packet filtering applications (e.g. [4,6]). In these approaches, some representation of the rulebase is stored in RAM, either within the FPGA or on RAM chips and an FPGA is used to prototype an algorithm to perform rule lookup on the RAM. An alternative approach used software to decide initially whether a connection should be set up, and then use the FPGA to manage the connection from that point [7]. Our approach is orthogonal to this technique.

Our approach differs from other FPGA-based approaches because rulebases are directly implemented as circuits which do the classification. This uses the reconfigurability of FPGAs; hence we see the FPGA as an essential component of the solution, rather than just as a prototyping tool.

3   Proposed Filtering Technique

We propose that the packet filtering can be done by an FPGA acting as a coprocessor to a network card. In outline, our technique works as follows: (1) the access list is converted into a single, complex boolean expression; (2) the boolean expression is converted into a format suitable for entry into standard FPGA design tools; and (3) the standard FPGA design tool then converts the boolean expression into a bitstream which can be used to program the FPGA.

The result is an FPGA which takes as input the header bits of a network packet, and produces as a result a yes or no answer. These points are detailed below. We use the FPGA's ability to be reconfigured to enable us to cater for changes to the rule base, but we should emphasise that dynamic reconfiguration is unlikely to be needed.

Phase 1 – Representation as a boolean expression: For space reasons, only an outline of the method of conversion to a boolean expression can be shown here – interested readers are referred to [5,9]. The boolean expression is built in a hierarchical way. First, each component of each rule is represented as a boolean expression. For each rule, the component expressions are conjuncted together. This method deals with arbitrary masking and ranges of values efficiently and elegantly. Once we have expressions for each rule, these expressions are in turn combined, taking into account the order of the rules and the actions of the rules. The resulting boolean expression is semantically equivalent to the original rule list. In the work done so far there has been approximately 90 bits of interest in the packet header and so approximately 90 boolean variables.

Boolean expressions generated here are large in size, and our experiments show that the format chosen for representation is crucial. We use reduced, ordered binary decision diagrams (BDDs) [2]. BDDs have been used in a range of applications for the representation of boolean data; we believe that this is the first time they have been used in this application area.

Phase 2 – Conversion to design entry format: Once the boolean expression has been constructed and represented as a BDD, it must be converted into a format suitable for design entry to an FPGA design tool. In principle this is a trivial exercise. However, our experience is that how the conversion is done is critical practically. In the experiments presented in Section 4, we used a simple technique of converting from the BDD into a multiplexor based VHDL program. More detail can be found in [9].

Phase 3 – Implementing the FPGA: This step can be done using any standard FPGA design tool. For this research we used the Xilinx Foundation 1.5i tool.

4   Experiments and Results

For our experiments we created a number of sample rule sets, carefully constructed to be representative of real-world rule sets. The use of artificial sets enabled us to scale the sets to different sizes in meaningful ways, and so relate list size to lookup costs, which we would not have been able to do with real rule sets. The sample rule sets were converted to FPGA circuits, and the lookup performance and FPGA logic capacity requirements of the approach were determined.

The experiments were performed on the Xilinx XC4000XLA family of LUT-based FPGAs, a mid-end family that is cheaper than Xilinx's highest-performance Virtex family. The XC4013XLA used in this study is the cheapest, lowest-capacity member of the XC4000XLA family.

Lookup performance: Figure 1(a) shows a graph of the lookup time (in nanoseconds) of the filter for rule sets of sizes 25 to 300, with three sample rule sets per size. With 300 rules the average lookup time was 19 million lookups per second and the average lookup time for all the rule sets combined was 27 million lookups per second. This is at least two orders of magnitude faster than software filters and compares competitively with ASIC-based filters, which have similar performance.

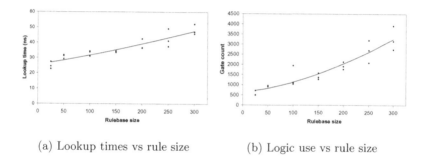

(a) Lookup times vs rule size   (b) Logic use vs rule size

Fig. 1. Experimental results

The rate of growth in lookup time is low. The best fitting line through the points, determined using non-linear regression, is $t = O(r^{1.2})$, where t is the lookup time (ns) and r is the rule set size. This model extrapolates well, and had an average error of 3.4% on rule sets of up to 500 rules.

Logic capacity requirements The approach has low FPGA capacity requirements. Figure 1(b) shows a graph of the logic capacity required, in number of equivalent gates, for different rule set sizes. For 300 rules the resulting circuit required only 54% of the 576 CLBs available on the XC4013XLA. The higher-end XC4085XLA can predictably store up to 1650 rules, which is adequate for most applications. For even larger rule sets, FPGAs with up to 10 times the capacity of the XC4085XLA are available.

The rate of growth of logic capacity required is also low. The best fitting model is $g = 0(r^{1.56})$ where g is the gate count and r is the rule set size (model error is 9% for extrapolations on rule sets of up to 500 rules).

Miscellaneous results: The approach is robust, with good results with different synthesis software, LUT-based FPGA families, hardware input languages (VHDL and XNF), and different rule sets of different sizes.

BDDs are a good representation for the boolean expression obtained from the rule set as they are compact and can be converted into much smaller and faster logic circuits than other representations such as sum of products. In other work we have done using real rule sets from commercial ISPs, the BDD representations were very compact, and so we believe that the good results we report here are generalisable.

Synthesis of 300-rule sets takes about 4 minutes using Foundation 1.5i on a 300MHz Pentium II. Rule set update thus cannot happen immediately, but this cost can obviously be reduced by using faster hardware and software.

An estimated high volume cost of the filter would be less than US$50. Most of the packet processing, as well as the filtering, can be done using FPGA resources. Hardware cost and complexity is considerably reduced as fewer glue logic and support chips are needed. An organisation using this approach would also need access to synthesis software, but this cost could be reduced by using free open source tools or by offering synthesis online as a web-based subscription service.

5   Conclusion

Initial experiments have shown that the proposed approach is not only feasible but has good performance characteristics. The approach is robust and scalable with regard to circuit size. With respect to time, the circuit's performance is very good. The technique is easily scalable as larger or newer FPGAs can be plugged in (provided they are pin compatible). Implementation does not require extra RAM or glue logic.

As future work, we are looking to continue the experimentation with a larger range of rule bases and different types of FPGAs. In addition we used fairly simplistic conversion algorithms and we believe improvement is possible. We also wish to assess the suitability of the approach to other types of packet classification, such as IP route lookup.

Acknowledgment of support: We gratefully the acknowledge the financial and equipment support of: Xilinx (through the Xilinx University Program), Avnett-Kopp Ltd, and the South African National Research Foundation.

References

1. S. Ballew. *Managing IP Networks with Cisco routers.* O'Reilly, 1997.
2. R.E. Bryant. Symbolic Boolean Manipulation with Ordered Binary-Decision Diagrams. *ACM Computing Surveys*, 24(3):293–318, September 1992.
3. P. Gupta and N. McKeown. Packet classification on multiple fields. In *Computer Communication Review*. ACM SIGCOMM, October 1999.
4. T. Harbaum, D. Meier, M. Zitterbart, and D. Brökelmann. Flexible hardware support for gigabit routing. In *Proc. Kommunikation in Verteilten Systemen (KiVS'99)*, Darmstadt, Germany, March 1999.
5. S. Hazelhurst, A. Attar, and R. Sinnappan. Algorithms for improving the dependability of firewall and filter rule lists. In *Workshop on the Dependability of IP Applications Platforms and Networks*, pages 576–585, New York, June 2000. In *Proc. IEEE Int. Conf. Dependable Systems and Networks*.
6. T. Lakshman and D. Stiliadis. High speed policy-based packet forwarding using efficient multi-dimensional range matching. In *ACM SIGCOMM '98*, pages 203–214, Vancouver, August 1998. ACM.
7. J. McHenry, P. Dowd, T. Carrozzi, F. Pellegrino, and W. Cocks. An FPGA-based coprocessor for ATM firewalls. In *Proceedings of the IEEE Symposium on FPGAs for Custom Computing Machines*, pages 30–39, April 1997.
8. David Newman. Firewall on a chip: Fore's FSA boosts throughput to multigigabit rates. *Data Communications*, 28(1):44–45, January 1999.
9. R. Sinnappan. A Reconfigurable Approach to TCP/IP Packet Filtering. MSc Research Report, School of Computer Science, University of the Witwatersrand, 2001.

FPGA-Based Modelling Unit for High Speed Lossless Arithmetic Coding

Riad Stefo[1], José Luis Núñez[2], Claudia Feregrino[2], Sudipta Mahapatra[3], and Simon Jones[2]

[1] Electronic and Electrical Engineering Department, Institut für Grundlagen der Elektrotechnik und Elektronik (IEE) TU Dresden, 01062 Dresden, Germany
stefo@iee.et.tu-dresden.de
[2] Electronic Systems Design Group, Loughborough University Loughborough, Leics., LE11 3TU, U.K.
{J.L.Nunez-Yanez, C.Feregrino-Uribe, S.R.Jones}@lboro.ac.uk
[3] Dept. of Computer Science Engineering & Applications, Regional Engineering College, Rourkela - 769 008, Orissa, India
Sudipta@rec.ori.nic.in

Abstract. This paper presents a hardware implementation of an adaptive modelling unit for parallel binary arithmetic coding. The presented model combines the advantages of binary arithmetic coding where the coding process is simplified, with the benefits of multi-alphabet arithmetic coding where any type of data can be compressed. The modelling unit adopts a simple method to store and modify the information, making it able to process 8 bits per clock cycle and to increase substantially the arithmetic coding speed. This model has been implemented in an A500K130 ProASIC FPGA and offers a throughput of 256 Mbits/s.

1 Introduction

Data compression allows representing data in a format that requires less space than is usually needed. It is particularly useful in communications because it enables devices to transmit the same amount of data in fewer bits. Data compression can be lossy or lossless [1]. Unlike lossy compression where the decompressed data may be different from the original, lossless compression requires decompressed data to be an exact copy of the original.

Arithmetic coding is one of the best algorithms that can be used in lossless data compression. It replaces a stream of symbols with a coding range of real numbers between 0 and 1. The low end of this coding range is then used as output code for this stream of symbols. At the beginning of the compression process, the coding range has 0 and 1 as its low and high ends, and a cumulative probability interval (Q_x , Q_{x+1}) is allocated to every possible input symbol. So, the symbol x has the probability $P_x = Q_{x+1}$ - Q_x. Every time a symbol is encoded, the coding range is narrowed to a portion allocated to the symbol according to its cumulative probability interval. The task of arithmetic coder is

G. Brebner and R. Woods (Eds.): FPL 2001, LNCS 2147, pp. 643–647, 2001.

to calculate the new low and high ends of the coding range using the equations (1) and (2), where $old\_range = old\_high - old\_low$.

$$new\_high = old\_low + old\_range \times Q_{x+1} \qquad (1)$$
$$new\_low = old\_low + old\_range \times Q_x \qquad (2)$$

Instead of the new high end of the coding range the new coding range can be obtained using equation (3) to execute the arithmetic coding task.

$$new\_range = old\_range \times P_x \qquad (3)$$

Arithmetic coding can be implemented for either multialphabet or binary alphabet. Because of the complexity of multialphabet arithmetic coding few implementations have been presented. One of them [2] presents a software implementation of arithmetic coding at byte level based on the equations (1) and (2). The complexity of computations in this implementation makes it impractical for real time applications. Other software implementation [3] presents a multialphabet arithmetic coding using a simpler algorithmic structure than the presented in [2], and offers similar compression ratio.

Due to the simplicity of binary arithmetic coding several binary arithmetic coding implementations have been presented. One of the best known, Marks [4], presents the Qx-coder which uses a 7th order binary model and processes a single bit per clock cycle. Kuang et al. [5] presents another implementation of arithmetic coder that uses a 10th order binary model and needs 8.5 clock cycles to process a bit.

In Section 2 we review a parallel implementation of arithmetic coding. Section 3 discusses the hardware architecture of the modelling unit. Section 4 reports the design's implementation and Section 5 concludes this paper.

2   Review of Parallel Arithmetic Coding

In [6] we proposed a parallel implementation of arithmetic coder that follows the scheme showed in [7]. The model is 0th order and processes symbols of 8 bits using a binary tree of $n = log_2 N$ levels to store the frequency information of the symbols, where N is the size of the alphabet. Part of such tree is shown in Fig. 1. The complete tree has 8 levels for an alphabet of 256 symbols.

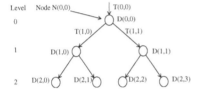

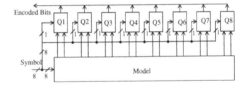

Fig. 1. Part of the binary tree   **Fig. 2.** Structure of the compressor

Each node N(i,j)stores frequency information of the symbol in a single variable D(i,j). The value of this variable splits the codespace of each node in two different halves. This codespace has zero as its left limit and the data received from the parent node T(i,j) as its right limit which is the total count of the symbols. The root node stores the size of the alphabet as the data from its parent node, which is increased after each symbol is encoded. It is assumed during the initialization operation that each symbol of the alphabet has occurred once.

Next we show the modelling algorithm, where b_i refers to the ith bit of the symbol to be encoded (b_0 is the MSB).

```
1 Initialize the nodes of the tree with the symbols frequency
  information D(i, j) and set T(0,0) to 256
  D(i, j) = 2^{n-i-1},  0 ≤ i ≤ n - 1,  0 ≤ j ≤ 2^i - 1,  n = 8
  T(0,0) = 2^n
2 Send T(0,0) to the root of the tree
3 Send the next symbol to be encoded to the first level and set
  j = 0
4 FOR i = 0 to n-1, execute the following operations:
   a) Receive the value T(i, j) from the parent node
   b) IF i < n - 1
         IF b_i = 0
            set T(i + 1, 2j) = D(i, j) and send it to the left child
            N(i + 1, 2j)
         ELSE
            set T(i + 1, 2j + 1) = [T(i, j) - D(i, j)] and send it to the
            right child N(i + 1, 2j + 1)
   c) Send the values D(i, j) and T(i, j) as the modelling
      information to the corresponding coder
   d) Update D(i, j) = D(i, j) + (1 - b_i)
      IF b_i = 0
         set j = 2j
      ELSE
         set j = 2j + 1
5 Update T(0,0) = T(0,0) + 1
6 IF there are more symbols to encode go to step 2
  ELSE
      EXIT
```

Fig. 2 shows the compressor model. The coders work in parallel such that each coder encodes one bit of the symbol. Each coder Q encodes either the left half or the right half of the code space according to the bit received from the symbol using the equations (2) and (3). The code bits generated by each coder Q are sent to the decompressor, which uses them to retrieve the original data. For details about the structure of the decompressor the reader is refered to [6]. A software implementation for the compressor and the decompressor has been done using C++. The average compression ratio for Canterbury Corpus files

[8] is 0.64, which is still a good compression ratio for a universal lossless data compressor.

3   Model Architecture

The fact that only one node in each level of the tree sends the modelling information to the corresponding coder makes the realisation of each tree level with one node possible. In this case each tree level contains one node and the corresponding memory to store the frequency information of the symbols for all the nodes in this level. The designed model works basically in two phases. The first phase is for initialization where the memory locations in the tree levels are initialized with the frequency information of the symbols. The second phase is for encoding where the model analyses the symbols in the input data and sends the modelling information to the coders. The model works in blockwise fashion, this means that the initialization phase is executed for each new block of data. Fig. 3 shows the architecture of the model. The total counter generates the data for the next phrase. The initialize counter generates the addresses to the memory locations during the initialization phase. Each tree level receives data from the previous level and the corresponding bit of the symbol from the symbol register. It analyses these data according to the modelling algorithm and sends data to the next level and modelling information to the corresponding coder. The signals mid point1...8 , range top1...8 in Fig. 3 form the modelling information that each tree level sends to its corresponding binary coder. Fig. 4 shows the architecture of a tree level. The intermediate logic updates the frequency information of the symbol and sends it to the RAM. It also calculates the data to be send to the next tree level. The index logic define which child node in the next level will receive the data sent from the current level. The comparator is used to avoid collisions between the read and write addresses of the RAM.

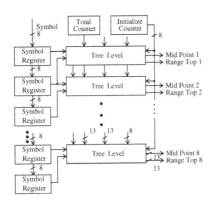

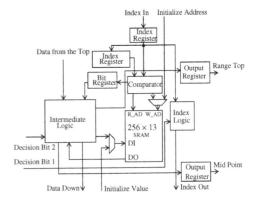

Fig. 3. Model architecture   **Fig. 4.** Tree level architecture

Table 1. Comparing our implementation with other available implementations

Implementation	Speed	Throughput	Symbol processed	Technology
Marks[4]	75 MHz	64 Mbits/s	0.8 bit/clock cycle	CMOS 5S 0.35 μm IBM
Kuang [5]	25 MHz	3 Mbits/s	0.12 bit/clock cycle	0.8 μm single poly double metal SPDM
Presented implementation	32 MHz	256 Mbits/s	8.0 bits/clock cycle	ProASIC A500K FPGA

4   Implementation

The model has been implemented in a non-volatile reprogrammable ProASIC A500K130 FPGA. The design only uses 32.6% of the device logic and 80% of the embedded RAM available. The device can be clocked at 32 MHz and processes a data block up to 256 Kbytes. Table 1 compares the results of our implementation with other available implementations. The results from Table 1 show clearly that the presented implementation outperforms other implementations.

5   Conclusions

A hardware implementation of a 0th order adaptive statistical modelling unit that is able to support parallel binary arithmetic coding is presented in this paper. The described model combines the advantages of binary arithmetic coding, with the benefits of multi-alphabet arithmetic coding. Parallel binary arithmetic coding increases the arithmetic coding speed substantially offering a throughput of 256 Mbits/s.

References

1. M. Nelson: The Data Compression Book, Prentice Hall (1991)
2. I.H.Witten et al: Arithmetic Coding for Data Compression , Communications of the ACM, Vol. 30, No.6, (1987), pp. 520-540
3. J. Jiang.: Novel Design of Arithmetic Coding for Data Compression, IEE Proceedings Computers and Digital Techniques, Vol. 142, No. 6, (1995),pp. 419-424
4. K. M. Marks: A JBIG-ABIC Compression Engine for Digital Document Processing, IBM Journal of Research and Development, Vol. 42, No.6, (1998), pp. 753-758
5. S. Kuang, J. Jou, Y. Chen: The Design of an Adaptive On-Line Binary Arithmetic Coding Chip, IEEE TCAS-I, Vol. 45, No. 7, (1998), pp. 693-706
6. S. Mahapatra, J. L.Núñez, C. Feregrino-Uribe and S. Jones: Parallel Implementation of a Multialphabet Arithmetic Coding Algorithm, IEE Colloquium on Data Compression: Methods and Implementations, IEE Savoy Place, London, (1999)
7. A. Moffat: Linear Time Adaptive Arithmetic Coding, IEEE Transaction on Information Theory, Vol. 36, No. 2, (1990), pp. 401-406
8. R. Arnold, T. Bell: A Corpus for the Evaluation of Lossless Compression Algorithms, Data Compression Conference,(1997), pp. 201-210

A Data Re-use Based Compiler Optimization for FPGAs*

Ram Subramanian** and Santosh Pande

[1] Xilinx Inc., 2100 Logic Dr., San Jose, CA 95124,
ram@xilinx.com
[2] College of Computing, Georgia Institute of Technology, Atlanta, GA 30332,
santosh@cc.gatech.edu

1 Our Approach

The speed at which a design could be tested (executed) really determines the use of FPGAs for rapid prototying. FPGAs provide reasonable routing resources, and a high capacity for mapping large hardware designs. However, profitable mapping of computations onto FPGAs is a complex task due to many trade-offs involved. We present an approach to customize FPGA-based co-processors to most profitably execute loops to speed-up the the execution. Our framework specifically addresses the issues of parallelism, reducing data transfer overheads through reuse, and optimizing the safe frequency at which design can be maximally clocked.

1.1 Motivating Example

We first illustrate our approach through an example and then present the framework developed.

Consider the example of a simple matrix multiplication code as shown below.

```
for I = 1 to 100
  for J = 1 to 100
    for K = 1 to 100
      C[I,J] = C[I,J] + A[I,K] * B[K,J];
```

As seen from the loop, we can exploit self-temporal data reuse for arrays A and B, since for all iterations of index J, A[I,K] is a constant, and similarly for all iterations of index I, B[K,J] is a constant. The loop thus has a self-temporal reuse factor of 100 for both indices I and J. Moreover, only loop K carries the dependency of C[I,J], and the variable is called a *reduction* variable since the same array location is being read and written into for all iterations of loop K. Suppose we unroll the inner loop by k and expand the reduction variable. The transformed loop is given below:

---

* This research was supported in part by DARPA award # ARMY DABT63–97–C–0029 and by NSF grant # CCR-0073512
** Work done as a part of Masters' thesis.

G. Brebner and R. Woods (Eds.): FPL 2001, LNCS 2147, pp. 648–652, 2001.
© Springer-Verlag Berlin Heidelberg 2001

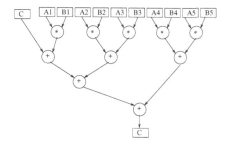

Fig. 1. Example loop unrolled five times

```
for I = 1 to 100
  for J = 1 to 100
    for K = 1 to 100 by k
      C[I,J] += A[I,K] * B[K,J]
          + ...
          + A[I,K+k-1] * B[K+k-1,J];
```

The computation graph for the statement inside the loop for $k = 5$ is given in Figure 1. Similarly for any k, a parallel computation graph is created. This graph has the nice property of directly translating to hardware, where the rectangular modules are registers and the circular modules are hardware implementations of the operator and the arrows are input and output buses connecting the operators and registers. For any other k, the graph changes in width and depth. As the depth increases, the maximum register to register latency also increases. As the width increases, so does the number of operands to be brought into hardware before the start of computations. As seen in the figure, registers $A1, A2 \ldots, A5$ and registers $B1, B2, \ldots, B5$ take values of array A and B as given by the iterations. The input register C takes the value of the previous C result, and the output register C is stored into the memory as soon as the computation is done in hardware.

The array variable C is a reduction variable, carried by loop K. The loop nest is found to be a *fully permutable* nest, with loop K carrying a *doall reduction*. A fully permutable loop nest means that the loops in the nest can be legally interchanged without affecting the data dependencies. This means that if a reduction operation is carried out, the loop can be parallelized. Here, loop K is partially unrolled to carry out the reduction operation partially on hardware. Thus, the loop can be transformed and mapped on the hardware as follows:

```
for I = 1 to 100
  for K = 1 to 100 by k
    for J = 1 to 100 by j in parallel
      /* Statement S1 */
      C[I,J] = C[I,J] + A[I,K] * B[K,J]
          + ...
```

```
                + A[I,K+k-1] * B[K+k-1,J];
        :
        /* Statement Sj */
        C[I,J+j-1] = C[I,J+j-1]
                + A[I,K] * B[K,J+j-1]
                + ...
                + A[I,K+k-1] * B[K+k-1,J+j-1];
```

Statements $S_1,..., S_j$ are performed in parallel. Thus, a similar computation graph structure as shown in Figure 1 could be replicated on hardware j times. As can be seen from the transformed loop executing on hardware, all inputs for array A remain invariant for all J iterations of the loop (innermost). Hence self-temporal reuse is exploited here.

Consider mapping the above transformed loop on a XC6264 FPGA chip. Each multiplication and addition operator, including input registers and routing area, take 5% and 1% of the total chip space respectively. The multiplication operation takes an equivalent of 5 clock cycles in a 33 MHz clock, and the addition operation takes 1 clock cycle. Suppose the K loop is unrolled 5 times, i.e. $k = 5$, which means that there are 5 multiplication and 5 addition operators as given by the computation tree on chip. This takes a total of 30% of the XC6264 area, and to fill the chip completely, 3 such modules can be synthesized, i.e., $j = 3$ in the loop structure. Each module has a delay of 8 clock cycles, equivalent to the longest path delay, after all the input registers have been written with the corresponding values. Hence, the whole circuit can be safely clocked at $\frac{1}{8}^{th}$ of 33 MHz, i.e., 4 MHz, giving a delay time of 250 ns. Since the inner loop J executes in 34 steps, and for all 34 steps, array A values do not change, only 7 data elements (input C, B1, B2, B3, B4, B5 and output C) have to be transferred inside the chip at each step. Since there are 3 modules on chip, data transfer takes 21 clock cycles per step (data transfer delay for a single transfer is 1 cycle). Hence, complete execution of one step takes $(21 + 8) = 29$ clock cycles on an average. Total execution time for the loop is (100 I loop iterations * 20 K loop * 34 J loop) * 29 cycles * 250 ns/cycle = 0.493 sec on hardware. Thus, it can be seen that this optimization allows reducing the amount of data transfer, maximizes parallelism on hardware and if we reduce the height of the tree, allows it to be clocked at the best frequency. This motivates our approach described in next section.

2   Outline of Solution

Based on the ideas illustrated, we have developed a compiler-based framework to automatically configure the hardware to program needs. Our framework is developed under the SUIF compiler infrastructure.

Input to the compiler framework apart from the source program is a FPGA architectural model. This model has been compiled by designing and creating a macro library of arithmetic and logic functions on the FPGAs. The input program (in C or FORTRAN) is parsed and converted to SUIF after various front end optimizations. The next pass recognizes reduction variables and statements and adds annotations to the SUIF instructions. The annotation includes the type of reduction, summation, product, minimum or maximum, and the reduction variable. Later passes use the annotations to unroll and expand reductions. The next pass finds DOALL loops (every iteration of the loop can execute in any order), fully permutable loops (any permutation of the loop nest gives a legal order of execution), and reorders the loops such that DOALL loops are innermost. DOALL loops should be innermost so that the body of the loop can be parallelized and mapped on hardware. The *reuse analysis and transformation* pass determines the amount of data reuse (self-temporal reuse) present in all loops of the innermost fully permutable nest and moves the maximum reuse loop that is also a DOALL as the innermost loop. This pass also generates maximally parallel computation trees of all the statements using a tree height reduction algorithm so as to reduce the length of the critical path using expression tree transformations (commutative and associative). With the reduction variables already identified in the second pass, the next pass unrolls the loop (in the innermost fully permutable loop nest) that carries the maximum reductions and expands each reduction statement. The pass uses two cost based algorithms, *space constrained* and *time constrained* reduction unroll to expand and convert the reductions to their maximum parallel form. The next pass generates the hardware configurations of all the loop nests that have to be mapped using the hardware macro library and produces a netlist form. This pass also determines reused data and the iterations in which they are reused and converts the computation tree forms of the statement to the actual computation graph on hardware by definition-use connections of register variables. The final pass places and routes the configurations on the FPGA hardware, and passes on the register addresses to the software. The software determines whether to use the data from the on-board memory or stream the data from the main memory to feed the computation on hardware.

3   Results

The compilation framework uses the hardware architectural cost model which describes the space and time costs of operator modules on hardware. The hardware model was generated through actual implementations of the macros using Xilinx Foundational Series for Virtex FPGAs.

Table 1 shows the results of benchmark program execution on the Virtex chip XCV400 with 8 bit operands for multiplication and division and 16 bit operands for additions and subtractions. Ths table shows speedups over unoptimized program. In the above table, the computation time shows the time of execution of the optimized loop, including data transfer times. The reconfiguration time is given by the column titled **rec. time**. The **total time** of execution includes reconfiguration overheads also. The **unoptimized total time** is the total time, including data transfer overheads, and reconfiguration overheads, that is needed, if the loop were not optimized for reduction unrolls and data reuse. The unoptimized time, however, assumes that the loop is parallelized and directly mapped

Program	data saved (in %)	no. of reconf.	comp. time	rec. time	total time (opt)	total time (unopt)	speed up (unopt)
Livermore:							
HF	42.9	1	19.35	6.36	25.71	39.16	1.52
IP	47.5	1	23.8	6.36	30.16	52.31	1.73
BLE	47.5	1	26.95	6.36	33.31	49.10	1.47
2DP	Data transfer in every iteration is too large to warrant execution						
EHF	32.3	3	117.62	19.08	136.7	153.06	1.12
ESF	80	1	8.68	6.36	15.04	19.84	1.32
IPR	0	1	8.54	6.36	14.9	15.26	1.02
Lapack:	39.4	6	14.28	38.16	52.44	65.73	1.25
DCT	43.7	1	119.01	6.36	125.37	212.92	1.70
Sig. Proc.:							
FIR	37.5	1	6.41	6.36	12.77	17.56	1.37
Quant.	66.67	1	30.14	6.36	36.50	95.75	2.62
NAS	24	11	442.6	69.96	512.56	992.4	1.93
Mat Mult	45.8	1	42.1	6.36	48.46	83.59	1.72

Table 1. Speed-ups for the XCV400 (speed grade 5) Virtex chip

on the chip. We believe that this would give a better measure of speedup and also prove how important data reuse and reduction unroll optimizations are isolating the gains due to of parallelism (in other words, we wanted to measure the impact of data re-use and unroll and that is why we compare parallel versions both in optimized and unoptimized cases). The last column shows the **speedup** attained when compared with the unoptimized time. In general we achieve good speedups ranging from 1 to 2.62 are observed. The tree height reductions play an important part in the reduction of latencies and improvement in maximum clock frequency at which the circuit can be driven. As a direct consequence of the reduction algorithm, frequency speedups range from 1.1 to 1.56 for the benchmarks, with an average increase in driving frequency being 1.4. As the effects of parallelism are isolated, one can see that these gains come from data re-use and better clocking frequency due to tree height reduction.

3.1   Conclusion

In order to use the power of configurable systems in terms of creating a 'speedy design' one must optimize the design generated on the hardware. We have presented a framework that exposes parallelism in loop nests, transforms loop nests to exploit available self-temporal data reuse and optimizes the design to clock it at the best possible frequency. We evaluated our work on several loops from several benchmarks and showed that their performance can be improved using our framework. This work complements other approaches proposed in literature to speed up designs which use pipelining. In this work, we contend that the DOALL parallelism found in DSP codes could be mapped with speed-ups provided one optimizes data re-use and clocking frequency of the design.

Dijkstra's Shortest Path Routing Algorithm in Reconfigurable Hardware

Matti Tommiska and Jorma Skyttä

Signal Processing Laboratory
Helsinki University of Technology
Otakaari 5A
FIN-02150, Finland
{Matti.Tommiska, Jorma.Skytta}@hut.fi

Abstract. This paper discusses the suitability of reconfigurable computing architectures to different network routing methods. As an example of the speedup offered by reconfigurable logic, the implementation of Dijkstra's shortest path routing algorithm is presented and its performance is compared to a microprocessor-based solution.

1 Introduction

The uses of reconfigurable logic have increased both in number and scope. The combination of reconfigurability and high-speed computing has given birth to a new field of engineering: reconfigurable computing which ideally combines the flexibility of software with the speed of hardware. [1]

Increased Quality of Service (QoS) poses tough requirements on network routing. The increase in computational complexity is exponentially related to an increase in QoS, and to achieve acceptable network performance, additional computing resources are required [2]. A promising solution to computational bottlenecks in network routing is reconfigurable computing.

This paper presents a brief overview of the applications of reconfigurable computing in network routing. As a case study, an FPGA-based version of Dijkstra's shortest path algorithm is presented and the performance differences between the FPGA-based and a microprocessor-based versions of the same algorithm are compared.

2 Classification of Routing Methods and Suitability to Reconfigurability

There are a number of ways to classify routing algorithms [3,4]. One of the simplest routing strategies is static routing, where the path used by the sessions of each origin-destination pair is fixed regardless of traffic conditions.

Most major packet networks use adaptive routing, where the paths change occasionally in response to congestion. The routing algorithm should change its routes and guide traffic around the point of congestion.

G. Brebner and R. Woods (Eds.): FPL 2001, LNCS 2147, pp. 653–657, 2001.

In centralized routing algorithms all route choices are made at the Routing Control Center (RCC). In distributed algorithms, the computation of routes is shared among the network nodes with information exchanged between them as necessary. Because computation is distributed evenly across the whole network, the network is not vulnerable to the breakdown of the RCC.

The applicability of reconfigurable computing in routing varies according to the routing method. In static routing, reconfigurable computing methods help in accelerating the computations to fill the lookup tables. In adaptive routing, reconfigurable computing allows the routing algorithm to run in hardware where parallelism is exploited to the fullest, and when network conditions change, a different routing algorithm is swapped in to run in the same hardware. Traditionally, adaptive routing algorithms have been run in software, but running these algorithms in reconfigurable hardware brings speed advantages.

Whether the routing method is centralized or distributed is not essential to the applicability of reconfigurable computing, since both central and distributed algorithms can be adaptive. The pros and cons of routing methods and the applicability of reconfigurable computing are presented in Table 1 [5].

Table 1. Characteristics of routing methods

Routing method	Advantages	Disadvantages	Applicability of reconfigurable computing
Static	Simple, fast	Inflexible	Precomputation of the routing tables
Adaptive	Adapts to network changes	Complex, requires careful planning	Good
Centralized	Relieves nodes from computation	Vulnerability of the RCC	Depends on the routing algorithm
Distributed	Large tolerance to link failures	Vulnerability to oscillations	Depends on the routing algorithm

3 Dijkstra's Shortest Path Algorithm in Route Computation

The problem of finding shortest paths plays a central role in the design and analysis of networks. Most routing problems can be solved as shortest path problems once an appropriate cost is assigned to each link, reflecting its available bandwidth, delay or bit error ratio, for example.

There are various algorithms for finding the shortest path if the edges in a network are characterized by a single non-negative additive metric. The most popular shortest path algorithm is Dijkstra's algorithm [6], which is used in Internet's Open Shortest Path First (OSPF) routing procedure [7].

Dijkstra's shortest path routing algorithm is presented below in pseudocode:

Given a network $G = (N, E)$, with a positive cost D_{ij} for all edges $(i, j \in N)$, start node S and a set P of permanently labeled nodes, the shortest path from start node S to every other node j is found as follows:

Initially $P = \{S\}$, $D_S = 0$, and $D_j = d_{Sj}$ for $j \overset{j \neq S}{\in} N$.

Step 1: (Find the closest node.) Find $i \notin P$ such that

$$D_i = \min_{j \notin P} D_j$$

Set $P = P \cup \{i\}$. If P contains all nodes then stop; the algorithm is complete.

Step 2: (Updating of labels.) For all $j \notin P$ set

$$D_j = \min[D_j, D_i + d_{ij}]$$

Go to Step 1.

Since each step in Dijkstra's algorithm requires a number of operations proportional to $|N|$, and the steps are iterated $|N - 1|$ times, the worst case computation is $O(|N|^2)$ [8]. Using priority queues the runtime of Dijkstra's algorithm is $O(|E| \lg |N|^2)$, which is an improvement over $O(|N|^2)$ for sparse networks [9]. However, the space requirement increases and operations on priority queues are difficult to implement in reconfigurable logic, and for these reasons priority queues have not been dealt with in this paper.

4   FPGA-Based Dijkstra's Shortest Path Algorithm

A parameterizable version of Dijkstra's shortest path algorithm was designed in VHDL [10] with Synopsys' FPGA Express design software version 3.4 [11]. The design was targeted for Altera's FLEX10K device family [12] with the Quartus design software [13].

The parameterizable features of Dijkstra's shortest path algorithm were compiled into a separate VHDL package which was included in the main design file. This way the design of other versions of Disktra's algorithm with different accuracy and for networks of different sizes is made easier, since all the changes are made only in the VHDL package.

The block diagram of the FPGA-based Dijkstra's shortest path algorithm is presented in Fig. 1. The network structure is presented in the internal ROM block of the logic device. In the block diagram of Fig. 1, there are six address lines. This is sufficient to represent all node-to-node links of networks of size upto eight nodes, if the network is represented as an adjacency matrix [9]. The internal RAM blocks of the logic device represent the known status of nodes, the distance to this node and the previous node. There are separate address and data lines for the ROM and RAM blocks, which allows the parallel transfer of information to/from the memory blocks. To speed up the computations for finding the closest node from the set of unknown nodes, all node-to-node links whose other pair is the last known node are prefetched from ROM. Then the next known node is computed by the parallel comparator bank.

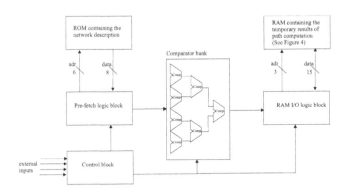

Fig. 1. The top-level block diagram of the FPGA-based Dijkstra's shortest path algorithm. The ROM block contains the network description and the RAM block contains the temporary results of shortest path computation. The comparator bank selects the smallest distance from the prefetched edge lengths.

As an example, the compiled version of Dijsktra's algorithm for networks of maximum sixe eight nodes fitted into an EPF10K20TC144-3 device, which has 1152 logic elements (LEs) corresponding to approximately 20000 available gates. The design required 72 per cent of all LEs and 5 per cent of available memory bits. Additional compilation results are summarized in Table 2. Logic element requirements increase linearly, since the size of the comparator bank grows linearly. On the other hand, memory requirements increase quadratically, since the network description of a network of size N nodes requires NxN memory locations. If the network description requires an external memory chip, all that is needed is to add an external data and address bus and to change the memory handling functions to handle external memory instead of internal memory.

To compare the performance of an FPGA-based Dijsktra's algorithm with a microprocessor-based version, an identical algorithm was coded in C and compiled with gcc in Linux Redhat 6.2. The same network descriptions were then tried in both the FPGA-based and software-based versions of the same algorithm. The speedup factor in favor of the FPGA-based version depended on the number of network nodes. As network sizes grew, the average execution time of the FPGA-based version grew only linearly, whereas the average execution time of the microprocessor-based version displayed quadratic growth (See Table 2). This can be attributed to the more effective FPGA-based execution of Step 1 in Dijkstra's algorithm, since multiple comparators are used in parallel (See Fig. 1).

Table 2. FPGA resources required by the implementation of Dijkstra's shortest path algorithm and a comparison between the execution times of FPGA-based and microprocessor-based versions of the same algorithm.

Nodes (edge cost @ 8 bits)	Logic Elements	Memory bits	Device	Execution time (FPGA-based)	Execution time (μP-based)	Average speedup factor
8	834	632	EPF10K20	$10.6\mu s$	$250\mu s$	23.58
16	1536	2116	EPF10K30	$13.4\mu s$	$434\mu s$	32.39
32	2744	8287	EPF10K50	$17.2\mu s$	$802\mu s$	46.63
64	5100	32894	EPF10K250	$21.6\mu s$	$1456\mu s$	67.41

5   Conclusions

Reconfigurable architectures have many applications in network routing. Depending on the routing algorithm or method, reconfigurability may assist in speeding up network routing.

The FPGA-based version of Dijkstra's shortest path algorithm was tens of times faster than a microprocessor-based version. This can be attributed to the following factors: multiple assignments to variables are executed concurrently, multiple arithmetic operations, including comparisons, are executed in parallel and the data structures and tables are implemented in the internal memory blocks.

References

1. N. Tredennick: "Technology and Business: Forces Driving Microprocessor Evolution", Proceedings of the IEEE, Vol. 83, No. 12, December 1995, pp. 1641-1652.
2. A. Alles: ATM Internetworking. Cisco Systems, Inc. 1995.
3. W. Stallings: Data and Computer Communications. Prentice-Hall, 1999.
4. A. Tanenbaum: Computer Networks. Prentice-Hall, 1996.
5. M. Tommiska: "Reconfigurable Computing in Communications Systems", Licentiate of Sciences Thesis, Helsinki University of Technology, 1998, pp. 46-50.
6. E. Dijkstra: "A Note on Two Problems in Connexion with Graphs", Numerische Mathematik, Vol. 1, 1959, pp. 269-271.
7. J. Moy: "OSPF Version 2, RFC 2328", May 1998.
8. D. Bertsekas, R. Gallager: Data Networks. Prentice-Hall, 1987, pp. 297-421
9. M.A. Weiss: Data Structures and Algorithm Analysis in C. The Benjamin/Cummings Publishing Company, Inc. 1993, pp. 281-343
10. M. Zwolinks: "Digital System Design and VHDL", Prentice-Hall 2000.
11. FPGA Express User's Manual, 2000, Synopsys Corporation.
12. FLEX 10K Embedded Programmable Logic Family Data Sheet, ver. 4.02, May 2000, Altera Corporation.
13. Quartus Programmable Logic Development System & Software, ver. 1.01, May 1999, Altera Corporation.

A System on Chip for Power Line Communications According to European Home Systems Specifications[1]

Isidoro Urriza, José I. García-Nicolás, Alfredo Sanz, Antonio Valdovinos

Department of Electronics and Communications Engineering
Centro Politécnico Superior, University of Zaragoza, Spain
C/ María de Luna 1, Zaragoza 50015-E
{urriza, jign, asmolina, toni}@posta.unizar.es

Abstract. This paper describes a System on Chip (SoC) implementation of a complete node for the European Home Systems specifications (EHS). The Power Line medium of EHS provides a narrow band network for home appliances. This SoC node, the EHS on a Chip (EHSoC), includes an 8051 microcontroller as Logic Link Control unit (LLC), a Medium Access Controller (MAC) and a Modem circuit for the EHS Power Line medium specifications. The MAC circuit included in EHSoC reduces the LLC computational load.

1 Introduction

Interest in home networking has increased significantly in the last years. The work in the CE has offered the EHS open specification [1]. A number of requirements have been considered in this specification: Inter-operability, Expandability, Flexible placement, Automatic configuration and Interworking. All these requirements lead to the plug and play capability.

The protocol supports several media. The power line media is the most actually developed. These media have different transmitting speeds. For the power line media EHS defines a Minimum Shift Keying modulation (MSK or FSK with low frequency deviation). The central frequency is 132.5 kHz ± 0.2% (0.25 kHz) with ± 0.6 kHz deviation, the upper/lower frequency are 133.1/131.9 kHz ± 0.2%.

The bit period is 416.67 μs (2400 baud, 1200 baud is also supported), and the lowest frequency codes data '1'.

2 System Overview

The standard EHS node is composed of two IC's, a microcontroller and a modem. The presented system, EHSoC, adds a hardwired implementation of the MAC layer; and joins the microcontroller, the MAC and the modem in a single digital chip. This will provide a very small size solution for power line communications (Fig.1).

[1] This work has been supported by the Spanish Government (CICYT) under grant TIC99-0941

G. Brebner and R. Woods (Eds.): FPL 2001, LNCS 2147, pp. 658-662, 2001.
© Springer-Verlag Berlin Heidelberg 2001

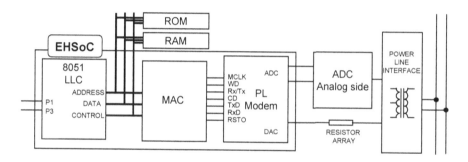

Fig. 1. The EHS Power Line System includes an 8051 microcontroller, a Medium Access Controller (MAC) and a Modem circuit for the EHS Power Line medium specifications

The microcontroller included in the system is a 8051 compatible core [2], with 256 bytes of internal RAM memory, two timers (T0, T1), six interrupts (RI, TI, T0, T1, INT0, INT1) and the Standard Serial Interface. The microcontroller executes the LLC (Logic Link Control Sub layer) and the applications tasks.

The MAC is used as a coprocessor by the microcontroller. The MAC circuit provides a reduction of 60% in size code of EHS communication library and a reduction from 95% to 5% in the CPU used time for communications purpose. The microcontroller interfaces with the MAC addressing it as external data RAM.

The power line modem uses a multi-bit sigma-delta converter [3] to implement the ADC and DAC. The DAC uses mismatch-shaping multi-bit and a D class output amplifier to improve EMC and energy efficiency. The modulator of ADC is implemented using a continuos time modulator with external passive components.

3 MAC Tasks and MAC Circuit

The MAC interconnects the LLC and the Physical Layer. Its functional capabilities involve the construction of messages datagrams, adding Forward Error Correcting Code (FEC) to bytes and Frame Check Sequence (FCS) to datagrams, the access control to the power line complaints a Carrier Sense Multiple Access (CSMA) protocol, and the selection and correction of the incoming datagrams. The MAC circuit complaints EHS V1.3.

The data packet is encapsulated with long preamble and header fields to avoid mistaking noise into datagrams. Further, frequency related burst noise can seriously affect the channel. To protect each byte against this a 6 bits FEC is added (polynomial $G(x)=x^6+x^5+x^4+x^3+1$), and finally a 16 bits FCS (polynomial $G(x)=x^{16}+x^{15}+x^2+1$) detects loss of synchronization and excessive errors. The FCS is appended at the end of the message.

Datagrams don't use end frame delimiter, the packet end is detected using byte count in normal messages, or is intrinsic in ACK (Acknowledge) messages. The data field of the ACK datagram is the FCS of the previously received message.

The access control uses Carrier Sense Multiple Access Protocol (CSMA), and datagram acknowledge (ACK) is used to detect reception.

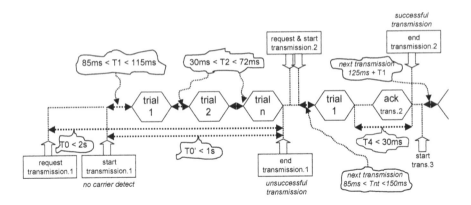

Fig. 2. CSMA Protocol. The figure shows an unsuccessful transmission, a successful one, and the different timing slacks involved in the CSMA protocol.

As Fig.2 shows a device wishing to transmit a message has a time limit t0' to complete the transaction. Initially t0 is set to 2s, and this time is reduced to 1s after starting the transmission. To start transmission on the line, or to retry, devices must wait a random time t1, or t2. If the ACK is not received, the device is allowed to retry if there is enough remaining t0' time. After a correct transmission a device is not allowed to perform a new transmission in the next 125ms.

The MAC circuit is mapped in the memory space of the microcontroller as external data RAM. The MAC memory space is divided in four blocks, they are assigned in the following way:

- [Ox00:Ox15] for management, to store EHS address (individual, group, house, source and destination). The MAC will receive all messages that have been send to any of those sixteen addresses.
- [Ox16:Ox5B] for request (transmission), to store the message to be sent, and the delay of transmission start.
- [Ox5C:OxA2] for indication (reception), to store the received message.
- [OxFE:OxFF] these two registers are for MAC configuration (OxFF CONFIG register) and operation (OxFE CONTROL register).

When the MAC successfully receives a message it stores the content in the indication zone and it asserts the LLC. Further reception is avoided until the message has been read by the LLC.

4 Modem Architecture

The modem included in EHSoC uses multi-bit sigma-delta converters [3] in both the Analog to Digital Converter (ADC) and the Digital to Analog Converter (DAC). The DAC uses multi-bit mismatch shaping.

We have used a non-traditional demodulation method to decrease the hardware complexity and the power consumption. A standard FSK demodulation needs more that 1Mflop for the reception and demodulation sections. The method that we have used is the measure of period time. The filtered output of the ADC is connected to a zero crossing block. The logic unit counts the numbers of clock cycles between N zero crossings to decide if a logic '1', a logic '0' or no logic value is received. This architecture needs less than 300Kflop for the reception and demodulation sections.

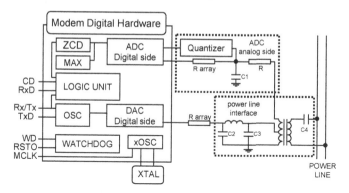

Fig. 3. Modem architecture

The analog converters are the design key points of this modem. The different types of topologies and the different types of loads connected to the power line, make necessary a large dynamic range in reception [5],[6]. The traditional approach to this problem is to use an Automatic Gain Control (AGC). To avoid the need of an analog AGC we have used a new approach.

The modem for the power line medium uses a multi-bit sigma-delta converter [3] in the ADC and DAC. The DAC transmitting stage uses a sigma-delta architecture with a fifth order modulator, a quantizer of fifteen non regular levels and mismatch-shaping. As Fig.3 shows, this DAC uses the digital CMOS output to control a resistors array in D class configuration. The resistors array and the input impedance of power line interface configure a non-uniform quantizer.

The Fig.4 left shows the output of DAC, with load impedance of 10Ω, without mismatch shaping to control the external resistors array. The noise floor is lower bounded by the fifth order modulator. The Fig.4 right shows the output of DAC, with load impedance of 10Ω, with mismatch-shaping to control the external resistors array. The noise floor is lower bounded by the mismatch-shaping noise. The result is a DAC with Equivalent Number of Bits (ENOB)=7.7, BandWidth (BW)=1MHz and 11 Mega Samples per Second (MSPS). When the power line interface is connected to the DAC the noise floor is further reduced, and the result is a DAC with ENOB=8.9, BW=1MHz & 11MSPS.

To provide the necessary large dynamic range in reception the ADC uses a multi-bit sigma-delta converter with a continuos time modulator and few external analog components (Fig.3). The ADC modulator uses a DAC with a fifteen non-uniform levels quantizer and mismatch shaping.

EHS, in the transmission stage for power line medium, sets a maximum output level of 116dBµV (631mVrms). The traditional solution uses a B class amplifier powered by a 10V supply and a line adapter with a voltage transformation rate of 5. The power efficiency is 70%. We have used the digital CMOS output to control an array or seven resistors in a D class configuration, the use of D class output amplifier increases the power efficiency to 90%. Moreover using a D-class output amplifier, the whole system is powered by a 3.3V DC supply.

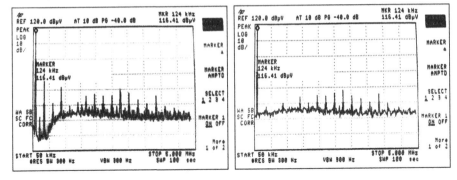

Fig. 4. The left hand side figure shows the Output DAC spectrum without mismatch-shaping, the right hand side figure shows the Output DAC spectrum with mismatch-shaping

5 Results

Each module has been tested as stand-alone circuit. The 8051 microcontroller core has been fully tested, it agrees with the standard 80C51 architecture [2], only the power-saving modes of operation are not implemented. The MAC has been tested by the authors and by EHS software providers. The modem has been tested and the measured Bit Error Rate (BER) is better that 10^{-5} in the condition of use in a home. For a 52dBµV (281µVrms) signal the measured BER is better than 10^{-4}. The dynamic range is greater than 60db.

To test the whole system we have designed a specific test board that includes a Xilinx FPGA (XC4085XLA). These board has been used to test the whole system (microcontroller, MAC and a simplified version of the modem) mapped into the FPGA. The final version of the modem has been mapped, with the MAC, into the FPGA and it has been tested using an external microcontroller. The size of the EHSoC is 3192 CLB in a XC4000 FPGA, (1050 for the 8051, 486 for the MAC and 1656 for the modem).

References

1. EHSA: EHS Specification Release 1.3. EHSA Zavenem, Belgium (1997)
2. Philips: 80C51-Based 8-Bit Microcontrollers, Data Handbook IC20. Philips (1998)
3. S. R. Norsworthy, R. Schreier, G. C. Temes. D. Liu, E. Flint, B.Guacher, Y. Kwark: Delta-Sigma Data Converters. Theory, Design, and Simulation. IEEE Press, New York (1996)
4. Leon W. Couch II: Digital and Analog Communication Systems. Prentice Hall Inc. (1997)
5. J. B. B'Neal: The Residential Power Line Circuit as a Communication Medium. IEEE Transactions on Consumer Electronic, vol 45 n.4, IEEE Press, New York (1999) 1087-1097
6. D. Liu, E. Flint, B. Guacher, Y. Kwark: Wide Band AC Power Line Characterization. IEEE Transactions on Consumer Electronic, vol 45 n.4, IEEE Press, New York (1999) 1087-1097

Author Index

Lecture Notes in Computer Science

For information about Vols. 1–2048
please contact your bookseller or Springer-Verlag